Nepal

THE ROUGH GUIDE

There are more than eighty Rough Guide titles covering
destinations from Amsterdam to Zimbabwe

Forthcoming titles include
China • Corfu • Jamaica • New Zealand • South Africa
Southwest USA • Vienna

Rough Guide Reference Series
Classical Music • The Internet • Jazz • Opera • Rock Music • World Music

Rough Guide Phrasebooks
Czech • French • German • Greek • Indonesian • Italian • Mandarin Chinese
Mexican Spanish • Polish • Portuguese • Spanish • Thai • Turkish

Rough Guides on the Internet
http://www.roughguides.com/
http://www.hotwired.com/rough

Rough Guide credits

Editor:	Annie Shaw
Series editor:	Mark Ellingham
Editorial:	Martin Dunford, Jonathan Buckley, Samantha Cook, Jo Mead, Alison Cowan, Amanda Tomlin, Lemisse Al-Hafidh, Catherine McHale, Paul Gray, Vivienne Heller
Online editors:	Alan Spicer (UK), Andrew Rosenberg (US)
Production:	Susanne Hillen, Andy Hilliard, Melissa Flack, Judy Pang, Link Hall, Nicola Williamson, David Callier, Helen Ostick
Marketing & Publicity:	Richard Trillo, Simon Carloss (UK), Jean-Marie Kelly, Jeff Kaye (US)
Finance:	John Fisher, Celia Crowley, Catherine Gillespie
Administration:	Tania Hummel, Margo Daly

This book is dedicated to Krysia, who was with me when I first set foot in Nepal, and has never wavered since.

Special thanks for help in this edition must again go first to Dadi Ram Sapkota, researcher, translator, fact-checker and friend. Other people who provided invaluable insights and assistance are: Om Charan Amatya, for help in Bhaktapur; Rajendra M. Bajracharya, for his excellent and inspiring efforts at NETWAC; Chief Sub-Inspector S.K. Basnet and the crew at Palung Police Station; Basanta Bidari of the Lumbini Development Trust, for authoritative archeological information; Hikmat Bisht, ever the gracious host in Mahendranagar; Abhijaya Dhakal, who is doing great work at Bardia; Sadhu Ram Dhakal, for unstinting hospitality in Kathmandu; Andrew Duncan, for conversation and all the San Miguel we could hold in Butwal and Thakurdwara; Colin Izod of the Bhutanese Refugee Support Group; Yogendra Kayastha and the staff of KEEP for trekking information; G.P. Kharel of NARA for rafting information; Arjun Lamsal, Panchbhaiya Danda's friendliest innkeeper; Govinda Prasad Neupane in Bhairawa; Chandi Prasad Pandey and family, for a lovely time at Rani Ghat; Gorakh Pyera Shrestha of Janakpur's tourist office; Nirmal Shrestha, for help and advice in Tansen; and S.K. Suman, for putting up with me at Koshi Tappu. Thanks, also, to readers of the previous edition for comments and updates – see p.x for credits.

Thanks, too, to all at Rough Guides who helped produce this book, especially Annie Shaw; Samantha Cook for help with editing; Micromap for spot-on cartography; Susanne Hillen for patient production; Helen Ostick for typesetting; Robin Sawers for proofreading, and Cameron Donald for Australasian research.

The publishers and authors have done their best to ensure the accuracy and currency of all the information in *The Rough Guide to Nepal*; however, they can accept no responsibility for any loss, injury or inconvenience sustained by any traveller as a result of information or advice contained in the guide.

This third edition published August 1996 by Rough Guides Ltd, 1 Mercer Street, London WC2H 9QJ.
Reprinted in February 1997.

Distributed by the Penguin Group:

Penguin Books Ltd, 27 Wrights Lane, London W8 5TZ
Penguin Books USA Inc, 375 Hudson Street, New York 10014, USA
Penguin Books Australia Ltd, 487 Maroondah Highway, PO Box 257, Ringwood, Victoria 3134, Australia
Penguin Books Canada Ltd, 10 Alcorn Avenue, Toronto, Ontario, Canada M4V 1E4
Penguin Books (NZ) Ltd, 182–190 Wairau Road, Auckland 10, New Zealand

Previous edition published in the United States and Canada as *The Real Guide Nepal*.

Typeset in Linotron Univers and Century Old Style to an original design by Andrew Oliver.
Printed in the UK by Cox & Wyman, Reading, Berks.

Illustrations in the Guide by Hal Aqua; Incidental illustrations in Part One and Part Three by Edward Briant. Illustration on p.1 by Tommy Yamaha; Illustration on p.379 by Sally Davies.

464pp
includes index

A catalogue record for this book is available from the British Library

ISBN 1-85828-190-3

Nepal

THE ROUGH GUIDE

Written and researched by
David Reed

Contributors
Andy Balestracci, Charles Leech, Anna Robinson,
Carol Tingey, Kesang Tseten and Gopal Yonjan

THE ROUGH GUIDES

LIST OF MAPS

MAP SYMBOLS

Railway		Lodge	
Main road		Ancient monument	
Minor road		Mountain range	
Steps		Mountain peak	
One-way street		Pass	
Path		Tourist office	
River		Post office	
Chapter division boundary		Gate	
Ridge line		Building	
Airport		Park	
Camp		National park	

CONTENTS

Introduction vi

INTRODUCTION

Nepal forms the very watershed of Asia. Landlocked between India and Tibet, it spans terrain from subtropical jungle to the icy Himalaya, and contains eight of the world's ten highest mountains. Its cultural landscape is every bit as diverse: a dozen major **ethnic groups**, speaking as many as fifty languages and dialects, coexist in this narrow, jumbled buffer state, while two

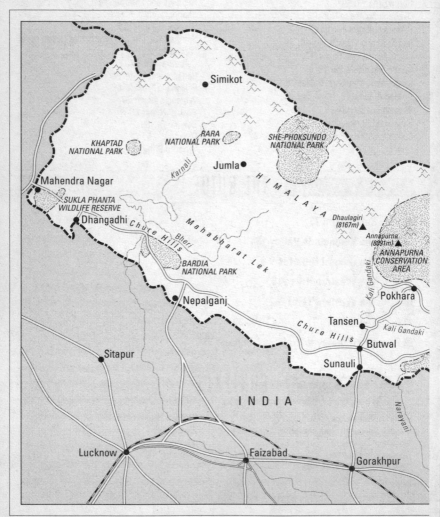

of the world's great **religions**, Hinduism and Buddhism, overlap and mingle with older tribal traditions – yet it's a testimony to the Nepalis' tolerance and good humour that there is no tradition of ethnic or religious strife. Unlike India, Nepal was never colonized, a fact which comes through in fierce national pride and other, more idiosyncratic ways. Founded on trans-Himalayan trade, its dense, medieval **cities** display a unique pagoda-style architecture, not to mention an astounding flair for festivals and pageantry. But above all, Nepal is a nation of unaffected **villages** and terraced hillsides – more than eighty percent of the population lives off the land – and whether you're trekking, biking or bouncing around in packed buses, sampling this simple lifestyle is perhaps the greatest pleasure of all.

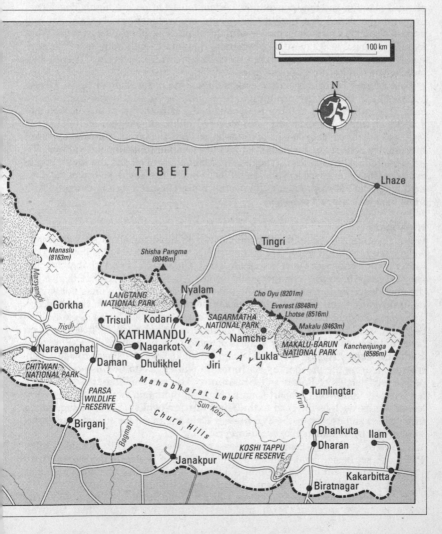

But it would be misleading to portray Nepal as a fabled Shangri-la. One of the world's poorest countries (if you go by per capita income), it suffers from many of the pangs and uncertainties of the Third World, including overpopulation and deforestation; **development** is coming in fits and starts, and not all of it is being shared equitably. Heavily reliant on its big-brother neighbours, Nepal was, until 1990, run by one of the last remaining absolute monarchies, a regime that combined China's repressiveness and India's bureaucracy in equal measure. The **people's movement** (*jana andolan*) of 1990 ushered in democracy and tapped a vast reservoir of idealism; yet a new constitution has changed little for the average struggling Nepali family.

Travelling in Nepal isn't a straightforward or predictable activity. **Getting around** is tough and time-consuming; certain tourist areas are highly developed, even overdeveloped, but facilities elsewhere are rudimentary. Nepalis are well used to shrugging off inconvenience with the all-purpose phrase, *Ke garne?* ("What to do?"). Nepal is also a more fragile country than most – culturally as well as environmentally – so it's necessary to be especially sensitive as a traveller. Tips for minimizing your impact are given in *Basics*.

Topography is obviously a key consideration when travelling in Nepal. Generally speaking, the country divides into three altitude zones running from west to east. The northernmost of these is, of course, the **Himalayan chain**, broken into a series of *himal* (permanently snow-covered mountain ranges) and alpine valleys, and inhabited, at least part of the year, as high as 5000m. The largest part of the country consists of a wide belt of middle-elevation **foothills** and **valleys**, Nepal's traditional heartland; two ranges, the Mahabharat Lek and the lower, southernmost Chure (or Siwalik) Hills, stand out. Finally, the **Tarai**, a strip of flat, lowland jungle and farmland along the southern border, has more in common with India than with the rest of Nepal.

Highlights

Given the country's primitive transport network, most travellers stick to a well-worn circuit, with the result that certain sights and trekking routes have become rather commercialized. Don't be put off. The beaten track is remarkably thin and easy to escape in Nepal – and this guide is intended, first and foremost, to give you the confidence to do just that. It's the out-of-the-way places, the ones not written up in any book (even this one), that you'll remember most fondly on your return.

Everyone touches down in **Kathmandu** at some point, but for all its exotic bustle, the capital is rather rough going these days – logistically it makes a good base, but you won't necessarily want to spend lots of time there. Hindu temples, Buddhist stupas, rolling countryside and huddled brick villages provide incentives for touring the prosperous **Kathmandu Valley**, as do the historically independent city-states of **Patan** and **Bhaktapur**. The surrounding central hills are surprisingly undeveloped, apart from a couple of mountain view points, yet a few lesser routes, such as the road to the **Tibet border** (which is, if anything, falling into disuse) and especially the **Tribhuwan Rajpath**, make for adventurous travel – especially by mountain bike or motorcycle.

The views get more dramatic, or at least more accessible, in the **western hills**. **Pokhara**, set beside a lake under a looming wall of peaks, is the closest thing you'll find to a resort in Nepal. Other hill towns – notably **Gorkha** and its impressive fortress and laid-back **Tansen** – offer scenery with history to boot.

It's in the teeming jungle and ethnic villages of the **Tarai** that Nepal's diversity really becomes apparent. Most travellers venture no further than **Chitwan**

National Park, where endangered Asian one-horned rhinos are easily viewable, but **Bardia National Park** and two other rarely visited wildlife reserves are out there for the more adventurous. **Lumbini**, Buddha's birthplace in the western Tarai, is stunningly peaceful and unwesternized, as is **Janakpur**, a Hindu holy city in the east. Rolling tea plantations, weekly markets and a rich cultural mix figure prominently in the spectacular and little-visited **eastern hills**, most easily reached from the Tarai.

The **Himalaya** are covered separately in the last chapter of the guide, along with all hill areas that fall within the government's prescribed **trekking regions**. Special rules apply in this roadless half of Nepal: distances are reckoned in days of walking, and shelter is provided by trailside inns. The terrain can vary from infernal valley bottoms and cultivated foothills to lush rhododendron forests and glacial deserts. You'll encounter people everywhere you walk, and the cultural interactions are often, in retrospect, the most rewarding part of a trek.

Some words of warning

The 1990s have brought great upheaval to Nepal, and there's probably more still to come. The country's political system, economic development and mercurial relationship with India all seem to be in a worrying state of flux. While some people are prospering from economic liberalization, most aren't.

But while political instability is unlikely to have much of a direct effect on your plans, other changes inevitably will. No guidebook can reliably predict quite how things will be by the time you get to Nepal, but the following recent trends give an idea of what's in store:

• New **road-building** is moving trailheads further into the hinterland, making some treks shorter and the transport to them longer. This year's great trek or bike ride is next year's dirt road, and the following year's paved road (and a few years later, it may be a trail again).

• **Tourist bus** services are proliferating, making travel to certain places easier, but also turning those places into tourist traps.

• Nepal is getting more and more **packaged**: for no good reason other than heavy marketing, guided tours, organized treks and safaris have become common, even for budget travellers.

• The growth of **budget tourist ghettos** has been a major theme of the past decade. The commercialization is really dismaying in some areas, leading many returning travellers to complain that Nepal is "ruined". It's not, but parts of it are, so avoid them.

• Fortunately, a **Nepali cultural revival** seems to be emerging, fuelled in part by a backlash against Westernization but more significantly by Nepalis' realization that they need not toss out traditional ways to cater to foreigners. Thus travellers dissatisfied with pseudo-Western food and facilities now have a growing range of good, indigenous alternatives to choose from.

• **Rural electrification** is proceeding steadily, bringing not only lights but also videos, satellite TV and a whole lot more contact with the outside world.

• **Ripoffs and hustle** are on the rise, owing to an influx of Indian (especially Kashmiri) immigrants and high unemployment. Nepal is still one of the mellowest countries in the world, but it's no longer the hassle-free paradise it once was.

• **Prices** have historically risen faster than average in the tourist areas, though oversupply is beginning to reverse this trend. Off the beaten track, prices if anything tend to decline in real terms.

GIVE SOMETHING BACK TO NEPAL

If you would like to contribute materially to Nepal and its people, please join us in supporting the following non-profit organizations. The author and Rough Guides will each donate a portion of the proceeds from this book to:

Action Aid, Amlyn House, MacDonald Road, London N19 5PG (☎0171/ 281 4101). Promotes a variety of community development programmes in Nepal.

Building With Books, P O Box 16741, Stamford, CT 06905 (☎203/961-5042). Mobilizes American high-school students to raise money to build schools.

Nepal Social Service Fund, c/o Rt 1, Box 79, Clarks Grove, MN 56016. Works with far western villages to introduce agricultural innovations.

Seva Foundation, 8 N San Pedro Rd, San Rafael, CA 94903. Supports an eye clinic in Bhairawa.

Voluntary Service Overseas (VSO), 317 Putney Bridge Rd, London SW15 2PN (☎0181/780 2266). Places volunteers in health, education, agriculture, technical and other projects.

THANKS

Special thanks to the following readers for their letters: Phil Anslow; Barry Arthur; Gabriel Best; D Broby and A Hayles; Catherine Champion; Lee Chantrell, Stuart Colley; Avril Corbett; Dr Andrew Cordell; Valerie Dewar; Tina Dunne; Mick Edwards; Stephen Fairchild and Isabelle Lippitsch; Nathan Funk; A R Gallagher; Peter and Susan Goldie; Deborah Hammond; Rosenlund Hössna; Matt Jarrett; Nicholas Jones; Chad Leech; Susie Loger; Alexander W Kindness; Francine Marshall; Philip Robinson and Rene MacDonald; K M M Ross; Ben Rupinder; Isabelle Sénéchaud; Michel Van Dam.

HELP US UPDATE

We've gone to a lot of effort to ensure that this third edition of *The Rough Guide to Nepal* is completely up-to-date and accurate. However, things do change – places get "discovered", transport connections change, restaurants and guest houses get renamed – and any suggestions, comments or corrections would be much appreciated. We're particularly keen to hear of accounts of travels to remote and untried destinations.

We'll credit all contributions, and send a copy of the next edition (or any other Rough Guide if you prefer) for the best letters. Please mark letters "Rough Guide Nepal Update" and send to:

Rough Guides, 1 Mercer Street, London WC2H 9QJ or
Rough Guides, 375 Hudson Street, 9th Floor, New York NY 10014 or
nepal@roughtravl.co.uk

Online updates about this book can be found on Rough Guides' website at
http://www.roughguides.com/

PART ONE

THE
BASICS

GETTING THERE BY AIR

If Nepal is your only destination, flying direct to Kathmandu is the logical option. However, only a few airlines serve this route, so you may well find yourself making several hops with two or even three different carriers. Flights in the autumn and spring high seasons (early October to mid-November, and late February to early March) fill up months ahead, so make sure you book well in advance if you plan to travel at these times.

Since it's a long way to Nepal, consider **stopping over** on the way there or back. If you're coming from North America or Australasia, it should cost little or no extra to stop in Hong Kong, Bangkok, Singapore or a number of other Asian cities. From Europe, a stop in Karachi, Delhi or Dhaka may be free. Another option is an **"open jaw" ticket**, which entails flying into one city (in this case Kathmandu) and returning from another (say, Delhi), allowing you to travel overland in between. The price is usually calculated by halving the return fares to each destination and adding the two figures together.

If Nepal is only one stop on a longer journey, you might save money with a **round-the-world ticket**. Many discount travel agents can sell you an "off-the-shelf" RTW ticket that will have you touching down in about half a dozen cities including Kathmandu or at least Delhi (customized RTW tickets are apt to be more expensive). For greater flexibility, if not economy, buy a **one-way ticket** to Hong Kong, Bangkok or Singapore, where onward tickets are very cheap. For typical airfares from other Asian cities to Kathmandu, see "Asian Connections" (p.13).

SHOPPING FOR TICKETS

Airline tickets are sold through many channels, and there's no magic rule of thumb for predicting which will be cheapest. For fares to Kathmandu and most of Asia, however, the best deals generally come from "consolidators" and other discount-type agents. You'll probably save time if you conduct your search in the following order.

Consolidators buy up large blocks of tickets that airlines don't think they'll be able to sell at their published fares, and sell them at a discount. Besides being cheap, consolidators normally don't impose advance purchase requirements, but they do often charge very stiff fees for date changes; note also that airlines generally won't alter tickets after they've gone to a consolidator, forcing you to make changes only through the consolidator. Also, these companies' margins are pretty tiny, so they make their money by dealing in volume – don't expect them to entertain lots of questions.

Discount agents also sell consolidated tickets, but in addition they typically offer a range of related services such as travel insurance, youth and student ID cards, car rentals and tours. These agencies tend to be most worthwhile to students and under-26s, who can often benefit from special fares and deals.

Try the firms listed in the boxes on the following pages, or check out the ads in the Sunday newspaper travel sections. Call as many as you can, since each one will have contracts with different airlines. Make sure to check the restrictions carefully before buying any ticket. And remember, price isn't the only consideration: some companies are more reputable than others. Deal only with those that belong to an official travel trade association (such as ABTA in Britain or ASTA in the US) – they must uphold certain professional standards, and if they go bust you will probably be protected. Never deal with a company that demands cash up front, refuses to accept payment by credit card, won't provide written confirmation of flight details, or can't guarantee a full refund in the event of a cancellation.

Once you've found the best discounted fare, it's probably still worth checking out what the **airlines** themselves are offering. Any local travel agent will be able to access published fares, but in practice they may not have time to search out special promotions and the like, so it's worth doing your own research. Ordinarily, the cheapest way to go is with an **Apex** (Advance Purchase Excursion) ticket, although this will carry certain restrictions: you have to book – and pay – at least 21 days before departure and return within three months, and you tend to get penalized if you change your schedule. Many airlines don't offer Apex fares to Kathmandu, but their standard excursion fares often cost no more, and they carry no advance purchase restrictions.

FROM THE UK AND IRELAND

The half-dozen airlines that fly direct between London and Kathmandu all make two stops en route, resulting in a minimum of sixteen hours' total travel time. None flies daily. Many other airlines fly from London and other regional cities to Delhi, where you can change planes for

---

MAJOR AIRLINES IN THE UK & IRELAND

AIRLINES SERVING NEPAL

Aeroflot, 70 Piccadilly, London W1 (☎0171/355 2233). London or Shannon to Kathmandu via Moscow and Dubai.

Biman Bangladesh – Tickets sold through *Jumbo Travel*, 95 Praed St, London W2 (☎0171/ 258 0295). London to Kathmandu via Paris/ Frankfurt/Rome and Dhaka.

Lufthansa, 10 Old Bond St, London W1; 78 St Vincent St, Glasgow G2 (☎0345/737 747). London, Birmingham, Glasgow or Manchester to Kathmandu via Frankfurt and Dubai.

Pakistan International Airways (PIA), 45 Piccadilly, London W1 (☎0171/287 2582). London to Kathmandu via Karachi.

Royal Nepal Airlines Corporation (RNAC) – Tickets sold through *Brightsun Travel*, 4 New Burlington St, London W1 (☎0171/287 4949). London (Gatwick) to Kathmandu via Frankfurt and Dubai.

Singapore Airlines, 143–147 Regent St, London W1 (☎0181/747 0007). London to Kathmandu via Singapore and Dhaka.

Thai International, 41 Albemarle St, London W1 (☎0171/499 9133). London to Kathmandu via Delhi and/or Bangkok.

OTHER USEFUL AIRLINES

Air France, 177 Piccadilly, London W1 (☎0181/ 742 6600). London, Dublin or various other regional cities to Delhi via Paris.

Air India, Lansdowne House, 55 Berkeley Square, London W1 (☎0171/436 8361). London to Delhi nonstop, with connections to other Indian cities.

British Airways, 156 Regent St, London W1 (☎0181/897 4000). London to Delhi nonstop, with connections to Calcutta and other Indian cities.

Egyptair, 296 Regent St, London W1 (☎0171/734 2395). London to Delhi via Cairo.

Emirates Airlines, 125 Pall Mall, London SW1 (☎0171/808 0808). London or Manchester to Delhi via Dubai.

Finnair, 14 Clifford St, London W1 (☎0171/408 1222). London to Bangkok via Helsinki.

Gulf Air, 10 Albemarle St, London W1 (☎0171/ 408 1717). London or Manchester to Delhi via various Gulf cities.

KLM, Terminal 4, Heathrow (☎0181/750 9000). London, Manchester or other regional cities to Delhi via Amsterdam.

Kuwait Airlines – Tickets sold through *Jetair*, 188 Hammersmith Rd, London W6 (☎0181/970 1522). London to Delhi via Kuwait.

LOT Polish Airlines, 313 Regent St, London W1 (☎0171/580 5037). London to Bangkok via Warsaw.

Qantas, 182 The Strand, London WC2 (☎0345/ 747 767). London to Bangkok.

Royal Jordanian Air, 177 Regent St, London W1 (☎0171/734 2557). London to Delhi via Amman.

Swissair, Swiss Centre, Leicester Square, London W1 (☎0171/434 7300). London or Dublin to Delhi via Zurich.

Tarom Romanian Air – Tickets sold through *Skydeal Travel*, 12 Rathbone St, London W1 (☎0171/396 9933). London to Delhi or Calcutta via Bucharest.

Kathmandu – this won't get you there any faster, and it probably won't save you any money either, but it expands your options for getting a seat on the day of your choice.

Fares to Kathmandu are **seasonal**, with airlines generally charging full whack for departures in October–November, around Christmas and in February–April. During these months a return ticket will cost £50–200 more than during less popular times of the year, depending on the airline. (A notable exception is *Biman Bangladesh*, whose high season is mid-December to mid-January.) Handily, though, *indirect* tickets routed through Delhi are cheapest in the spring and autumn. Flying on weekends will add £50 or more to a return fare; prices quoted below assume midweek travel.

FROM LONDON

You'll get the best deal if you can fly **from London**, of course. *Royal Nepal Airlines Corporation* (*RNAC*), *Lufthansa* and *Pakistan International Airways* (*PIA*), which all offer reasonably direct routings (see box), sell their tickets through consolidators for around £500 in low season, £560 in high season (RNAC's high-season fare goes up to £680). *Biman Bangladesh* is even cheaper – as little as £430 – although you may have to spend the night in Dhaka. Consolidated fares with *Singapore* are also in the £500–600 range, but these entail an even longer detour via Singapore.

The cheapest fares of all are usually with *Aeroflot*, which charges around £400 return. Note, however, that this weekly flight requires a long, late-night stopover in Moscow, and *Aeroflot* also has a reputation for abruptly cancelling flights and leaving passengers stranded for days.

Flights **to Delhi** can run as low as £325 on such airlines as *Royal Jordanian Air* and *Tarom Romanian Air*, but expect to pay more like £400/550 (low/high season) for discounted fares with more reliable carriers like *Air India*, *British Airways* or *Air France*. A connecting flight to Kathmandu and back on *RNAC* or *Indian Airlines* will add about £180 to the final tab (if you're trying to save money, go overland – see below).

Several of the travel agents listed in the box below sell **round-the-world** tickets including Delhi, Kathmandu and Bangkok for £900–1000. Typically you have to travel the Delhi–Kathmandu leg overland at your own expense. Returning to Delhi overland and then flying Delhi–Bangkok may save some money, but not much.

FROM OTHER BRITISH CITIES

From Manchester, *Lufthansa* provides the most direct service to Kathmandu (via Frankfurt), and the fare is the same as from London. *KLM*, *Air France*, *Emirates* and *Gulf Air* all fly to Delhi (via their capital cities), where you can pick up a

---

DISCOUNT AGENTS AND CONSOLIDATORS IN THE UK AND IRELAND

Alpha Flights, 173 Uxbridge Rd, London W7 (☎0181/579 8444). Consolidator.

Campus Travel, 52 Grosvenor Gardens, London SW1 (☎0171/730 8111), with branches in several other cities and on university campuses all over Britain. Discount travel agency specializing in student/youth fares.

Council Travel, 28a Poland St, London W1 (☎0171/437 7767). General student/youth discount agent.

Flight Bookers, 177 Tottenham Court Rd, London W1 (☎0171/757 3000). Consolidator.

Flight File, 49 Tottenham Court Rd, London W1 (☎0171/323 4203). Consolidator.

Holiday Planners, 111 Bell St, London NW1 (☎0171/724 2255). *Lufthansa*'s principal consolidator.

STA Travel, 86 Old Brompton Rd, London SW7 (☎0171/361 6262) and branches in a dozen other

UK cities. Worldwide discount travel firm specializing in student/youth fares and travel services.

Trailfinders, 42–50 Earls Court Rd, London W8 (☎0171/938 3366), with other locations in Manchester, Glasgow, Birmingham and Bristol. Discount travel agent.

Travel Bug, 597 Cheetham Hill Rd, Manchester M8 (☎0161/721 4000). Consolidator.

Travel CUTS, 295a Regent St, London W1 (☎0171/255 2082). Discount agent specializing in student fares and other travel services.

USIT, Aston Quay, O'Connell Bridge, Dublin 2 (☎01/679 8833); 13b College St, Belfast BT1 (☎0232/324 073). Ireland's main outlet for discounted, youth and student fares.

Welcome Travel, 55–57 Wells St, London W1 (☎0171/439 3627). *Air India*'s principal consolidator.

Kathmandu connection on *RNAC* or *Indian Airlines*. *Lufthansa* also offers flights out of **Glasgow** and **Birmingham**, and *Air France* from Glasgow, Birmingham, **Bristol** and **Edinburgh**. However, from most regional cities it will probably still work out cheaper to take a shuttle flight or train to London to take advantage of the much cheaper fares from there.

FROM IRELAND

There are no direct flights to Kathmandu **from Ireland**, and indeed flights from here are indirect at best. Most travel agents will recommend flying to London to connect with one of the cheap flights from there (see above); figure on £70 for the Dublin–London or Shannon–London connection. Alternatively, you could fly with *Air France* or *Swissair* via their respective capitals to Delhi, and

then on to Kathmandu on *RNAC* or *Indian Airlines*. *Aeroflot* flies from Shannon to Moscow, where you can connect with the once-weekly flight to Kathmandu, but it's not particularly cheap nor, as explained above, very reliable.

FROM NORTH AMERICA

Nepal is basically on the other side of the planet from North America. If you live on the East Coast it's somewhat shorter to go via Europe, and from the West Coast it's shorter via the Far East; but either way it's a long haul, involving one or more intermediate stops, and you'll arrive fresher and less jet-lagged if you can manage to fit in a few days' stopover somewhere en route.

Several airlines fly to Kathmandu from North America, although as this is a fairly low-volume route none operates a daily service. Plenty of other

---

MAJOR AIRLINES IN NORTH AMERICA

AIRLINES SERVING NEPAL

Aeroflot (☎1-800/995-5555). Flights from several US cities and Montréal to Kathmandu and Delhi (via Moscow).

Lufthansa (☎1-800/645-3880). Many US and Canadian cities to Kathmandu (via Frankfurt and Karachi); also connections to Delhi.

Pakistan International Airlines (PIA) (☎1-800/221-2552 or 212/370-9158). New York to Kathmandu (via Karachi); also connections to Delhi and Bombay.

Royal Nepal Airlines Corporation (RNAC) (☎1-800/266-3725). Various US and Canadian

cities (through a co-operative agreement with *Northwest*) to Kathmandu (via Hong Kong, Singapore, Bangkok or London).

Singapore Airlines (☎1-800/742-3333). Los Angeles, San Francisco and Vancouver to Kathmandu (via Singapore), New York to Kathmandu (via Amsterdam or Frankfurt).

Thai International (☎1-800/426-5204 in US; ☎1-800/668-8103 in Canada). Los Angeles to Kathmandu (via Bangkok); also connections to Delhi and Calcutta.

OTHER USEFUL AIRLINES

Air Canada (toll-free number varies by province). Toronto to Delhi (via London); Vancouver to Hong Kong.

Air India (☎1-800/223-7776 or ☎212/751-6200). New York and Toronto to Delhi and Calcutta (via London).

British Airways (☎1-800/247-9297 in US; ☎1-800/668-1059 in Canada). Many US and Canadian cities to Delhi (via London).

Canadian Airlines (☎1-800/665-1177). Vancouver to Hong Kong and Bangkok.

Cathay Pacific Airways (☎1-800/233-2742). Los Angeles and Vancouver to Bombay (via Hong Kong).

China Air Lines (☎1-800/227-5118). Los Angeles and San Francisco to Bangkok and Delhi (via Taipei).

Finnair (☎1-800/950-5000). New York and Miami to Bangkok (via Helsinki).

Garuda Indonesia (☎1-800/342-7832 in US; ☎1-800/663-2254 in Canada). Los Angeles to Bangkok (via Jakarta).

KLM (☎1-800/374-7747 in US; ☎1-800/361-5073 in Canada). Major US and Canadian cities to Delhi and Calcutta (via Amsterdam).

Korean Air (☎1-800/438-5000). Several US and Canadian cities to Bangkok (via Seoul).

Kuwait Airways (☎1-800/458-9248). New York and Chicago to Delhi (via London).

LOT Polish Airlines (☎1-800/223-0593 in US; ☎1-800/361-1017 in Canada). New York and Chicago to Bangkok (via Warsaw).

airlines fly to Delhi, Bangkok and other Asian cities, where you can catch a connecting flight to Kathmandu, so when seat availability is tight it's well worth asking about alternative routings.

Seasonal considerations may help determine your route. Most airlines flying east (over the Atlantic) consider high season to be summer and the period right around Christmas; low season is winter (excluding Christmas), spring and sometimes autumn. Flying west (over the Pacific), high season is generally summer and midwinter, with everything else being low season. The difference between high- and low-season fares is $100–200. Note that flying on weekends ordinarily adds $100 or so to a round-trip fare; prices quoted below assume midweek travel in low season.

A **round-the-world ticket** originating in the US and including stops in Delhi and Bangkok will typically cost $1500 and up. From Canada, figure on Can$2000. Most off-the-shelf tickets don't include Kathmandu in the itinerary, forcing you to buy a separate Delhi–Kathmandu ticket (US$250/Can$300) or travel overland (see below). Some agents may be able to put together a ticket that has you travelling overland at your own expense from Delhi to Kathmandu and then flying from there to Bangkok.

FROM EAST AND CENTRAL USA

Flying eastwards, you'll stop over somewhere in Europe (usually London), and probably again somewhere in the Gulf. Figure on at least twenty hours' total travel time.

The cheapest deals going east tend to be with *PIA* out of **New York** (via Karachi). Sold through several New York consolidators (see box below),

Malaysia Airlines (☎1-800/421-8641). Los Angeles and Vancouver to Delhi and Bangkok (via Kuala Lumpur).

Northwest Airlines (☎1-800/447-4747). Los Angeles and Seattle to Hong Kong, Bangkok and Singapore (via Tokyo).

United Airlines (☎1-800/538-2929). Los Angeles and San Francisco to Bangkok (via Tokyo or Taipei).

DISCOUNT AGENTS IN NORTH AMERICA

Air Brokers International, 323 Geary St, Suite 411, San Francisco, CA 94102 (☎1-800/883-3273 or 415/397-1383). Consolidator, RTW specialist.

Airtech, 584 Broadway, Suite 1007, New York, NY 10012(☎1-800/575-TECH or 212/219-7000). Standby seat broker/consolidator.

Amsag Travel, 292 Madison Ave, New York, NY 10017 (☎1-800/683-4200 or 212/696-5200). Discount agent/consolidator.

Council Travel, 205 E 42nd St, New York, NY 10017 (☎1-800/226-8624 or 212/661-1450), and branches in many other US cities. Student/youth discount travel agency.

Educational Travel Center, 438 N Frances St, Madison, WI 53703 (☎1-800/747-5551 or 608/256-5551). Student/youth and consolidated fares.

Fly Time, 45 W 34th St, Suite 305, New York, NY 10001 (☎212/760-3737). Consolidator.

Maazda Travel, 9100 Wilshire Blvd, Suite 423, Beverly Hills, CA 90212 (☎310/273-9100). Consolidator.

Skylink, 265 Madison Ave, 5th Floor, New York, NY 10016 (☎1-800/AIR-ONLY or 212/599-0430) with branches in Chicago, Los Angeles, Toronto, and Washington DC. Consolidator.

STA Travel, 48 East 11th St, New York, NY 10003 (☎1-800/777-0112 or 212/627-3111), and other branches in the Los Angeles, San Francisco and Boston areas. Worldwide discount travel firm specializing in student/youth fares and travel services.

Third Eye Travel, 33220 Sandpiper Place, Fremont, CA 94555 (☎1-800/456-3393 or 510/487-9010). Travel agent specializing in Nepal.

Town & Country Travels, 6603 Sunset Blvd, Hollywood, CA 90028 (☎213/464-1214). Consolidator.

Travel CUTS, 187 College St, Toronto, ON M5T 1P7 (☎416/979-2406), and other branches all over Canada. Discount firm specializing in student fares, IDs and other travel services.

Travel Universe, 104 E 40th St, Suite 111, New York, NY 10016 (☎212/867-4303). Agent/consolidator.

these tickets can be had for as little as $1100 in low season. Marked-down tickets on several other carriers (notably *Air India, British Airways, Air France, KLM* and *Lufthansa)* are frequently sold by consolidators starting at around $1250. These tickets often have you crossing the Atlantic with one airline and then switching to another – there are any number of permutations, but it's common to change at London, Frankfurt or Delhi to connect with *RNAC. RNAC*'s low-season fare from New York, which includes a connecting flight on *Northwest*, is $1400.

The story is similar from **other Eastern and Midwestern cities**, but fares are $150–300 higher. In many cases the cheapest option will be to go via New York to take advantage of the rock-bottom consolidated fares from there. From the Midwest, flying west via Los Angeles (see below)

may not cost any more, in case you've got a Far Eastern stopover in mind.

FROM WEST COAST USA

From the West Coast, it takes about the same time to fly eastwards or westwards – a minimum of 24 hours' total travel time – but westbound airfares are generally cheaper. *Singapore* and *Thai* fly direct from **Los Angeles** to Kathmandu via their respective capitals; tickets on *Thai* are heavily discounted through a couple of West Coast consolidators (see box). Many other airlines (*Cathay Pacific, Malaysia, Korean, China Air Lines, United* and *Northwest*) can take you as far as Hong Kong, Bangkok or Singapore, where you'll typically switch to *RNAC* or *Thai*. The best deals through consolidators start at around $1150. *RNAC* charges $1400 in low season.

MAJOR AIRLINES IN AUSTRALIA AND NEW ZEALAND

AIRLINES SERVING NEPAL

Royal Nepal Airlines, 456 Kent St, Sydney (☎02/9264 7346); NZ Agent: Adventure World, 101 Great South Rd, Remuera, Auckland (☎09/524 5118). Flights to Kathmandu from Bangkok, and Singapore.

Singapore Airlines, 17–19 Bridge St, Sydney (local-call rate ☎13 1011); Lower Ground Floor, West Plaza Building, cnr Customs and Albert streets, Auckland (☎09/379 3209). Flights to

Kathmandu from Singapore, and numerous connecting flights from Australasian cities.

Thai Airways, 75–77 Pitt St, Sydney (☎02/9844 0999; toll-free 1800/422 020); Kensington Swan Building, 22 Fanshawe St, Auckland (☎09/377 3886). Flights to Kathmandu from Sydney, Auckland and Perth, with a one-night stopover in Bangkok required.

OTHER USEFUL AIRLINES

Air France, 12 Castlereagh St, Sydney (☎02/321 1000); 57 Fort St, Auckland (☎09/303 1229).

Air India, Level 18, 44 Market St, Sydney (☎02/9299 1983); 57–59 Customs St East, Auckland (☎09/303 1301).

Air New Zealand, 5 Elizabeth St, Sydney (☎02/9223 4666); Quay St, Auckland (☎09/357 3000).

Alitalia, Orient Overseas Building, 32 Bridge St, Sydney (☎02/9247 1308); 6th Floor, Trustbank Building, 229 Queen St, Auckland (☎09/379 4457).

British Airways, Level 26, 201 Kent St, Sydney (☎02/9258 3300); 154 Queen St, Auckland (☎09/356 8690).

Cathay Pacific, Level 12, 8 Spring St, Sydney (☎02/931 5500); 11f Arthur Andersen Tower, 205–209 Queen St, Auckland (☎09/379 0861).

Garuda, 55 Hunter St, Sydney (☎02/334 9900); 120 Albert St, Auckland (☎09/366 1855).

Gulf Air, 403 George St, Sydney (☎02/9321 9199). No NZ office.

Lauda Air, 143 Macquarie St, Sydney (☎02/9251 6155); Lufthansa House, 36 Kitchener St, Auckland (☎09/303 1529).

MAS Malaysian Airlines, 16 Spring St, Sydney (local-call rate ☎13 2627); Floor 12, Swanson Centre, 12–26 Swanson St, Auckland (☎09/373 2741).

Merpati, 146 Smith St, Darwin (☎08/8941 1030). No NZ office.

Olympic Airways Floor 3, 37–49 Pitt St, Sydney (☎02/9251 2044). No NZ office.

Philippine Airlines, 49 York St, Sydney (☎02/9262 3333). No NZ office.

FROM CANADA

From **Toronto** or **Montréal**, you'll almost certainly fly east. The cheapest discounted deals tend to be out of Toronto on *Air India* (connecting with *RNAC* in London, Delhi or Calcutta), and start at around Can$1600 in low season. Consolidators can also route you through London on any number of airlines to connect with the *Air India–RNAC* route, or use various European carriers (*British Airways*, *Air France*, *Lufthansa*, *KLM* or *Aeroflot*, to name a few) to get you to Delhi or Kathmandu via their respective capitals.

From **Vancouver**, flying west is the clear choice. *Singapore* flies direct to Kathmandu (via Singapore), while several other airlines (*Air Canada*, *Canadian*, *Cathay Pacific*, *Korean* and *Malaysia*) fly to Hong Kong or Bangkok to connect with *RNAC*. Other options are to fly via Seattle (served by *Northwest*), San Francisco (for *China Air Lines* or *United*) or Los Angeles (*Thai*'s US gateway). The cheapest fares are likely to come in at around $1450.

From **other central and eastern cities**, you can go via Toronto, Vancouver or possibly New York or Los Angeles. The latter two are worth considering because of the extremely cheap consolidator flights from there (see above). Most connecting flights to Toronto or Vancouver will add $150–300 to the above fares.

FROM AUSTRALIA AND NEW ZEALAND

Flying to Nepal from Australia and New Zealand invariably means stopping over in a Southeast Asian city. As ever, prices depend on the season. These vary slightly from airline to airline, but

---

Qantas, Chifley Square, cnr Hunter and Phillip streets, Sydney (☎02/957 0111); Qantas House, 154 Queen St, Auckland (☎09/357 8900).

Royal Brunei Airlines, Suite 5208, MLC Centre, Sydney (☎02/9223 1566); Unit 9, 25 Mary St, Brisbane (☎07/3221 7757). No NZ office.

DISCOUNT AGENTS IN AUSTRALIA AND NEW ZEALAND

Accent on Travel, 545 Queen St, Brisbane (☎07/3832 1777).

Anywhere Travel, 345 Anzac Parade, Kingsford, Sydney (☎02/9663 0411).

Brisbane Discount Travel, 260 Queen St, Brisbane (☎07/3229 9211).

Budget Travel, 16 Fort St, Auckland; other branches around the city (☎09/366 0061; toll-free 0800/808 040).

Destinations Unlimited, 3 Milford Rd, Milford, Auckland (☎09/373 4033).

Flight Centres Australia: Circular Quay, Sydney (☎02/9241 2422); 19 Bourke St, Melbourne (☎03/9650 2899); other branches nationwide. New Zealand: National Bank Towers, 205–225 Queen St, Auckland (☎09/209 6171); Shop 1M, National Mutual Arcade, 152 Hereford St, Christchurch (☎03/379 7145); other branches countrywide.

Harvey World Travel, 631 Princes Highway, Kogarah, Sydney (☎02/9567 6099); branches nationwide.

Northern Gateway, 22 Cavenagh St, Darwin (☎08/8941 1394).

Passport Travel, Kings Cross Plaza, Suite 11a, 4010 St Kilda Rd, Melbourne (☎03/9824 7183).

STA Travel, Australia: 855 George St, Ultimo, Sydney (☎02/9212 1255; toll-free 1800/637 444); 256 Flinders St, Melbourne (☎03/9654 7266); other offices nationwide. New Zealand: Travellers' Centre, 10 High St, Auckland (☎09/309 0458); 90 Cashel St, Christchurch (☎03/379 9098); other branches countywide.

Thomas Cook, Australia: 321 Kent St, Sydney (☎02/9248 6100); 330 Collins St, Melbourne (☎03/9602 3811); branches in other state capitals. New Zealand: Shop 250a St Luke's Square, Auckland (☎09/849 2071).

Topdeck Travel, 65 Glenfell St, Adelaide (☎08/8232 7222).

Trailfinders, Hides Corner, Shield St, Cairns (☎07/041 1199).

Tymtro Travel, 428 George St, Sydney (☎02/9223 2211).

UTAG Travel, 122 Walker St, North Sydney (☎02/956 8399); branches throughout Australia.

generally low season runs from mid-January to late February, and from early October to the end of November; high season is mid- to late May, June through August, and early December to mid-January; shoulder season comprises the rest of the year.

Return fares to Kathmandu start at about A$1200/NZ$1300, but a cheaper option is to fly to Bangkok for about A$700/NZ$650 (the cheapest return flight from Sydney is currently *Olympic*'s at A$620) and pick up an onward ticket to Nepal from there. These can be had for around US$140, even in peak season, although obviously this option lacks the certainty of a through ticket, and you might be turned back if you don't have sufficient funds.

Fares to Delhi are about the same as to Kathmandu, so another possibility – although not the most economical one – is to fly into India and fly or travel overland into Nepal from there.

Round-the-world tickets start at A$2300/NZ$2100. For all tickets, the best prices are usually found through the discount agents listed on p.9.

FROM EAST COAST AUSTRALIA

From **Sydney**, *Thai Airways* serves Kathmandu with an obligatory one-night stopover in Bangkok for A$1429/1779, depending on the season. *Singapore Airlines* also flies the whole way, going through Singapore, for A$1465/1850. It often works out cheaper if you change airlines during your journey: several airlines, among them *Air New Zealand*, *Qantas* and *British Airways*, connect with *Royal Nepal* in Bangkok or Singapore, the cheapest combination being the *Alitalia/Royal Nepal* package at A$1190/1645.

FROM WEST COAST AUSTRALIA

From **Perth**, *Thai Airways* flies directly to Kathmandu, wth an overnight stop in Bangkok,

---

SIGHTSEEING TOUR OPERATORS

NORTH AMERICA

Abercrombie & Kent (☎1-800/323-7308 or 708/954-2944).

Adventure Center (☎1-800/227-8747 or 510/654-1879 in US; ☎1-800/661-7265 or 416/922-7584 in Canada).

Cox & Kings (☎1-800/999-1758 or 212/935-3935).

InnerAsia (☎800/777-8183 or 415/922-0448).

Journeyworld International (☎1-800/635-3900 or 212/247-6127).

Mercury Travels Limited (☎1-800/223-1474 or 212/661-0380).

Rascals in Paradise (☎1-800/872-7225). Independent family tours.

UK & IRELAND

Abercrombie & Kent, Sloane Square House, Holbein Place, London SW1W 8NS (☎0171/730 9600).

Cox & Kings, St James Court, 45 Buckingham Gate, London SW1E 6AF (☎0171/873 5000).

Explore Worldwide, 1 Frederick St, Aldershot, Hants GU11 1LQ (☎01252/344 161).

Mercury Travels, 1 Thames Place, Richmond Rd, London SW15 1HF (☎0181/780 3022).

AUSTRALIA & NEW ZEALAND

Abercrombie & Kent, 90 Bridport St, Albert Park, Melbourne 3206 (☎03/699 9766); and 14th Floor, Brookfield House, 17 Victoria St W, Auckland NZ (☎09/358 4200).

Asia and World Travel, cnr George and Adelaide streets, Brisbane (☎07/3229 3511).

Asian Travel Centre, 126 Russell St, Melbourne (☎03/9654 8277).

Creative Tours, Level 3, Grafton St, Woollahra, Sydney (☎02/386 2111).

Far East Travel Centre, 50 Margaret St, Sydney (☎02/9262 6414).

India/Nepal Adventure Travel, 1st Floor, 132 Wickham St, Brisbane (☎07/3854 1022).

India/Nepal Travel Centre, 262 Adelaide St, Brisbane (☎07/3221 4788); branches in Melbourne and Perth.

for A$1319/1609. A ticket on *Singapore Airlines*, via Singapore, is A$1395/1695. A combined *Qantas/Royal Nepal* flight costs A$1370/1760 via Bangkok, A$1412/1686 via Singapore or A$1554/1936 via Hong Kong.

FROM NEW ZEALAND

From **Auckland**, all flights to Nepal go via Sydney. A *Thai Airways* flight entails an overnight stop in Bangkok, and costs NZ$1800/2000, according to season. A combined *Air New Zealand/Royal Nepal* flight, also calling at Sydney and Bangkok, is NZ$1950/2050.

PACKAGE TOURS

Most **tours** of Nepal are based around trekking, rafting, cycling or wildlife-viewing, which are described later in "Outdoor Pursuits". Sightseeing packages do exist, although most treat Nepal as an add-on to India. For a longer (not to mention cheaper) tour, wait till you get to Kathmandu and arrange a customized itinerary with one of the travel agents there. As with trekking, booking a sightseeing tour from your home country can cost as much as ten times what you'd spend by doing things independently (at least £600/US$1000 a week, excluding airfare), but this is the price of peace of mind. A few sightseeing tour operators are included in the box on p.10 (you should note that although phone numbers are given, you're better off booking through your local travel agent, who will make all the phone calls, sort out the snafus and arrange flights, insurance and the like – all at no extra cost to you). You could also try the travel agents listed earlier.

OVERLAND ROUTES TO NEPAL

Several **overland expedition operators** (see box on p.12) run 6- to 18-week trips in specially designed vehicles all the way through to Kathmandu. Expect to pay between £700 and £1500 for the one-way trip from London, depending on the level of luxury.

FROM INDIA

Transport connections between **India** and Nepal are well developed, with travel agents in Delhi, Darjeeling and other major train junctions in the north selling **bus** packages to Kathmandu. However, these are often ripoffs, and in any case it's an easy matter to ride to the border and make your own way from there – you'll almost certainly end up on the same Nepali bus anyway.

Three **border crossings** are of principal interest to travellers: **Sunauli**, the most popular entry point, reachable from Delhi, Varanasi and most of north India (via Gorakhpur); **Birganj**, accessible from Bodh Gaya and Calcutta (via Patna); and **Kakarbitta**, serving Darjeeling and Calcutta (via Siliguri). These crossings are described fully in the relevant sections of the guide. At the time of writing, three others (near Nepalganj, Dhangadhi and Mahendranagar) were also open to tourists,

The classic Asia overland trip is still alive and kicking, despite periodic political reroutings. Leaving Europe behind at Istanbul, the usual route traverses Turkey, angles down through Iran, crosses Pakistan and enters India at Amritsar; Iran is off-limits to US passport holders, however, who have to fly from Istanbul to Karachi.

A list of **adventure travel** operators and agents appears on p.55.

OVERLAND OPERATORS AND AGENTS

UK & IRELAND

Adventure Travel Centre, 131–135 Earls Court Rd, London SW5 9RH (☎0171/370 4555).

Encounter Overland, 267 Old Brompton Rd, London SW5 9JA (☎0171/370 6845).

Exodus Travels, 9 Weir Rd, London SW12 0LT (☎0181/673 0859).

Silk Road Travel, 64 S William St, Dublin 2 (☎01/677 1029).

NORTH AMERICA

Adventure Center (☎1-800/227-8747 or 510/654-1879 in US; ☎1-800/661-7265 or 416/922-7584 in Canada).

Safaricentre (☎1-800/223-6046 or 310/546-4411).

AUSTRALIA & NEW ZEALAND

Adventure World, 73 Walker St, North Sydney (☎02/956 7766); 8 Victoria Ave, Perth (☎09/221 2300); 101 Great South Rd, Remuera, Auckland (☎09/524 5118).

Exodus Expeditions, Suite 5, Level 5, 1 York St, Sydney (☎02/9251 5430; toll-free 1800/800 724).

Top Deck Travel, 8th Floor, 350 Kent St, Sydney NSW (☎02/299 8844).

and others near Janakpur and Biratnagar sometimes seemed to let foreigners through; but public transport to these points is patchy, and you can't be sure ahead of time that you'll be allowed through. Enter the country via one of the conventional crossings to avoid a wasted journey, and if you're up for adventure on the way out, check with Central Immigration in Kathmandu before setting off to find out what else is open.

BY PRIVATE VEHICLE

Nepal used to be *the* place to sell **vehicles** – particularly vans – but an official crackdown on the trade has removed the financial incentive to drive in Nepal (reportedly, however, there are still ways round this). Needless to say, bringing a

vehicle into Nepal is a hell of a commitment, and requires nerves of steel to cope with precarious roads, drunk drivers, slow-moving vehicles, nonexistent law enforcement, horrendous city traffic, parking nightmares, sacred cows and fatalistic pedestrians. The tradeoff is that you don't have to deal with Nepali buses, and you get to go at your own pace, bring lots more gear and have your own personal space.

To import a car or other four-wheeled vehicle into Nepal you'll have to show a **carnet de passage**, a document intended to ensure you don't illegally sell the vehicle in the country. A *carnet* is available from the *AA* or similar motoring organization in your home country or the country where you purchased the vehicle. You'd

CYCLING INTO NEPAL

If you're entering Nepal by bike, here's a brief look at the main routes:

Birganj–Kathmandu. Distance 185km, elevations ranging from 90m above sea level to 2490m. A tremendous introduction to Nepal along the spectacular Tribhuwan Rajpath. Birganj is unpleasant, though, and you'll want to bus it on the final, heavily used stretch.

Kakarbitta–Kathmandu. Distance 540km, elevations 80m–2490m. Adventurous route from Darjeeling through little-visited country, with an obligatory stopover in Janakpur and possible side trips up into the eastern hills.

Sunauli–Pokhara. Distance 185km, elevations 90–1300m. A scenic, reasonably cycle-friendly route offering side trips to Lumbini and Tansen.

Mahendranagar–Pokhara. Distance 750km, elevations 80–1500m. The most rural way from Delhi, passing two great wildlife parks and then joining the Sunauli-Pokhara route.

Kodari–Kathmandu. Distance 230m, elevations 630m–1640m. The only route from Tibet. This Nepal stretch will seem tame compared to the ride from Lhasa to the border.

also do well to come equipped with an **international driving licence**.

You can enter Nepal via any official border crossing (see above). If you've made it this far with a vehicle, Nepal border formalities will seem a breeze – customs might spend an hour or two over your carnet, but you shouldn't have to pay any money. For tips on driving in Nepal, see p.32.

BY BICYCLE

Entering Nepal by **bicycle** involves no special paperwork. The main routes are summarized in the box opposite. "Outdoor Pursuits" (pp.56–58) tells you what you need to know about biking in Nepal.

FROM TIBET

Any advice to do with travelling in **Tibet** is liable to be out of date by the time it's in print, so seek current information before going to Tibet in anticipation of being able to cross into Nepal. However, at the time of writing, China was allowing individual travellers to exit Tibet at Zhangmu (Kodari on the Nepal side) on the Lhasa–Kathmandu highway, but was only allowing groups to enter. Charter **buses** ply a standard three- or four-day quasi-sightseeing route from Lhasa via Shigatze, Gyantse and Tingri to the border, where you'll have to walk a bit (or, if the road is washed out, a lot) and then spend another full day on a Nepali bus to Kathmandu.

If you've managed to **cycle** all the way to Lhasa, you ought to be fit and acclimatized enough to make it the rest of the way to Nepal – but needless to say, this is an extremely arduous journey along an unpaved road, crossing two passes of at least 5000m, and should only be attempted in good weather.

CLIMATE AND WHEN TO GO

It's hard to generalize about the climate of a country ranging in elevation from near sea level to Mount Everest. About the only thing that can be said is that all but a few parts of Nepal are governed by the same monsoonal pattern (see box on p.15), with temperatures varying according to elevation (see chart p.14).

Five **seasons** prevail in Nepal, but these are based on more than just weather: whenever you choose to go, you'll have to weigh other factors, both positive (mountain visibility, festivals, wildlife) and negative (crowds, disease).

Probably half of all tourists visit Nepal in the **autumn** (October to November), and for good

AVERAGE TEMPERATURE AND RAINFALL

	FEB			APR			JUN			AUG			OCT			DEC		
	°C Min Max		rain cm	°C Min Max		rain cm	°C Min Max		rain cm	°C Min Max		rain cm	°C Min Max		rain cm	°C Min Max		rain cm	
Ilam (1200m)	10	18	0	16	25	6	18	25	32	19	25	28	16	25	8	8	18	0	
Janakpur (70m)	9	24	1	16	35	4	24	36	23	25	34	24	20	29	5	10	24	0	
Jumla (2420m)	-3	13	4	3	22	3	13	24	7	15	24	17	6	24	4	-5	15	0	
Kathmandu (1300m)	4	20	3	11	27	6	19	29	29	20	28	36	13	26	6	2	20	0	
Namche (3450m)	-6	6	2	1	12	3	6	15	14	8	16	24	2	12	8	-6	7	4	
Pokhara (800m)	8	21	3	15	30	9	20	29	57	21	29	71	17	26	22	7	20	0	
Sunauli (90m)	10	26	1	18	37	6	24	38	28	26	35	41	21	30	8	10	25	0	

reasons. The weather is clear and dry, and temperatures aren't too cold in the high country nor too hot in the Tarai. With the air washed clean by the monsoon rains, the mountains are at their most visible, making this the most popular time for trekking. Two major festivals also fall during this season. The downside, however, is that the tourist quarters are heaving and hustley, prices are higher and it may be hard to find a decent room, you'll wait ages for food and for trekking permits, and people are short on ready smiles and chat.

Winter (December and January) is not especially cold at lower elevations, but, while it never snows in Kathmandu, the "mists of Indra" make mornings dank and chilly (especially in unheated budget lodgings). Most travellers head down into India, leaving the trekking routes and guest houses fairly quiet – too quiet, sometimes, as many restaurants pare down their menus for the season. This is an excellent time to visit the Tarai, where temperatures are relatively mild.

Spring (February to mid-April) brings warmer temperatures, longer days, weddings and more festivals. The rhododendrons are in bloom in the hills towards the end of this period, and in the Tarai the thatch has been cut, so depite the increasing heat this is the best time for viewing wildlife. All of which creates another tourist crush, albeit not quite as bad as in the autumn. The one factor that keeps people away is a disappointing haze that obscures the mountains from lower elevations, though it's usually possible to trek above it.

The **pre-monsoon** (mid-April to early June) is stifling at lower elevations, and dusty wind squalls are common. People get a little edgy with the heat; this is the time for popular unrest, but also for the Kathmandu Valley's great rain-making festival. Trek high, where the temperatures are more tolerable.

Nepalis welcome the **monsoon** (June to September), which breaks the enervating monotony of the previous months, and makes the fields come alive with rushing water and green shoots. The rains rinse and renew the land. This can be a fascinating time to visit, when Nepal is at its most Nepali, but there are many drawbacks: mountain views are rare, leeches come out in force along the mid-elevation trekking routes, roads become impassable, flights get cancelled, and disease runs rampant as the rising water table brings the entire contents of Kathmandu's sewers to the surface.

THE MONSOON

*Listen to these humming downpours in the night
and the doors to godly pleasures will unfold themselves.*

Lekhnath Poudyal (1885–1966), "Thoughts on the Rainy Monsoon"

Nepal's climate is governed by the **monsoon**, one of the world's great weather phenomena. A seasonal wind (the word derives from the Arabic for "season"; the Nepali word for monsoon is *barkhaa*), the monsoon is driven by extreme temperature fluctuations in Central Asia. As air over the Asian land mass warms in late spring and early summer, it rises, sucking air in from the ocean periphery to take its place. The air drawn from the south, passing over the Indian Ocean, is laden with moisture; as soon as it's forced aloft and cooled (whether by updrafts over hot land, or by a barrier, such as the hills and mountains of Nepal), it reaches its saturation point and drops its moisture. With the arrival of autumn, the flow reverses: cooling over the continent blows dry air outwards, bringing clear, stable conditions.

That's the theory, though in practice this huge, complex system is affected by countless variables such as land temperatures, jet-stream patterns, topography and late-season typhoons. The further inland you are, the harder it is to predict the outcome. Nepal is at the end of the line of the eastern arm of the South Asian monsoon sweeping up from the Bay of Bengal, which means it gets a month or so of **pre-monsoon** – a period of false storms and dry lightning – before the moist air arrives.

In Nepal, the **rains** generally advance from east to west in early to mid-June, and drop more precipitation overall in the east than in the west. They build slowly, reaching a peak in July and early August, then taper off again until clear weather returns by early October. Even at the monsoon's height, however, it doesn't bring continuous torrential rain – more usually it's intermittent showers and longer overnight soaks. Local terrain and other factors can affect rainfall considerably: areas lying in the "rain shadow" north of the Himalaya see very little monsoon moisture, while south-facing slopes may receive precipitation long before the plains to the south do. The latter effect is most dramatic where monsoon winds slam into high ranges with few intervening foothills, as they do around Pokhara.

RED TAPE AND VISAS

All foreign nationals (except Indians) need a visa to enter Nepal. Tourist visas are issued on arrival with a minimum of fuss at Kathmandu airport and at official overland entry points. Have a passport-size photo at the ready, and if possible bring exact change for the visa fee.

Fees change often and without warning, but visas currently **cost** $15 (or equivalent) for fifteen days, $25 for thirty days ($40 for a double-entry visa), and $60 for a sixty-day multiple-entry visa. If you plan on border-hopping between Nepal and India (or Tibet), the double- or multiple-entry option may save some time and money, but it's not essential as you can get a re-entry stamp at any official border crossing (same prices as visas).

Getting a visa from an overseas **Nepalese embassy or consulate** will cut down on paperwork on arrival, but it's really only worth doing if you happen to be in the neighbourhood or if you're one of those people who has to have everything sorted out before you go. The fees are supposed to be the same as those given above, but there are some anomalies. See the box overleaf for addresses.

Tourist visas can be **extended**, up to thirty days at a time, for a maximum of 120 days in a calendar year (150 days given extenuating circumstances). Extensions are granted only at the Kathmandu or Pokhara **Central Immigration** offices – a simple procedure, although high-

NEPALESE EMBASSIES AND CONSULATES

Australia: 441 Kent St, 3rd Level, Sydney 2000 (☎02/264 5909); Moncroft House, 93 Rose St, Essendon 3040, Victoria (☎03/337 0444); 16 Robinson St, Suite 2, Nedjands 6009, WA (☎09/386 2102).

Bangladesh: Road No. 2, Baridhara Diplomatic Enclave, Baridhara, Dhaka (☎02/601790).

Belgium: 149 Lamorinierstraat, B-2018 Antwerp (☎03/230 8800).

Canada: 3/0 Duport St, Toronto, ON M5 RIV9 (☎416/226-8722).

Denmark: 2 Teglgardsstr, DK-1452, Copenhagen (☎3312 4166).

France: 45 rue de Acacias, 75017 Paris (☎4622 4867); 7 bis Allée des Soupirs, 31000 Toulouse (☎6132 9122).

Germany: Im Hag 15, D-5300 Bonn 2 (☎0228/343097).

India: Barakhamba Rd, New Delhi 110001 (☎11/332 9969); 19 Woodlands, Sterndale Rd, Alipore, Calcutta 700027 (☎33/452024).

Italy: Piazzale Medaglie d'Oro 20, 00136 Rome (☎06/345 1642).

Netherlands: Prinsengracht 687-1017-Jv, Amsterdam (☎020/241 530).

Norway: Haakon Viis Gate 5B, PO Box 1483, Vika, 0116 Oslo (☎02/283 5510).

Pakistan. 419 Qamar House, M.A. Jinnah Rd, Karachi 2 (☎021/201 113).

Sweden: Eriksbergsgatan 1A, S-114 30, Stockholm (☎08/679 8039).

Switzerland: Asylstrasse 81, 8030 Zurich (☎01/475993).

Thailand: 189 Soi 71, Sukhamvit Rd, Bangkok 10110 (☎2/391 7240).

UK: 12a Kensington Palace Gdns, London W8 4QU (☎0171/229 1594).

USA: 2131 Leroy Pl NW, Washington DC 20008 (☎202/667-4550); 820 Second Ave, Suite 202, New York, NY 10017 (☎212/370-4188).

---

season queues can run to two hours or more, especially just before and after the week-long festival of *Dasain* in October. The cost is $1 per day, payable in Nepalese currency only. Submit one passport-size photo with your application (instant photos are available from studios near Central Immigration offices). The fine for overstaying is double the amount that you would have paid had you properly extended your visa.

TREKKING PERMITS

A tourist visa is technically valid only in the fraction of Nepal served by roads. To visit anywhere more than about a day's walk off a main road you need to get a **trekking permit** from Central Immigration – even if you don't intend to trek. For most trekking areas, the fee is the rupee equivalent of $5 per week, plus you need to submit two identical passport photos. Central Immigration offices will process simultaneous applications for visa extensions and trekking permits, but you still have to pay both fees.

A trekking permit isn't required for any of the places described in this book *except* the areas covered in Chapter Seven, *The Himalayan Trekking Regions*. You'll find a more detailed discussion of trekking permits there.

COSTS, MONEY AND BANKS

Your money goes a long way in Nepal. Off the tourist routes, it can actually be hard to spend US$5/£3 a day, however willing you might be to pay more. On the other hand, Kathmandu and some of the other tourist traps can burn a hole in your pocket rather faster than you might have expected in the Third World. While even in the capital it's still possible to keep to $7/£5 a day, the figure can effortlessly balloon to $20/£13 or more simply by trading up to slightly nicer hotels and restaurants. The cost of seeing Nepal, then, depends in large part on the proportion of time you spend on and off the beaten track.

The price of **accommodation** varies considerably, depending on where you stay and when. Really basic rooms can almost always be found for $1.50/£1 or less. Prices aren't automatically higher in tourist areas, but most travellers take up the option of paying more for a few creature comforts: figure on $4–10/£2.50–6.50 for a double room in the high season. Off-season rates can plummet by fifty percent or more, but it's up to you to bargain. Prices for single rooms are usually lower, and dorm beds are often available, but you'll generally save money by doubling up.

Food, cheap as it is, tends to be the biggest daily expense for budget travellers. Normally, a tourist dinner will run to $2–4/£1.50–2.50, rising to $8/£5 or more in a really posh place. However, *daal bhaat*, the all-you-can-eat national meal of rice, lentils and curried vegetables, costs less than $1/70p just about anywhere, and you can fill up on road snacks for just pennies.

As long as you stick to buses, the cost of **transport** is trifling. An all-day bus journey will cost $2/£1.30 or less, and the buses are so uncomfortable that you probably won't want to move around very often anyway. However, the stakes go up dramatically if you fly (one-way fares are generally in the region of $50–150/£33–100).

No matter how tight your budget, it would be foolish not to **splurge** now and then on some of the things that make Nepal unique: trekking on your own is quite cheap, but you might prefer to hire a porter for $4/£2.50 a day, or even pay upwards of $20/£13 a day for a fully catered trek; rafting and wildlife trips also work out to be relatively expensive, but well worth it. And few will be able to resist buying at least something from Nepal's rich range of handicrafts.

You'll inevitably pay over the odds for things at first, but don't think of it as being ripped off. So what if you pay Rs100 too much for your first night's lodging? It's all part of the process of learning the going rate of things, which you can't be expected to know right away.

A final point: Some travellers make a wild show of pinching pennies, which Nepalis find pathetic: they know how much an air ticket to Kathmandu costs. Others throw money around too freely, which only proves they deserve to be parted from it. Bargain where appropriate, but don't begrudge a few rupees to someone who's worked hard for them, and try to spend your money where it will do the most good.

THE ALMIGHTY DOLLAR

Nepal's annual inflation rate has been running at 10–20 percent during the 1990s, so by the time you get there rupee prices will probably be higher than those quoted in this book. However, prices in US dollars – still the most coveted foreign currency in Nepal – tend to remain fairly constant from one year to the next, since the exchange rate compensates for inflation. For this reason, hotels and travel operators in Nepal invariably quote their prices in dollars – and in fact most tourist businesses tend to express prices over Rs1000 or so in dollars.

NEPALESE MONEY

Nepal's unit of currency is the **rupee**, which is divided into 100 paisa. At the time of writing, the **exchange rate** was Rs56 to the US$ (£1=Rs84). The Nepalese rupee floats freely against most other currencies but is generally pegged to a fixed rate against the Indian rupee, which at the time of writing was 160 Nepalese rupees to 100 Indian rupees. (Where confusion might arise, it's common practice to refer to the two currencies as NC and IC respectively.)

Almost all Nepali money is paper: **notes** come in denominations of Rs1, 2, 5 10, 20, 50, 100, 500 and 1000. **Coins** are 25 and 50 paisa and 1, 2, 5 and 10 rupees. The smaller, aluminum coins are used mainly for almsgiving.

One minor annoyance of travelling in Nepal is **getting change**. In tourist areas it's no problem, but trying to pass a Rs100 (or larger) note to a village merchant or a riksha driver is sure to invite delays, since few Nepalis can afford to keep much spare change lying around. It gets to be a game of bluff between buyer and seller, both hoarding a wad of small notes for occasions when exact change is vital.

TRAVELLERS' CHEQUES AND CREDIT CARDS

Travellers' cheques are of course more secure than cash, and they bring a slightly higher official exchange rate. Any major brand will do. If at all possible, bring **US dollar** cheques, which are more widely accepted: other hard currencies can only be exchanged at major banks and luxury hotels. The usual fee when buying travellers' cheques is one or two percent, and it pays to get a selection of denominations. (A small amount of hard-currency cash may also come in handy – again, US dollars are best.) Make sure to keep the purchase agreement and a record of cheque serial numbers safe and separate from the cheques themselves. In the event that cheques are lost or stolen, the issuing company will expect you to report the loss immediately to their office in Kathmandu (see "Police and Trouble"). Most companies claim to replace lost or stolen cheques within 24 hours.

Luxury hotels and some of the midrange guest houses accept major **credit cards**, but budget outfits don't. An increasing number of retailers take plastic, but they are likely to use the issuing bank's five-percent commission as a bargaining chip (you can, too). Be wary if a proprietor insists on taking your card out of sight for processing: a con artist can make duplicate impressions to bill fictitious transactions against your account.

BANKS AND CHANGING MONEY

Using **banks** in Nepal is, by Asian standards, surprisingly hassle-free. One national bank (*Nepal Rastra Bank*), two quasi-government ones (*Rastriya Banijya Bank* and *Nepal Bank*) and numerous private ones all vie for tourists' business, as do a horde of government-registered **moneychangers**. The government banks give slightly better rates and/or charge less commission than the private ones. The private banks and moneychangers offer very similar rates once you've factored in commissions, which vary considerably, but some work out better for large transactions, others for small ones.

Private banks are found mainly in larger cities, with government banks typcially providing the only service in smaller places. **Hours** for foreign exchange vary: at least one Kathmandu airport branch operates around the clock, *Nepal Bank*'s central Kathmandu (New Road) branch stays open seven days a week and some private banks keep extended hours, but lesser branches generally change money only Sunday through Thursday 10am–2pm, Friday 10am–noon. Specific timings are given in the guide where they're notable. Moneychangers, confined to tourist areas, keep generous hours – twelve hours a day (usually 8 am–8pm), seven days a week.

Hold onto all exchange receipts, as you'll need them for **changing money back** when you leave. Some private banks in Kathmandu will buy rupees back, as will banks at the Kathmandu airport and at official border crossings. However, they may have trouble giving the exact change equivalent in foreign currency, and they're unlikely to be able to give anything but US dollars. If you're entering India, changing NC into IC is no problem.

Nepal's currency **black market** has been all but killed off by the government's move to make the rupee fully convertible and its lifting of a ban on Nepalese citizens taking hard currency out of the country. All that's left of the black market now is a few touts offering no better than the official rate, and usually a bit worse. The only reason to change unofficially would be if all official outlets were closed. If you do, haggle hard (make sure you know the official rate) and be on your guard for sleight-of-hand tricks.

If you run low on funds in Nepal, by far the best way to replenish them is with a **credit card cash advance**. At least one bank (*Nepal Grindlays*) issues cash advances against *Visa/ Mastercard*, and it charges no commission if you take the money in rupees (of course you'll still end up paying interest on the advance to your credit card company). *American Express* cardholders can similarly draw money at the *Amex* office in Kathmandu.

Having money wired from home is never cheap or convenient, and should be considered a last resort. Funds can be sent via *Western Union* (☎0800/833 833 in the UK; ☎1-800/543-4080 in the US or Canada), and can be collected at *Sita World Travel* (opposite Central Immigration) in Kathmandu. It's also possible to have money wired directly from a bank in your home country to a bank in Nepal, although this is somewhat less reliable because it involves two separate institutions. If you go this route, the person wiring the funds to you will need to know the fax or telex number of the bank the funds are being wired to (see p.124 for a list of major banks in Kathmandu).

HEALTH AND INSURANCE

Health is not one of Nepal's strong points. Sanitation is a problem, and a lot of bugs make the rounds, especially during the monsoon and immediately after it. But don't panic – by coming prepared and looking after yourself while you're in the country, you're unlikely to come down with anything worse than the local version of Delhi belly.

This section deals with health matters mainly in the context of Western-style medicine. Traditional ayurvedic and Tibetan practices are discussed later in the "Spiritual Pursuits and Alternative Therapies" section. For more detailed health advice, refer to the books recommended on p.428.

No **inoculations** are required for Nepal, but hepatitis A, typhoid and meningitis jabs are recommended, and it's worth ensuring that you're up to date with tetanus, polio, mumps and measles boosters. Malaria tablets and injections for Japanese B encephalitis and rabies may also be in order, depending on where and when you go. All of these can be obtained in Kathmandu, often more cheaply than at home, but obviously it's better to get nasty things like injections out of the way before starting your trip.

If you have any medical conditions or concerns about your health, don't set off to a place like Nepal without first seeing a **doctor**. Also, consider seeing a **dentist** before you go – you don't want to have dental work done in Nepal if you can help it.

RECOMMENDED INOCULATIONS

Hepatitis A isn't the worst disease you can catch in Nepal, but the frequency with which it strikes travellers makes a strong case for immunization. Transmitted through contaminated food and water, it can lay a victim low for several months with exhaustion, fever and diarrhoea – and may cause liver damage if mixed with alcohol. Immunoglobulin (gammaglobulin), a serum of hepatitis antibodies, is still the most common inoculation for travellers. Its protection wears off quickly, so the injection should therefore be had as late as possible before departure. The standard dosage is 2ml for one month, up to 5ml for four months. The new hepatitis A vaccine is more effective and lasts longer than immunoglobin, but it costs quite a bit more. A single injection provides

MEDICAL RESOURCES FOR TRAVELLERS

UK

British Airways Travel Clinic, 156 Regent St, London W1 (☎0171/439 9584), with other branches throughout the country. Gives inoculations and sells travel-related health accessories.

Hospital for Tropical Diseases, Queen's House, 180–192 Tottenham Court Rd, London W1

(☎0171/636 6099). Travel clinic offering inoculations and travel health advice.

Medical Advisory Service for Travellers Abroad (MASTA), London School of Hygiene and Tropical Medicine, Keppel Street, London WC1. Operates a 24-hour travellers' health line (☎0891/224100), giving written information tailored to your needs by return of post.

NORTH AMERICA

Canadian Society for International Health, 170 Laurier Ave W, Suite 902, Ottawa, ON K1P 5V5 (☎613/230-2654). Distributes a free pamphlet, "Health Information for Canadian Travellers."

International Association for Medical Assistance to Travellers (IAMAT), 417 Center St, Lewiston, NY 14092 (☎716/754-4883), and 40 Regal Rd, Guelph, ON N1K 1B5 (☎519/836-0102). A non-profit organization supported by donations, it can provide a list of English-speaking doctors in Nepal, climate charts and leaflets on various diseases and inoculations.

International SOS Assistance, PO Box 11568, Philadelphia, PA 19116 (☎1-800/523-8930; in Canada, ☎1-800/363-0263). Members receive pre-trip medical referral information, as well as over-

seas emergency services designed to complement travel insurance coverage.

Medic Alert, 2323 Colorado Ave, Turlock, CA 95381 (☎1-800/432-5378; in Canada, ☎1-800/668-1507). Sells bracelets engraved with the traveller's medical requirements in case of emergency.

Travel Medicine, 351 Pleasant St, Suite 312, Northampton, MA 01060 (☎1-800/872-8633). Sells first-aid kits, mosquito netting, water filters and other health-related travel products.

Travelers Medical Center, 31 Washington Square, New York, NY 10011 (☎212/982-1600). Consultation service on immunizations and treatment of diseases for people travelling to developing countries.

AUSTRALIA & NEW ZEALAND

Auckland Hospital, Park Road, Grafton (☎09/797 440).

Travellers' Medical and Vaccination Centre, Level 7, 428 George St, Sydney (☎02/9221 7133); Level 3, 393 Little Bourke St, Melbourne (☎03/9602 5788); Level 6, 29 Gilbert Place, Adelaide (☎08/8212 7522); Level 6, 247 Adelaide St, Brisbane (☎07/3221 9066); 1 Mill St, Perth (☎09/321 1977). General info/health line (☎1/902/9261 560), inoculations/medications, area-specific advice, lists of English- speaking doctors in Nepal, first-aid/medical kits and post-travel examinations.

Travellers Immunization Service, 303 Pacific Hwy, Sydney (☎02/416 1348). Offers inoculations and general advice.

Travel Health and Vaccination Clinic, 114 Williams St, Melbourne (☎03/9670 2020). Vaccine and anti-malarial advice from continually updated US database, inoculations, first-aid/medical kits and post travel examinations.

Travel-Bug Medical and Vaccination Centre, 161 Ward St, North Adelaide (☎08/8267 3544). Consultations, inoculations, first-aid/medical kits, post-travel examinations.

---

protection for a year; a booster shot within the year increases the protection to ten years.

Typhoid is endemic in Nepal and is also spread through contaminated food and water, but outside of the monsoon it's fairly rare. It produces a persistent high fever, headaches, abdominal pains and diarrhoea, but is treatable. Vaccination

can be by injection (two shots are required if you haven't been inoculated before) or orally – the tablets are somewhat more expensive, but a lot easier on the arm.

The risk-benefit decision on the **meningitis** jab is more debatable. Spread by airborne bacteria (through coughs and sneezes, for example), this is indeed a very unpleasant disease that attacks the lining of the brain, and can be fatal. However, while localized epidemics are occasionally reported in Nepal, normally the chances of catching meningitis are fairly remote. The injection causes few side effects, and lasts for three years.

You should have a **tetanus** booster every ten years, whether you travel or not. Assuming you were vaccinated for **polio** in childhood, only one (oral) booster is necessary during your adult life. Immunizations against **mumps** and **measles** are recommended for anyone who wasn't vaccinated as a child and hasn't already had these diseases.

MALARIA PROPHYLAXIS

Malaria hasn't been eradicated in Nepal – as is sometimes claimed – and the effectiveness of mosquito-control measures appears to be waning. Fortunately, malaria doesn't occur above 1000m, and Kathmandu and most hill areas are higher than this. However, you need to guard against it if you're planning to travel in the Tarai, especially between April and October. It has a variable incubation period of a few days to several weeks, so you can become ill long after being bitten. The best prevention is mosquito netting or repellent (see below). There is no vaccination against malaria, but taking regular "prophylactic" doses of tablets will provide a fair degree of immunity.

Advice on malaria **prophylaxis** changes from year to year, so seek the latest information from one of the medical organizations listed in the box opposite. The basic drug used is chloroquine (trade names include Nivaquin, Avloclor and Resochin), a weekly tablet which you must start taking one week *before* entering the malarial area and continue until three weeks *after* leaving it. However, Nepal has chloroquine-resistant strains, so doctors there also recommend taking daily doses of proguanil (Paludrine) or weekly doses of mefloquine (Lariam). Note that these drugs may cause **side effects** including itching, rashes, hair loss and even sight problems, and it is not advisable to use them for more than two or three months at a stretch. Chloroquine is safe during pregnancy, but the others should be avoided. Incidentally, all these medicines are much cheaper and more readily available in Kathmandu than in Europe or North America.

OPTIONAL MEASURES

Like malaria, **Japanese B encephalitis** is carried by mosquitoes. While it's a potentially

> For advice on **altitude sickness** and other trekking hazards, plus a **first-aid checklist**, see pp.347–350.

fatal disease, it's confined to the more jungly portions of the Tarai during the monsoon, when few foreigners are likely to go there. The inoculation is in the form of two injections, one to two weeks apart.

Although **rabies** is a problem in Nepal, the best advice is just to give dogs and monkeys a wide berth. Vaccination against it is expensive and time-consuming, and probably only worth it if you expect to be spending an unusual amount of time around animals. The pre-exposure ("human diploid cell") vaccine involves a series of three injections over a four-week period, which produces a protective antibody level for three years; if you get bitten, you'll still have to get two more shots, but that's better than the six you'd have to get without the pre-exposure course.

Don't bother with the **cholera** inoculation – few authorities now believe it's worthwhile.

PRECAUTIONS

The lack of sanitation in Nepal is sometimes overhyped – it's not worth getting too uptight about it or you'll never enjoy anything, and run the risk of rebuffing Nepalese hospitality.

A few common-sense precautions are in order, though, starting with the **water**: stick to tea or bottled drinks, or purify water with iodine (for more on this, see the trekking chapter). Many guest houses provide water in drip-filter units, but make sure it's been boiled. Clean or dirty, water is regarded as a purifying agent, and plates, glasses and cutlery are customarily rinsed just before use: if you're handed wet utensils it might not be a bad idea to give them a discreet wipe.

When it comes to **food**, usually it's flashy tourist restaurants and "Western" dishes that bring the most grief: more people get sick in Kathmandu than anywhere else. Be particularly wary of prepared dishes that have to be reheated – the lasagne may look fantastic, but just ask yourself how long it's been sitting there. Nepali food is usually fine and you can probably trust anything that's been boiled or fried in your presence, although meat can sometimes be dodgy. Raw, unpeeled fruit and vegetables should always be viewed with suspicion, and you should always verify that salads in tourist restaurants have been soaked in an iodine or potassium permanganate solution.

You need to be particularly vigilant about **personal hygiene** while travelling in Nepal. That means, above all, washing your hands often. Keep any cuts clean, and treat them with iodine to prevent infection. If you're staying in cheap guest houses, bring a sleeping sheet to keep fleas and lice at bay. Wear shoes at all times, since scabies and hookworm can be picked up through bare feet. Take the usual precautions to avoid sunburn and dehydration.

When travelling in the Tarai, minimize your exposure to malaria by depriving **mosquitoes** of the opportunity to bite you. They're hungriest from dusk to dawn: during these times, wear repellent and/or long-sleeved clothes (watch out especially for ankles), and sleep under netting or burn mosquito coils. Remember, though, that very few mosquitoes carry malaria, so you don't need to worry over every bite. If you do get bites or itches, try not to scratch them as infection may result. Tiger balm and even dry soap may relieve the itching.

Asthmatics and others with **breathing problems** should avoid Kathmandu, where exhaust fumes can be debilitating. Bringing a filter mask of the kind worn by cyclists would be a wise precaution.

AIDS

AIDS is not, as yet, a significant health problem in Nepal, although a small number of Nepali prostitutes returning from India have been identified as HIV positive. Prostitution is not common in Nepal itself, but young Nepali women are frequently lured (or kidnapped) from their homes to Indian brothels, where they are in great demand (see p.411). Your main sexual threat, however, is apt to be other foreigners – use the same precautions that you would at home. Carry condoms with you (preferably brought from home as Nepali ones may be less reliable) and insist on using them.

If you get a shave from a barber, make sure he uses a clean blade, and don't submit to processes such as ear-piercing, acupuncture or tattooing unless you can be sure the equipment is sterile. Should you need an injection or a transfusion, make sure that new, sterile equipment is used; any blood you receive should be from voluntary rather than commercial donor banks.

SELF-DIAGNOSIS

Chances are, at some point during your travels in Nepal you'll feel ill. In the vast majority of cases, it won't be something you need to see a doctor about, and sod's law says it will happen somewhere remote and inconvenient anyway. The following information should help with **self-diagnosis**, although it is *not* presented as a substitute for professional medical advice.

Antibiotics definitely shouldn't be taken lightly: they pre-empt the body's ability to develop its own immunity to the disease, and can increase susceptibility to other problems by killing off "good" as well as "bad" organisms in the digestive system (curd can replenish them to some extent). Some may cause allergic reactions or other unpleasant side effects. Also, the more a particular antibiotic is used, the sooner organisms build up a resistance to it. It's not a bad idea to travel with a course of one or more of the drugs mentioned here, but make sure you have the dosage explained to you. In the case of serious or persistent intestinal problems, you're strongly urged to have a **stool test** done at a clinic (see below), where the doctor can make an authoritative diagnosis and prescription.

INTESTINAL TROUBLES

Diarrhoea is the most common bane of travellers. If it's mild and not accompanied by other major symptoms, it probably won't require any treatment and should pass of its own accord within a few days. In the meantime, however, it's essential to replace the fluids and salts you're losing down the drain – Jeevan Jal, sold in packets everywhere, is a cheap and effective oral rehydration formula. Some people recommend starving the bug, which will at least slow the flow, but the best advice is simply to follow your appetite. Diarrhoea tablets such as Lomotil and Immodium will at least plug you up if you have to travel, although this undermines the body's efforts to rid itself of the infection.

If the diarrhoea comes on suddenly and is accompanied by bad **cramps** and **vomiting**, there's a good chance it's food poisoning, which is brought on by toxins secreted by foreign bacteria. There's nothing you can do for food poisoning other than keep replacing fluids, but it should run its course within 24 to 48 hours. If it doesn't, a course of antibiotic such as ciprofloxacin, norflox-

Some of the illnesses and parasites you can pick up in Nepal may not show themselves immediately. If you become ill within a year of returning home, tell the physician who treats you where you have been.

acin or cotrimoxazole may be necessary (note that resistence to the latter has reduced its effectiveness in Nepal).

If the diarrhoea is more severe, or if you see **blood** or **mucus** in your stools, the cause may be amoebic dysentery or giardiasis (giardia). These also frequently produce a **temperature** alternating with **chills**. Occasionally, dysentery can even produce **constipation**, while giardiasis is often recognizable by **rotten-egg belches** and **farts**. Giardia is more commonly contracted while trekking, and involves one to two weeks' incubation time, which may help you rule it out if you haven't been in the country that long. Both giardia and dysentery are treatable with tinidazole or metronidazole. Again, be sure to keep rehydrating.

Finally, bear in mind that oral drugs, such as malaria pills or the contraceptive pill, are rendered less effective or completely ineffective if taken while suffering from diarrhoea.

FLU AND FEVER

Flu-like symptoms – fever, headache, runny nose, aching muscles – may mean nothing more serious than the latest virus floating around on Kathmandu's bad air. Respiratory infections are easy to catch in Kathmandu and in smoky trailside inns on less developed trekking routes. Rest and aspirin or other pain reliever should do the trick. However, strep throat or a bronchial infection will require an antibiotic course such as erythromycin or amoxycillin. Flu symptoms and **jaundice** (yellowing of the eyes) point to hepatitis, which is treated with rest and a plane ticket home.

A **serious fever** or delirium is cause for real concern. Diagnosis is tricky, but safe to say the sufferer needs to be got to a doctor as quickly as possible. To begin with, try bringing the fever down with aspirin or paracetamol. If the fever rises and falls dramatically every few hours, it may be malaria, which, in the absence of medical help, can be zapped with three tablets of pyralfin (Fansidar). If the fever is consistently high for four or more days, it may be typhoid – again, only if no doctor is available, treat with ciprofloxacin/norfloxacin or chloramphenicol.

MINOR SYMPTOMS

Minor **muscle cramps**, experienced after heavy exercise or sweating, may indicate you're low on salt – a teaspoon of salt will bring rapid relief. Likewise, a simple **headache** may just mean you're dehydrated. (However, a severe headache, accompanied by eye pain, neck stiffness and a temperature, could mean meningitis – in which case get to a doctor pronto.)

Itchy skin is often traced to insect bites – not only obvious ones like mosquitoes, but also fleas, lice or scabies picked up from dirty bedclothes. The latter, a burrowing mite, goes for the webbed spaces between fingers and toes. Shampoos and lotions are available locally. Air out your bedding and wash your clothes thoroughly.

Worms may enter your body through the skin (especially the soles of the feet) or food. An itchy anus is a common symptom, and you may even see them in your stools. They are easy to treat with worming tablets, available from any pharmacy.

ANIMAL BITES

For **animal bites** or scratches, *immediately* wash the wound with soap and water for as long as half an hour, depending on severity, then treat it with iodine, 40–70 percent alcohol or 0.1 percent quaternary ammonium compound (brand name Cetrimide), then hightail it to one of the Kathmandu clinics for a series of five very expensive rabies injections over the course of a month. The disease's incubation period is between ten and ninety days. Ideally, you're supposed to capture the animal alive for observation.

GETTING MEDICAL HELP

In a non-emergency situation, make for one of the traveller-oriented **clinics** in Kathmandu. Run to Western standards, these can diagnose most common ailments, write prescriptions, and also give inoculations. A veritable cornucopia of Indian-manufactured medicines is available without prescription from **pharmas** (pharmacies) in all major towns, but always check the sell-by date.

In the event of a serious injury or illness, contact your embassy (see p.125) for a list of recommended **doctors** in Kathmandu, which is where virtually all qualified GPs and specialists are based. Most speak English.

TRAVEL INSURANCE COMPANIES

Most travel agents will arrange travel insurance at no extra charge. The following insurance companies can be called directly.

UK

Columbus Travel Insurance (☎0171/375 0011).
Commercial Union Travel Insurance (☎01903/893 333).
Endsleigh Travel Insurance (☎0171/436 4451).
Frizzell Insurance, Frizzell House, County Gates, Bournemouth, Dorset BH1 2NF (☎01202/292 333).

International Student Insurance Service (**ISIS**) – sold by *STA Travel* (☎0171/361 6262).
Worldwide Travel Insurance Services (☎01732/773 366).

NORTH AMERICA

Access America (☎1-800/284-8300).
Carefree Travel Insurance (☎1-800/323-3149).
Desjardins Travel Insurance – Canada only (☎1-800/463-7830).
International Student Insurance Service (**ISIS**) – sold by *STA Travel* (☎1-800/777-0112).

Travel Assistance International (☎1-800/821-2828).
Travel Guard (☎1-800/826 1300).
Travel Insurance Services (☎1-800/937 1387).

AUSTRALIA & NEW ZEALAND

AFTA, 144 Pacific Hwy, North Sydney (☎02/956 4800).
CIC Insurance – offered by *Cover-More Insurance Services,* Level 9, 32 Walker St, North Sydney (☎02/9202 8000) branches in Victoria and Queensland.

Ready Plan, 141–147 Walker St, Dandenong, Victoria (☎1800/337 462) and 10th Floor, 63 Albert St, Auckland (☎09/379 3329)
UTAG, 347 Kent St, Sydney (☎1800/809 462).

Hospitals are listed in the Kathmandu and Pokhara sections of the guide; other hospitals are located in Patan, Tansen and the bigger Tarai cities. Most are poorly equipped and the standard of care is variable. Should you be unlucky enough to have to spend time in a Nepali hospital, note that nursing staff do not perform many of what we would consider to be routine functions: relatives are expected to feed patients, change bedpans, monitor IVs and so on.

INSURANCE

In the light of all this, **travel insurance** is too important to ignore. Your travel agent can usually recommend a company, otherwise see the box above.

Policies vary: some are comprehensive while others cover only certain risks (accidents, illnesses, delayed or lost luggage, cancelled flights, etc). In particular, ask whether the policy pays for medical evacuation to your home country. One of the rare policies that pays your medical bills directly is better than one that reimburses you on your return home. For policies that include lost or stolen luggage, check exactly what is and isn't covered, and make sure the per-article limit will cover your most valuable possession (a camera, for instance). Conversely, don't pay for coverage that you don't need, such as too much baggage or a huge sum for personal liability.

The best **premiums** are usually to be had through student/youth travel agencies – *ISIS* policies, for example, cost £38–46/$48–69 for fifteen days (depending on coverage), £44–55/$80–105 for a month, £77–101/$149–207 for two months, on up to £351–484/$510–700 for a year. If you plan to go **trekking or rafting**, check whether the policy specifically excludes such "dangerous activities". You might have to pay extra for this coverage, but without it you could be left footing the bill for an expensive helicopter rescue – worse, the chopper might not even be sent if it looks like you won't have the funds to pay for it.

Before you spend money on a travel insurance policy, though, find out what coverage you already have or might qualify for. For example, if you're eligible for certain student/teacher/youth **ID cards**, by all means sign up, as the health insurance benefit more than pays for the cost of the card (inquire at student travel agencies such as *STA, Council Travel* or *Travel CUTS* – see the earlier "Getting There" sections for addresses). Students also may find that their **student health coverage** extends for one term beyond the date of last enrolment. **Bank and credit cards** (particularly *American Express*) often provide certain levels of medical or other insurance, and travel insurance may also be included if you use a major credit card to pay for your trip (but usually only while you're actually travelling to and from

your destination). **Homeowners' or renters' insurance** may cover theft or loss of documents, money and valuables while overseas. **Canadian provincial health plans** include some overseas medical coverage, although this is unlikely to pick up the full tab in the event of a mishap.

Keep **receipts** for any treatment or medicines that your insurance doesn't cover on the spot. Similarly, should you have anything stolen, report the theft to the police (see "Police and Trouble") as soon as possible, and keep a copy of your statement to substantiate any later claim.

INFORMATION, MAPS AND GUIDES

Nepal's Tourism Department runs on a shoe-string budget, letting the free market fill the gap with a confusing welter of advertising. There are no tourist offices outside the country, and those few in Nepal are chronically starved of printed materials and generally

bereft of maps. They can, however, some-times come up with information on festival dates, local bus schedules and the like.

You'll always get the most useful information from other travellers. Check the informal **notice boards** in restaurants around the tourist quarters for news of upcoming events or to find travelling or trekking companions. In Kathmandu, the neighbour-ing offices of the **Kathmandu Environmental Education Project** and the **Himalayan Rescue Association** can help out with information on trekking routes and conditions. Despite its unabashed advertorialism, *Travellers' Nepal*, a free monthly magazine handed out at the airport and distributed to the big hotels and travel agen-cies, is the best of several sources of what's-on information.

MAPS

The best **country map** you'll find in the tourist bookshops is one produced by *Mandala* on a scale of 1:800,000, which is reasonably reliable

A NOTE ON PLACE NAMES

Even though Devanaagari (the script of Nepali and Hindi) spellings are phonetic, transliterating them into the Roman alphabet is an inexact science. Some places will never shake off the erroneous spellings bestowed on them by early British colonialists – for instance Durbar Square, which according to widely accepted phonetic rules (see p.430) should be spelled "Darbaar". Where place names are Sanskrit- or Hindi-based, the Nepali pronunciation sometimes differs from the

accepted spelling – the names Vishnu (a Hindu god) and Vajra (a tantric symbol) sound like "Bishnu" and "Bajra" in Nepali. This book follows local pronunciations as consistently as possible, except in cases where this would be out of step with every map in print. Having said that, it's often hard to get a consensus on pronunciation – some people say Hetauda, others Itaura; some say Trisuli, others Tirsuli – so keep an open mind while map-reading.

MAP AND TRAVEL BOOK SUPPLIERS

BRITAIN

Daunt Books, 83 Marylebone High St, LondonW1 (☎0171/224 2295).

John Smith and Sons, 57–61 St Vincent St, Glasgow G2 5TB (☎0141/221 7472).

National Map Centre, 22–24 Caxton St, London SW1 (☎0171/222 4945).

Stanfords, 12–14 Long Acre, London WC2 (☎0171/836 1321); 52 Grosvenor Gardens, London SW1W 0AG; 156 Regent St, London W1R 5TA.

Thomas Nelson & Sons Ltd, 51 York Place, Edinburgh EH1 3JD (☎0131/557-3011).

The Travel Bookshop, 13–15 Blenheim Crescent, London W11 2EE (☎0171/229 5260).

Maps by **mail or phone order** are available from *Stanfords* (☎0171/836 1321).

IRELAND

Easons Bookshop, 40 O'Connell St, Dublin1 (☎01/873 3811).

Fred Hanna's Bookshop, 27–29 Nassau St, Dublin 2 (☎01/677 1255).

Hodges Figgis Bookshop, 56–58 Dawson St, Dublin 2 (☎01/677 4754).

Waterstone's, Queens Bldg, 8 Royal Ave, Belfast BT1 1DA (☎01232/247355).

UNITED STATES

Book Passage, 51 Tamal Vista Drive, Corte Madera, CA 94925 (☎415/927 0960).

Chessler Books, PO Box 399-122, Kittridge, CO 80457 (☎303/670-0093). Mail-order mountaineering books and trekking maps.

The Complete Traveler Bookstore, 199 Madison Ave, New York, NY 10016 (☎212/685-9007); 3207 Fillmore St, San Francisco, CA 92123 (☎415/923- 1511).

Forsyth Travel Library, 9154 W 57th St, Shawnee Mission, KS 66201 (☎1-800/367-7984).

Map Link Inc, 25 E Mason St, Santa Barbara, CA 93101 (☎805/965-4402).

Phileas Fogg's Books & Maps, #87 Stanford Shopping Center, Palo Alto, CA 94304 (☎1-800/233-FOGG in California; ☎1-800/533-FOGG elsewhere in US).

Rand McNally, 444 N Michigan Ave, Chicago, IL 60611 (☎312/321-1751); 150 E 52nd St, New York, NY 10022 (☎212/758-7488); 595 Market St, San Francisco, CA 94105 (☎415/777-3131); 1201 Connecticut Ave NW, Washington, DC 2003 (☎202/223-6751).

The Savvy Traveller, 310 S Michigan Ave, Chicago, IL 60604 (☎312/913-9800).

Sierra Club Bookstore, 730 Polk St, San Francisco, CA 94109 (☎415/923-5500).

Travel Books & Language Center, 4931 Cordell Ave, Bethesda, MD 20814 (☎1-800/220-2665).

Traveler's Bookstore, 22 W 52nd St, New York, NY 10019 (☎212/664-0995).

Maps by **mail or phone order** are available from *Rand McNally* (☎1-800/333-0136, ext 2111).

CANADA

Open Air Books and Maps, 25 Toronto St, Toronto, ON M5R 2C1 (☎416/363-0719).

Ulysses Travel Bookshop, 4176 St-Denis, Montréal (☎514/289-0993).

World Wide Books and Maps, 714 Granville St, Vancouver, BC V6Z 1E4 (☎604/687-3320).

AUSTRALIA & NEW ZEALAND

Bowyangs, 372 Little Bourke St, Melbourne, VIC 3000 (☎03/9670 4383).

The Map Shop, 16a Peel St, Adelaide, SA 5000 (☎08/8231 2033).

Perth Map Centre, 891 Hay St, Perth, WA 6000 (☎09/322 5733; ☎08/9322 5733 from May 1997).

Specialty Maps, 58 Albert St, Auckland (☎09/307 2217).

Travel Bookshop, 20 Bridge St, Sydney, NSW 2000 (☎02/9241 3554).

NEPAL ONLINE

A growing amount of information about Nepal can be found on the **Net**. For interactive advice from fellow travellers, try the Usenet discussion groups. To surf for interesting titbits and tales, check out the home pages created by Nepalis studying overseas and by returning travellers; it's also easy to strike up e-mail pen-pal friendships through these sites. In the commercial domain, many of the trekking and adventure travel companies have web sites, and you can get the latest news from Nepal from a couple of Kathmandu newspapers that post their local stories.

Needless to say, the following list of recommended addresses won't remain current for long, but you only have to find one Nepal site to find the rest, since they're well linked.

Ayo-Gorkhali Nepal Link Page <http://www.fiu.edu/~bajracha/pub/nlinks.html> – A great place to start: comprehensive links to other Nepal-related sites on the Web.

Discussion groups <soc.culture.nepal> and <rec.travel.asia> – Unmoderated Usenet groups: excellent for getting answers to specific questions, though bear in mind that firsthand information isn't necessarily accurate or up-to-date information.

Great Outdoors Recreation Pages (GORP) <http://www.gorp.com/gorp/location/asia/nepal.html> – Travellers' tales.

Kathmandu Home Page <http://www.math.grin.edu:80/~pradhan/> – Useful mainly for its Chanakya Page, which contains scholarly articles, economic stats and a list of aid organizations.

Mercantile Communications <http:/www.south-asia.com> – Commercial site representing the *Kathmandu Post*, *Independent Weekly*, *Himal Magazine* and other Nepal-based publications.

Nepal Home Page <http://www.cen.uiuc.edu/~rshresth/nepal.html> – The premier Nepal site, giving access to discussion groups, newspapers, travel information, a festival calendar, photos, development background and even recipes.

Nepal Tourist Office <http://tol.com/govnepal> – Pretty slim pickings.

Nepal Trekking Home Page <http://bena.com/nepal.trek/> – A commercial site offering a mix of useful info and links to trekking companies.

Stego's Little FAQ on Nepal Travel <http://www.cfn.ist.utl.pt/~stego/NEPAL1/> – A topical selection of postings to discussion groups: like the groups themselves, there's a lot there but you have to sift through a large amount of dross.

US State Department travel advisory <ftp://ftp.stolaf.edu:/pub/travel-advisories/advisories/nepal> – Warns of epidemics or unrest when appropriate.

for roads and towns but not at all helpful for trails. A larger (1:500,000) three-sheet version of the same is available through *Maps of Nepal* in Baneswar in Kathmandu (near the *Everest Hotel*). They also sell a series of five 1:250,000 maps put out by the Suspension Bridge Division which, though of no use to trekkers, is highly recommended for mountain-bikers venturing beyond the Kathmandu Valley (a 1:125,000 set is also available, but only a few are available in English). The prettiest map of the country, published by *Nelles*, is appallingly inaccurate – much of it is pure fiction.

Free city maps of Kathmandu, available at the airport and through tourist offices, are adequate for most purposes. Bookshops and street vendors sell somewhat better Kathmandu maps and also ones of Pokhara. Maps of other cities simply don't exist. The Geo-Buch (or Schneider, named after its cartographer) "Kathmandu Valley" is getting out of date, but still indispensable if you plan to do any serious exploring of that area. Free brochures containing sketch maps of national parks and wildlife reserves are available from the Department of National Parks and Wildlife Conservation, Thapathali, Kathmandu, although the office is not used to dealing with tourist queries. For most parks and reserves these maps are the only ones in existence, and they are hard to come by in the parks themselves. The exception is Chitwan National Park, where tourist maps are available. Trekking maps are detailed in Chapter Seven.

All of the above maps are available in the bigger Kathmandu bookshops, and many of them (or at least the Western-published ones) can be found in the overseas outlets listed in the box on p.26.

GUIDES

Hiring a **guide** is a great way to get under the skin of Nepal. You'll have instant introductions everywhere you go, and will probably be invited home to meet the family, which will give a perspective on Nepalis' lives that you couldn't possibly gain on your own. You'll also learn all sorts of things you won't get from a book (Nepali swear words, for instance).

Most people only think of hiring a guide for a **trek** (more on this in Chapter Seven), but a guide is even more essential when tracking **wildlife** in the Tarai parks. A growing number of travellers are discovering that they can escape the crowds of Chitwan by hiring a guide there and then moving on to remoter parks, which are otherwise accessible only on an expensive pack-age. A guide can also save you money when **shopping**.

Would-be guides often position themselves strategically at temples and palaces, but these "pay me what you will" characters often end up blackmailing you for more than they're worth. Better to find one through an innkeeper, travel agent or someone you've already done business with.

An inexperienced guide hired informally may accept as little as Rs200 a day; someone with better English will demand upwards of Rs500 a day, and an agency will charge even more for a licensed guide. Generally, you get what you pay for.

For a list of recommended **books** on Nepal, see p.425.

GETTING AROUND

(or vice versa). Whenever and wherever you travel, the route will probably be new in parts, disintegrated in parts, and under construction in parts.

The usual way to get anywhere is by bus (apart from one short line around Janakpur, Nepal has no rail network), although the odd internal flight, if you can afford it, can save a good deal of time and discomfort. But the best way to experience Nepal is to walk or cycle – which often doesn't take a whole lot longer than going by bus.

BUSES

Travel in Nepal expands to fill the time allotted to it: no matter where you're going, it always seems to take all day (or night) to get there. Distances aren't great, but in a mountainous country there's no such thing as a straight line.

Nepal has one of the least developed **road** networks in the world. Of the few highways that are paved, only one is wide enough for two buses to pass without having to slow down or go over onto the shoulders. Highways are irregularly maintained, and each monsoon takes a toll on road surfaces, so in the space of one year a stretch of road can go from wonderful to hellish

Public **buses** ply every paved road in Nepal, as well as quite a few of the unpaved ones, and tourist services cover a few well-worn routes. The bus network is completely and chaotically privatized – there seem to be as many bus companies as there are buses – but all fares are fixed for public services (not for tourist ones). Fares depend less on distance than on the state of the road and the time it takes to make the journey; for express buses it works out to about Rs10–15 per hour, somewhat less for local buses (see box on p.30).

Open-air **bus stations** (*bas park* or *bas istand* in Nepali, and referred to as "bus parks" throughout the *Guide*) are typically located in the smelliest, dustiest and muddiest parts of town. Some cities have more than one bus park to handle services along different routes. Tickets are often sold through syndicates – for example, all night bus tickets from one window or booth, all day buses from another. Destinations may not be written in English, in which case you just have to ask around. In Kathmandu and Pokhara you may find it easier to make arrangements through a ticket agent (but heed the warnings given in the box below), while in other cities with inconveniently located bus stations you can ask your hotel to send someone to buy a ticket for you.

Few travellers are ever quite prepared for the sheer **slowness** of bus travel in Nepal. Allowing for bad roads, overloaded buses, tea stops, meal stops, police checks, constant picking up and letting off of passengers, and the occasional flat tyre or worse, the average speed in the hills is barely 25km per hour; in the Tarai it's more like 40kph; on remote, unpaved roads it can be as little as 10kph.

TOURIST BUSES

Regularly scheduled **tourist buses** connect Kathmandu with Pokhara, Chitwan National Park and Nagarkot, and Pokhara with Chitwan and Sunauli. Additional services may start up in time.

The vehicles are usually in good condition and the drivers know what they're doing, making for a much **safer** ride than in a public bus. Tourist buses aren't supposed to take any more passengers than there are seats (though they usually pick up a few anyway), so the journey should also be more comfortable and somewhat faster. Those billed as minibuses are slightly faster still. There

should be just two **seats** on either side of the aisle ("2x2"), making for a roomier ride than on 2x3 buses, and the seats should be reasonably well padded **Luggage** is kept safely stowed under a tarpaulin on the roof, but lock it just to be sure, and keep valuables with you inside.

Tickets are widely touted in Kathmandu and Pokhara. Buses depart from the tourist quarters of those cities, which saves you the trouble of hoofing it down to the bus station (or the expense of taking a taxi). Book seats one or two days in advance. Since tourist fares aren't regulated, and ticket agents often add an undisclosed commission onto the price, it's worth shopping around.

PUBLIC EXPRESS BUSES

Public long-distance services generally operate on an **express** basis. Not that they don't make any stops: besides calling at all major towns en route, an express bus will stop as often as necessary on the way out of town until it's full, and will also let passengers off all over the place as it approaches its final destination. Still, this is a lot better than a local bus (see below), and an express bus will also be much less crowded. Vehicles are reasonably comfortable and drivers reasonably safe.

In addition to those operated by private companies, quasi-government *Sajha* ("cooperative") buses run limited express services between the major cities in central Nepal. Donated by Japan, these converted city buses have less comfortable seats and they can't take luggage on the roof, but they are said to be safer, and in a few cases (noted in the *Guide*) they offer particularly useful connections.

SAMPLE BUS FARES

These express bus fares were compiled when the exchange rate was Rs56=$1. Use them for relative purposes only. **Kathmandu to**:

Barhabise	Rs33	Janakpur	Rs137/156	Pokhara	Rs85/96
Birganj	Rs93 (day)/	Jiri	Rs108	Sunauli	Rs118
	Rs113 (night)	Kakarbitta	Rs255	Tansen	Rs126
Gorkha	Rs50	Nepalganj	Rs178/221	Trisuli	Rs32

Express buses fall into two functional categories. **Day buses** usually cover the medium-distance routes (approximately 6–12 hours) and set off in the morning to arrive at their destination before nightfall or not long after. That means if a given journey takes, say, eight hours, you can be pretty sure that the last bus will depart no later than midday. Day buses may be 2x2s or 2x3s and can vary a lot in comfort level – some are fiendishly short on legroom. **Night buses**, which operate on the longest routes (10–20+ hours), depart in the afternoon or early evening to arrive the following morning. On these you're assured of 2x2 reclining seats with adequate legroom. Between all the lurching, honking, tea stops and blaring music you won't get much sleep, but it does free up time during the day and saves on the cost of accommodation (a prime consideration for Nepali passengers).

Like tourist buses, and unlike local buses, express buses allow you to **reserve seats** in advance. Do this, or you could end up in one of the whoopee seats along the back bench. Fortunately Nepalis don't plan very far ahead, so you can usually get away with buying a ticket just a few hours beforehand; the exception is during the big autumn festivals, when buses are packed with people heading back to their villages and seats get booked up several days in advance. Check the seating chart to see what's available – there will always be one for night buses, though not necessarily for day buses. The ticket should indicate the vehicle number, which is useful for verifying that you're on the right bus. Normally seats can be reserved only at the bus's point of origin; getting on at a major junction along the route may be possible, but you'll probably have to stand.

Express buses usually have a special hold where you can stow your **baggage** upon payment of a fee (up to fifty percent of the seat price). This is a very worthwhile insurance policy against theft, especially on night buses. You'll have to make the arrangements at the bus's point of origin; make sure you get a receipt for your bag, and have any valuables noted on the receipt.

LOCAL BUSES

Serving mainly shorter routes or slow, remote roads, **local buses** are ancient, battered contraptions with seats designed for midgets. Lack of safety is a real concern in these buses, which are often overworked, overloaded and poorly maintained. When you read a newspaper story about a bus plunging into a river, drowning some infeasibly large number of people, chances are it was a local.

With local buses, the idea is to cram as many passengers in as possible – indeed, a bus isn't making money until it's nearly full to bursting, and it can get awfully suffocating inside. This can lead to infuriating false starts, as the driver inches forward and the conductor runs around trying to round up customers, since no local bus will leave the station with empty seats. Once on the road, the bus will stop any time it's flagged down.

Almost all local buses are day services, so as with express day buses, departures tend to be in the early part of the day to arrive at the final destination before dark. They often depart from a different bus park from express buses. Tickets are usually bought on board. Since seats can't be reserved, the only way to be sure of getting one is to board the bus early and wait.

Unless your **bag** is small, it will have to go on the roof; during daylight hours it should be safe there so long as it's locked, but again, keep all valuables on your person. **Riding on the roof** can actually be quite pleasant in good weather, but it's illegal and you'll only be allowed to do it in remote areas between checkposts (except during big holidays, when the rules are relaxed).

TRUCKS

If no buses are going your way, you may be able to get there by **truck**. Mostly they're ungainly

Indian-built Tatas, ferrying fuel to Kathmandu or building materials to hill boomtowns; many in the Tarai are "Public Carriers" – gaily decorated hauliers-for-hire from India. Many do a sideline in hauling passengers, and charge set fares comparable to what you'd pay on a bus. Fully laden, they go even slower than buses. The ride is comfortable enough if you get a seat in the cab, and certainly scenic if you have to sit or stand in the back – either way, the trip is bound to be eventful.

However, trucks aren't licensed as passenger vehicles, and so take little interest in passenger **safety**: watch your luggage. Women journeying by truck will probably prefer to join up with a companion.

If you're really stuck, you could try **hitching**. There aren't many private vehicles in Nepal, though, and anyone you manage to flag down will expect money.

PLANES

Internal flights aren't such a bargain now that tourists are charged inflated dollar prices on all routes. Even so, there may be times when $75 seems a small price to pay to avoid spending 24 hours on a bus, or a week retracing your steps along a trail. The so-called **mountain flight** – an hour-long scenic loop out of Kathmandu – is also very popular among tourists who want to get an armchair view of Everest.

Given Nepal's mountainous terrain, aircraft play a vital role in the country's transport network, especially in the west, where planes are often used to carry in food during the winter. Of the 37 cities and towns with **airstrips**, almost half are two or more days' walk from a road. Most flights begin or end in Kathmandu, but two other **airports** in the Tarai – Nepalganj in the west, Biratnagar in the east – serve as secondary hubs. Popular destinations, such as Lukla in the Everest region, get up to six flights a day, while obscure airstrips may receive only one flight a week. Some operate only seasonally. For frequencies and flight times, see "Travel Details" at the end of each chapter.

Government deregulation of the domestic air sector in the early 1990s has made life easier for air travellers in Nepal. No fewer than four **airlines** – *RNAC*, *Nepal Airways*, *Everest Air* and *Necon Air* – now provide services within the country, and competition between them has helped reduce the delays and uncertainty that marked *RNAC*'s former monopoly. The choice of airlines is greatest on tourist routes, since they're the most lucrative ones; for more obscure destinations, *RNAC* may still be the only option. The airlines use a variety of small propeller **planes** designed for mountain flying. Thermals can make the ride bumpy, and landings on mountain airstrips are always eye-opening.

Book **tickets** through a travel agent, who will have a handle on who's flying where, and when.

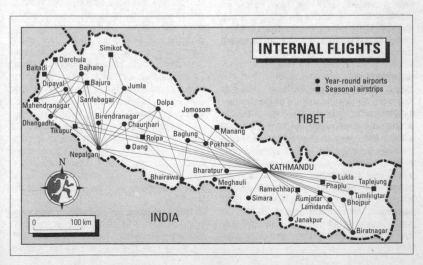

SAMPLE INTERNAL AIR FARES

The following are one-way fares on *RNAC* – other carriers' prices may vary slightly, and they're all bound to go up.

Kathmandu to:					
		Jumla	$127	Pokhara	$61
Bharatpur	$50	Lukla	$83	Taplejung	$110
Biratnagar	$77	Mahendra Nagar	$150	Tumlingtar	$44
Dhangadhi	$149	Meghauli	$72	**Pokhara to:**	
Janakpur	$55	Nepalganj	$99	Jomosom	$50

At off-peak times or away from the trekking routes – in the Tarai, for instance – you shouldn't have any trouble getting a seat. However, during the trekking season, flights out of airstrips along the popular trails may be booked up months in advance by trekking agencies. If you're finding you can't get a seat, all is not lost. Agencies often overbook, releasing their unused tickets on the day of departure, so you may be able to buy a returned ticket from the airline that morning. Otherwise, adjust your schedule and go a week or two later, by which time the agency peak should have tapered off.

Any number of things can delay or cancel a flight, **weather** being the most common. Pilots will not fly if they can't see the ground (sensibly enough, considering some of the places they're expected to land). When planes are grounded, **delays** multiply throughout the system. Since clouds usually increase as the day wears on, delays often turn into **cancellations**. If your flight is cancelled, rather than getting on the next available flight, you may be placed at the bottom of a waiting list; in busy times or during extended periods of bad weather, the wait can be several days. Pad your schedule accordingly.

HELICOPTERS

Charter **helicopter** services have arrived in Nepal in a big way, despite what most travellers would regard as prohibitive costs. *Nepal Airways, Everest Air, Himalayan Helicopters* and *Asian Airlines Helicopters* all offer flights to and from the major trekking areas, as well as scenic tours. Most companies operate French-made Ecureuils, which seat four or five passengers and are designed for mountain flying. *Nepal Airways* also has bigger Russian Mi-17s, which carry up to 27 passengers. Most flights cost $150–250 per person, based on full occupancy, although one-hour mountain flights cost the same as by plane ($99).

CARS

Rented cars generally come with a driver in Nepal. Arranged through a travel agent in Kathmandu or Pokhara, a chauffeur-driven car will cost about $50 a day, but you can hire a taxi (see below) by the day for about $25. Self-drive **jeeps** are increasingly available in Tarai cities, again for about $25 a day, which may be a wise investment if you're planning to explore the remoter game parks. Elsewhere, you're better off not having to grapple with Nepal's treacherous roads and daunting traffic laws (for example, killing a cow carries the same penalty as killing a person – up to twenty years in prison).

If you've brought your **own vehicle** into the country, here are some driving tips. First, drive defensively: Nepalis, normally so good-natured, become impatient maniacs behind the wheel (it has to do with status). Fortunately, it's only in Kathmandu that things get really hairy. Use your horn liberally – when overtaking other vehicles, when rounding mountain bends, or just to remind other vehicles and pedestrians you're there. Observance of traffic signals is fairly lax, and at some four-way junctions you may find the signal only controls traffic coming from two directions. On roundabouts, confusion arises (for visitors) because priority officially goes to vehicles *entering* the intersection, not those already going around it. Drivers use their turning indicators only haphazardly; tempos (see p.33) and minibuses will often pull over without warning, so you have to learn to anticipate their moves. Finally, take special care around pedestrians, who, even in cosmopolitan Kathmandu, sometimes behave as if they've just walked out of the forest.

Filling stations can be found on main roads at the outskirts of all major towns, so it's generally no problem getting fuel. At the time of writing, the cost of petrol was Rs30 per litre.

MOTORCYCLES

You won't exactly be helping Nepal's smog problem by renting a **motorcycle**, but you may well decide that if you can't beat 'em, you might as well join 'em – and there's no denying that motorcycling is a tremendously liberating way of getting around. It's just about the fastest way to travel moderate distances, allowing you to explore more country in less time than on a bicycle, and giving you much more flexibility about where and when to stop than on buses. Almost all rentals are just 100cc models, which aren't suitable for covering hundreds of kilometres a day but are quite sufficient for doing day trips or even touring the country at a leisurely pace.

Motorcycles can be rented in Kathmandu and Pokhara for about Rs400 a day; petrol is extra. You're supposed to produce a driving licence from your home country or an international driving licence, and you'll be expected to leave an air ticket, passport or large sum of money as a deposit. Check brakes, horn, lights and indicators before setting off, and make sure to get a helmet.

Motorcycling carries some **risk**. See the previous section on cars for safety tips, which apply doubly for motorcyclists. Also note that rented bikes carry no insurance – if you break anything, you pay for it. Stick to back roads (they're more pleasant anyway), and beware of wet dirt roads, which can be extremely slick.

BICYCLES

A rented **bicycle** (*saikal*) is the logical choice for most day-to-day getting around. One-speeders (usually Indian-made *Hero* models) are good enough for most around-town cycling: they're incredibly heavy and their brakes are poor, but they're sturdy and have built-in locks.

For a few rupees more, a **mountain bike** will get you there in greater comfort, and is essential for longer distances or anything steep. Even a one-speed mountain bike, with its fatter tyres, better leverage and grabbier brakes, makes an improvement over the old sit-up-and-beg design. However, the models available in Nepal are cheap Indian and Taiwanese imitations of their Western namesakes, and they do not stand up well to rough roads or off-road use – for that you'll need to bring your own. (More tips on mountain-biking are given on p.56.)

Cycles are rentable in Kathmandu, Pokhara and a few other tourist bases. Elsewhere, rental shops are rare, but you may be able to strike a deal with a lodge owner or cycle repairman. Check brakes, spokes, tyres and chain carefully before setting off – the last thing you want is for something to break on a remote mountain road. Repair shops are everywhere, but they won't have mountain bike parts. A bell is pretty well essential if you plan to do any city pedalling. Theft is a concern, especially with a flashier bike – be sure to bring it inside your guest house compound at night.

CITY TRANSPORT

Taxis, identified by black number plates, are confined mainly to Kathmandu and Pokhara, and you'll find details on their idiosyncrasies in the relevant sections. A metered ride should cost about Rs10–15 per kilometre, but on popular tourist routes, fixed fares work out to be around twice that. You can hire a taxi by the day for around $20–40, depending on distance – worth considering to get to certain trekking trailheads with your wits intact.

Tempos – three-wheeled, passenger-carrying scooters also known as *autorikshas* – are nasty little beasts, putting out noxious fumes and jamming city streets, but they're a force to be reckoned with. They come in two forms. The ones with meters, manufactured by *Bajaj*, have room for two passengers (or one with luggage) and are more common than taxis, though only slightly cheaper. *Vikram* tempos, which operate on fixed routes, fit six (barely), set off when they're full, and usually charge only a few rupees per head.

Pedal-powered **rikshas**, common in Kathmandu and the Tarai, are slow and bumpy, but may come in handy for short distances along narrow, crowded streets. Be sure to establish the fare before setting off (Rs5–20 per kilometre, depending on how touristy the place is).

Few cities in Nepal are so large that you're dependent on public transport. Where available, **city buses** and minibuses are usually too crowded, slow or infrequent to be worthwhile, but you may find yourself using them to visit outlying sights in the Kathmandu Valley. Fares are just a few rupees.

ACCOMMODATION

Finding a place to sleep is hardly ever a problem in Nepal, although only the established tourist centres offer much of a choice.

GUEST HOUSES

Most places to stay in Nepal call themselves **guest houses** (this is for the benefit of foreigners; the Nepali word is "lodge"). This category covers everything from primitive flophouses to fairly well-appointed small hotels. By and large, those that cater to foreigners do so very efficiently: most innkeepers speak excellent English, and can arrange anything for you from laundry to bus tickets to trekking-porter hire. Those that serve a mainly Nepali clientele are usually (though not always) more basic, and are less attuned to the peculiar needs of Westerners.

Most guest houses offer a choice of **common bath** or **attached bath**. This is an important distinction in Nepal. It can cost twice as much or more to get a room with an attached bath, but the advantages are obvious: you don't have to wait when the "common" bath is in use (a disaster if you've got the runs), leave your valuables while you shower, or walk up and down halls in partial undress. Note, however, that in cheaper places an attached bath isn't necessarily an asset, as it can make the room damp and smelly if not properly maintained.

The cheeriest and most efficiently run guest houses are highlighted throughout the guide, but remember that recommendations are often self-defeating and can result in instant price hikes. Also, watch out for name changes, which suggest a change in ownership or an attempt to escape a bad reputation.

TOURIST GUEST HOUSES

Kathmandu and Pokhara have their own tourist quarters where fierce competition among **budget guest houses** ensures great value for money – typically Rs100–200 for a double room with common bath. In these enclaves, all but the very cheapest places provide hot running water (though perhaps only sporadically), flush toilets, foam mattresses and (usually) clean sheets and quilts. Most also offer some sort of roof terrace or garden, a supply of (supposedly) boiled and filtered water and a phone. They're never heated, however, which makes them rather cold in winter.

Upmarket guest houses (for lack of a better term) are becoming increasingly popular. These tend to be more spacious, private buildings where there's a lobby of sorts (often with a TV), the rooms have carpeting, furniture and maybe a fan and a phone, toilet paper is provided in the bathrooms, and daily maid service is available; the better ones will provide a portable electric heater in winter. But even in this class, despite assurances to the contrary, you can't necessarily count on constant hot water (many rely on solar panels) nor uninterrupted electricity (power cuts are common). Most quote their prices in dollars (about $5–15 for a double with attached bath) and add ten percent tax on top. Many of them even accept payment by credit card.

Nepal has only a couple of **youth hostels**, in Patan and Pokhara. **Trekking inns** are another matter altogether, and are described in Chapter Seven.

NEPALI-STANDARD LODGES

Off the beaten track, lodgings are geared for **Nepali** travellers. Some are luxurious – in bigger Tarai cities there will usually be at least one upscale place with creature comforts (even air conditioning) – but for the most part Nepalis are more concerned about the quality of the rice than the cleanliness of the bathrooms, so you may have to settle for something less salubrious. Stark concrete floors, cold-water showers and smelly squat toilets are the rule, and often not much

---

ROOM PRICE SCALES

All guest houses and hotels in this book have been price-graded according to the scale outlined below. The rates quoted represent the cheapest available double room in high season – at other times, you should be able to secure a room at a rate of one or even two grades below that given. You should also be able to negotiate a better rate for longer stays. In the lowest categories, the cheapest rooms will generally be those with a "common" (shared) bathroom. Where all rooms come with their own attached bath, this is denoted by a B prefix to the code. Where both common and attached baths are available, two codes are given – for example, ①/B②.

Single travellers can usually expect a discount of 20 to 40 percent off the price of a double.

① Less than Rs100 ($1.75 if quoted in US dollars)

② Rs100–175 ($1.75–3)　　③ Rs175–300 ($3–5)　　④ $5–8　　⑤ $8–12

⑥ $12–20　　⑦ $20–40　　⑧$40–70　　⑨ Over $90

English is spoken. Sheets and cotton quilts are usually provided, but it's a good idea to bring your own sleeping sheet to protect against bedbugs and lice. Noise is always a problem: bring earplugs. In the Tarai, mosquito netting (or mosquito coils) and a ceiling fan that works are crucial.

This is not to say that Nepali lodges are to be avoided. Sometimes the most primitive places – the ones with no electricity, where you sit on the mud floor by a smoky fire and eat with your hosts – can be the most rewarding of all.

HOTELS AND JUNGLE LODGES

It's hard to generalize about the more expensive **hotels**. Most – usually the bigger ones – are overpriced and insulate guests from the Nepal they came to see, but there are a few admirable exceptions which, in their own way, offer unique experiences of the country. After a trek or a long spell of roughing it, a night or two in one of these hotels can be just what the doctor ordered. A government rating system awards hotels from one to five stars, but this is a vaguer guide to quality than price. Rated hotels add between ten and fifteen percent tax, depending on the number of stars.

Jungle lodges and tented camps inside the Tarai wildlife parks are the most expensive

hotels of all. A stay in one is indeed the experience of a lifetime, but if $100–200 a night is beyond your reach there are plenty of more affordable outfits just outside Chitwan and Bardia national parks.

CAMPING

Perhaps surprisingly, **camping** doesn't come high on the agenda in Nepal. Much of the country is well settled, every flat patch of ground is farmed, and rooms are so cheap that camping offers little saving. The only developed commercially operated campground is in Pokhara.

It's a different story, of course, if you're rafting or trekking, and camping is (theoretically) permitted in the Tarai wildlife parks. Long-distance cyclists might also find it useful to bring a **tent** along, to avoid spending nights in roadside flea-pits en route to more interesting places. Between October and May many terraces are left fallow, and you can pitch a tent if you ask permission and you keep out of the owner's way. Set up well away from villages, unless you want to be the locals' entertainment for the evening. Don't burn wood. An unattended tent will probably be safe if zipped shut, but anything left outside is liable to be pinched.

EATING AND DRINKING

Nepal – specifically Kathmandu – is renowned as the budget eating capital of Asia. Sadly, its reputation is based not on Nepali food, but on the skilful aping of Continental and other cuisines: pizza, chips (fries), "buff" (buffalo) steaks and apple pie are the staples of tourist restaurants. Outside the popular areas, travellers' chief complaint is the blandness of the diet.

Yet Nepal lies at the intersection of two great culinary traditions, Indian and Chinese, and if you know what to look for you'll find good, native renditions of everything from tandoori to stir-fried dishes. The simple cooking of the hills – Nepal's heartland – is essentially a regional variation of north Indian, comprising rice, lentils, curried vegetables and meats, and chutneys. In the Kathmandu Valley, the indigenous Newars have their own unique cuisine of spicy meat and vegetable dishes. In the Tarai, *roti* (bread) and the vast range of Indian curries, snacks and sweets comes into play, while in the mountains the diet is essentially Tibetan, consisting of soups, pastas, potatoes and breads.

WHERE TO EAT

Enterprising budget **tourist restaurants** in Kathmandu and Pokhara show an uncanny knack for sensing exactly what travellers want and simulating it with the most basic ingredients. Some specialize in Italian, "Continental", Chinese, Tibetan, Indian, Mexican or even Japanese food, but the majority attempt to do a little of everything; display cases full of extravagant cakes and pies are a standard come-on.

There's no denying that the food is tasty – especially after a trek – but the scene has grown progressively more gross and surreal over the years, and quite a few travellers end up getting sick from the food in such places (see "Health"). And while they won't necessarily admit it, virtually all tourist restaurants rely heavily on monosodium glutamate as a flavour enhancer, which tends to make all tourist food taste the same (and can cause allergic reactions: if MSG gives you trouble, you can try asking for food without "tasting powder").

Tourist restaurants are notoriously hard to recommend, as chefs are forever jumping ship and taking their menus with them. And don't assume that a crowded place must have good food: tourists tend to judge restaurants by their ambience, and in any case the more diners there are, the slower the service will be. That said, a popular restaurant's high turnover should ensure fresher ingredients.

Local **Nepali restaurants** (*bhojanalaya*) are traditionally humble affairs, offering a limited choice of dishes (or no choice at all). Menus don't exist, but the food will normally be on display or cooking in full view, so all you have to do is point. Utensils should be available on request, but if not, try doing as Nepalis do and eat with your hand – the right one only (see "Cultural Hints" for more on social taboos relating to eating). In towns and cities, eateries tend to be dark, almost conspiratorial places, unmarked and hidden behind curtains. On the highways they're bustlingly public and spill outdoors in an effort to win business. Tarai cities always have a fancy (by Nepali standards) restaurant or two, patronized by businessmen and Indian tourists. Confusingly, Nepali restaurants are often called "hotels".

It might take some time before you start appreciating the fine differences between *bhojanalaya* and other traditional establishments. **Teahouses** (*chiya pasal*) really only sell tea and basic snacks, while the simple **taverns** (*bhatti*) of the Kathmandu Valley and the western hills put the emphasis on alcoholic drinks, but also serve basic Nepali meals. Trailside, both *chiya pasal* and *bhatti* are typically modest operations run out of family kitchens. **Sweet shops** (*mithai pasal*), found in bigger towns and identified by their display cases of sweets, also do tea and perhaps yoghurt (usually called curd; *dahi* in Nepali) and beaten rice.

Street vendors sell fruit, nuts, roasted corn, fried bread and, in the Tarai, various fried specialities. But when you're travelling, as often as not the food will come to you – at every bus stop, vendors will clamber aboard or hawk their wares through the window.

Vegetarians will feel at home in Nepal, since meat is considered a luxury. Imaginative preparations are rare, though: rice, lentils, vegetable curry and noodles are the standard offerings everywhere. As a rule, vegetarian dishes get more interesting and varied the closer you get to India, with some orthodox Hindu restaurants near the border billing themselves as vegetarian-only. Tourist menus invariably include meatless items, which are often excellent.

Nepalis generally start the day with nothing more than a cup of tea, eat a full meal around midmorning, then carry on until the second big meal of the day at dinnertime. The Western concept of **breakfast** doesn't tie in very well. Again, tourist restaurants have this covered – many do excellent set breakfast deals, with eggs, porridge, muesli and the like – but out in the sticks you'll have to adjust your eating schedule, or make do with a greasy omelette or packet noodles.

NEPALI FOOD

Daal bhaat tarkaari (lentil soup, white rice and curried vegetables) isn't just the most popular meal in Nepal – for many Nepalis it's the *only* meal they ever eat, twice a day, every day of their lives. Indeed, in much of hill Nepal, *bhaat* is a synonym for food. It's a potentially boring dish, admittedly, and if you spend much time trekking or travelling off the beaten track you'll probably quickly tire of it. That said, a good *achhaar* (chutney) – made with tomato, radish or whatever's in season – can liven up a *daal bhaat* tremendously. The food will be served on a gleaming steel platter divided into compartments; one price covers unlimited refills, except in a few establishments that adhere to the "plate system". Add the *daal* and other condiments to the rice in the main compartment, a little at a time, knead the resulting mixture into mouthsized balls with the right hand, then push it off the fingers into your mouth with the thumb.

You'll often be able to supplement a plate of *daal bhaat* with small side dishes of **maasu**

(meat), marinated in yoghurt and spices and fried in oil or **ghiu** (clarified butter). In Indianinfluenced Tarai towns you can often get *taareko daal*, fried with *ghiu* and spices to produce a tastier variation, and *roti* instead of rice. **Sokuti** (dried, spiced meat fried in oil) is popular in eastern hill areas. **Soups** (*surwa*) are sometimes available: *tama surwa*, made with bamboo shoots, is a favourite. You could make a meal out of rice and **sekuwa** (kebabs of spicy marinated meat chunks) or **taareko maachhaa** (fried fish), both common in the Tarai. If you're invited into a peasant home in the hills you might be served **dhedo** (a dough made from water mixed with toasted corn, millet or wheat flour) instead of rice.

Nepali **desserts** include *khir* (rice pudding), *sikarni* (thick, whipped yoghurt with cinnamon, raisins and nuts) and versions of Indian sweets (see below). Other traditional Nepali dishes are more localized, or reserved for special occasions, but well worth the effort of tracking them down.

NEWARI FOOD

Like many aspects of Newari culture, **Newari food** is all too often regarded as exotic but too weird for outsiders. It is indeed like no other cuisine on earth: complex, subtle, delicious and devilishly hard to make (most dishes require absolutely fresh ingredients and/or very long preparation times).

Most Newari specialities are based around four mainstays, buffalo, rice, pulses and vegetables (especially radish). The Newars use every part of the buffalo: **momocha** (meat-filled steamed dumplings), **choyila** (buff cubes fried with spices and greens), **palula** (spicy buff with ginger sauce) and **kachila** (a paté of minced raw buff, mixed with ginger and mustard oil) are some of the more accessible dishes; others are made from tongue, stomach, blood, brain, bone marrow and so on. Rice, besides being boiled, is also made into **chiura** (beaten rice, a common dry substitute for cooked rice) and **chataamauri** (rice bread). Pulses and beans play a role in several other preparations, notably **woh** (fried lentil-flour patties), **kwati** (a soup made with several varieties of sprouted beans), **musya palu** (a dry mix of roasted soyabeans and ginger) and **bhuti** (boiled soya beans with spices and herbs). Various vegetable mixtures are available seasonally, including **pancha kol** (a curry made with

A GLOSSARY OF FOOD TERMS

The following list should give an idea of what to ask for in restaurants, although tourist places will usually have an English menu.

Basics

Bread	*Roti*	Innkeeper (male)	*Sahuji*	Rice (uncooked)	*Chaamal*
The bill	*Bil*	(female)	*Sahuni*	Rice (beaten)	*Chiura*
Butter	*Makhan*	Knife	*Chakku*	Salt	*Nun*
Chutney, Pickle	*Achhaar*	Milk	*Dudh*	Spoon	*Chamchaa*
Egg	*Phul*	Oil	*Tel*	Sugar	*Chini*
Food	*Khaanaa*	Pepper (ground)	*Marich*	Sweets, Candy	*Mithaai*
Fork	*Kaata*	Plate	*Plet*	Water	*Paani*
Glass	*Gilaas*	Rice (cooked)	*Bhaat*	Yoghurt, Curd	*Dahi*

Common Nepali Dishes

Daal bhaat tarkaari	Lentil soup, white rice and curried vegetables.	*Samosa*	Pyramids of pastry filled with curried vegetables.
Dahi chiura	Curd with beaten rice.		
Pakauda	Vegetables dipped in chickpea-flour batter, deep fried.	*Sekuwa*	Spicy, marinated meat kebab.
		Taareko maachhaa	Fried fish.

Common Newari Dishes

Alu achhaar	Boiled potato in spicy sauce, often eaten with *woh*.	*Kwati*	Soup made with sprouted beans.
		Momocha	Meat-filled steam dumplings.
Choyila	Buff cubes fried with spices and greens.	*Pancha kol*	Curry made with five vegetables.
Kachila	Paté of minced raw buff meat mixed with ginger and oil.	*Woh*	Fried lentil-flour patties served plain (*mai woh*) or topped with minced buff (*la woh*) or egg (*khen woh*).

Common Tibetan Dishes

Momo	Pasta shells filled with meat, vegetables and ginger, steamed.	*Thukpa*	Soup containing pasta, meat and vegetables.
Kothe	The same, fried.	*Tsampa*	Toasted barley flour.

Vegetables (*Saabji* or *Tarkaari*)

Aubergine	*Bhanta*	Coriander	*Dhaniyaa*	Peas	*Kerau, Matar*
Beans	*Simi*	(Cilantro)		Potato	*Alu*
Cabbage	*Banda Kobi*	Corn	*Makai*	Pumpkin	*Pharsi*
Carrot	*Gaajar*	Garlic	*Lasun*	Radish	*Mulaa*
Cauliflower	*Kaauli*	Lentils	*Daal*	Spinach, Greens	*Palungo,*
Chickpeas	*Chaana*	Mushroom	*Chyaau*		*Saag*
Chili pepper	*Khursaani*	Onion	*Pyaaj*	Tomato	*Golbheda*

Meat (*Maasu*)

Beef	*Gaiko maasu* (rare: taboo for most Nepalis)	Chicken	*Kukhuraako maasu*
		Mutton	*Khasiko maasu*
Buffalo ("Buff")	*Raangaako maasu*	Pork	*Bungurko maasu*

Fruit (*Phalphul*) and Nuts

Apple	*Syaau*	Lemon	*Kagati*	Peanut	*Badaam* (*Mampale*
Banana	*Keraa*	Lime	*Nibuwaa*		near India)
Cashew	*Kaaju*	Mango	*Aaph*	Pineapple	*Bhuikatahar*
Coconut	*Nariwal*	Orange,	*Suntalaa*	Pistachio	*Pista*
Date	*Chhokada*	Mandarin		Raisin	*Kismis*
Guava	*Ambaa*	Papaya	*Mewaa*	Sugar cane	*Ukhu*

Spices (*Masaala*)					
Aniseed	*Sop*	Chili	*Khursaani*	Ginger	*Aduwaa*
Cardamom	*Sukumel,*	Cinnamon	*Daalchini*	Saffron	*Kkesari*
	Elaaichi	Clove	*Lwang*	Turmeric	*Besaar*

Some common terms			
A little	*Alikati*	Hot	*Taato*
A lot	*Dherai*	I'm full	*Pugyo*
Another	*Aarko*	More	*Aru*
Boiled (water)	*Umaaleko (paani)*	Spicy	*Piro*
Cooked	*Paakeko*	Stir-fried	*Bhuteko*
Cold	*Chiso*	Sweet	*Guliyo*
Deep-fried	*Taareko*	Vegetarian	*Sahakaari*
Delicious	*Mitho*	I don't eat meat	*Ma maasu khaanna*

five vegetables) and **alu achhaar** (boiled potato in a spicy sauce). Radish turns up in myriad forms of *achhaar*. Order two or three of these dishes per person, together with *bhaat* or *chiura*, and share them around.

INDIAN FOOD

A full description of Indian dishes isn't possible here. The ones you're most likely to encounter in Nepal are from **northern India**, such as **mughlai** curries (thick, creamy and mildly spiced) and **tandoori** meats (baked in a clay oven, called a *tandoor*, with special spices). **Roti** is the accompaniment to north Indian cuisine: *chapati* (round, flat pieces of unleavened bread) are always available in Indian restaurants, *naan* (bigger, chewier and puffier versions of the same), *paratha* (fried bread) usually so. In the Tarai the best bets are **masaala** (meaning spicy, although it isn't really) curries, and you generally can't go wrong with **kofta**, spiced vegetable dumplings in curry.

In Kathmandu you'll also run across **south Indian** canteens, which serve a completely different and predominantly vegetarian cuisine. The staple dish here is the **dosa**, a rice-flour pancake rolled around curried potatoes and vegetables, served with **sambar** (a savoury tamarind sauce) and coconut chutney. You can also get *idli* (mashed rice, usually accompanied with *sambar*), *dahi vada* (lentil-flour dumplings in curd) and various vegetable curries.

And as for the incredible array of Indian **sweets**, well, that could fill a book in itself. A selection: *laddu*, yellow and orange speckled chewy balls; *jelebi*, deep-fried pretzels of sweetened batter; *barphi*, fudgy diamonds made from reduced milk, often decorated with edible silver leaf; *koloni*, a softer version of the same *kudpak*, a thick molasses pudding; *lal mohan*, brown spongy balls in sweet syrup; and *ras malai*, sweet curd cheese blobs in cream. Really good sweets are only found in Kathmandu and the bigger Tarai towns.

TIBETAN FOOD

Strictly speaking, "Tibetan" refers to nationals of Tibet, but the people of the Nepal Himalaya, collectively known as Bhotiyas, together with the people of several other highland ethnic groups, all eat what could be called Tibetan food.

Momo, arguably the most famous and popular of Tibetan dishes, are available throughout hill Nepal. Distant cousins to ravioli, the half-moon-shaped pasta shells are filled with meat, vegetables and ginger, steamed, and served with hot tomato *achhaar* and a bowl of broth. Fried *momo* are called *kothe*. Put the same stuffing ingredients inside a flour pastry shell and fry it and you get *shyaphagle*, a sort of Tibetan meat pie. Tibetan cuisine is also justly celebrated for its excellent hearty soups, usually called **thukpa** or **thenthuk**, consisting of homemade pasta strips or noodles, meat and vegetables in broth.

For a special blow-out, try **gyakok**, a huge meal for two that includes chicken, pork, prawns, fish, tofu, eggs and vegetables, and which gets its name from the brass container it's served in; *gyakok* is only found in tourist restaurants and has to be ordered several hours ahead. In trekking lodges you'll encounter frisbee-shaped items called **Tibetan bread** which, though unappealing on their own, are made more interesting by the addition of honey or peanut butter.

The average Bhotiya peasant seldom eats any of the above: the most common standbys in the high country are **potatoes**, boiled or made into pancakes (*riki kur*), and **tsampa** – toasted barley flour, mixed with milk or tea to make a sort of paste, or eaten plain.

ROAD FOOD AND SNACKS

There's certainly no need to go hungry when you're travelling – fast food and snacks are available at every stop. Since these dishes are prepared ahead of time, what you see is what you get. Common sit-down fare includes **pakauda**, fried, bready nuggets of battered vegetables, served with hot sauce, and **tarkaari ra roti**, vegetable (usually bean) curry served with a few pieces of fried bread that in India would be called puris. Another refreshing possibility is **dahi chiura**, a mixture of yoghurt and beaten rice that isn't so different from the "muesli curd" served in tourist restaurants. If you're in more of a hurry, you can grab a handful of **samosa**, fried pyramids of pastry filled with curried vegetables, or carry away *papar* (pappadums – crispy fried discs made from chickpea flour), *daal paara* (fried lentil patties), *chap* (potato and garlic, battered and fried), *chana* (curried chickpeas), *taareko phul* (boiled egg, battered and fried) or other titbits on a leaf plate.

If nothing else, there will always be packet **noodles** (usually referred to by brand name: Rara, Maggi, Waiwai or Yum Yum), which can either be boiled as a soup or stir-fried as **chow mein**. Roadside vendors peddle *chatpate* (a mixture of peas or soya beans, radish, chilli, salt and lemon, all whisked together and served in a paper cone or on a leaf), roasted peanuts, coconut slivers, corn on the cob and *sel roti* (doughnuts).

FRUIT

Which fruits are available depends on the season, but there's usually a good choice. Lovely mandarin **oranges** (*suntalaa*), which ripen throughout the late autumn and winter, grow from the Tarai up to around 1200m and are actually sweetest near the upper end of their range. Winter also brings **papaya** (*mewaa*) in the Tarai and lower hills, **apples** (*syaau*), grown in higher valleys but widely sold lower down, and **sugar cane** (*ukhu*), a low-elevation crop that requires strong jaw muscles to appreciate. **Mangoes**

(*aaph*) from the Tarai start ripening in May and are available throughout most of the summer, as are **lichis**, **watermelons** and **guavas** (*ambaa*). **Bananas** (*keraa*) are harvested year-round at the lower elevations and range in size from little stubbies to jumbo plantains.

OTHER PROVISIONS

Imported **chocolates** are sold in Kathmandu and Pokhara, and waxy Indian substitutes can be found in most towns. **Biscuits** and cheap boiled sweets are sold at roadside stalls everywhere. *Kwality* **ice cream**, available throughout the Kathmandu Valley and Pokhara, is safe. **Cheese**, a relatively recent innovation produced from buffalo and yak milk, comes in several styles and is sold in tourist areas and "factories" along trekking routes. (In the hills you might also come across *churpi*, a native version of cheese made from dried buttermilk or yoghurt – it's inedibly hard, and is normally softened by being added to soup.)

DRINKS

Tea (*chiya*), something of a national beverage in Nepal, is traditionally brewed with milk (*dudh*) and heaps of sugar (*chini*). Tourist restaurants will make it either way, but you have to specify "black" or "milk" tea (you can also ask for lemon tea – "hot lemon"). Tibetans and Bhotiyas take their tea with salt and yak butter, which is definitely an acquired taste. **Coffee** (*kaphi*), made with instant, is also very milky, almost like a latté. Indian-made espresso machines are getting to be in vogue, but they're usually only used to boil the milk.

Water (*paani*) is automatically served with food in Nepali restaurants – unless you really know what you're doing, stick to the bottled stuff (*Bisleri* and *Star*). Inexpensive **soft drinks** are safe and sold in "cold stores" just about everywhere, but prices rise steadily as you move into roadless areas; *Coke*, *7-Up* and most other international brands are available. Fresh lemon soda, made with lemon (or lime) juice and soda water, makes a good alternative if you want to cut out sugar. Some tourist restaurants serve freshly squeezed **fruit juices**, according to the season, but the mark-up on these is enormous, and roadside juice shacks have turned it into a real racket. Tinned juice and fruit drinks in cartons are widely available. A **lassi**, a blend of yoghurt, water or ice (beware), sugar and fruit (or salt), always goes down nicely, and helps take the heat out of a curry.

Beer (*biyar*) makes another fine accompaniment to Nepali and Indian food. *San Miguel*, *Carlsberg* and *Tuborg*, foreign lagers brewed locally with foreign assistance, have captured much of the market previously held by domestic brands. Of the local beers, *Iceberg* is full-bodied but heavy, while *Star*, the cheapest, is on the rough side. All of these come in 650ml bottles and less often in (non-recyclable) aluminium cans.

An amazing and amusing selection of ersatz **spirits** is bottled in Nepal, ranging from *Ruslan* vodka to *Ye Grand Earl* whisky ("Glasgow – London – Kathmandu"). They're cheap and on the whole nasty, but tolerable if disguised by liberal quantities of soft drinks. *Khukuri 'XXX'* rum is actually quite palatable with Coke. Imported spirits and wine are exorbitant. Look out for regional specialities like the apricot and apple brandies of Marpha, north of Pokhara, and the aniseed-based *dudhiya* (so called because it goes milky when added to water) of the eastern Tarai. Unless you're desperate, give so-called "country liquors" such as *Urvashi* a miss. Shops sell spirits in convenient quarter-litre bottles, restaurants by the "peg" (measure). You can even get improvised **cocktails** in tourist bars.

Nepalis are avid home brewers and distillers. *Chhang* is the generic term for any beer made from rice or other grains, typically fermented in cast-off mountaineering expedition barrels; cloudy (sometimes almost porridgy) unfiltered *chhang* is called *jaand*. *Raksi*, the most popular alcoholic drink in Nepal, is a distilled version of the same and bears a heady resemblance to tequila. Harder to find, but perhaps the most pleasant drink of all, is a brew-it-yourself highland concoction called **tongba**. The ingredients are a jug of fermented millet, a straw and a flask of hot water: you pour the water in, let it steep, and suck the mildly alcoholic brew through the straw until you reach the bottom; repeat four or five times. Two *tongba* can easily lubricate an entire evening.

TOBACCO AND *PAAN*

Nepalis love their **cigarettes** (*churot*). Even if you don't smoke, consider carrying a pack – cigarettes are much appreciated as tips. Factories in Janakpur and Birganj manufacture dozens of cheap brands, most of them from a mixture of Nepali and Indian tobacco. The most popular filter cigarettes are *Surya*, *Shikhar*, *Yak* and *Khukuri*; cheap non-filters such as *Bijuli* and *Deurali* are big with porters. Cheapest of all are **bidi**, rolled single leaves of the poorest tobacco, tied together in bundles of twenty (ask for *ek muthaa*). After the evening meal, old men will often be seen smoking tobacco in a **hookah** (hubble-bubble), or occasionally passing around a **chillam** (clay pipe).

Many Nepali men make quite a production of preparing tobacco **snuff** (*surti*), slapping and rubbing it in the palm of the hand and mixing it with lime before placing a pinch behind the lower lip. *Surti* comes in little foil packets hung outside *kiraana pasal*, village stalls that sell cigarettes, matches, biscuits and the like.

At least as popular, particularly near India, is **paan**, the digestive and mild stimulant that Westerners often wrongly call **betel**. *Paan* sellers sit like priests in their little booths, and ordering *paan* is a hallowed ritual. The *paan* wallah starts with a betel leaf, upon which he spreads four basic ingredients: *katha* (a paste that produces *paan*'s characteristic red colour), *supaari* (chopped or shredded areca nut), *mitha masaala* (a mixture of sweet spices) and *chuna* (slaked white lime, to leach the other ingredients). After that, the possibilities are endless, although in general most *paan* will be either of the *jharda* (tobacco) or *mitha* (sweet) variety. For those who haven't got time for the whole performance, *paan* wallahs also sell foil packets of *paan parag*, a simple, ready-made mix.

COMMUNICATIONS: POST, PHONES AND THE MEDIA

Nepal isn't nearly as isolated as it once was. The post is still slow and patchy, and English-language newspapers and magazines are often hard to find, but satellite TV, international direct dialling, faxes and even e-mail now all make keeping in touch relatively easy.

POST

Mail takes at least ten days, sometimes a lot longer, to get to or from Nepal. Nepal's main **Poste Restante** service, in Kathmandu, is reasonably efficient, the one in Pokhara less so. Mail should be addressed: Name, Poste Restante, GPO, Kathmandu (or Pokhara), Nepal. Letters are filed alphabetically in self-serve pigeonholes. To reduce the risk of misfiling, your name should be printed clearly with the surname underlined or capitalized; it's still always a good idea to check under your first initial, too. Parcels can be received, but they may not arrive intact, so anything of value should be sent registered. Mail is held for about two months, and can be redirected on request.

American Express handles mail only in Kathmandu (see p.124). You need to be carrying *Amex* cheques or a card to use the service. US citizens can receive mail c/o the Consular Section of the **American Embassy** in Kathmandu.

When sending mail home, there's rarely a need to deal directly with the Nepalese postal system. **Private postal services**, found in larger cities, sell stamps and deliver letters for no service charge. **Book and postcard shops** in tourist areas also sell stamps and take mail to the post office for a small (usually 10 percent) fee — just make sure they're reliable. Where no such services or shops exist, take your letters or cards to the **post office** and have the stamps franked before your eyes, or wait to send them from Kathmandu, where they've got a higher probability of reaching their destination. Never use a letterbox: the stamps will be removed and resold, and your correspondence will be used to wrap peanuts.

SENDING PARCELS

Parcels can be sent by air or sea. Obviously sea mail is cheaper, but of course it takes a lot longer (three months or more) and, as it first has to go by land to Calcutta, there are more opportunities for it to go astray.

Again, the private sector is much easier to deal with than the offical postal service. **Shipping agents** and **air freight services** in Kathmandu will shield you from much of the frustration and red tape, and they provide packing materials to boot, but for this they charge almost twice as much as the post office. Be sure you're dealing with a reputable company, though (a few are recommended at the end of the Kathmandu chapter). Don't entrust shipping to a handicrafts shop.

Sending parcels through the post office is thoroughly exasperating. Bring your parcel packed, but open for inspection, to the **Foreign Post Section**, around the corner from the Kathmandu GPO (Sun–Fri 10.15am–1.30pm). You begin by filling out a customs form and paying a small tax on the value of the item (no prizes for being truthful). Then a wizened old man stitches the parcel up in cheesecloth (Rs100–150) and you have it officially sealed with wax, and finally the parcel is weighed (surface rates are Rs500–700 for the first kg and Rs100–250 for each additional kg, depending on destination). The whole business takes an hour and a half even if there's no queue, and you'd be wise to set aside the whole morning.

TELECOMMUNICATIONS

There can be no better illustration of the emerging electronic village than the private **telecom-**

munications **centres** sprouting in Kathmandu and other tourist areas. Like glittering electronic oases, they offer international direct dialling, "call back", fax, "fax back" and e-mail services. Most accept payment by credit card, too. Simpler telephone-only outfits, which advertise themselves with the acronyms **ISD/STD/IDD** (international subscriber dialling/standard trunk dialling/international direct dialling), can be found in nearly every town of consequence. Many **tourist guest houses** also make their phones available to guests. Most district headquarters have government-operated **telephone offices**, which are slightly cheaper but considerably less user-friendly.

INTERNATIONAL SERVICES

Phoning home from Nepal is expensive: about Rs 180–200 per minute from Kathmandu, Rs200–230 from other parts of Nepal. At the time of writing it was only possible to **call collect** from Nepal to the UK, Canada and Japan, but other nationalities can simply have their party **call back** on the same line. Either way, phone centres charge about Rs10 per minute while you're on the phone.

Sending a **fax**, you'll be charged by the minute of transmission time, not by the page. Rates for international faxes are usually Rs10 per minute more than the applicable telephone rate. A standard page takes less than a minute to go through, but you'll probably end up paying for an extra minute if someone answers the phone. It costs Rs25–50 per page to collect an incoming fax (**fax back**) from a private communications centre. You can receive faxes at the Kathmandu GPO (☎977-1/225145) for just Rs5 per page; have the sender spell out your name clearly, underlining the surname, and you'll get a notification of the fax's arrival at Poste Restante. Private centres offering **e-mail** access charge around Rs75 per 1k of data (about half a page of text), which works out slightly cheaper than sending a fax.

TRUNK AND LOCAL CALLS

Private phone centres charge Rs15–50 per minute for **trunk** (domestic long-distance) calls, depending on the distance. Your guest house should let you make **local calls** for a few rupees. (Public phones in Nepal are for now confined to the airport, but this could change.)

While this guide gives local **phone numbers** where they exist, the likelihood that the number will have changed or the other person won't speak English means that you'll seldom use them. If the number has changed, **directory enquiries** (☎197 throughout Nepal) might be able to help, but have a Nepali translate.

THE MEDIA

Despite only forty-percent literacy, Nepal boasts nearly 800 **newspapers** – an outgrowth of two noble Brahmanic traditions, punditry and gossip. A growing number are published in English. Of these, however, only two dailies – the *Kathmandu Post* and the *Rising Nepal* – are widely circulated, and outside the Kathmandu Valley they're usually a day or more out of date. The *Post* is marginally the better of the two; the government-owned *Rising Nepal* carries mainly HMG and palace press releases. Several English-language weeklies are stronger on analysis than news, and are aimed principally at political insiders. The *Independent* (published Wednesdays), the *Sunday Despatch* and the *Commoner* (Tuesdays) are the most readable.

A number of **magazines** are published in English, the most interesting and easy to find being *Himal*, a bimonthly journal of environmental and development issues that's published in Kathmandu but covers all of South Asia. *Face to Face*, *Voice of Child Workers* and *Everest Voice*, all published by nonprofit organizations, tackle development issues on a quarterly basis, while *Spiny Babler* and *Nepal Letters* are literary anthologies.

Foreign publications such as the *International Herald Tribune*, *USA Today*, *Asian Wall Street Journal*, *Time* and *Newsweek* are sold in Kathmandu and Pokhara, but nowhere else. For British newspapers, try the British Council in Kathmandu.

The government-run **Radio Nepal** is by far the most influential of the nation's media, catering to the illiterate majority of Nepalis and reaching villages well beyond the reach of any newspaper. With a daily format of traditional and pop music, news bulletins, English language lessons, dramas and development messages, it has been a powerful force for cultural and linguistic unity, though in

The *Kathmandu Post* posts its Nepal-based reports to its Web site the day after publication. The address is: <http://www.south-asia.com/news-ktmpost.html>

recent years various ethnic groups have pressured the government to provide programming in their native tongues. The station carries English-language news bulletins daily at 8am, 1.10pm and 8pm, and relays the **BBC World Service** in Kathmandu from 11pm to 12.15am. If you're travelling with a short-wave radio, you can pick up the World Service at 15.31 MHz (19.6m) between about 8.45am and 10.45pm. Alternative frequencies include 11.75 and 9.74 MHz.

Nepal-TV, with transmitters in Kathmandu, Pokhara and Biratnagar, broadcasts Nepali and Indian shows mainly in the early morning and evening, with the news in English at 10.15pm – check the daily schedule in the daily papers. Rupert Murdoch's **STAR satellite TV**, out of Hong Kong, beams BBC World Service TV, Channel V (a sort of Hindi MTV), Zee TV (Hindi films), Star Plus (American talk shows and sitcoms) and Star Movies (mostly second-rate).

OPENING HOURS AND HOLIDAYS

Shops in Nepal keep long hours, and in tourist areas usually stay open seven days a week. But when dealing with officialdom remember that Saturday, not Sunday, is the day of rest – and bureaucrats like to knock off early on Friday, too.

In theory, **government offices** and **post offices** are open Sun–Thurs 10am–5pm, Fri 10am–3pm; in winter (mid-Nov to mid-Feb), the Sun–Thurs closing time is 4pm. These schedules often get truncated at either end, though. Most **museums** keep roughly the same hours, except some close on Tuesdays instead of Saturdays.

Moneychangers and some **banks** in tourist areas are generous with their hours, but elsewhere you'll have to do your transactions between 10am and 2pm Sun–Thurs, 10am–noon on Fri. **Travel agents** tend to work a five-day week, 9 or 10am to 6pm, Mon–Fri; airline offices are the same but they take a lunch break at 1–2pm. **Embassy** and consulate hours are all over the place: see the Kathmandu chapter for a rundown.

Complicating matters is Nepal's hectic calendar of **festivals** and **holidays**, which can shut down offices for up to a week at a time. Dates vary from year to year – Nepal has its own calendar, beginning in mid-April and consisting of twelve months that are completely out of step with the Western ones. (The Vikram Sambat calendar began in 57 BC. Thus the Nepali year beginning in April 1997 is 2054 VS.) Religious festivals, meanwhile, are calculated according to the *lunar* calendar (see the next section). Tibetan festivals follow yet a different calendar.

NATIONAL HOLIDAYS

Prithvi Narayan Shah's Birthday – January 10 or 11.

Basanta Panchami – late January or early February.

Shiva Raatri – late February or early March.

Democracy Day – February 18 or 19.

Nawa Barsa (Nepali New Year) – April 13 or 14.

Janai Purnima – late July or early August.

Dasain – a full week off in October.

Tihaar – three days off in late October or early November.

Queen's Birthday – November 7 or 8.

Constitution Day – December 15 or 16.

King's Birthday – December 28 or 29.

Guru Purnima – late June or early July.

FESTIVALS AND ENTERTAINMENT

Stumbling, perhaps accidentally, onto a village festival may prove to be the highlight of your travels in Nepal (and given the sheer number of them, you'd be hard pressed not to). Though most are religious in nature, merrymaking, not solemnity, is the order of the day, and onlookers are always welcome. However, some celebrations, while public, are also personal: don't photograph worshippers without asking permission.

Music and dance are also integral parts of the culture – so much so that they can only be briefly introduced here; for more detailed coverage, see p.397.

FESTIVALS AND OTHER RITES

Festivals are a sophisticated brand of performance art in Nepal, as exotic as the religions that underlie them, which may be Hindu, Buddhist, animist or a hybrid of all three (see *Contexts*). **Hindu events** can take the form of huge pilgrimages and fairs (*mela*), or more introspective gatherings such as ritual bathings at sacred confluences (*tribeni*) or special acts of worship (*puja*) at temples. Many involve animal sacrifices and jolly family feasts afterwards, with priests and musicians usually on hand. Parades and processions (*jaatra*) are common, especially in the Kathmandu Valley, where idols are periodically ferried around on great, swaying chariots. **Buddhist festivals** are no less colourful, typically bringing together

maroon-robed clergy and lay pilgrims to walk and prostrate themselves around stupas (dome-shaped monuments, usually repainted specially for the occasion), chant from sacred texts and make splendid, otherworldly music.

Festival **dates** vary from year to year, as most are governed by the lunar calendar, and determining them more than a year in advance is a highly complicated business best left to astrologers. Each lunar cycle is divided into "bright" (waning) and "dark" (waxing) halves, which are in turn divided into fourteen lunar "days". Each of these days has a name – *purnima* is the full moon, *astami* the eighth day, *aunsi* the new moon, and so on. Thus lunar festivals are always observed on a given day of either the bright or dark half of a given Nepali month. Confused? The easiest strategy is just to consult a current Nepali calendar (sold in tourist bookshops) or, less reliably, a tourist information office. If you've got access to the Internet, you can check the Nepali calendar on the Nepal Home Page (see p.27) before you go.

Similarly jubilant (and public), Nepali **weddings** are always scheduled on astrologically auspicious days, which fall in the greatest numbers during the months of Faagun, Magh, Chaitra and Baisakh (see the festival box overleaf). The approach of a wedding party is often heralded by the sound of a hired brass band – one of colonialism's stranger legacies, sounding like a Dixieland sextet playing in a pentatonic scale – and open-air feasts go on until the early hours. The bride usually wears red – an auspicious colour – and for the rest of her married life she will colour the parting of her hair with red *sindur*.

Funeral processions are understandably sombre and should be left in peace. The body is normally carried to the cremation site within hours of death by white-shrouded relatives; white is the colour of mourning for Hindus, and the eldest son is expected to shave his head and wear white for a year following the death of a parent. Many of the hill tribes conduct special shamanic rites to guide the deceased's soul to the land of the dead.

MUSIC AND DANCE

Music is as common as conversation in Nepal. In the hills, travelling minstrels (*gaaine*) make their

NEPAL'S MAJOR FESTIVALS

Nepal doesn't have any truly national festivals, but the following are the most widely observed events, plus a few notable local ones worth trying to coincide with. Many other local festivals are listed in the relevant chapter.

MAGH (Jan–Feb)

Magh Sankranti – Looking forward to warmer weather and lengthening days, the first day of Magh (Jan 14 or 15) is an occasion for ritual bathing at all sacred river confluences. More bathing takes place on the new-moon day after Magh Sankranti, especially at Devghat.

Basanta Panchami – A one-day spring festival celebrated on the fifth day after the new moon in most Hindu hill areas. School playgrounds are decorated with streamers and children have their books and pens blessed.

FAAGUN (Feb–March)

Losar – **Tibetan New Year** falls on the new moon of February and is celebrated with three days of drinking, dancing and feasting. This is the highlight of the calendar in Buddhist highland areas, as well as in Boudha and other Tibetan settlements near Kathmandu and Pokhara.

Shiva Raatri – Falling on the new moon of Faagun, "Shiva's Night" is marked by bonfires and evening vigils in all Hindu areas, but most spectacularly at Pashupatinath, where tens of thousands of pilgrims and sadhus (holy men) gather for Nepal's best-known *mela* (religious fair). Children collect firewood money by holding pieces of string across the road to block passers-by – foreigners are considered easy prey. Nepalis say the festival is usually followed by a final few days of winter weather, which is Shiva's way of encouraging the Indian sadhus to go home.

Faagun Purnima (or **Holi**) – Nepal's version of the spring water festival, common to many Asian countries, is an impish affair lasting about a week. During this period, anyone – bus passengers included – is a fair target for water balloons and coloured powder (usually red, the colour of rejoicing), and it culminates in a general free-for-all on the full-moon day of Faagun.

CHAITRA (March–April)

Seto Machhendranth Jaatra – Four-day chariot procession through Kathmandu, starting on the eighth day after the new moon; similar to Patan's Machhendranath Raath festival.

BAISAKH (April–May)

Nawa Barsa – **Nepali New Year**, which always falls on the first day of Baisakh (April 13 or 14), is observed with local parades and the like. Bhaktapur's celebration, known as Bisket Jaatra, is the most colourful, combining religious processions with a rowdy tug-of-war.

Machhendranath Raath Jaatra – Arguably Nepal's most spectacular festival: thousands gather to watch as the image of Machhendranath, the Kathmandu Valley's rain-bringing deity, is pulled around the streets of Patan in a swaying, sixty-foot-high chariot. It moves only on astrologically auspicious days, taking four weeks or more to complete its journey.

Buddha Jayanti – Anniversary of the Buddha's birth, enlightenment and death, celebrated at Swayambhu and Boudha on the full-moon day of Baisakh.

SAAUN (July–Aug)

Janai Purnima – The annual changing of the sacred thread (*janai*) worn by high-caste Hindu men takes place at various sacred bathing sites throughout the country on the full-moon day of Saaun. Mass observances are held at Gosainkund, a holy lake high in the mountains north of Kathmandu, and Patan, where it's an occasion for serious splashing.

Gaai Jaatra – A Kathmandu festival in honour of cows (*gaai*), who are said to guide dead souls to the underworld with their tails. On the day after Janai Purnima, revelers wear whimsical costumes and young boys are dressed up in fanciful cow costumes and followed by family and friends through the streets of the old city.

BHADAU (Aug–Sept)

Tij – On the third day after the new moon of Bhadau, Hindu women fast and ritually bathe to wash away their sins and make offerings to their husbands. The most popular bathing site is Pashupatinath, near Kathmandu.

Indra Jaatra – A wild week of chariot processions and masked-dance performances in Kathmandu, held around the full moon of Bhadau.

On the last day, the king receives a special *tika* (an auspicious mark on the forehead) from the "living goddess" and beer flows from the mouth of an idol in Durbar Square.

Yartung – A swashbuckling fair held at Muktinath, in the Annapurna trekking area, featuring horse-racing, dancing, drinking and gambling.

ASHOJ (Sept–Oct)

Dasain (known as **Dashera** near India) – Although Hindu in origin, Nepal's greatest festival is enthusiastically embraced by members of almost all religious and ethnic groups. It stretches over ten days leading up to the full moon of Ashoj, but the liveliest action, as far as outside observers are concerned, takes place on Durga Puja, the ninth day, when animals are sacrificed to the goddess Durga in honour of her victory over demons. On Bijaya Dasami (the "Victorious Tenth Day"), elders bestow *tika*, which on this day consist of a red paste mixed with rice. Dasain is a time for families to gather (buses can get very crowded with homeward-bound passengers), and you'll see swings and miniature ferris wheels set up to entertain the kids.

KARTIK (Oct–Nov)

Tihaar (**Diwali** near India) – The "Festival of Lights" lasts for five days, starting two days before the new moon of Kartik. On the first, crows are honoured as the messengers of death, while on the next three days dogs, cows and bulls are garlanded. More significantly, houses throughout the hills and Tarai are trimmed with hundreds of candles and oil lamps on the third night, called Lakshmi Puja, in the hope of attracting Lakshmi, the goddess of wealth. Trusting in her, many Nepalis gamble on street corners and student groups make the rounds singing "*Diusire*", a form of musical fundraising, during this festival. On the fifth day, Bhaai Tika, sisters give their younger brothers *tika* and sweets. Firecrackers have become a big part of the fun for kids (and a source of stress for everyone else) for weeks around Tihaar time.

MANGSIR (Nov–Dec)

Biwaha Panchami – As many as 100,000 pilgrims converge on Janakpur for this five-day gathering, five days after the new moon of Mangsir. The highlight is the re-enactment of the wedding of Ram and Sita, the divine, star-crossed lovers of the *Ramayan*, one of the great Hindu epics.

Mani Rimdu – Held at Tengboche in the Everest trekking region around the full moon of the ninth Tibetan month (usually Nov), this colourful Sherpa masked dance dramatizes Buddhism's victory over the ancient Bon religion in eighth-century Tibet. A similar event is held in May or June at Thami.

living singing ballads and accompanying themselves on the *sarangi*, a hand-carved, four-stringed fiddle. Teenagers traditionally attract the attention of the opposite sex by exchanging teasing verses. After-dinner singalongs are popular, even in sophisticated Kathmandu, and of course music is indispensable in all festivals.

Traditional Nepali music often gets drowned out by the rising tide of **Indian film music**, with its surging strings and hysterically shrill vocals, and *ghazal*, a more languorous, crooning style of music often performed live in Indian and Nepali restaurants. Yet Nepali folk music still gets a good airing; in contrast, it sounds mercifully calm and villagey. A few tourist restaurants in the budget quarters of Kathmandu and Pokhara host regular free performances by local folk groups.

Nepali music is almost inseparable from **dance**, especially at festivals. Nepali dance is an unaffected folk art – neither wildly athletic nor subtle, it depicts everyday activities like work and courtship. Each region and ethnic group has its own distinct traditions, and during your travels you should get a chance to join a local hoedown or two, if not a full-blown festival extravaganza. Look out, too, for the muscular stick dance of the lowland Tharus, performed regularly at lodges outside Chitwan National Park.

Staged **culture shows** in Kathmandu and Pokhara are a long way from the real thing, but they do provide a sampling of folk and religious dances, and hint at the incredible cultural diversity contained in such a small country. Most troupes perform such standards as the dance of the *jhankri* (shaman-exorcists still consulted by many, if not most, hill Nepalis); the sleeve-twirling dance of the Sherpas; the flirting dance of the hill-dwelling Tamangs; the Tharus' fanciful peacock dance; perhaps a formal priestly dance, to the accompaniment of a classical *raga* (musical piece); and at least one of the dances of the Kathmandu Valley's holiday-loving Newars.

CINEMA AND THEATRE

Nepal's love-hate relationship with India is perhaps best illustrated by its **cinema**: Nepalis might grouse about India's cultural imperialism, but that doesn't stop them rushing to see the latest schmaltz and pyrotechnics from Bombay. Nepali and Hindi are similar enough that movies aren't usually dubbed. Nepali films are still the exception, and are less slick than Indian productions, but much more popular when they're on. **Video** parlours and rental shops are now commonplace in Kathmandu, where kung-fu epics from Hong Kong are almost as popular as Indian imports. Some tourist restaurants screen Hollywood flicks on video, many of them amazingly current – bootleg tapes often hit the streets in Kathmandu long before their official release.

Theatre is poorly developed in Nepal. Occasional (and unpublicized) plays are performed at the National Theatre and, even less frequently, at the Royal Nepal Academy, both in Kathmandu.

SHOPPING

Nepal's handicrafts scene is as rich and varied as its culture, having been influenced by hundreds of years of trade and religious exchange with Tibet and India. In addition, the influx of Tibetan artisans since 1959 has enriched the marketplace immeasurably, while tourist demand, ironically, has helped fuel something of an artistic renaissance. You can pick up distinctive gifts, souvenirs and clothes for a song, or if your budget runs to it, spend a fortune on carpets and *objets d'art*.

WHERE TO SHOP

Ninety-nine percent of crafts outlets are concentrated in the Kathmandu Valley and Pokhara: that's where the buyers are, and just about all of the mass-produced stuff is actually made there. Competition is intense. You can't stroll the tourist strips without being importuned by **curio sellers** cradling "priceless" goods in white cloths, or be beckoned from the sidelines by operators of makeshift stalls; their overheads are low and so, at least in theory, should be their prices. More reputable **shops**, galleries, "emporiums" and boutiques have better selections and aren't as hard-driving (many have fixed prices). In Patan – Nepal's handicrafts capital – you'll also find **"factory" showrooms**, where you can watch the wares being made.

One of the most encouraging developments in recent years has been the rise of **non-profit shops** in Kathmandu and Patan. By providing outlets for women, disadvantaged people and workers' cooperatives in some of Nepal's remotest hill areas, they increase employment and channel money where it's most needed. They also appear to avoid the pitfalls of other development projects in the hills, where lavish foreign aid has often led Nepalis to expect something for nothing.

Quite a few items sold in tourist areas are made elsewhere, though, and needless to say it's more fun (and cheaper) to pick them up at their source. Best buys are noted in the relevant sections of the *Guide*, along with a few local specialities that can't be found anywhere else.

No matter what the seller says, very few items are older than last week. Genuine **antiques** – anything over 100 years old, or anything customs officials might think is that old – have to be cleared for export by the Department of Archeology, Lainchaur, Kathmandu. Get the dealer to take care of the paperwork.

BARGAINING

Except where prices are clearly marked as fixed (and sometimes even then), you'll be expected to **bargain**. Bargaining is very much a matter of personal style, but in Nepal it's always lighthearted, never acrimonious. Sellers always speak English in tourist areas, but everywhere else you'll need some rudimentary Nepali to bargain properly.

There's no firm guide as to what to expect to have knocked off, although prices are usually softer on the street than in shops. The initial asking price may be anywhere from 10 to 1000 percent over the going rate, depending, to a certain extent, on how much like a tourist you look. All the old chestnuts still hold true: never show the least sign of interest, let alone enthusiasm; and walking away will usually cut the price dramatically. But most important is to know what you want, its approximate value, and how much you're prepared to pay. Never start to haggle for something you definitely don't intend to buy – it'll end in bad feeling on both sides. Similarly, don't let a figure pass your lips that you're not prepared to pay. Having mentioned a price, you are obliged to pay it.

If you're contemplating making a big purchase, hiring a knowledgeable **guide** may save you money many times over what you spend on the guide's fee – but make absolutely sure you're getting independent counsel, and not just being taken on a tour of brother-in-laws' shops.

STATUES AND OTHER METALWARE

Artisans of the Kathmandu Valley have been casting bronze, brass and copper **statues** of Buddhist and Hindu deities for at least 1300 years – an unbroken artistic tradition with few parallels worldwide. The images are produced by the lost-wax process, in which a model is carved out of wax, surrounded by clay and then fired, melting the wax and leaving a terracotta mould. Small pieces can be cast from a single mould, but larger ones have to be assembled from up to a dozen pieces, the joins concealed by ornate embellishments.

Statues are cast mainly in the **style** of Tibet (Nepal's main customer for centuries), depicting a tremendous variety of Buddhas, *bodhisattva* and defenders of the *dharma*, as well as Hindu and indigenous deities. Each is characterized by a certain posture, weapon or other identifying feature. If you're shopping for a metal statue, the Handicraft Association of Nepal's inexpensive booklet, *A Short Description of Gods, Goddesses and Ritual Objects of Buddhism and Hinduism in Nepal*, sold in some bookshops, can help in figuring out the iconography.

Patan is the traditional casting centre. **Prices** depend on size, metal and workmanship, but are never cheap – at least Rs5000 for a 20cm-tall image. The best-quality images will have carefully detailed fingers and eyes, and the metal will be without pits or spots.

Many brass **pots** and **vessels** are wonderful pieces of design. *Ghada*, the brass water jugs that Nepali women cradle against one hip, may be too big to tote home, but small incense holders, *raksi* pourers, *puja* trays, oil lamps and *jal* urns are all attractive and relatively cheap.

So-called **singing bowls** are popular both as domestic and ritual objects. Made from an amalgam of various (traditionally seven) metals, these vessels produce a continuous harmonic ringing when rubbed around the rim with a wooden pestle. When held near the navel, the singing bowl is said to resonate with the body and aid in meditation.

JEWELLERY

Every hill bazaar has its metalsmiths who sell **gold** and **silver** at the going rate and, for a modest charge, will tap it into an earring, nose ring, necklace clasp, bracelet or any other form in which a woman wants to display the family wealth. Common to almost all hill women are *pote*, a necklace consisting strands of glass beads drawn together with a cylindrical gold ornament. Shops in Kathmandu sell **jewellery** made of silver, white metal and semiprecious stones, which, though designed entirely for the tourist market, are nonetheless attractive.

Gem sellers in Kathmandu deal in a wide range of cut and uncut stones at reasonable prices (though they're cheaper in Agra in India). Garnet, tourmaline, ruby, aquamarine, citrine ("golden topaz") and cat's eye come from mines in Nepal's Ganesh Himal and eastern hills; turquoise, amethyst and sapphire come from Tibet, coral from India and lapis lazuli from Afghanistan. Most stones are cut and polished in India. Take care when buying, as gem quality and cut can make a vast difference to value. Turquoise is often fake (bite it to see if the colour comes off).

WOOD, PAPIER MÂCHÉ AND PAPER

Nepali **woodcarving** reaches its apex in Bhaktapur, where you'll find everything from modest Buddha busts and Ganesh figures to exquisite, full-size window frames. Miniature replicas of Bhaktapur's famed Peacock Window are ubiquitous, and artisans are increasingly turning out non-traditional items such as animals, cassette boxes and chess sets. Pieces are carved with mallet and chisel out of one of several types of wood, most of them from the Tarai. The most common are *sal*, a hard, heavy, chocolate-coloured wood like teak; *sisu*, similar but with more grain to it; *chaab*, a cheaper, softer, honey-coloured wood; and *korma*, also light in colour but harder than *chaab*. Prices depend not only on size but also the type of wood and the quality of carving: Rs1000 should get you a finely detailed 20cm figure.

Wooden masks are used by Tibetans and highland Nepalis in religious dances and shamanic rituals. The genuine articles are rarely sold, but replicas are widely available in tourist areas; in the never-ending battle for tourists' attention, craftsmen are now souping up their masks with overlain metal designs.

Thimi is famous for its **papier mâché masks**, copies of those used in the masked dances of the Kathmandu Valley in which dancers take on the persona of the deity represented. The Nawa Durga (Nine Durgas) and their attendant deities Ganesh, Shiva and Bhairab are the ones most commonly recreated for tourist consumption, ranging from full size down to bite size. The Nawa Durga also take the form of **puppets** with clay or papier mâché heads and multiple wooden arms.

Lokta, an indigenous form of **handmade paper**, makes a fine, portable purchase. In winter, when there's little else going on, hill people gather the bark of the *daphne* bush, boil it, beat it to a pulp, mix it with water, pour the mixture into floating frames, and finally sun-dry it on fallow terraces. The result is a rough but richly textured parchment which is then block-printed to produce calendars, stationery and greeting cards.

CARPETS

Tibetan-style hand-woven **carpets** have come a long way from their folk roots. What started out, thirty years ago, as a modest income-generator for Tibetan refugees has become far and away Nepal's biggest export item – and a multi-ethnic creative collaboration. The traditional Tibetan form has been reinvented, with a unique look and lustrous, hard-wearing texture brought about by the use of synthetic dyes, blended Tibetan and New Zealand wool, standardized manufacture and modern chemical washing processes. In recent years the field has been enlivened by an explosion of contemporary colour schemes and designs.

Many foreigners prefer carpets in earthy, pastel **colours**, assuming them to be traditional and presumably coloured with vegetable dyes. Actually, traditional Tibetan carpets come in bright, almost gaudy hues – the earth tones are in vogue because of foreign demand. Synthetic dyes can produce any colour or shade, whether muted or bright, whereas vegetable dyes have a more limited range. Carpets made of all-Tibetan wool and/or vegetable dyes are rare, and more expensive.

Traditional Tibetan **designs** are bold and simple – angular dragons, flowers, clouds or various auspicious symbols, usually against a plain field and contained within a geometric border. Most carpets being produced these days are further simplified, using large, open fields, and combining traditional motifs with abstract patterns.

Carpets are woven throughout the Kathmandu and Pokhara valleys. Compared to Middle Eastern makes, Tibetan-style carpets have deeper, more luxuriant pile, but lower knot densities and coarser patterns. The best **shopping** is in the Jaulakhel area of Patan, and you'll find more information about their manufacture in that section. The choice is vast, so take your time: compare carpets in different price ranges for subtlety of colour and design, quality of finish and embossing, and knot count (usually 40 to 100 per square inch). Make sure the ratio of vertical to horizontal knots isn't less than 2 : 3.

Prices are dependent on all these factors, plus of course **size**. To give a relative idea of price, figure on paying Rs500 apiece for *khakama* (50cm squares), which make fine seat covers, or Rs6000 for a standard *khaden* (1m x 2m).

Imported **Kashmiri carpets** and **chain-stitch tapestries** are recent introductions to the Nepal handicraft scene, brought by traders fleeing the tourist meltdown in Kashmir. Kashmiri rugs are among the world's finest, but Kashmiri rug salesmen are among the world's wiliest, so proceed with great caution. A *pukka* carpet should have a label on the back stating that it was made in Kashmir, what it is made of (wool, silk, or "silk touch" – wool combined with a little cotton and silk to give it a sheen), its size, number of knots per inch, and the name of the design. To tell if it really is silk, scrape the carpet lightly with a knife and burn the fluff – real silk shrivels to nothing and leaves a distinctive smell.

TEXTILES AND CLOTHING

Nepali designers are applying their creative talents to **textiles** and, as with carpets, adapting indigenous designs in stylish new ways. Most of these items are produced by tiny cottage-industry outfits and have yet to find their way overseas, but the fleeting success of certain fashions shows there's a receptive market.

Dhaka, a brightly patterned cotton weave made on hand looms in the eastern and western hills, has long been used to make *topi* (men's caps), *cholo* (women's half-length blouses) and shawls. Palpali *dhaka*, the preferred make for *topi*, comes from Tansen (Palpa), and you'll find more about it in that section. Women's cooperatives are now producing *dhaka* in colour schemes and patterns aimed squarely at Western tastes, and turning it into scarves, ties, placemats, jackets, handbags – you name it. At least one group also markets ***allo***, a wool-like material woven from the pounded bark of nettle stems.

Other cotton weaves, including ***khadi*** (traditional homespun) and many forms of sari material, are produced locally all over Nepal. These, too, turn up in innovative incarnations – block-printed, quilted and hand-stitched – from pot holders and tea cosies to cushion covers and bedspreads. Less impressive are the cheap cotton dresses and drawstring pants sold in all the tourist areas.

Pashmina, a cashmere-like wool gleaned from the softest hair of goats, is made into shawls which are worn by many Kathmandu Valley residents in winter. These are good purchases, but be sure you're not buying acrylic. Rub off some fibres and burn them: *pashmina* will smell like burning hair, acrylic won't smell of anything.

Sweaters, socks and other **woollens**, knitted by women everywhere, are amazingly cheap and sold all over tourist areas. The cheaper ones suffer from quality-control problems – many will quickly fall apart at the seams. Ask which grade of wool the garment is made from. For more durability and better styling, it's worth paying more at one of the pricier boutiques in Kathmandu or Patan. Tibetan-style black **felt** with rainbow trim is another budget-wear staple, finding its way into not only caps but also jackets, bags and the like.

Tibetan wrap-around dresses, called ***chuba***, can be bought off the peg or custom-made by shops in Kathmandu and Boudha. Intricate (and expensive) **Bhutanese embroidery** also turns up in specialist shops in Kathmandu and Boudha.

Silk is a relatively new industry in Nepal, with just a few manufacturers in the Kathmandu Valley producing thread and raw material. Others weave Indian thread into *dupian*, which looks like raw silk but is softer, shinier and more expensive, or fine *crepe de Chine*.

Nepal's burgeoning garment industry has been quick to experiment with all these materials and more, producing cheap designer **ready-made** Punjabis and the like – the sort of clothes you wouldn't feel silly about wearing again back home. High **fashion** has hit Nepal, too, and is patronized not only by foreigners but also by a growing clientele of wealthy Nepalis. Boutiques in Kathmandu and Patan display some stunning original pieces melding Western and local influences; in global fashion terms, these are quite cheap, and all the more exciting for their obscurity.

PAINTINGS

Like so many things in Nepal, ***thangka*** – Tibetan ritual paintings – are now cranked out for the tourist market, yet the best ones remain undiminished by commercialization, and even the cheapest can't hide the dense Buddhist symbolism inherent in the form. The production process and subject matter of these vibrant, intricate paintings is discussed on p.120.

Thangka are produced not only by Tibetans but also by Tamangs and, increasingly, by artisans of other Nepali ethnic groups. In addition, ***paubha*** – paintings in the style of the Kathmandu Valley's Newars – are undergoing a modest revival after near-extinction earlier this century. *Paubha* are created in much the same way as *thangka*, but they tend to contain less background detail, focusing instead on a central deity, who may just as easily be Hindu as Buddhist.

Before **buying** a *thangka* or *paubha*, first watch a painter at work in Patan or Bhaktapur – the main production centres – to get an appreciation for how painstaking the art is, and try to get someone to explain the imagery and the meanings behind it. When you see one you like, examine the detail of the eyes, facial expression and fingers of the main figure; background figures should also stand up to scrutiny. Many paintings aimed at tourists make a great show of their "gold" paint: real gold won't come away when a moist finger is pressed against it. Most "old" *thangka* have been aged with wood smoke. A halfway decent small (15cm x 30cm) *thangka* will **cost** at least Rs1200, though poor ones will go for much less than that. A large (90cm x 120cm) one, using microscopic brushstrokes and genuine gold paint, will cost hundreds or thousands of dollars.

So-called **Maithili art** has caught on in the past few years. These brightly coloured folk paintings, which keep alive age-old religious and fertility symbols, are created by women in the villages surrounding Janakpur in the eastern Tarai; you can read more about them in that section. However, they're most easily bought in the non-profit shops of Kathmandu or Patan, where Maithili motifs are reproduced not only on paper but also pottery and papier mâché.

Batiks, depicting typical Nepali scenes, are an inexpensive artform introduced in the past two decades as an income-generator for disabled people in the Kathmandu and Pokhara valleys.

MISCELLANEOUS CRAFTS AND POTTERY

Khukuri, the deadly knives of Nepal's feared Gurkha soldiers, are Nepal's most ubiquitous souvenirs. Bhojpur, in the eastern hills, is the traditional forging centre, but knives are heavily peddled in Kathmandu. An authentic one will have a moon-shaped notch at the base of the blade to channel the blood away, and its sheath will contain two small tools for sharpening and honing. Prices start at Rs300, but a city-slicker model with a buffalo-horn handle will cost several times that.

The Kathmandu Valley and Pokhara are awash with **Tibetan curios**, though the vast majority of these are manufactured in Nepal or India. The range of items is formidable: prayer wheels, amulets, charm boxes, bracelets (usually inscribed with the mantra, *Om mani padme hum*), prayer-flag printing blocks, *chhang* pots, masks, turquoise and coral jewellery, musical instruments and many other bizarre artefacts. Much of it has been artificially aged, and the turquoise is often fake. The sale of human skulls and bowls (which are quite real), ornamented with metalwork and baubles and traditionally used for tantric purposes, is illegal and such items are now sold only in secret; decorated goat skulls are easy enough to come by. A couple of shops in Kathmandu sell nothing but **musical instruments**, including *sarangi* (Nepal's version of a fiddle) and *jhankri* (shaman) drums.

Simple, unglazed **pottery** is produced by *kumal* (potters) throughout the hills. Very little of it rises above the level of mundane implements, but the potters of Bhaktapur and Thimi turn out a few ornamental items – candlesticks, elephant-shaped plant pots and so on. Some of the non-profit shops sell non-traditional, glazed pieces. Ceramics don't travel well, though, so you'll have to wrap them carefully.

OTHER ITEMS

Attractive embroidered pouches and wooden "caddies" of Nepali **tea** make great presents or souvenirs. They're sold mainly in the Kathmandu Valley, but the tea itself is cultivated in the eastern hills around Ilam (just over the border from Darjeeling), and you'll find an account of processing and grading in that section. Two principal varieties are grown for export: Ilam, which has a full flavour much like Darjeeling, and Kanyam, smokier but considered superior by many. If you're not bothered about presentation, loose tea is much cheaper than the packaged stuff and can be sealed in plastic for travelling.

Incense can also bring back fond memories of Nepal after your return. Sweet-smelling Indian sticks are available in every bazaar. Tibetan mixtures, made in Nepal and sold mainly in Tibetan neighbourhoods such as Boudha and Swayambhu, are redolent of juniper.

There's no need to lug a library along when travelling in Nepal: Kathmandu and Pokhara each have dozens of **bookshops** devoted to travel, fiction and classics, new and used, in English and other European languages, Western imports and cheaper Indian imprints. Kathmandu, especially, seems to have more booksellers per capita than anywhere in the English-speaking world. Most will buy books or trade as well. The bigger tourist outlets also stock compilation **cassettes** of Nepali and other regional music which, though relatively expensive, give an overview of musical styles with English titles (see "Music and Dance" in *Contexts*). Cheaper tapes produced for the home market are available in local shops and stalls.

Things not to bring home include *shaligram* (fossil-bearing stones), ritual objects made from human bones (or even animal bones that a customs officer might mistake for human ones), and anything made from a rare or protected species (including ivory, certain furs and peacock feathers). All of these are illegal to export from Nepal. As for drugs, see "Police and Trouble".

OUTDOOR PURSUITS

It hardly needs to be said that Nepal is ideal for outdoor enthusiasts. Most come to trek, but rafting, cycling and wildlife- and bird-watching are also well developed. None requires any previous experience.

TREKKING AND HIKING

Even if you're not the outdoor type, **trekking** is a rare pleasure that shouldn't be passed up: it's the only way to get *into* the Himalaya, as opposed to looking at them from a distance, and is by far the best way to experience Nepal's constantly changing landscape and people-scape. Though trekking can be physically demanding and sometimes uncomfortable, few people experience any real difficulties. A trek normally lasts at least a week, but you'll get more out of it if you can set aside two or more weeks. Most people don't trek with a group, and wait until they get to Kathmandu before making any arrangements, but those with lots of money and little time may want to book through a trekking agency in their home country (see box). Equipment can be rented cheaply in Nepal, and it's no problem to store unneeded stuff while you're on the trail. Note that travel insurance is all the more essential if you plan to trek.

Day hikes – which offer many of the rewards of trekking without the red tape – are described throughout the guide. While the scenery on a day hike will seem rather tame compared with a trek, the cultural interactions on these uncommercialized trails are often more genuine.

Trekking is such a big topic that it needs its own chapter. For a full rundown on **trekking preparations and routes**, see Chapter Seven, *The Himalayan Trekking Regions*.

RAFTING

Of all the outdoor activities on offer in Nepal, **rafting** probably tops the list for excitement. Nepal's whitewater is fine for first-timers, and from the river you can get fresh angles on villages and religious gatherings at sacred confluences. Most rafting companies offer a standard three-day trip, and provide all camping gear; some organize longer trips and raft-wildlife or raft-trek packages.

Unfortunately, rafting is also the single biggest source of disappointment for many travellers, who too often get duped by shady or inexperienced **river operators**. Trip prices and quality vary enormously – as a rule, the only difference between cheap companies and expensive ones is that the latter usually can be relied on to do what they promised. A few of the more reputable operators are listed on pp.128–129; these deal mainly with groups booked from overseas, but they'll take walk-in clients, and if you can muster up a few friends you can arrange your own customized trip. Some of the cut-price outfits in Kathmandu and Pokhara aren't bad, but making recommendations would be misleading – companies come and go, and standards rise and fall from one season to the next. Shop around, and press operators hard on the criteria given below.

Many places advertising rafting trips are merely **agents**, who usually don't know what they're talking about. But if you're having trouble finding an operator who has a trip scheduled for when you want to go, an agent may be able to hook you up with one.

COSTS AND RED TAPE

Trips **cost** from $15 to $75 a day, depending on the river, number of people in the party, and standard of service. For trips on the Trisuli, Nepal's most popular river, upmarket companies typically charge $30–40 a day, which should include transport to and from the river by private van and good, hygienic meals. Budget outfits offer this trip for around $20 a day, but at that price you can expect to travel by regular bus and be served pretty unappetizing food; anyone charging less than $20 is likely to make you buy your own bus tickets and meals. These prices assume full rafts, which hold up to seven paying passengers each – five or six is safer, but smaller group sizes mean a higher price per head. Other rivers cost $10–20 a day extra.

Your rafting company is responsible for arranging the trip **permit**, which costs $5 per person and is normally included in the package (one passport photo required). Fly-by-night operators sometimes collect permit fees and pocket the money – a risky proposition, since as far as the government is concerned, unpermitted trips

RAFTING RIVERS IN NEPAL

Perhaps eighty percent of all raft trips are done on the **Trisuli River**, west of Kathmandu. The normal itinerary is three days: given that it takes three or four hours to drive each way, two-day trips are a waste of time, and four-day trips are often just the three-day trip in slow motion. The Trisuli contains a good mix of whitewater (Class 3+) and scenery, though it's hardly wilderness – a road follows it the entire way. In October and November you'll have to share the river with many other parties and perhaps compete for campsites. Operators' boasts of "road support" mean the overnight gear is kept in a van, which precludes camping on the river's less crowded north side. All the best rapids are above Mugling and many Pokhara-based companies miss these out. Ask where the put-in point is: anything much below Baireni isn't a proper whitewater trip; most companies pull out between Mugling and Narayanghat. Many operators misleadingly advertise trips to Chitwan National Park; though these almost always end at Narayanghat, it's a pleasanter way of getting to the Chitwan than by bus.

Recently opened up to rafting by the construction of a new road, the **Kali Gandaki** provides an intense five-day itinerary out of Pokhara. Serious whitewater (Class 3–4) starts almost immediately after the put-in point at Baglung and continues for much of the first three days, with some more on the final day before pulling out at Radmi Ghat on the Siddhartha Highway. Upriver views of the Annapurnas and Dhaulagiri are excellent early on, and there's the possibility of adding this raft trip onto the end of a trek in the Annapurna region. Another river most easily reached from Pokhara, the **Seti** is a fairly tame (Class 2) but picturesque river, taking three days from Damauli to near Narayanghat.

Next in popularity comes the **Sun Kosi**, an eight-day run beginning at Dolalghat, three hours east of Kathmandu, and ending at Chatara, near Dharan in the eastern Tarai. If you're planning to go on from Nepal to Darjeeling, this raft trip cuts out most of the twenty-hour bus ride to the eastern border. Fewer companies do scheduled trips on the Sun Kosi, so you're less likely to see other parties and the camping is great. Providing a steady diet of increasingly exciting whitewater (Class 3–4), the river traverses a remote, roadless part of the country, flowing through a varied landscape of jungle-clad canyons, arid, open valleys and sparse settlements. Some operators also run a gentle, one-day stretch of the **Bhote Kosi**, which joins the Sun Kosi at Dolalghat.

Other rivers are harder to get to – budget operators don't run them, and the few companies that do charge through the nose. Rafting the **Karnali** in far western Nepal involves a two-day walk-in, but it's an adventurous twelve-day trip with big whitewater (Class 3–5), pristine jungle and plenty of wildlife. A tributary of the Karnali, the easy (Class 2) **Bheri** can be run from the Surkhet road to Bardia National Park. The little-rafted **Arun**, reached by flying to Tumlingtar in the eastern hills and raftable from Tumlingtar to Chatara, offers three or four days of good whitewater (Class 3–4) and unspoilt scenery; a tributary, the **Tamur Kosi**, is good for an exhilarating (Class 4) one- or two-day run from Mulghat to Dharan. If you're considering any of these or other off-the-beaten-track trips, you'll definitely want to get yourself a copy of *White Water Nepal* (see "Books" in *Contexts*).

---

don't exist and therefore don't need rescuing. In theory, you're supposed to be **insured** in order to get a permit.

EQUIPMENT

Most companies use "paddle" **rafts**, in which everyone paddles and the guide steers from the rear; on less exciting "oar" trips, the guide does all the work. Tents, sleeping bags, foam mattresses and kit bags should be provided and each raft should come with a waterproof "ammo" box for storing clothes, cameras and valuables. Some rafting companies also have **kayaks**. Those experienced enough to organize their own trip will want to weigh the benefits of bringing

kayaks from home versus renting them in Kathmandu (about Rs750/day) – but note that the supply is limited in high season.

Bring two sets of clothes (one to remain dry), two sets of shoes (one that you don't mind getting wet: sport sandals are best), a bathing suit, towel, hat, sunglasses, suntan lotion, insect repellent and torch (flashlight). Birdwatchers will want to bring binoculars.

SAFETY AND THE ENVIRONMENT

Lack of **safety** is a perennial complaint. Make sure the company supplies life vests, helmets (not required in "oar" rafts) and a full first-aid kit, and satisfy yourself that the rafts are in good running

ADVENTURE TRAVEL OPERATORS AND AGENTS

The following are some of the most established overseas companies running trekking, rafting, mountain-biking and wildlife-viewing trips in Nepal, along with a few big sales agents. Booking directly with operators in Kathmandu (see pp.128–130) will save money but may increase complexities.

NORTH AMERICA

Adventure Center (☎1-800/227-8747 or 510/654-1879 in US; ☎1-800/661-7265 or 416/922-7584 in Canada). Trekking, trekking peaks, rafting, wildlife.

Above the Clouds Trekking (☎1-800/233-4499 or 508/799-4499). Trekking, rafting, family treks.

Himalayan Travel (☎1-800/225-2380 or 203/359-3711). Trekking, rafting, wildlife, customized trips.

InnerAsia (☎1-800/777-8183 or 415/922-0448). Trekking, trekking peaks, wildlife, customized trips.

Journeys (☎1-800/255-8735 or 313/665-4407). Trekking (including women's, alternative health and tree-planting treks), rafting, wildlife; some trips suitable for children.

Mountain Travel-Sobek (☎1-800/227-2384 or 510/527-8100). Trekking, wildlife.

Overseas Adventure Travel (☎1-800/221-0814 or 617/ 876-0533). Trekking, rafting, wildlife.

Safaricentre (☎1-800/223-6046 or 310/546-4411). Trekking, wildlife, rafting.

Wilderness Travel (☎1-800/368-2794 or 510/548-0420). Trekking, trekking peaks.

Worldwide Adventures (☎1-800/387-1483 or 416/221-3000). Trekking, rafting, wildlife.

UK & IRELAND

Adrift Whitewater Rafting, Collingbourne House, Spencer Court, 140-142 High Street, London SW18 4JJ (☎0181/874 4969). Rafting.

Adventure Travel Centre, 131–135 Earls Court Rd, London SW5 9RH (☎0171/370 4555). Trekking, mountain-biking, wildlife.

Classic Nepal, 33 Metro Ave, Newton, Derbyshire DE55 5UF (☎01773/873497). Trekking, trekking peaks, rafting, wildlife.

Encounter Overland, 267 Old Brompton Rd, London SW5 9JA (☎0171/370 6845). Trekking, rafting, wildlife.

Exodus Travels, 9 Weir Rd, London SW12 0LT (☎0181/673 0859). Trekking, trekking peaks, rafting, mountain-biking, wildlife.

Explore Worldwide, 1 Frederick St, Aldershot, Hants GU11 1LQ (☎01252/344 161). Trekking, trekking peaks, rafting, wildlife.

High Places, Globe Works, Pennestone Rd, Sheffield S6 5AE (☎0114/275 7500). Trekking, rafting, wildlife.

Himalayan Kingdoms, 20 The Mall, Clifton, Bristol BS8 4DR (☎0117/923 7163). Trekking, trekking peaks, expedition peaks, rafting, wildlife.

Sherpa Expeditions, 131a Heston Rd, Hounslow, Middx TW5 0RD (☎0181/577 2717). Trekking, rafting, wildlife.

Silk Road Travel, 64 S William St, Dublin 2 (☎01/677 1029). Trekking, trekking peaks, rafting, mountain-biking, wildlife.

AUSTRALIA & NEW ZEALAND

Adrift, PO Box 354, Ngongotaha, NZ (☎07/347 2345). Rafting.

Adventure World, 73 Walker St, North Sydney NSW 2060 (☎02/9956 7766) and 101 Great South Rd, Remuera, Auckland NZ (☎09/524 5118), with other offices in Adelaide, Brisbane, Melbourne and Perth. Trekking, trekking peaks, rafting, wildlife.

Destinations Adventure, 2nd Floor, Premier Bldg, Auckland NZ (☎09/309 0464). Trekking, mountain-biking, wildlife.

Exodus Travels, Suite 5, Level 5, 1 York St, Sydney NSW 2000 (☎02/251 5430). Trekking, trekking peaks, rafting, mountain-biking, wildlife.

Journeys Worldwide, Adelaide St, Brisbane (☎07/221 4788). Trekking, trekking peaks, rafting, wildlife.

Outdoor Travel, PO Box 286, Bright, Victoria 3741 (☎057/551 743); 55 Hardware St, Melbourne 3000 (☎03/ 9670 7252). Trekking, rafting, wildlife.

Peregrine Adventures, 258 Lonsdale St, Melbourne 3000 (☎03/9663 8611). Trekking, trekking peaks, rafting, wildlife.

Sun Travel, 407 Great South Rd, Penrose, Auckland (☎09/525 3074). Trekking, trekking peaks, rafting, wildlife.

Sundowners Adventure Travel, Suite 15, 600 Lonsdale St, Melbourne (☎03/ 9670 1123; Encounter Overland). Trekking, trekking peaks, rafting, wildlife.

Ultimate Descents, PO Box 208, Riwaka, Motueka, NZ (☎03/528 6792). Rafting.

order and that there will be a safety demonstration before entering the river. The minimum number of rafts is two, in case one capsizes. Most important of all, **guides** must be trained, certified, have experience guiding on the stretch of river in question, and speak adequate English (there should be an opportunity to meet guides before departure). Use only a company belonging to the *Nepal Association of Rafting Agents*, a trade body that sets safety standards, requires its members to employ only trained and licensed guides, and handles complaints. Companies not belonging to *NARA* are unregulated, so you've got no recourse if things go wrong.

Rafters have the same responsibilities to **the environment** as trekkers, particularly regarding firewood, sanitation and litter – see the tips on p.351.

WHEN TO GO

Time of year makes an enormous difference to water volumes. The major rivers are off-limits to all but experts during the monsoon, and if you're a beginner you probably won't want to try rafting until mid- or late October, when things have calmed down. The rapids are more manageably exciting in November, becoming mellower from December through to April or May, when snow-melt begins to add to flows. However, different rivers are at their best at different times of the year, so which river you go on will depend to a large extent on when you're in Nepal. Also note that a given trip will take less time in high water than when the water is running more slowly. March and April are the best months for long, warm days and excellent birdwatching. Winter can be chilly, though not so bad as you might think: most raftable river sections are below 500m elevation.

MOUNTAIN-BIKING

Nepal was made for **mountain bikes**: most roads are uncrowded and spectacular, the cycling is challenging, and the alternative – buses – is unpleasant. On a bike you can stop where you like, enjoy the scenery, make detours and amaze the locals. A degree of fitness is required, but if you can handle a *Hero* you should have no trouble with a mountain bike.

However, the riding in Nepal is probably not like what you're used to back home. Although there are zillions of **trails**, most are not suitable

for biking because they're too steep, stepped and heavily used by humans and animals. There are some excellent single-track rides, but it takes a lot of exploring to find them (this is a good reason to go with a tour – see below). If you do go off-road, give other people and livestock priority on the trail, and be prepared to carry your bike a lot of the time.

But you'll probably spend most of your time on **roads**. Nepal has a surprising number of paved and unpaved secondary highways, most of which see very little traffic. Many other primitive, half-completed or half-washed-out roads can also be found, although these often peter out after a short distance. If you're adventurous, the possibilities for exploring off the beaten track, especially in the Tarai, are almost unlimited. Try to stay off the main highways in central Nepal, which carry most of the heavy-vehicle traffic – the Prithvi Highway between Kathmandu and Pokhara should be avoided at all costs. Highway traffic diminishes as you get further from Kathmandu (especially in the Tarai), but you're still going to take in lungfuls of exhaust fumes and eyefuls of dust on the main arteries.

Bear in mind that you don't have to pedal all the way from A to B. If you want to skip a busy section or a steep climb, or avoid backtracking, take the bus. It's usually no problem to load your bike on the roof, although you will be charged up to twice the price of a seat for it.

RENTAL BIKES

As already mentioned (see p.33), **rental mountain bikes** in Nepal are generally flimsy and unreliable. If you take one off-road, it's likely to break and you'll be stuck pushing it back. Worse, rental bikes aren't very safe – you can't quite be sure they'll perform the way they're supposed to when you're descending a steep, rough pitch, where a malfunction could spell disaster – and helmets are rarely available.

Given those limitations, you probably won't be going off-road on a rental, nor will you be touring long distances. What you *can* do perfectly well is there-and-back day rides and perhaps modest overnight loops on paved or graded unpaved roads. Since you'll need to return the bike to where you rented it, and mountain bikes are really only rentable in Kathmandu and Pokhara, you'll probably end up just doing excursions from those places. However, there are a number of other fine mountain-biking bases around the

WHERE TO MOUNTAIN-BIKE

Great Bases

Bhaktapur – Ideally situated in the very ridable eastern Kathmandu Valley, with excursions to Changu Narayan, Nagarkot, Nala, Dhulikhel, Panauti and beyond.

Dhulikhel – A very popular base for exploring the Kathmandu Valley's eastern rim area, especially Namobuddha and Panauti.

Patan – A springboard for the southern Kathmandu Valley, including Dakshin Kali, Phulchoki and the Lele Valley.

Kakani – A fine destination in itself, it gives access to the scenic Trisuli Road and, with a bit of carrying, to the Shivpuri Watershed and Budhanilkantha.

Pokhara – Day trips abound from here, as well as overnights along the Baglung and Siddhartha highways.

Sauraha – The main tourist village outside Chitwan National Park, it offers gentle riding through villages and some jungle.

Thakurdwara – Just outside Bardia National Park, within reach of villages, jungle and the Karnali River.

Janakpur – A holy city in the Tarai surrounded by lots of interesting villages.

Hile – A bazaar in the remote eastern hills, offering several off-the-beaten-track routes.

Great Destinations

Nagarkot –A brisk (700m) paved ascent to the hill station of Nagarkot, and a fun, bumpy return to Kathmandu via Sankhu (2 days, round-trip).

Namobuddha/Panauti – A classic loop out of Dhulikhel on fairly easy dirt roads, visiting a stupa and a sacred confluence (1 day, round-trip).

Trisuli/Nuwakot – A long (1500m) descent from the Kathmandu Valley's north rim at Kakani to a subtropical valley with a historic fort (2 days, one way).

Daman – A classic, challenging ride that gains 1400m as it climbs up a spectacular paved road to a mountain viewpoint (2–4 days, round-trip).

Kodari (Tibet border) – An adventurous 1000m climb on a deteriorating road, with hot springs, a deep gorge and views of Tibet (4–5 days, round-trip).

Baglung – A pleasant pedal along a newly paved road into the heart of the Annapurna trekking region, gaining and then losing 800m each way (4 days, round trip).

Tansen – A strenuous ride from Pokhara along a winding, scenic highway, involving three separate climbs, the last one 1000m (2–3 days, one way).

For recommended long-distance routes, see "Cycling Into Nepal" (p.12).

---

country (see box), so you might consider lugging a rental bike along by bus.

BRINGING YOUR OWN

A mountain bike **brought from home** will be superior to anything you can rent in Nepal. It will enable you to do fun single-track rides in greater safety and with much less risk of breaking down. With a set of panniers, you'll be able to tour long-distance and see parts of Nepal (especially the Tarai) that few travellers see. However, don't bring a bike unless you have the time, energy and commitment to use it most of the time – otherwise it will just be a millstone that you have to lug everywhere and keep safe.

Airlines will accept a bicycle as baggage at no extra charge, so long as it doesn't put you over the weight limit. No special container is needed, but you'll be expected to deflate the tyres and swivel the handlebars to be parallel with the frame.

Accessories are scarce in Nepal, so bring the following items from home: helmet; water bottle; pump; all relevant tools, puncture repair (patch) kit, extra tubes and spare parts; security cable; panniers (if you're planning to travel long-distance); shock cords (bungie cords); a bell; and breathable waterproof clothing (such as *Gore-Tex)*, cycling gloves and shorts.

MOUNTAIN-BIKE TOURS

There are two main reasons for joining an organized bike **tour**, the first being ease of logistics. Good bikes and all the necessary gear are provided, and guides take care of bike maintenance and ensure that the bikes are safe at night. On longer tours, a "sag wagon" will tote heavy gear, provide emergency backup, and whisk you past the busier or less interesting stretches of road to ensure that you spend as much time as possible hitting the highlights.

Secondly, if you're into single-track riding, a tour guide will show you trails you'd never find on your own. And, like trekking guides, biking guides can interpret the culture and answer any questions.

Of course joining a tour means you have to stick to a fixed itinerary, and it costs quite a bit more than doing it yourself: **prices** are comparable to organized treks, or about $40 per day. The "Adventure Travel Operators and Agents" box on p.55 includes some overseas companies that offer mountain-bike tours. Almost all tours booked through these companies are organized by *Himalayan Mountain Bikes* in Kathmandu, and you can book directly with them (see p.129).

WILDLIFE VIEWING

Viewing **wildlife in the Tarai** is safariing with a distinctly Asian flavour: the animals most commonly seen include rhinos, monkeys, several kinds of deer and the occasional bear – tigers are spotted only rarely – and the most fun way to see them is atop an elephant. **Bring** lightweight clothes (neutral colours are best), a sun hat, swimsuit, sunscreen, insect repellent, shoes you don't mind getting wet, and binoculars if you have them. From November to February you'll also need warm clothes and a jacket for chilly evenings and early-morning walks.

Chitwan National Park (p.266) is the easiest game reserve to get to, and the one most geared for budget travellers, although it's heavily used: **Bardia National Park** (p.297) and **Sukla Phanta Wildlife Reserve** (p.305) are untouristed alternatives. Bird-watchers can notch up hundreds of species around Phulchowki at the southern edge of the Kathmandu Valley, or explore seldom-visited **Koshi Tappu Wildlife Reserve** (p.323).

Mammals aren't as easy to see **in the hills** and mountains, most of the interesting ones being nocturnal or extremely reclusive. While trekking you might see monkeys, various small rodents or (if you're lucky) goat-like tahr or blue sheep.

For an overview of Nepal's wildlife, see "Natural History" in *Contexts*.

SPORTS

It's often said that Nepalis are a martial race. Certainly military parade grounds are more common than playing fields, and the **martial arts** are big among urban youth. Nepali athletes have placed well in international karate and taekwando competitions, and **boxing** is also quite popular.

Team sports aren't common, though district-level **football (soccer)** teams often square off at the National Stadium in Kathmandu – check the English-language daily papers for news of upcoming matches. Children and some adults play *kabbadi*, a sort of organized game of tag indigenous to the Indian subcontinent, and basketball is beginning to catch on in schools. **Elephant polo** is a joke sport invented by and for expats, but the "world championships" each December at Chitwan certainly make for a fun spectator event.

The big tourist hotels in Kathmandu have **swimming** pools and **tennis** courts, and some of them allow outsiders to use their facilities for a fee (usually steep). There's also a health club in Kathmandu, as well as two **golf** courses in the Kathmandu Valley and a third in Dharan.

SPIRITUAL PURSUITS AND ALTERNATIVE THERAPIES

Nepal is a great place to go to challenge your Western assumptions, study other systems of thought and open yourself to other ways of experiencing life. The tolerant atmosphere encourages experimentation and provides several traditional disciplines to delve into.

Moreover, Nepal is turning into quite a spiritual supermarket. The past few years have seen an explosion of outfits teaching yoga and meditation in the Kathmandu Valley, and centres in the other tourist watering holes can't be far behind. The allied health fields of ayurvedic and Tibetan medicine are also attracting a growing interest among travellers in Nepal. Many programmes are designed for those who are just starting out and don't require a lengthy commitment, although some do. Note that it's advisable to book any residential courses well in advance – fax numbers/addresses are given where possible.

This section provides a quick introduction to a few major practices. For general background on Hinduism and Buddhism, which provide their philosophical bases, be sure to see the section on religion in *Contexts*.

YOGA

Contrary to what's often put about in Western manuals, **yoga** is not just exercises – it's a system of spiritual, mental and physical self-discipline, designed to bring about mastery of the self and true awareness of the self's oneness with the universe. There are several classical schools of yoga, but the ones that fit most easily into Western lifestyles come under the category of **raja yoga** and share eight "limbs" or steps (*astanga*), which represent an ascending path to self-control. The first two are the moral limbs, divided into dos and don'ts; after that come the three external limbs, *asana* (correct posture), *pranayama* (correct breathing) and *pratyahana* (control of the senses); followed finally by the three internal limbs, *dharana* (concentration), *dhyana* (meditation) and *samadhi* (super-consciousness).

Yoga's reputation for headstands and the like comes from **hatha yoga**, which places special emphasis on the three external methods to purify the body as an aid to developing the self. The term comes from the syllables *ha* and *tha*, representing inhalation and exhalation, since breath-control techniques, along with various postures, form an important part of this practice. Another popular variant, **kundalini yoga**, stresses meditation. The individual visualizes the process of enlightenment as a serpent, coiled near the base of the spine, rising through six psychic centres (*chakra*) in an ascending progression of consciousness, finally reaching the seventh, highest level.

Several **yoga centres** are located in and around Kathmandu, and are rounded up on p.123.

BUDDHIST MEDITATION AND STUDY

Meditation is closely related to yoga, and the two often overlap: much of yoga (*kundalini*, for example) involves meditation, and Buddhist meditation draws on many Hindu yogic practices. However, meditation centres in Nepal generally follow the Buddhist – particularly Tibetan Buddhist – tradition.

Buddhist meditation is a science of mind. To Buddhists, mind is the cause of confusion and ego, and the aim of meditation is to transcend these. **Vipassana** ("insight") is the kernel of all forms of Buddhist meditation; related to *hatha yoga*, it emphasizes the minute observation of physical sensations and mental processes to achieve a cool, clear understanding of mind. Another basic practice common to most schools of Buddhism, **shamatha** ("calm abiding" – co-opted by New Agers as "be here now") attunes and sharpens the mind by means of coming back again and again to a meditative discipline (breathing, visualization, etc). Theravada Buddhists consider *vipassana* to be sufficient for the attaining of enlightenment. At least two centres in the Kathmandu Valley run rigorous residential courses in this practice – see p.122 for details on one that caters to foreigners.

Tibetan Buddhist centres start students out with *vipassana* and *shamatha*, which form the foundation for a huge armoury of elaborate meditation practices. An adept will cultivate Buddha-like qualities through visualization techniques – meditating on the deity that manifests a particular quality, while chanting the *mantra* and

For information on **astrology**, see p.394.

performing the *mudra* (hand gesture) associated with that deity. The Tibetan Buddhist path also involves numerous rituals, such as prayer, offerings, circumambulation and other meritorious acts, and committed followers will also take vows. Kathmandu has several centres offering introductory courses.

A big part of Tibetan Buddhism is the teacher–disciple relationship; more advanced students of the *dharma* will want to **study** under one of the lamas at Boudha (see p.145), some of whom give discourses in English.

AYURVED

Ayurved (often spelled *ayurveda*) is the world's oldest form of medicine still being practised. Dating back five thousand years, the "knowledge of life" is a holistic medical system that assumes the fundamental sameness of self and nature. Unlike the allopathic medicine of the West, which is all about finding out what's ailing you and then killing it, *ayurved* looks at the whole patient: disease is regarded as a symptom of imbalance, so it's the imbalance that's treated, not the disease.

Ayurvedic theory holds that the body is controlled by **three forces** (*tridosha*), which are a reflection of the forces within the self: *pitta*, the force of the sun, which is hot and rules the digestive processes and metabolism; *kapha*, likened to the moon, the creator of tides and rhythms, which has a cooling effect and governs the body's organs, fluids and lubricants; and *vata*, wind, which relates to movement and the nervous system. The healthy body is one that has the three forces in balance. To **diagnose** an imbalance, the ayurvedic doctor goes not only by the physical complaint but also family background, daily habits and emotional traits.

Treatment of an imbalance is typically with **herbal remedies** designed to alter whichever of the three forces is out of whack. Made according to traditional formulas using indigenous plants, ayurvedic medicines are cheaper than imports, which is why the Nepali government is encouraging their production. In addition, the doctor may prescribe various forms of **yogic cleansing** to rid the body of waste substances. To the uninitiated, these techniques will sound rather offputting – for instance, swallowing a long strip of cloth, a short section at a time, and then pulling it back up again to remove mucus from the stomach.

You'll find **ayurvedic doctors** and clinics throughout the Hindu parts of Nepal, but those who are able to deal with foreigners are confined mainly to Kathmandu.

TIBETAN MEDICINE

Medicine is one of the traditional branches of study for Tibetan Buddhist monks, and **Tibetan medicine** is based on the same philosophical and magical principles as Tibetan Buddhism.

Like *ayurved*, from which it derives, Tibetan medicine promotes health by maintaining the correct balance of **three humours**: *beken*, inert matter or phlegm, which when out of balance is responsible for disorders of the upper body; *tiba*, heat or bile, which is associated with intestinal diseases; and *lung*, meaning wind, which may produce nervousness or depression.

Tibetan medicine is as much a spiritual discipline as a physical one. Part of a Tibetan doctor's regular practice is to meditate on the "medicine Buddha", a manifestation of the Buddha's compassion, wisdom and healing power. The physician **diagnoses** the patient's imbalance by examining the tongue, pulse and urine, and by determining the patient's psychological state through questioning. He'll then prescribe a **treatment** to counteract the imbalance, which initially may only be a change of diet or behaviour (for instance, "cold" disorders – those to do with wind – are treated with "hot" foods and activities). For quicker relief, he'll prescribe one of a range of herbal-mineral tablets, which have been empowered by special rites.

Recommended **clinics** specializing in Tibetan medicine are listed in the Kathmandu and Boudha sections.

MASSAGE AND OTHER THERAPIES

Nepal, like many Asian countries, has its own indigenous form of **massage**. So-called Nepali "hard" massage is a deep, therapeutic treatment that works mainly on the joints and insertions (the places where muscles meet bones). It's not all that relaxing, but it can be just the job for sore shoulders after a trek. Nepalis themselves rarely receive massages after the age of about three, and would find it hard to conceive of paying for one, but numerous masseurs ply their services to foreigners in Kathmandu and Pokhara. A few practitioners also offer yogic, shiatsu and Swedish or Thai massage.

Dubious-looking signs in the tourist areas frequently advertise "Yoga & Massage", which has become a sort of shorthand for a long menu of un-Nepali services: steam baths (usually a jury-rigged box with a hole in the top for your head to stick out), reflexology, herbal treatments and the like. Caveat emptor.

PHOTOGRAPHY

Everyone's a National Geographic photographer in Nepal – ethnic peoples, mountains, wildlife, temples and festivals all make winning subjects. But beware of experiencing your trip through a lens. The camera can provide great memories, but don't hesitate to put it away when it's getting in the way of the real thing.

EQUIPMENT

The first rule of packing photo gear is to keep it to what you can realistically carry. For many, if not most, people, this will mean sticking to a pocket-sized 35mm **point-and-shoot** model with a built-in flash. These cameras are unobtrusive, lightweight and easy to use; the fancier ones with automatic zooms can do just about everything. The drawback is a lack of versatility, since you can't usually override the automatic functions.

Bringing an **SLR (single lens reflex) camera** involves a tradeoff between higher performance versus extra bulk and security precautions. To get the most out of your SLR you'll want to bring a decent selection of accessories. Zoom **lenses** lighten your load, minimize lens changes and give you a whole range of focal distances to choose from. Two or three should do it: something in the 35–80mm range, an 80–200mm, and a wide angle (24mm works well). On longer lenses, the lower the f-stop available, the more flexibility you'll have but the greater the bulk (and price). You'd also do well to bring polarizing or split-density **filters** to cut down on glare, plus UV filters to protect lenses. A **flash** is useful for filling in shadows, and a **tripod** for long exposures indoors. And if you're carrying all that booty, you'll want to make sure it's protected in some sort of **bag** – either over the shoulder, strapped to the chest or around the waist – which you shouldn't let out of your sight.

If you think you might go rafting, a **waterproof camera** could save you some grief; a regular camera will have to be kept stowed away in a storage box most of the time while on the river.

Most major brands of **film** (prints and slides) are easily obtainable in Kathmandu for slightly more than what they cost back home; in other tourist areas the selection is pretty thin and often out of date, while off the beaten track you'll be lucky to find any film at all. Have a selection of both fast (ASA/ISO 200–400) and slow (100, 64 or even 25) film on hand to deal with different conditions. If you're bringing film into the country, pack it in a lead bag (available in camera shops) or carry it as hand baggage and have it hand-checked – the dosage of checked-luggage X-ray machines may damage film. Labs in Kathmandu and Pokhara **process** most types of film (but not Kodachrome), many offering a one-hour service.

Shops in Kathmandu sell many camera **accessories** – batteries, lens filters, tripods – but you can't count on them having the thing that fits your particular camera, so you're better off bringing spares with you. Remember that batteries go flat quickly in cold temperatures.

All the comments about bulk and security for still cameras apply even more so to **video cameras**. Note that Nepal's electricity is 220V/50 cycles, which means North Americans won't be able to recharge battery packs without a transformer.

TECHNIQUE

People always make good photos, but be sensitive. Always ask first, and if they say no, don't press it. Try to make photography a fun, two-way process: let people take pictures of their friends, or of you with their friends; it also helps if you can show pictures of your own family or home. Take time to establish intimacy, rather than just barging in and "taking" pictures. Unless you've got a Polaroid, don't mislead people into thinking they'll get an instant portrait of themselves. Never offer money, and if someone demands *bakshish* for a photo, just put the camera away – this is a form of begging (see below) and should be discouraged. That said, sadhus in certain tourist spots make their living from the *bakshish* they earn posing for photos (and if you try to steal a photo they'll visit holy wrath upon you). Never photograph masked festival dancers, who are believed to embody the deities they represent.

Postcard-perfect shots of **scenery** with clear blue skies aren't always the ones that stand out when you get home. Clouds, fog and rain often add more drama. Look for unusual images, things you've never seen before. Rather than trying to make big, sweeping statements with your photos, try zooming in on **details** that capture something essential about the scene or culture. Go for

action shots that will serve as a springboard for a story.

Light levels and contrast can be very high on sunny days in Nepal – especially at high elevations. To get around this, plan on doing most of your shooting in the early morning or late afternoon. Tones are especially mellow at these times, producing the best results, and in any case some of the most interesting scenes occur just after dawn. If you can't avoid midday conditions, use a flash to fill in shadows on faces, especially if the subject is relatively dark against a bright background. To get the correct exposure without a flash, walk up close or zoom in, so the subject fills the frame, before reading the meter. For snow shots, meter off something of a neutral shade, like your hand or the darkest part of the sky.

CULTURAL HINTS

Customs and traditions run deep in Nepal. Few Nepalis get the chance to travel abroad, or even to see foreign films or media, so their only exposure to the outside world is through travellers. This puts a great responsibility on visitors to be sensitive to Nepali ways and values, and to project a favourable image of foreigners.

Many different ethnic groups coexist in Nepal, each with their own complex customs. In the Kathmandu Valley, where they mix the most, there's a necessarily high degree of tolerance of different clothes and lifestyles – a fact that travellers sense, and often abuse. Away from the tourist areas, however, these groups are quite parochial, and foreign ways may cause offence.

The dos and don'ts listed here aren't as inflexible as they might sound. You'll make gaffes all the time and Nepalis will rarely say anything. The list is hardly exhaustive, either: when in doubt, do as you see Nepalis doing. The important thing is to show a willingness to adapt and learn.

COMMON COURTESIES

Namaste ("I salute the god within you"), the standard Nepali greeting for strangers, acquaintances and friends, is traditionally delivered with palms together as if praying. *Namaskar* is a very formal or subservient variant. The height to which

the pressed-together hands are raised roughly corresponds to the degree of deference being shown. Nowadays younger Nepalis are pretty informal about their *namaste*-ing, and often just flip the right hand in front of the forehead like a vertical salute. Returning a *namaste* with the appropriate gesture is a complex social calculation, but as a foreigner you need not worry about it – a middle-of-the-road *namaste* with hands at chest level will suffice for most situations.

One of the many delightful aspects of Nepali culture is the familiar **forms of address** that Nepalis use when speaking to each other: *didi* ("older sister"), *bhai* ("younger brother"), *bua* ("father") and so on. To a large extent these are used to avoid speaking another person's name, which Nepalis are somewhat superstitious about, but they are also used between strangers.

Nepalis don't automatically **thank** people for rendering services that they're paid to do, especially not servants or employees. The word *dhanyabaad* is normally reserved for a person of higher rank or someone who has gone above and beyond the call of duty – it's inappropriate to toss it around as casually as we say "thank you". Nepalis who aren't used to dealing with foreigners find it a bit disconcerting to be thanked for simply bringing a plate of food.

The gestures for **"yes"** and **"no"** may also cause confusion, since Nepalis don't nod or shake their heads. To indicate agreement, rock your head slightly to one side and then back the other way. To tell a tout or a seller "no", hold one hand in front of you, elbow pointing towards the ground, and swivel your wrist subtly, as if you were adjusting a bracelet. (Shaking the head in the Western fashion looks too much like "yes".)

CASTE AND STATUS

In Nepal, where Hinduism is tempered by Buddhist and other influences, **caste** doesn't dominate social interactions to quite the extent that it does in India. Nevertheless, caste *is* deeply engrained in the national psyche, as even non-Hindus were historically assigned places in the hierarchy based on ethnic affiliation or occupation. Following India's lead, Nepal "abolished" the official caste system in 1963, but a millennia-old system cannot be dismantled overnight. For most Nepalis, caste and status continue to determine what they do for a living, whom they may (or must) marry, where they can live and whom they can associate with.

In a Hindu society, foreigners are technically **casteless**, and their presence is polluting to orthodox, high-caste Hindus. In Nepal, this is really only a big deal in the remote far western hills, but wherever you travel you should be sensitive to minor caste restrictions: for example, you will not be allowed to enter the kitchen of a high-caste Hindu home.

However, **status** (*ijat*) is an equally important factor in Nepalese society, and as a foreigner you have a lot of it: you are fabulously wealthy, in the eyes of most Nepalis, and your culture dominates the world. Status adds extra complexity and nuance to interactions between strangers. Meeting for the first time, Nepalis observe a ritual of asking each other's name, home town, education, profession and age, all to determine relative status and therefore the correct form of address and level of deference. When you meet Nepalis you, too, will be subjected to this twenty-questions treatment. Incidentally, business cards now streamline this process, so it might not be a bad idea to bring a handful with you to Nepal (and indeed to most Asian countries).

EATING

Probably the greatest number of Nepali taboos – to an outsider's way of thinking – have to do with **food**. One underlying principle is that once you've touched something to your lips it's polluted (*jutho*) for everyone else. If you take a sip from someone else's canteen, try not to let it touch your lips (and the same applies if it's your own canteen – you're expected to share). Don't eat off someone else's plate or offer anyone food you've taken a bite out of (with one exception: a wife may eat her husband's leftovers), and don't touch cooked food until you've bought it.

Another all-important point of etiquette is **eat with your right hand only**. In Nepal, as in most Asian countries, the left hand is reserved for washing after defecating; you can use it to hold a glass or utensil, but don't eat, wipe your mouth, pass food or point at someone with it. It's considered good manners to give and receive everything with the right hand – or, to convey respect, with both hands. Sherpas and some other highland groups regard the family hearth as sacred, so don't throw rubbish or scraps into it.

TEMPLES

Major Hindu **temples** or their inner sanctums are usually off-limits to non-believers, who are technically outcastes. Respect this: what seems like elitism is just Hindus' way of keeping a part of their culture sacred in a country where nearly everything is open to inspection by outsiders. In most cases, you can see everything from outside anyway. Where you are allowed in, be respectful, take your shoes off before entering, don't take photos unless you've been given permission, and leave a few rupees in the donation box. The same goes for Buddhist monasteries. If you're granted an audience with a lama, it's traditional to present him with a *kata* (a ceremonial white scarf, usually sold nearby). Walk around Buddhist stupas and monuments clockwise – that is, keep the monument on your right.

CLOTHING AND THE BODY

Nepalis are innately conservative in their attitudes to **clothing**. Not a few are still shell-shocked from the hang-loose styles of the hippy era, and wary of all budget travellers as a result. A woman is expected to dress modestly, with legs and shoulders covered, especially in temples and monasteries: a dress or skirt that hangs to mid-calf level is best; trousers are acceptable, but shorts or a short skirt are offensive to many. A man should always wear a shirt in public, and long trousers if possible (men who wear shorts are assumed to be of a low caste). It's equally important to look clean and well groomed – travellers are rich, Nepalis reckon, and ought to look the part. You can flout these traditions, but you'll only shut yourself off from the happy encounters with locals that make travelling in Nepal so pleasant.

Nudity is a sensitive issue. Only women with babies or small children in tow bare their breasts. When Nepali men bathe in public, they do it in their underwear, and women bathe fully clothed. Foreigners are expected to do likewise. Nepal has some idyllic hot springs, but most are heavily used as bathing areas; don't scare the locals off by stripping. Paradoxically, it's deemed okay to defecate in the open, as in many villages there are no covered toilets – but out of sight of others, in the early morning or after dark. Men may urinate in public away from buildings – discreetly – but women have to find a sheltered spot.

Still other conventions pertain to **the body**. In Nepal, the forehead is regarded as the most sacred part of the body and the feet the most unclean. It's impolite to touch an adult Nepali's head, and it's an insult to kick someone. Take your shoes off when entering a private home, or follow the example of your host. When sitting, try not to point the soles of your feet at anyone. On a related note, it's bad manners to step over the legs of someone seated: in a crowded place, Nepalis will wait for you to draw in your feet so they can pass.

Nepali views about **displays of affection** are the opposite of what most of us are used to. It's considered acceptable for friends of the same sex to hold hands or put their arms around each other in public, but not for lovers of the opposite sex. Couples shouldn't cuddle or kiss in public, nor in front of a Nepali host.

PRIVACY

Nepalis do not have the same concept of **privacy** that Westerners do. Nepali families are large and close-knit, and houses are small. Nepalis grow up constantly surrounded by other people (and noise). They like to be with other people, and they will assume you do too.

Moreover, as a foreigner you will be an object of great curiosity as soon as you step off the beaten track. People may stare, point at you and even talk about you (in Nepali) among themselves. Nepalis will constantly be befriending you, wanting to exchange addresses and extracting solemn promises that you will write to them. Sometimes they will ask you point-blank to help them travel to your country, assuming you to be wealthy enough to pay their airfare and powerful enough to fix their visa.

There will be days when you feel like if you're asked the question "What is your country?" one more time you'll hit someone. Give yourself time off when you need it. But Nepalis are the best thing about Nepal, so don't close yourself off to meeting them.

OTHER THINGS

Try to convey an accurate impression of your home country – both its good and bad points – and play down materialistic standards of success. Don't rub Nepalis' noses in technology and fashions they can't afford. Nepali society is rich in the traditions of family and community that are so often mislaid in the West, but like traditional societies worldwide it is under attack, and we are only now beginning to see that tourism is a major corrupting agent.

Finally, **be patient**. Nepal is a developing country and things don't always work or start on time.

It's unrealistic to expect things to be like they are at home, even if the menu or brochure makes them sound like they will be. If a restaurant is slow in filling your order, you have to remember they've probably only got one stove. Getting angry or impatient will only confuse Nepalis and won't resolve the problem. The Nepali way of dealing with setbacks isn't to complain, or even to keep a stiff upper lip, but to laugh. It's a delightful, infectious response.

You can't change Nepal, and even if you could, it is not yours to change. Many things in Nepal are slow, inefficient or downright nutty, but that's just the way things are. Taking the attitude that "somebody's got to teach them a lesson" or "if nobody complains it'll never change" (real-life dialogue overheard in Kathmandu) will only make you and everyone around you miserable. Go with the flow. It's Nepal you've come to experience – let it be Nepal.

To get by with a minimum of disappointment, the best strategy is to scale back your expectations, always double- and triple-check important arrangements, take all assurances with a pinch of salt (Nepalis will sometimes tell you what they think will make you happy rather than the truth), and find something fun to do while you're waiting.

BEGGARS AND TOUTS

Dealing with beggars is part of travelling in Nepal, as in most developing countries. The pathos might initially get to you, as well it should, but you will probably adjust to it fairly quickly. A thornier dilemma, which will plague you as long as you're in Nepal, is how to cope with panhandling kids and pushy touts.

A small number of bona fide **beggars** make an honest living from *bakshish* (alms). Hindus and Buddhists alike have a long and honourable tradition of giving to lepers and the disabled, as well as sadhus and monks. Destitute women make up another large contingent of the begging population: it's terrifyingly easy for a Nepali woman to find herself alone in the world, either widowed or divorced – perhaps for failing to bear a son or because of a dowry dispute. There are no unemployment or social security benefits in Nepal; anyone who can't work and has no family for support generally turns to begging. Few would choose to do so if they had an alternative.

Giving is, of course, a personal decision. You might resolve only to give to the most needy-looking, or the most persistent, or the most dignified. You might conclude that almsgiving only treats the symptoms of poverty, and decide to support a charity trying to address the causes instead. On the other hand, you could argue that direct giving gets one hundred percent of the money to the target, with no administration, red tape or corruption. At any rate, it's important to give the matter some thought (see also "Development Dilemmas" in *Contexts*).

In the hills, ailing locals will occasionally approach foreigners for **medicine**, knowing that they usually carry first-aid kits. It's probably best not to make any prescriptions unless you're qualified to diagnose the illness. However, before leaving the country you can donate unused medicines to the dispensary at Kathmandu's Bir Hospital (see p.125), which distributes them to the destitute, or to the Himalayan Yogic Institute (p.122), which gives them to Buddhist monks.

CHILDREN

Throughout Nepal – but principally along the tourist trails – **children** will hound you for money, candy and pens. Sometimes they're cute, usually they're a pain. They're not orphans or beggars, they're just ordinary Nepali schoolkids having a go. Unless they're collecting money for a festival – which is a legitimate tradition – **don't give them anything**. It will only encourage obnoxious behaviour, take away their dignity and start them on a life of toadying to tourists. Don't even try to rationalize it by thinking you'll give only to well-behaved kids: that's how monsters are created. It's natural and noble to want to share your wealth with less well-off people, but dispensing rupees and pens only leads Nepalis to expect something for nothing and saps the country's traditional self-reliance.

Saying no isn't easy. Kids will sometimes tag along for hours, giving you the Chinese water-torture treatment. In groups they can be unbearable. Remember that for them it's a game – they're just out for entertainment. The best defence is a sense of humour. If you can speak a little Nepali, try teasing them back. They're either going to laugh *at* you or *with* you, and you might as well make it the latter.

Kathmandu's **street children** are another matter. They're begging for real, but you should still think twice before giving to them – see p.96.

TOUTS AND OTHER MIDDLEMEN

Indian-style hustle is on the rise in Nepal. You'll get a major dose of it at the airport or any major bus station, where packs of **touts** lie in wait to accost arriving tourists with guest-house cards. They also cruise the tourist strips of Kathmandu, offering drugs. However, Nepali touts for the most part aren't as parasitic as their Indian brethren, and if you're entering Nepal from north India, where aggressive touts have to be dealt with firmly, adjust your attitude: they'll usually leave you alone if asked nicely, whereas they'll take a

rude brush-off personally. That said, many touts in Nepal these days are in fact Indian, and may require more drastic measures.

Kathmandu and Pokhara are full of other lone entrepreneurs and middlemen – touts by any other name. **Ticket agents** (see p.29), riksha wallahs, innkeepers and guides are ever anxious to broker services and information. Naturally they take a cut, but as with touts, they usually get their commission from the seller; your price is bumped up correspondingly. Is it a ripoff? Ripoff is a relative term. If you don't know where to spend the night or change money, a tout's services are certainly worth a few rupees. In general, though, cutting out the middleman gives you more control over the transaction – and you should find, without being too mercenary about it, that a few rupees (and smiles) given to people whose services you may require again will grease the wheels and make your stay much more pleasant.

POLICE AND TROUBLE

Nepal is one of the safest countries in the world, which is all the more remarkable when you consider the gulf between rich and poor. However, reports of theft seem to be on the rise, and political instability may be bringing a general rise in lawlessness.

The only real concern is **petty theft**, and then chiefly from fellow travellers. Common sense suggests a few precautions. Carry valuables in a money belt or pouch around your neck at all times. Bring along a padlock for securing your

room and baggage; it doesn't have to be big – deterrence is the main thing. In a dormitory, keep your kit locked up and any expensive items with you. A bag stowed on the roof of a bus is probably safe if it's lashed under the luggage tarpaulin (see "Getting Around"), but have all your valuables with you inside.

If you're robbed, report it as soon as possible to the police headquarters of the district in which the robbery occurred. They're apt to be friendly and consoling, if not much help. For insurance purposes, go to the Interpol Section of the police headquarters in Durbar Square or Naksal, Kathmandu, to fill in a report, a copy of which you'll need to keep for claiming from your insurer once you're back home. Bring a photocopy of the pages in your passport containing your photo and your Nepalese visa, together with two passport photos. Dress smartly and expect an uphill battle – they're jaded by stolen-travellers'-cheque scams.

Violent crime is extremely rare. The danger of getting raped or assaulted in a populated area is statistically insignificant, the only real concern being a certain amount of hooliganism in the Kathmandu tourist bars. The countryside is for the most part equally safe although several Western women have been raped by trekking guides in recent years (see p.343). There has always been a small risk of violent attack by bandits on remote trekking trails, so it's advisable not to walk alone.

There are several ways to get on the wrong side of the law, none of them worth it. **Smuggling** is the usual cause of serious trouble – drugs and gold are the big no-nos, and if you get caught with commercial quantities of either you'll be looking at a more or less automatic five to twenty years in prison (see p.98 for a description of that edifying experience). Give a wide berth to anyone in Hong Kong or Singapore offering "courier" jobs to Kathmandu: smuggling illicit electronics into Nepal, or antiques out, could also land you behind bars.

While it would be incredibly stupid to go through immigration control with **drugs**, discreet possession inside the country carries virtually no risk; flash dope around, though, and you could conceivably get shopped by an innkeeper.

In Nepal, where government servants are poorly paid, a little **bakshish** sometimes greases the wheels. Nepalese police don't make busts simply in order to get bribes, but if you're accused of something it might not hurt to make an offer, in an extremely careful, euphemistic and deniable way. This shouldn't be necessary if you're the victim of a crime, although you may feel like offering a reward.

WOMEN'S NEPAL

Nepal is a relatively easy place for a woman to travel. In most parts of the country you'll be of interest mainly as a foreigner rather than as a woman, and, as such, the atmosphere is tolerant and inquisitive rather than threatening or dangerous.

DEALING WITH MEN

Nepali society is on the whole chaste, almost prudish; **men** are almost universally respectful, and perhaps a little in awe, of foreign women. **Sexual harassment** is on the whole low-key, and need rarely upset your travels. Staring and catcalling are on the increase in Kathmandu –

mostly by groups of young lads who seem to have acquired the stereotype, gleaned from imported videos, of all Western women as sexually available – but it's nowhere near as bad as in India, or indeed most of Asia, and it rarely goes any further than words. Your chief danger comes from a few predatory trekking guides (see p.343).

A woman travelling or trekking **alone** won't be hassled so much as pitied. Going alone (*eklai*) is most un-Nepali behaviour. Locals (of both sexes) will ask if you haven't got a husband – the question is usually asked out of genuine concern, not as a come-on. Teaming up with another female stops the comments as effectively as being with a man. Again, you'll ensure a better reception if you wear a long skirt and a modest top – shorts and skimpy clothes are considered offensive.

If you find yourself without a reserved seat on a **public bus**, you can make your way to the front compartment, where preference is usually given to women and children. About the only form of discrimination you'll encounter is during toilet stops, when you'll have to hunt around for a sheltered place while men are free to pee by the side of the road (yet another reason to wear a long skirt).

Tarai cities and border towns are another matter, unfortunately. Some men here, as in northern India, have some real misconceptions about Western women, and may try for a surreptitious grope or even expose themselves. Travelling with a man generally shields you from this sort of behaviour. If that isn't possible, or if you resent having to do so, don't be afraid to make a public scene in the event of an untoward advance – that's what a Nepali woman would do. Though he'll pretend it wasn't him, all eyes will be upon him and he'll never try it again.

Of course, you may find you want to strike up a **relationship** with a Nepali man. If so, you should have no trouble finding eligible candidates in the bars of Kathmandu's Thamel quarter, but be aware that these gentlemen are not without their own agendas: exotic romance, conquest, perhaps even a ticket out of Nepal. If you suspect ulterior motives, let him down gently but firmly and he'll usually retreat gracefully. Quite a few women travellers fall for trekking or rafting guides – the men of highland ethnic groups, such as Sherpas, have very similar views to ours on sexual equality – and Kathmandu has a small but growing community of women who have married and settled there.

MEETING WOMEN

A frustrating aspect of travelling in Nepal is the difficulty of making contact with **Nepali women**. The tourism industry is controlled by men; women, who are expected to spend most of their time in the home and are given fewer educational opportunities, have little contact with foreigners and speak much less English. If you're lucky enough to be invited to a Nepali home for a meal, chances are the women of the house will remain in the kitchen while you eat, only emerging to clear the plates and eat the leftovers. Upper-class women are free of these restrictions and are often well educated, but of course they don't have to work so they, too, have few dealings with travellers.

The sexual politics are different among highland ethnic groups, which is as good a reason as any for going **trekking**. Along trekking routes, many women run teahouses single-handedly while their husbands are off guiding or portering. Proud, enterprising and flamboyant, these "didis" are some of the most wonderful women you're likely to meet anywhere. Language may be a problem off the popular trails, but that doesn't rule out all communication. On buses, women will be much more approachable in the front compartment. And anywhere you go, having a child with you will always open doors.

For more on **women's issues** in Nepal, see "Development Dilemmas" (p.411). The Rough Guide Special, *More Women Travel: Adventures, Advice and Experience*, gives one Western woman's account of travelling in the country.

SPECIAL NEEDS

If you plan to travel with children, or if you have a disability, you'll face extra challenges in Nepal. But don't let that stop you.

TRAVELLING WITH CHILDREN

Travelling with **children** can be extremely rewarding. Kids always help break the ice with strangers, and in Nepal they unleash even more than the usual hospitality (although the lack of privacy may prove to be a problem). They can also open a door into the often closed world of Nepali women.

However, parents will have to take extra **precautions** in the light of Nepal's poor sanitation, dogs, crowds, traffic and steep slopes. It may be very hard to sterilize bottles, or to keep hands clean and yucky stuff out of mouths. Small children will have to be kept a firm grip on most of the time.

Naturally you'll want to plan a more **modest itinerary** and travel in greater comfort with children than you would on your own. Nepal's winding, bumpy roads are likely to make kids travel sick, so take bus journeys in very small doses, or rent a car. Most cheap lodgings will be out of the question on account of their bathroom arrangements. In tourist areas it should be no problem finding food that kids will eat, but older ones may turn their noses up at Nepali food. Baby food and disposable nappies/diapers are available in Kathmandu, but are hard to come by elsewhere.

Trekking is logistically awkward with children, especially ones who are too old to ride in a backpack and too young to hike on their own. You'll need one or more porters for all the kiddie paraphernalia; porters can also carry young ones in modified *doko* (wicker baskets). Trekking with an agency can alleviate some of the hassles.

DISABLED ORGANIZATIONS

Australia *ACROD*, PO Box 60, Curtain, ACT 2605 (☎06/682 4333); 55 Charles St, Ryde (☎02/9809 4488).

Canada *Jewish Rehabilitation Hospital*, 3205 Place Alton Goldbloom, Montréal, PQ H7V 1R2 (☎514/688-9550). Guidebooks and travel information.

Ireland *National Rehabilitation Board*, 25 Clyde Rd, Ballsbridge, Dublin 4 (☎01/668 4181).

New Zealand *Disabled Persons Assembly*, PO Box 10-138, The Terrace, Wellington (☎04/472 2626).

UK *Royal Association for Disability and Rehabilitation* (*RADAR*), 250 City Rd, London EC1V 8AS (☎0171/250 3222)

USA *Mobility International USA*, PO Box 10767, Eugene, OR 97440 (☎503/343-1284).

Society for the Advancement of Travel for the Handicapped (*SATH*), 347 5th Ave, New York, NY 10016 (☎212/447-7284).

A few companies run treks and tours especially for families with children – see the earlier "Getting There" and "Outdoor Pursuits" sections.

DISABLED TRAVELLERS

Although disability is common in Nepal, it's a poor country without the means to cater for **disabled travellers**. If you walk with difficulty, you will find the steep slopes, stairs and uneven pavements hard going. Ramps and other wheelchair facilities are non-existent. Open sewers, potholes, crowds and a lack of proper street crossings will all make it hard for a blind traveller to get around.

That said, Nepalis are likely to be very helpful. **Guides** are readily available and should be prepared to provide whatever assistance you need. If you rent a taxi for the day, the driver is certain to help you in and out, and perhaps around the sites you visit. A safari in one of the Tarai wildlife parks should be feasible, and even a trek, catered to your needs by an **agency**, might not be out of the question. Try *Himalayan Holidays*, PO Box 5513, Kathmandu (☎01/228933; fax 272866).

Organizations for the disabled have little information on travel in Nepal, but they may be able to recommend tour operators or put you in touch with travelling companions.

STAYING ON

Volunteering, studying or working while in Nepal can add a satisfying focus to your trip, and deepen your understanding of another way of life.

Unfortunately, the Nepalese government doesn't make it easy to stay on legitimately, the main obstacle being that you can't stay longer than four months at a time on a tourist visa. To stay longer than this, you generally have to get a non-tourist visa through a recognized work or study programme *before* entering the country.

ON A TOURIST VISA

If you feel you've received a lot from Nepal, **volunteering** is a good way to give something back. Mother Teresa's Sisters of Charity run old people's hospices in Pashupatinath and Chabahil, and welcome walk-in help on a day-to-day basis. Tulsi Meher Ashram, a training centre for destitute women located out beyond the international airport, can use people with design experience or creative handicraft ideas – contact them through *Mahaguthi* outlets in Kathmandu or Patan. The

Kathmandu Environmental Education Project and *Himalayan Rescue Association* offices in Kathmandu need volunteers during the trekking season. Tashi Palkhel, one of the former Tibetan refugee camps near Pokhara, welcomes help, and no doubt many other aid organizations wouldn't say no to a willing dogsbody.

People with **medical qualifications** are always needed. The *Himalayan Rescue Association* accepts four doctors each autumn and spring to staff its high-altitude aid posts; the waiting list is two or three years long, but it can't hurt to write to Dr David Shlim, Director, Himalayan Rescue Association, GPO Box 495, Kathmandu, Nepal.

Numerous language schools in Kathmandu offer intensive **courses** in Nepali, Newari or Tibetan – see p.125. Opportunities to study yoga and Tibetan Buddhism are summarized in "Spiritual Pursuits and Alternative Therapies", above.

It's against the rules to work on a tourist visa, but plenty of people do anyway – notably as **trekking and rafting guides**. However, you'd have to have made several trips to Nepal, or already be experienced and well connected in the adventure-travel business, to find work as a guide. Guides are usually hired on a freelance basis, so the work is only seasonal, and immigration restrictions make it hard for non-Nepalis to stay in the country for more than two or three treks in a row. Qualified **masseurs** and **yoga/meditation instructors** may be able to find work in Kathmandu or Pokhara – try contacting the places listed towards the end of those sections.

If you haven't got any particular skills and just want an open-ended arrangement for a few weeks or so, **teaching English** is a good way to become a temporary local. Language schools in Kathmandu and Pokhara take people on with no previous experience, although the pay is negligible.

STAYING LONGER

Postings with the **Peace Corps**, **VSO** and other national voluntary agencies abound, providing you've got the relevant skills and the determination to stay two or more years. People with experience in education, health, nutrition, agriculture, forestry and other areas are preferred. Such organizations don't instigate their own projects, but place volunteers in existing projects where technical help is needed. Many other **aid agencies** (such as Action Aid, Save the Children, CARE and Oxfam) operate in Nepal and occasionally take on specialists. See "Development Dilemmas" (p.405) for an idea of what to expect.

Several American universities run **study programmes** in Nepal. The University of Wisconsin-Madison's School of South Asian Studies places students in Nepal for a full year. The School for International Training in Brattleboro, Vermont has its own campus in Naksal, Kathmandu (☎414516). The Naropa Institute in Boulder, Colorado runs a thirteen-week course on Tibetan Buddhism each autumn at Boudha.

The only known way to get a non-tourist visa after you've already arrived in Nepal is to study at Tribhuwan University's Campus of International Languages in Kathmandu. One-year courses in Nepali, Tibetan, Sanskrit and Newari begin in July, which isn't climatically convenient, although they're considering offering a six-month Nepali course starting in February. Classes run for two hours a day, five days a week, and a year's tuition costs $525. Apply no later than June with a letter of recommendation from your embassy or university to: Campus Chief, Campus of International Languages, Exhibition Road, Bhrikuti Mandap, Kathmandu, Nepal (☎226713). The university will sort out your visa.

DIRECTORY

Airport departure tax is Rs700 (Rs600 if flying within South Asia).

Addresses don't exist in Nepal: few streets even have names, and houses are never numbered. In cities, though, intersections or neighbourhoods (*tol*) usually have names and these are gradually lending themselves to the major streets nearby.

Contraceptives Condoms and birth-control pills are available in pharmacies everywhere. Consult one of the clinics in Kathmandu for other contraceptive advice.

Customs Officers are fairly lax on entry, but they might note fancy video gear in your passport so you can't sell it in Nepal. They check more thoroughly on departure, mainly to make sure you're not smuggling antiques out.

Drugs Cannabis grows wild throughout hill Nepal, and old folks sometimes smoke it as an evening tonic. Touts in Kathmandu – shady characters, but not informants – mostly peddle local hash, and also whisper offers of opium and heroin from the Golden Triangle. See the section on "Police and Trouble" for legalities.

Electricity is 220 volts/50 cycles per second, where you can get it. The bigger hill towns and most of the Tarai are electrified, as are an increasing number of villages. Virtually all power is generated by hydroelectric projects, so power cuts ("load shedding") are common in spring when water levels get low.

Embassies and consulates are all in Kathmandu: see p.125.

Emergencies Where there's a phone, dial ☎100 for the police or ☎102 for an ambulance – but it's better to get a Nepali-speaker to do the talking. Registering with your embassy can expedite things in the event of an emergency.

Gay Nepal Nepalis will tell you gay sex doesn't happen, or it's "something that Indians do". There are no gay bars or meeting places or any support network whatsoever, even in the capital. Yet in a society where the sexes are kept well apart before marriage, and men routinely hold hands and sleep together, it obviously goes on. Gay couples will certainly feel a certain freedom in being able to be close in public – but obviously not *too* close. The only approach a gay traveller is likely to get is from touts who might offer, at the end of a long inventory of drugs, "nice Nepali girls", and if that doesn't work, boys. But it's nothing like the scene in, say, Thailand.

Laundry Tourist guest houses generally take laundry, although the turn-around time depends on the weather. Rates are reasonable. If you're doing your own, detergent is sold in inexpensive packets in Kathmandu, although a concentrated liquid brought from home is less messy.

Left luggage Guest houses will always store bags for you, an invaluable service if you go trekking or any time you just want to travel light. The usual charge is a few rupees per item per day, but some places waive this if you take a room when you return.

Time Nepal is 15 minutes ahead of India – just to be contrary, one suspects. That makes it 5 hours 45 minutes ahead of London, 12 hours 45 minutes ahead of New York, 15 hours 45 minutes ahead of Los Angeles, and 21 hours 45 minutes ahead of Sydney. However, daylight-saving time in those places reduces the time difference by one hour.

Tipping Not expected, except in the classier restaurants where service is often added to the bill anyway (figure on ten percent), but a few rupees on a dinner at a budget tourist place is appreciated. Don't tip taxi drivers.

Toilets Where they exist, these range from "Western" (sit-down) flush jobs to two planks projected over a stream. In lodges – tourist ones aside – the norm is a squat toilet, usually pretty stinky and flyblown. When travelling by bus, there will almost always be a bathroom available at rest stops, but sometimes the public toilet will be nothing but a designated field. When in doubt, ask *Chaarpi kahaa chha?* (Where is the toilet?). Don't throw paper down squat toilets:

put it in the basket provided. Toilet paper is not provided in more basic guest houses and restaurants, so bring your own. Nepalis use a jug of water and the left hand (try it yourself – it's no more or less disgusting than the toilet paper method).

WHAT TO BRING

As a rule, travel light. You can buy or rent most things in Kathmandu. This box goes over the essentials that are worth bringing from home or picking up specially in Nepal. (If you think you might go **trekking**, see p.346 for an additional list of recommended items.)

An internal-frame **backpack** is probably best for heaving your things around on buses and rikshas, especially if you're also travelling in other parts of Asia as well. A travel pack, with shoulder straps that can be zipped out of sight, will help dispel lingering "hippy" prejudices when dealing with officialdom; best of all is one in which all compartments can be secured with a single padlock. A lightweight daypack also comes in handy for short excursions.

The **clothes** you bring will depend very much on the time of year, and where you expect to be going. For warm weather you'll want lightweight cotton garments – loose-fitting but modest, and covering enough to ward off sun and bugs. Shorts and a swimsuit are worth bringing (especially for rafting), but heed the advice given in "Cultural Hints", p.63. A lightweight waterproof jacket or poncho is advisable at any time of year. For cooler seasons, try to dress in layers: a T-shirt, long-sleeved shirt, sweater or polyester pile jacket and shell will set you up for almost any weather. Trainers or any sort of durable, lightweight **foot-wear** will be adequate for most conditions in Nepal, even on a trek, though higher up you'll need something sturdier. You'll also need a backup pair of shoes in case those get wet. Flipflops, available locally, will do in warm weather; sport sandals are better, and perfect for rafting.

For the sun, bring **sunscreen**, **lip balm**, **sunglasses** and a brimmed **hat**; an umbrella (available locally) acts as an effective parasol at low elevations, and is indispensable during the monsoon. If you're heading to the Tarai, especially between April and October, bring **mosquito repellent** and/or **mosquito netting** (you can buy coils locally). **Toiletries** are pretty easy to come by in Kathmandu, but bring anything out of the ordinary. Medicines, covered in the health section and the trekking chapter, are sold over the counter everywhere, but obviously bring any prescribed **medications**. If you wear **glasses** or contact lenses, make sure to pack a spare pair.

Carry valuables in a **money belt** or neck purse; a small **padlock** (available locally) is an effective deterrent to would-be thieves. **Earplugs** are a must for shutting out the ubiquitous honking vehicles, barking dogs and general commotion at night. In cheap lodgings, a **sleeping sheet** is an insurance policy against bedbugs and the like (unnecessary if you bring a sleeping bag for trekking). A **musical instrument**, portable **game** or **photos of home** will help break the ice and while away some dead hours.

And finally, some odd essentials: a **flashlight** (**torch**), **small towel**, **sewing kit**, a length of **cord** for drying clothes, a universal sink plug (few sinks have them), a pocket **alarm clock** (for early-morning departures), sealable **plastic bags** for keeping things separate in your pack, passport-size **photos** for visa and trekking applications, and **photocopies** of the pages in your passport containing personal data and your Nepalese visa.

PART TWO

THE

GUIDE

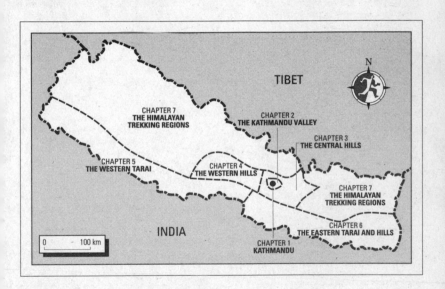

TIBET

N

CHAPTER 7
**THE HIMALAYAN
TREKKING REGIONS**

CHAPTER 2
THE KATHMANDU VALLEY

CHAPTER 3
THE CENTRAL HILLS

CHAPTER 5
THE WESTERN TARAI

CHAPTER 4
THE WESTERN HILLS

CHAPTER 7
**THE HIMALAYAN
TREKKING REGIONS**

INDIA

CHAPTER 6
THE EASTERN TARAI AND HILLS

CHAPTER 1
KATHMANDU

0 — 100 km

CHAPTER ONE

KATHMANDU

Flooded with foreign aid, beset by tourism and Indian profiteering, **Kathmandu** couldn't have been expected to remain untouched, yet it's surpassing itself in its haste to join the global village. Only a few years ago, you could just about dismiss its tourist quarters and modern buildings as aberrations in an otherwise medieval city of breathtaking architecture, dark alleys and sacred cows. Now, the picture is more confused. Not that Nepal's capital has entirely abandoned its traditional identity, but the rapid pace of change has produced a stressful, often overwhelming, urban environment.

There are, in fact, a thousand Kathmandus, layered and dovetailed and piled on top of one another in an extravagant morass of chaos and refinement. With half a million people, Kathmandu is Nepal's biggest and most cosmopolitan city: a meeting place of a dozen ethnic groups, and the home town of the Newars, Nepal's master craftsmen and traders extraordinaire (see p.86). Trade, indeed, created Kathmandu – for at least a thousand years it controlled the most important cara-

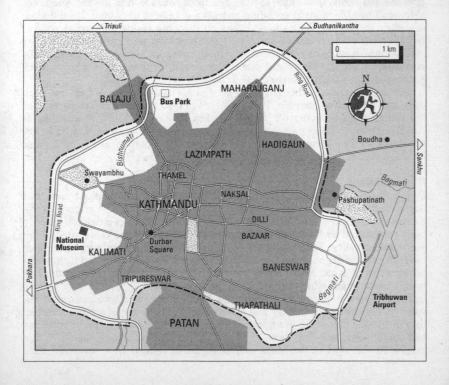

van route between Tibet and India – and trade has always funded its Newar artisans. Little wonder, perhaps, that Kathmandu has so deftly embraced the tourist business.

The Kathmandu most travellers know, **Thamel**, is like a thumping, Third World theme park, all hotels and hoardings and promises, promises, with touts flogging carpets and hashish to holiday hippies, while the words "Cake and Pie" blaze from restaurant windows like a mantra. The shrinking **old city**, though squeezed by traffic and commercial pressures, is still studded with ageless temples and shrines. Its narrow lanes seethe with an incredible crush of humanity, echoing with the din of bicycle bells, religious music, construction and car horns, reeking of incense, spices, sewage and exhaust fumes. There are, too, the outcaste shantytowns down by the river, the decrepit ministry buildings, the swanky five-star shopping streets, the sequestered suburbs, the burgeoning bazaars. But above all, the predominant images of contemporary Kathmandu are those of growth, in all its familiar and dispiriting forms: traffic jams and choking fumes; coolies stacking bricks and shovelling sand; a jostling skyline of rooftop water-storage tanks, TV antennas and satellite dishes; mobs of tourists; gangs of leather-jacketed *goondas*, Nepal's angry young men; suburban sprawl, student demonstrations, riot police, power cuts, chauffeured Land Cruisers, families on motorbikes, advertisements for kitchen appliances. Kathmandu is acquiring many of the trappings of other Asian metropolises, albeit with a uniquely Nepali slant.

Nevertheless, Kathmandu is likely to be your first port of call in Nepal – all international flights land in the capital, and most roads lead to it – and you probably won't be able to avoid spending at least a couple of days here. It's the obvious place to sort out your affairs: it has all the **embassies** and airline offices, Nepal's main **poste restante**, and a welter of **trekking and travel agencies**. At least as important, in the minds of long-haul travellers anyway, are the capital's **restaurants** and the easy social scene that surrounds them, all of which makes Kathmandu the natural place to get your initial bearings in Nepal.

All things considered though, you'd be well advised to get your business here over with as soon as possible. If you're intending to do any sightseeing around the valley, you'd be better off basing yourself in the healthier surroundings of Boudha, Patan or Bhaktapur (see Chapter Two), or even further out in Nagarkot or Dhulikhel (see Chapter Three). These days, the smart money is on staying *outside* Kathmandu and making day trips *in*, not vice versa.

A little history
People must have occupied what is now Kathmandu for thousands of years, but chroniclers attribute the city's founding to Gunakama Deva, who reigned in the early eighth century – by which time sophisticated urban centres had already been established by the **Lichhavi** kings at Pashupatinath and other sites in the surrounding valley. Kathmandu was originally known as Kantipur, but it later took its present name from the Kasthamandap ("Pavilion of Wood") that was constructed as a rest house along the main Tibet–India trade route in the late twelfth century, and which still stands in the city centre.

The city rose to prominence under the **Malla** kings, who took control of the valley in the thirteenth century and ushered in a golden age of art and architecture that lasted more than five hundred years. All of Kathmandu's finest buildings and monuments, including those of its spectacular Durbar Square, date from this period. At the start of the Malla era, Kathmandu ranked as a sovereign state alongside the valley's other two major cities, Bhaktapur and Patan, but soon fell under the rule of Bhaktapur. The cities were again divided in the fifteenth century, and a long period of intrigue and rivalry followed.

Malla rule ended abruptly in 1769, when Prithvi Narayan Shah of Gorkha, a previously undistinguished hill state to the west, captured the valley as the first conquest in his historic unification of Nepal. Kathmandu fared well in defeat, being made capital of the new nation and seat of the new **Shah** dynasty. The Shahs rule to this day, although from 1846 to 1951 they were politically outmanoeuvred by the powerful **Rana** family, who ruled as hereditary prime ministers and left Kathmandu with a legacy of enormous white (now mouldy grey) Neoclassical palaces. The capital remains the focus of all national political power – the 1990 democracy movement led, inevitably, to the palace gate – while its industrial and financial activities continue to fuel a round-the-clock building boom.

Orientation and arrival

Despite chaotic first appearances, Kathmandu is surprisingly easy to get to grips with; the touts, like everything else, become much more manageable once you've dumped your bags. The following, along with the map overleaf, should help with **orientation**.

Tradition has it that old Kathmandu was laid out in the shape of a *khukuri* knife. Positioned at what would be the hilt of the knife is **Durbar Square** – a non-stop carnival set amidst temples, monuments and the former royal palace – while the city's oldest neighbourhoods stretch northeast and (to a lesser extent) south-west. **New Road,** the city's best-known shopping street, runs east from the square. Kathmandu's budget hotels are concentrated in two areas: **Thamel**, north of Durbar Square in a new part of town, and Jhochhen, better known as **Freak Street**, immediately south of the square.

Suburban Kathmandu sprawls mainly east of **Kantipath**, the main north–south thoroughfare, and is dominated by two landmarks, the **Royal Palace** and the **Tudikhel** (parade ground). Most of the expensive hotels, restaurants and airline

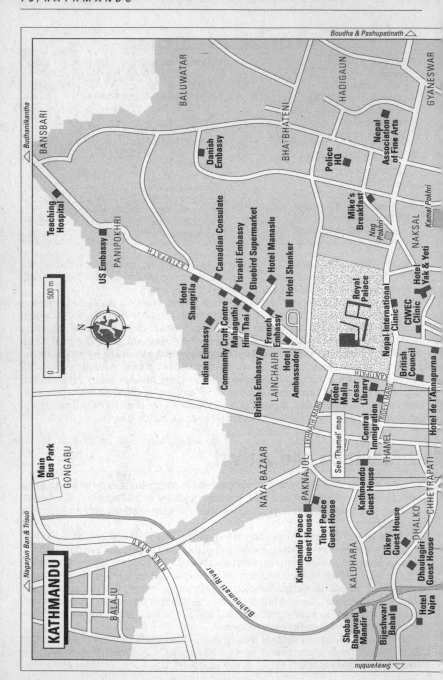

KATHMANDU

Airport & Pashupatinath Airport Bhaktapur & the Airport

German Embassy

MAITIDEVI

DILLI BAZAAR

BANESWAR

Everest Hotel

Maps of Nepal

Jail

Dhobi Khola

American Library

Singha Durbar

Royal Nepal Academy

RAM SHAH PATH

Supreme Court

Archaeology Dept

Ministry of Tourism

Dept. of National Parks

Bhanchha Ghar

KAMALADI

French Cultural Centre

Clocktower

BAGH BAZAAR

EXHIBITION ROAD

City Park

City Hall

PRITHVI PATH

Exhibition Ground

Army Camp

THAPATHALI

AIRPORT ROAD (ARNIKO RAJMARG)

Bluebird Supermarket

KALAMOCHAN

Patan

DURBAR MARG

KAMAL

Rani Pokhri

Ratna Park

Tudikhel

Bhadrakali Mandir

National Stadium

Bhaktapur Trolley Bus Stop

Delicatessen Centre

THAHITI

American Express

National Theatre

KANTIPATH

Martyrs' Gate

Central Telegraph Office

ASAN

Bir Hospital

RNAC

GPO

Jails

TRIPURESWAR

Bagmati River

INDRACHOWK

SHUKRA PATH

NEW ROAD

Nepal Bank

Bhimsen Tower

BHOTE BAHAL

Patan

See 'North of Durbar Square' map

Nepal Market

JHOCHHEN (FREAK ST)

LAGAN

TRIPURESWAR MARG

GHATS

See 'South of Durbar Square' map

DURBAR SQUARE

BASANTAPUR SQUARE

Hanuman Dhoka

MARU

BHIMSEN THAN

TEKU

Kiripur

TAHACHAL

Peace Guest House

KALIMATI

Swayambhu National Museum Pokhara

offices huddle along **Durbar Marg**, the broad boulevard running south from the palace gate. West of the Bishnumati River is not, strictly speaking, part of Kathmandu, but the hilltop temple of **Swayambhu** is close enough to be reached easily on foot.

Arriving by air

Arriving by air at **Tribhuwan International Airport**, 5km east of the city centre, you'll first have to deal with **immigration**. If you haven't already got a visa, fill out a visa application form and join the queue; you'll need one passport-size photo and $25 or hard-currency equivalent in cash – and worn notes aren't accepted. An exchange window in the immigration hall cashes travellers' cheques. Having a visa already will save a few minutes on the immigration process. Baggage claim is downstairs, where if you're quick you might be able to grab a trolley. The **bank**, to the right as you exit customs, changes money at rates slightly lower than those in town. Nearby is a government **tourist information** desk and a desk operated by *Travellers' Nepal*, which hands out free magazines and city maps.

The guest house **touts** outside the airport can be awful. Brace yourself before leaving the building, and have a plan. One strategy is to fix on a particular guest house and immediately hire a taxi to take you there; phone ahead using a white courtesy phone (if it's working), or just name a place where you know there'll be other fallbacks nearby if it's full. Alternatively, entertain offers from touts, choose one, and see what kind of room you end up with (you can always change the next day). Either way, as soon as you've made a decisive action the other touts will back off. **Taxi** fares into town are quasi-fixed at Rs150 (supplement charged for extra passengers) – buy a coupon from the cooperative association desk and present it to one of the member drivers. **Blue (Sajha) buses** offer a cheap (Rs3) but inconvenient alternative. They depart from the main intersection at the end of the airport drive (a 200m walk) and drop passengers off at the City Bus Park, a good 1km from most guest houses. Touts may offer a "free" ride if you stay in their lodge, but of course the fare will just get added on to the room price.

Arriving by bus

Tourist **buses** from Pokhara and Chitwan let passengers off at Thamel and Bhimsen Tower, an easy walk from guest houses. Coming from the Indian border or Pokhara by public bus, you'll arrive at the Main Bus Park, located at Gongabu at the extreme north end of the city; taxis and tempos (see below) charge Rs40–60 to most tourist destinations. If you happen to be travelling by *Sajha* bus, stay on board and the bus will continue on to Bhimsen Tower. Buses from the Tibet border terminate at the City Bus Park, east of the city centre and a Rs25–40 taxi ride to lodgings.

Information and maps

The government **tourist offices** at the airport and just off Durbar Square (Sun–Thurs 9am–5pm, 4pm in winter; Fri 9am–3pm) give out general brochures and can answer easy questions. They're most useful for information on upcoming festivals and public transport. The Ministry of Tourism (Sun–Thurs 11am–4pm, Fri 11am–3pm), located in Babar Mahal on the Airport Road, provides free colour posters and mediocre country maps, subject to availability. By the time you read

The telephone code for Kathmandu and the Kathmandu Valley is ☎01.

this, the new **Kathmandu Tourist Service Center** should have opened at Bhrikuti Mandap, the exhibition ground east of the Tudikhel, and may eventually take the place of the other tourist offices.

For nuts-and-bolts practical information, bypass the government offices and make for the **Kathmandu Environmental Education Project (KEEP)** and the **Himalayan Rescue Association (HRA)**, which have offices on Tridevi Marg, near Central Immigration. These nonprofit organizations specialize mainly in trekking tips, but staff may be able to help with other matters, and the notice board in the hall outside is useful for finding trekking partners, selling or buying equipment, and hearing about events. (Similar notice boards can be found in many tourist guest houses and restaurants, notably the *Kathmandu Guest House* and *Pumpernickel Bakery*.) Another nonprofit organization, the **Nepal Tourist Watch Centre (NETWAC)**, can help with questions about local culture and festivals. It has no permanent premises, but its director can be contacted through one of the curio shops opposite the entrance to the Hanuman Dhoka palace.

The advertiser-supported city **maps** given away at the airport and tourist information offices should suffice for most purposes. More detailed maps, as well as country and trekking maps, are sold in bookshops and by street vendors; *Pilgrim's Book House* in Thamel has a comprehensive selection. For avid cartographers, *Maps of Nepal*, 300m west of the *Everest Hotel* on the Airport Road, carries an intriguing range of political and resource maps.

Getting around

Getting around the old city is easiest on **foot**. Traffic and pollution make **cycling** something of a chore these days, but it's the best way to get to many outlying sights. One-speed bikes can be rented from numerous outlets in Thamel and Freak Street and from some guest houses (Rs50–75 a day). **Mountain bikes**, often of disappointing quality (see p.33 and p.56), range from about Rs80 a day for a one-speed model to Rs150–200 for an eighteen-speeder. There are a few proper American mountain bikes for rent in Thamel for Rs300 per day, plus Rs50 for a helmet – try *Hotel Star*, just south of the *Kathmandu Guest House*. Shop for bikes early, or even the night before, and try to bargain for long-term discounts.

Riding a **motorcycle** isn't much fun inside the Ring Road, but it's a great way to explore the Kathmandu Valley. Several operators in Thamel and Freak Street rent out 100cc motorcycles (a *great* way to explore the Kathmandu Valley) for about Rs400 a day, not including petrol. You'll need to leave a plane ticket or passport as security, and you're supposed to show a driving licence.

If you're in your own car or van, beware – central Kathmandu is a nightmare for **driving**. Do not attempt to enter with a camper or other large vehicle. The streets are too narrow and crowded, and you'll be constantly defeated by the one-way system.

Taxis, tempos and buses

Vehicles with more than two wheels make slow progress through the old part of town, but have their place for longer journeys. Lured by generous tax breaks, a large number of **taxi companies** operate in Kathmandu. Taxis that display a company logo or light are newer, more comfortable and equipped with tamper-proof meters, which drivers are legally required to use. Older, **freelance cabs** still use mechanical meters, which are usually out of date (ask your guest house what percentage they're currently adding to the meter), and drivers will often try to quote a fixed price. Company taxis can be requested by phone; freelances can usually be found at the main Thamel intersection, north of the *Kathmandu Guest House* and at the top of Freak Street. Taxis get scarce after about 8pm – try the night taxi service (☎224374).

Like freelance taxis, **metered tempos** (auto rikshas) add a percentage to the displayed fare, if you can get them to go by the meter at all. The fare is likely to be only slightly less than what a taxi would charge. **Fixed-route tempos** shuttle on various routes, generally starting from near the *Air India* office on Kantipath, where they create the most almighty jams; the only ones you're likely to use are the white battery-powered *safaa* ("clean") tempos that ply between Kathmandu and Patan. Pedal **rikshas** are really only worthwhile for short distances on narrow, crowded streets; the price should be about the same as for a tempo, but they charge whatever they can, so establish terms before setting off.

Public **buses** and **minibuses** are cheap (no more than Rs5), but slow and extremely crowded. They run along regular but unnumbered routes, and are easiest to cope with if you can get on at the starting point (usually the City Bus Park) and stay on till the end. Details of services are given where relevant in this chapter and the next.

The City

The scene on Thamel avenue today: a very pretty pale-brown cow standing on the sidewalk, between a cigarette stand and an umbrella repairman, her head lifted straight up, perpendicular with the ground, while a ten-year-old boy heading home from school stood there, reaching up and scratching the animal's neck. Meanwhile all the tourists pointing to the fruit-bats hanging in the trees. The smell of bat shit and garbage and day-old murk, literally Another Shitty Day in Paradise. Shangri-la's getting wasted, but you can still stand on the street corner in Kathmandu and scratch her heavy velvet throat.

Jeff Greenwald, *Mister Raja's Neighborhood*

The Kathmandu most travellers come to see is the old city, a tight tangle of narrow alleys and numerous temples immediately north and south of the central **Durbar Square**. It's a bustling, intensely urban quarter where tall, extended-family dwellings block out the sun, while dark, open-fronted shops crowd the lanes, and vegetable sellers clot the intersections. Though the city goes to bed early, from before dawn to around 10pm there's always something happening somewhere. Early morning is the best time to watch people going about their daily religious rites (*puja*), adorning idols with red paste (*sindur*) and marigold petals. If you walk around after dinner, especially in the neighbourhoods of Indrachowk, Asan and Chhetrapati, you'll frequently run across mesmerizing devotional hymn-sings (*bhajan*).

This is only one side of Kathmandu, though, and not necessarily representative of the rest. Across the Bishnumati River, just **west** of town, is a more newly settled and rapidly developing area; the famous Swayambhu stupa, magnificently set on a conical hill here, has attracted a large community of expatriate Tibetans, whose culture is a world apart from that of Kathmandu's indigenous Newars.

Most commerce these days is conducted **east** of the old quarter: the boulevards around the Royal Palace are wide and businesslike, lined with airline offices and five-star hotels, while tinny, congested bazaars sprawl further to the south and east. The northeast is given over to quiet, shaded suburbs.

Durbar Square

Teeming, touristy **Durbar Square** is the natural place to begin sightseeing. The old royal palace (*durbar*), running along the eastern edge of the square, takes up more space than all the other monuments here combined. Kumari Chowk, home of Kathmandu's "living goddess", overlooks the square from the south. The square itself is squeezed by the palace into two parts: at the southern end is the Kasthamandap, the ancient building that probably gave Kathmandu its name, while the northern part is taken up by a varied procession of statues and temples.

The *Nepal Tourist Watch Centre* (*NETWAC*), which operates out of a handicrafts shop across the square from the palace entrance, sells an excellent **map** of the square that contains a wealth of archeological and historical detail (Rs20 donation).

Hanuman Dhoka

The rambling **old royal palace** (Mon, Wed, Thurs & Sun 10.30am–4pm, 3pm in winter; Fri 10.30am–2pm; closed Tues; Rs50) is usually called **Hanuman Dhoka**, after its main entrance. Its oldest, eastern wings date from the mid-sixteenth century, but in all likelihood there was a palace on this spot before then. Malla kings built most of the rest by the late seventeenth century, and after capturing Kathmandu in 1768, Prithvi Narayan Shah added (in characteristically martial fashion) four lookout towers at the southeastern corner. Finally, the Ranas left their mark with the garish Neoclassical facade along the southwestern flank. Nepal's royal family last lived here in 1886, before moving to the northern end of town, retaining the complex for ceremonial and administrative purposes.

Only a fraction of the five-acre palace and grounds is open to the public; entrance is through **Hanuman Dhoka** (Hanuman Gate), a brightly decorated doorway at the east side of the northern part of Durbar Square. The gate is named after the popular monkey god Hanuman, whose statue stands outside – you won't recognize him, smothered under a layer of *sindur* paste, but that's the way Nepalis like him. Ram's right-hand man in the Hindu *Ramayan* epic, Hanuman has always been revered by Nepalese kings, who, like Ram, are held to be incarnations of the god Vishnu. On the left as you enter stands a masterful sculpture of another Vishnu incarnation, the man-lion Narasimha, tearing apart a demon, followed by the Malla kings' audience hall, now adorned with a series of portraits of Shah kings, beginning with Prithvi Narayan Shah.

The entrance opens to **Nassal Chowk**, the large central courtyard that provided the setting for King Birendra's coronation in 1975, and which is still used for important royal functions. The brick wings that form its southern and eastern flanks date from the sixteenth century and boast painstakingly carved wooden doorways, windows and struts – check out the door jambs beaded with

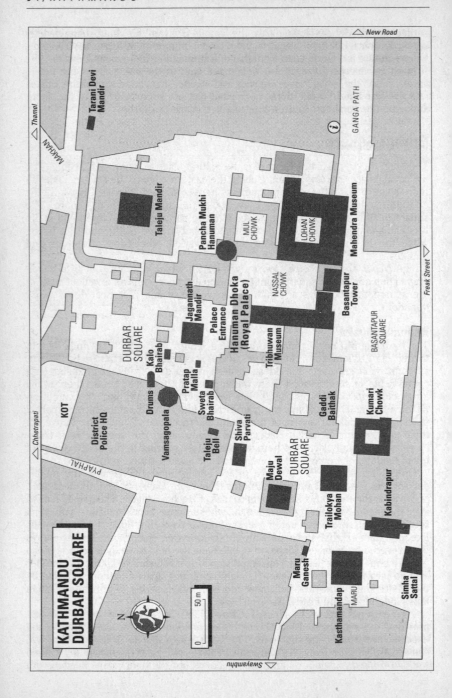

KATHMANDU
DURBAR SQUARE

0 50 m

New Road

Thamel

MAKHAN

Tarani Devi
Mandir

GANGA PATH

Taleju Mandir

Pancha Mukhi
Hanuman

MUL
CHOWK

LOHAN
CHOWK

Mahendra Museum

Jagannath
Mandir

NASSAL
CHOWK

Basantapur
Tower

Palace
Entrance

DURBAR
SQUARE

Hanuman Dhoka
(Royal Palace)

Kalo
Bhairab

Tribhuwan
Museum

BASANTAPUR
SQUARE

Freak Street

KOT

Drums

Pratap
Malla

Sweta
Bhairab

District
Police HQ

Vamsagopala

Taleju
Bell

Shiva
Parvati

Gaddi
Baithak

Kumari
Chowk

PYAPHAL

Chhetrapati

Maju
Dewal

DURBAR
SQUARE

Kabindrapur

Trailokya
Mohan

Maru
Ganesh

Kasthamandap

MARU

Simha
Sattal

Swayambhu

tiny skulls. At the northeast corner of the square, the five-tiered pagoda-like turret, notable for its round roofs, is the **Pancha Mukhi Hanuman Mandir**.

Two equally ornate courtyards, **Lohan Chowk** and **Mul Chowk**, are visible through doorways to the east; the latter is closed to the public.

THE MUSEUMS AND BASANTAPUR TOWER

Housed in the west and south wings overlooking Nassal Chowk, the **Tribhuwan Museum** features a collection of memorabilia from the reign of the present king's grandfather, Tribhuwan. Often referred to as *rashtrapita* ("father of the nation"), Tribhuwan is fondly remembered for his pivotal role in restoring the monarchy in 1951 and opening up Nepal to the outside world. Looking at the photos and newspaper clippings in this exhibit, you get a sense of the upheavals and high drama of 1950–51, when the king sought asylum in India and then, having served as the figurehead for resistance efforts against the crumbling Rana regime, returned triumphantly to power. Also on display are jewel-studded coronation ornaments, royal furniture, guns, trophies and even a casket. The exhibit ends with a small selection of salvaged wooden temple carvings.

The museum leads to the massive nine-storey **Basantapur Tower**, the biggest of the four raised by Prithvi Narayan Shah in honour of the four main cities of the Kathmandu Valley (Basantapur – "Place of Spring" – refers to Kathmandu). You can ascend to a kind of crow's nest enclosed by pitched wooden screens to get fine views in four directions, while the sound of flute sellers drifts up from the square below. The highest mountains visible are those of the Langtang Himal, just peeking up above the Gosainkund Lekh.

From the tower you can descend directly to Nassal Chowk, but carry on through labyrinthine corridors to the **King Mahendra Memorial Museum**, dedicated to the present king's late father. Like the Tribhuwan exhibit, this one marches chronologically through the life and times of a monarch, the most interesting attractions being a hunting scene, recreations of Mahendra's office and cabinet room, items from his library (including a book of his poetry) and two thrones (one for the king's immediate ascension, the other for his formal coronation). The museum exits onto Lohan Chowk.

THE PALACE EXTERIOR

Two sights along the outer walls of the palace are worth mentioning. Just to the north of the entrance is a **stone inscription** in fifteen languages, carved in 1664 by King Pratap Malla, the prime architect of Durbar Square's temples, who also fancied himself something of a linguist. The inscription is supposed to be a poem to the goddess Kali, and the story goes that if anyone can read the whole thing, milk will gush from the tap. Look for the two words in French and one in English.

Stuck onto the palace's southwestern end like a barnacle is the **Gaddi Baithak**, a ponderous addition from 1908 that pretty much sums up Rana-era architecture. If you didn't know Nepalese history you might say it had a whiff of the Raj about it, and in a way you'd be right: while India was under British rule, Nepal was labouring under its own home-grown colonialists, the Rana line of isolationist prime ministers. Purists bemoan the building's distorting effect on Durbar Square's proportions, but while it's admittedly out of step with traditional Nepali architecture, it certainly peps up the square with a dash of mock bravado.

KATHMANDU CULTURE: THE NEWARS

Although only a minor ethnic group in national terms, the **Newars** account for three-quarters of Kathmandu's population and exert a cultural influence in Nepal far beyond their numbers. Some scholars make the Newars out to be descendants of the Kiratas, who ruled the Kathmandu Valley between the seventh century BC and the second century AD, while others say they go back even further than that. In any case, the Newar community has had to absorb successive waves of immigrants, refugees, traders and usurpers ever since, resulting in a complex cultural matrix.

Centuries of domination by foreign rulers have, if anything, only accentuated the uniqueness of Newar culture. For 1500 years the Newars have sustained an almost continuous artistic flowering: under the Lichhavis they produced acclaimed stone carvings, and under the Mallas and Shahs they've excelled in wood, metal and brick. They're believed to have invented the pagoda, and it was a Newar architect, **Arniko**, who led a Nepali delegation in the thirteenth century to introduce the technique to the Chinese. The pagoda style of stacked, angled roofs finds unique expression in Nepali (read Newar) temples, and is echoed in the overhanging eaves of Newar houses.

The shape of Newar settlements goes right to the roots of Newar civilization: farming and trade. As farmers, Newars build their **villages** in compact, urban nuclei to conserve the fertile farmland of the valley. As traders, they construct their houses with removable wooden shutters, so that the ground floor can double as a shop. Scattered, in part, by the shortage of land in the valley, Newar traders have colonized lucrative crossroads throughout Nepal, recreating bustling **bazaars** wherever they go.

But above all, Newars are consummate city-builders. The fundamental building block of old Newar **cities** is the **bahal** – a set of buildings joined at right angles around a central courtyard. Kathmandu is honeycombed with *bahal*, many of which were originally built as Buddhist monasteries but have reverted to residential use during two centuries of state-sponsored Hinduism. (*Bahal* architecture was applied to palaces as well, as a look at a map of Durbar Square will readily demonstrate.) Another uniquely Newar invention is the **guthi**, a benevolent community trust based on caste or kinship links that handles the upkeep of temples (*mandir*) and fountains (*hiti*), organizes festivals, arranges cremations and, indirectly, ensures the transmission of Newar culture from one generation to the next. Kathmandu's *guthi* have been on the decline since the 1960s, however, when land reform deprived them of much of their income from holdings around the valley, and with young Newars losing interest in traditional ways they are gradually being marginalized into social clubs.

Newars are easily recognized. Traditionally they carry heavy loads in baskets suspended at either end of a **shoulder pole** (*nol*), whereas other Nepali hill people carry things on their backs, supported by a tumpline from the forehead. As for **clothing**, you can usually tell a Newar man by his waistcoat, and a woman by her shawl (it used to be the fashion for Newar women to wear their saris in complicated pleats, requiring upwards of twenty-five metres of material, but these days most follow the Indian style). Most Newars still speak among themselves in **Newari** (known among purists as Nepal Bhasa), a Tibeto-Burman language with many borrowings from Nepali (see p.436), and several Newari newspapers are published in Kathmandu. Repressed by the pre-1990 regime, Newari is now undergoing a strong revival, with schools offering courses in it and Radio Nepal broadcasting Newari programming.

For a detailed description of Newar **religion**, see *Contexts*, p.393.

Kumari Chowk

Immediately south of the Gaddi Baithak stands **Kumari Chowk**, the gilded cage of the Raj Kumari, Kathmandu's "living goddess". In case there was any doubt, Kumari Chowk proves Kathmandu is no stuffy, dead museum: no other temple better illustrates the living, breathing and endlessly adaptable nature of religion in Nepal, with its freewheeling blend of Hindu, Buddhist and indigenous elements.

A Newar and his *nol*

The cult of **the Kumari** – a prepubescent girl worshipped as a living incarnation of Durga, the demon-slaying Hindu mother goddess – probably goes back to the early Middle Ages. Jaya Prakash, the last Malla king of Kathmandu, institutionalized the practice when he built the Kumari Chowk in 1757. According to legend, the king either committed some sexual indiscretion against a Kumari, or disbelieved a girl who claimed to be the goddess – in any case Jaya Prakash, who is remembered as a particularly paranoid and weak king, was so consumed by guilt that he erected the building as an act of atonement. He also established the tradition – continued to this day – that each September during the festival of Indra Jaatra, the Kumari should bestow a *tika* (auspicious mark) on the forehead of the king who was to reign for the coming year. In 1768, the hapless Jaya Prakash was driven into exile on the eve of Indra Jaatra, and the conquering Prithvi Narayan Shah slipped in and took the *tika*. Kathmandu's Raj Kumari is the pre-eminent of eleven in the valley.

Although the Kumari is supposed to be a Hindu goddess, she is chosen from the Buddhist Shakya clan of goldsmiths, according to a **selection process** reminiscent of the Tibetan Buddhist method of finding reincarnated lamas. Elders interview hundreds of Shakya girls, aged three to five, short-listing those who exhibit 32 auspicious signs: a neck like a conch shell, a body like a banyan tree, eyelashes like a cow's and so on. Finalists are placed in a dark room surrounded by freshly severed buffalo heads, while men in demon masks parade around making scary noises. The girl who shows no fear and can correctly identify belongings of previous Kumaris, and whose horoscope doesn't clash with the king's, becomes the next Kumari. She lives a cloistered life inside the Kumari Chowk and is only carried outside on her throne at Indra Jaatra and four or five other festivals each year; her feet are never allowed to touch the ground. Durga's spirit leaves her when she menstruates or otherwise bleeds, whereupon she's retired with a modest state pension. The transition to life as an ordinary mortal can be hard, and she may have difficulty finding a husband, since tradition has it that the man who marries an ex-Kumari will die young. The present Kumari was installed in 1993, when she was four and a half years old, so she's likely to make the millennium.

Non-Hindus aren't allowed past the Kumari Chowk's **interior courtyard**, which is decorated with exquisitely carved (if weathered) windows, pillars and doorways. When she feels like it, the Kumari, decked out in exaggerated eye makeup and jewellery, shows herself at one of the first-floor windows, at which time one of her handlers generally whips round for donations. She's believed to answer her

For background information on the various gods, their symbols and styles of worship, see "Religion" in *Contexts* (p.388). Definitions of various Nepali religious terms are also given in the glossary on p.437.

visitors' unspoken questions with the look on her face. Cameras are okay inside the courtyard, but photographing the Kumari is strictly forbidden.

Temples and monuments

Dozens of freestanding temples (*mandir*), stepped platforms (*dewal*) and statues litter Durbar Square; the following stand out as highlights.

THE KASTHAMANDAP

If legend is to be believed, the **Kasthamandap**, standing at the southwestern end of the square, is Kathmandu's oldest building, and one of the oldest wooden buildings in the world. It's said to have been constructed from the wood of a single tree in the late twelfth century (Simha Sattal, the smaller version to the south, was made from the leftovers), but what you see is mostly the result of several renovations since 1630. An open, pagoda-roofed pavilion (*mandap*), it served for several centuries as a rest house (*sattal*) along the Tibet trade route, and probably formed the nucleus of early Kathmandu. This corner of the square, called Maru Tol, still has the look of a crossroads, with sellers hawking fruit, vegetables and flowers, and the city's indigents still sleep in the Kasthamandap at night.

The Shah kings converted the Kasthamandap into a temple to their protector deity*, **Gorakhnath**, whose statue stands in the middle of the pavilion. A Brahman priest usually sets up shop here to dispense instruction and conduct rituals. In four niches set around are shrines to Ganesh, the elephant-headed god of good fortune, which supposedly represent the celebrated Ganesh temples of the Kathmandu Valley (at Chabahil, Bhaktapur, Chobar and Bungamati), thus enabling Kathmandu residents to pay tribute to all four at once.

The building to the southeast of the Kasthamandap is **Kabindrapur**, a temple to Shiva in his role as Nataraj ("Lord of the Dance"), which is mostly patronized by musicians and dancers.

THE REST OF THE SOUTHERN SQUARE

Immediately north of the Kasthamandap stands yet another Ganesh shrine, the unassuming but ever-popular **Maru Ganesh**. A ring on Ganesh's bell is usually the first stage in any *puja*, and the shrine is the first stop for people intending to worship at the other temples of Durbar Square, royalty included. Ganesh's trusty "vehicle", a rat, is perched on a plinth of the Kasthamandap, across the way.

---

*A word about the confusing matter of royal deities. Gorakhnath, a mythologized Indian guru, is revered as a kind of guardian angel by all the Shah kings. Taleju Bhawani, to whom many temples and bells are dedicated in the Kathmandu, Patan and Bhaktapur Durbar Squares, played a similar role for the Malla kings. The Kumari has been worshipped by the kings of both dynasties, but mainly as a public gesture to secure her *tika*, which lends credibility to their divine right to rule. Finally, the present king, Birendra, exercising the prerogative of all Hindus, has taken as his own family deity Dakshin Kali, whose shrine is at the southern edge of the Kathmandu Valley.

The three-roofed temple between the Kasthamandap and the Kumari Chowk is the seventeenth-century **Trailokya Mohan,** dedicated to Vishnu. The *das avatar* dance takes place here during the September Indra Jaatra celebrations, in which masked dancers portray the ten incarnations of Vishnu. A much-photographed statue of the angelic **Garud,** Vishnu's man-bird vehicle, kneels in his customary palms-together *namaste* position in front of the temple.

The large doors just south of the Trailokya Mohan conceal the chariot that ferries the Kumari around during Indra Jaatra. The broad, bricked area to the east is **Basantapur Square,** once the site of royal elephant stables, where souvenir sellers now spread their wares.

Moving north, the huge seventeenth-century **Maju Dewal** sits high atop a pyramid of nine stepped levels. Climb to the top for a sweeping, god's-eye view of the square and all its hubbub, but don't expect to escape the roving bangle-sellers and students anxious to practise their English. From this height you can look straight across at the rectangular **Shiva Parvati Mandir,** erected in the eighteenth century by one of the early Shah kings. Painted figures of Shiva and his consort Parvati lean out of the first-floor window, looking like they're about to toss the bouquet and dash off to the honeymoon suite.

SWETA BHAIRAB AND KALO BHAIRAB

North of the Shiva Parvati temple, the square narrows and then opens out to another temple-clogged area. Ranged along the left (western) side are the **Taleju Bell,** the octagonal **Vamsagopala,** and a pair of ceremonial **drums** from the eighteenth century. To the right, set against the palace wall but not very visible behind a wooden screen, is the snarling ten-foot-high gilded head of **Sweta Bhairab** (White Bhairab), a terrifying, blood-swilling aspect of Shiva. One day a year, during Indra Jaatra in September, the screen comes down and men jostle to drink rice beer flowing out of a pipe in Bhairab's mouth. The column nearby supports a gilded statue of **King Pratap Malla** and family, a self-congratulatory artform that was all the rage among the Malla kings of the late seventeenth century.

North of this, on the other side of the small Degu Taleju Mandir, the massive, roly-poly image of **Kalo Bhairab** (Black Bhairab) dances on the corpse of a demon. Carved from a single twelve-foot slab of stone, it was found in a field north of Kathmandu during the reign of Pratap Malla, but probably dates to Lichhavi times. It used to be said that anyone who told a lie in front of it would vomit blood and die; one story has it that when the chief justice's office stood across the way, so many witnesses died while testifying that a temple had to be erected to shield the court from Kalo Bhairab's wide-eyed stare.

THE JAGANNATH AND TALEJU TEMPLES

Between Pratap Malla's column and his multilingual inscription on the palace wall stands the sixteenth-century pagoda-style **Jagannath Mandir,** dedicated to the god whose runaway-chariot festival in India gave us the word "juggernaut". The struts supporting the lower roof of this temple contain Kathmandu's most tittered-about **erotic carvings,** although such carvings are actually quite common in Nepali temples: once you know where to look, you start noticing them everywhere. Scholars can't seem to agree on the significance of these little vignettes, which often feature outrageous athletics, threesomes and bestiality. Some suggest that sex in this context is being offered as a tantric path to enlightenment, and as evidence they note that such scenes generally appear on the lower portions of struts, separated from the gods and goddesses above by lotuses (symbolic of transcendence). A more popular belief is that the goddess of lightning is a chaste virgin who wouldn't dare strike a temple so decorated. In any case, Hanuman, who guards the nearby palace entrance, is spared the sight by the globs of *sindur* over his eyes.

Set atop a twelve-tiered plinth and rising 40m above the northeast end of the square, the **Taleju Mandir** was erected in the mid-sixteenth century by King Mahendra Malla, who built it to outdo the Taleju temples of his rivals in Patan and Bhaktapur, and decreed that no building should exceed it in height – a ban that remained in force until the middle part of this century. Kathmandu's biggest temple, it looks down on you with haughty grandeur. It's open only on the ninth day of Dasain, and then only to Nepalis, who make sacrifices to Durga in the courtyard. Taleju Bhawani, a south Indian goddess imported in the fourteenth century by the Mallas, is considered by Hindus to be a form of the mother goddess Durga, while Buddhist Newars count her as one of the Taras, tantric female deities. Behind the Taleju Mandir, reached by a doorway from Makhan Tol (see below), sits the brick god-house of **Tarani Devi**, Taleju's "older sister".

Other, minor temples dotting the northern square belong mainly to Shiva. Inside each, the god is worshipped as a *linga*, a stone phallus that to a Shaiva (follower of Shiva) is as potent a symbol as the cross is to a Christian. The infamous **Kot Courtyard**, which once lay northwest of the square, is now taken up by a walled police compound. It was here that the Machiavellian general Jang Bahadur Rana engineered a grisly massacre of 55 of the king's top brass in 1846, thereby clearing the way to proclaim himself prime minister and establish the hereditary line that was to rule Nepal until 1951.

North of Durbar Square

Kathmandu's oldest, liveliest streets lie north and northeast of Durbar Square. You could make a more or less circular swing through the area (as this section does), but you'll almost certainly be diverted somewhere along the way. At any rate, the sights described here are only a backdrop for the old city's fascinating street life.

Indrachowk and Kel Tol

The old trade route to Tibet passes through Durbar Square and becomes a narrow lane where it rounds the Taleju Mandir. Passing through **Makhan Tol** – the name harks back to a time when butter (*makhan*) was sold here – it runs a gauntlet of *thangka* (Buddhist scroll painting) sellers and then takes a northeasterly bearing toward Kathmandu's traditional goldsmiths' neighbourhood. The first big intersection you reach is **Indrachowk**, named in honour of the original Hindu king of the gods. A sort of Asian Zeus, complete with thunderbolt, Indra fell from grace in India centuries ago, but in the Kathmandu Valley he's still revered as a rainmaker and rates his own festival (Indra Jaatra). The gaudy house-like temple on the west side of the crossroads – its front decorated with European ceramic tiles, a common practice earlier this century – is that of **Akash Bhairab** (Sky, or Blue, Bhairab), who in the best anything-goes spirit of Hinduism sometimes trades places with Indra. The upstairs temple is out-of-bounds to non-Hindus, but you can see the scary black mask of Bhairab paraded around Kathmandu during Indra Jaatra.

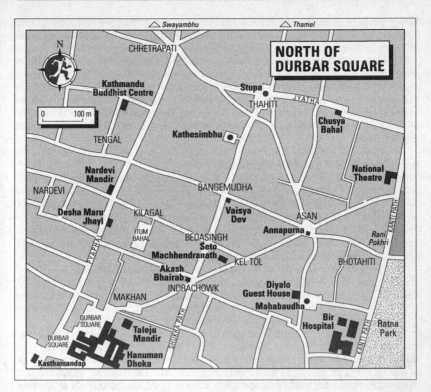

Shopping is good around Indrachowk. *Pashmina* shawls are sold from the steps of shrines in the intersection, and colourful bead necklaces (*pote*) and tassels (*dhaago*) hang in curtains from the stalls of the **Pote Pasal**, a small market area to the southeast. *Pote*, worn by virtually all married women in hill Nepal, typically consist of numerous strands of glass beads, all of the same colour, drawn together with a cylindrical gold ornament known as a *tilhari*. The beads are strung with deft speed, each strand anchored with a big toe or a nail. Many married women also weave *dhaago* into their hair – these are always red, a colour that indicates married status. The stalls here are owned mainly by Muslims, descendants of Kashmiri traders who migrated to the valley three centuries ago.

The tumultuous street heading north from Indrachowk is the direct route to Thamel, but the old Tibet road continues diagonally to the small square of **Kel Tol** and the seventeenth-century temple of **Seto Machhendranath** (White Machhendranath), one of two main shrines to the protector god of the Kathmandu Valley (the other is in Patan). Newars call this god Karunamaya, but the Nepali/Indian name prevails generally. Machhendranath's white mask, which you can see from the threshhold of the temple, is wheeled around the city on a chariot in late March or April. The well-concealed building features some beautiful gold and brass work on the outside, but an iron grille, installed to thwart temple thieves, robs it of its aesthetic appeal. This kind of precaution is still unusual in Nepal, a country whose artistic riches are all the more remarkable for being so public, but theft, driven by demand from Western collectors, has become an increasingly common occurrence in the past decade or so. The entrance is a gate at the west side of the square.

Beyond Kel Tol, the street is known mainly for its brass, copper and stainless steel wares: you'll see a bewildering array of incense holders, *thaal* (trays), water jugs, and vessels designed to hold water or cow's urine for *puja*. On the left, **Tilang Ghar**, a former Rana general's residence, is decorated with a stucco frieze of marching soldiers. The three-tiered octagonal **Krishna Mandir** just beyond is no longer active, and has been half obscured by the encroachments of surrounding buildings.

Asan, Mahabaudha and Bangemudha

The last and most exuberant intersection along this route is **Asan Tol**, Kathmandu's principal gathering point and hiring centre for labourers (*kuli* in Nepali and Hindi – hence "coolie"). Until recently Asan was better known as the old city's main fruit and vegetable market, but authorities now bar such trade in an effort (often futile) to prevent gridlock. Some produce is still sold in the streets leading east and north from here, while the trade in spices, homemade balls of soap, candles, oil, incense and other household wares has shifted to Kel Tol and Indrachowk.

The brass-roofed pagoda at the south side of the square is the temple of **Annapurna**, the goddess of grain and abundance, and a manifestation of Lakshmi, the popular goddess of wealth. A lavish little affair, the pagoda bristles with icons and imagery, and its roof is strung with electric bulbs like a Christmas tree. Annapurna is represented by a silver *kalash*, or vessel.

From Asan, the trade route angles up to Kantipath and the modern city, and an alley heading south leads to **Mahabaudha**. This plain white stupa, stuck in a rather unattractive square, takes its name from the big, harlequin-painted statue of the Buddha in an adjacent shelter. Just east of Mahabaudha, Kathmandu's removal men wait for work: you see them all over town, pushing loads around on rubber-wheeled flatbed carts (*thela gadhi*), almost always in bare feet and shorts – like porters, they are usually of the Tamang tribe (see p.208).

Walk westwards from Asan and you'll return to the main Indrachowk–Thamel lane at **Bangemudha**. Just south of this square is the odd shrine to **Vaisya Dev**, the Newar toothache god. Commonly billed as the "Toothache Tree", it's actually the butt end of a log, embedded in the side of a building, and locals believe you can cure toothache by nailing a coin to the log. (Bangemudha – "Crooked Stick" – refers to the legendary tree from which the log was cut.) Fans of ancient sculpture might appreciate the tiny fifth-century figure of the Buddha at the north end of Bangemudha, though its tacky tiled niche does it no favours.

Kathesimbhu, Thahiti and Thamel

Kathesimbhu, central Kathmandu's biggest stupa, stands in a square off to the left about 200m north of Bangemudha. The temple is only a modest replica of the more impressive Swayambhu stupa (its name is a contraction of "Kathmandu Swayambhu"), but for those too old or infirm to climb to Swayambhu, rites performed here earn the same merit. According to legend it was built from the earth left over after Swayambhu's construction; Lichhavi-era sculptures roundabout attest to the antiquity of the site, but the stupa itself probably dates to the seventeenth century. The square doubles as the playground for a local school, so watch out during playtime.

Traffic circulates around another stupa at **Thahiti**, the next square north on the way to Thamel. Because they're continually replastered, stupas never look very old and are hard to date, but this one probably goes back to the fifteenth century. One of Kathmandu's finest old *bahal*, the seventeenth-century **Chusya Bahal** stands about two blocks east of Thahiti. You'll recognize it by the two stone lions out in front and a meticulously carved wooden *torana* (decorative shield) above the doorway, both standard features of a *bahal*. The building is now privately owned, but you can get a look at the courtyard from the threshhold.

Playing a *maadal*

In the tourist zone north of Thahiti, old buildings are few and about the only sights are the goodies in the restaurant windows. To find a monument in the vicinity of **Thamel**, you could visit **Bhagwan Bahal**, a little-used pagoda that lends its name to an area north of Thamel (a sign in front calls it "Bikrama Sila Mahabihar"). A feature of this temple is the collection of kitchen pans and utensils nailed to the front wall, placed there as offerings to the deity.

Chhetrapati south to Durbar Square

At the southwestern fringe of Thamel lies boisterous **Chhetrapati**, a six-way intersection of almost perpetual motion. Though the neighbourhood lacks any ancient monuments, it supports a central *pati* (open shelter) resembling an Edwardian bandstand around which religious processions and impromptu musical jamborees are frequent occurrences. During Shiva Raatri in February, sadhus build fires on the platform and light up their chillums, and during Tihaar the iron railings are decorated with oil lamps.

From Chhetrapati it's a straight run south to the Kasthamandap; this street is favoured as an assembly point for protest marches, since the police can't easily secure it. The **Nardevi** area, to the west of the temple of the same name, has acquired quite a reputation as an important centre of ayurvedic medicine, with a college, hospital and many doctors' practices and pharmas. To the east, **Bhedasingh** is the domain of fruit and vegetable sellers, and a few potters who sell their wares from the steps of a squat Mahadev temple erected in memory of King Tribhuwan. The name Bhedasingh, which means "Sheep Horn", is a legacy of the days when livestock was traded here. Just to the south of Kilagal, the large flagstoned piazza of **Itum Bahal** is still used for grain-drying during the harvest, but the old buildings that surround it are steadily being replaced and the traditional *bahal* ambience is ebbing.

Continuing south towards Durbar Square you get back into atmospheric eighteenth-century neighbourhoods, with several large *bahal* dating back as far as the fourteenth century tucked away down dark alleys. Keep an eye out on the east side of the street for the **Desha Maru Jhayl** – literally, the "Country Nowhere Window" – a window grille of staggering complexity which, even in a country abounding in outstanding woodwork, is considered unique. Carved from a single block of wood, it predates the house in which it's now set.

South of Durbar Square

Except for the zone from Freak Street across to the GPO, the area **south of Durbar Square** is relatively untouristed and in parts desperately poor – a fair representation of reality in modern, urban Nepal. The older parts of it are less picturesque and commercial than the quarters north of Durbar Square, but New Road, which bristles and throbs with high-end consumerism, is as lively a street as any in Kathmandu.

Bhimsenthan and Jaisi Dewal

A small square southwest of the Kasthamandap, down a lane leading to the Bishnumati River, **Bhimsenthan** is named after one of Nepal's favourite gods. Bhimsen was one of the famous five brothers of the Hindu *Mahabharat*, a mortal hero who has been adopted as the patron saint of Newar merchants: you'll see pictures of him in shops everywhere. According to legend, Bhimsen came to Kathmandu as the manservant of a bride from eastern Nepal, who was married off to a farmer who lived on the west bank of the Bishnumati. Unaware of his new servant's identity, the farmer put Bhimsen to work in the fields; Bhimsen proceeded to work miracles with the rice, and the farmer, finally recognizing the god, granted him a plot of land he could reach in three strides. Bhimsen bounded across the river and settled at Bhimsenthan. The temple here was built in the early eighteenth century, but is frequently renovated to look much newer. The shrine on the upper floor is open only to Hindus, while the ground floor is, fittingly, occupied by shops.

Jaisi Dewal, a seventeenth-century Shiva temple, stands in a square several blocks south of the Kasthamandap down a different road. A three-tiered pagoda without much ornamentation, its size alone is impressive. *Linga*-spotters can ogle the eight-foot-high monster at the foot of the temple, which, though only a raw, uncarved stone, has to be the biggest in the kingdom. The road continues south to **Tripureswar Marg**, an important east–west thoroughfare.

Pachali Bhairab and the ghats

The most interesting part of south Kathmandu begins with **Pachali Bhairab**, an open-air shrine marooned near the city dump south of Tripureswar Marg (follow the road to Patan and bear left at a fork marked by a small park). The tiny gilded idol of Bhairab stands in a peaceful courtyard, dwarfed by a huge pipal tree and a brass, life-sized human figure laid out like a pharaoh's casket. This is a *betal*, Bhairab's vehicle and a likeness of death which, in Nepali Hinduism, is believed to protect against death (the old principle of fighting fire with fire); *betal* normally take the form of miniature skulls or skeletons at temple entrances, and this one is unusual for being so large. An esoteric parade involving Bhairab and other gods converges here on the fifth day of Dasain.

Continuing south along the path from Pachali Bhairab, you'll reach the **ghats** of the Bagmati River, which stretch as far as the eye can see in either direction. Statues, temples and all manner of neglected artefacts are jumbled along the shore – especially to the west, where the Bishnumati joins the Bagmati – and you could easily spend several hours picking around among them. The entire area is the subject of a proposed restoration project and may eventually enjoy a

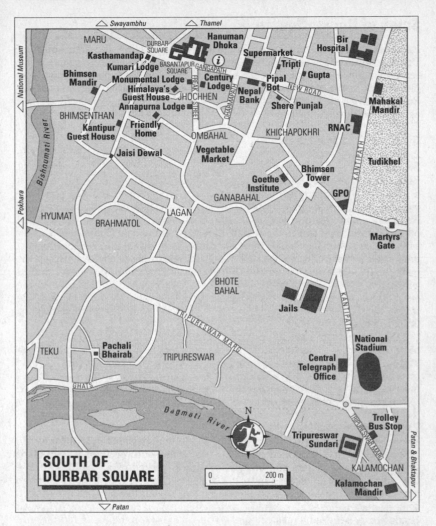

long-overdue renaissance. Cremations are often held at Teku *masan*, the cremation ground near the confluence, and kites wheel overhead in large numbers. The buffalo you see along the river banks today will be your sizzling steak or *momo* tomorrow – they're slaughtered here in the early mornings. A new bridge crosses the river to the suburban north end of Patan.

The biggest riverside temples are more than 1km to the east of the bridge, but to get to them you're faced with two equally unappealing prospects. One is to join the buzzing, sputtering stream of crosstown traffic along **Tripureswar Marg**, Kathmandu's strongest entry in the Bangkok lookalike sweepstakes. The other is to follow a trail along the riverbank, where you'll see scenes of utter deprivation.

SURVIVORS: KATHMANDU'S STREET CHILDREN

Street children, like so many urban problems, are a relatively recent phenomenon in Kathmandu. Ground down by rural poverty, abetted by new roads and bus services, growing numbers of children are running away to the capital in search of a better life. Some are lured there by men promising high-paying jobs in tourism. These promises often prove false.

The charity Child Workers in Nepal (CWIN) estimates that more than a thousand children – some as young as five, and invariably male – live on Kathmandu's streets, and their number is rising daily. They call themselves *khate*, a word that may be translated as "survivor". Most are lone runaways or orphans, though some live with their squatter families. The young **beggars** who roam Thamel and Durbar Marg, barefoot and clutching dirty cloths for warmth, are perhaps the more "acceptable" face of homelessness. Living relatively well off tourist handouts, however, they spurn training programmes and education, and grow up illiterate, unskilled and unemployable – your alms will do more good if given to a charity working with beggars, rather than to the beggars themselves. The majority of street children scrounge a meagre existence as **rubbish pickers**, selling what salvageable materials they can find. Some wangle work as casual labourers or *kanchha* (errand boys), but in such a vulnerable position they run a high risk of exploitation. Some pick pockets, or drift into drugs or prostitution. The best a *khate* can hope for is to find steady work as a labourer, bus conductor or perhaps a riksha wallah.

In a country where sixty percent of the population is living below the poverty line, it's easy to overlook the plight of street kids. Yet the conditions Kathmandu's *khate* endure are far more debilitating than mere rural poverty. **Homeless**, they sleep in doorways, *pati* (open shelters) or unfinished buildings. **Hungry**, they often subsist on food thrown out by tourist restaurants, and many suffer from malnutrition. Weakened by toxic chemicals in the rubbish piles, pollution and contaminated water, few are without **disease** (CWIN reports that 20 percent have tuberculosis). They're regularly **beaten** by the police, who regard them as bad for tourism, and during visits by foreign delegations they may be thrown in prison or loaded into buses bound for India. And perhaps most damaging of all, they are deprived of the traditionally supportive environment of family and community, and instead must deal with daily rejection.

CWIN, one of several organizations working with Nepali street children, operates a "common room" near its office off Tripureswar Marg to provide food, education, health care and play for children. Volunteers and donations are needed. For more information, contact CWIN at PO Box 4374, Bafal, Kathmandu (☎271658).

Kathmandu's very poorest – rubbish-pickers, butchers, sweepers – live here in makeshift shanties amid piles of trash and channels of raw sewage.

Lurking inside a crumbling courtyard near the junction of Tripureswar Marg and Kantipath, the massive pagoda of **Tripureswar Sundari** has been squatted by a collective of low-caste families; it was erected in the early nineteenth century in memory of an assassinated king by his widow. Further south, the marvellously hideous **Kalamochan Mandir** is a study in Rana excess and faded glory. Resembling a grotesque white wedding cake, it was completed in 1852 by the first of the Rana prime ministers, the homicidal Jang Bahadur, who is said to have buried the ashes of those killed in the Kot massacre in its foundation, mafia-style; the brass gargoyles snarling at its four corners are fitting testaments to his ambition.

New Road, Freak Street and Bhimsen Tower

Rebuilt after the disastrous 1934 earthquake, **New Road** (Juddha Sadak) cuts a swathe of modernity through the old city. Wealthy Nepalis and Indian tourists regard it as a magical duty-free bazaar and swarm its shops for perfume, kitchen appliances, consumer electronics and myriad other imported luxury goods. Security guards stand watch in front of department store entrances, well-heeled matrons stroll the pavements with shopping bags, and peasants visiting the capital stand transfixed at the sight of holiday snaps rolling off automatic photo-processing machines. This is what economic prosperity looks like in one of the world's poorest nations: materialistic, elite and very localized.

The statue at the west end of New Road commemorates Prime Minister Juddha Shamsher Rana, who is credited with rebuilding the road (and much of Kathmandu) after the earthquake. **Pipal Bot**, a venerable old tree about midway along the road's south side, provides a natural canopy for newspaper and magazine vendors, and is a favourite gathering place for Kathmandu's intelligentsia and gossip mongers.

THE JAILS

One of the more thought-provoking things you can do while in Kathmandu is to visit Westerners held in the capital's four **jails**. Since families are expected to provide for most of the prisoners' needs, foreigners are particularly badly off. Most are held in one of the jails south of the GPO (Central, Badragol or Women's); a fourth facility is located in Dilli Bazaar.

At any given time, as many as half a dozen **Westerners** may be imprisoned or awaiting trial in Kathmandu, mainly on charges of smuggling drugs or gold. Five years is a typical sentence, with no time off for good behaviour: a favourable appeal verdict usually doesn't result in freedom, only a shortened sentence, and every prisoner can tell a sorry tale or two about shady lawyers and indifferent embassy officials. **Nepalis** receive the same rough justice, plus they are liable to be imprisoned for political reasons. Although human rights in Nepal appear to be slowly improving under democracy, Amnesty International noted in its 1995 annual report that the Nepalese government continues to detain its people by the hundreds for participating in strikes and demonstrations, and occasional reports of torture and ill-treatment by police continue. Nepal also does not hesitate to imprison **children** when the family breadwinner is jailed and the family is without any other means of support; a charity, Prisoners Assistance Mission (PO Box 1649, Kathmandu; ☎233440) provides a "nesting home" for children of prisoners.

Conditions are grim. For food, inmates receive a half-kilo of "black" (fermented) rice and *daal* each day, plus a few rupees with which to buy vegetables at the prison shop. They sleep on the floor, with up to fifty to a room. No clothes or bedding are provided. Still, the prisoners here can consider themselves lucky they aren't locked away in provincial jails, beyond the normal range of human-rights organizations.

Daily **visiting hours** are 10am–5pm (but check: times may vary). You must ask for prisoners by name – check posters around Thamel and Freak Street to find out who's being held where. Inmates appear at the barred doorway of what looks like an animal stable, while visitors stand behind a chain, so conversations are far from private. Most prisoners will be grateful just for a chat, but don't go without bringing something tangible: food, vitamins, toiletries, books, clothes, blankets and cash are all appreciated.

Freak Street (Jhochhen Tol), like Thamel, isn't prime sightseeing territory, although nowadays tour groups come in search of the hippies that gave the street its name – you still get the occasional sighting – or just to take a trip down memory lane. On a cultural note, the pair of *chaitya* in front of the *Paradise Restaurant* illustrate the unique synthesis of Hindu and Buddhist imagery that's so common in the Kathmandu Valley: the Buddha would probably be appalled, but his images are carved around suggestively phallic *linga*, and set atop bases that symbolize the female genitalia (*yoni*).

The lane heading east from here leads to Kathmandu's main **vegetable market**, located in an unpaved compound; fish and other smelly items are sold in the street in front. Further east, **Bhimsen Tower** ("Dharahara" in Nepali), the tall minaret-like tower overlooking the GPO, is of no earthly use to anyone except land surveyors. It was built in 1832 by the prime minister, Bhimsen Thapa, possibly in imitation of Calcutta's Ochterlony Monument, which had been erected only four years earlier. A story is told that Bhimsen Thapa, sitting astride his horse, leapt off the tower, creating the nearby **Sun Dhara** (Golden Water Tap) where he landed. Three of Kathmandu's four **jails** are located south of here, down a side street off Kantipath – turn right just after the Ministry of Finance.

Swayambhu and around

Even if temple-touring makes your eyes glaze over, don't miss **Swayambhu** (or Swayambhunath), perched on a hill 2km west of Thamel. To begin with, it's a great place to get your bearings, geographically and culturally, in your first few days in Nepal: the hill commands a sweeping view of the Kathmandu Valley, and the temple complex, overrun with pilgrims and monkeys, is a real eye-opener.

But there's much more if you dig for it. The two-thousand-year-old stupa is the most profound expression of Buddhist symbolism in Nepal (all *bahal* in the valley contain a replica of it), and the source and central location of the valley's creation myth. There's evidence to believe the hill was used for animist rites even before Buddhism arrived in the valley two thousand years ago. Tantric Buddhists consider it the chief "power point" of the Kathmandu Valley, and one chronicle states that an act of worship here carries thirteen billion times more merit than anywhere else.

Since the Chinese invasion of Tibet in 1959, the area surrounding Swayambhu has become home to hundreds of Tibetans in exile. You'll see them and many other Buddhist pilgrims making a full circuit around the hill, queueing up to spin gigantic fixed prayer wheels and frequently twirling their own hand-held ones. The place is so steeped in lore and pregnant with detail that you'll never absorb it all in a single visit. Try going early in the morning at *puja* time, or at night when the red-robed monks pad softly around the dome, murmuring mantras and spinning the prayer wheels. Make a final visit on your last day in Nepal and see how your perceptions of it differ from your initial trip.

Swayambhu's main **festivals** are Buddha Jayanti (April or May) and Losar (in February or March), when pilgrims throng around the stupa and monks splash arcs of saffron paint over it in a lotus-flower pattern. Many also flock here each morning during the month-long Gunla festivities (August or September) to mark the "rain's retreat" with music and offerings to the monks.

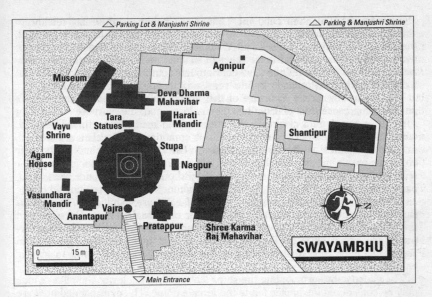

Parking Lot & Manjushri Shrine — Parking & Manjushri Shrine

Agnipur

Museum

Deva Dharma Mahavihar

Tara Statues — Harati Mandir

Vayu Shrine

Shantipur

Stupa

Agam House

Nagpur

Vasundhara Mandir

Vajra

Anantapur

Pratappur

Shree Karma Raj Mahavihar

0   15 m

SWAYAMBHU

Main Entrance

Getting there

The main entrance is at the eastern foot of the hill and **getting there** is a simple matter on foot or cycle. From Thamel the easiest way is via Chhetrapati, where a small road heads straight towards Swayambhu, passing the *Hotel Vajra* en route. From Freak Street or Durbar Square, take the rustic lane running northwest-wards from the Kasthamandap. Either way, it should take about twenty minutes to walk it. If you're cycling, the local kids will expect you to cough up a few rupees' protection money for your bike – failure to comply invites a flat tyre. A city bus also runs at irregular intervals between Ratna Park (north of the Tudikhel) and the eastern entrance, and taxis drive up to a small car park near the top, just west of the stupa.

A paved road circles the base of the hill. Although there are several other ways up the hill, the steep main path from the **eastern entrance**, with its 365 centuries-smoothed steps, is the most dramatic. The **Buddha statues** near the bottom are seventeenth-century, while a second group further up was donated in the early part of this century. The slates heaped up along the path are *mani* stones, inscribed, in Tibetan script, *Om mani padme hum* ("Hail to the jewel in the lotus"), the ubiquitous Buddhist mantra.

For **food**, follow the road around to the south side of the hill, where you'll find plenty of Nepali–Tibetan eateries, among them the *Iko* and *Green Hills* cafés, sedate descendants of the hippy hangouts that once thrived here.

The stupa

According to Buddhist scriptures, the Kathmandu Valley was once a snake-infested lake (geologists agree about the lake: see "Natural History" in *Contexts*). Long ago – 91 eons ago, to be exact – a perfect, radiant lotus flower appeared on the surface of the lake, which the gods proclaimed to be Swayambhu ("Self-created"), the abstract essence of Buddhahood. Manjushri, the *bodhisattva* of knowledge, drew his sword and cut a gorge at Chobar, south of Kathmandu, to drain the lake and allow humans to worship Swayambhu. As the water receded, the lotus settled on top of a hill and Manjushri established a shrine to it, before turning his attention to ridding the valley of snakes* and establishing its first civilization. Another legend tells how, when Manjushri cut his hair at Swayambhu, the hairs that fell on the ground grew into trees, and the lice turned into monkeys.

The apparently simple structure of **the stupa** belies an immensely complex physical representation of Buddhist cosmology, and the purpose of walking round it – always in a clockwise direction – is to meditate on this. The solid, whitewashed dome symbolizes the womb or creation. Set in niches at the cardinal points, statues of **dhyani (meditating) Buddhas** correspond to the four elements (earth, air, fire and water) and a fifth, placed at an angle, to the sky or space. Like the rainbow colours produced by the refraction of pure white light, each represents a different aspect of Buddhahood: the hand positions, colours and "vehicles" (the animal statues below) of each are significant. The *dhyani* Buddhas are the same characters who appear on virtually every *chaitya* around the Kathmandu Valley. At each of the sub-cardinal points sit **female counterparts**, who according to the Buddhist tantric view of things represent the wisdom aspect that must be sexually united with the compassionate male force to achieve enlightenment.

The gilded cube surmounting the stupa surrounds a thick wooden pillar, which may be considered the phallic foil to the female dome. The **eyes** painted on it are those of the all-seeing Adi-Buddha (primordial Buddha), staring in all four directions; what looks like a nose is actually the Nepali figure "one", conveying the unity of all things. A **spire** of thirteen gold disks stacked above the pillar represents the thirteen steps to enlightenment. The *torana*, or gold plaques above the painted eyes, also show the five *dhyani* Buddhas, known collectively as the *panchabuddha*. Finally, the umbrella at the top symbolizes the attainment of enlightenment: some say it contains a bowl filled with precious gems.

Shrines around the stupa

The stupa is surrounded by an incredible array of shrines and votive whatnots, most of which have been donated over the past four centuries by merit-seeking kings and lamas. The bronze sceptre-like object at the top of the steps is a vastly oversized **vajra**, a tantric symbol of power and indestructibility; its pedestal is carved with the twelve animals of the Tibetan zodiac. The twin bullet-shaped *shikra* on either side of this, known as **Pratappur** and **Anantapur**, were installed by King Pratap Malla during a seventeenth-century dispute with Tibet, on the advice of an Indian guru. The story of the king's gift, and his subsequent victory over the Tibetans, is engraved on the twin bells in front of the *shikra*.

Moving around clockwise, as is the custom at all stupas, the brick hut to the south of Anantapur is **Vasundhara Mandir**, dedicated to the earth goddess Vasundhara, who's more or less synonymous with Annapurna and Lakshmi, the

*The Kathmandu Valley harbours a powerful and abiding *nag* (snake spirit) cult. During the summer festival of Nag Panchami, emblems are placed above each doorway to appease the *nag*, who are able to release or withhold the life-giving monsoon rains. They're also considered the rightful owners of everything under the earth, which explains why the authorities are loath to allow archeological excavations. Upset a *nag* and you could bring on an earthquake.

goddesses of grain and wealth respectively. Further on – past the priests' quarters and a number of *chaitya* – is a small marble-faced shrine to **Vayu**, the Vedic god of wind and storms. The **museum** behind (daily except Sat 10am–5pm; donation) contains a formidable range of bas-relief statues of gods, Hindu as well as Buddhist, which, though beautiful to look at, are so tersely identified that they'll leave you hopelessly confused by the Nepali pantheon. Next door and up a flight of steps, the **Deva Dharma Mahavihar** is a small, uneventful monastery that's open to the public, and in front of this, close to the stupa behind protective caging, stand two acclaimed bronze statues of the **White and Green Taras**, princess wives of an eighth-century Tibetan king.

At the far side of the stupa squats a gilt-roofed temple built to appease **Harati**, the smallpox goddess, whom Newars worship as a form of **Ajima**, or Grandmother, a more general protectress of children. A legend relates how Harati was originally an abductor of children: when the people complained to the Buddha, he stole one of Harati's own children, forcing her to realize the pain she caused humans and repent of her ways. Harati/Ajima's shrine is extremely popular, and you'll see queues of mothers with kids in tow, waiting to make offerings. The nineteenth-century idol was carved to replace an earlier one smashed by King Rana Bahadur Shah after his wife died of smallpox. Following rites observed throughout hill Nepal, petitioners toss handfuls of flower petals and rice at the image, sprinkle a bit of consecrated water (*jal*) onto the image and themselves, and finally receive a *tika* from the resident priest.

The **International Buddhist Library**, housed upstairs in a former *bahal* behind the Harati Mandir, always seems to be closed, but the roof above is good for an overview of the stupa area.

Agnipur, an insignificant-looking lump on the pavement in the extreme northwest corner of the complex, marked by two tiny lions in front, is a seldom-visited shrine to the Vedic fire god Agni, the relayer of burnt offerings to heaven. **Nagpur**, a bathtub-sized tank at the north point of the stupa, propitiates the valley's snake (*nag*) spirits, and when it's not filled with water you can see the idol (looking more like a draught excluder than a snake) at the bottom. Finally, the **Shree Karma Raj Mahavihar**, an active monastery at the northeast corner of the compound, contains a big Buddha and numerous butter candles, which Tibetan Buddhists light in much the same way Catholics do; you can catch the sonorous chanting of the monks at around 3 or 4pm every day.

Shantipur

A 1500-year-old mystery surrounds **Shantipur**, the otherwise plain, box-like building northwest of the stupa. Shanti Shri, a fifth-century holy man, is supposed to have sealed himself in a vault beneath the temple to meditate, vowing not to emerge until the valley needed him. Commentators write that he subsequently attained a mystic state of immortality, and according to devout believers he's still in there.

King Pratap Malla, who entered the chamber in 1658 to seek magical help in ending a drought, experienced

A *chaitya*

adventures worthy of Indiana Jones. According to scholar Keith Dowman, the king recounted how he entered alone and descended to the second subterranean level. In the first room "bats as large as kites or hawks came to kill the light", while in the second room "ghosts, flesh-eating spirits and hungry ghosts came to beg", clutching at anyone who failed to pacify them. Of the third room he said, "if you cannot pacify the snakes by pouring out milk, they chase and bind you. Having pacified them you can walk on their bodies". Finally, Pratap Malla found the saint in an almost skeletal form, and was rewarded with a *nag* rain-making emblem. Faded frescoes on the walls of the outer sanctum show scenes from the *Swayambhu Purana*, a recent (seventeenth-century) scripture that recounts the story of Manjushri's sword act and other creation myths. Shantipur, also known as Akashpur ("Sky-place"), completes a cycle of shrines to the five elemental spirits: earth, air, fire, water (snakes) and sky.

Other sights around the hilltop

The **Manjushri Shrine**, located on a western spur of the hilltop, comes second only to the main stupa in antiquity – the canopied *chaitya* is reckoned to be 1500 years old. Manjushri, the Buddhist god of wisdom and founder of civilization in the valley, is traditionally depicted by an empty niche in the *chaitya*, but an image of Saraswati, the Hindu goddess of learning, was placed in the niche three hundred years ago, and so the shrine is now on the pilgrimage circuit for Hindus as well. Schoolchildren make a special trip here on Basanta Panchami, in late January or early February, to have their books and pencils blessed.

The rest of the hilltop is littered with other obscure monuments. In addition, several **Tibetan monasteries**, which as a rule welcome visitors, have been built in the area since 1959, and more seem to be going up all the time. Many Westerners study Tibetan Buddhism here (see "The Dharma Scene", p.145).

The morbidly amusing **Natural History Museum** (daily except Sat 10am–4pm; Rs10) also lurks nearby, on your right as you follow the road from the car park down the south side of Swayambhu hill. Its jumbled collection of stuffed birds and shrivelled animals in old-fashioned display cases looks like it was cobbled together from the trophy rooms of hoary old Rana hunters. The weirdness is fun for its own sake though, and the specimens might give you an idea of what to look for when you get to the mountains or jungle. (See also "Natural History" in *Contexts*.)

East of Swayambhu: Bijeshwari

Bijeshwari, along the west bank of the Bishnumati on the way to Swayambhu, used to be Kathmandu's execution ground; Henry Ambrose Oldfield, one of the few Europeans allowed to tour Nepal in the last century, attended a beheading here and pronounced the place "a regular Golgotha". While Tibetan immigrants have broken the taboo against settling near the cursed ground, a fear of ghosts still endures, as do two important but little-visited temples.

Bijeshwari Bahal, perched at the top of a flight of steps above the river, is the centre of worship of an esoteric Buddhist goddess, Bijeshwari (Lord of Victory), who is also known as Akash (Sky) Jogini and sometimes counted as the fifth of the valley's Bajra Joginis, the wrathful aspects of the tantric Tara goddesses. The inner courtyard is thick with *chaitya* and stone figures, and doors around the perimeter are painted with probing pairs of eyes – a reminder to worshippers that the Buddha is watching, and an injunction to look inward.

Just upstream stands a new cremation pavilion, and beyond that, the Hindu **Shobha Bhagwati Mandir**. Bhagwati is a common Nepali name for the mother goddess, and this idol of her is considered to be among of the most powerful in the valley: early in the morning you might see political candidates, students preparing for exams, or anyone requiring quiet strength coming here to do *puja* to her. According to legend, the sculptor of the Shobha Bhagwati image here carved it with his feet, his hands having been cut off by a jealous king to prevent him from reproducing an earlier masterwork in the king's collection.

South of Swayambhu: the National Museum

Museums may seem redundant in Nepal, given the wealth of heritage displayed out in the open. But theft and modernization are forcing a belated move to safe-guard national treasures, many of which can be seen in the **National Museum**, based in an old Rana armoury 1km south of Swayambhu (Mon, Wed, Thurs & Sun 10.30am–4pm, 3pm in winter; Fri 10.30am–2.30pm; closed Tues; Rs5, Rs10 extra for camera). It's no curatorial coup, and shouldn't be considered a substitute for the valley's countless living exhibits, but you'll come away with a better apprecia-tion of the intertwining of religion, art, myth and history in Nepal.

Count on spending most of your time in the **art building**, the white plaster one on your left as you enter. The collection of **stone sculptures** showcases an amazing artistic consistency spanning almost two thousand years, from the Lichhavi period through the tantric-influenced Malla dynasties: though motifs and styles change, the common element is a wild diversity of gods and themes inspired by the vast and imaginative canon of Hindu mythology. The images seem to celebrate not only the power of the deities, who loom up in their "universal" forms or act out Herculean labours, but also the divinity that resides within each worshipper. The **metalwork** exhibit pays tribute to a later art form which blossomed under patronage from Tibet. A trio of absolutely stunning fourteenth-century bronzes of the tantric deity Samvara and his consort form the centrepieces of this exhibit. To Western eyes, the tantric *yab yum* (sexual intercourse) motif and its gory attendant imagery (skull cups, daggers, blood) may seem pretty peculiar, yet on some intuitive level it's a powerful celebration of life in all its creativity, weirdness and danger. Other exhibits feature images, window frames and *torana* (ornate shields mounted over the doors of temples) carved from **wood**, as well as terra cotta images and a few Tibetan Buddhist ritual objects. A final room displays a couple of dozen rare **paubha** (Nepali scroll paintings) from the sixteenth century on, and a later series of miniatures exhibiting a marked Rajasthani influence.

The **history building**, a Rana-style mansion across the compound, is hardly worth the walk. It's almost as if the downstairs was meant to be a joke: the hodge-podge natural history section includes, among other things, the bones of a blue whale (why?) and an assortment of shrivelled mammals and birds, while another room features an international doll collection (check out the embarrassing speci-mens donated by your country!) and a moon rock. Upstairs, endless displays of weaponry do little to dispel the stereotype of the Nepalis as a "martial" race (although a pair of leather cannon, captured during a skirmish with Tibet in 1856, is a genuine rarity). More interesting than what's included, perhaps, is what's left out. This is Nepalese history as rewritten by the Shahs and Ranas, who've ruled Nepal for the past two centuries; the country's lower classes and ethnic groups, and any history prior to the Shah conquest, are given hardly a mention.

A third building houses the **National Numismatic Museum**, displaying coins from the Lichhavi, Malla and Shah dynasties, and even a few dating back to the Buddha's time from the kingdom of Kapilvastu.

Eastern neighbourhoods

For travellers, the area east of Kantipath is mainly of interest for airline offices and restaurants, not sightseeing. But while you're in the neighbourhood it's worth stopping to take a closer look at a few odds and ends.

The Kesar Library, Royal Palace and Durbar Marg

The **Kesar (Kaiser) Library** (Sun–Thurs 10am–5pm, Fri 10am–3pm; free), located in the compound marked "Ministry of Education and Culture", east of Thamel, is your best shot at seeing the inside of a former Rana palace. The library of Field Marshal Kesar Shamsher Rana (1891–1964) looks like a featured spread in the Nepali edition of *Better Homes and Gardens*: long shelves of European books, a suit of armour, a stuffed tiger and portraits of all the famous people the field marshal ever shook hands with shed intriguing light on a member of Nepal's pre-1951 ruling elite. Another sort of colonial landmark, **Fora Durbar**, the swish R&R compound for American expats, hides behind high brick walls just north of the British Council.

An architectural travesty from the 1960s, the creepy new **Royal Palace** looks like something out of Buck Rogers, with echoes of the Mormon Tabernacle. Built on the site of an earlier palace dating from the turn of the century, it was inaugurated in 1970 for King (then Crown Prince) Birendra's wedding; its Nepali name, **Narayanhiti Durbar**, refers to a water tap (*hiti*) east of the main entrance. Guarded by soldiers, the palace is open to the public only on the tenth day of Dasain, when Nepalis queue up to receive *tika* from the king and queen. The things that resemble black handbags dangling from the trees out front are bats; at dusk, they and about a million crows wheel overhead, creating an almighty racket.

Running south from the palace, **Durbar Marg** is the capital's premier commercial address: a single building on one *ropani* of land (about an eighth of an acre) here sold in the early 1990s for the staggering sum of Rs96 million.

Rani Pokhri and around the Tudikhel

Rani Pokhri (Queen's Pool), the large square tank east of Asan, is older than it looks. It was built in the seventeenth century by King Pratap Malla to console his queen after the death of their favourite son; the shrine in the middle, which is opened one day a year during the Tihaar festival, is more recent. The pool and nearby **Ratna Park** are active centres for small-time trade (including prostitution).

West of Rani Pokhri stands the mouldering edifice of **Durbar High School**, established in 1853 to educate the children of the Rana aristocracy and their hangers-on for jobs in a nascent bureaucracy. To the east rise the turn-of-the-century **Ghanta Ghar** (clocktower) – like Bhimsen Tower, a landmark only in the functional sense – and Kathmandu's two **mosques**. Muslims first settled in Kathmandu as traders five centuries ago, and now represent only a tiny fraction of Nepal's half-million "Musalmans". Nearby Trichandra College, whose students have a reputation for militancy, was a flashpoint of anti-government riots in 1990, when its walls were painted with such slogans as "Do or Die for Democracy".

Kathmandu's **Tudikhel** is the biggest military parade ground in Nepal; Percival Landon, an early twentieth-century traveller, proclaimed it "level as Lord's", and indeed the expanse seems quixotically flat in so mountainous a country. An institution rooted in Nepal's warring past, the *tudikhel* is a feature of every town of consequence throughout the hills. The king turns out to review occasional displays of pomp and circumstance here (notably during Ghoda Jaatra in March or April), and bronze statues at each corner of the parade ground depict past Rana prime ministers on horseback striking suitably swashbuckling poses.

On the Kantipath side of Tudikhel stands the **Mahakal Mandir**, whose modern surroundings have in no way diminished the reverence of its worshippers: passing pedestrians and motorists almost always touch a hand to the forehead. Mahakal – to Hindus a form of Bhairab, to Buddhists a defender of *dharma* – is depicted here trampling a corpse (signifying ignorance), holding a skull-cup of blood and wearing what look like glacier goggles. The **Bhadrakali Mandir**, at the southeast corner of Tudikhel, has been turned into a traffic roundabout but remains a popular wedding venue. The nearby **Martyrs' Gate** commemorates the four ringleaders of a failed 1940 attempt to overthrow the Rana regime.

Singha Durbar

Undoubtedly the most impressive structure ever raised by the Ranas, **Singha Durbar** dominates the governmental quarter in the southeastern part of the city. Once the biggest building in Asia, the prime ministers' palace of four hundred rooms was built in 1901 by Chandra Shamsher Rana, who employed workers round the clock for two years to complete the pile and fill it with such European extravagances as Carrera marble floors, crystal chandeliers and gilt mirrors, all for the then unconscionable sum of Rs2.5 million. It's said that the entire population of Kathmandu abstained from *daal*, an ingredient in traditional mortar, during the construction. While it was in use as a palace, up to 1500 servants were required to maintain the prime minister and his household in the style to which they were accustomed.

The complex was mostly destroyed by fire in 1973, but has since been partially rebuilt. You can go right past the guards at the sweeping front gate to have a look at the luxurious gardens and the gleaming white colonnaded main wing. Numerous governmental ministries and departments are housed here and in crumbling old mansions nearby.

Dilli Bazaar, Baluwatar and Maharajganj

Kathmandu's eastern and northeastern neighbourhoods have absorbed the lion's share of recent city growth, and while these areas don't have much of scenic interest, they certainly provide insights into suburban Nepal.

Crowded **Bagh Bazaar** and **Dilli Bazaar** pretty much sum up one end of the spectrum, with their typing institutes, lawyers' cubbyholes and shops selling office furniture and "suitings and shirtings". ("Fine Art", incidentally, means signpainting – there's always work for sign-painters in ever-changing Kathmandu.) Dilli Bazaar is also the home of Nepal's budding stock exchange. The other extreme is found further north in the shady lanes of **Baluwatar** and **Maharajganj**, where old money, new money and foreign money hide in walled compounds, and caretakers water the flowers for absentee development consultants.

Between the two lie the hopeful settlements of a burgeoning middle class, who build their houses one floor at a time, as funds allow, and send their children off in uniforms to "English boarding schools" with names like "Bright Future" and "Little Flower". An "English" education is almost universally viewed as the key to success in the capital: an encouraging trend for Nepal's development in the next generation.

Hadigaun and Dhum Barahi

Another world away, **Hadigaun**, on the edge of the northeastern suburbs, is the nearest place to Thamel to find typical Newar village life in action. You'll see better as you go further out into the valley, but Hadigaun's old brick houses, dirt streets and farm animals are remarkably well insulated from the hurlyburly of the city. Indeed, archeological excavations suggest that the settlement is probably as old as Kathmandu.

Evidence of Hadigaun's age comes from the overgrown shrine of **Dhum Barahi**, a further 1km northeastwards (head north out of Hadigaun, and when in doubt always take the right fork). Inside the small brick shelter, which is completely engulfed in the roots of an enormous pipal tree, a whimsical fifth-century image illustrates the tale of Barahi (Vishnu in his incarnation as a boar) rescuing the earth goddess Prithvi from the bottom of the sea. Scholars rave about this sculpture because it dates from a time when there were no established rules for depicting Vishnu as a boar, nor for how a boar should look while fishing the earth from the sea. Locals say the shrine was built at the same time as the nearby Boudha stupa to appease Vishnu, who out of jealousy had caused the stupa's spire to collapse while under construction.

Accommodation

Kathmandu is well stocked with all kinds of **accommodation**. At the budget end of the spectrum, it's just a matter of hitting the guest houses: they're all cheek by jowl, so if one's full you can just try the next. In the autumn high season the prominent Thamel lodges fill up early, but there'll always be vacancies at smaller places nearby.

To avoid the tourist scene, consider staying outside Kathmandu – for possibilities, see the sections on Boudha (p.142), Patan (p.154) and Bhaktapur (p.179).

Budget places

Budget tourism in Nepal was born on **Freak Street** (Jhochhen Tol) in the late 1960s, and, being the least modern area nowadays, its prices are the lowest (double rooms start at less than Rs100). In the 1980s, **Thamel** emerged as a smarter, more respectable alternative both for basic guest houses (rooms from Rs150) and more upmarket establishments (rooms usually $8–20, plus tax). In the past few years, with land prices in Thamel going through the roof, guest houses have started springing up in unlikely **off-the-beaten-track** locales, and these may well be your best bet for avoiding the tourist treadmill.

Prices are influenced by supply and demand, and thus fairly fluid. Rates given here are for high season, but in slow times expect discounts of up to fifty percent or more. You should also be able to negotiate a better rate for longer stays. Take all recommendations with a pinch of salt, because maintenance in the budget category is pretty much nonexistent and so anywhere that's clean and good value one year may not be the next.

ROOM PRICE SCALES

All guest houses and hotels have been price-graded according to the scale outlined below, which represents the cheapest available double room in high season; codes prefixed by B denote the cost of a room with attached bathroom. See p.35 for a fuller explanation of the system.

① Less than Rs100 ($1.75 if quoted in US$)
② Rs100–175 ($1.75–3)
③ Rs175–300 ($3–5)
④ $5–8

⑤ $8–12
⑥ $12–20
⑦ $20–40
⑧ $40–70
⑨ Over $70

As a rule, Kathmandu innkeepers are tremendously helpful and good-humoured people. During the winter, when Kathmandu can be cold and clammy, guest houses will provide kapok quilts, but only the most upmarket places have heaters. Finally, try to get a room that doesn't overlook the street: Kathmandu's barking dogs, banging pots and clattering shutters are enough to wake the dead.

Freak Street

Little remains to remind you of **Freak Street's** hippy heyday. Bona fide hippies have been an endangered species in Nepal ever since 1974, when the present king, then new to the throne, passed a series of immigration and drug laws that made life more difficult for them. Yet the lodge area in and around Freak Street certainly comes out better these days in a comparison with Thamel – it's quieter and less crowded, and it generally retains more traditional buildings and ways. And while it trails in the tourist restaurant department, it's within easy walking distance of New Road's many excellent Indian eateries. Some have rightly pointed out that the traditional buildings here would be more dangerous in the event of an earthquake, but then if you've observed modern Nepali construction methods you wouldn't necessarily have much faith in the city's new buildings either.

For locations, see the South of Durbar Square map (p.95).

Annapurna Lodge (☎213684). The biggest of the old Freak Street pack, with a large in-house restaurant. ②/B③.

Century Lodge (☎214341). A warren of tiny cubicles with plywood walls, but the building has some fine traditional features. ②/B③.

Friendly Home (☎220171). Kathmandu's longest-running guest house, and invariably packed in high season. A nice place to be for Christmas, when the owners throw a party on the roof. ②/B③.

Himalaya's Guest House (☎215416). Freak Street's finest: a very spiffy, friendly place in a secluded location, with a small in-house restaurant and great views from the roof. ③/B③.

Kantipur Guest House (☎222953). Unpretentious place in a less touristed street, although rooms in this old building are chilly in winter. ②/B②.

Kumari Guest House (☎222498). Right on Durbar Square, it's as grotty as they come, but friendly and ideally located (especially during festivals). ③.

Monumental Lodge (☎214864). A dive, albeit a traditional one, whose chief recommendation is its low prices. ①/B②.

Traveller's Paradise Guest House (☎240602). Dumpy but central, and with a good vegetarian restaurant (the *Paradise*). ③/B③.

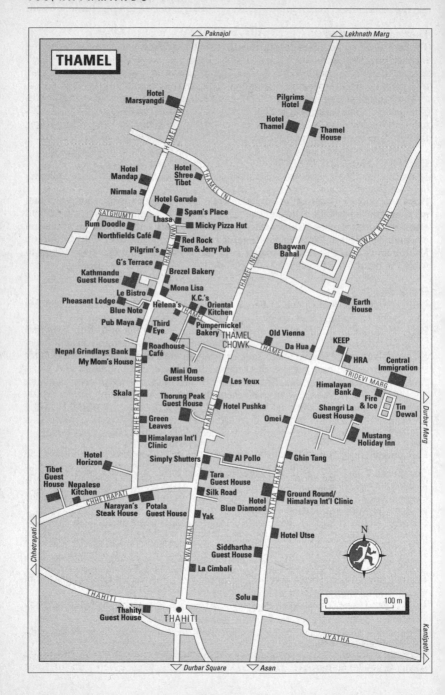

Thamel and around

Thamel used to be a restful, if unreal, haven – a place you genuinely looked forward to after some hard travelling or trekking. Now, at least in the high season, there's so much hype, and so little that has anything to do with Nepal, that you may wonder why it remains as popular as it does.

That said, if you've just arrived and your brain is still six time zones out to sea, Thamel can help ease you into things until you feel ready to sally forth. It's painting by numbers here, with every imaginable convenience at your fingertips, though bear in mind it's a rather long, jostling walk to the sights of Kathmandu.

INEXPENSIVE GUEST HOUSES

Hotel Horizon, Chhetrapati Thamel (☎220904). Very secluded down a quiet side lane, with decent rooms and plenty of rooftop seating. ③/B⑤.

Hotel Puska, Thamel South (☎225027). A bit of a monolith, but cheap, central, and with a small courtyard restaurant. ③/B④.

Mini Om Guest House, Thamel (☎229288). Basic, but cheap and, considering its central location, admirably insulated from the Thamel hurlyburly. ②.

My Mom's House, Chhetrapati Thamel (no phone). The way Thamel guest houses used to be, before everything got so damned fashionable: basic, sociable and cheap. ②/B③.

Pheasant Lodge, off Chhetrapati Thamel (☎417415). One of several modest outfits tucked away in a quiet yet central cul-de-sac. ③.

Sagarmatha Guest House, Thamel (☎410214). Economical choice if you want to be right in the trendy heart of things. ②/B③.

Siddhartha Guest House, Jyatha Thamel (☎227119). Clean and very quiet, with a peaceful courtyard shaded by pomelo trees. ④/B⑤.

Tara Guest House, Thamel South (☎220634). Small but pleasant garden, and basic rooms. ③/B④.

UPMARKET GUEST HOUSES

Earth House, Bhagwan Bahal (☎418436). Comfortable place with a nice roof terrace, located near the Bhagwan Bahal on an interesting (but rapidly modernizing) street. ④/B⑤.

Hotel Garuda, Thamel Northwest (☎416776). A smart place with friendly staff. B⑥.

Hotel Shree Tibet, Thamel North (☎419902). Nice rooms and a rooftop garden. B⑤.

Kathmandu Guest House, Thamel North (☎413632). Thamel's original guest house is still the best, set well back from the noisy street, with efficient management and a gorgeous garden. It's a huge and social place: exciting or pretentious, depending on your outlook. Rooms are always in demand, and booked up well ahead during the high season. Old wing ④/B⑥; new wing B⑦.

Mustang Holiday Inn, Jyatha Thamel (☎226538). Immaculate and professional, a long-standing favourite with a quiet location, garden and roof seating, and phones in rooms. B⑦.

Pilgrims Hotel, Thamel Northeast (☎416910). Cosy, with a delightful garden restaurant and an indoor cafe with lots of books. ⑤/B⑥.

Potala Guest House, Chhetrapati (☎226566). Central, with a garden. B⑥.

Thorung Peak Guest House, Thamel South (☎224656). Friendly, efficient and quiet, with well-appointed rooms (all with phones) and a great roof terrace. ⑥/B⑥.

Tibet Guest House, Chhetrapati (☎214383). Friendly, and with a really lovely roof garden. ⑤/B⑥, or B⑥ with a/c.

Off the beaten track

Here are a few out-of-the-way options to help you steer clear of the tourist-ghetto scene. If you've just arrived, see if any of these names rings a bell with the touts at the airport or bus station (they're often employed by places tourists wouldn't easily find on their own), and if so, you'll save yourself some grief getting settled in.

INEXPENSIVE GUEST HOUSES

Hotel Shrestha, Tahachal – off the main Kathmandu map, about 1km west and south of *Peace Guest House* (☎270528). Quiet and out of the way, this might be a good choice if you've got kids with you. ③/B④.

Peace Guest House, Tahachal – see main Kathmandu map (☎271093). This place outfreaks Freak Street: it attracts a real budget-minded crowd, but it's friendly and has generous rooms and a big roof terrace. A short but fairly wretched walk to Durbar Square. ①/B②.

Swoyambhu Restaurant, Thahiti – just off the main Kathmandu map, on the southerly road to Swayambhu (no phone). Clean rooms, interesting location. B③.

Thahity Guest House, Thahiti – see Thamel map (no phone). Clean rooms, laid-back management, high rooftop terrace, good central location on an as-yet-uncommercialized street with several good *bhojanalaya*; the guest house has a quirky tourist restaurant of its own. B⑤.

UPMARKET GUEST HOUSES

Dhaulagiri Guest House, Dhalko – see main Kathmandu map (☎213393). Reasonably clean, sequestered from the humdrum neighbourhood it's in. ⑤/B⑤.

Dikey Guest House, Dhalko – see main Kathmandu map (☎215996). Friendly, helpful, clean. ③/B⑤.

Kathmandu Peace Guest House, Paknajol – see main Kathmandu map (☎415239). Secluded, friendly place, with a garden, parking and good views north and west from rooftop. ④/B⑥.

Tibet Peace Guest House, Paknajol – see main Kathmandu map (☎415026). Similar to the nearby *Kathmandu Peace Guest House*, with a better garden but poorer views. ④/B⑥.

Camping

Kathmandu has no developed **campsites**, which is probably just as well since it would be pretty nerve-wracking to drive a camper into the city. If you're determined to camp, try Nagarjun Ban (see p.153), which has zero facilities but a wonderful jungly setting (Rs50–100 per vehicle). Or drive up to Changu Narayan (Chapter Two), Nagarkot, Dhulikhel or Kakani (Chapter Three), all within an hour or so of Kathmandu.

Listed hotels

Kathmandu's **listed hotels** are more spread out, so it's advisable to have a particular place in mind before setting off. Most are members of the *Nepal Hotel Association*, which operates a reservation desk at the airport. Tax of twelve to fifteen percent (rising with the number of stars) is extra. All have air conditioning and should be able to provide heat in the winter. The expensive ones generally have top-notch restaurants, TVs in the rooms, and other facilities as mentioned. Except where indicated, refer to the main Kathmandu map for locations.

Moderate

Hotel Ambassador, Lazimpath (☎410432). All mod cons at a reasonable price. Two stars. B⑦.

Hotel Blue Diamond, Jyatha Thamel – see Thamel map (☎226320). No great shakes, but it's cheap for this class and centrally located. Two stars. B⑦.

Hotel Manaslu, Lazimpath (☎410071). Pleasant oasis with a nice front lawn, popular with aid workers and their visitors. Two stars. B⑦.

Hotel Mandap, Thamel Northwest – see Thamel map (☎413321). Comfortable retreat in a popular part of Thamel, which for some people might represent the best of both worlds. Two stars. B⑦.

Hotel Vajra, Bijeshwari (☎272719). Unquestionably the best in its class: beautifully appointed, with a library, theatre and art gallery, and tremendous views of Swayambhu from the roof terrace. Definitely worth a splurge. Two stars. ⑥/B⑦.

Expensive

Dwarika's Hotel, Battisputali – off the main Kathmandu map, east of the German Embassy near Pashupatinath (☎470770). Unique bungalow-style accommodation with traditional touches. Four stars. B⑨.

Everest Hotel, Baneswar (Airport Road; ☎220567). Pool, tennis, gym, disco. Five stars. B⑨.

Hotel de l'Annapurna, Durbar Marg (☎221711). Pool, sauna, the works. Five stars. B⑨.

Hotel Marshyangdi, Thamel Northwest – see Thamel map (☎414105). Swanky hotel that sits strangely amidst the budget fracas of Thamel. Three stars. B⑧.

Hotel Shangrila, Lazimpath (☎412999). Tucked away in embassyland. Four stars. B⑨.

Hotel Shanker, Lazimpath (☎410151). Converted Rana palace with an entrance that has to be seen to be believed. Three stars. B⑨.

Hotel Yak & Yeti, Durbar Marg (☎413999). Kathmandu's finest: pool, tennis, opulent restaurants. Five stars. B⑨.

Malla Hotel, Lekhnath Marg (☎418383). Small and personal, with a pool and health club. Four stars. B⑨.

Eating

Scores of **restaurants** and **cafés** line the lanes of Kathmandu's tourist quarters, and more spring up after each monsoon. Quite a few carry on in a funky, student-coffee-house style – they're like time capsules from the early 1970s – but a growing number are emulating French bistros, American diners and even English pubs. While **Tibetan**, **Chinese** and **Indian** food have long been taken for granted in Kathmandu, **European** specialities predominate these days; American-style **pies and cakes**, though overrated, are ever-popular; and even **Japanese**, **Thai** and **Mexican** dishes are available. Sometimes the food is ingeniously authentic, sometimes you have to use your imagination. The best news of all is that fine **Nepali** and **Newari** food – traditionally only served in private homes – is increasingly available not only in tourist restaurants but also in reasonably sanitary local eateries, and is slowly taking its place among the other distinguished regional Indian cuisines. The listings that follow are unabashedly biased in favour of these indigenous offerings.

As with lodgings, **Thamel** has all the newest, trendiest and most credible budget restaurants – though some are getting so stylish they're pricing themselves out of the budget category. **Freak Street** is noticeably cheaper for eating, but it's got a smaller and less interesting selection of establishments. Kathmandu's best and most expensive restaurants are generally found near, or sometimes inside, the deluxe hotels around **Durbar Marg** and **Kantipath**. Except where indicated, refer to the Thamel map for locations (unfortunately, restaurants on Freak Street, Durbar Marg and Kantipath couldn't be squeezed onto the other maps).

Even at the top end, **prices** are reasonable. As a guide, places decribed here as cheap will charge less than Rs100 per person for a full dinner; inexpensive restaurants will run to Rs100–200; moderately priced ones Rs200–400, and expensive ones Rs400–800. Restaurants move or go out of business often, so don't set off for a far-flung place without first verifying it's still there. Phone numbers are given for restaurants where it's advisable to book ahead for dinner.

It's all too easy to overemphasize food in Kathmandu – it can also be the greatest peril of staying here. More travellers get **sick** in the capital than anywhere else, and eating in "reputable" restaurants is no guarantee of hygiene. Indeed, Nepali restaurants are arguably safer, since chefs know what they're doing when they prepare Nepali food. Heed the words of caution given in *Basics* (p.21), and don't be taken in by an apparently clean dining room or shiny cutlery.

Nepali and Newari

The Nepali and Newari places listed below are geared for tourists and tend to be on the expensive side, but worth it. At the other extreme are Kathmandu's many dirt-cheap *bhojanalaya*, which advertise themselves with a curtain (usually green) hung over the entrance and are impossible to recommend by name. Most are merely the Nepali equivalents of a greasy spoon, but the best ones are fantastic. Ask your innkeeper for suggestions, or try the places north and east of Asan or along the lane from Asan to Chhetrapati. Many tourist restaurants advertise "special Nepali meals", which usually turn out to be rather ordinary *daal bhaat*. See *Basics* (p.37) for a rundown of Nepali and Newari dishes.

Bhanchha Ghar, Kamaladi, east of the Clocktower – see main Kathmandu map (☎225172). Nepali nouvelle cuisine, featuring such delicacies as wild boar, wild mushroom curry and buckwheat chapatis – truly wonderful. Expensive.

Las Kus, in the *Kathmandu Guest House*, Thamel North. Does a set meal that provides a good introduction to Newari cuisine. Moderate.

Naachghar, in the *Hotel Yak & Yeti* off Durbar Marg – see main Kathmandu map (☎413999). Top-flight Nepali, Indian and Western cooking; set dinner in a palatial setting with nightly culture shows in season. Expensive.

Nepalese Kitchen, Chhetrapati. A serviceable budget version of the others listed here, demonstrating that there's more to Nepali cuisine than *daal bhaat*. Outdoor seating, a fireplace and live music some evenings. Inexpensive to moderate.

Thamel House, Thamel Northeast (☎410388). A clone of *Bhanchha Ghar*, offering marginally cheaper vegetarian and non-vegetarian set menus. Expensive.

Tibetan and Chinese

Tibetan restaurants offer some of the cheapest tourist food in Kathmandu; cheaper still are the many *momo* kitchens throughout the old city, notably around Mahabaudha. Again, see *Basics* for descriptions of popular Tibetan dishes. Chinese food can be reasonably priced, although the best restaurants are found in deluxe hotels like the *Malla*.

Da Hua, Bhagwan Bahal. Good all-round Chinese. Inexpensive to moderate.

Lhasa, north Thamel. Excellent Tibetan soups, fiery *momo* and – best of all – *tongba* (do-it-yourself millet beer). Cheap.

Mountain City, in the *Hotel Malla* on Lekhnath Marg – see main Kathmandu map. Delicious Chinese food; Szechuan a speciality. Moderate.

Nanglo, Ganga Path (east of Durbar Square). Reliable Chinese food in a well-appointed setting. Inexpensive to moderate.

New Mandarin, Freak Street. Cramped but cosy, and good for both Chinese and Tibetan dishes. Cheap.

Omei, Jyatha Thamel. Convincing Beijing, Cantonese and Szechuan cuisine on white linen. Moderate.

Solu, Jyatha Thamel. A locals' hole-in-the-wall that does *tongba*. Very cheap.

Utse, Jyatha Thamel. Reasonably priced Tibetan and Chinese food. Cheap.

Yak, Kwa Bahal. Great value for standard Tibetan offerings, plus a fair range of Indian dishes. Cheap.

Indian

Perhaps the best measure of the Indian population in Kathmandu is the number of Indian restaurants – they're popping up everywhere. The more expensive ones serve food every bit as good as you'll find in India, and even the cheapies (mostly around New Road) do some fine pure vegetarian dishes. Indian cuisine is also summarized in *Basics*.

Ghar-e-Kebab, Durbar Marg (☎221711). Superlative north Indian food, *ghazal*, strange nightclub interior. Expensive.

Ghoomti, New Road, in the Supermarket compound – see South of Durbar Square map. Good Mughlai and south Indian food, *ghazal* most evenings, lounge ambience. Inexpensive.

Gupta Bhojanalaya, off New Road – see South of Durbar Square map. Hole in the wall serving vegetarian south and north Indian dishes. Cheap.

Mangalore Coffee House, corner of Jamal and Durbar Marg, near *American Express*. Great south Indian vegetarian food in an efficient upstairs canteen – authentic, right down to the toilets. Very cheap.

Moti Mahal, Durbar Marg. Tandoori food rivalling that of *Ghar-e-Kebab*, though the decor isn't as swanky. Moderate.

New Kebab Corner, Jyatha, in the *Hotel Gautam* just off Kantipath. Expats swear by this place. Moderate.

Shere Punjab, off New Road – see South of Durbar Square map. Basic in-and-out Punjabi canteen. Cheap.

Tansen, Durbar Marg (☎224707). Top-notch tandoori and other Indian dishes served on burnished copper in minimalist surroundings. Expensive.

Tripti, off New Road – see South of Durbar Square map. Lively little pure vegetarian place serving south Indian fare. Cheap.

European

Keep telling yourself: this is not what I came to Nepal for . . . Still, there are times when you feel like you've eaten a lifetime's worth of lentils and you could just murder a pizza. Many of these places serve wine, though it's expensive.

G's Terrace, Thamel North. High-cholesterol Bavarian specialities (would you believe *Zwiebelrostbraten*?). Moderate.

La Cimbali, Kwa Bahal, Thamel. A small café with a nice (if simple) atmosphere and a good range of Italian fare. Inexpensive.

La Dolce Vita, Thamel. Kathmandu's most upscale Italian restaurant. Inexpensive to moderate.

Micky Pizza Hut, Thamel Northwest. Small dining room, good atmosphere and really rather good thin-crust pizza. Inexpensive.

Old Vienna, Thamel. Schnitzel, crêpes and other rich, tasty Austrian dishes. Moderate to expensive.

Simply Shutters, Thamel South. Classy bistro with a *menu du jour*, featuring French and other Continental specialities. Good place for a romantic meal. Expensive.

Japanese and Thai
Sushi is out of the question, but Nepali-style sukiyaki comes fairly close to the mark. Try miso soup if your stomach's acting up.

Fuji, Kantipath. Good food, beautiful decor. Expensive.

Him Thai, Lazimpath – see main Kathmandu map (☎418683). The food won't astound anyone who's just flown in from Bangkok, but it's tasty and reasonably authentic. Moderate.

Koto, Durbar Marg (☎226025). Probably the best value for money on the Japanese front. Moderate.

Kushi Fuji, Durbar Marg (☎220545). More authentic, but more expensive.

Vegetarian
There are only a few all-vegetarian tourist restaurants worthy of recommendation, but every restaurant serves at least a few meatless dishes; even Tibetan places will usually do vegetable *momo*. See also Indian restaurants.

Nirmala, Thamel Northwest. Tasty meals from a short but varied menu. Inexpensive.

Paradise, Freak Street. Italian, Mexican, Indian and cheesy dishes. Cheap.

Skala, Chhetrapati Thamel. Nice garden seating, reasonably creative savoury pies, roulades, soups and salads. Inexpensive.

All-rounders
The overwhelming majority of budget places fall into this catch-all category: jacks of all trades and usually masters of none. The old standbys are "buff" (water buffalo: cows are sacred, remember) steaks, pastas (creamy and gooey), pizza, cakes and pies.

Al Pollo, Thamel South. A cosy atmosphere makes this place popular, despite unremarkable offerings. Inexpensive.

Café de la Cabine, Thahiti, in the *Thahity Guest House*. Snug wood-and-rattan décor, mellow music, little-of-everything menu; the offbeat location is a plus. Inexpensive.

Cosmopolitan, Freak Street. The best pasta and steaks south of Durbar Square; salad with every dish, if you dare. Inexpensive.

Green Leaves, Chhetrapati Thamel. Organic salads, lovely outdoor seating under a big banyan tree and nightly live music are the main attractions; the main dishes are run of the mill. Inexpensive.

Ground Round, Jyatha Thamel. The menu has something for everybody, all of it quite tasty, and the clientele is refreshingly local. Live music and dance some evenings. Inexpensive.

Helena's, Thamel. The cake display window here is Thamel's most popular tourist sight; the usual menu, but a gloomy decor. Inexpensive.

K.C.'s, Thamel. A perennial favourite: cosy surroundings, reliable menu, generous portions; big on "sizzling" dishes and killer desserts. Moderately priced.

Narayan's Steak House, Chhetrapati. Popular for steaks, pasta and pies. Inexpensive.

Oasis, Freak Street. The only patio dining on Freak Street. Inexpensive.

Rum Doodle, Satghumti. Trusty buff, chicken and vegetarian dishes, salads and proficient desserts. Moderate.

Third Eye, Chhetrapati Thamel. Steaks, soups, salads and some very decent north Indian food. The retro-1970s "Rice Terrace" room in the back is hugely social. Inexpensive to moderate.

Breakfast and lunch places
You can't beat Kathmandu's cafés for breakfast or lunch on a warm day, though in winter you'll want to head indoors. Besides the places listed below, many all-rounders offer set breakfasts, which often represent great value for money (especially if you like eggs).

For **picnic** ingredients, the *Delicatessen Center* beats all. "Cold stores" in tourist areas sell biscuits, beer, chocolate and other imported items. The *Bhatbhateni Supermarket*, north of *Mike's Breakfast*, sells fantastic trail mix, tinned food and things you won't find anywhere else. Other supermarkets in Thamel (on the corner of Bhagwan Bahal), Lazimpath and Tripureswar Marg also stock a wide range of goodies. For fruit and vegetables, hit the open-air markets east of Asan and south of New Road.

Le Bistro, Thamel. A fully fledged restaurant, but its strong suit is café seating – it's popular, so get there early. Inexpensive.

The Gourmet, Thamel (inside *Old Vienna*). Spotless German deli, serving authentic wurst and pâté. Inexpensive.

Brezel Bakery, Thamel Northwest. Does a fair range of breads and buns; the rooftop terrace is ideal for a snack or tea. Inexpensive.

Delicatessen Center, Kantipath. An eye-popping cornucopia of deli meats, cheeses, breads, pastries, salads and fixings. Inexpensive to moderate.

Fire and Ice, Tridevi Marg. Really good pizza from an authentic oven, plus soft-serve ice cream. Moderate.

Mike's Breakfast, Naksal – see main Kathmandu map. Absolute bliss for breakfast – garden tables, classical music and spot-on food. Americans' eyes will mist over at the huevos rancheros, waffles and fresh coffee. Moderate.

Narayan's, Thamel Northwest. Secluded yet central breakfast spot. Inexpensive.

Northfields Café, Thamel Northwest. A somewhat less accomplished cousin of *Mike's*. Inexpensive to moderate.

Oasis, Freak Street. Probably the most pleasant breakfast/lunch spot in this area, with indoor and outdoor seating. Cheap to inexpensive.

Oriental Kitchen, Thamel. Clean and serene indoor seating. Good for breakfast. Cheap.

Pumpernickel Bakery, Thamel. A sort of Mecca for skinflints. Immensely popular for croissant sandwiches and sticky buns, with seating in a pleasant garden out back. Cheap.

Desserts

K.C.'s, Helena's, Narayan's Steak House and many other restaurants listed above produce spectacular confections, some of which actually taste as good as they look. If none of those hits the spot, try one of the following.

Angan, corner of New Road and Shukra Path. Divine Indian-style sweets (buy them by the piece), also ice cream. (Other purveyors of fine Indian sweets include *Dudh Sagar* on Kantipath and *Trishna Mithai* on Lazimpath.) Inexpensive.

Delicatessen Center, Kantipath. Really decadent cake and pie slices, pastries, crème brulée, chocolates and ice cream. Inexpensive.

Hot Breads, Durbar Marg. Pastries, cake slices and ice cream, as well as savoury baked items. Inexpensive.

Nirula's, locations on Durbar Marg and New Road. American ice cream parlour meets Indian bureaucracy. The ice cream's pretty good, though. Inexpensive.

Nightlife and entertainment

For a capital, Kathmandu is pretty sleepy: most restaurants start putting up their chairs around 9.30pm, and drinking is supposed to stop at 10pm. **Bars** are still a speciality item, found only in Thamel and the big hotels. Attending a **culture show** is probably a more enlightening alternative – but perhaps the best idea of all is to retire early and rise early the next morning, when the city is at its best.

Bars

Thamel's **bar** scene is small, but growing. The area around the *Kathmandu Guest House* has mutated into quite a throbbing little scene in the evenings, with duelling sound systems blaring across the alleyways, noisy bands of revellers looking for action, and the cops and the riksha wallahs waiting outside for closing time.

A handful of nightspots serve up beer, improvised cocktails and music. As with the restaurants, they're more like a Nepali's imagined idea of what a bar must be like than the real thing, but on the whole they're fine for meeting, mixing and prolonging an otherwise short evening. Many have "happy hours" in the early evening, which generally means free popcorn. In the high season, bars often keep serving until the wee hours behind drawn curtains and locked doors. Don't forget to warn your innkeeper if you think you're going to stay out late, or you could get locked out. Reputations rise and fall from season to season, but the establishments listed below appear to be in for the duration.

A warning: unlike Thamel's restaurants, which are frequented almost exclusively by travellers, the bars here attract a fair share of well-off Nepali lads, who aren't very representative of Nepalis in general. They're apt to latch onto any unescorted foreign female, and sometimes pick fights with other men (an Italian tourist was stabbed to death in a Thamel bar in 1995).

Blue Note, Chhetrapati Thamel. A rabbit warren of cosy rooms, plus a roof terrace. Rock, blues, jazz.

Carpe Diem Music Café, Freak Street. Bar and table seating, snacks, big sound system, eclectic tunes.

Maya Cocktail Bar, Thamel, just behind the *Pumpernickel Bakery*. Two bars on two floors, relaxed atmosphere. Rock.

Pub Maya, Chhetrapati Thamel. Next door to the *Blue Note* and very similar to it. Rock.

Roadhouse Café, Chhetrapati Thamel. More like a restaurant than a bar, but offers frequent live gigs. Rock/pop.

Rum Doodle Restaurant's "40,000 $1/_2$-Foot Bar", Satghumti. Kathmandu's oldest nightspot (but recently relocated), cultivating a cluttered *après trek* atmosphere. The story behind the name is a long one (a novel, in fact).

Silk Road Café & Bar, Kwa Bahal. Live music venue on weekends, featuring aspiring Nepali rock bands.

Spam's Place, Thamel Northwest. Ersatz pub, with garden seating.

Tom and Jerry Pub, Thamel Northwest. An established and surprisingly bar-like bar. Rock.

Culture shows

Music and dance are essential parts of Nepali culture, and perhaps nowhere more so than in Kathmandu, where neighbourhood festivals and parades (not to mention weddings) are an almost daily occurrence. Touring other regions of the country, you'll encounter other, markedly different styles of music and dance (see p.397), and while it's more fun to see these performances in their native context, it's worth checking out a **culture show** before you leave the capital to get a taste of Nepal's folk and performing arts. Or better yet, catch an authentic evening music session at Kel Tol, Chhetrapati or several other spots in the old city.

The shows listed below cost about Rs275; call for times. In addition to these, several Thamel restaurants (notably *Green Leaves*, *Ground Round* and *Nepalese Kitchen*) host regular folk music performances in the high season. Most of the deluxe hotels do pricey dinner shows.

KATHMANDU'S FESTIVALS

Your chances of coinciding with a festival while in Kathmandu are good, since the capital spends about a month out of every year partying. Those listed here are just the main events; neighbourhood festivals happen all the time. Dates are determined according to the lunar and Nepalese calendars, and vary from year to year – enquire at a tourist office for dates, or consult a Nepalese calendar (*patro*), available in main bookshops.

MAGH (Jan–Feb)
Basanta Panchami – The spring festival is marked by a VIP ceremony in Durbar Square on the fifth day after the full moon. Children celebrate Saraswati Puja on the same day at Swayambhu.

FAAGUN (Feb–March)
Losar – Tibetan New Year, observed at Swayambhu on the full moon of February, but more significantly at Boudha (see p.142).
Shiva Raatri – "Shiva's Night" is celebrated with bonfires in Kathmandu on the new moon of Faagun, but the most interesting observances are at Pashupatinath (see p.136).
Faagun Purnima (Holi) – Popular week-long water-splashing festival, reaching a climax on the full moon.

CHAITRA (March–April)
Seto Machhendranath Jaatra – A flamboyant four-day procession in which the white mask of Machhendranath is placed in a towering chariot and pulled from Jamal to an area south of Freak Street. The festival starts on the eighth day after the full moon.
Ghora Jaatra – Equestrian displays at the Tudikhel.

BAISAKH (April–May)
Nawa Barsa – Nepali New Year (April 13 or 14): Kathmandu holds parades, but Bhaktapur's festivities are more exciting (see Chapter Two).
Buddha Jayanti – The anniversary of the Buddha's birth, enlightenment and death, celebrated on the day of the full moon at Swayambhu.

SAAUN (July–Aug)
Ghanta Karna – Demon effigies are burned on street corners throughout the city on the new moon of Saaun.
Nag Panchami – A day set aside for the propitiation of snake spirits with offerings and worship on the fifth day after the new moon.
Gaai Jaatra – The Cow Festival, marked by processions through the old city, led by garlanded boys costumed as cows, on the day after the full moon.

BHADAU (Aug–Sept)
Indra Jaatra – A week of chariot processions and masked-dance performances held around the full moon of Bhadau. On the last day, the king receives a special *tika* from Kathmandu's "living goddess" and beer flows from the mouth of Sweta Bhairab in Durbar Square.

ASHOJ (Sept–Oct)
Dasain – A mammoth ten-day festival celebrated in most parts of Nepal, concluding on the full moon of Ashoj. In Kathmandu, mass sacrifices are held at the Kot courtyard near Durbar Square on the ninth day, Durga Puja, and the king bestows *tika* on all and sundry at the Royal Palace on the last day.

KARTIK (Oct–Nov)
Tihaar – The Festival of Lights, celebrated here (as in most places) with masses of oil lamps throughout the city and five days of special observances. Lakshmi Puja, falling on the full moon of Kartik, is the highlight.

Everest Cultural Center, at the *Hotel de l'Annapurna*, Durbar Marg (☎221711). Fairly conventional performances, nightly in high season.

Holistic Culture Show, at the *Holistic Yoga Ashrama*, just south of the *Kathmandu Guest House* (☎419334). Folk and classical dances in a very small and acoustically not very brilliant space, nightly in high season.

Hotel Vajra, Bijeshwari (☎271545). The *Vajra*'s own Kalamandapa ensemble and other visiting troupes put on the most authentic and varied programmes, two or three times a week. The resident Studio 7 company also presents occasional dramatic productions.

New Himalchuli Cultural Group, at the *Hotel Shanker*, Lazimpath (☎410151). Nightly performances in high season.

Ghazal

An Indian style of music, **ghazal** has recently started catching on in Nepal, or at least in the capital. Troupes tend to work the better Indian restaurants, where they provide dinnertime accompaniment from a platform over to the side somewhere. A typical ensemble consists of amplified tabla, harmonium and guitar; the singer, who gets top billing, croons in a plaintive voice. Love is the theme, and the sentimental lyrics – typically in Urdu or Hindi, but increasingly in Nepali – draw from a long tradition going back to the great Persian poets.

In Thamel, the most authentic *ghazal* **venues** are *Ghin Tang* on Jyatha Thamel and *Gorkha Palace Restaurant* on Tridevi Marg. *Rimini Pizzeria*, on Chhetrapati, hosts young, rock-influenced acts whose style could best be described as garage *ghazal*. For really high-class *ghazal*, make for *Amber* or *Ghar-e-Kebab* on Durbar Marg.

Theatre and cinema

Outside the tourist arena, scheduled performances of the arts are rare, but that's hardly surprising considering how much goes on all the time in public. Groups allegedly rent out the **National Theatre** on Kantipath for dance, drama and musical events, although the box office seems to be perpetually shut.

Despite stiff competition from video parlours, Kathmandu's several **cinemas**, showing the latest Indian blockbusters in Hindi, are still popular. The easiest ones to get to are the *Jai Nepal Chitra Ghar*, one block east of the Royal Palace entrance, and the *Bishwa Jyoti* on Jamal. Showtime is generally noon, 3pm and 6pm daily and tickets cost just pennies. Some Thamel restaurants show free Hollywood **videos** to bring in customers.

Shopping

Kathmandu is the obvious place to do some serious **shopping**, especially if it's your last stop before leaving the country. For an overview of handicrafts available in Nepal, see *Basics*; just about all of them are sold in or around Kathmandu. Usually items will be cheaper where they're actually made, but keen competition keeps prices low in the capital. The majority of wool, metal and wood items are made in the valley anyway, and many "Tibetan" items are imported from India.

Traditional souvenirs and curios

If you're in the market for a **khukuri** knife, you won't have to go far: street vendors and shops sell them wherever there are tourists, and there's a whole shop devoted to them next to the *Rum Doodle* in Thamel. Brass sets of **bagh chal**, Nepal's own "tigers and goats" game, are almost as common. Stalls and shops between Indrachowk and Asan sell all manner of household **brassware**. A couple of small shops in Thamel and Khichapokhri (south of New Road) are devoted to Nepalese **musical instruments**, while hack minstrels peddle *sarangi* (traditional fiddles) around Thamel and cheap bamboo flutes in Durbar Square.

Vendors in Basantapur Square and Thamel flog vast arrays of **Tibetan-style curios**. It's all attractive stuff, but much of what is claimed to be silver, turquoise, coral or ivory is fake, and virtually none of it is antique. Gold- and silversmiths in the old city (mainly north and west of Indrachowk) produce fine ethnic **jewellery**; tourist shops sell cheaper but perhaps more wearable ornaments, usually made with white metal. **Gem** sellers are grouped mainly at the east end of New Road. The *pote pasal* near Indrachowk is the place to go for traditional **glass beads**. Boxes and embroidered bags of Nepalese **tea**, sold in many shops in the tourist areas, make good gifts.

Countless boutiques sell identical ranges of **Kashmiri handicrafts**, predominantly silk carpets, chain-stitch tapestries, and various items made out of papier mâché, soapstone and sandalwood. These guys are particularly adept at fleecing unwary tourists. They also sell **furs** – fox, jungle cat, "snow" cat and the like, most hunted in the wild in India and technically legal. Snow leopard, clouded leopard and other endangered species are also said to be obtainable, despite being protected under international conventions. The trade persists because of lax regulation, but it can be stopped, or at least slowed, if enough travellers raise hell.

Certain handicrafts, though widely sold in Kathmandu, are better bought elsewhere in the valley: **metal statuettes** are a Patan speciality, **wood carvings** are best in Bhaktapur, and **papier mâché masks**, **puppets** and **pottery** are all better represented in Thimi and Bhaktapur. Kathmandu **carpet**-sellers offer some good deals, but don't buy until you've had a chance to see carpets being made in one of the many factories in the Kathmandu Valley or around Pokhara (see p.168–169 for background on the carpet industry). The best selection is in Patan's Jaulakhel district.

Contemporary crafts

Nepali artisans are turning out an ever-expanding range of **contemporary crafts** that adapt traditional materials or motifs to foreign tastes: unusual forms of *dhaka* and other textiles, beautiful greeting cards of handmade paper, Maithili-style paintings and papier mâché items, toys, dolls in ethnic dress, ready-made clothes, woollens, leather goods, batiks, scented candles, and ingenious articles out of bamboo and pine needles. The impetus for most of these innovations has come from a few income-generation projects supported by aid organizations, although many products are now widely imitated.

Each of the following outlets features a good range of crafts at fixed prices, but of course bazillions of other shops in Thamel sell many of the same items. For the best selection of all, go to Patan's "Fashion Row" (see p.167).

Community Craft Centre, Lazimpath. Woollens, *dhaka* and other textiles, also ceramics, toys and paper.

Mahaguthi, Durbar Marg (just north of *Hotel de l'Annapurna*) and Lazimpath. Aided by Oxfam, it supports a home for destitute women; mainly textiles, some jewellery and other gift ideas.

Didi's Boutique, Chhetrapati. A for-profit shop that carries a savvy selection of wares, all with a slight feminist undercurrent.

Clothing and fashion

Thamel and Freak Street are full of shops selling **wool sweaters**, jackets, mittens and socks, which are among Nepal's best bargains – just steer clear of the cheap garments, which fall apart at the seams. Similarly inescapable around here are **kit bags**, **caps** and other fashion items made from black felt with Tibetan rainbow fringes. Hardly fashionable, though many people lap them up, are **T-shirts** and **ready-made clothes**; watch out when you wash them because the cheap fabrics shrink and the colours run. **Tailors**, usually found inside the same clothing shops, are skilled at machine-embroidering designs on clothing.

Shawls and scarfs made of **pashmina**, the Nepali equivalent of cashmere, are cheapest at Indrachowk. **Topi**, the caps that Nepali men wear in much the same way Westerners wear ties, are sold around Asan Tol. You'll find **sari material** in shops around Indrachowk, although for discriminating textile buyers, Patan and Bhaktapur are the places to go. Other traditional textiles are sold in the non-profit shops (see above).

For really attractive Western clothes with a Nepali flavour – especially **silks** – try the following outlets.

Kee, Chhetrapati. Readymade cotton, silk and wool fashions.

Nepalese Handloom Silk, Chhetrapati Thamel. Silk and *pashmina* garments; silk by the metre.

Rage, Durbar Marg. Designer fashions.

THANGKA

A good **thangka** is the product of hundreds or even thousands of hours of painstaking work. A cotton canvas is first stretched across a frame, gessoed and burnished to a smooth surface that will take the finest detail. The desired design is next drawn or traced in pencil using a grid system and precise proportions; there is little room for deviation from accepted styles, for a *thangka* is an expression of religious truths, not an opportunity for artistic licence. Large areas of colour are then blocked in, often by an apprentice, and finally the master painter will take over, breathing life into the figure with lining, stippling, facial features, shading and, finally, the eyes of the main figure. Mineral- and vegetable-based paints are still used for the best paintings, but most nowadays are acrylic.

For discussion purposes, *thangka* can be grouped into four genres. The **Wheel of Life**, perhaps the most common, places life and all its delusions inside a circle held firmly in the clutches of red-faced Yama, god of death. The wheel's "rim" depicts the twelve causes of misery, while its "spokes" show the six sensual realms, where dwell the damned, ghosts, animals, humans, demigods and gods; all are caught in Yama's grip – even the gods – and only the Buddha exists outside the wheel. A second standard image is the **Buddha's life story**, tracing the major events of his life starting in the upper right and proceeding clockwise, dominated by an enlightened Buddha in the centre. Many *thangka* feature tantric **deities**, either benign or menacing; Avalokiteshwara, the Lord of Compassion, is a favourite. Such an image serves as a meditation tool in visualization techniques, in which the subject identifies with the deity's godly attributes or recognizes its demonic ones in him or herself. **Mandala**, too, are used in meditation. Symbolically, the subject moves through the three rings of the outer circle (representing the three parts of human nature that must be controlled), through the inner hexagram, towards the figure of the Buddha at the centre.

Silk Palace, Durbar Marg. Factory showroom with Kathmandu's widest selection of silk material, Western designs (men's and women's) and saris.

Wheels, Durbar Marg. Designer fashions.

Yasmine, Durbar Marg. Designer fashions.

Thangka and other fine art

It's hard to say where to look for bargains on **thangka** and **paubha** (ritual paintings in the Tibetan and Newari styles, repectively), since there are so many standard depictions and levels of quality that any comparison of prices is often an apples-and-oranges exercise. The biggest grouping of dealers is in Makhan Tol, north of Durbar Square, but there are many others along Tridevi Marg and elsewhere in Thamel. As with carpets, don't commit yourself to a *thangka* until you've shopped around and seen them being painted in Patan or Bhaktapur. To get a grounding in styles and prices with less pressure, visit one of the handicrafts emporiums on New Road or Jamal, or *Indigo Gallery*.

Indigo Gallery, at *Mike's Breakfast*, Naksal (daily except Mon 9am–4pm). Top-of-the-line *thangka* and *paubha*, and occasional special exhibits.

Nepal Association of Fine Arts (NAFA) Gallery, Naksal (daily except Sat 11am–3pm; Rs15). Contemporary works by Nepali painters and sculptors.

October Gallery, inside the *Hotel Vajra*, Bijeshwari (daily except Sat 9–11am & 5–8pm). Nepali paintings.

Sirjana Contemporary Art Gallery, Jamal (daily 10am–5pm). Features the work of young non-traditional artists.

Books

Kathmandu has a great collection of English-language **bookshops**, and browsing them is one of the city's main forms of nightlife – many stay open till 10pm. Most are nameless holes-in-the-wall. Don't forget that they'll buy back books at half price.

Kailash Book Distributors, Durbar Marg on the way to the *Hotel Yak & Yeti*. A branch of *Pilgrim's* (see below), with the same range of books and supplies, plus a whole floor of antiquarian books.

Mandala Book Point, Kantipath. Good selection of reference, fiction and maps.

Pilgrim's Book House, Thamel, north of the *Kathmandu Guest House*. Extensive reference sections on all things Nepali: religion, mysticism, health, travel, language, development; also maps, postcards, paper, cassettes, incense, supplies.

Music

There's no lack of **music** around Kathmandu to keep your Walkman humming. Several shops in Thamel sell cheap rock/pop reissues and new agey East-West mood music on tape and CD, as well as some traditional Nepali folk and classical compilations on tape. Countless cassette stalls throughout the city sell Nepali folk and pop, and Indian pop and movie soundtracks. Prices at these stalls will be less than half what the tourist places charge, but finding what you're looking for will be harder if you don't speak (or read) Nepali.

Outdoor equipment

Kathmandu trekking shops sell some new, name-brand **outdoor equipment**, clothing and footwear for considerably less than what you'd pay for it back home. You can also get second-hand gear and nearly new expedition castoffs, commonly given to porters as tips and promptly resold. However, the selection is patchy, so you might not able to find the size or style you're looking for.

Almost anything for a trek can be **rented** in Thamel or Freak Street, including climbing gear. Figure on about Rs40 per day for a good sleeping bag, pack or parka. Bring small items like water bottles and sunglasses from home, where they're cheaper. As for woollens, you might as well buy. For a full trekking equipment checklist, see p.346.

Meditation, yoga and astrology

Not surprisingly, Kathmandu is an important centre for spiritual pursuits. This section sketches out the general possibilities, concentrating on established outfits that cater specifically for Westerners; a scan through the posters in the popular lodges and restaurants will no doubt turn up others. See also the organizations listed in the next section on alternative therapies, as there's a lot of overlap between all these disciplines. You'll find brief introductions to meditation and yoga in "Spiritual Pursuits" (p.59).

Meditation

The Mahayana Buddhist **Himalayan Yogic Institute** (PO Box 817, Kathmandu; ☎413094), located in Baluwatar, conducts regular evening meditations and weekly *dharma* teachings (donation), hosts a revolving schedule of day-long workshops and courses on Tibetan Buddhist meditation and related Tibetan arts (Rs275), and has a library and meditation room. HYI is affiliated with Kopan Monastery, north of Boudha, where it offers seven- to ten-day meditation courses during the autumn and spring (about Rs400 per day, including food and lodging).

Nepal Vipassana Centre (PO Box 133, Kathmandu; ☎225490) runs ten-day courses on *vipassana*. These aren't for the frivolous: daily meditation begins at 4.30am, and silence is kept for the full ten days. To register or pick up a pamphlet on the course, visit the centre's Kathmandu office (Sun–Fri 10am–5.30pm) in the courtyard of Jyoti Bhawan, behind *Nabil Bank* on Kantipath. All courses are funded by donations.

The **Kathmandu Buddhist Centre** (PO Box 5336, Kathmandu) holds introductory talks on Western Buddhism a few times a week during the tourist seasons – check at the *Nepalese Kitchen* or on notice boards for the location. It also conducts one-day courses in Buddhism and two-day meditation workshops (both Rs450 per day) at its premises next door to *Hotel Ganesh Himal*, about 200m south and then west of Chhetrapati Chowk, overnight retreats at Nagarkot (Rs1600), and five-day residential courses in a restored *bahal* in Patan (Rs4500).

Opportunities also exist for individual study under Tibetan lamas – see "Boudha" (p.145).

If you're of the Rajneesh persuasion, you'll be pleased to learn that Kathmandu supports a thriving Osho industry which includes a travel agency, a bimonthly magazine and three meditation centres. The **Asheesh Osho Meditation Centre** (☎271385) in Tahachal and a second site in Lazimpath conduct one-hour dynamic meditation sessions every morning; these are open to all and the fee is a donation. The third venue, **Osho Tapoban Forest Retreat Centre** (PO Box 278, Kathmandu; ☎271385), located in a beautiful setting north of Nagarjun Ban, hosts occasional retreats as well as daily meditations and discourses, charging about Rs175–250 per night for basic accommodation and meals. If you can't get through to the centres themselves, contact *Osho World Travel* on Tridevi Marg (☎223758).

Yoga

Patanjali Yoga Centre (☎278437; fax 229459), east of the National Museum in Chhauni, has a highly respected director in Yogacharya Sushil Bhattacharya, and offers classes and residential courses in pure *astanga yoga*, a balance of the eight traditional yoga systems. Daily early-morning and afternoon meditation/*hatha yoga* sessions are open to all (Rs100). Residential study in *hatha yoga*, yoga philosophy, diet and health costs about Rs500 per day. Month-long yoga/ trekking programmes and yoga teacher-training courses are also offered.

The Yoga Studio (☎417900; fax 220143) teaches *hatha yoga* in the Iyengar method, a gradual path espoused by BKS Iyengar, a key figure in bringing yoga to the West. The resident instructors teach a regular schedule of classes year-round, as well as one- and two-week intensive courses in season. The studio is located in Tangal, about a ten-minute bike ride east of Thamel: follow the road north of the Royal Palace eastwards until it becomes dirt, and it's between the Ganesh shrine and a small *pokhri* (pond).

Ananda Yoga Centre, a retreat facility in a lovely setting in the valley 8km west of Kathmandu, caters for both beginners and advanced students of yoga. The teacher is Shri Vikashananda, who brings an eclectic approach to *hatha yoga*, *pranayama*, meditation, yogic cleansing, diet and naturopathy. You can set your own itinerary and the cost is $15 a day, including room and board. For information contact *Travellers Service* (☎ & fax 225184) on the corner of Jamal and Kantipath.

The only real yoga centre in Thamel, **Holistic Yoga Ashrama** (PO Box 4783; ☎419334), just south of the *Kathmandu Guest House*, offers daily morning and afternoon yoga/meditation sessions (Rs200). Simple accommodation is available here and at another branch near Pashupatinath.

The **Himalayan Yogic Institute** (see "Meditation" above) also does one-day beginners' workshops on *hatha yoga* (Rs275).

Astrology

It's best not to single out **astrologers** in the Kathmandu area, partly because few of them speak English, but mostly because they all have their own flocks to look after and it wouldn't be fair to rain hordes of foreign horoscope-seekers down on them. Try offering your innkeeper or a guide a commission to take you to his astrologer and to translate for you – you'll get a fascinating glimpse into an extremely important but behind-the-scenes aspect of Newar life (see p.394).

To have a **horoscope** prepared you'll need to make an appointment first, and when you go you'll be expected to provide the exact time and place of birth (if you don't know the time, the astrologer may be able to improvise by reading your palm). It'll take the astrologer up to a week to produce an annual chart, even longer for a full span-of-life chart. You'll need to schedule a separate session for him to interpret it for you and answer any questions you may have; the fee for the entire service may run to Rs500 or more. Whatever you may think of astrology or your particular reading, at the least you'll come away with a beautiful and unique work of art.

Alternative therapies

Many of what we in the West call alternative therapies are, of course, established practice in Nepal. The full range of remedies is actually quite a bit greater than what you see in this section, which, like the previous one, focuses on what's accessible to the average visitor. Again, refer to "Spiritual Pursuits" in *Basics* for a bit of background on these practices.

Ayurved

For private consultations, try **Dr Mana Bajra Bajracharya**, who operates a small clinic and dispensary in Mahabaudha. He also sells books on ayurvedic medicine. To find his practice, head north of the Mahabaudha stupa towards Asan and take the first left, then look for the sign on the left. **Dr Ram Narayan Shah** at the Ayurvedic Hospital in Nardevi, about 200m west of the Nardevi Mandir on the left, will also treat foreigners.

To fill ayurvedic prescriptions, visit the **Gorkha Ayurved Company**, south of Chhetrapati Chowk, or if your Nepali is up to standard, try any of the ayurvedic pharmas lining the lane running west from the Nardevi Mandir.

Tibetan medicine

Kunphen Tibetan Medical Centre (☎213820) has two locations in Kathmandu: the main clinic, due north of Chhetrapati Chowk, keeps daytime hours, while a branch clinic in the *Hotel Star*, next door to the *Kathmandu Guest House*, treats patients in the evenings. Both are basically front offices for a Tibetan medicine company, whose products they sell, but their services come highly recommended.

There's also a Tibetan medicine clinic out in Boudha – see p.148 for details.

Massage

Many of the numerous signs around Thamel advertising **"massage"** have been put there by complete charlatans attracted by the princely sums tourists will pay to have their bodies rubbed. However, there are some professional masseurs around, though they come and go; ask to see their credentials, which should be from a certified yoga school. The price of an hour's massage should be somewhere around Rs200–300. Two centres that can be recommended are **Holistic Yoga Ashrama**, which offers yogic massage as well as various yogic therapies, and **The Yoga Studio**, which holds courses in Thai-style massage (phone numbers and locations given above).

Listings

Airlines – see p.131.

American Express c/o *Yeti Travels Pvt Ltd*, Hotel Mayalu, Ground Floor, Jamal (daily except Sat 10am–1pm & 2–5pm; ☎226152). As usual, you can receive mail at the office if you can produce an *Amex* card or travellers' cheques.

Banks and Moneychangers In Thamel, the main option is *Nepal Grindlays Bank*, with branches on Chhetrapati Thamel (Sun–Fri 9.45am–4.15pm) and Kantipath (Sun–Thurs 9.45am–3.15pm, Fri 9.45am–12.30pm). *Rastriya Banijya Bank* operates inside the Central Immigration office (Sun–Fri 10am–4pm). In the Freak Street area, your best bet is *Nepal Bank* on New Road (daily 10am–4pm, limited service available 7.30–10am & 4–7.30pm). Also useful is *Himalayan Bank*, with branches in the Sanchaya Kosh Building on Tridevi Marg (opposite

Central Immigration) and in the Supermarket plaza on New Road (both Mon–Fri 10am–3pm). Many other private banks can be found along Durbar Marg and Kantipath. Several registered moneychangers in Thamel and Freak Street keep longer hours (generally daily 8am–8pm). See "Costs, Money and Banks" in *Basics* for details on having funds wired to Nepal.

Car rental Exorbitantly expensive: a Toyota Corolla with driver costs $50–75 a day. Better to hire a taxi (upwards of $20 a day, depending on mileage).

Central Immigration Tridevi Marg, just east of Thamel. For general information on trekking permits and visa extensions, see "Red Tape and Visas" in *Basics*. Application hours are Sun–Thurs 10am–2pm (1pm in winter), Fri 10am–noon. The queues can be distressingly long in the busy seasons – the wait tends to be shorter later in the day (a trek or ticket agent will do the waiting for you, for a fee). You can retrieve your passport later the same day. Beware Dasain in October, when the office closes for at least a couple of days. All fees are payable in rupees (there's a bank inside Central Immigration for changing money). National park entry permits can be purchased at a separate office across the street. Nearby studios do instant passport photos for Rs150 (24-hr places on New Road are cheaper).

Credit cards *Amex*, *Visa* and *Mastercard* are accepted at major hotels and many boutiques. You can draw **cash** against *Visa* or *Mastercard* at *Grindlays* in Thamel and on Kantipath.

Drugs All kinds are sold by "hello friend" touts in Thamel and Freak Street. Foreign buyers are invariably overcharged, but the price is still low by any standard. Obviously, don't be conducting transactions in public, nor somewhere so private that you could be mugged.

Embassies and consulates *Australia*, Bansbari (☎411578); *Belgium*, Durbar Marg (☎228925); *Canada*, Lazimpath (☎415193); *Denmark*, Baluwatar (☎413010); *Finland*, Lazimpath (☎416636); *France*, Lazimpath (☎412332); *Germany*, Gyaneswar (☎416832); *Israel*, Lazimpath (☎411811); *Italy*, Baluwatar (☎412280); *Netherlands*, Kumaripati, Patan (☎522915); *Poland*, Ganabahal (☎221101); *Spain*, Battisputali (☎472328); *Sweden*, Khichapokhri (☎220939); *Switzerland*, Jaulakhel, Patan (☎523468); *UK*, Lainchaur (☎414588); *US*, Panipokhari (☎411179). For visas for other Asian countries, see pp.132–133.

Emergencies Police ☎100; Tourist Police ☎211293; Ambulance ☎211959; Red Cross ☎228094.

Fitness *Kathmandu Fitness Centre*, Lazimpath (☎412473), offers aerobics classes and weight-training sessions.

Hospitals, clinics and pharmas For emergencies, *Bir Hospital* (☎223807) on Kantipath is the most central; *Teaching Hospital* (☎412303) in Mahrajganj and *Patan Hospital* (☎522266) in Lagankhel, Patan, are further afield. For inoculations, stool tests and other diagnostics, make for the *CIWEC Clinic*, off Durbar Marg on the way to the *Yak & Yeti* (Mon–Fri 9am–noon & 1–4pm; ☎228531), *Nepal International Clinic*, a block east of the Royal Palace entrance (Sun–Fri 9am–5pm; ☎412842), *Himalayan International Clinic* on Chhetrapati Thamel (daily 9am–5pm; ☎216197) or *Himalaya International Clinic* on Jyatha Thamel (Sun–Fri 9am–5pm; ☎225455). All offer Western-standard facilities, but are expensive. *CIWEC* also sells some excellent information sheets on health matters. *Kalimati Clinic* (Mon & Fri 10–11.30am & 12.30–2.30pm, Wed 11am–2pm;☎271873) in southwest Kathmandu is cheaper for inoculations, and your fee helps subsidize a local immunization programme. Pharmas are in every neighbourhood; *Sajha Swastha Sewa*, opposite the Mahakal temple on Kantipath, is open 24hr.

Language courses *Namaste Language Institute* (☎215660) in Chhetrapati is highly recommended. The Peace Corps (☎410019) or Experiment in International Living (☎414516) might be able to suggest other outfits. For longer-term study opportunities, see "Staying On" in *Basics*.

Laundry Most lodges will send laundry out – in by 9am, back by 6pm (weather permitting). There are a few laundry services, but it's safer to use your own guest house.

Libraries The *British Council* on Kantipath has an admirable little collection, where you can pore over recent UK papers and magazines (summer Mon–Fri 9.30am–6pm; winter Mon–Fri 10am–5pm). The *American Cultural Center*, east of Kamal Pokhri, has a smaller library (Mon–Fri 11am–6pm).

Newspapers and magazines The *Kathmandu Post, Rising Nepal* and other local English-language publications sell out early at the main bookstores, supermarkets and at Pipal Bot on New Road. *The International Herald Tribune, USA Today, Time* and *Newsweek* are available at most bookshops.

Photography Print and slide film is widely available at only slightly higher than Western prices; shops along New Road are competitive. High-quality processing labs in Thamel and on New Road offer same-day service on print and E6 transparency films.

Police Report thefts to the district police headquarters, which in Kathmandu is in Durbar Square; ask for the Interpol section. The national police HQ and Interpol office is in Naksal.

Post Private postal services perform all the functions of the government post office at no extra charge – the one most convenient to tourist areas is located downstairs in the Sanchaya Kosh Building on Tridevi Marg. Plenty of book and postcard shops sell stamps (10 percent surcharge) and handle outgoing mail. The GPO is open for selling stamps, aerogrammes and such Sun–Thurs 9am–7pm, Fri 9am–3pm, and for Poste Restante Sun–Thurs 10.15am–4pm (winter to 3pm), Fri 10.15am–2pm. Send parcels from the Foreign Post Section, around the corner from the GPO on Kantipath (Sun–Fri 10.15am–1.30pm) – see *Basics* for the procedure – or use a shipping agent (below).

Radio and TV *Radio Nepal* reads English-language news bulletins at 8am and 8pm. *Nepal TV* broadcasts the news in English at 10.15pm and also carries BBC World Service and CNN feeds. STAR satellite TV provides continuous Indian music videos, BBC news and recycled English-language dross.

Shipping agents *Sharmasons Movers*, Kantipath (☎222709); *Mountain Packers & Movers*, Thamel (☎416697); *Atlas Cargo Service*, Thamel (☎412335); *Atlas Packers & Movers*, Durbar Marg (☎224254).

Sports The *National Stadium*, at the southern end of Kantipath, hosts frequent **football (soccer)** matches, and is also the headquarters for various martial arts clubs. The *Soaltee Holiday Inn, Everest Hotel* and *Yak & Yeti* all have **tennis** courts, open to non-residents for a fee. For **golf**, make for the *Royal Nepal Golf Club*, near the airport, or *Gokarna Safari Resort* (see p.149).

Swimming pools Kathmandu's public pool, behind the National Stadium, is open daily (except winter) for morning and afternoon sessions (Sun women only), and admission is Rs20. *Hotel de l'Annapurna* charges non-guests Rs350 to use its pool and Rs300 for the sauna, while use of the *Yak & Yeti*'s pool costs Rs250. *Hotel Woodlands'* facilities are less appealing (Rs175). If you can afford to wait three weeks for security processing, you can swim at Phora Durbar on an ICS membership (see "Cultural/Sightseeing Tours" on p.130).

Telephones Wherever two or three tourists are gathered together, ISD/STD/IDD outfits (see p.43) will be also – they're generally open daily 8am–11pm and accept credit cards. The *Central Telegraph Office*, opposite the National Stadium, is open 24 hours a day, seven days a week; the queue can range from a few minutes to over an hour.

Moving on from Kathmandu

Life in Kathmandu is easy – too easy. Get out before you start gathering moss; later, you'll wonder why you stayed so long. What follows is a full rundown on buying tickets, arranging transport and trips, and getting visas. If you can't find what you're looking for here, try the "Listings" above.

Travel within Nepal

For better or worse, most people make Kathmandu their base for travels within Nepal. The country is so centralized, with Kathmandu its transport hub, that a grand tour easily becomes a series of trips out from the capital and back again.

BUS SERVICES FROM KATHMANDU

TOURIST BUSES	Frequency (per day)	Time (minimum)
Nagarkot	1	2hr
Pokhara	2–12*	6hr
Sauraha/Chitwan	0–2*	6hr

EXPRESS BUSES	Frequency (day)	Frequency (night)	Time (minimum)
Barhabise	21		7hr
Bhairawa	9#	19#	9hr
Biratnagar		12	18hr
Birganj	8#	26#	10hr
Butwal	5	17	8hr
Dhangadhi		2	21hr
Dhankuta/Hile		2	21hr
Dharan		10	18hr
Dhulikhel	21		2hr
Dhunche	2		8hr
Gorkha	10#		6hr
Hetauda	1#		8hr
Janakpur	2#	10#	12hr
Jiri	4		11hr
Kakarbitta		21	18hr
Mahendra Nagar		2	24hr
Meghauli	1#		6hr
Narayanghat	9#		5hr
Nepalganj	1#	6#	15hr
Pokhara	21#	14#	8hr
Sunauli	8	17	10hr
Tadi Bazaar (Chitwan)	1#		6hr
Tansen (Palpa)	1#	6	13hr
Tatopani	2		9hr
Taulihawa	1#		12hr
Trisuli	9#		4hr

LOCAL BUSES	Frequency	Time
Balaju	2/hr	20min
Bhaktapur**	3/hr	45min
Boudha	2–3/hr	30min
Budhanilkantha	2/hr	40min
Dakshinkali	2/hr	1hr
Kirtipur (Tribhuwan U.)	2–3/hr	40min
Panauti	6/day	2hr
Pashupatinath	2–3/hr	20min
Patan	4/hr	20min
Sankhu	4/day	1hr
Thimi	2/hr	30min

*Depending on season.
Sajha service available.
** A separate electric trolley bus service also operates to Bhaktapur every 15min.

This, admittedly, has its advantages: you can make good use of the tourist bus services and choose from the most reputable trekking, rafting and cycle-touring companies. It's also easy to leave luggage in Kathmandu, allowing you to travel lightly around the country.

Buses

About a dozen companies operate regular **tourist buses** to Pokhara, and at least three go to Sauraha (for Chitwan National Park). Consider using one of these services if your destination is somewhere en route. Tickets cost about double the public bus fare, and are available through any agent (although not every agent will be able to sell tickets for every bus); book as far in advance as possible during the busy seasons. Buses depart from the north end of Kantipath, usually in the early morning.

Most private **express and night buses** depart from the Main (Gongabu) Bus Park, 3km north of Thamel on the Ring Road. Those serving destinations along the Arniko Highway (such as Dhulikhel, Barhabise, Tatopani and Jiri) leave from the City Bus Park on the east side of the Tudikhel. Buses operated by the quasi-government *Sajha* service originate at Bhimsen Tower near Freak Street, but you can also catch them at Gongabu as they're heading out of town. It's worth paying an agent or an innkeeper to buy your ticket for you.

Local buses (including buses to all destinations in the Kathmandu Valley) originate at the City Bus Park, east of the Tudikhel. Get on there to have any hope of getting a seat.

See the box on p.127 for bus frequencies and approximate journey times.

Flights

Flight schedules are seasonal and fairly volatile, so consult a travel agent for the latest information. The box opposite gives a rough idea of services to the most notable of the thirty-odd airstrips that can be reached directly from Kathmandu (others require plane changes, usually in Pokhara, Nepalganj or Biratnagar).

Locations and telephone numbers for the domestic airlines are as follows, but you're better off making bookings through a travel agent.

Everest Air, Babar Mahal (☎226941).

Necon Air, Kamal Pokhari (☎475231).

Nepal Airways, Kamal Pokhari (☎412388).

RNAC, New Road, located down the first alley west of *RNAC*'s main international office (☎214862). Note that services to Pokhara, Lukla, Meghauli and Bharatpur, plus the mountain flight, are handled by the international office.

Rafting operators

Unless you *really* know what you're doing, you'll have to join a group to go **rafting** in Nepal. Most rafting operators are based in Kathmandu; there are a few inexpensive outfits in Pokhara, but their trips are run on a more sedate stretch of river. Smaller Kathmandu companies tend to offer only three-day trips on the Trisuli River for around $15–20 a day, but for reasons explained in the rafting section (p.53), companies in this price bracket are hard to recommend. The ones listed here are more reputable, hence more expensive.

Equator Expeditions, Thamel Northwest, immediately north of the *Kathmandu Guest House* (Box 8404, Kathmandu; ☎416596; fax 414083;). Experienced guides, good equipment, communal cooking. Trips on the Trisuli, Kali Gandaki, Seti, Sun Kosi and Karnali for $35–50 a day. Kayaks available.

INTERNAL FLIGHTS FROM KATHMANDU

	Frequency	Time	Fare ($)
Bhairawa	1–2/day	45min	72
Bharatpur	2–3/day	25min	50
Biratnagar	3–5/day	50min*	77
Dhangadhi	1–2/week	1hr 50min	159
Janakpur	1–2/day	35min	55
Lamidanda	3/week	35min	66
Lukla	2/day	40min	83
Jomosom	0–2/week	40min*	110
Jumla	1–2/week	1hr 15min*	127
Mahendra Nagar	1–2/week	2hr 30min	160
Meghauli	0–1/day	30min	72
Mountain flight	3–6/day	1hr	99
Nepalganj	2–4/day	1hr 10min*	99
Phaplu	4/wk	25min	77
Pokhara	5–8/day	35min	61
Simara	1–2/day	30min	44
Tumlingtar	3–4/week	55min	44

* Indirect flights will take longer.

Great Himalayan Rivers, Lazimpath (☎410937). Established company offering Trisuli trips for $35 a day and Sun Kosi trips for $55 a day.

Himalayan Encounters, Thamel Northwest, in the forecourt of the *Kathmandu Guest House* (☎417426; fax 417133). Trips encourage group participation and appeal to gung-ho types. Three-day Trisuli trip costs $99, ten days on the Sun Kosi $450.

Shiva's River Adventure, Thamel Northwest (☎417685). A more affordable Nepali-run outfit that has a good track record. Does the Sun Kosi, Kali Gandaki, Seti, Trisuli and Karnali for $25–50 a day.

Ultimate Descents, at *Northfields Café*, Thamel Northwest (☎ & fax 411933; same number for fax). Specializing in the Sun Kosi, Kali Gandaki, Marsyangdi and Karnali, generally priced at $45 per day.

Trekking companies

For a full discussion of the pros and cons of trekking with a group versus doing it independently, see Chapter Seven. As with rafting companies, individual budget trekking companies can't be recommended because the quality of their service can vary so much from year to year (or trip to trip). The following higher-priced outfits have reputations for maintaining high standards.

Asian Trekking, Bhagwan Bahal (PO Box 3022; ☎415506).

Journeys Mountaineering & Trekking, Maharajganj (PO Box 2034; ☎412898; fax 419808).

Rover Treks & Expeditions, Naksal (PO Box 1081; ☎416817; fax 226820).

Sherpa Co-operative Trekking, Durbar Marg (PO Box 1338; ☎224068; fax 223520).

Summit Nepal Trekking, *Summit Hotel*, Kopundol, Patan (PO Box 1406; ☎521810; fax 523737).

Yangrima Trekking & Mountaineering, Kantipath (PO Box 2951; ☎225608; fax 227628).

Mountain-bike tours

At present only one company operates **mountain-bike tours** out of Kathmandu, although others may soon follow suit. *Himalayan Mountain Bikes* (PO Box 2247;

☎416596; fax 411055), based in Thamel just north of the *Kathmandu Guest House*, runs trips of one to four days around the Kathmandu Valley and rim, plus some longer vehicle-supported tours of the hills and Tarai. Prices work out to be about $30 for a day-long outing and $40 per day for the overnighters. The company also boasts Nepal's only proper mountain bike repair shop and the only real fleet of high-quality mountain bikes and accessories. Unfortunately it doesn't rent out its bikes to individuals, except on an informal basis on Saturdays in season to participants in the weekly rides organized by the Kathmandu-based Gear Wallah Club.

For information on renting mountain bikes, see "Getting Around" (p.33). Tips for touring on your own are given in "Outdoor Pursuits" (p.56).

Wildlife package tours
Although most of the **budget lodges** near Chitwan and Bardia national parks are represented by agents in Kathmandu, their packages are not recommended. See the Chitwan and Bardia sections (pp.266 & 297) for full details on doing it yourself.

For **luxury jungle lodges and tented camps**, you do need to book ahead. See the relevant listings for Chitwan National Park (p.276), Bardia National Park (p.300), Sukla Phanta Wildlife Reserve (p.307) and Koshi Tappu Wildlife Reserve (p.325).

Cultural/sightseeing tours
Various operators run half- and full-day tours to Pashupatinath, Dakshin Kali and other cultural sights around the valley. You can book through any agent. The following, which can't be booked through agents, offer unique tours.

Getaway Himalayan Eco-Trekking, Gyaneswar (PO Box 3606; ☎411790; fax 228467). Day hikes around the valley with a cultural slant.

Insight Nepal (PO Box 6760; ☎418964; fax 223515). Homestays, cultural tours, language instruction and volunteer work placement.

International Community Services (ICS), Kantipath, in the British Library compound (☎220598). A nonprofit educational organization that runs cultural tours and hikes guided by recognized authorities. To participate in ICS activities you have to take out an annual membership, which costs Rs500. Office hours are Mon–Fri noon–3pm.

Leaving Nepal

Overland connections between Nepal and India are well developed, not to say comfortable; Kathmandu is the usual setting-off point, since it's the only place in Nepal to get an Indian visa. For all other countries you'll almost certainly fly: see the box opposite for details on recommended travel agents and international airline offices. It's worth shopping around, as even supposedly standard airfares may vary from one agent to the next.

If you're flying out of Nepal, remember that there's an astronomical Rs700 **airport tax** (Rs600 if you're flying within south Asia). Also, don't forget to **reconfirm** your return flight at least 72 hours prior to departure or you'll lose your seat. It's best to reconfirm in person, but this can be a hassle (especially with *RNAC*). A travel agent will do it for you for about Rs100.

Overland to India
Many travellers get burned by scams involving **tickets to India**. Given that a typical bus–train package involves three different tickets and as many as six

RECOMMENDED TRAVEL AGENTS

Everest Travel Service, with branches on Kantipath (☎221216) and Ganga Path, just off Durbar Square (☎222217).
Kathmandu Travels & Tours, Tripureswar (☎222511).
Marco Polo Travels, in the forecourt of the *Kathmandu Guest House* (☎414192).

Mountain Voyages Nepal, Thamel South (☎224049).
Natraj Tours & Travels, Durbar Marg (☎222014).
President Travels & Tours, Durbar Marg (☎220245).
Yeti Travels, Durbar Marg(☎211234).

INTERNATIONAL AIRLINES

See p.13 for sample air fares between Kathmandu and other Asian cities.
Aeroflot, Kamaladi (☎227399).
Air Canada, Durbar Marg (☎222838).
Air France, Durbar Marg (☎223339).
Air India, Nag Pokhri (☎415637). Flights from Kathmandu are handled by *Indian Airlines* (see below).
Biman Bangladesh, Kamal Pokhri (☎416582).
British Airways, Durbar Marg (☎222266).
Cathay Pacific, Kamaladi (☎411725).
China Southwest Airlines, Kamaladi (☎419770).
Dragon Air, Durbar Marg (☎223162).
Emirates, Kantipath (☎220579).
Indian Airlines, Nag Pokhri (☎419649).

KLM, Durbar Marg (☎224895).
Korean Air, Kantipath (☎216080).
Kuwait Airways, Kantipath (☎222884).
Lufthansa, Durbar Marg (☎223052).
Northwest, Lekhnath Marg (☎410089).
Pakistan International Airways (PIA), Durbar Marg (☎223102).
Philippine Airlines, Kantipath (☎226262).
Qantas, Durbar Marg (☎220245).
RNAC, corner of Kantipath and New Road (☎220757).
SAS, Kopundol, Patan (☎524232).
Singapore Airlines, Durbar Marg (☎220759).
Swissair, Durbar Marg (☎222452).
Thai, Durbar Marg (☎221316).
TWA, Kamaladi (☎411725).

companies or agents, the chances of something going wrong are high. Ticket sellers in Kathmandu know that few travellers will come back to complain.

All **bus–train packages** to India involve travelling by public bus to the border at Sunauli, and then by Indian bus to Gorakhpur, the nearest broad-gauge train station to Kathmandu. It's probably worth paying double in Kathmandu to have a confirmed sleeper out of Gorakhpur, since tickets are hard to obtain there, but Kathmandu ticket sellers require at least a week to arrange train tickets and they demand money up front. When you return to pick up your ticket, you may be told that it's being held at the border – and when you get to the border, you may be told it's in Gorakhpur. If the ticket isn't ready when it was promised, demand your money back and take your chances with the ticket scalpers in Gorakhpur. Be particularly careful when booking first-class sleepers, as there's a racket in replacing them with second-class sleepers or first-class seats. Never surrender your receipt to anyone – without it, you've got no proof of what you paid for.

Bus-only deals to Darjeeling, Delhi and a few other Indian cities are less chancey. On the other hand, there's less reason to book an Indian bus so far in

Not quite full yet

advance; if you want to save money, take any bus to the border and book your seat on the Indian bus there. At least one company runs a regular **direct bus** to Delhi; other outfits lay on occasional direct services to Goa and such places, but they're overpriced and must be horrendously long journeys.

Just a handful of companies package tickets to India from Nepal, and all other agents deal through them. Of these, the most reliable appear to be:

Pagoda Travels & Tours, Basantapur Square (☎216871).
Shikhar Nepal Tours & Travels, Chhetrapati (☎228163).
Shiva Travels, Chhetrapati (☎215650).
Student Travels & Tours, Chhetrapati (☎220334).

The Indian visa two-step

Those geniuses at the Indian embassy (☎410900), off Lazimpath in Lainchaur, have come up with a new and improved **visa** application process – allow *one week* to work your way through it.

Application hours are 9.30 to 11am, Monday to Friday. The time-consuming part of the procedure is obtaining "clearance" from Delhi, which is needed before your visa application can even be considered. Queue up at Counter B, where they'll take a fee off you (Rs300 at the last count) and send a fax with your details to Delhi. Wait three to four days for the reply. Then come back, collect your clearance document and report to Counter A (why B first, then A? you'll understand when you get to India), where you actually apply for your visa. Visas for most nationalities cost Rs1000 for three months, or Rs250 for fifteen days, and you'll need to supply a couple of passport photos. Note that a multiple-entry visa costs no more than a single-entry one. Your visa should be ready for collection later the same day.

Attention British, French, German, Dutch, Austrian, Spanish and Italian passport holders! Still more adventures await you. *Before* going through the above process, you must first get a "recommendation letter" from your embassy.

Travelling to Tibet

Officially, travellers are not allowed to enter **Tibet** from Nepal independently: you have to join a tour, although once in Tibet you can strike off on your own. Many tours are based around a five-day overland journey from Kathmandu to Lhasa, two days in Lhasa, and then a flight back to Kathmandu, costing a minimum of $350. Flying both ways adds $190. Travel agents arrange your Chinese visa and Tibet endorsement for an extra $30–80, depending on your nationality.

Tour prices go up slightly during the Tibet high season, May to September. Overland travel between Nepal and Tibet is generally not possible due to snow between the second week in December and the second week in March. *China Southwest Airlines* also suspends its twice-weekly flights to Lhasa between late November and early March. See p.210 for advice on crossing the border.

Arniko Travel, Bhatbateni (☎414594; fax 411878).
Green Hill Tours, Thamel Northwest, just north of the *Kathmandu Guest House* (☎414803).
Marco Polo Travels, Gyaneswari (☎418832; fax 418479).
Nepal Travel, Ramshah Path (☎412899; fax 227782).
Shiva Travels, Chhetrapati (☎212256).
Tibet Travels & Tours, corner of Jyatha Thamel and Tridevi Marg (☎212130; fax 228986).

Visas for other Asian countries

If you're moving on to other parts of Asia, the following embassies and consulates in Kathmandu issue **visas**. Formalities often change, so it's worth calling ahead.

Bangladesh, Mahrajganj (☎414943). Apply Mon–Fri 9–10.45am; visa ready in two or three days.

Burma (Myanmar), Chakpat, Patan (☎521788). Apply Mon–Fri 9.30am–4.30pm; visa ready later the same day or early the next.

China, Baluwatar (☎411740). Visas issued only through travel agents.

Pakistan, Panipokhri (☎411421). Apply Mon–Thurs 10–11.30am; visa ready in two or three days.

Thailand, Bansbari, north of the Ring Road on the way to Budhanilkantha (☎420410). Apply Mon–Fri 10am–2pm; visa ready in 24 hours.

CHAPTER TWO

THE KATHMANDU VALLEY

Few places on earth can rival the **Kathmandu Valley**'s combination of natural and man-made beauty. Despite suburbanization and industrialization, the fertile, terraced valley maintains its traditional ways in a hundred huddled brick villages, most of which rarely see foreigners; much of the valley floor still shimmers in an undulating patchwork of paddy fields – brown, golden or brilliant green, depending on the season – crisscrossed by rutted paths and country lanes. But above all it's the valley's incredible wealth of art and architecture that overwhelms visitors, just as it did the early explorers. "The valley consists of as many temples as there are houses, and as many idols as there are men," gushed William Kirkpatrick, the first Englishman to reach Kathmandu, and generations of travellers since have accurately (if patronizingly) described it

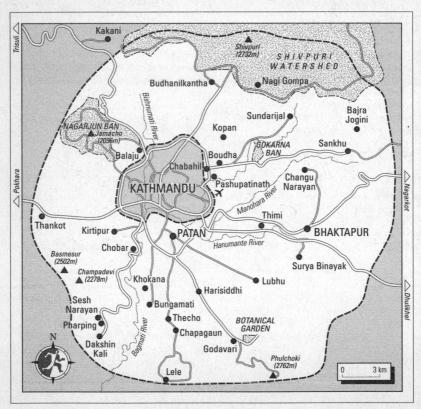

as a "living museum". If most of this chapter is devoted to temples and holy sites – there are no forts, you'll notice – it's because religion is the best and most fascinating window on Nepali culture.

Until two hundred years ago, this protected bowl *was* Nepal (and for many hill people outside the valley, it still is). At that time, Kathmandu was only one of three major city-states constantly battling for dominance: **Patan**, just across the Bagmati River, controlled the southern part of the valley, while **Bhaktapur** ruled the east. These historical divisions are profoundly ingrained in valley society, and they live on in distinct religious practices, festivals and even dress. This chapter divides the valley into three sections, as much for practical reasons as historical ones, since roads and transport developed out of the old patterns of settlement.

The sheer density of sights in the valley is phenomenal. Roads radiate out to dozens of towns and villages, and you won't go wrong with any of them. Hindu holy places abound: the great pilgrimage complex of **Pashupatinath**, the sleeping Vishnu of **Budhanilkantha**, the sacrificial pit of **Dakshin Kali** and the hilltop temple of **Changu Narayan** are the most outstanding. If Buddhism is your main interest, head for the great stupa of **Boudha**, the centre of Tibetan Buddhist worship and study in Nepal, or the *bahal* of **Patan**, the valley's most Buddhist city. For medieval scenes, try **Kirtipur**, **Bungamati** or, best of all, **Bhaktapur**. For views, you're spoilt for choice – the protected areas of **Shivpuri**, **Nagarjun Ban** and **Godavari** stand out, but almost any hill will do.

Getting around the valley is generally easiest by **bike** or **motorcycle**. In the sections that follow, bus routes are mentioned where they exist (fares are usually just a few rupees), but unless it's stated otherwise, take it as given that the quickest way to get there is with your own wheels. **Walking**, on the other hand, is often more rewarding: distances are small, trails are everywhere, and people will usually be happy to give directions. The *Schneider* colour **map** of the valley is by far the best for serious walking, although the cheaper *Mandala* or *Nepa* versions will probably suffice. For suggested itineraries and detailed route descriptions, pick up a copy of *Kathmandu Bikes & Hikes* (see "Books" in *Contexts*).

GREAT HIKES AND BIKES IN THE VALLEY

Although the hiking and biking will be good in any rural part of the Kathmandu Valley, you might want to have a destination in mind. Here are a few; later sections give more details.

Shivpuri – Hike up to the crest of the valley's north rim for views, or ride along the traffic-free roads within the Shivpuri Watershed.

Nagarjun Ban – Hike or bike to a hilltop stupa and explore sacred caves.

Champa Devi – Another hike to a high point along the valley rim.

Dakshin Kali – A varied ride through the southern valley, taking in several sacred sites.

Bungamati and beyond – A ride along rural byways to a very traditional village, with the option of carrying on all the way to Lele.

Phulchoki – A trail and a rough, winding road pass through splendid forest to the highest point along the valley rim.

East of Bhaktapur – Pastoral lanes lead to Nala and a number of other small villages.

Changu Narayan – Hike or bike up to this ancient temple site; hiking trails also connect to Nagarkot and Sankhu.

NORTH OF KATHMANDU

Chapter One covered Kathmandu within the Ring Road; this section deals with the remainder of the northern valley. Most people will treat the sights described here as **day trips** from Kathmandu – some places are theoretically even within walking distance – but if you're interested in Buddhism, or you're just getting fed up with Kathmandu, an **overnight stay** in Boudha would be a smart move.

> The telephone code for the Kathmandu Valley is ☎01.

Pashupatinath

Often likened to Varanasi in India, **PASHUPATINATH** (pronounced Posh-*potty*-not) is Nepal's holiest Hindu pilgrimage site: a time-warp enclave of exotic temples, cremation ghats, ritual bathers and half-naked sadhus. The sacred complex lies just beyond the Ring Road, 4km east of Kathmandu – incongruously close to the modern airport, but fortunately sheltered from it in a wooded ravine. Pashupatinath, together with the associated temples of Gorakhnath and Ghujeshwari, is a heady cocktail of Hindu (and to a lesser extent Buddhist) proceedings, spiked with some of the most bizarre mythology in the world.

Buses from Kathmandu's City Bus Park drop you off southwest of the temple area at Gaushala, a busy, modern intersection on the Ring Road; the lane angling downhill from the northeast corner of the intersection leads to the western side of the temple area. If you're **cycling**, follow Tridevi Marg east past the Royal Palace, take the first right after Durbar Marg, then a left on the first main road (Kamal Pokhari), and follow that road over the Dhobi Khola and all the way to Gaushala, where there are signs. You'll probably have to pay a few rupees to have your bike "watched".

The site's layout favours an anticlockwise circuit on foot, first around Pashupatinath's temples and ghats, then up to Gorakhnath, on to Ghujeshwari and back. Instead of returning to Pashupatinath, however, you might want to continue on to Boudha (see p.142), about 2km further northeast along a quasi-paved road.

The Pashupatinath complex

The **temples of Pashupatinath** straddle the Bagmati River, which is thought by Hindus to be the holiest in the Kathmandu Valley, and this specific stretch the most sacred of all. To die and be cremated here is to be released from the cycle of rebirths, according to tradition. Wives used to commit *sati* on their husbands' funeral pyres here, and although the practice was outlawed early this century, it's still widely believed that husbands and wives who bathe here together will be remarried in the next life. **Bathing** is considered especially meritorious on full-moon days, on Magh Sankranti (usually Jan 14) and Bala Chaturdashi (late Nov or early Dec), and, for women, during the festival of Tij (late Aug or early Sept). The entire complex overflows with pilgrims from all over the subcontinent during the **festival** of Shiva Raatri (held on the new moon of late Feb or early

△ *Boudha*

PASHUPATINATH, GORAKHNATH & GHUJESHWARI

Ring Road

Bagmati River

Gauri Ghat

Kailash Hill

GHUJESHWARI

Pashupati Mandir

Gorakhnath Mandir

PASHUPATINATH

Arya Ghat

Terrace

GORAKHNATH

Bachhareshwari Mandir

Pancha Dewal

Ram Ghat

Ram Mandir

Ram Janaki Mandir

Lakshmi Narayan Mandir

Bishwarup Mandir

Bagmati River

Raj Rajeshwari Nawa Durga

Gaushala & Ring Road

N

0   100 m

March). Devout locals also come for special services on full moon days and on the eleventh lunar day (*ekadashi*) after each full and new moon.

Foreigners are free to observe most of these rituals, but it's essential to respect the privacy of bathers and worshippers. Be especially sensitive about photographing people and cremation pyres: you wouldn't want tourists snapping away at your mother's funeral, would you?

Shiva is the principal deity here, in one of his more benign forms: **Pashupati, Lord of the Animals**, in whose name the king of Nepal ends all his public addresses, and to whom praises are sung on Radio Nepal at the start of each broadcasting day. Several tales are told of how Shiva came by this title. Nepali schoolchildren are taught that Shiva, to escape his heavenly obligations, assumed the guise of a one-horned stag and fled to the forest here. The other gods pursued him and, laying hold of him, broke off his horn, which was transformed into the powerful Pashupati *linga*. The *linga* was later lost, only to be rediscovered at its present site by a cow who magically began watering the spot with her milk.

PASHUPATI MANDIR

Approaching from the west through the hamlet of Pashupathinath, a lane leads past trinket stalls and sweet shops to the main gate of the **Pashupati Mandir** – the holy of holies for Nepali Shaivas, followers of Shiva. Like many orthodox Hindu temples, it's only open to Hindus (in Nepal, Buddhists, Sikhs and Jains are included as Hindus). From the outside, though, you can glimpse the two symbols that are found in front of almost every Shiva temple, their gargantuan proportions here a measure of the temple's sanctity: a two-storey-high *trisul* (trident), and the enormous brass backside of Nandi, Shiva's faithful bull, who is yet another reminder of the god's procreative power. The best view of the whole compound can be had from a terrace high above the opposite (east) bank of the river.

Hidden inside, the famous **Pashupati linga** is supposed to display four carved faces of Shiva, plus a fifth, invisible one on the top; Buddhists claim one of the faces is that of the Buddha. Hindus associate this *linga* with yet another Shiva

---

SADHUS, YOGINS AND GANJA

Sadhus, those dreadlocked, ashen waifs usually seen lurking around Hindu temples, are essentially an Indian phenomenon. However, Nepal, being the setting for many of the amorous and ascetic exploits of Shiva (the most popular deity among sadhus), is a favourite sadhu stomping ground – and nowhere more so than Pashupatinath, which is rated as one of the four most important Shaiva pilgrimage sites. During the festival of Shiva Raatri, Pashupatinath hosts a full-scale sadhu convention, which draws pilgrims from all over the subcontinent. The government lays on free firewood for the festival.

Shaiva sadhus follow Shiva in one of his best-loved and most enigmatic guises – the wild, dishevelled **yogin**, the master of yoga, who sits motionless atop a Himalayan peak for eons at a time and whose hair is the source of the mighty Ganga (Ganges) River. Sadhus live solitary lives, always on the move, subsisting on alms and owning nothing but what they carry. They bear Shiva's emblems: the *trisul* (trident), *damaru* (two-sided drum), a necklace of furrowed *rudraksha* seeds, and perhaps a conch shell for blowing haunting calls across the cosmic ocean; some smear themselves with ashes, symbolizing Shiva's role as the destroyer, who reduces all things to ash so that creation can begin anew; and on their foreheads is usually painted a trident-shaped *tika*. (In addition to the trident, sadhus employ scores of other *tika* patterns, each with its own cult affiliation and symbolism.)

Given Shiva as a role model, Shaiva sadhu theology – insofar as it exists – is a bloody-minded business. As befits followers of a mountaintop ascetic who is also the god of the phallus, sadhus practice celibacy, performing diverse contortions and mortifications of the flesh to free themselves from sensual passions, yet radiate a smouldering sexuality. Of one famous sadhu it was said that he had so completely marshalled his sexual energies that he bled semen; and until recently a popular sadhu at Pashupatinath publicly performed feats of hoisting large stones with a string tied to his penis. Similarly, sadhus refrain from alcohol, but blithely get stoned out of their heads on **ganja**, whose transcendental powers were supposedly discovered by Shiva. Marijuana, which grows wild throughout hill Nepal, is smoked by sadhus in a *chillam*, and with each toke on the vertical clay pipe they intone "*Bam Shankar*" – "I am Shiva".

myth, in which the god transformed his phallus into an infinite pillar of light and challenged Brahma and Vishnu – the other members of the Hindu trinity – to find the ends of it. Brahma flew heavenward, while Vishnu plumbed the depths of hell; both were forced to abandon the search, but Brahma falsely boasted of success, only to be caught out by Shiva. Shaivas claim that this is why Brahma is seldom worshipped, Vishnu gets his fair share, and Shiva is revered over all.

The gold-clad pagoda dates from the early seventeenth century, but inscriptions indicate that a temple has stood here since at least the fifth century, and some historians suspect it goes back to the third century BC, when the ancient village of Deopatan is said to have been founded just west of here. The temple apparently emerged as a hotbed of tantric practices in the eleventh century and remained so for four hundred years, until King Yaksha Malla reined things in by importing conventional Brahman **priests** from south India – an arrangement that continues to this day. Wearing the ceremonial orange robes of the Pashupata sect, the priests array the *linga* in brocade silk and bathe it with curd, ghee, honey, sugar and milk.

Hindu pilgrims are expected to distribute offerings to the priests and then make a circuit of the temple and the 365 *shivalinga* and other secondary shrines scattered about the precinct. Most also distribute alms to beggars lined along some of the nearby lanes. If you choose to give, arm yourself with a sufficient stockpile of small change (*saano paisa*), available from vendors.

ALONG THE WEST BANK

Many of the buildings around the main temple, including the tall, whitewashed ones overlooking the Bagmati's west bank, are *dharmsala* (pilgrims' rest houses), set aside here for devout Hindus approaching death. In their final hour, the dying will be laid out on a sloped stone slab with their feet in the Bagmati and given a last drink of the holy river water. Cremations are held continuously on two **burning ghats** along the embankment: Arya Ghat, north of the footbridges, is reserved for the royal family and VIPs, while Ram Ghat, to the south, is used by other members of the higher castes. The cremations are carried out by the families of the deceased.

The small pagoda between the two footbridges is the **Bachhaleshwari Mandir**, dedicated to Shiva's consort Parvati in one of her mother-goddess roles. Next to it stands a newish ten-foot terracotta frieze of Narayan (alias Vishnu) and other sculptures of Ganesh and Gauri (Parvati). Running south along the west bank is another string of metal-roofed *dharmsala*, which you can explore in a limited way. Sticking out of the embankment in front of the next-to-last is a small but priceless seventh-century **Buddha statue**, looking rather out of place in this Hindu Lourdes. Hindus hold the image to be of **Kalki**, the tenth and final incarnation of Vishnu, a sort of messiah figure who will bring the evil Kali Yuga (Age of Kali) to a close and usher in a new, virtuous cycle of history; some claim that the idol is gradually emerging from the earth, marking the flourishing of the Kali Yuga. Ensconced in a round brick battlement just to the south is a neglected bumper-sized *linga* which may be of even greater antiquity. The southernmost building shelters two temples in its courtyard, the oval **Raj Rajeshwari** and the gilded pagoda of **Nawa Durga**.

Behind the *dharmsala* broods the gothic bulk of **Pancha Dewal**, whose five Mughal-style cupolas are visible from high up on the opposite bank. This now serves as an old people's home, one wing of which is operated by **Mother**

Theresa's Missionaries of Charity (the government runs the rest), and though emphatically not a tourist site, it is an excellent place to experience a different side of Nepal as a volunteer. The sisters need help each morning changing and cleaning sheets, helping residents wash, clipping nails, scrubbing pots and so on – real humble work, but that's the whole idea of it. They also run a second nursing home in nearby Chabahil. The entrance to the compound is on the north side; look for the sisters (who speak English) in their trademark white saris with blue trim.

THE EAST BANK

Crossing over to the east bank along the southernmost bridge, the first thing you'll reach is a pockmarked slope: a **burial ground**, where plots are reserved for sadhus, infants and people too poor to afford wood for a funeral pyre.

A *sadhu*

Moving northwards and uphill, you'll enter a wide, paved enclosure which during Shiva Raatri is chock-a-block with sadhus doing mysterious and sometimes gruesome penances. Two small temples are found here: the one with a statue of Garud in front is called **Lakshmi Narayan**, in honour of Vishnu (aka Narayan) and his wealth-bringing wife Lakshmi; the other is the **Ram Janaki**, containing statues of Ram – Vishnu's incarnation as a mortal in the *Ramayan* epic – and his whole family, including Hanuman the monkey king, who helped rescue Ram's wife Sita from the clutches of a Sri Lankan demon. Sita is popular among Nepali Hindus, since she was born in Janakpur in the eastern Tarai (see p.316). These temples, along with the **Ram Mandir** in the next compound, are disappointingly recent and un-Nepali. Temples at Pashupatinath are built and rebuilt often, renovations being the standard way of winning favour with gods and men, and wealthy Indian patrons are among the principal contributors to the development fund. Further north along the river, the eleven great **shivalaya** (boxy *linga* shelters) were erected in honour of women who committed *sati* on the pyres opposite.

Gorakhnath

The main stairway up the east bank carries on up through Mrigasthali Ban, the forest where Shiva is supposed to have cavorted as a stag, to the mellow **Gorakhnath Mandir** at the top of the hill. Visiting this compound, after the sensory overload below, is like entering a soundproofed room. The temple itself, a medium-sized *shikra* structure dedicated to the patron deity of the Shah kings, isn't interesting – what will amaze you is the sight of scores of **shivalaya** arranged in crumbling rows in the forest, mottled by shade and shafts of sunlight. The place has the romantic, ruined feel of an overgrown cemetery, with broken statuary lying undisturbed and stone inscriptions recording long-forgotten decrees. You could easily mistake the *shivalaya* for tombs, but their iconography – the *trisul*, statues of Nandi and Shiva (always with an erection), the *linga* atop the *yoni* – proclaims them to be Shiva shrines. It's a fine spot for a picnic, though you have to watch out for the thieving monkeys.

The onion dome rising above the trees to the southeast of Gorakhnath is the **Bishwarup Mandir** (entrance only to Hindus), dedicated to Vishnu in his many-limbed "universal form". Dominating the sanctum, however, is a six-metre-tall statue of Shiva and Parvati in the state of *yab-yum* (sexual union).

THE KATHMANDU VALLEY'S MAJOR FESTIVALS

Some of the festivals listed in the Kathmandu chapter are also celebrated in the valley. Again, most are reckoned by the lunar calendar, so check locally for exact dates.

MAGH (Jan–Feb)
Magh Sankranti – The first day of Magh (Jan 14 or 15), marked by ritual bathing at Patan's Sankhamul Ghat; more bathing takes place at Sankhu on the day of the full moon of Magh.

FAAGUN (Feb–March)
Losar – Tibetan New Year, the new moon of February, celebrated at Boudha with processions, horn-blowing and *tsampa*-throwing on the big third day.
Shiva Raatri – On the full moon of Faagun, the Pashupatinath *mela* (fair) attracts tens of thousands of pilgrims and holy men, while children everywhere collect money for bonfires on "Shiva's Night".

BAISAKH (April–May)
Bisket Jaatra – Bhaktapur's celebration of Nepali New Year (April 13 or 14), in which chariots are pulled around the city for several days and a *linga* pole is ceremonially toppled to mark the start of the new year. Thimi and Bode have their own idiosyncratic festivities.
Balaju Jaatra – Ritual bathing at the Balaju Water Garden on the day of the full moon in April.
Buddha Jayanti – The anniversary of the Buddha's birth, enlightenment and death, celebrated at Boudha.
Machhendranath Raath Jaatra – An amazing, uniquely Newar extravaganza in which an immense chariot is pulled through old Patan in stages over a period of several weeks (see p163).
Lalit Festival – A four-day exposition of arts and culture in Patan in late April.

ASAAR (June–July)
Dalai Lama's Birthday – Observed informally at Boudha (July 6).

SAAUN (July–Aug)
Janai Purnima – The annual changing of the sacred thread worn by high-caste Hindu men, involving bathing and splashing at Patan's Kumbeshwar Mahadev on the day of the full moon of Saaun.

BHADAU (Aug–Sept)
Krishna Jayanti – Krishna's birthday, marked by an all-night vigil at Patan's Krishna Mandir on the seventh day after the full moon.
Gokarna Aunsi – Nepali "Father's Day", observed at Gokarneswar with bathing and offerings on the new-moon day of Bhadau.
Tij – A day of ritual bathing for women on the third day after the new moon, mainly at Pashupatinath.

KARTIK (Oct–Nov)
Haribondhini Ekadashi – Bathing and *puja* on the eleventh day after the new moon. The main action takes place at the Vishnu sites of Budhanilkantha, Sesh Narayan, Bishanku Narayan and Changu Narayan.

MANGSIR (Nov–Dec)
Indrayani Jaatra – Deities are paraded through Kirtipur on palanquins on the new-moon day of Mangsir.
Bala Chaturdashi – All-night vigil at Pashupatinath on the night of the new moon, involving candles and ritual seed-offerings to dead relatives.

Ghujeshwari and back

The **Ghujeshwari** (or Guhyeshwari) **Mandir** sits at the bottom of the path that continues downhill from Gorakhnath. Here, too, non-Hindus can only peek from outside, but the legend behind this temple is one of the all-time masterpieces of Hindu surrealism. The story goes that Shiva's first wife, Sati, offended by some insult, threw herself onto a fire (giving rise to the term *sati*, or *suttee*); Shiva retrieved her corpse and, blinded by grief, flew to and fro across the subcontinent, scattering parts of the body in 51 sacred places. Ghujeshwari is where Sati's vagina (some say her anus) fell. As a consequence, the temple here represents the female counterpart to Pashupatinath and is held to be every bit as sacred, its chief focus being a *kalash* (vessel) kept in a sunken pit and containing an "odiferous liquid". Buddhists consider Ghujeshwari to be one of the valley's four mystic Bajra Joginis – powerful tantric goddesses – and the site to be the seed from which the Swayambhu lotus grew.

From Ghujeshwari a lane follows the river back around to Pashupatinath, passing **Gauri Ghat**, a peaceful spot where the river enters the Pashupatinath ravine and monkeys leap from branches and cliffs into the water. The road crosses the river here and circles around to the village of Pashupatinath, while a trail past the river crossing takes a more direct route up and over **Kailash Hill**. This grassy, grotty knoll, named after the Tibetan mountain where Shiva does his meditating, gives good views of the mountains (smog permitting) as well as the Pashupatinath area.

Practicalities

Pashupatinath village would be a wonderful place for a simple tourist **guest house**. Unfortunately none exists (but keep an ear out in case this changes), and the only lodging in the immediate vicinity is provided by the riverside *dharmsala*, which are reserved for Hindu pilgrims. There are a few guest houses near the Gaushala intersection (*Khumbila Hotel* and *Hotel Maharaj*, for example, both ③/ B④), but these are mentioned only for their proximity to the airport and lack any sort of ambience. For **food**, it's *daal bhaat*, noodles, snacks and sweets in Pashupatinath.

Handicrafts peddlers sell the usual range of Tibetan curios and *khukuri* knives, all of which are totally irrelevant here. If you're looking for an authentic souvenir of Pashupatinath, check out the things Nepalis buy: cheap votive icons, statuettes, *linga* replicas, conch shells, *rudraksha* necklaces, offertory vessels and bangles. *Shaligram* (fossil-bearing stones associated with Vishnu) are also widely sold, but bear in mind that it's illegal to export these from Nepal.

Boudha (Boudhanath)

To ancient travellers along the Kathmandu–Tibet trade route, the ten-kilometre corridor from Pashupatinath to Sankhu was known as the zone of *siddhi* (supernatural powers), where guardian deities dwelt and all wishes were granted. The biggest, most auspicious landmark along this route was – and still is – the great stupa at **BOUDHA** (or **BOUDHANATH**), about 5km east of downtown Kathmandu.

One of the world's largest stupas, Boudha is generally acknowledged to be the most important Tibetan Buddhist monument outside Tibet – Tibetans simply call

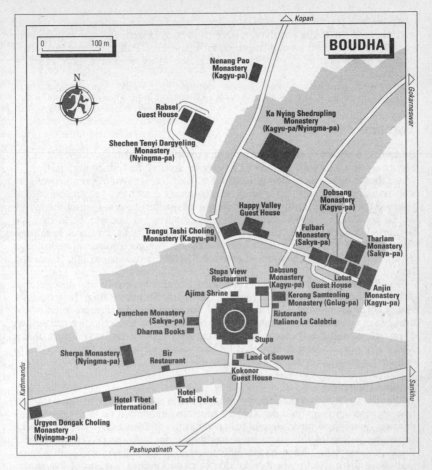

it Chorten Chempo, "Great Stupa" – and since 1959 it has become the Mecca of **Tibetan exiles** in Nepal. Tibetans now run most of the businesses along the main road and around the stupa, while the construction of monasteries has created a regular suburban sprawl to the north: despite the coach parties and souvenir sellers, Boudha gives you a thorough dunking in Tibetan culture, both its proud past and anxious present. Dusk is the best time to be here, after the day-trippers and overflying helicopters have gone, when the resonant chanting of monks and the otherworldly cacophony of their music drifts from the upper rooms of the houses that ring the stupa, and pilgrims perform *kora*, shuffling and prostrating their way around the dome.

If you want an extra helping, go during the **festival** of Losar in February, when Boudha hosts the biggest celebration of the Tibetan New Year in Nepal. Other busy times are Buddha Jayanti (the Buddha's birthday), the full moon of April–May, when an image of the Buddha is paraded around the stupa aboard an elephant, and the full moon of March–April, when ethnic Tamangs – the original guardians of the stupa – converge here to arrange marriages, and hundreds of eligible brides are sat around the stupa for inspection. Full moon and new moon days in general attract more pilgrims, since acts of worship earn more merit on these days.

Crowded **minibuses** and buses depart frequently for Boudha from Kathmandu's City Bus Park, but you're better off going by bike or taxi.

The site

Assigning a reliable age to Boudha is impossible, and historians are left at the mercy of legends, which seem to fix its origins around the fifth century AD.

A **Tibetan text** relates how a daughter of Indra stole flowers from heaven and was reassigned to earth as a lowly poultryman's daughter, yet prospered and shamed the valley's wealthy folk by building a gigantic stupa to honour the mythical Buddha of the Previous Age. Tibetans attach great importance to this tale because it's attributed to Guru Padma Sambhava, Tibet's first and best-loved evangelist. Interestingly, in the same manuscript the guru warns of an invasion by a giant enemy, which would scatter the Tibetan people south into Nepal and India.

The **Newar legend** has a firmer historical grounding, involving a drought that struck Kathmandu during the reign of the early Lichhavi king, Dharmadeva. When court astrologers advised that only the sacrifice of a virtuous man would bring rain, Dharmadeva commanded his son Manadeva to go to the royal well on a moonless night and decapitate the shrouded body he would find there. Manadeva obeyed, only to find that he had sacrificed his own father, and so to expiate his guilt he erected the Boudha stupa.

Around the stupa

While less embellished than Swayambhu, Boudha is in its own way more interactive: you can climb up onto **the stupa**'s base, and kids often fly kites from it. The dome is elevated on three *mandala*-shaped plinths of decreasing size, which reinforce the notion of the stupa as a meditation tool. As usual, the primordial Buddha's searching blue eyes are painted on the four sides of the central spire, and above them rise the thirteen golden steps to *nirvana*. Instead of five *dhyani* Buddhas, however, 108 (an auspicious number) much smaller images are set in niches around the dome.

The small **Ajima shrine** at the far side of the stupa shelters the image of a nasty goddess dining on a hapless victim. Ghoulish though she may look, Buddhist Newars worship Ajima as a grandmother-protectress of children; she is also known as Harati, goddess of smallpox. Next door is a room-sized prayer wheel – all are welcome to spin it – and on the other side of the shrine you'll see the tanks where whitewash is mixed during festivals.

Boudha's **pilgrims** are arguably its greatest attraction, as the stupa is famed throughout the Himalayan region for its wish-fulfilling properties. Prayer wheels, heavy silver jewellery and rainbow-striped aprons are good general indicators of Tibetan origins. The men of Kham, in eastern Tibet, wear red tassels in their long hair, as do the Dolpo-pa of northwest Nepal, many of whom winter here. Nomads from the central Tibetan plateau wear sheepskin *chuba* (coats) with extra-long sleeves. Bhutanese men and women keep their hair cropped short and wear

THE DHARMA SCENE

Boudha's Western community is well established, though to become a part of it you need either an introduction or a lot of time, since serious Western students of *dharma* tend to regard tourists as spiritual interference. But as those in the know say, if you're ready you will find a teacher here. Many Westerners rate Boudha as the best place in the world to **study** Tibetan Buddhism, for although Dharmsala in India is better known because the Dalai Lama is based there, the presence of the Tibetan government-in-exile creates a politically charged atmosphere that can distract from serious study. Moreover, Dharmsala is heavily dominated by the Dalai Lama's Gelug-pa order, whereas at Boudha all four sects are well represented, making it easier to sample the different traditions.

The Chinese occupation of Tibet killed or drove away an entire generation of teachers, and Boudha's line-up of **lamas**, though formidable, reflects this: most are either very old or rather young. By far the most popular among the *dharma* set is **Chokyi Nyima**, abbot of Ka Nying Shedrupling Monastery, who speaks excellent English and holds open teachings most Saturday mornings. He also runs meditation courses during the tourist season (for a profile of Chokyi Nyima, see "Tibetan Exiles in Nepal" in *Contexts*). His younger brother, **Tsokney Rinpoche**, who's abbot of a monastery near Swayambhu, is also accessible and frequently gives teachings at Ka Nying Shedrupling. The death in 1992 of **Dingo Khyentse** of Shechen Tenyi Dargyeling Monastery has left a large gap, but this may in time be filled by his grandson, **Rabjam Rinpoche**, and **Trangu Rinpoche** of the Trangu Tashi Chökorling Monastery, who teaches a course each December–January. Kopan Monastery (north of Boudha, off the map), whose **Yeshe Lama** passed away in 1986, remains as busy as ever with a full schedule of Gelug activities; a Spanish boy is being groomed as Yeshe's *tulku* (reincarnation). Other teachers include **Choge Trichen**, who runs Jyamchen Monastery and is also abbot of the Tibetan *gompa* at Lumbini, and **Kenpo Tsultrim Gyamtso** of the Marpa Institute on Mahakal Road (the road that forks left about 1km west of Boudha and leads to Kopan).

Western monks wear the same maroon robes and have taken the same monastic vows as Tibetan monks but, partly because of visa restrictions, aren't expected to make the same commitment to a monastery. While Tibetan monks live at their monastery, maintaining the building and making visits to the local community, Westerners are free to come and go. Given a four-month visa, most cram as much personal instruction as possible into their time, and then try to maintain a long-distance teacher–disciple relationship from home. Some follow their lama on speaking tours overseas, which are conveniently scheduled during the soggy monsoon months. In any case, a lifestyle with one foot in the West and the other in the East requires either sponsorship or independent means. A separate wing of the *dharma* crowd consists of Westerners living in Boudha for a season of **individual study**. Some are just trying Buddhism on for size, others are earnestly shopping around for a lama. Most lamas and teachers at Boudha give occasional open talks – with or without English translation – and normally agree to one-on-one meetings with anyone who shows a keen interest. If you go to a teaching, present the lama with a **kata**, a ceremonial white scarf, which he will then return to you. Pick up a cheap rayon *kata* in any shop that deals in Tibetan clothing, and they'll show you how to fold it.

To find out about upcoming teachings, check out the notice board at the *Bir Restaurant*, or try asking some of the regulars there. But if you've had no prior experience with Buddhism, you'd probably want to test the waters first by enrolling in a **meditation course**. The retreats run by the *Himalayan Yogic Institute* and the *Kathmandu Buddhist Centre* are the usual place to start; Kopan Monastery (affiliated with *HYI*) also holds a month-long course each November (see p.122).

distinctive embroidered robes. Ladakhi women are distinguished by their velvet dresses, and high-crowned silk hats with small wings on either side. In addition, Nepali Bhotiyas (p.358) and Tamangs (p.208) visit Boudha in force, although the stupa has no special attraction for Buddhist Newars.

The monasteries and back lanes

The past decade has seen quite a spate of monastery-building at Boudha, and at the last count there were 37 *gompa* (monasteries) scattered around the neighbourhood. All four of the major Tibetan Buddhist sects (see "Religion" in *Contexts*) are represented at least twice – for a partial listing of names and sects, refer to the Boudha map.

The older, smaller **monasteries** around the stupa keep their doors open most of the time, and welcome spectators during their morning and dusk *puja*. Furnishings and icons are broadly similar in each. The gilded statues at the front of the assembly hall (*lhakang*) will usually represent the Buddha, various *bodhisattva*, or the founder of the monastery's sect. Spread out in front of these are likely to be oil lamps, which monks and pilgrims continually replenish; heaps of rice piled onto three-tiered silver stands, which are objects of meditation; conical dough-cakes (*torma*) symbolizing deities; and offerings of fruit, coins, flowers and incense. Frescoes on the walls depict fearsome guardians of the faith, symbolic deities and

Painting of a *dharmapala* (protector of the faith) in a Buddhist monastery

historical figures, or, like *thangka* (see p.120), express the complex cosmology of Tibetan Buddhism.

If you follow either of the two lanes heading **north of the stupa**, the romance evaporates in short order: this is Boudha the boomtown, an unplanned quagmire of garbage-strewn lanes, unlovely new buildings, schools, carpet factories and the mansions of their nouveau riche owners. The area from Boudha to Gokarneswar accounts for the largest share of the valley's carpet manufacture, a dubious distinction that contributes to serious water pollution as well as pretty awful congestion out on the main road in front of the stupa. Yet the carpet industry has brought undreamt-of wealth to the Tibetans of the Kathmandu Valley, who are piously donating much of it for the construction of new monasteries here. Sequestered behind high walls and iron gates, these monasteries have been deliberately named after *gompa* in Tibet that were destroyed by the Chinese, and it's hoped that, besides keeping the flame of Tibetan Buddhism alight and preserving traditional art forms, they'll help bring about the resurrection of their namesakes. It's a telling picture of the bittersweet present – and forseeable future – of the Tibetan diaspora. With each new carpet factory or monastery, Boudha's Tibetans find themselves more comfortable in exile, and more deeply enmeshed in the difficult development-related dilemmas of their hosts.

Further afield

Boomtown aside, Boudha makes a good springboard for several walks and bike rides in this part of the valley. **Kopan Monastery**, occupying a beautifully leafy

---

ROOM PRICE SCALES

All guest houses and hotels have been price-graded according to the scale outlined below, which represents the cheapest available double room in high season; codes prefixed by B denote the cost of a room with attached bathroom. See p.35 for a fuller explanation of the system.

① Less than Rs100
($1.75 if quoted in US$)
② Rs100–175 ($1.75–3)
③ Rs175–300 ($3–5)
④ $5–8

⑤ $8–12
⑥ $12–20
⑦ $20–40
⑧ $40–70
⑨ Over $70

---

ridge about 3km due north of the stupa, is an easy target. Further along this ridge to the east lies **Pulahari Monastery** (also accessible from Gokarneswar – see below), where a stupa containing the remains of the recently deceased abbot, Jamyung Kongtrol Rinpoche, has the makings of an important pilgrimage stop. From either of these points, it's a delightful two- or three-hour hike north along the ridge to **Nagi Gompa**, and another hour's descent to Budhanilkantha.

In the opposite direction, Pashupatinath is only about a half-hour's walk south of Boudha. A path sets off from the main road almost opposite the entrance to the stupa. Sankhu and Gokarneswar, described in the next section, make fine excursions on a bike.

Accommodation

There's a good range of budget and moderately priced **accommodation** in Boudha, so it's well worth staying overnight – especially as the place is much pleasanter after hours (the coach-party crush is at its worst between mid-morning and late afternoon). Budget options are conveniently located close to the heart of things, whereas most of the pricier places are so far-flung you practically need to take a taxi to get to the stupa.

Budget places

Bir Restaurant, on the main road just west of the stupa entrance (☎470790). Good location and camaraderie, but often booked up by long-term *dharma* types. ③/B③.

Hotel Tashi Delek, across the street from the *Bir* (☎471380). The south-facing rooms have balconies that overlook paddy fields, but they're perilously close to the public latrines. ③.

Kokonor Guest House, at the main stupa entrance (no phone). Pretty grotty and noisy, and no hot water. ②.

Lotus Guest House, down a lane north and east of the stupa (☎472320). Operated by the next-door monastery, this clean but minimalist guest house offers Boudha's best value and location. ③/B④.

Rabsel Guest House, in the compound of the Shechen Tenyi Dargyeling Monastery (☎470721). Quiet and good for making contact with monks, but it seems a million miles from the interesting part of Boudha. B④.

Snowlion Lodge, on the main road about 400m east of the stupa entrance, off the map (☎470341). Comparable to the *Tashi Delek*, but further from the stupa. ②/B④.

Moderate and expensive hotels

Happy Valley Guest House, north of the stupa (☎471241). Cavernous five-storey tower with fabulous views of the stupa (and the airport, unfortunately) from its rooftop terrace. B⑦.

Maya Guest House, east of the *Snowlion* (☎470266). Gorgeous garden; the price includes breakfast and transport from Kathmandu. B②.

Stupa Hotel, east of the *Maya* (☎470400). Large and efficient, but on the sterile side. B②.

Tara Gaon Regency, off the main road nearly 1km west of the stupa. A planned new resort hotel expected to open in 1996 or 1997.

Eating

Although Western **food** is readily available in the places listed here, you'd be foolish to miss trying Tibetan specialities such as the ravioli-like *kothe* and *momo*, chunky *thukpa* soup, and *tongba* (hot millet grog) – check out the many cheap and cheerful local eateries along the main road or northeast of the stupa.

Bir Restaurant, west of the stupa on the main road (north side). Still the main meeting place for long-term Westerners in Boudha, with a cosy atmosphere and inexpensive (though unremarkable) food.

Double Dorjee Restaurant, east of the stupa on the main road (south side), 300m east of the stupa. A cosy hole-in-the-wall with quirky food.

Land of Snows Restaurant, overlooking the stupa. Good Tibetan and Indian dishes in a clean setting, with rooftop seating available.

Ristorante Italiano La Calabria, overlooking the stupa. Excellent homemade pasta, risotto and other Italian fare. There's limited rooftop seating, too.

Stupa View Restaurant, overlooking the stupa. Boudha's premier restaurant, with prices to match. All-vegetarian and fairly imaginative dishes (good pasta and tofu), plus there's a full bar and a roof terrace.

Shopping and other practicalities

Run-of-the-mill souvenirs at Boudha are notoriously overpriced, but this is the place to come if you're seeking genuinely obscure or **antique** items. Keep an eye out for Tibetan musical instruments, jewellery, flasks, butter-tea churns and prayer-flag printing blocks. Boudha is also a good place to buy incense and prayer flags.

For **books** on Buddhism, try *Dharma Books*, overlooking the stupa. Cassette **tapes**, not only of music but also teachings by local lamas, are sold at a couple of places around the stupa and on the main road. Near the entrance you can buy **film**, and there are even travel agents and international telephone offices.

For **Tibetan medicine**, there's a branch of the *Kunphen Tibetan Medical Centre* on the main road just opposite the stupa entrance. Dr Kelsang Dolma has a practice located in the same building as *Dharma Books*. Long-term guests at the *Bir* might be able to recommend other doctors who treat foreigners.

The Sankhu road

The paved road past Boudha – the old trade route to Tibet – begins at Chabahil on the Ring Road and rolls eastwards as far as Sankhu. It's a gentle ride on a **bicycle** once you get past noxious Jorpati, the carpet-industry conurbation east of Boudha, and it can be combined with visits to Nagarkot or Changu Narayan. From the City Bus Park, an erratic **minibus** service plies the whole way to Sankhu; four buses a day go as far as Gokarna Ban; and dozens cover the stretch to Chabahil and Boudha.

Chabahil

You'll probably experience **CHABAHIL** merely as a traffic jam on your way to Boudha. Straddling the Ring Road, part Kathmandu suburb and part Boudha Tibetan spillover, it appears as a cluster of shops and concrete buildings without much character, though it's one of the valley's older settlements.

Tibetans have long been drawn to Chabahil's **stupa** (known locally as **Dhando Chaitya**), which despite its newish appearance dates to Lichhavi times. An ancient chronicle states it was constructed by Dharmadeva, a fifth-century king, although legend attributes it to Charumati, who settled here and married a local prince after accompanying her father Ashoka on his apocryphal pilgrimage to the Kathmandu Valley in the third century BC. The prince, Devapala, is credited with founding Deopatan, one of the valley's ancient capitals and now the site of Pashupatinath. In a brick shelter at the south end of the compound stands a sixth-century statue of Padmapani Lokeshwar, carved in black stone.

Chabahil's Nepalis rally round the **Chandra Binayak**, one of the valley's four principal Ganesh temples, located in the reasonably atmospheric bazaar west of the main Chabahil intersection.

Gokarna Ban

Gokarna Ban, just beyond the Bagmati River 3km east of Boudha, looks and feels more like an English country estate than a **royal game reserve**. The "game" in this onetime royal hunting preserve consists mainly of tame deer, monkeys, plenty of birds and a few tigers safely penned up in a three-acre enclosure, so promises of "safari adventure" are fairly hyperbolic. On Saturdays the park is mobbed with picnicking locals. *Gokarna Safari Resort* (☎410063) manages all activities – which include golf, elephant rides and horse rides – and also operates a **hotel** (⑦). However, the place seems to be closed indefinitely – you should check before turning up.

Five kilometres beyond here, a trail to the south crosses the Manohara River on a temporary bridge (dry season only) and ascends the ridge to Changu Narayan.

Sankhu

An important trade and spiritual centre in ancient times, **SANKHU**, 20km east of Kathmandu, now drifts on as a Newar backwater in a far corner of the valley. You could easily pedal out here on a one-speeder, but Sankhu is best seen as a stopover along the back route down from Nagarkot, for which you need a proper mountain bike. A few shops sell cold soft drinks, but food is scarce.

Sankhu's abiding claim to fame is its temple to **Bajra Jogini**, whose gilded roof glints from a grove of trees on the otherwise barren hillside above town. To make the two-kilometre hike, follow the dirt road northwards out of town and then bear left on a stony path that heads straight for the temple. Sankhu Bajra Jogini is the most senior of a ferocious foursome of tantric goddesses specially venerated in the Kathmandu Valley. To Buddhist Newars, her main devotees, she represents the wrathful, corpse-trampling, female aspect of Buddhahood; her implicitly sexual role in a supernatural union of opposites earns her the esoteric "tantric" label.

The slightly dilapidated **temple** dates from the seventeenth century, but inscriptions elsewhere record that a shrine stood here a thousand years earlier. Next to the temple is a small shrine containing a replica of the Swayambhu stupa. The compound is pleasantly shaded, but overrun by monkeys – the place literally stinks of them. Animal sacrifices performed in front of a triangular stone representing Bhairab, just below the temple, sadly don't include monkeys.

The Sundarijal road

Branching off from the Sankhu road at Jorpati, 1km east of Boudha, a second road rumbles along as far as Sundarijal in the extreme northeastern corner of the valley. The stretch from Jorpati to Gokarneswar is becoming increasingly blighted by carpet-industry build-up, and the road receives relatively heavy traffic (and wear) as a result, but things become more rural beyond that. Four **buses** a day leave from the City Bus Park for Sundarijal.

Gokarneswar

Located 4km up the Sundarijal road, **GOKARNESWAR** overlooks the Bagmati River where it cuts through a low ridge (the Gokarna Ban game reserve is just across the river, but there's no access from here). A tranquil spot, it has been an important cremation and pilgrimage site since ancient times, and is marked by the imposing **Gokarna Mahadev**, dedicated to Shiva. Despite UNESCO conservation efforts, the fourteenth-century temple appears slightly worse for wear. Its most unusual feature is an outdoor gallery of stone **sculptures** representing an unorthodox cross-section of the Nepalese pantheon – you'll see a bearded Brahma and a skeletal Chamunda (a form of Kali), among others. Inside the temple stands a beefy *linga*, while the smaller temple nearby contains a beautiful eighth-century statue of Parvati, Shiva's consort. The highlight of the **festival** calendar here is Gokarna Aunsi, Nepali "Father's Day", held in late August or early September.

From Gokarneswar you can **hike** up to Pulahari Monastery on the long ridge to the west, and from there northwards to Nagi Gompa or westwards to Kopan.

Sundarijal

Although **SUNDARIJAL**, 15km from Kathmandu, isn't a brilliant destination in itself, it's the most accessible trailhead for treks in the Helambu region. The steep climb up alongside the cascading Bagmati River – no more than a stream here – would be much prettier without the hulking iron pipe that crisscrosses the trail: much of Kathmandu's water supply comes from the upper Bagmati. After a half-hour or so, the trail leaves the pipe and civilization behind and enters the forested Shivpuri Watershed (see below; admission Rs250).

Sundarijal is the home of the **Himalayan Rescue Dog Training Centre**, located at the west end of the village. Founded in 1989 by Dutchman Ingo Schnabel, the centre provides the only search and rescue service in Nepal. It is also a good source of up-to-date **trail information**, can arrange **guides**, and supplies basic **room and board** (①). The centre relies on donations.

Budhanilkantha and Shivpuri

A paved road leads 8km north from Kathmandu to **BUDHANILKANTHA**, site of the Jalasaya Narayan (Sleeping Vishnu), one of the valley's most impressive reminders of its semi-mythic early history. There's a small village with basic teahouses nearby, but the Vishnu statue, set in a walled compound, is the only attraction of the place. Try to make it here in time for the morning *puja* (9–10am), when things are most interesting.

Jalasaya Narayan

Buses to Budhanilkantha leave from the City Bus Park in Kathmandu every half-hour or so. **Cycling**, you'll want a mountain bike for the last steep bit (and for any longer rides – see below). Or bring your boots: from Budhanilkantha you can **hike** to the summit of Shivpuri, the second-highest point of the valley rim.

The Sleeping Vishnu (Jalasaya Narayan)

The five-metre **Sleeping Vishnu (Jalasaya Narayan)** reclines in a recessed water tank like an oversized astronaut in suspended animation. The figure's origins are obscure: local people say it was unearthed by a farmer two thousand years ago, having been carved and dragged here at some remote point in time, but most art historians believe its style pinpoints it to the seventh or eighth century AD. In the fields to the east, piles of bricks and a lone statue provide further evidence that this must have been a substantial settlement in ancient times.

Budhanilkantha's name has been a source of endless confusion and not a little religious rivalry. It has nothing to do with the Buddha (*budha* here means "old"), though that doesn't stop Buddhist Newars from worshipping the image as Lokeshwar, the *bodhisattva* of compassion. The real puzzler is why Budhanilkantha (literally "Old Blue-Throat"), a title which unquestionably refers to Shiva, has been attached here to Vishnu. The myth of **Shiva's blue throat**, a favourite in Nepal, relates how the gods churned the ocean of existence and inadvertently unleashed a poison that threatened to destroy the world. They begged Shiva to save them from their blunder and he obliged by drinking the poison. His throat burning, the great god flew up to the range north of Kathmandu, struck the mountainside with his trident to create a lake, Gosainkund, and quenched his thirst – suffering no lasting ill effect except for a blue patch on his throat. Shaivas claim a reclining image of Shiva can be seen under the waters of Gosainkund during the annual Shiva festival there in August, which perhaps explains the association with the waterborne figure of Budhanilkantha.

Nonetheless, the Budhanilkantha sculpture bears all the hallmarks of Vishnu or, as he's often called in Nepal, **Narayan** (pronounced Nuh-*rai*-n): "having waters for his abode". It depicts Vishnu at his most cosmic, floating in the ocean of existence upon the snake Sesh (or Ananta, which in Sanskrit means "never-ending"); from his navel will grow Brahma and the rest of creation. Each year the god is said to "awaken" from his summer slumber during the Haribondhini Ekadashi **festival** in late October or early November, an event that draws thousands of worshippers.

One person who never puts in an appearance, as a matter of policy, is the king of Nepal. Some say the boycott goes back to the seventeenth-century king Pratap Malla, who was visited by Vishnu in a dream and warned that he and his successors would die if they ever visited Budhanilkantha; others say it's because the king, who is half-heartedly held to be a reincarnation of Vishnu, must never gaze upon his own image.

Up to Shivpuri

At 2732m, **Shivpuri** (or Sheopuri) offers excellent views of the Himalaya off to the west, from Jugal and Ganesh Himal out to Himalchuli, not to mention intense rhododendron blossoms in March and April. The summit can be reached in about four hours by one of at least two trails from Budhanilkantha. You'll need to pack a lunch and sufficient water, and the vertical gain, nearly 1300m, shouldn't be taken lightly. You can **camp** on the flat, grassy summit to catch the best views first thing in the morning; clouds often move in by lunchtime.

Shivpuri and the Shivpuri Lek (the ridge that forms the northern rim of the Kathmandu Valley) lie within the **Shivpuri Watershed and Wildlife Reserve** (Rs250), a huge walled area set aside to protect the valley's water supply and critical forest. As with several other parks and reserves in Nepal, this one was initially created without much regard for the needs of local people, who were summarily prohibited from gathering wood and other forest products. More recently, the government and foreign aid agencies have recognized the need to add social programmes to their original environmental agenda; various alternative income-generating schemes now target women and the poor, who have been most affected by the creation of the reserve.

From Budhanilkantha, follow the paved road straight uphill until it veers to the right and crosses a stream, where the more **direct trail** to the summit leaves the road and continues up the west side of the stream before entering the walled Shivpuri Watershed. Climbing steadily, it crosses a dirt road, enters the forest and meets the ridge; from here, a less-used trail branches off from the main one and follows the ridge eastwards for another two hours to the top. The **other route** sticks to the paved road until the main Shivpuri Watershed gate, and from there follows the dirt road to the right, contouring around and up the ridge to the east.

BIKING IN THE SHIVPURI WATERSHED

The Shivpuri Watershed and Wildlife Reserve contains some superb, and still largely untested, mountain biking possibilities. The wide-reaching and little-used road network begins at the Budhanilkantha entrance, where a signboard map gives an overview of the system (to date, no published maps of the valley indicate the full extent of it).

Two main routes present themselves. The dirt road to the left snakes generally westwards for at least 15km, at which point the hill resort of Kakani (see p.211) is only about 2km further east along the ridge by trail (some carrying required). For a shorter day ride, descend from the Tokha Hospital (marked "Sanitorium" on the *Schneider* map) along a steep, sandy road that brings you back to Budhanilkantha.

The road to the right (east) is even longer and offers even more adventure: it contours and climbs out of the valley, reaching Chisapani and Pati Bhanjyang on the main Helambu trekking route after about 25km. It then descends to the Malemchi Khola, where it joins another road coming up from the Arniko Highway. That alone would be a two- or three-day cycle trek, and could lead to further explorations in the Dhulikhel area (see p.202).

These two roads are eventually supposed to connect around the back (north) side of Shivpuri, but for the time being this route is impassable.

Where the road finally rounds this ridge, take a trail up to **Nagi Gompa**, a former Tamang monastery now run by the renowned lama Urgyen Rinpoche, and continue along the ridge to Shivpuri (when in doubt, bear left). Another trail leads back down from Nagi Gompa, following the ridge south to Boudha or Gokarneswar.

Balaju and Nagarjun Ban

The road to Trisuli (see p.211) passes a couple of worthy sights before it climbs out of the valley. **Buses** (departing from the City Bus Park) and **tempos** (from near the *Air India* office on Kantipath) follow fixed routes to Balaju and almost as far as the Nagarjun Ban gate, but both of these destinations are within easy **cycling** distance of Kathmandu – and a mountain bike will stand you in good stead once you get to Nagarjun Ban.

Simple **food** – snacks, *momo* and *daal bhat* – is available from diners in Balaju. If you're cycling or walking to Nagarjun Ban, you can eat in more pleasant surroundings at a couple of outdoor cafés located along the main road 1km and 4km beyond the forest entrance (the latter being the Rajneeshis' idiosyncratic vegetarian restaurant *Zorba the Buddha*).

Balaju

If **BALAJU**'s "Water Garden" isn't as ravishing as its name suggests, neither is the Balaju Industrial Estate as awful as it sounds. The water garden is where Kathmandu comes to picnic and paddle on Saturdays, and for the jaded traveller it can provide some welcome relief from the commotion of the city. The park is only 2km northwest of Thamel along the road to Trisuli, behind a municipal-looking fence at the foot of a wooded hill. Admission is Rs2.50, plus a few rupees to park your bike.

In the northeast corner of the grounds lies a **Sleeping Vishnu**, a smaller version that scholars now believe to be contemporaneous with the one at Budhanilkantha. An earlier theory held that it was only a copy, commissioned in the seventeenth century by King Pratap Malla when he was barred from visiting the original, leading to its nickname Balanilkantha ("Young Blue-Throat"). Balaju's other claim to fame – for Nepalis, at least – is **Baaisdhaara**, a bathing tank fed by twenty-two (*baais*) stone spouts (*dhaara*), which really rocks with bathing worshippers on the day of the full moon in April.

Nagarjun (Rani) Ban

Once in Balaju, you might as well continue on up the road another 2km to the entrance of **Nagarjun Ban** (also known as **Rani Ban**), a large and surprisingly wild royal forest preserve (daily 7am–10pm; pedestrians and cyclists Rs5, motorcyclists Rs15, cars and elephants Rs50). An unpaved road winds to the summit of 2096-metre **Jamacho**, but you can hike more directly up the ridge along a five-kilometre trail starting at the entrance. The north side of this ridge is riddled with limestone **caves**, including one where the famous second-century Buddhist saint Nagarjuna meditated and died, or so it's said. At the summit, a **stupa** decorated with fluttering prayer flags and penetrating eyes marks the spot where the Buddha sat during an apocryphal visit to the Kathmandu Valley, and a small **lookout tower** commands a panoramic (but usually smoggy) view of the valley and the Himalaya towards Ganesh Himal.

Several **alternative routes** return to the valley below. If you can find it, the most interesting one is an obscure trail that starts from the road southeast of the lookout tower and descends in a southeasterly direction through thick forest and past several limestone caves, one of which contains a large image of the Buddha. The trail eventually meets the Jamacho road, which you can either follow back to the entrance (3km), or part of the way to a military post (1km), from where you can leave the forest reserve for the village of Rani Ban and muddle back down to Balaju or Swayambhu. Another trail from Jamacho makes for the slightly higher summit 1km to the west, then curves south down to the rather seedy temple of **Ichangu Narayan**, from which a rough road leads east to the Ring Road behind Swayambhu.

PATAN AND THE SOUTHERN VALLEY

The southern valley is as well endowed with sights as the north, and no less accessible. Once you cross the Bagmati River you're in **Patan** – even the cows commute. Good roads fan out from Kathmandu and Patan to the hilltop outpost of **Kirtipur**, the holy places of **Chobar** and **Dakshin Kali**, and the wilds of **Godavari**, while rougher roads strike out towards a dozen other rural settlements.

Although everything is within day-tripping range of Kathmandu by bus or bike, **staying in Patan** will give you a head start. The valley's second city – a world apart from Kathmandu – deserves more than just an afternoon's visit, and is increasingly geared up for overnight guests. Except for a few luxury operations in the hills south of Patan, however, accommodation isn't available anywhere else in the southern valley.

Patan (Lalitpur)

PATAN (*Paa*-tun) likes to recall its old name **LALITPUR** ("City of Beauty"), and although now largely absorbed by greater Kathmandu, this once-powerful independent kingdom still maintains a defiantly distinct identity. Compared to Kathmandu it's quieter, less frenetic and more Buddhist (there may be a correlation). Sophisticated and, in a Nepali sort of way, bohemian, it's like Kathmandu's Left Bank: while Kathmanduites are busy amassing power and wealth, Patan's residents appreciate the finer things of life. Above all, it remains a proud city of **artisans**: Patan produces nearly all Nepal's fine metalwork (the sounds of tapping and filing ring out from workshops all over town), and its craftspeople have created some of the most extraordinarily lavish temples, *hiti* and *bahal* in the country. *Bahal* – their doorways here always guarded by cuddly stone lions with unscary overbites – are a particular feature of Patan, and a few still function as active monasteries. In the past two decades, Patan has also emerged as the de facto **foreign aid** capital of Nepal: the UN delegation and diverse smaller organizations are scattered around the western suburbs, as are the residences of many expats who commute to the big USAID headquarters just across the river.

In legend and fact, Patan is the oldest city in the valley. **Manjushri**, the great lake-drainer, is supposed to have founded Manjupatan, the forerunner of Patan,

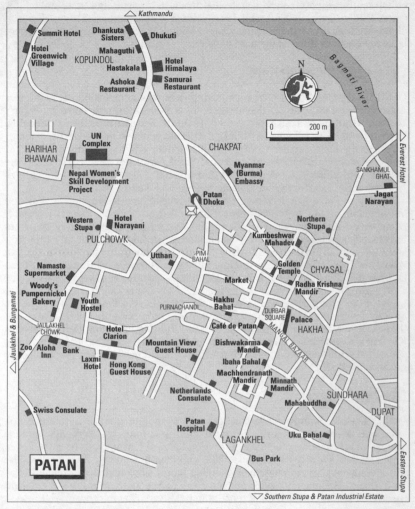

right after he enshrined Swayambhu, while the so-called Ashokan stupas, earthen mounds standing at four cardinal points around Patan, seem to support the legend that the Indian emperor **Ashoka** visited the valley in the third century BC (historians are sceptical). More reliable legend ascribes Patan's founding to **King Arideva** in 299 AD. By the seventh century Patan had emerged as the cultural and artistic capital of Nepal, if not the entire Himalayan region. It maintained strong links with the Buddhist centres of learning in Bengal and Bihar – thereby playing a role in the transmission of Buddhism to Tibet – and when these fell to the Muslims in the twelfth century, many scholars and artists fled to Patan, setting the stage for a renaissance under the later **Malla kings**. Patan existed as part of a unified valley kingdom until the late fifteenth century, then enjoyed equal status with Kathmandu and Bhaktapur as a sovereign state until 1769, when Prithvi Narayan Shah and his Gorkhali band conquered the valley and chose Kathmandu for their capital. One of Patan's charms is that its historic core is frozen much as it was at the time of defeat.

Orientation and arrival

Old Patan developed along two intersecting axes, which extended out to the four **Ashokan stupas**. The northern route, now pedestrianized, takes in Patan's **Durbar Square** and also the famed **Golden** and **Kumbeshwar temples**. Patan's western axis (known as **Mangal Bazaar** where it meets Durbar Square) serves as the main way into town from Kathmandu. The busy southern road runs past the **Machhendranath Mandir** and the **Lagankhel bus park**, while the eastern road skirts the temple of **Mahabuddha**. The Tibetan crafts centre of **Jaulakhel** is located at the southwestern edge of the city.

Getting to Patan has become a bit more civilized and less polluting since the introduction of the battery-powered **Safaa Tempo** ("Clean Tempo") service. Donated by a multilateral aid programme, the white three-wheelers run from Kathmandu's northern suburbs to Patan's Mangal Bazaar via the City Bus Park and Martyrs' Gate. They operate daily except Saturday from 8am to 8pm (7pm in winter) at approximately fifteen-minute intervals. Frequent **minibuses** also shuttle from the City Bus Park to Lagankhel in Patan, but they're always crowded.

By **bike**, it shouldn't take more than half an hour. Coming over the main bridge from Kathmandu, you can enter the city via the Western Stupa or more directly via Patan Dhoka (Patan Gate) – the latter route is a little confusing, though. A less stressful alternative is to cross the Bagmati from the Teku area of Kathmandu, entering Patan through its northwestern suburbs. Patan itself has some **taxis** and metered tempos, but within the old part of town you can easily get around on foot.

Durbar Square

Patan's **Durbar Square**, while smaller and less monumental than Kathmandu's, comes across as more refined, not to mention less touristy. Maybe it's because the city of artisans has a better eye for architectural harmony; or because Patan, which hasn't been a capital since the eighteenth century, has escaped the continuous meddling of monument-building kings. That said, the formula is similar to that in Kathmandu, with a solemn royal palace looming along one side and assorted temples grouped in the remaining public areas of the square.

The Royal Palace

Patan's richly decorated **Royal Palace** was largely constructed during the second half of the seventeenth century, but substantially rebuilt after the Gorkhali invasion of 1769 and the 1934 earthquake. It consists of three main wings, each enclosing a central courtyard and reached by a separate entrance.

The courtyard of the small, southernmost wing, **Sundari Chowk**, contains what must surely be one of the grandest bathtubs in the world. **Tusha Hiti**, the seventeenth-century sunken royal bath, is done up like a hall of fame of Hindu gods and goddesses. Its brass spout, the only bit of metal here, is decorated with Shiva and Parvati, while the bath itself is shaped like a *yoni*, the symbol of female

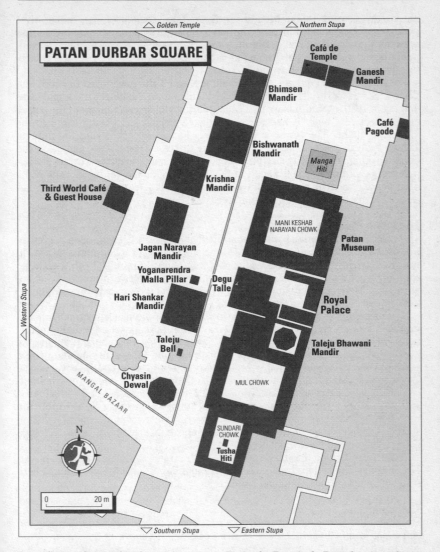

PATAN DURBAR SQUARE

△ Golden Temple △ Northern Stupa

Café de Temple

Ganesh Mandir

Bhimsen Mandir

Café Pagode

Bishwanath Mandir

Manga Hiti

Krishna Mandir

Third World Café & Guest House

MANI KESHAB NARAYAN CHOWK

Patan Museum

Jagan Narayan Mandir

Yoganarendra Malla Pillar

Degu Talle

Hari Shankar Mandir

Royal Palace

Taleju Bell

Taleju Bhawani Mandir

Chyasin Dewal

MANGAL BAZAAR

MUL CHOWK

N

SUNDARI CHOWK

Tusha Hiti

△ Western Stupa

0   20 m

▽ Southern Stupa   ▽ Eastern Stupa

sexuality, and ringed with *nag* (serpents). Fittingly, Bernardo Bertolucci used it as Prince Siddhartha's bath in his 1994 film *Little Buddha*. At one end of the basin stands the obligatory statue of Hanuman the monkey god, plus a "holy stone" on which the kings of Patan performed *puja* after bathing, and at the other end a replica of the Krishna Mandir, one of the temples outside. The courtyard is covered in ornate woodwork, including many fabulous carved doorways, windows, *torana*, and images of deities individually set into niches like icons.

Mul Chowk, the next wing to the north, served as the actual royal family residence. A sadly deteriorated gilt door in the right-hand wall of the courtyard, leading to the private Taleju Mandir, is flanked by statues of the Indian river goddesses **Ganga** and **Jamuna**, the latter riding a *makana* – a mythical cross between a crocodile and an elephant, whose curling snout decorates almost every public water spout in Nepal. Behind and to the left of Mul Chowk rises the octagonal, three-tiered **Taleju Bhawani Mandir**.

Yet another Taleju temple, the monolithic **Degu Talle** towers just north of Mul Chowk. Seven storeys high and the tallest building on the block, the temple was erected in 1640 by Siddhi Narsingh Malla, during whose reign much of the palace and square were built. It had to be completely rebuilt after being razed in the 1934 earthquake. The tower is permanently locked except during the autumn Tihaar festival, when a priest is supposed to refill a pipe with ganja for the departed king. Behind it, just off a small *chowk* once used for courtly performances, you'll find a small branch of the non-profit *Mahaguthi* handicrafts shop. This *chowk* retains its connection with dance since it also contains the headquarters of Patan's autumn festival committee.

The Patan Museum

The palace's northernmost wing, Mani Keshab Narayan Chowk, once served as the palace of another noted seventeenth-century king, Yoganarendra Malla. It, too, suffered in the 1934 quake and was only clumsily rebuilt. With assistance from the Austrian government, it has recently been restored to house the splendid **Patan Museum**, scheduled to open in late 1996 (hours and admission price hadn't been decided at the time of writing).

A tasteful space that does honour to this city of artisans, the museum will display a well-curated permanent collection of important bronzes, stone sculptures, wood carvings and a gilded Malla throne, as well as archival photographs and temporary exhibits. If that's not enough for you, there's the building itself, which, with its newly stuccoed walls and arty lighting, suggests the royal palace Yoganarendra Malla might have built if he had reigned at the end of the twentieth century. You can ascend to the corner belfries, their eaves decorated with *kinkinimali*, leaf-shaped tin cut-outs designed to flutter in the breeze, or stroll the carved-wood balconies and overlook the courtyard below and its central Lakshmi shrine. Outside, a stunning gold window above the exterior main entrance depicts Vishnu and a heavenly host.

A courtyard behind the museum serves as the venue for Patan's **Lalit Festival**. The four-day exposition, held in late April, highlights Patan's rich cultural heritage with music, dance, food and handicrafts exhibits.

The square

Starting at the newer – eighteenth-century – southern end of Durbar Square, the octagonal stone **Chyasin Dewal** in front of Sundari Chowk is the lesser of the square's two Krishna temples. Some say the temple was raised in memory of the eight wives that committed sati on a king's funeral pyre, but others say it spontaneously appeared the day after the cremation. As it happens, Krishna temples almost always have eight sides to commemorate Krishna's role as the eighth *avatar* (incarnation) of Vishnu. The cast-iron **Taleju Bell** was the first to be erected in the valley, in 1736; keen civic rivalry among the three valley capitals prompted Bhaktapur and Kathmandu to follow suit with their own bells.

North of here, the finely carved **Hari Shankar Mandir** is dedicated both to Vishnu (sometimes called Hari) and Shiva (alias Shankar), while the statue mounted on a pillar and praying to the Degu Talle depicts **Yoganarendra Malla**. An angry cobra rears up like a halo behind the king, and atop the cobra's head perches a gilded bird. Like all god-fearing rulers of the valley, Yoganarendra would have made sure to appease the *nag*, animist snake spirits who deliver or withhold the valley's rains. As for the bird, chroniclers state that the king, upon commissioning the statue, told his subjects that as long as the bird remained they would know he was still alive; accordingly, a bed is made and a meal prepared daily for the absent king in an upper chamber of the palace.

If the two-tiered **Jagan Narayan**, built in 1565, is the oldest temple in the square, the most unusual one is the seventeenth-century **Krishna Mandir**. Its central structure, a Mughal-style *shikra*, is girdled by three levels of stone verandas, with detailed scenes from the great Hindu epics, the *Mahabharat* and *Ramayan*, carved along the lintels. An incarnation of Vishnu, Krishna is one of the best-loved characters of the *Mahabharat*: superhuman baby, mischievous lad, seducer of milkmaids and heroic slayer of the evil king Kamsa. The upstairs sanctum (closed to non-Hindus) displays images of the whole cast of the *Mahabharat*. *Bhajan* is sung here most nights, and devotees gather at the temple on Krishna's birthday in August or early September.

The **Bishwanath Mandir** contains a copy of the Shiva *linga* of the same name in Varanasi, India. The temple collapsed in 1990, but has been seamlessly restored. Last but not least, the seventeenth-century **Bhimsen Mandir** is dedicated to the ever-popular god of Nepali traders. Non-Hindus aren't allowed inside, but you can often see and hear *puja* being performed in the open upstairs sanctuary. Across the way, one of the valley's best-preserved bathing tanks, **Manga Hiti**, has been flowing since the sixth century.

North and west of Durbar Square

Some of Patan's most interesting sights – the Golden and Kumbeshwar temples and the ghats – lie north of Durbar Square, but there's also plenty of serendipitous exploring to be done among the back alleys west of the square.

Hiranyavarna Mahavihara (The Golden Temple)

Dark and masonic (if it weren't for the sign, you'd never think of entering), the **Hiranyavarna Mahavihara** – that's Sanskrit for **"Golden Temple"** – is the most opulent little temple in Nepal. The three-tiered pagoda occupies one side of the cramped courtyard of Kwa Bahal, a still-active twelfth-century Buddhist Newar monastery and the spiritual hub of old Patan. During early-morning *puja*, the *bahal* is a fascinating theatre of Nepali religion in all its perplexing glory. A donation is expected, and note that you're not allowed to bring anything made of leather inside.

The temple's brass-clad facade, embossed with images of Buddhas and Taras, is regarded as the pre-eminent example of large-scale repoussé **metalwork** in Nepal, while in the middle of the courtyard a small, lavishly ornamented shrine contains a priceless silver and gold *chaitya*. Both the shrine and the main temple are draped with what look like long brass neckties; these *pataka* are supposed to provide a slide for the gods when they descend to answer the prayers of their worshippers. Buddha is the main image in the temple, and various Buddhas and *bodhisattva* are represented in alcoves around the courtyard. Mounted on the wall to your left as you enter, a chalkboard lists the astrological year and festivals in Newari.

Shiva

One block to the east, the three-tiered **Radha Krishna Mandir** has been restored by the Kathmandu Valley Preservation Trust, an organization which has now moved on to saving several other derelict temples and residences in Patan. The lovers Krishna and Radha, to whom this temple is dedicated, are a favourite subject for sandalwood carvers.

Kumbeshwar Mahadev

The **Kumbeshwar Mahadev**, Patan's oldest temple and one of only two freestanding five-tiered pagodas in Nepal (the other is in Bhaktapur), was built as a two-roofed structure in 1392, and despite the addition of three more levels it remains well proportioned and to all appearances sturdy. Shiva is the honoured deity here: inside you can see a stone *linga* and a brass one with four faces; Nandi,

Shiva's patient mount, waits outside. The temple apparently owes its name to an episode in which a pilgrim at Gosainkund, the sacred lake high in the mountains north of Kathmandu, dropped a pot (*kumbha*) into the water there. Much later, the same pot appeared in the water tank here, giving rise to the belief that the tank is fed by an underground channel from Gosainkund, and adding to Shiva's roll of titles that of Kumbeshwar – Lord of the Pots.

Thanks to this connection, Kumbeshwar's water tank is regarded as an alternative venue during Gosainkund's great annual **festival**, Janai Purnima. Falling on the full moon day of late July or early August, Janai Purnima is the ceremony in which Brahmans and Chhetris formally change the sacred thread (*janai*) that distinguishes them as members of the "twice-born" castes. At Kumbeshwar, thousands come to pay respect to a *linga* erected in the middle of the tank, and a big part of the festivities is for bathers to see how much water they can splash at spectators.

Elsewhere in the temple courtyard stands the shrine of **Bangalamukhi**, a local manifestation of the popular Newar protectress Ajima, whose tiny idol is encased in an ornate silver frieze. Women come here in droves on Thursday afternoons to pray for offspring and conjugal bliss.

The Northern Stupa ... and on to the ghats

Just northeast of the Kumbeshwar Mahadev, the **Northern Stupa** is the smallest and most central of the Ashokan mounds, and the only one that's been sealed over with plaster. Although it doesn't look wildly interesting for a 2200-year-old monument, you can let your imagination dwell on what treasures or relics Ashoka might have buried here – the contents are unlikely ever to see the light of day, since archeological digs are prohibited in the valley.

The stupa stands at the abrupt edge of the city. From here the road south plunges back between brick tenements and neglected temples to Durbar Square; northwards, it wends through receding farmland towards Patan's **Sankhamul Ghat, a** kilometre-long embankment near the junction of the Manohara and Bagmati rivers. Confluences are regarded as auspicious locations, and Sankhamul Ghat serves as Patan's main cremation site and, during the spring festival of Magh Sankranti, an important spot for ritual bathing. Atop the bank behind the ghats stands the brick *shikra* of **Jagat Narayan**, named after its builder, the nineteenth-century prime minister Jagat Shamsher.

West of Durbar Square

From **Mangal Bazaar**, which these days sells mainly cloth and tourist odds and ends, central Patan's main drag heads out towards the Western Stupa. One of Patan's less touristed former monasteries, **Hakhu Bahal**, rises on the left after 300m. Its courtyard crowded with lotus pedestals, indicative of divinity, the *bahal* is the home of Patan's Kumari.

Though little more than a grassy mound beside a busy intersection, the **Western Stupa** comes alive on one day a year when it serves as the starting point of the great chariot procession of Rato Machhendranath (see p.163). A nearby shelter displays retired *ghama* – long, upward-curving chariot yokes – from past festivals.

The northwestern quarter of old Patan is a jumble of *bahal*, none particularly worth singling out; the lane leading from the Golden Temple west to Patan Dhoka takes you past quite a few. The next lane further south, which parallels the main road to the Western Stupa, is the site of Patan's small fruit and vegetable **market** and eventually opens out into Pim Bahal, a large and less than glamorous square that contains what some hold to be a **fifth Ashokan stupa**, although no records mention it before the fourteenth century.

A small bazaar area surrounding an unremarkable city gate, **Patan Dhoka** had its finest hour during the 1990 *jana andolan* (people's movement), when it stood on the front line of an all-out revolution. Nearly a month before the government's final capitulation Patan was declared "liberated", with ditches dug across every road into the city, and defiant residents vowing to kill any opponent of the *andolan* who dared enter. Several police cars and buses met their end at narrow Patan Dhoka – and throughout the uprising the banned Nepali Congress Party flag flew from the gate.

South and east of the square

South of Durbar Square you essentially have two choices. The southbound street passes the Machhendranath temple and other sights en route to the Lagankhel bus park, while the continuation of Mangal Bazaar leads southeastwards to Mahabuddha. The area directly east of Durbar Square, though short on specific sights, is an active artisans' quarter.

Bishwakarma Mandir and Ibaha Bahal

One of Patan's most charming streets runs parallel to Mangal Bazaar, a block to the south. This is an area of metalsmiths and sellers, which perhaps accounts for the **Bishwakarma Mandir**'s facade of hammered brass and froggy copper lions standing guard. The name Bishwakarma refers both to the god of artisans and to members of the occupational caste of blacksmiths (more commonly known as Kami).

Patan's second-oldest monastery, **Ibaha Bahal**, stands one block further to the south. Founded in 1427, the *bahal* was latterly converted into a school and finally fell into disrepair. In 1990 the Nippon Institute of Technology began restoring it, and by the time you read this it should be up and running again as a fully functional Buddhist centre and school.

Machhendranath Mandir

Outwardly, Patan's **Machhendranath Mandir** resembles many others: a huge seventeenth-century pagoda adorned with beautifully carved struts, elegant *torana* and an ill-advised layer of modern tiles. It stands in an extra-large grassy compound called Ta Bahal, about 300m south of Durbar Square, reached by following a lane west from the main street.

What makes this temple so extraordinary, however, is its idol, **Rato Machhendranath** (Red Machhendranath), a painted shingle of sandalwood which, for several weeks beginning in late April, is the object of one of Nepal's most extraordinary festivals (see box). Older than his white counterpart in Kathmandu, Rato Machhendranath is a god of many guises. To Newars he's Bunga Deo, the androgynous god of agricultural prosperity and a manifestation of the great cult figure Karunamaya. To Buddhists of other ethnic groups he's Avalokiteshwara or Lokeshwar, the *bodhisattva* of compassion. As Machhendranath, the progenitor of the *nath* (lord) cult, he's the spirit of a seventh-century Hindu guru who once taught the Shah kings' beloved saint, Gorakhnath. Legend has it that Gorakhnath once visited the valley and, offended that he wasn't accorded a full reception, caused a drought by rounding up all the rain-bringing snakes. The locals sent a posse to fetch Machhendranath from Assam, who came to their rescue in the form of a bee. Wishing to pay tribute to his guru, Gorakhnath had to release the snakes, whereupon the rains returned and Machhendranath came to be revered as a rain-maker.

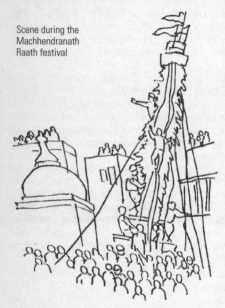

Scene during the Machhendranath Raath festival

Minnath and on to the Southern Stupa

Set behind a *hiti* (sunken bathing tank) across the street, the smaller sixteenth-century **Minnath Mandir** is dedicated to yet another mythologized Indian saint. Historically supposed to have been Machhendranath's guru, Minnath has been transmuted by popular tradition into his sister, brother or even daughter, and his likeness follows Machhendranath in a smaller chariot of its own during the procession.

The main road continues south from here past the chaotic minibus park at **Lagankhel**, then jogs left; straight ahead lies an army base and a pair of over-grown water tanks that feed Patan's many *hiti*. It's not really worth travelling another kilometre south to visit the grassy **Southern Stupa** – the biggest of the four – although anyone bound for the Patan Industrial Estate (see "Shopping") will pass right by it.

RATO MACHENDRANATH'S BIG RIDE

The Kathmandu Valley's oldest, lengthiest and most spectacular festival, the **Machhendranath Raath Jaatra**, begins the day after the full moon of Baisakh (April–May), when priests ritually bathe Rato Machhendranath's sandalwood idol outdoors in Patan's Lagankhel square. Moved back to its temple at Ta Bahal, the idol then spends the next ten days undergoing the life-cycle rituals of Buddhist Newars, both male and female. Meanwhile, just south of the Western Stupa at Pulchowk, Machhendranath's **chariot** (*raath*) is assembled and its sixty-foot-high tower of poles and vegetation constructed; a smaller chariot to carry Minnath is built at its temple.

After a few more preliminaries, the idols are installed in their chariots and the great procession is ready to begin. It is an electrifying event. Scores of men heave at the ropes; Machhendranath's unwieldy vehicle rocks and teeters and suddenly lurches forward, its spire swaying and grazing buildings as it passes. The crowd roars, people leap out of the way, and the chariot comes to a stubborn stop until the pullers regroup and try to budge it again. It goes on like this, in stages, for four or more weeks, until the chariots reach Jaulakhel, a journey of about four kilometres. At three designated resting spots – Hakhu Bahal, Sundhara and Lagankel – neighbourhood residents celebrate the gods with offerings, music and other auspicious acts.

When the chariots reach Jaulakhel the stage is set for the dramatic **Bhoto Jaatra**. At noon on a day ordained by the astrologers, a huge crowd assembles at Jaulakhel. The king and queen arrive in their limousine, and Patan's Kumari is carried by palanquin. At last a priest climbs aboard Machhendranath's chariot and holds aloft the god's magical jewelled vest, a relic of some ancient dispute. The king then pays homage to the gods and departs, after which the crowd charges the chariots for *prasad* (consecrated food offerings). Since the procession culminates during the showery pre-monsoon, Machhendranath usually obliges with rain: bring an umbrella.

Machhendranath's idol is then carried to Bungamati, 6km to the south (see p.176), where it is welcomed "home" with great fanfare – the cult of Rato Machhendranath is believed to have originated in Bungamati, accounting for the god's Newar name, Bunga Deo ("God of Bunga"). The idol spends the summer months in Bungamati before being transported back to Ta Bahal, but once every twelve years it is kept in Bungamati all winter and the chariot procession begins and ends there. That will next happen in 2003.

Mahabuddha

Nicknamed "Temple of a Thousand Buddhas", **Mahabuddha** is not your average Nepali temple. Constructed entirely of terracotta tiles – each one bearing the Buddha's image – this remarkable rococo structure mimics the famous Mahabodhi Temple of Bodhgaya in India, where its builder, an enthusiastic seventeenth-century Patan architect, had previously meditated for several years. Although the likeness is only approximate, the temple introduced to Nepal the Indian *shikra* form, which to this day remains prevalent around Patan. Reduced to rubble during the 1934 earthquake, it was put back together rather like Humpty Dumpty; the smaller temple beside it was built from the spare parts.

Mahabuddha stands about 500m southeast of Durbar Square (follow the signs); so tightly is it hemmed in by residences, the temple is like a casket that's been upended to fit in a hole. For the best view, follow a sign to the top floor of one of the surrounding buildings, which – surprise, surprise – is a metal handicrafts studio.

Other eastern sights

Uku Bahal lies just south of Mahabuddha, behind an arch guarded by large, curly-maned lions. The now-defunct Buddhist monastery, though it's undergone a recent renovation, is believed to be Patan's oldest – the wooden struts on the north side of the courtyard date from the thirteenth century. Its ornate principal temple, known as **Rudravarna Mahavihara** ("Red Monastery"), is surrounded by a small menagerie of bronze animals and mythological beasts.

North and east of Mahabuddha, **Dupat** is a poor and not altogether welcoming neighbourhood whose close, dark alleys are nevertheless crawling with atmosphere. The **Eastern Stupa** is way out in the sticks, beyond the Ring Road.

Jaulakhel and the zoo

Patan's Tibetan ghetto, **Jaulakhel** (often transliterated as Jawalakhel) is arguably the best place in the valley to watch carpets being made, although as a cultural experience it doesn't compare with Boudha or Swayambhu. Tour groups tend to spoil the atmosphere. Everything revolves around the modern **weaving and sales centre**, 1km south of the Western Stupa (weaving daily except Sat 8am–noon & 1–8pm; sales office closes at 5pm). See pp.168–169 for information on the carpet industry.

Tibetans started pouring into the Kathmandu Valley immediately after the Chinese annexation of Tibet and the flight of the Dalai Lama in 1959. By 1960 their plight prompted the International Red Cross to set up a transit camp at Jaulakhel, later assigned to the Swiss Red Cross, which in turn formed the Swiss Association for Technical Assistance (offices just north of here) to help Tibetans on a long-term basis. SATA encouraged carpet-making and other cottage industries, and by 1964 the Jaulakhel "transit camp" was a registered company. A generation on, Jaulakhel's Tibetans are prospering from the booming carpet industry that was born here, and many have left the centre to establish businesses and live closer to the Buddhist holy places.

Those who remain have created a sprawling suburb of solid brick residences east of the sales centre. About the only sight worth seeing is a small **gompa** with a big prayer wheel right beside the main road; wander beyond it and someone will probably take you to their house and show you carpets or woollens, which will be far more memorable than visiting a monastery. There's scant **food** in the immediate vicinity save *Bakena Batika* (see "Eating", below), but it's not far up the hill to the eateries of Jaulakhel Chowk.

The zoo

Nepal's only **zoo** (summer daily 10am–5pm; winter daily 10am–4pm; Rs20) – often rendered "jew" by Nepali-speakers – lies en route to Jaulakhel, just past the big Jaulakhel Chowk roundabout. Conditions for the animals leave much to be desired (if only the admission fee went to pay for better facilities), but a visit might be in order for close-up views of species that can otherwise only be glimpsed in the mountains or the Tarai. The resident tiger is a man-eater that attacked a young woman near Bardia National Park in 1994; it's now serving a life sentence here in the zoo. Other highlights include almost-tame rhinos, graceful blackbuck antelope, ungainly nilgai, beautiful clouded leopards, and a bevy of birds (for an account of Nepal's wildlife, see "Natural History" in *Contexts*).

Animals aside, the zoo is the closest thing to a park in Patan, and the shady shore of the central lake makes a pleasant place for a picnic. For Rs100 you can even take a spin around the grounds on an elephant. The playing field in front of the entrance is popular with street performers, storytellers and palm readers.

Accommodation

While Patan welcomes day-trippers, it seems less keen on visitors staying overnight. There's a distinct lack of good budget **accommodation** in the old part of town, and such as there is is generally priced higher than its Kathmandu equivalent. This situation is changing, however, as more and more Thamel refugees find their way here. Arrive early and you should have no trouble finding a room. The picture is better for hotels in the middle and high range, most of which are located comfortably close to the aid offices northwest of town.

Budget places

Café de Patan, Mangal Bazaar (☎525499). Friendly, with well-maintained rooms, rooftop views and a highly regarded restaurant. Central location. ④/B⑤.

Hong Kong Guest House, east of Jaulakhel Chowk (☎523089). Spacious rooms, but not accustomed to dealing with Westerners. ③/B③.

Laxmi Guest House, east of Jaulakhel Chowk (☎523968). A very stark option, only worth considering if you're desperate. ③/B③.

Mahendra Youth Hostel, just north of Jaulakhel Chowk (☎521003). Lonely but quiet dorms (①); some private rooms (②). Ten percent off for HI members – whoopee.

Mountain View Guest House, east of Jaulakhel Chowk (☎524168). Similar to *Hong Kong Guest House*, but closer to the old city. ③.

Pizza Palace Restaurant & Guest House, Mangal Bazaar, next door to *Café de Patan* (☎526374). A grungier, cheaper, but still friendly alternative to *Café de Patan*. Good rooftop views. ③.

Moderate and expensive hotels

Aloha Inn, Jaulakhel Chowk (☎522796). Small and functional. Two stars. B⑦.

Bakena Batika, just north of the Ring Road, Jaulakhel (☎523998). A small, rusticated place with stylish nouveau Nepali decor and a good in-house restaurant. One star. B⑦, including breakfast.

Hotel Clarion, east of Jaulakhel Chowk (☎524512). Small, with restaurant and gardens. No stars. B⑧.

Hotel Greenwich Village, Kopundol (☎521780). Idiosyncratic, with a pool and good views. Two stars. B⑨.

Hotel Himalaya, Kopundol (☎523900). Really posh, with a/c and swimming pool. Four stars. B⑨.

Hotel Narayani, Pulchowk (☎525015). Another deluxe choice, also with a/c and pool. Four stars. B⑨.

Summit Hotel, Kopundol (☎521894). Beautiful Nepalese architecture, terrific view, beautiful grounds. Two stars. ⑦/B⑨ (discounts in low season).

Third World Guest House, Durbar Square (☎522187). Unbeatable location: all rooms look directly out on the square. No stars. ⑥/B⑦.

Deluxe resorts south of Patan

Godavari Village Resort, Godavari (☎522399). Swimming pool, health club, acres of gardens. Five stars. B⑨.

Himalayan Heights Resort, Pikhel (☎220622). Views and pleasant piney surroundings. Four stars. B⑨.

Malla Alpine Resort, near Tika Bhairab (☎410966). Pool, sauna, views. Five stars. B⑨.

Eating

When it comes to **eating**, the choice in Patan is definitely smaller than in Kathmandu. This can be a problem at lunchtime, when places around Durbar Square get packed by day-trippers, but at night you'll feel like you've got the place to yourself. Sitting at a table overlooking the square on a balmy evening, with the temples lit from within, it can be magical.

Cafés and lunch places

Café de Patan, Mangal Bazaar. Consistently good (tourist) food plus great Newari dinner specials on weekends, phenomenal lassis, courtyard and roof terrace seating.

Café Pagode, northeast corner of Durbar Square. The usual Durbar Square overlook: the sunny rooftop terrace is literally a tourist trap, but understandably so.

Café de Temple, north side of Durbar Square. All-rounder menu, featuring very good Indian food. Head for the roof for great views.

Third World Restaurant, west side of Durbar Square. Superb food and the best views of Durbar Square. Somewhat pricey, but worth it.

Woody's Pumpernickel Bakery, Jaulakhel Chowk. Passable sandwiches, croissants and cakes.

Other tourist restaurants

Ashoka Restaurant, Kopundol. Basic Indian food, sahib service, reasonable prices.

Bakena Batika, Jaulakhel, 100m south of the carpet-weaving sales centre. Lovely garden restaurant specializing in Westernized Nepali dishes. Expensive, by Patan standards.

Bakery Café, Jaulakhel Chowk. Nepali yuppie hangout, serving pizza, *momo*, ice cream, etc.

Samurai Restaurant, Kopundol. Rather poor attempt at a Japanese restaurant (most items are Chinese anyway), but inexpensive.

Youth Green Garden Restaurant, Jaulakhel Chowk. Simple diner adjoining the youth hostel.

Bhojanalaya

Patan's most famous **bhojanalaya**, *Woh Naacha* is renowned for its *woh*, a sort of fritter made from soaked and pounded lentils (see "Eating", p.37). The place doesn't have a sign, of course, but it's just off Durbar Square, behind the Krishna Mandir.

For a night out, Patan residents head for one of several (relatively) fancy *bhojanalaya* around Patan Dhoka or Jaulakhel Chowk – in the latter area you'll also find Nepali-style snack bars that do espresso coffee, sweets, and that odd local speciality, roast chicken. Places around Lagankhel are pretty dingy, but will suffice if you're waiting for a bus.

Shopping

Even if you're not in the market to buy anything, Patan is the best place in Nepal to watch **handicrafts** actually being made. The Patan Industrial Estate does a little of everything, Jaulakhel mainly produces carpets, while Patan's many non-profit shops, supported by the local aid community, stock some excellent contemporary crafts made by disadvantaged workers.

Film is sold near Durbar Square and Lagankhel, and there are quick photo-processing places east of Jaulakhel Chowk and north of Lagankhel.

Traditional handicrafts and carpets

Despite its forbidding name, the **Patan Industrial Estate** is industrious in the nicest possible way. Located just beyond the Southern Stupa, the laid-back "estate" consists of a dozen or so factory showrooms, mainly pitched at coach parties, which means that independent travellers are generally left to mosey round the work areas without any pressure. The fixed prices are rarely undercut anywhere else (a prayer wheel will be as little as half what it costs at Jaulakhel), but then the money you spend here isn't going to a good cause. Most shops are open daily from 9am to 5pm.

Perhaps the most fascinating workshops are those of the **metalsmiths**, who mass-produce statuettes by the lost-wax process, and do repoussé and filigree work with a hammer and punch. You can also watch craftspeople painting **thangka** and chiselling **wood** statuettes, doors and windows. This is also a good place to shop for **gems**: the outlets here are reputable, and are usually happy to go over the subtleties of stone quality and cuts.

For **carpets**, the obvious place to start is the Jaulakhel Tibetan centre, where you can observe the actual weaving process. The sales centre's fixed prices are useful for gauging the market, although you'll probably get away with paying less in one of the private shops along the road leading back up to Patan, where they'll do deals. Profits from the Jaulakhel sales centre benefit elderly and poor Tibetans. Similarly, the Kumbershar Technical School, near the Kumbeshwar Temple, sells woollens and pure Tibetan wool carpets made by women, orphans and disadvantaged youths.

Contemporary crafts and fashion

The main drag from Kathmandu, where it passes through the Kopundol area, is known to English-speakers as "Fashion Row". Most of Patan's many non-profit outlets are clustered along here, as are several for-profit handicrafts shops and boutiques specializing in contemporary fashions; the following list is just for starters. The selection of items is much the same as in Kathmandu (see p.118).

Dhaka Weaves Ltd, Kopundol. Factory showroom with a full range of locally produced *dhaka* shawls, cushion covers and other accessories.

Dhankuta Sisters, Kopundol. Small non-profit outlet for village women in the eastern hills, selling *dhaka* clothes and place settings, plus some *allo*, wickerwork and Maithili paintings.

Dhukuti, Kopundol. Run by a village and low-income project marketing association, Patan's biggest non-profit shop stocks a wide variety of cotton and quilted-cotton crafts, wool sweaters, dolls, copper vessels, basketry and leather.

Dzambala Boutique, Kopundol, north of the *Hotel Himalaya*. Hand-painted silk garments, silver jewellery, leather bags and garments.

Hastakala, Kopundol, opposite the *Hotel Himalaya*. Good selection and display of woollens, *dhaka*, quilted cottons, ceramics, paper, Mithila art and general gift items.

Koseli, Kopundol, south of *Hotel Himalaya*. "Museum"/sales outlet with a wide range of regional arts and crafts.

Mahaguthi, branches in Kopundol and inside the Royal Palace. Aided by Oxfam, this supports a home for destitute women with a good selection of textiles, plus pine-needle crafts, toys and other items.

Utthan, southeast of Pulchowk. Outlet for women's crafts projects, selling garments, textiles, candles and other gift items.

Women's Skills Development Project, Pulchowk, just west of the UN Complex. The sales outlet for the Nepal Women's Organization (offices behind) specializes in block-printed cottons, with some quilted cotton items, woollens, toys and paper.

Other practicalities

Patan is not Kathmandu (thank the gods). It has tourist sights, but not, as yet, tourist quarters. This means that facilities are comparatively limited, but you won't lack for anything – and if you do, Kathmandu is just a short ride away.

Official moneychangers near Durbar Square offer reasonably competitive rates. For full **banking** facilities, including credit card cash advances, go to *Nepal Grindlays*, just east of Jaulakhel Chowk (Sun–Thurs 9.45am–3pm, Fri 9.45am–12.30pm). Several international **phone** and fax services can be found in the same neighbourhood. The **post office** is at Patan Dhoka (Sun–Thurs 10am–5pm, Fri 10am–3pm), but you'd be better off using the one in Kathmandu. At the time of writing the only place to rent **bikes** was in front of *Hotel Narayani* in Pulchowk, although *Café de Patan* has plans to get into the business.

Kirtipur

Once-proud **KIRTIPUR** ("City of Glory") occupies a long, low battleship of a ridge 5km southwest of Kathmandu. An historic stronghold commanding a pano-

THE CARPET INDUSTRY

If you've read the section on shopping in *Basics*, you'll know that there's not much Tibetan about so-called Tibetan carpets. Nonetheless, they do have their origin high up on the Tibetan plateau, where sheep are bred for their unusually long, high-tensile **wool**. Brought into Nepal by yak and mule train over passes in the far west, the Tibetan wool is blended with processed New Zealand wool and then carded and spun into yarn. Although **carding** machines are increasingly being used, **spinning** is still done exclusively by hand to produce a distinctive, slightly irregular look. The yarn is then taken to a **dyeing** plant, where it's dipped in vats of boiling dye (chemical dyes are used almost exclusively nowadays) and sun-dried before being rolled into balls, coded for colour and batch, and stored in warehouses. Weavers can then order up their colours by number, as instructed by a pattern or their carpet master.

As throughout Asia, weavers sit on benches in front of tall looms – but that's as far as the similarity goes. Tibetan-style carpets are produced by the **cut-loop method**, which bears little relation to the process employed by Middle Eastern and Chinese artisans. Rather than tying thousands of individual knots, the weaver loops the yarn in and out of the vertical warp threads and around a horizontally placed rod; when the row is finished, the weaver draws a knife across the loops, freeing the rod. The loops, cut in half, form the pile. This method enables relatively speedy production – one person can produce a 1m x 2m carpet in about seven working days – but it results in a rather low density of forty to one hundred "knots" (cut loops) per square inch. Rather than **beating** each row down with an iron mallet, which in Middle Eastern carpets helps to create a tight weave, Tibetan-style weavers deliberately use wooden mallets for a looser, blanket-like feel.

The weaving done, carpets are taken off the looms and **trimmed** with shears to give an even finish. **Embossing**, an optional stage, subtly separates the colours to

ramic view of the valley, the town is ideal for wandering, yet seldom visited – outsiders tend to get stared at. Poor Kirtipur is still shunned and pitied in the Kathmandu Valley, more than two centuries after its spirit was broken by an act of spectacular cruelty and humiliation.

Established as a western outpost of Patan in the twelfth century, Kirtipur had gained nominal independence by the time Prithvi Narayan Shah began his final conquest of the Kathmandu Valley in 1767. The Gorkha king, who had himself been born and raised in a hilltop fortress, considered Kirtipur the strategic lynch-pin of the valley and made its capture his first priority. After two separate attacks and a six-month siege, with no help forthcoming from Patan, Kirtipur surrendered on the understanding it would receive a total amnesty – instead, in an **atrocity** intended to demoralize the remaining opposition in the valley, Prithvi Shah ordered his troops to cut off the noses and lips of every man and boy in Kirtipur. "This order was carried out in the most exact way," wrote the early twentieth-century traveller Percival Landon, "and it adds rather than detracts from the savagery of the conqueror that the only persons spared were men who were skilled in playing wind instruments. The grim statistic is added that the weight of the noses and lips that were brought to Prithvi Narayan in proof that his order had been obeyed amounted to no less than eighty pounds." The rest of the valley fell within a year.

Kirtipur's hilltop position, once a strategic asset, has become a serious handi-cap to development, for although a road was belatedly pushed up to the neglected upper town, almost all of Kirtipur's commerce has shifted to **Naya Bazaar** (New

highlight the design. Finally, carpets must be **washed** to remove dirt and excess dye, an industrial process which, in the absence of effective controls, pollutes local streams with chemicals that have been linked with birth defects.

Marketing is more sophisticated than it might at first appear. The carpets so haphazardly displayed in tourist shops represent only a tiny tip of the iceberg – most are in fact made to order for the export market and air-freighted to wholesal-ers in Frankfurt and London. A handful of export traders, led by the Carpet Trading Company, founded in 1966 with help from the Swiss Association for Technical Assistance (SATA), handle international distribution.

In thirty years, Nepal's carpet industry has grown into a $200 million industry, accounting for two-thirds of the country's exports and **employing** (directly and indirectly) 300,000 people. Having long ago outstripped the Tibetan exile labour pool, it now provides work for members of every ethnic group, especially the poor and landless who might otherwise be forced into bonded labour or prostitution. It's an economist's dream – but some observers fear it may be a nightmare in the making.

In recent years the industry has seen a worrying **decline in overseas sales**, generally attributed to poor quality control. Manufacturers now seem chastened and anxious to restore their reputations, but it's their employees who have paid the price in reduced hours and wages. Worse, carpet manufacture appears to be responsible for an alarming rise in **child labour** in Nepal, even as other carpet-producing countries are enacting laws to stop exploitation. And the carpet industry is far too concentrated in the Kathmandu Valley, which lacks the infrastructure to cope with it, resulting in air and water **pollution**, traffic, social dislocation and land speculation. Yet as long as carpets continue to bring in so much foreign exchange, the government is unlikely to take the industry to task over these issues.

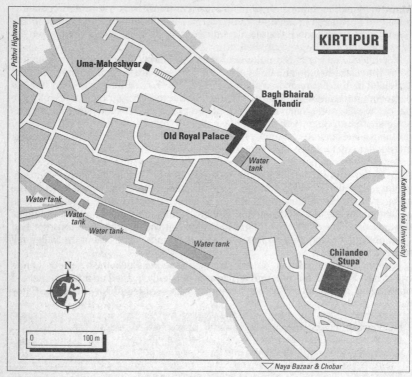

Market) at the southern base of the hill. Many residents are Jyapus (members of the Newar farming subcaste), who work the fields below the town and in spring and autumn haul their sheaves up and thresh the grain in the narrow streets. Others, whose land was appropriated for the building of **Tribhuwan University** (Nepal's largest, with 5000 students), now commute to jobs in Kathmandu or produce handicrafts behind closed doors. The village's unpaved, narrow lanes and mainly low-income inhabitants seem out of place so close to the prosperous capital, and in recent years it has been singled out by some tour companies as an example of picturesque poverty. Fortunately, prosperity is coming even to Kirtipur, as new health clinics, roads and electricity attest.

Frequent **minibuses** run from the City Bus Park to a point just short of Naya Bazaar, from where it's a ten-minute walk up to the village. If you're **cycling**, follow the Dakshin Kali road about 1km beyond the Ring Road, turn right at the red-brick Tribhuwan University gate, and take the left fork another 1km later – there's a steep, uphill slog at the end. Other footpaths lead to Kirtipur from the Prithvi (Kathmandu–Pokhara) Highway and Chobar. For **food**, you can't expect much more than *daal bhaat* or a plateful of chow mein in Naya Bazaar.

Bagh Bhairab Mandir

The road from the university ascends to the saddle of Kirtipur's twin-humped ridge and deposits you in a weedy square outside the prodigious **Bagh Bhairab**

Mandir (donation requested), which serves double duty as a war memorial and a cathedral to Bhairab in his tiger (*bagh*) form. Mounted on the outside is a collection of rusty weapons captured during the siege of Kirtipur – either by the Gorkhalis or the defenders, depending on whom you ask. Local musicians perform *bhajan* early in the morning and around dinnertime near the shrine just left of the main door, and on Tuesdays and Saturdays people sacrifice animals to it. Also kept in this courtyard is an image of Indrayani, one of the Kathmandu Valley's eight mother goddesses (*ashta matrika*), who, according to one Cinderella-like legend, was bossed around by the other goddesses until she miraculously turned a pumpkin into gold. Kirtipur's biggest **festival** is in late November or early December, when Indrayani and Ganesh are paraded through town on palanquins and a pair of pigeons are ceremonially released.

Uma-Maheshwar Mandir and Chilandeo Stupa

A pleasantly confusing maze of stony alleys, Kirtipur is great for wandering, and navigating isn't hard so long as you stick to the ridgeline. The northwestern end of town is predominantly Hindu, the southeastern Buddhist.

At the top of the northern, Hindu hump stands the elephant-guarded **Uma-Maheshwar Mandir**, mainly of interest for its sweeping view of Kathmandu, Swayambhu and the distant whitecaps of the Jugal Himal. Kathmandu's quaint **aerial ropeway** runs just north of here; built in 1925, before any roads connected the valley to the outside world, it's since been upgraded and is still used for ferrying heavy freight. The atmospheric **Chilandeo Stupa** crowns the southern hill, its exposed brickwork lending a hoary antiquity generally lacking in better-maintained stupas. Chilandeo (also known as Chilancho Bahal) is commonly believed to have been erected by Ashoka – though if Ashoka really built every stupa attributed to him he would have had little time for anything else. The ridge that rears up so impressively to the southwest is Champadevi (see below), one of the high points along the valley rim.

Naya Bazaar and the Theravada temple

Naya Bazaar's only attraction sits below the road where it rounds the southeast flank of the Kirtipur ridge. A Thai-style Theravada temple, the **Nagara Mandapa Kirti Vihara** was completed in 1989 with money donated by the Thai king and an array of the great and good of Thailand. In the minimalist Theravada tradition, the main sanctuary is unadorned except for an altar groaning with assorted gilded Buddhas and *bodhisattva*. A statue outside honours Pragyananda Mahastho Viraya, the elderly patriarch of all Nepali Theravada Buddhists, who lives in Patan. A separate image hall, rather shamelessly emblazoned with the *Thai Airways* logo, supports on its roof replicas of the four holy sites of Buddhism: Lumbini, Bodh Gaya, Sarnath and Kushinagar.

Hikes to Champadevi and Bhasmesur

It takes three to four hours to hike from Kirtipur to the crest of **Champadevi**, the prominent ridge that forms the southwestern rim of the Kathmandu Valley. Bring food and plenty of water for the all-day round trip. Start by following the dirt road southwest from Naya Bazaar and then west to Machhegaun ("Fishville"), from where a trail switchbacks up to a saddle on the ridge just north of **Bhasmesur**, the highest of several summits (2502m). The views of the high Himalaya from this knoll are excellent.

In Hindu myth, Bhasmesur was a demon who extracted a boon from Vishnu that everything he touched would turn to ash. Emboldened by his apparent invincibility, the demon proceeded to make a heavenly nuisance of himself until Vishnu, having taken the form of a fair maiden, seduced Bhasmesur into imitating a dance. Vishnu concluded the dance by touching his forehead, and Bhasmesur, following suit, incinerated himself. This mountain is reputed to be the pile of ashes left by the demon's demise.

To return you could follow the ridge eastwards, up and over a lower summit and down to the Dakshin Kali road at several points (see below). However, flagging down full-to-bursting buses along this road isn't great fun, so the full circuit is more easily done in reverse.

The Dakshin Kali road

The longest and most varied of the valley's roads begins in Kathmandu and ends at the famous sacrificial shrine of Dakshin Kali, a distance of 18km. En route it passes several temples, some beautiful stretches of forest, pleasant rest stops and fine views as it rises more than 300m above the valley floor.

Appallingly crowded **buses** and minibuses depart for Dakshin Kali from Kathmandu's Central Bus Park roughly every hour, more often (and even more crowded) on Saturdays. Kathmandu travel agents offer guided **tours** on Tuesday and Saturday mornings (about Rs250), or you could hire your own **taxi** (about Rs600 round trip to Dakshin Kali with stops). For real independence, though, go by **mountain bike**, which takes at least two hours one way.

Chobar Gorge

When Manjushri drained the Kathmandu Valley of its legendary lake, **Chobar Gorge** was one of the places he smote with his sword to release the waters, and as the Bagmati River slices through a wrinkle in the valley floor here it really does look like the work of a neat sword stroke. A path along the west bank scrambles up to the main entrance of **Chobar Gupha** (Chobar Cave), which Hindus associate with Shiva and Tibetan Buddhists with the saint Guru Padma Sambhava. A Czech team explored the cave in 1985 for at least 1.2km before pronouncing it the third-

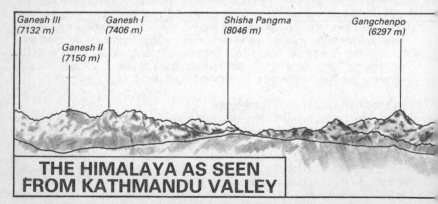

Ganesh III (7132 m)　　Ganesh I (7406 m)　　Shisha Pangma (8046 m)　　Gangchenpo (6297 m)

Ganesh II (7150 m)

THE HIMALAYA AS SEEN FROM KATHMANDU VALLEY

largest cave in South Asia; locals claim it's connected to Chobar's Adinath Mandir, the Shantipur temple at Swayambhu, or even Tibet or Varanasi. If you want to go inside, hire a guide locally and be prepared for a lot of stooping and crawling.

Jal Binayak, a seventeenth-century Ganesh temple, stands where the Bagmati, swollen with the accumulated gunge and sewage of the valley, emerges from the gorge. Built on a rocky outcrop, the tip of which is worshipped as Ganesh, it's full of the usual bells and bell-ringing. High above the river, an iron **footbridge**, custom-cast by a Glasgow foundry and assembled here in 1907, gives a good view of the chasm and Jal Binayak. The vista would be better if it weren't for the unfortunate siting of the Himal Cement Factory (the source of much of the valley's modern concrete construction and pollution) just downstream from the temple.

Chobar

Various paths lead from the main road up to **CHOBAR**, a former outpost of Patan at the top of the deceptively tall hill west of the gorge. The walk begins unpromisingly – the lower slopes look like they're being carried away by earth-movers – but higher up the northern valley spreads out handsomely.

Chobar huddles around its idiosyncratic **Adinath Mandir**, the front of which is completely decorated with pots, pans and jugs. Various explanations are cited for the practice of offering kitchen utensils to Lokeshwar, the temple's deity: newlyweds will say it ensures a happy union, others claim it's a necessary rite to send a recently departed loved one off to a prosperous next life. Like so many traditions, the act has become independent of its origins, and may hark back to a time when metal implements were new technology and decorating a temple with them was a way to keep it looking spiffy and up-to-date – just as other temples are often graced by mirrors, photographs and European tiles. Lokeshwar is worshipped here in the form of a red mask, which bears a close resemblance to Patan's Rato Machhendranath.

Taudaha and hikes to Champadevi

Beyond the cement plant, the road begins climbing through attractive countryside and after 2km passes **Taudaha**, the Kathmandu Valley's only lake of note. According to legend, when Manjushri drained the valley he left Taudaha as a home for the snakes, and the belief persists that the serpent king Karkatoka still lives at the bottom, coiled around a heap of treasure. Jang Bahadur Rana, prime minister in the middle of the last century, is said to have tried to dredge the lake

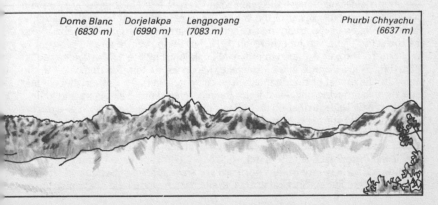

Dome Blanc (6830 m)   Dorjelakpa (6990 m)   Lengpogang (7083 m)   Phurbi Chhyachu (6637 m)

for booty but gave up because of its depth. Nowadays Taudaha is considered sacred and is off-limits to hunters and fishermen.

The road ascends steadily for another 6km to its highest point, a little beyond Pikhel. The villages of Khokana and Bungamati rest in tight whorls on the plateau across the river. Trails to **Champadevi**, the ridge to the west, start from near Taudaha, Pikhel and Pharping (see below). A hike up one and down another will take four to six hours, not including time spent at the top. The first trail begins where the road makes an abrupt bend beyond Taudaha, climbing steeply southwestwards to gain the ridge and then more gradually along it to the nearest, stupa-marked summit (2278m). From Pikhel, a trail heads north to the ridge, passing the four-star *Himalayan Heights Resort* and entering a splendid pine forest, then tracks northwest to join the first trail. The Pharping route (best taken going down if you intend to get a seat on the bus) follows a dirt road up a valley south of the ridge as far as a duck pond, where it veers northwards straight up to the ridge. You can continue westwards along the ridge to the highest summit, Bhasmesur (see above), and from there down to Kirtipur.

Sesh Narayan (Yanglesho)

Cool, quiet and shady, **SESH NARAYAN** crouches under a wooded hillside 2km beyond Pikhel and is regarded as a holy spot by both Hindus and Buddhists. Hindus worship Vishnu here as the mighty creator, who formed the universe out of the cosmic ocean; the snake Sesh (or Ananta), the "remainder" of the cosmic waters after Vishnu's creation, is symbolized by the four tranquil **pools** beside the road.

Steps from there lead to Narayan's **temple** at the base of a limestone overhang, whose serpentine rocks and roots no doubt inspired Vaishnavas to make the Sesh connection. Buddhists, meanwhile, call this grotto **Yanglesho** and hold it to be the place where Guru Padma Sambhava, the eighth-century founder of the Nyingma-pa sect of Tibetan Buddhism, wrestled with a horde of *nag* and turned them to stone. This episode marked a turning-point in Padma Sambhava's career – allegorically, it probably refers to the saint's struggle to introduce his brand of tantric Buddhism from India – which accounts for the presence of a **gompa** next to the Sesh Narayan temple.

Pharping

PHARPING is located a few hundred metres beyond Sesh Narayan, straight ahead up a side road where the main road swerves left. Unexpectedly large and lively for this distant corner of the valley, the town is only just beginning to register the changes of electricity and concrete construction. Ironically, Nepal's first hydroelectric plant was built here, in 1911, but the power generated all went to light Singha Durbar. A fifteen-minute walk uphill brings you to the golden-roofed **Pharping Bajra Jogini**, one of the valley's four tantric temples dedicated to the angry female aspect of Buddhahood. You can go upstairs – a rare privilege – and view the two prancing images of Bajra Jogini, each holding a skull cup and knife.

A short path leads further up the hill to a monastery sometimes used as a retreat by Buddhist Westerners. Introduce yourself and the monks will show you the **Padma Sambhava Cave** in the courtyard; the irrepressible guru, whose image stands among butter candles, apparently meditated in this grotto as well as at Yanglesho. Buddhists say the handprint to the left of the cave entrance and the "footprints" in the centre of the courtyard are those of Padma Sambhava (Hindus claim they were left by Gorakhnath). The site has grown to be a major pilgrimage stop for Tibetan Buddhists, and has spawned several other nearby *gompa* of Padma Sambhava's Nyingma-pa sect.

Dakshin Kali

The best and worst aspect of **DAKSHIN KALI** is that everything happens out in the open. The famous sacrificial pit of Southern Kali – the last stop for hundreds of chickens, goats and pigs every week – lies at the bottom of a steep, forested ravine, affording an intimate view of Nepali religious rituals; unfortunately, the public bloodbath also attracts busloads of camera-toting tourists. For the full show in all its Technicolor gore, go on a Saturday or Tuesday morning, but get there *early* (before 8 if possible). If you're squeamish or wish to avoid the crush, try visiting in the afternoon or on another day. Whenever you go, respect the privacy of worshippers, especially if you're taking pictures.

Motorists and motorcyclists have to pay a small fee before the final switchback descent into the ravine, and then pay again to park. From the parking lot a path leads to a small bazaar of stalls selling food, drinks and sacrificial accessories. The **shrine** is directly below the bazaar, positioned at the auspicious confluence of two streams. Tiled like an abattoir (for easy hosing down) and covered with a brass canopy, the sacred area consists of little more than a row of short statuettes, Kali being the heavily decorated one on the right. You can get a good view of the whole area from a secondary shrine on a promontory high above the far side of the ravine.

Dakshin Kali is as much a picnic area as a holy spot. The sacrifice done, families make for the pavilions that surround the shrine and merrily cook up the remains of their offerings.

A NOTE ON HINDU ANIMAL SACRIFICE

Hindu animal **sacrifice** is superficially similar to what the Old Testament patriarchs did, but Hindus don't kill animals to prove their loyalty to a deity so much as to propitiate it. Kali, the usual recipient, doesn't care about the personal sacrifice her worshipper has made in order to get an animal, all she wants is the blood. Nepalis lead their offerings to the slaughter tenderly, often whispering prayers in the animal's ear and sprinkling its head with water to encourage it to shrug in assent; they believe that the death of this "unfortunate brother" will give it the chance to be reborn as a higher life form. Only uncastrated males, preferably dark in colour, are used. At Dakshin Kali, men of a special caste slit the animals' throats and let the blood spray over the idols. Brahman priests (referred to as *bahun, pandit* or *pujari*) oversee the butchering and instruct worshippers in all the complex rituals that follow – the priests like to make things obscure to keep themselves in demand. However, you don't need to speak Nepali to get the gist of the explanations.

The Bungamati and Chapagaun roads

Two minor roads south of Patan make for some easy, off-the-beaten-track cycling through rustic villages and countryside. The first, mostly unpaved road leads directly to delightful Bungamati, summer home of Rato Machhendranath. The second is paved as far as Chapagaun and its nearby forest temple.

You can **cycle** to either town on a one-speeder, but with a mountain bike you'll be able to make a circuit of both as well as roam all over the southern end of the valley. **Buses** depart from the Ring Road near Jaulakhel for Bungamati (only 2–3 per day) and from Lagankhel for Chapagaun (hourly).

Bungamati and Khokana

From a distance, you could almost mistake **BUNGAMATI** for a well-preserved Tuscan village: scrunched together on a hillock, its tall, brick houses, with their tiled roofs sloping in different directions, look distinctly Romanesque. The bus stops along the road a short walk northeast of the town.

Close up, Bungamati is quintessentially Newar, and what at first looks like a tiny village quickly envelops you in its self-contained universe. All alleys eventually lead to the broad, teeming central plaza and the great white *shikra* of **Machhendranath**, whose more ancient Newar name is Bunga Deo ("God of Bunga"). According to legend, Bungamati marks the spot where Machhendranath, having arrived in the valley in the form of a bee to save it from drought, was "born" as the valley's protector-rainmaker. Each summer at the end of Patan's Rato Machhendranath festival, the god's red mask is brought to the Bungamati temple for a six-month residency, but every twelfth year it is kept here through the winter and then pulled by lumbering chariot all the way to Patan (see p.163).

One kilometre to the north, **KHOKANA** resembles Bungamati in many ways, but somehow lacks the character and magnetism of its neighbour. It's locally renowned for its mustard oil, and in season the presses run full tilt. Khokana's pagoda-style **Shekali Mai Mandir**, a massive three-tiered job, honours a local nature goddess. Midway between Khokana and Bungamati stands the poorly maintained **Karya Binayak**, another of the valley's four Ganesh temples. Marijuana grows in profusion around here.

Thecho and Chapagaun

THECHO, 8km south of Patan, is the largest town in this rural, undulating end of the valley, while **CHAPAGAUN**, 1km further south, is a smaller but similarly brick-built settlement. Thecho has a touch more atmosphere, Chapagaun more to eat.

More attractive than either town, the seventeenth-century **Bajra Barahi Mandir** is secreted in a small wood 500m east along a track from Chapagaun. Despite Shiva imagery, the temple is dedicated to a tantric goddess: like the Bajra Joginis, Bajra Barahis represent the female, creative power of divinity. This goddess receives her share of worship and sacrifice on Saturdays, but most visitors come to picnic in the park.

From Chapagaun, you've several options for **cycling on**. The Bajra Barahi track continues eastwards and eventually meets the Godavari road (see below), while a trail heading west from Chapagaun crosses the pretty Nakhu Khola and bends north to join the Bungamati road. The main Chapagaun road carries on to the Lele Valley, home of the mildly interesting **Tika Bhairab Mandir**, housing a colourful abstract mural of Bhairab.

The Godavari road

The greenest, most pristine part of the valley is its southeastern edge, where you'll find something now all too rare in Nepal, or at least around the Kathmandu Valley: virgin forest, once the dominant feature of the middle hills, which has

AGRICULTURE IN THE VALLEY

Agriculture employs two out of three residents of the Kathmandu Valley, the **farmers** a mixture of Newars, Brahmans, Chhetris and Tamangs (see p.86, 204 and 208 for background on these ethnic groups). Newar farmers, called *Jyapus*, dig their fields with two-handed spades called *kodaalo* (*ku* in Newari) – it's back-breaking work – and live in close, brick settlements on the valley floor, while the other groups tend to use bullock ploughs and build detached, mud-walled houses around the fringes. Many are tenant farmers and are expected to pay half their harvest as rent.

Low enough in elevation to support two or even three main crops a year, and endowed with a fertile, black clay – *kalimati*, a by-product of sediment from the prehistoric lake – the valley floor has been intensely cultivated and irrigated for centuries. **Rice** is seeded in special beds shortly before the first monsoon rains in June, and seedlings are transplanted into flooded terraces no later than the end of July. Normally women do this job, using their toes to bed each shoot in the mud. The stalks grow green and bushy during the summer, turning a golden brown and producing mature grain by October.

Harvest time is lazily anarchic: sheaves are spread out on paved roads for cars to loosen the kernels, and then run through portable hand-cranked threshers or bashed against rocks. The grain is gathered in bamboo trays (*nanglo*) and tossed in the wind to winnow away the chaff, or, if there's no wind, *nanglo* can be used to fan away the chaff. Some sheaves are left in stacks to ferment for up to two weeks, producing a sort of baby food called *hakuja*, or "black" rice. The rice dealt with, terraces are then planted with **winter wheat**, which is harvested in a similar fashion in April or May. A third crop of pulses or maize can often be squeezed in after the wheat harvest, and vegetables are raised year-round at the edges of plots.

The lot of valley farmers has improved in recent years. **Land reform** in the 1950s and 1960s, which didn't work too well in most parts of the country, was more rigorously implemented near the capital, helping to get landlords and moneylenders off the backs of small farmers. However, Kathmandu's **prosperity** is bringing problems. In the past decade, while the valley's population has nearly doubled to 1.2 million, housing (and the brick "factories" that make it possible) has been chewing up farmland at an alarming rate – a trend that threatens to accelerate, as ever more hill people flock to the valley for a piece of the action. At the same time, skyrocketing land prices and the declining quality of life in the capital are only adding to the pressure on farmland. Those who can are fleeing the inner city, just as they have every other city in the world, and are rapidly creating a **suburban** commuter culture. In the absence of any greenbelt regulations, valley farmers and *guthi* (temple trusts) are steadily selling out, as their valuable farmland becomes even more valuable as real estate.

come under increasing pressure in recent years from an exploding population desperate for fuel and farmland. One way to take in the greenery is by visiting the Royal Botanical Garden; another is to hike or ride up Phulchoki, the highest point on the valley rim. The starting point for both is **Godavari** (pronounced Go-*daa*-vari), 10km southeast of Patan near the end of a straight, tree-lined paved road.

Local **buses** depart infrequently for the botanical gardens from the City Bus Park in Kathmandu. Hourly minibuses from Patan's Lagankhel bus park go as far as the Jesuits' St Xavier School in Godavari. Since the road gains more than 200m along the way, **cyclists** will need gears.

The Royal Botanical Garden

To reach the **Royal Botanical Garden** (daily 10am–5pm; Rs2), follow the main road to the left of the St Xavier School for 1km, then turn left again at the shops (some food available) to the car park and main gate. Despite their modest size, the grounds contain some idyllic paths, streams and picnic areas; highlights are the orchid house and fern shed. If you're expecting well-labelled plants and trees you'll be disappointed, but the Department of Medicinal Plants publishes a map (Rs2 at the ticket booth) and guide booklet in English (Rs10) that are of some help in identifying species. The garden receives fairly enthusiastic support from the government – not surprising, perhaps, in a country where flowers play a major part in worship and medicine is largely based on plants.

Another pleasant spot nearby is the spring-fed water tank of **Godavari Kunda**, 300m past the botanical garden turning on the Godavari road, which hosts a big *mela* every twelve years during July and August (last held in 1991). Alternatively, you can leave the garden via a back way on the western side, and keep following it for a long walk around the small valley to the north. The three- or four-hour circuit takes you past **Bishanku Narayan**, a Vaishnava pilgrimage cave high up in a notch at the far end of the valley. Kathmandu seems incredibly far away.

Phulchoki

The road bearing straight ahead to the right of the St Xavier School switchbacks and spirals right to the top of **Phulchoki** – a rough, 1200-metre ascent that would challenge even the most experienced mountain-biker. The trail to the summit starts behind the shrine to **Phulchoki Mai**, the mother goddess of these parts, 500m up the road and just opposite the entrance to an unsightly marble quarry. This hike takes about three hours, and crosses the road a few times; the trail can be very slippery. Set off as early as possible to beat the afternoon clouds.

Phulchoki means **"Place of Flowers"**, which is entirely apt. If you know what to look for, you'll see orchids, morning glories, corydalis and, of course, rhododendrons; March and April are best for catching them in bloom. The whole mountain is covered by tall, luxuriant **forest**, and as you climb from its subtropical base to its temperate summit you pass through mixed stands of oak, chestnut, walnut, bamboo, laurel and rhododendron. It's a great place for **birdwatching** – a trained eye is supposed to be able to spot a hundred or more species in a day – and even better for **butterflies**, which are apparently attracted to the flowers during spring.

If the **summit** (2762m) isn't wreathed in clouds, you'll have a magnificent view of a wide swathe of the Himalaya and practically the entire Kathmandu Valley (smog permitting). The effect is only slightly marred by the presence of a microwave relay station, erected with Canadian assistance, which is the summit road's *raison d'être*.

BHAKTAPUR AND THE EASTERN VALLEY

The valley's eastern arm maintains a discreet cultural, as well as geographical, distance from Kathmandu. Perhaps because it lay off the main India–Tibet trade route all those years, its Hinduism has scarcely been diluted by Buddhism. Creeping Westernization has been slower to take root here, too, and concrete has made fewer inroads against native brick. Fashions at this end of the valley remain conservative, especially among Jyapu women: most still wear the traditional black and red-trimmed *pataasi*, wrapped around the waist in tiers, giving the effect of a flamenco skirt; hitched up in back, these often reveal tattoos above the ankles, believed to be necessary for a woman to enter heaven.

Everywhere is within day-tripping range of Kathmandu, but for more detailed exploration a stay in the medieval time capsule of **Bhaktapur** is a must. Trails radiate in all directions from here, the temple complex of **Changu Narayan** making an immensely rewarding excursion, particularly for fans of Nepali sculpture. Bhaktapur is also a staging post for Nagarkot, and can serve as a springboard for trips up the Arniko Highway to Dhulikhel and beyond (see Chapter Three).

Bhaktapur (Bhadgaun)

> *In the soft, dusty light of evening the old city of Bhaktapur, with its pagoda roofs and its harmonious blend of wood, mud-brick and copper, looked extraordinarily beautiful. It was as though a faded medieval tapestry were tacked on to the pale tea-rose sky. In the foreground a farmhouse was on fire, and orange flames licked like liquescent dragon's tongues across the thatched roof. One thought of Chaucer's England and Rabelais's France; of a world of intense, violent passions and brilliant colour, where sin was plentiful but so were grace and forgiveness . . .*
>
> Charlie Pye-Smith, *Travels in Nepal*

Kathmandu's field of gravity weakens somewhere east of the airport; beyond, you fall inexorably into the rich, heady atmosphere of **BHAKTAPUR** (also known as **BHADGAUN**). A medieval world unto itself ("remote – willingly remote – from her neighbours, and one of the most picturesque towns in the East," wrote Percival Landon), Bhaktapur is Nepal's most perfectly preserved city. Bricks everywhere, streets paved with bricks in herringbone and parquet patterns, houses built of bricks and carved wood: brick and wood, the essential media of Newar city-builders. Well clear of the Ring Road, with no industrial zone, no diplomatic enclave and few suburbs, Bhaktapur feels more like a big village than a small city. Its streets and alleys are all the more suited for wandering, thanks to a fifteen-year restoration and sanitation programme led by the German-funded Bhaktapur Development Project and to the local council's progressive policy of charging vehicles to enter the municipality.

The "City of Devotees" was probably founded in the ninth century, and by 1200 it was ruling Nepal. In that year Bhaktapur witnessed the launch of the Malla era when, according to the Nepalese chronicles, King Arideva, upon being called out of a wrestling bout to hear of the birth of a son, bestowed on the prince the hereditary title Malla ("wrestler") – to this day, beefy carved wrestlers are the city's trademark temple guardians. Bhaktapur ruled the valley until 1482, when Yaksha Malla divided the kingdom among his three sons, setting in train three centuries of continuous squabbling. It was a Bhaktapur king who helped to bring the Malla era to a close in 1766 by inviting Prithvi Narayan Shah, the Gorkha leader, to aid him in a quarrel against Kathmandu. Seizing on this pretext, Prithvi Narayan conquered the valley within three years, Bhaktapur being the last of the three capitals to surrender.

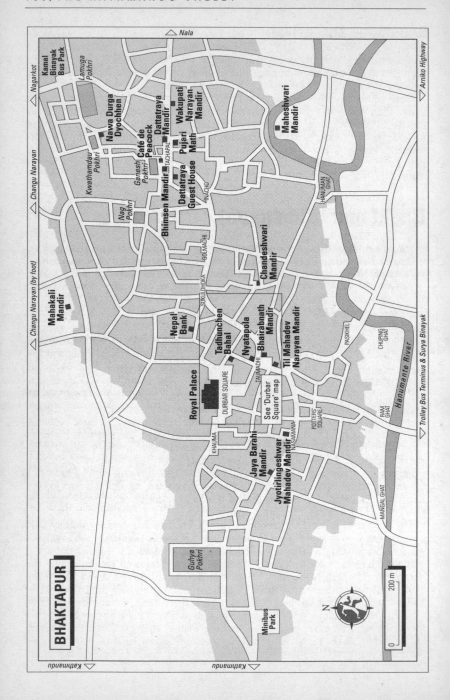

BHAKTAPUR

Nala

Nagarkot

Amiko Highway

Changu Narayan

Kamal Binayak Bus Park

Lamuga Pokhri

Nawa Durga Dyochhen

Wakupati Narayan Mandir

Maheshwari Mandir

Café de Peacock

Dattatraya Mandir

Changu Narayan (by foot)

Kwathandau Pokhri

Ganesh Pokhri

Pujari Math

TACHAPAL

Dattatraya Guest House

Bhimsen Mandir

Nag Pokhri

HANUMAN GHAT

INACHO

GOLMADHI

Chandeshwari Mandir

Mahakali Mandir

SUKULDHOKA

Nepal Bank

Tadhunchen Bahal

Nyatapola

Bhairabnath Mandir

Til Mahadev Narayan Mandir

PASIKHEL

CHUPING GHAT

Hanumante River

Royal Palace

DURBAR SQUARE

See 'Durbar Square' map

TAUMADHI

POTTERS' SQUARE

RAM GHAT

Trolley Bus Terminus & Surya Binayak

KHAUMA

NASAMANA

Jaya Barahi Mandir

Jyotirlingeshwar Mahadev Mandir

MANGAL GHAT

Guhya Pokhri

Minibus Park

N

200 m

0

Kathmandu

Kathmandu

Orientation and arrival

Bhaktapur drapes across an east–west fold in the valley, its southern fringe sliding down towards the sluggish Hanumante River. Owing to a long-term westward drift, the city has two centres (residents of the two halves stage a boisterous tug-of-war during the city's annual Bisket festival) and three main squares. In the west, **Durbar Square** and **Taumadhi Tol** dominate the post-fifteenth-century city, while **Tachapal Tol** presides over the older east end.

You'll arrive by one of two routes. The handy **trolley bus**, departing from the National Stadium south of Kathmandu's GPO every fifteen minutes or so, drops you on the main road about ten minutes' walk south of town, as do the frequent Barhabise-bound **buses** from Kathmandu's City Bus Park. Arriving by **minibus** from the City Bus Park, you'll be deposited near Sidha Pokhri, a five-minute walk west of Durbar Square. Local buses from Nagarkot terminate at Kamal Binayak, five minutes northeast of Tachapal; tourist buses from Nagarkot continue to the main intersection just north of Durbar Square.

Bhaktapur has no rikshas and just a few resident taxis, but it's compact enough to be explored on foot. One-speed **bikes** can be rented along the road east of the minibus park (west of Durbar Square). Foreigners are charged a one-time **fee** of Rs300 to enter the city – keep your ticket in case you need to show it later.

Durbar Square

Bhaktapur's **Durbar Square** hasn't got quite the same gusto as its namesakes in Kathmandu and Patan. Isolated near the city's edge, it's neither a commercial nor a social focal point, and consequently the only locals you see here are either preying on tourists or cutting across the square to somewhere else. The 1934 earthquake, which knocked the stuffing out of Bhaktapur, claimed a number of the square's temples and left a great void in its middle. Despite all that, it boasts one of Nepal's proudest artistic achievements – the Golden Gate – plus the National Art Gallery.

The square enjoyed one brief, magnificent renaissance during the shooting of Bernardo Bertolucci's 1994 film **Little Buddha**, when it was used as the location for many of the ancient flashback scenes. Bertolucci transformed the area beyond recognition: high, simulated brick walls were erected to block modern sightlines, the palace front was extended with false balconies and columns, and the dead space in the middle was taken up with a raised water tank. Residents won't soon forget that Hollywood facelift – nor the handsome fees Bertolucci paid them for the use of their houses and shopfronts.

The Royal Palace

Bhaktapur's **Royal Palace** originally stood further east, near Tachapal Tol, but was shifted westwards (like the city) in the fifteenth century; the present structure, dating from the eighteenth century, was renovated and greatly scaled down after 1934. Its superbly carved eastern wing, known as the **Panchapanna Jhyale Durbar** ("Palace of Fifty-Five Windows"), was raised around 1700 by Bupathindra Malla, Bhaktapur's great builder-king, whose *namaste*-ing figure kneels on a stone **pillar** opposite.

While the **Golden Gate** (Sun Dhoka) probably wouldn't be so famous if it were made of wood or stone – it is, in fact, made of brass – its detail and sheer

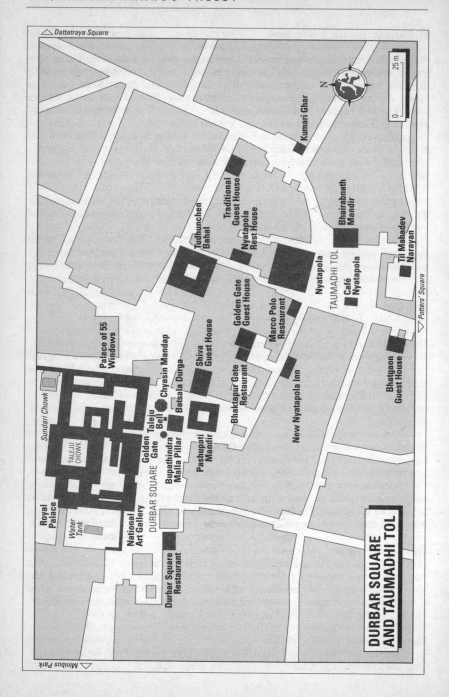

DURBAR SQUARE AND TAUMADHI TOL

exuberance raise it to the level of a masterpiece. The *torana* above the door features a squat Garud and a ten-armed, four-headed Taleju, the Mallas' guardian deity, but to locals the most powerful figures are those of Bhairab and Kali, situated chest-high on either side of the gate. Upon entry, you follow an outdoor passage around to another impressive doorway, depicting Taleju and her heavenly host in wood, beyond which lies the ornate and sacrosanct **Taleju Chowk**. A sentry bars the way to non-Hindus, and guards the store of gold treasures contained within. Sacrifices take place here during festivals. Another old doorway nearby leads to **Sundari Chowk**, Bupathindra Malla's regal bathing tank fed by an ornate stone spout and protected by a gilded *nag* figure, once the centrepiece of a now-obliterated palace section.

THE NATIONAL ART GALLERY

The palace's western wing houses the excellent **National Art Gallery** (daily except Tues 10.15am–3.45pm, Fri closes 2.45pm; Rs5), displaying an extensive permanent exhibit of tantric *paubha* and *thangka*, plus a small number of oblong book covers and illuminated pages of religious texts. An English-speaking guide employed by the museum gives occasional free tours, which are well worth joining to get the most out of this rich collection. There are some terrifically old paintings here (some date to the fifteenth century), including such paradigms of tantric art as the "Sata Chakra Darsan", a medical chart showing the location of the seven power points (*chakra*) of the human body. Stone friezes at the entrance portray Vishnu Varahi and Narasimha, Vishnu's boar and man-lion *avatar*.

The square

The square itself won't detain you for long. Near the main gate at the west end you can admire a pair of multiple-armed statues of **Bhairab** and **Ugrachandi**, whose sculptor reportedly had his hands cut off by order of the Bhaktapur king to ensure that he wouldn't reproduce the images in Kathmandu or Patan. Among the clutch of minor temples opposite, a Shiva *shikra* showcases the often overlooked Newar art of brickwork.

In the entire square, only the fifteenth-century **Pashupati Mandir** at the busier, more touristy eastern end receives much in the way of reverence. The oldest structure extant here, the temple houses a copy of the exalted Pashupatinath *linga*, and its roof struts sport some wildly deviant erotic carvings. Next door stands the mid-eighteenth-century stone *shikra* of **Batsala Durga** and the obligatory **Taleju Bell**, plus a smaller replica known generally as the **"Bell of Barking Dogs"**, so called because its toll evidently inflicts ultrasonic agony on local curs.

Behind the bell rises the **Chyasin Mandap**, the Pavilion of the Eight Corners, erected in 1990 as an exact replica of an eighteenth-century structure destroyed in the 1934 earthquake. The restorers did a first-rate job of relocating original pillars and lintels and integrating them into a sturdy new structure – the steel reinforcing may clash a bit, but this pavilion is going to stay standing when the next quake hits. The upper floor makes a fine vantage point for observing the square. East of here are another fine stone *shikra* to Durga and the platforms of other demolished and half-heartedly rebuilt temples.

Rare for predominantly Hindu Bhaktapur, the well-preserved **Tadhunchen Bahal**, east of the square, attracts Buddhist as well as Hindu worshippers, and is a gathering place for neighbourhood metalsmiths in the evening; you might also hear languorous music performed on harmonium and tabla.

Taumadhi Tol

One hundred metres southeast of Durbar Square, **Taumadhi Tol** is a livelier place to linger, if only to admire the view from the balcony of *Café Nyatapola*. In mid-April this square serves as the assembly point for the high-spirited **Bisket Jaatra**, Nepal's foremost New Year celebration.

Dominating Taumadhi and all of Bhaktapur, the graceful, five-tiered **Nyatapola** is Nepal's tallest and most classically proportioned pagoda. So obscure is its honoured deity, a tantric goddess named Siddhi Lakshmi, that she apparently has no devotees, and the sanctuary has been barred to all but priests ever since its completion in 1702. The Nyatapola's five pairs of temple guardians – Malla wrestlers, elephants, lions, griffins and two minor goddesses, Baghini (Tigress) and Singhini (Lioness) – are as famous as the temple itself. Each pair is supposed to be ten times as strong as the pair below, with Siddhi Lakshmi herself, presumably, being ten times as strong as Baghini and Singhini. Bisket chariot components, including the solid wooden wheels, are stored in an empty lot behind the temple.

The heavy, thick-set **Bhairabnath Mandir** is as different from the slender Nyatapola as one pagoda could possibly be from another. The funniest thing of all about this hulk of a building, in fact, is the tiny Bhairab idol mounted on a sort of mantel on the front of the temple (several other figures are kept inside, including the one that leads the Bisket parade). A story is told that Bhairab, travelling incognito, once came to Bhaktapur to watch the Bisket festivities. Divining the god's presence and hoping to extract a boon, the priests bound him with tantric spells, and when he tried to escape by sinking into the ground they chopped off his head. Now Bhairab, or at least his head, gets to ride in the Bisket parade every year – inside a locked box on board the chariot.

Hidden behind recent buildings southeast of the square, the seventeenth-century **Til Mahadev Narayan Mandir** displays all the iconography of a Vishnu (Narayan) temple: a gilded *sankha* (conch), *chakra* (wheel) and Garud are all hoisted on pillars out in front, in a manner clearly imitating the great temple of Changu Narayan, 5km north of Bhaktapur. The temple's name, it's said, derives from an incident involving a trader from Thimi who, upon unfolding his wares here, magically discovered the image of Narayan in a consignment of sesame seeds (*til*).

A block northeast of the Bhairabnath Mandir stands Bhaktapur's **Kumari Ghar**. An image of the goddess is kept upstairs and is only displayed publicly for nine days during Bisket. The living goddess herself resides in another building north of Tachapal Tol.

The western city

Like a brick canyon, Bhaktapur's main commercial thoroughfare runs from Taumadhi west to the city gate. Roughly 150m along, you'll reach a kind of playground of sculptures and shrines, and a *shikra* that rejoices in the name of **Jyotirlingeshwar Mahadev**, freely translatable as "Great God of the Resplendent Phallus" – a reference to a myth in which Shiva challenges Brahma and Vishnu to find the end of his organ (they never do). Further west, where the street's brick cobbles temporarily give way to flagstones, the **Jaya Barahi Mandir** commemorates the *shakti* (consort) of Vishnu the boar; you have to stand well back from this broad edifice to see its pagoda roofs. Non-Hindus aren't barred from entering the upstairs sanctuary, but this intimate space wasn't designed for spectators.

Dark, damp alleys beckon on either side of the main road – north towards Durbar Square and south to the river. The most promising destination in this area is Kumale Tol, the **potters' square**, a sloping open space southwest of Taumadhi Tol. Although you may be buttonholed by the occasional potter's wife angling for a sale, for the most part this low-key production centre has few retail pretensions. The output here consists mainly of simple water vessels, stovepipes, disposable yoghurt pots and ever-popular piggy banks (called *kutrukke*, a word that imitates the sound of a coin being dropped in). For more decorative items, pay a visit to nearby Thimi, the valley's pottery capital – information on production processes is given in that section.

Tachapal Tol (Dattatraya Square)

From Taumadhi, the eastern segment of Bhaktapur's main artery snakes its way to the original and still-beating heart of the city, **Tachapal Tol** (or **Dattatraya Square**). Here again a pair of temples looms over the square, older than those of Taumadhi if not as eye-catching. More notably, though, Tachapal conceals Nepal's most celebrated masterpiece of woodcarving, the Pujari Math's Peacock Window, and a superb woodcarving museum. You'll also find the finest woodwork studios in Nepal here, which are well worth a browse, even if you haven't got room in your rucksack for an eight-foot, Rs50,000 peacock-window reproduction.

Just north of Tachapal, a second open space around Ganesh Pokhri is equally busy with *pasal* (shops) and street vendors. South of the square is even better for exploring, as Bhaktapur's medieval backstreets spill down the steep slope to the river like tributaries.

Dattatraya and Bhimsen temples

Rearing up behind an angelic pillar-statue of Garud, the **Dattatraya Mandir** (accent on the second syllable of Dattatraya) is Bhaktapur's oldest structure. The temple was raised in 1427 during the reign of Yaksha Malla, the last king to rule the valley from Bhaktapur, and like the Kasthamandap of Kathmandu, which it resembles, it was allegedly built from a single tree (the front portico was probably added later). Dattatraya, a sort of one-size-fits-all deity imported from southern India, epitomizes the religious "syncretism" (as anthropologists call it) that Nepal is famous for: to Vaishnavas Dattatraya is an incarnation of Vishnu, while Shaivas hail him as Shiva's guru and Buddhists even fit him into their pantheon as a *bodhisattva*.

The oblong temple at the opposite end of the square belongs to **Bhimsen**, the patron saint of Newar merchants, whose territory Tachapal is. As usual for a Bhimsen temple, the ground floor is open and the shrine is kept upstairs.

The Pujari Math

Behind and to the right of the Dattatraya temple stands the sumptuous eighteenth-century **Pujari Math**, one of a dozen priests' quarters (*math*) that once ringed Tachapal Tol. Given the nature of the caste system, perhaps it's not surprising that the grandest houses in the city traditionally belonged to priests. Similar to Buddhist *bahal*, these *math* typically sheltered communities of Hindu devotees loyal to a single leader or sect; and like *bahal*, most have now been converted to other, secular uses. The Pujari Math's awesome windows can be seen on two sides; the often-imitated **Peacock Window**, overlooking a narrow lane on the building's far (east) side, has for two centuries been acclaimed as the zenith of Nepalese window-lattice carving.

The woodcarving and brass museums

Don't miss the small **Woodcarving Museum** (daily except Tues 10am–4pm, Fri closes 3pm; Rs5) inside the Pujari Math. Well displayed and lit, it enables you to inspect a small collection of exquisite temple carvings that in their normal surroundings are often too high up to fully appreciate. Highlights of the collection are an alluring Nartaki Devi of the fifteenth century, a seventeenth-century Bhairava (Bhairab), several magnificent steles and *torana*, and various abstractly weathered temple struts. The courtyard itself contains possibly the greatest concentration of woodcarving virtuosity in the country.

Somewhat misleadingly, the **Brass and Bronze Museum** (daily except Tues 10am–4pm, Fri closes 3pm; Rs5) across the square contains none of the flamboyant religious art that one might expect, consisting instead of domestic and ritual vessels and implements. For statues and the like, go to the National Museum in Kathmandu or the Patan Museum.

Nawa Durga Dyochhen and points east

North of Tachapal, the **Nawa Durga Dyochhen** looks like a haunted house, Nepali-style. A tantric temple only open to initiates, it honours the nine manifestations of Durga, who are especially feared and respected in Bhaktapur. According to legend, the Nawa Durga used to eat solitary travellers, turning the area east of Bhaktapur into a Bermuda triangle until a priest managed to cast a tantric spell on them. The Nawa Durga occupy a special place in Bhaktapur's spiritual landscape: the city is said to be delimited by symbolic Nawa Durga stones (*pith*), and most *tol* (neighbourhoods) have adopted one of the nine as their protector goddess.

Most famous of all are the **Nawa Durga dancers**, a troupe whose members are drawn from the caste of flower sellers. Each wears a heavy painted clay mask which, empowered by tantric incantations, enables the wearer to become the very embodiment of the deity. Every September a new set of masks is moulded and painted, each with its own iconography – there are actually thirteen in all, the Nawa Durga plus four attendant deities. On Bijaya Dasami, the "victorious tenth day" of Dasain, the dancers and accompanying musicians gather at Brahmayani Pith, about 1km east of town, and dance all the way to the Golden Gate, where they re-enact the legend of Durga's victory over a buffalo demon. The troupe is available for hire throughout the winter and spring wedding and festival seasons until the month of Bhadra (Aug–Sept), when their masks are formally retired and burned; the ashes are saved and added to clay to form the next year's masks.

East along the main road from Tachapal, the **Wakupati Narayan Mandir**, where local Jyapus worship Vishnu as a harvest god, displays no fewer than five Garuds mounted on pillars in a line.

The ghats and beyond

The Hanumante River is Bhaktapur's humble tributary of the River Ganga, its name deriving from the monkey god Hanuman who, locals like to think, stopped here for a drink on his way back from the Himalaya after gathering medicinal herbs to heal Ram's brother in an episode from the *Ramayan*. Several bathing and cremation ghats flank the river as it curls along the city's southern edge, although unfortunately there's no riverside path connecting them. The most active is **Hanuman Ghat**, located straight downhill from Tachapal Tol: morning *puja*, bathing and tooth-brushing are a daily routine for many, while old-timers come here just to hang out. A peaceful spot, the ghat packs an eyeful of cluttered *linga*, statues and trees into a small area. A priest is usually set up in front of the main Hanuman image to prescribe the Hindu equivalent of Hail Marys.

Downhill from Taumadhi Tol, **Chuping Ghat**'s array of temples and statuary is more of the mouldering-ruins school. The long, sloping area above the ghat is the focal point on New Year's Day (Nawa Barsa) in April, when a 25-metre *linga* pole is ceremonially toppled by the throng. **Ram Ghat**, below the potters' square, has little to offer beyond a run-of-the-mill Ram temple, but **Mangal Ghat**, further downstream, boasts a more atmospheric selection of neglected artefacts, and by following the trail of *linga* across the river you'll end up at a forbidding Kali temple in one of Bhaktapur's satellite villages.

Once south of the Hanumante, a ramble up to the forested ridge overlooking Bhaktapur might be in order, and **Surya Binayak** makes a worthy target. This most pleasantly situated of the valley's four main Ganesh shrines – catching the valley's first rays of sun – is reached by a steep, kilometre-long paved road from the trolley bus terminus. The temple itself is just an ordinary plaster *shikra*, surrounded by usual Ganesh trappings; smeared with red *sindur* paste, the god's image looks like a warm fire in an ornate Victorian hearth. Ganesh is regarded as a divine trouble-shooter and this particular image specializes in curing children who are slow to walk or speak.

Accommodation

Although Bhaktapur is usually regarded as a day trip from Kathmandu, it has perfectly adequate facilities for a longer stay – and you really ought to spend at least one night to do the place justice. The city's **lodges** all fall into the guest house category. Most are exceptionally well located, friendly, and priced about the same as comparable lodgings in Kathmandu. Try to arrive as early as possible in the day. You might also consider staying up at Changu Narayan (see below).

Bhadgaon Guest House, Taumadhi Tol (☎610488). Personable management, clean rooms and a super view from the three-level roof terrace. B⑤.

Bhaktapur Guest House Country Resort, Chandevisthan, about 1km west of the trolley bus terminus (☎610670). Nice place, nice views, but nowhere near town. ④/B⑥.

Dattatraya Guest House, just off Dattatraya Square (no phone). Rooms are stark but spacious; good view of the square from the roof terrace. ③.

Golden Gate Guest House, between Durbar Square and Taumadhi Tol (☎610534). Secluded and tidy, but rather cavernous. Rooftop restaurant planned. ③/B⑤.

New Nyatapola Inn, between Durbar Square and Taumadhi Tol (☎611323). Minimal atmosphere and facilities. B⑤.

Nyatapola Rest House, just north of the Nyatapola (no phone). A good cheapie: quiet, rustic and friendly, with rooftop seating. ②.

Shiva Guest House, Durbar Square (☎610740). Clean and reasonably cheerful, with a good location overlooking the Pashupati Mandir. ②.

Traditional Guest House, east of Durbar Square (☎611057). A laid-back, family-run place: it's the management that's traditional, not the building. B③.

Eating

Food is basic, but sufficient. All the guest houses have their own restaurants serving the usual line-up, and there are plenty of cheap *bhojanalaya* west of Durbar Square and around the bus park. If nothing else, you can always load up on thick, sweet yoghurt (Bhaktapur's "king of curds"), available by the clay pot or glass from local stalls at a fraction of the price charged in tourist restaurants. As for **nightlife**, forget it.

Bhaktapur Gate Restaurant, adjacent to *Golden Gate Guest House*. Not much atmosphere, but it serves palatable *kothe* and other pasta dishes.

Café de Peacock, in a former *math* overlooking Dattatraya Square. You can't beat the surroundings, but it's overpriced for what amounts to fairly primitive tourist grub.

Café Nyatapola, in a former temple in the middle of Taumadhi Tol. Another place with a great location and middling food.

Durbar Square Restaurant, west end of Durbar Square. Popular with daytrippers and tour groups and consequently overpriced, but the food (especially the Indian) is competent.

Marco Polo Restaurant, overlooking Taumadhi Tol. Enjoy the view over a cup of tea or a bowl of curd – but steer well clear of the food.

Nyatapola Restaurant, just north of the Nyatapola. Serviceable Western, Nepali, Indian and Tibetan food. Rooftop seating with an up-close view of the Nyatapola.

Rooftop Café, in *Shiva Guest House* overlooking Durbar Square. Unexciting tourist menu. It isn't actually on the roof, although it commands a fine vantage of the square.

Shopping and other practicalities

Bhaktapur's best buys are in **wood**: browse around the workshops along the south side of Dattatraya Square to get a feel for different styles, woods and techniques, then haggle for bargains with the traders along the lane that contains the Peacock Window. See *Basics* for more on what's available. Several shops around Durbar Square and Taumadhi sell quality **thangka**, and artists can often be seen painting them.

Nepalis recognize Bhaktapur for its traditional **textiles**, such as black and red *pataasi* material and black *Bhadgaonle topi*, formal headgear now worn mainly by traditionalists and government officials. Foreigners will be more attracted by the locally produced *dhaka* in original designs, as well as block-printed, quilted cotton items, *pashmina* shawls and Rajasthani-style tapestries.

Nawa Durga **puppets** and **masks** are widely sold in Bhaktapur, but they're cheaper in Thimi (see below) where they're made. Thimi is better for **pottery**, too.

Film is sold in many tourist shops. There's a film processing lab just west of the Durbar Square gate.

At the time of writing there were no moneychangers in Bhaktapur and the only **bank** (*Nepal Bank*, signed only in Nepali) was unequipped to do foreign exchange transactions. This is likely to change, but bring enough cash just in case. There are no private **telephone** services, but you should be able to make international calls from your guest house's phone.

Changu Narayan

Art and history buffs will get the most out of **CHANGU NARAYAN**, but this beautiful, tranquil site, reached by a delightful walk, is a must for anyone. Perched at the abrupt end of the ridge north of Bhaktapur, the ancient temple complex

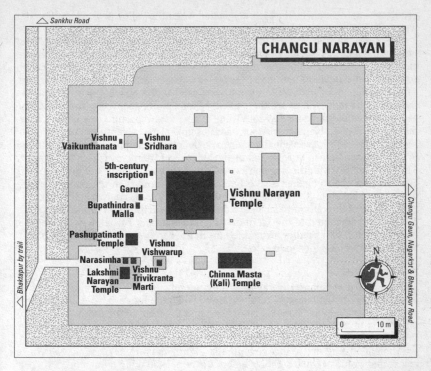

commands an extraordinary view of the valley in three directions – especially in late afternoon, when the meandering Manohara River turns into a golden ribbon. A simple guest house offers the prospect of staying overnight here, removed from the valley's noise and smog, and makes a potential stopover in a circuit to or from Nagarkot (see p.195).

The site

"One remembers all the wealth of carving of the rest of the Valley," wrote Percival Landon in 1928, ". . . but when all is recalled it is probably to the shrine of Changu Narayan that one offers the palm. Perhaps one drives back home from Bhatgaon more full of thought than from any other expedition to the many outlying places of this crowded centre of holiness and history and art." Protected by its remote location, Changu Narayan has changed little since Landon's day, with relatively few travellers, or even worshippers, making the effort to visit it. It is, on the face of it, just another pagoda, yet Changu Narayan's palpable age and its collection of the finest, oldest statues outside the National Museum seem to make it the archetypal Nepalese pagoda. Ideally, you should see it before you've burned out on the others.

The valley's **oldest Vaishnava site**, Changu Narayan's documented history goes back to the fourth century AD, and its sculptures attest to continuous worship here ever since. Some historians suspect an even greater antiquity, postulating that Changu Narayan and Swayambhu were built on the foundations of prehistoric animist shrines which originated when the valley floor was still under water. Changu is an ancient word meaning "shaking or swinging hill".

The **main temple**, rebuilt around 1700, stands in a quiet quadrangle of rest houses and pilgrims' shelters. A measure of the temple's importance is the exaggerated size of the four traditional emblems of Vishnu – the wheel (*chakra*), conch (*sankha*), lotus (*padma*) and mace (*gada*) – mounted on pillars at its four corners. The brass repoussé work on the front (west side) of the building is as intricate as any you'll find in Nepal, as are the carved, painted struts supporting the roofs. The *torana* above the main door depicts Vishnu in his *sridhara* posture (see below), brandishing the four emblems in his four hands. A gold-plated seventh-century image of Vishnu is allegedly kept inside the sanctuary, but only the temple priests are allowed to view it. From time to time, the statue is said to sweat miraculously, indicating that Vishnu is battling with the *nag* spirits, and the cloth used to wipe the god's brow is considered a charm against snake bites. **Smaller temples** in the compound are dedicated to Lakshmi (the goddess of wealth, Vishnu's consort), Kali and Shiva.

The base of the *chakra* pillar bears the **oldest inscription** in the valley. Dated 454 AD and attributed to the Lichhavi king Manadeva, it relates how Manadeva, upon the death of his father, dissuaded his mother from committing sati by promising to conquer his foes to the east.

The statues

The courtyard of Changu Narayan is an outdoor museum of priceless works of art, displayed in an almost offhand manner and all the more exciting for it. You'll find the oldest, famous statues grouped around the front of the temple (see map) plus loads of other, more recent (but still centuries-old) pieces in the vicinity. With few exceptions, they all pertain to Vishnu or his faithful carrier, Garud.

Probably dating from the seventh or eighth centuries, Changu Narayan's celebrated statue of **Garud** kneels before the temple, looking human but for a pair of wings and a cobra scarf. He used to be mounted on a pillar, the broken base of which is lying just to his right. Garud's association with snakes is legendary. It's said that when his mother was kidnapped by his stepmother, Garud appealed to his serpentine stepbrothers to free her, which they did on condition that Garud brought them ambrosia from Indra's heaven. Although Indra later flew down and reclaimed his pot of nectar (leaving the snakes to split their tongues as they licked up the few drops spilt on the grass), Vishnu was so impressed that Garud hadn't been tempted to consume the ambrosia that he immediately hired him as his mount. The brass statues inside a screened cage next to Garud commemorate **King Bupathindra Malla** of Bhaktapur and his queen Bubana Lakshmi, who ruled during the late seventeenth and early eighteenth centuries.

Though damaged, the eighth-century image of **Vishnu Vishwarup** (Vishnu of the Universal Form) is an awesome example of Hindu psychedelia. The lower portion of this composite image shows Vishnu reclining on the snake of infinity in the ocean of existence, echoing the sleeping statues of Budhanilkantha and Balaju. Above, the god is portrayed rising from the waters before a heavenly host, his thousand heads and arms symbolizing sheer omnipotence. The latter image is borrowed from an episode in the *Mahabharat* in which the warrior Arjuna lost his nerve and Krishna (an incarnation of Vishnu) appeared in this universal form to dictate the entire *Bhagavad Gita* by way of encouragement.

Two notable statues rest on the platform of the Lakshmi Narayan temple. The eighth-century **Vishnu Trivikranta Murti**, Vishnu of the Three Strides, illustrates a much-loved story in which the god reclaimed the universe from the demon king Bali. Disguised as a dwarf (another of his ten incarnations), Vishnu petitioned Bali for a patch of ground where he could meditate, which need only be as far as the dwarf could cover in three strides; when Bali agreed, Vishnu grew to his full divine height and bounded over the earth, sky and heavens. (An even older version of this statue is held in the National Museum.) The adjacent eleventh- or twelfth-century image depicts Vishnu in yet another of his incarnations, that of the man-lion **Narasimha**.

At the northwest corner of the compound, the twelfth- or thirteenth-century **Vishnu Vaikunthanata** – reproduced on the Nepalese ten-rupee note – shows a purposeful Vishnu riding Garud like some sort of hip space traveller. Nearby stands a **Vishnu Sridhara** of the ninth or tenth century, an early example of what has since become a stereotypical Vishnu representation.

Getting there and back

You can approach the temple complex from Bhaktapur, the Sankhu road or Nagarkot – time permitting, the ideal itinerary is to walk from Nagarkot to Bhaktapur via Changu Narayan.

From Bhaktapur, an asphalted **road** forks off from the Nagarkot road about 200m east of the hilltop Mahakali shrine (see the main Bhaktapur map) and climbs directly up to **Changu Gaun**, the village immediately east of the temple. The last 2km or so are steep: you'll need a mountain bike (and even then it's a fair old climb). Two **trails** set off from the north side of Bhaktapur towards Changu Narayan, but they soon converge, passing through rural villages before a steep ascent to reach the temple after 5km; the easternmost trail skirts the Mahakali shrine and a sleeping Vishnu water tank en route.

The ten-kilometre hike **from Nagarkot** is described on p.199. The trail **from the Sankhu road** is only 2km long, but it's hard to find at its lower end and the bridge over the Manohara River is only seasonal. Descending is no problem, although you'll probably end up walking halfway to Boudha before a minibus comes along to take you back to Kathmandu.

Accommodation and eating

Changu Narayan's only **accommodation** at the time of going to press is *Changu Narayan Hill Resort* (③), located about 500m east of Changu Gaun, along the unpaved road to Nagarkot. Facilities are pretty minimal and arguably overpriced, but you pay for the solitude and the fantastic views of Gauri Shankar. It's like Nagarkot, only better: there aren't any other lodges (yet) and there's a proper temple to look at. Brace yourself for no electricity or hot water, however, and something of a language problem. **Camping** is also possible.

Even if you don't stay at the "resort", you can **eat** in the dining room – breakfast after a cycle up from Bhaktapur, perhaps, or lunch on the way down from Nagarkot. Snacks and drinks are also available in and around the temple area and at the Changu Gaun parking lot.

Thimi

THIMI, the valley's fourth-largest town, lies on a plateau 4km west of Bhaktapur. The name is said to be a corruption of *chhemi*, meaning "capable people", a bit of flattery offered by Bhaktapur to make up for the fact that the town used to get mauled every time Bhaktapur picked a fight with Kathmandu or Patan. Its mainly Newar inhabitants are indeed very capable craftspeople, and Thimi is the place to go for papier mâché masks and pottery.

The Bhaktapur trolley bus will drop you off at the southern end of Thimi, but you'll get a far more favourable introduction by cycling in along the old road to Bhaktapur, which skirts the town to the north. Minibuses from Bhaktapur and Kathmandu also ply this back route. Several **handicrafts shops** – Thimi's only real attraction – are located along the north road. The **papier mâché masks** seen all over Kathmandu are made in Thimi, and you can count on getting the best deal here. Snarling Bhairab, kindly Kumari and elephant-headed Ganesh are most commonly represented by the masks, which are based on those worn by Bhaktapur's Nawa Durga dancers. Nawa Durga **puppets**, again associated with Bhaktapur, are also made and sold here for a fraction of their usual price. Salt and pepper shakers in the shape of the king and queen are quasi-contraband items, and you have to ask for them specially – though expensive, they make great, offbeat mementoes (don't let customs officers see them).

Pottery is an even older local speciality, and you can watch potters at work in alleys and courtyards at the north end of town; the busiest times are autumn and winter, when it's not so hot and the firing process is safer. The manufacture of traditional vessels and tiles is still strong in Thimi, though many potters now also churn out candlesticks, elephant flower pots and the like. As more producers learn how much money they can make from selling these to tourists, the simpler items for local consumption may well fall by the wayside.

The remainder of Thimi is grotty and unglamorously primitive – it's one of the few places in the valley where poverty isn't offset by quaintness. Thimi's only

Throwing pots

temple of note is that of **Balkumari**, a sixteenth-century pagoda located near the southern end of the main north–south lane. Couples pray to the "Child Kumari" for babies, presenting her with coconuts as a symbol of fertility. Balkumari's vehicle is a peacock, which stands upon a nearby pillar. The temple is the focus of frenzied Bisket **festivities** in April, when dozens of deities are ferried around on palanquins and red powder (red being the colour of rejoicing) is thrown like confetti.

Bode

A small, tight-knit Newar community, **BODE** is built on a bluff overlooking the Manohara River, 1km north of Thimi. The village's main shrine, the **Mahalakshmi Mandir**, stands at the northwest corner of the village, a modest and not partic-

THIMI'S POTTERS

Like their counterparts throughout Nepal, the **potters** (*kumal*) of Thimi employ low-tech techniques. The clay comes from flooded paddies, kneaded by hand. The solid wooden wheel – or, increasingly, a concrete-filled truck tyre – is literally hand-powered: spurning even a simple foot treadle, the potter uses a pole to spin the wheel to a dervish pitch, allowing four or five minutes' working time before the wheel gradually winds down to a slow wobble and needs to be cranked up again. The potter's creations – still grey at this stage – are set out in soldierly rows to dry in the sun for a day or two before firing. Kilns are uncommon. The usual procedure is to stack the vessels in an empty square, each layer packed with straw, sawdust or dung, then cover the mound with a coating of mud, and poke holes in the surface to let air in at just the right rate to sustain a slow burn. After being baked for a week or more, the wares will be ready for use – and bright red.

ularly well-maintained two-tiered pagoda. The goddess of wealth, Maha ("Great") Lakshmi is feted during a three-day festival beginning on New Year's Day (here called Baisakh Sankranti, meaning the first day of Baisakh – April 13 or 14). The highlight of the proceedings comes on the second day, when a volunteer has his tongue bored with a thin steel spike and, thus impaled and bearing a disc-shaped object with flaming torches mounted on it, accompanies the goddess as she's paraded around the village. Volunteers believe that they won't bleed if they've followed a prescribed three-day fast and have sufficient faith, and that by performing this act they'll go directly to heaven when they die.

CHAPTER THREE

THE CENTRAL HILLS

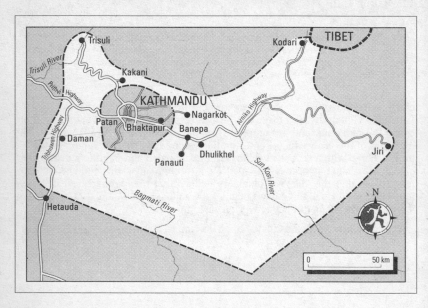

Beyond the Kathmandu Valley, major roads meander in three directions, making the **central hills** the most accessible – though not necessarily the most travelled – section of Nepal's jumbled, 700-kilometre band of foothills. To the northeast, the **Arniko Rajmarg** (Arniko Highway) follows the old Kathmandu–Lhasa trade route through broad valleys and misty gorges to the Tibet border; northwestwards, the **Trisuli Road** snakes its way down into a subtropical valley nearly 1000m lower than Kathmandu; and south, the **Tribhuwan Rajpath**, Nepal's first highway, cuts a tortuous cross-section through the hills on its way to the Tarai. If the scenery here is a shade less dramatic than what you'll encounter further west, the land is nonetheless varied and rugged, tamed only in pockets by defiant terraces. It's only when you leave the Kathmandu Valley that you appreciate how atypical it is of this hilly region.

The majority of places described here can be treated as easy overnights from Kathmandu. The most popular are those that involve mountain views and hill-walking: **Nagarkot** and **Dhulikhel**, with well-developed budget accommodation, are acknowledged classics; **Kakani** is equally scenic, though lacking in cheap lodgings, and **Daman** is splendidly off the beaten track. These vantage points can't compare with what you'll see on a serious trek, but they come into their own in winter, when trekking can be a chilly business. Although cultural attractions are relatively few outside the Kathmandu Valley, **Panauti** and **Nuwakot** are among Nepal's most intriguing villages – all the more because they're so seldom visited – and whether or not the most alluring destination of all, Tibet, is open to independent travellers entering from this direction, the **border** still beckons.

To an extent, the boundaries of this chapter are dictated by travel formalities: towns and **day hikes** are described here, while back country areas requiring a trekking permit are saved for Chapter Seven. Despite a relative abundance of roads, **buses** in the central hills are slow and infrequent, and indeed few travellers brave them except to get to the start of the Langtang/Helambu and Everest treks. All the more reason to go by **bike**, for indeed the region contains Nepal's most popular and rewarding mountain-biking destinations.

Nagarkot

Like many of Nepal's best highways, the road to **NAGARKOT** serves mainly strategic, not scenic, purposes: Nagarkot was originally developed as an army post, and tourist facilities came later, with government encouragement. Set on a ridge northeast of Bhaktapur, it commands a classic panorama of the Himalaya from Langtang Himal to Gauri Shankar, and on a good day you can see from Annapurna South to Everest. The best thing about Nagarkot is that you don't have to stay in an expensive hotel to get a view right out of your window. Hiking and mountain-biking routes up and back down are particularly worthwhile, although it has to be said that there's not much to do once you're here.

Nagarkot is often mentioned in the same breath as Dhulikhel and Daman, but chances are you'll only have time to visit one. Be sure to read the Dhulikhel and Daman sections later in this chapter before deciding.

Getting there

At least one **tourist bus** departs each afternoon for Nagarkot from the north end of Kantipath in Kathmandu and returns the following morning. Book through any ticket agent (the fare should be around Rs80 each way). The only **public buses** to Nagarkot depart from Bhaktapur's Kamal Binayak area (hourly; Rs10). If you're coming from Kathmandu or anywhere else by public bus, you'll not only have to change in Bhaktapur but also walk clear across town to make the connection: you might as well spend the night in Bhaktapur.

If you're **cycling**, the logical itinerary is to ride up from Bhaktapur and return the back way to Sankhu (see "Biking Down", below): this creates an eventful two- or three-day loop taking in Bhaktapur, Nagarkot, Sankhu and Boudha. The main road from Bhaktapur is consistently steep for the last 12km – the vertical gain is 650m – but paved all the way and relatively free of traffic. For a more interesting variation, first pedal up to Changu Narayan (see p.188). From there, a dirt road follows the ridge eastwards to intersect with the paved Nagarkot road at Phedi, near the start of the steep climbing. It's also possible to **walk** up from Changu Narayan or Nala, but most people prefer to do this in reverse (ie downhill) – see below.

Cycling or walking up, you can stop at Nepal's first-ever **snake farm**, a couple of kilometres beyond Phedi (Rs100 donation requested). Nepal is home to 56 snake species – thirty of them, including the extremely dangerous cobra and krait, poisonous and a significant hazard to rural Nepalis. The snakes featured in the modest

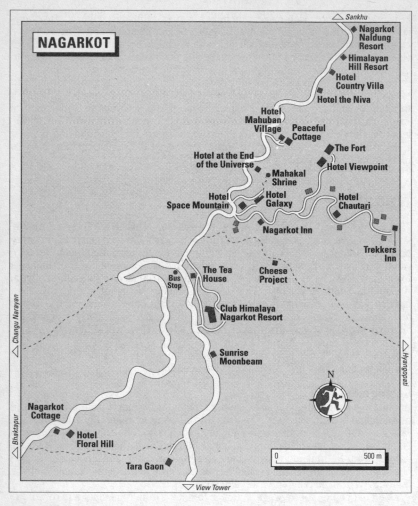

NAGARKOT

△ Sankhu
◆ Nagarkot
Naldung
Resort
◆ Himalayan
Hill Resort
Hotel
Country Villa
Hotel the Niva
Hotel
Mahuban
Village
Peaceful
Cottage
The Fort
Hotel at the End
of the Universe
Hotel Viewpoint
Mahakal
Shrine
Hotel
Space Mountain
Hotel
Galaxy
Hotel
Chautari
Nagarkot Inn
Trekkers
Inn
The Tea
House
Cheese
Project
Bus
Stop
Club Himalaya
Nagarkot Resort
△ Changu Narayan
▷ Hyangopati
Sunrise
Moonbeam
Nagarkot
Cottage
◆ Hotel
Floral Hill
◁ Bhaktapur
Tara Gaon
N
0   500 m
▽ View Tower

visitor display here are literally farmed for their venom, which when injected into animals produces antivenins that can be used to treat snakebite victims; the rather steep admission charge aids this work. Organizers hope eventually to have specimens of all but one of Nepal's snake species (pythons will not be represented, as the government bans their capture to discourage the trade in python skins). By the way, foreigners have little to fear from Nepal's poisonous snakes, as most are confined to the Tarai and are active only during the monsoon months.

Being there

Erase from your mind any picture of a quant hilltop village. There's no such town as Nagarkot – it's only a loose affiliation of guest houses and hotels stretching for

2km along a cultivated ridgetop at around 1950m. Almost all the budget places are grouped around the plunging north end of the ridge, reached by a dirt road that forks off to the left at the public bus stop. Two landmarks in this vicinity are a tiny **Mahakal shrine** and a small-scale **cheese-making project**.

Most guest houses have good views of their own, but you'll get much better ones – and a greater sense of having earned them – if you walk or ride to the **view tower** at the highest southern point of the ridge (2164m). Follow the main paved (later dirt) road south for 3km, which takes about an hour and a half on foot from most guest houses. When you get to the tower you'll understand why Nagarkot has been the site of a fort (*kot*) since Rana times: this hilltop controlled the eastern entrance to the Kathmandu Valley and the vital trade route to Tibet. It's still an **army base**, but nowadays the troops' primary responsibility is to regulate woodcutting in the area.

Many people set off before dawn to catch the sunrise at the tower and return to their lodgings in time to catch the midmorning tourist bus back to Kathmandu, but the programme is a lot more relaxed if you pack a lunch and set aside the whole day. For further hiking ideas, see "Walking Down", below.

Accommodation

Electricity has arrived in Nagarkot, turning the old trekking-standard lodges into Thamel-style guest houses and spurring the construction of a number of high-class hotels. With everything drifting upmarket, the quoted price of a room has risen markedly in the past few years – yet there's now such an oversupply of lodging that you can expect discounts of 50 to 75 percent or more. Always bargain. The map shows all the lodgings existing or under construction as of early 1996, but don't be surprised to find a few more when you get there. Views also are apt to change as new places are built in front of older ones, though it's not necessarily such a bad thing to have to hike a little bit to see the mountains.

The cheaper lodges are generally very small – just a few rooms each – so if you show up without a reservation be prepared to settle for a second or third choice. You'll greatly improve your chances if you get there before the tourist bus arrives. The more expensive places will arrange transport from Kathmandu for you.

All but the most deluxe places are unheated, and although quilts are provided, a sleeping bag might be worth bringing in winter. Water is generally heated by solar systems, and in budget lodges is often only available by the bucket – you'll pay considerably more for a room with its own solar hot water connection. Bring a torch (flashlight) for walking between buildings after dark.

ROOM PRICE SCALES

All guest houses and hotels have been price-graded according to the scale outlined below, which represents the cheapest available double room in high season; codes prefixed by B denote the cost of a room with attached bathroom. See p.35 for a fuller explanation of the system.

① Less than Rs100 ($1.75 if quoted in US$)	⑤ $8–12
② Rs100–175 ($1.75–3)	⑥ $12–20
③ Rs175–300 ($3–5)	⑦ $20–40
④ $5–8	⑧ $40–70
	⑨ Over $70

BUDGET

Hotel at the End of the Universe (no phone). Bamboo huts, a bank of other rooms and a welcome restaurant, with hot water by the bucket. At the high point of the ridge, with fine views. ③/B⑤.

Hotel Galaxy (Kathmandu office: ☎290870). Rooms and a dorm in the old building, classier rooms in a newer annexe. Hot running water and a partial view. B④, or B⑥ in the new building (dorm beds ②).

Hotel Madhuban Village (no phone). Robinson Crusoe-esque bamboo A-frames with common bath, or brick bungalows with attached baths. Hot water by the bucket. ④/B⑥.

Hotel The Niva (no phone). Good value: reasonably cheerful brick bungalows with running hot water, cosy dining room and good views. B④.

Sunrise Moonbeam (no phone). Great view, but forlorn and primitive facilities (no hot water). They're just killing time till they can sell out to a big developer. ②.

Trekkers Inn (no phone). Basic bungalows and some dorm accommodation. Hot water by the bucket. ③ (dorm beds ①).

MODERATE PLACES

Himalayan Hill Resort (no phone). A bit uninviting. View to the east. B④ with hot water by the bucket, B⑦ with hot running water.

Hotel Viewpoint (Kathmandu office: ☎417424). Tidy brick bungalows and a smart glassed-in dining room. Sits at a great high spot, but its view is marred by *The Fort*. B⑥ (B⑦ with running hot water).

Nagarkot Cottage (book through *Natraj Tours*: ☎222532). Rustic bungalows, but it's a long walk to the views. Hot water by the bucket. B⑦.

Nagarkot Naldung Resort (Bhaktapur office: ☎610963). Secluded bamboo huts in real *pukka* safari style, with a great view. Hot running water. B⑤ (dorm beds ③).

Nagarkot Inn (Bhaktapur office: ☎610874). Very small outfit (supposedly expanding) with rustic bamboo rooms and a dinky restaurant. ⑤.

Peaceful Cottage (Kathmandu office: ☎290877). Killer panorama of the mountains and the Kathmandu Valley from the glassed-in dining area. Call ahead or arrive early to get a room with a view. Hot water by the bucket in the common bath, attached baths have hot running water. ⑤/B⑦.

Tara Gaon Hill Resort (Kathmandu office: ☎290861). Nagarkot's original government-run outfit is a fair deal, despite befuddled service. B⑦, with discounts for longer stays.

EXPENSIVE PLACES

Club Himalaya Nagarkot Resort. Obscenely luxurious 50-room relative of the *Kathmandu Guest House*, scheduled to open in 1996. Expected to be B⑨.

Hotel Chautari (Kathmandu office: ☎419718). Medium-sized hotel with all mod cons. B⑧.

Hotel Country Villa (Kathmandu office: ☎228014). Nice rooms with east-facing balconies, but overpriced and faintly unsavoury. B⑧.

Hotel Floral Hill (Kathmandu office: ☎223311). Lifeless, overpriced and a 15-minute hike to views. B⑧.

Hotel Space Mountain (Kathmandu office: ☎231812). Second-rate hotel facing the wrong direction. B⑧.

Nagarkot Farmhouse (Kathmandu office: ☎272719). Located nearly 2km north of the bus stop on the road to Sankhu (way off the map). Run by the same folks who brought you the excellent *Hotel Vajra* in Kathmandu, this friendly and restful retreat places an emphasis on yoga and meditation. ⑦/B⑧.

The Fort (Kathmandu office: ☎232829). Imposing skyscraper with wood-panelled rooms, fancy restaurant with views, gardens and a sauna. B⑧.

100 Rough Guides*

Southwest USA THE ROUGH GUIDE
Greg Ward

India THE ROUGH GUIDE
David Abram, Devdan Sen, Harriet Sharkey and Gareth John Williams

China THE ROUGH GUIDE

Vietnam THE ROUGH GUIDE
Jan Dodd and Mark Lewis

Peru THE ROUGH GUIDE
Dilwyn Jenkins

Paris THE ROUGH GUIDE
Kate Baillie and Tim Salmon

Spain THE ROUGH GUIDE
Mark Ellingham and John Fisher

Norway THE ROUGH GUIDE
Jules Brown and Phil Lee

London THE ROUGH GUIDE
Rob Humphreys

Mallorca & Menorca THE ROUGH GUIDE
Phil Lee

Indonesian A ROUGH GUIDE PHRASEBOOK

French A ROUGH GUIDE PHRASEBOOK

Mandarin Chinese A ROUGH GUIDE PHRASEBOOK

Hindi & Urdu A ROUGH GUIDE PHRASEBOOK

Thai A ROUGH GUIDE PHRASEBOOK

The Internet AND WORLD WIDE WEB THE ROUGH GUIDE 2.0
Angus J. Kennedy from Tolpnet

Jazz THE ROUGH GUIDE

World Music THE ROUGH GUIDE
Salsa to Soukous... Cajun to Calypso... the complete handbook

Opera THE ROUGH GUIDE
Matthew Boyden

Rock THE ROUGH GUIDE
THE DEFINITIVE GUIDE TO 1000 ARTISTS AND BANDS FROM THEN...TO NOW

100% Reliable

Stay in touch with us!

ROUGH*NEWS* is Rough Guides' free newsletter.
In three issues a year we give you news, travel
issues, music reviews, readers' letters and the
latest dispatches from authors on the road.

I would like to receive ROUGH*NEWS*: please put me on your free mailing list.

NAME . . . .

ADDRESS . . . .

Please clip or photocopy and send to: Rough Guides, 1 Mercer Street, London WC2H 9QJ, England
or Rough Guides, 375 Hudson Street, New York, NY 10014, USA.

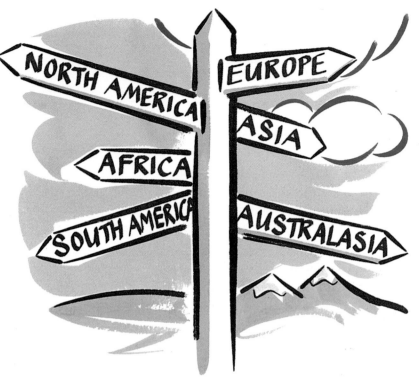

Travel the world
HIV *Safe*

Travel *Safe*

HIV, the virus that causes AIDS, is worldwide.

You're probably aware of the dangers of getting it from unprotected sex, but there are many other risks when travelling.

Wherever you're visiting it makes sense to take precautions. Try to avoid any medical or dental treatment, but if it's necessary, make sure the equipment is sterilised. Likewise, if you really need to have a blood transfusion, always ask for screened blood.

Make sure your travelling companions are aware of the risks and the necessary precautions. In fact, you should take your own sterile medical pack, available from larger high street pharmacies.

Remember, ear and body piercing, acupuncture and even tattoos could be risky, because they all involve puncturing the skin. And although you might not normally consider any of these things now, after a few drinks - you never know.

Of course, the things that are dangerous at home are just as dangerous when you travel. So don't inject drugs or share works.

Avoid casual sex and always use a good quality condom when having sex with a new partner (and each time you have sex with them).

And it's not just a gay disease' either. In fact, worldwide, it's most commonly transmitted through sex between men and women.

For information in the UK:

Ring for the TravelSafe leaflet on the Health Literature Line freephone 0800 555 777, or pick one up at a doctor's surgery or pharmacy.

Further advice on HIV and AIDS: National AIDS Helpline: 0800 567 123. (Cannot be reached from abroad).

The Terrence Higgins Trust Helpline (12 noon–10pm) provides advice and counselling on HIV/AIDS issues: 0171 242 1010.

MASTA Travellers Health Line: 0891 224 100.

Travel *Safe*

Travel the world HIV *Safe*

Eating

Food at guest house dining rooms takes a long time to prepare and usually doesn't live up to expectations. But as in trekking lodges, mealtimes are lively social occasions with an intimate, we're-all-in-this-together energy.

You can always try seeing if the grass is any greener at other guest houses or hotels, though this is more convenient for breakfast or lunch – eating dinner out means groping your way back in the dark. Some of the expensive hotels can offer some pretty fine dining, particularly *Club Himalaya*'s *Tea House* (located in a separate building above the public bus stop) and *The Fort*'s in-house restaurant. At the other end of the scale, you can get cheap, standard Nepali fare from any of several *bhojanalaya* in the small bazaar area around the bus stop.

Walking down

When people talk of **walking** down from Nagarkot they almost always mean **via Changu Narayan** (see p.188), a three- to four-hour hike. The main trail to Changu descends from the *Tara Gaon Hill Resort*, recrossing the Nagarkot road after about 600m. If you're starting from the north end of the ridge, a more convenient trail leaves from the big hairpin turn below the bus stop and joins up with the main trail 1km later. From there you keep descending, paralleling the road and at times walking on it, and passing the snake farm en route (see above). At Phedi, where the main road passes through a notch in the ridge, take the dirt road to the right and follow it generally along the wooded ridgeline to Changu Narayan. From there it's another hour down to Bhaktapur, or less to the Sankhu road.

A much less travelled trail heads eastwards from Nagarkot's small bazaar, down past the cheese project and through the village of Dhanar Gaun **to the Indrawati River** at Hyangopati, a three-hour hike. Buses trundle south from there to Panchkhal on the Arniko Highway, and some continue on to Dhulikhel and Kathmandu. In addition to the cycle route **to Nala**, there's a steeper, more direct hiking trail heading south from the view tower.

Biking down

The dirt road **to Sankhu**, which isn't marked on the *Schneider* map, is simply a continuation of the road past Nagarkot's northern lodges. It's very steep, rutted and good fun – vehicles can't use the track in its present state, although there are signs it might eventually be upgraded. A longer, somewhat smoother road branches off to the right after a few kilometres, ascending to Kattike before descending to rejoin the other track at Sankhu.

A second option is to ride south past the view tower **to Nala** (see below). This road isn't shown on any maps either, but it heads first west and then generally south, dropping a stiff 700m to Nala. From there you can head west to Bhaktapur or south to Banepa and Dhulikhel.

Banepa, Nala and Panauti

Leaving the Kathmandu Valley through a gap at its eastern edge, Nepal's only road to the Tibet border is officially known as the **Arniko Rajmarg** (Arniko Highway), appropriately named after the thirteenth-century Nepali architect who

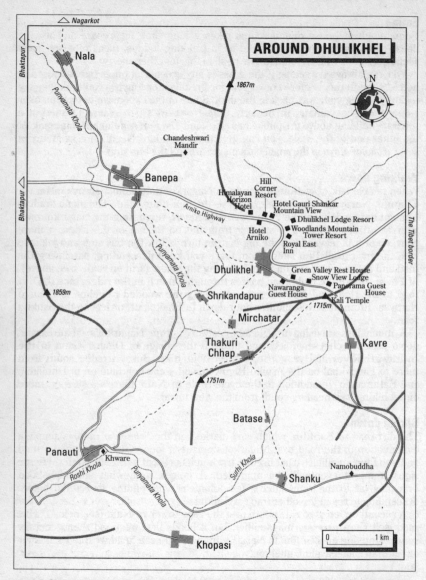

led a delegation to Beijing and taught the Chinese how to build pagodas. Three ancient Newar towns, which once comprised a short-lived independent kingdom, lie just east of the valley rim.

Loads of **buses** and minibuses ply the Arniko Highway as far as Banepa. However, it's much prettier and less stressful to ride a **mountain bike** from Bhaktapur, entering Nala from the east along a dirt road – see the *Schneider* map or similar. Other biking and hiking routes are discussed in the Panauti and Dhulikhel sections below.

Banepa

BANEPA, 26km east of Kathmandu, was for centuries an important staging post to Tibet, and now – such is progress – it's an obligatory pitstop for buses heading up the Arniko Highway. The roadside buildup is pretty unattractive, and unfortunately there's not much left of the old bazaar: a fire burned most of it down in the 1960s, and earthquakes have sorely weakened the rest. Cheap cotton cloth, woven here on semi-mechanized looms, is an important local industry. To **stay**, your choices are the basic *Banepa Guest House* (②), the better *Hotel Chandari* (③/B④) and the best *Hotel Anand* (③/B⑤), all near the main roundabout on the highway. For a **meal**, *Banepa Guest House* is said to have the best *bhaat*.

One kilometre northeast of town, the three-tiered **Chandeshwari Mandir** overlooks a set of cremation ghats at the bottom of a wooded ravine, and is best known for the psychedelic fresco of Bhairab decorating its exterior. The temple commemorates Bhagwati, who according to one of the *purana* (Hindu scriptures) slew a giant called Chandashur here, earning her the title Chandeshwari ("Lord of Chand"). Her image is the object of a chariot **festival** here coinciding with Nepali New Year (April 13 or 14). To get there, head north from the main roundabout on the Arniko Highway and then take a right at the next roundabout.

Nala

It's 3km northwestwards along an unpaved road from Banepa to **NALA**, a quiet, parochial village near the head of the meandering Punyamata Valley. Fanning out at the base of a hill, the classically Newar houses look like a landslide of bricks, frozen in mid-tumble. Nala's main temple, a seventeenth-century pagoda dedicated to Bhagwati, is unusual for having four tiers – even numbers are usually avoided as they're considered unlucky. The weathered image of eighteen-armed Bhagwati is ferried around on a chariot on the third day of Indra Jaatra.

From Nala you can continue west along a wide dirt track, passing a Lokeshwar temple on the outskirts of town, to reach Bhaktapur in 10km.

Panauti

More charming still, **PANAUTI** leads a sleepy, self-sufficient existence in its own small valley 7km south of Banepa. The most pleasant way to get there is by **bike**, either on the paved road from Banepa, which follows the lovely Punyamata Khola, or on the dirt road from Dhulikhel and Namo Buddha (see below). The latter route is also nice **on foot**. Another possibility would be to walk from Godavari or the summit of Phulchoki (see p.178) – you'll need a map and the whole day. **Minibuses** to Panauti depart from Kathmandu's City Bus Park about every two hours, calling at Bhaktapur and Banepa en route. You can stay **overnight** at the *Tribeni Guest House* (②).

Wedged between the Punyamata and Roshi streams, Panauti forms the shape of a triangle, with a serpent (*nag*) idol standing at each of its three corners to protect against floods. Buses pull up at the newish northwest corner, but the oldest and most interesting sights are concentrated at the streams' confluence at the east end of town. Pride of place goes to the massive, three-tiered **Indreshwar Mahadev**, dedicated to Shiva, the "Lord of Indra" in several myths. Some authorities believe this to be the original temple (albeit restored) that was raised here in

Carving from the Indreshwar
Mahadev Mandir

1294, which would make it the oldest surviving pagoda in Nepal. The graceful and sensuous roof struts have been dated to the fourteenth century, although they may have been recycled; each carved from a single piece of wood, they predate the Malla style of carving the arms separately and then attaching them to the strut figures. Unhappily, the building is showing its age, especially since the 1988 Dharan earthquake – which caused minor damage up to the edge of the Kathmandu Valley – shivered its timbers.

The shrine area at the sacred confluence, called the **Khware**, is one of those tranquil spots that can waylay a dreamer for hours. The large *sattal* (pilgrims' house) here, a favourite hangout for local pensioners, sports an eclectic range of frescoes depicting scenes from Hindu (and some Buddhist) mythology: Vishnu in cosmic sleep, Ram killing the ten-headed demon king Ravana, and even Krishna being chased up a tree by a pack of naked *gopi* (milkmaids). Krishna is the featured deity of the temple next door, too, where he's shown serenading his *gopi* groupies with a flute. Beside the river, the tombstone-shaped ramps laid into the ghats are where dying people are laid out, allowing their feet to be immersed in the water at the moment of death; on the opposite bank stands the recently restored seventeenth-century **Brahmayani Mandir**. The Khware has been regarded as a *tirtha*, a sacred power place, since ancient times, and on the first day of the month of Magh, which usually falls on January 14, it draws hundreds of people for ritual bathing. Every twelve years this date is celebrated with a full-scale *mela* (religious fair) – the next occurrence will be in 1998.

Dhulikhel

A well-preserved town as well as a mountain viewpoint, **DHULIKHEL** can keep you occupied for days – especially if you're into walking or biking. It sits in a saddle 5km east of Banepa, just off the Arniko Highway, at the relatively low elevation of 1550m, which makes it warmer than Nagarkot. You get a restricted view of the Himalaya from several places around the town, but for the full vista you have to walk to a small nearby summit. But perhaps more than for its views, Dhulikhel is known as the customary starting point for day hikes and bikes to Namobuddha and Panauti.

Dhulikhel requires more effort to reach than Nagarkot, at least until some sort of tourist bus service starts up. Local **buses** (every half-hour from Kathmandu's City Bus Park or from Bhaktapur's trolley bus stop) are exasperatingly slow. You can ask to be dropped off at any of the hotels along the highway, but for most of the cheap lodgings you'll want to stay on until the small **bus park**. It's a short walk from there to the main square at the new, east end of town – an unfortunately dismal introduction to Dhulikhel but straightforward for orientation.

Old Dhulikhel starts immediately to the west. A close, traditional Newar settlement of remarkable architectural consistency, it is comprised almost exclu-

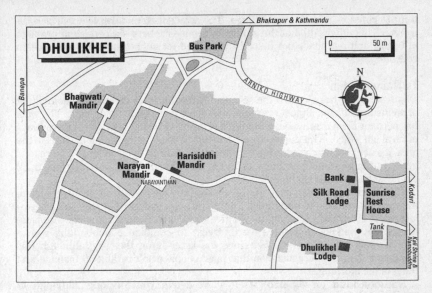

sively of four- and five-storey brick mansions, many with ornate wooden lattices in place of glass windows, affecting a stern, almost Victorian elegance. These huge houses are extended-family dwellings: some Dhulikhel clans number eighty or more members. The older buildings, which are only held together by mud mortar, show some fairly serious cracks from Kathmandu's infamous earthquake of 1934; Dhulikhel also experienced some damage during the 1988 quake centred near Dharan in the eastern Tarai. Wandering around Dhulikhel is basically a matter of following your nose (and occasionally holding your nose), but highlights include the central square of **Narayanthan**, containing a temple to Narayan and a smaller one to Harisiddhi (both emanations of Vishnu), and the **Bhagwati Mandir**, set at the high point of the village for a fine view of the mountains.

Be advised that the schoolchildren in Dhulikhel take a malevolent delight in taunting foreigners, and will sometimes even spit or throw stones. It's a game you cannot win – just don't betray any exasperation, and if you know any Nepali, tease them back.

The sunrise walk

The done thing in Dhulikhel is to hike to the high point southeast of town in time for sunrise over the peaks. To get to the top, take the road leading east from the *Dhulikhel Lodge* for about 1km to the big recreation area on the left (mountain views from here), then bear right and follow a gullied path straight up the hill. You'll need to allow about 45 minutes altogether. The summit (1715m) is marked by a small **Kali shrine** and, unfortunately, a small microwave tower. The peaks from Annapurna to (supposedly) Everest are visible from here, and the sight of Dhulikhel's brick houses, salmon in the dawn light and perhaps wreathed in mist, is pretty special, too.

On the way back down you can call in at a small, mossy temple complex, hidden down a flagstone path where the paved road gives out. The main **Shiva**

temple contains a large bronze *linga*. The adjacent **Ram temple**'s marble statues have been lopped off at the ankles by temple-robbers – a persistent problem in Nepal, and one that's not helped by demand for such treasures from foreign collectors.

To Namobuddha

Dhulikhel Lodge has elevated the so-called **Namobuddha circuit** into something of an institution, and almost everyone who stays there ends up doing it. The walk has perhaps been overhyped, although it remains a fine introduction to the byways of rural hill Nepal. With the rapid construction of roads and grading of paths in the area, it's actually much more fun for **mountain-biking** than walking. The road is graded (though sometimes quite sandy) to Namobuddha and more of a jeep track after that, but bikable all the way.

The full circuit takes most of the day on foot, and tea is available at villages along the way, but you should bring food. There's no point in describing the route here – just ask at *Dhulikhel Lodge* and they'll give you a sketch **map**, complete with landmarks and walking times. It's worth trying to combine Namobuddha with a sunrise walk to the Kali shrine, since the latter is on the way, although this requires a degree of organization that most people won't be able to manage first thing in the morning.

Namobuddha (or **Namro**) itself won't detain you for long, although to Tibetans it ranks right up there in the hierarchy of holy sites in Nepal. About two

---

BAHUNS, CHHETRIS AND OTHER HINDU CASTES

Nepal's human geography gets very confusing once you leave the Kathmandu Valley: over the course of millennia, waves of immigrants from Tibet and India have produced a complex overlay of cultures. Nearly half of all Nepalis are members of ethnic minorities and maintain distinct languages, customs and dress. The rest – the majority – are relative newcomers, descendants of Hindus who fled the Muslim conquest of northern India beginning in the twelfth century, or their converts. They are collectively referred to as **Parbatiyas** ("Hill-Dwellers") or, more generically, **Hindu castes**. In India, Hindus are divided into four primary castes, but nearly all the Hindu migrants to Nepal were of the two highest orders, Brahmans and Kshatriyas, who had the most to lose from the advance of Islam. These are sometimes called the "twice-born" castes, because males are symbolically "reborn" through an initiation rite at the age of thirteen and thereafter wear a sacred thread (*janai*), changed annually during the festival of Janai Purnima. Though originally only a small minority themselves, the refugee Hindus' high birth fuelled them with the ambition necessary to subjugate the rest, and in the process provide the country with much of its cultural framework, including its *lingua franca*, Nepali.

Although **Bahuns** (Brahmans) belong to the highest, priestly caste, they're not necessarily the wealthiest members of society, nor are they all priests. Most are farmers. Some are landlords and moneylenders, earning a reputation (by all accounts deserved) for subjecting their borrowers to crippling interest rates and swift foreclosures. Priests, who generally follow their fathers into the vocation, make a living administering rites for fixed fees. Most Brahmans observe a range of rules to maintain the purity of their caste (certain foods and alcohol are prohibited), and orthodox Brahmans won't eat with lower castes or permit them to enter the house. Extra restrictions are placed on orthodox women, who, for example, have to

and a half hours south of Dhulikhel on foot, the stupa rests on a red-earth ledge near the top of a jungly ridge. It's like a hick version of Swayambhu – smaller and pretty uneventful, except during the February–March pilgrimage season, when Tibetans and Bhotiyas arrive by the vanload to circumambulate it. Among the houses surrounding the stupa is a dinky Tamang *gompa*, which you can enter. A trail leads up to a bigger Tibetan *gompa* and a larger-than-life Buddha on top of the prayer-flag-festooned ridge behind, and in one of the outbuildings is preserved a famous stone relief **sculpture** depicting the legend of Namobuddha. According to the fable, the Buddha, in one of his previous lives as a hunter, encountered a starving tigress and her cubs here, and moved by compassion, offered his own flesh to her, a sacrifice that helped pave the way for his eventual rebirth as the historical Buddha. The stupa is supposed to contain the hunter's bones and hair.

To Panauti

Although the *Dhulikhel Lodge*'s map recommends returning to Dhulikhel by a different route, carrying on **to Panauti** from Namobuddha is equally enjoyable. A graded dirt road veers off to the left at Shanku and enters Panauti from the east, which if you're walking takes about an hour and a half. From there you can catch a minibus to Kathmandu or back to Dhulikhel (with a change at Banepa). By bike, you can pedal back to Dhulikhel on paved roads without encountering too much traffic.

keep strict seclusion during menstruation and for ten days after childbirth, when they're considered polluted.

The majority of Nepali Hindus are **Chhetris**, who correspond to Indian Kshatriyas, the caste of warriors and kings. While Nepali Brahmans usually claim pure bloodlines and exhibit the classic Aryan features of their caste, Chhetris are a more racially mixed lot and easily mistaken for members of other ethnic groups. Most of them are in fact the offspring of Hindus and the hill tribes they conquered, or of compliant hill dwellers who converted to Hinduism and were made honorary Chhetris (in the early days, Brahmans were willing to bend the rules to gain allies). Those of pure Kshatriya blood – notably the aristocratic Thakuri subcaste of the far west, who are related to the king – can be as twitchy about caste regulations as Brahmans. Significantly, it was a Chhetri who unified Nepal and gave the country its abiding martial character, and the old warrior-caste mentality remains a key in understanding the politics of modern Nepal, for Chhetris occupy the palace and command the army to this day.

India's two lower castes, Vaisyas (traders and farmers) and Sudras (menials) aren't really acknowledged in hill Nepal: indigenous Nepalis who would have fallen into these categories saw no advantage in becoming part of the caste system, and simply retained their ethnic affiliations. Those whose professions would have branded them as untouchables – principally leather-workers (Sarki), blacksmiths (Kami) and tailors (Damai) – obviously did the same. To orthodox Hindus these **occupational castes** still carry the threat of ritual pollution, but untouchability of the kind seen in India isn't observed in Nepal's more open social order. Traditionally the importance of the work performed by these castes largely offset their lowly status, but nowadays their wares are increasingly being marginalized by mass-produced items. Typically landless and uneducated, many are turning to tenant farming, portering and day-labouring to make ends meet.

A more direct walking route to Panauti from Dhulikhel leaves from just behind the statue in the main square, passing through terraced fields and the village of Chaukot before joining the paved Banepa–Panauti road after about an hour. It's then another hour's walk along the road to Panauti.

Accommodation

In busy times you'd be wise to book ahead for a room, or arrive early in the day, as Dhulikhel's accommodation market is volatile. Facilities in the budget range are modest, but a handful of fancy new hotels are leading a general move upmarket.

In 1990 Dhulikhel had just one **budget** lodge; in 1996 it had eight (only five of which are worth mentioning). None of the newcomers quite measures up to the trusty *Dhulikhel Lodge* – going strong since 1970. Dhulikhel's more **expensive** lodgings are all positioned along the highway to take advantage of the views – all can arrange transport from Kathmandu, as well as activities such as hiking, rafting and excursions to the Tibet border. For locations of accommodation options, refer to the "Dhulikhel" and "Around Dhulikhel" maps.

BUDGET LODGES

Dhulikhel Lodge, just off the main square (☎011/61114). Run by a large and likeable Shrestha family, it boasts peaceful garden seating, a retro-1960s dining room (cushions on the floor, leave your shoes at the door), passable food, hot running water and a phone (international calls possible) – but no view. ②.

Hotel Gauri Shankar Mountain View, on the main highway (Kathmandu office: ☎220645). Excellent views from from the patio and the upstairs dining room, nice gardens and hot running water. ④/B⑤.

Nawaranga Guest House, about 500m east of the main square (☎011/61226). Tolerable food, but uninviting rooms, and only one bathroom in the whole place (hot water by the bucket). Partial view from the roof. ②.

Panorama Guest House, near the Kali temple (no phone). Big new place in an improbable location: dynamite views, but getting there is a hassle. The cheaper common-bath rooms are in the primitive old building (hot water by the bucket); rooms in the new building have hot running water. ③/B⑤.

Snow View Lodge, 1km east of the main square (☎011/61229). Quieter and greener than other guest houses in this vicinity. No view, but it's relatively close to the Kali temple viewpoint. Hot running water. ③/B⑥.

MODERATE AND EXPENSIVE HOTELS

Dhulikhel Lodge Resort (Kathmandu office: ☎212988). Well-managed, tasteful architecture and grounds. B⑧.

Dhulikhel Mountain Resort (Kathmandu office: ☎428774). Very scenic, private grounds with individual cottages, but nowhere near Dhulikhel – it's 4km east along the highway (off the map). B⑨.

Hill Corner Resort. Scheduled to open in 1996. Will be B⑦.

Himalayan Horizon Hotel Sun-N-Snow (Kathmandu office: ☎225092). Attractive Newar-style buildings, spectacular back terrace. B⑧.

Himalayan Mountain Resort (☎011/61158). Garden and views, 4km east of Dhulikhel on the highway (off map). ③/B⑦.

Royal East Inn. New place with a great garden and nice rooms. ⑥/B⑦.

Woodlands Mountain Tower Resort (Kathmandu office: ☎220123). Under construction in early 1996. Will be five-star, with a revolving tower restaurant. Expected to be B⑨.

Eating and other practicalities

Dhulikhel has no tourist **restaurants**, other than those attached to guest houses and hotels. Of the cheapies, *Dhulikhel Guest House* does the best food, though the *Nawaranga* and others nearby have convenience going for them if you're looking for breakfast or lunch after a hard morning's mountain-viewing. Any of the hotel restaurants would be worth a splurge. For simple Nepali fast food, try the places around the bus park, or in the bazaar area east of the *Nawaranga*.

There's a **bank** just off the highway at the east end of town (Sun–Thurs 10.30am–2pm, Fri 10am–noon).

To Jiri and the Tibet border

Traffic along the **Arniko Highway** (Arniko Rajmarg) drops off drastically beyond Dhulikhel. Built by the Chinese in the mid-1960s – to India's great distress – the road was once a busy conduit for lorry loads of Chinese goods by way of Lhasa, but landslides north of the border have slowed trade to a trickle. Tour groups heading into Tibet follow the Arniko Highway to Kodari, the only official crossing from Nepal. However, the vast majority of travellers passing this way are bound for Jiri, the starting point of treks in the Everest region, located on a punishing side road off the Arniko Highway.

There are no scheduled tourist bus services on either of these routes. If you're heading from Kathmandu to the border, try for an express **bus** to Kodari (2 daily; 9hr), but you may have to settle for Tatopani (2 daily; 9hr) or Barhabise (every half hour; 7hr) and make connections from there. Four buses a day go directly to Jiri, a wretched journey taking anything up to thirteen hours – be wary if stowing luggage on the roof, as there have been many reports of thefts. All buses serving these routes depart from Kathmandu's City Bus Park (you can try getting on at Bhaktapur or Dhulikhel, but don't expect to get a seat). There are no views of the

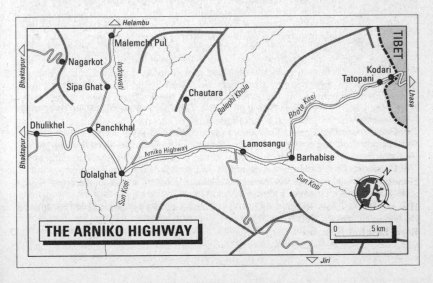

THE ARNIKO HIGHWAY

high peaks along the Arniko Highway past Dhulikhel, and only fleeting ones from the Jiri road.

After Dhulikhel, the road drops 600m into the broad Panchkhal Valley, a lush, irrigated plain cultivated with rice paddy, sugar cane and tropical fruits. The village of **Panchkhal** is a minor gateway to the Helambu trekking region: an unpaved road, served by local buses, heads north to the trailhead of Malemchi Pul. The highway reaches its lowest (and hottest) point 29km beyond Dhulikhel at **Dolalghat** (634m), a small market town clumped at either end of the bridge across the impressively vast and braided Indrawati River. Rafting parties put in here for the ten-day trip on the Sun Kosi, which joins the Indrawati just around the corner. **Chautara**, high on a ridge to the north and served by direct buses from Kathmandu, is an alternate trailhead for Helambu treks and the headquarters of a big Australian reforestation project.

The scenery changes abruptly after Dolalghat, as the highway bends northeast-wards up the deep, terraced **Sun Kosi Valley**. Nepal's terraces, while they're marvellous feats of engineering, are a sign of agricultural desperation: with so little flat land available and a growing number of mouths to feed, hill people have no choice but to farm ever steeper and less productive slopes. Terraces make

---

TAMANGS

Tamangs dominate Nepal's central hills between about 1500m and 2000m and constitute, numerically, the country's largest ethnic group: about one in every five Nepalis is a Tamang. The tribe is thought to have originated in Tibet and migrated south in prehistoric times, which accounts for their Mongoloid features but leaves the significance of their name, which means "horse trader" in Tibetan, intriguingly unexplained. Tamangs follow a form of Buddhism virtually indistinguishable from Lamaism – religious texts are even written in Tibetan script – but they also worship clan deities, employ *jhankri* (shamans) and observe major Hindu festivals.

Despite their numbers, Tamangs are one of Nepal's most **exploited** peoples, and have been ever since the Gorkhali conquest of the late eighteenth century. Geography has been the Tamangs' downfall. The new rulers of Nepal, requiring land to grant to their victorious soldiers, arbitrarily appropriated much of the vast Tamang homeland surrounding the Kathmandu Valley. Wrested from their lands, Tamangs became tenant farmers or bonded labourers for their new masters, or freelanced as porters or woodcutters. Many drifted down to the Kathmandu Valley, to fetch and carry for the new aristocracy. So efficiently did the Tamangs carry out these menial functions that the government came to view them as a strategic asset and prohibited them from serving in the Gurkha regiments. More recently, Tamangs are being deprived of another source of income – woodcutting – due to deforestation and the closing off of the Shivpuri Watershed.

Lacking land and opportunities, the Tamangs remain at the bottom rung of the economic ladder. They are the porters, the riksha wallahs, the cart-pullers of Kathmandu. They comprise an estimated 75 percent of the carpet industry's work force, and create many of the *thangka* and other "Tibetan" crafts sold in Nepal – for contract wages, of course. Tamang boys are lured to the capital to work as *kanchha* (tea boys), and Tamang girls are prime targets for brokers in the Indian flesh trade. Surveys show a disproportionate number of prison inmates in Nepal are Tamangs. A silent underclass in their own homeland, Tamangs often compare themselves to another displaced group, the Tibetans – only nowadays even the Tibetans are the Tamangs' bosses.

good farming and environmental sense – they stabilize the topsoil and form a stopgap against erosion on deforested slopes – but maintaining them is a tremendously labour-intensive chore that detracts from the actual business of growing food, and building more terraces inevitably brings about further deforestation.

The Jiri road

The **Jiri road** breaks off from the Arniko Highway at the 78-kilometre mark, passing close to a hydroelectric station built by the Chinese. The road climbs a merciless 1800m out of the Sun Kosi Valley, reaching an elevation of 2540m, then contours around two more small basins to the Newar pitstop of Charikot, from which it's a long descent to the Tamba Kosi (800m), another steep climb to a forested ridge (2500m) and finally a dip into the Jiri Valley at 1900m. Completed in 1985, the road was financed by the Swiss government to provide easier access to its long-term development works at Jiri. The presence of these Australian, Chinese and Swiss projects isn't unusual in the Nepalese hills, although as you approach the Everest region you'll be struck by how the most beautiful places often seem to attract the greatest number of aid workers.

Jiri

Once an insignificant hamlet, **JIRI** has somehow been singled out by fate and politicians to receive a booster shot of Western charity. Charlie Pye-Smith, in his book *Travels in Nepal* (see "Books" in *Contexts*), has called Jiri "the half-caste offspring of an impoverished Nepalese mother and a wealthy Swiss father". In 1958 the Swiss established the Jiri Multi-Purpose Development Project, a groundbreaking scheme based on the now widely accepted view that development needs – health, agriculture, education and so on – are interrelated and can't be tackled separately. The programme established a hospital, technical school, experimental farm and other facilities; most have since been handed over to HMG, and their subsequent deterioration raises troubling questions about development in Nepal (see *Contexts*). The road, in turn, has transformed Jiri into a busy little boomtown, where trucks constantly drop off supply shipments and porters assemble to carry them on to hill villages (it has all but put nearby **Those**, once the area's main bazaar and an important iron-smithing centre, out of business). Trekkers obviously add a few pennies to the local economy, although most are too eager to hit the trail or get back to Kathmandu to spend more than a night here.

At least a dozen **lodges** jostle on either side of the main street – *Cherdung Lodge and Valley Restaurant* (①) is comfortable enough, with a reasonable choice of food. Shops in the bazaar flog some trekker-oriented food and even rent clothing, although prices are naturally higher than in Kathmandu. Be sure to book **return bus tickets** from the booth on the main drag as soon as possible for the next day's departures, as seats go quickly.

To the border

Back on the Arniko Highway, 2km past the Jiri turning, **Lamosangu** (740m) is distinguished by a magnesite processing plant and a wasteland of castings. Soldiers sometimes ask to see foreigners' passports just beyond here, so bring yours even if you're not planning to cross the border. **Barhabise**, 8km north of Lamosangu, is as far as most buses from Kathmandu go. The highway and electricity have turned Barhabise, like Jiri, into an uncharismatic clutter of tall, slap-dash buildings and shops selling cassette tapes and readymade clothes. Several lodges let cheap rooms and serve noodles and *daal bhaat*. North of town you can visit a small mill producing traditional Nepali *lokta* paper, which is often confused with rice paper but is actually made from the bark of the native *daphne* bush. The permanent pavement ends north of Barhabise and the steep gradient to the border begins a few kilometres later. As dirt roads go, this one is pretty well-engineered, but it does its best to self-destruct with each monsoon. Afternoon rain is common up here, even in the dry season, and despite a general scarcity of trees near the river (here called the **Bhote Kosi**), everything is intensely green, with waterfalls splashing down cliff faces at every turn. The gorge is much deeper than it looks from the road.

Buses and minibuses make sporadic runs from Barhabise to Tatopani, 23km further on. Most passengers are bound for Khasa (Zhangmu), the first town in Tibet, which is as far as Nepalis can go without travel documents, to do a little innocent **smuggling**. They return the same day, after dark, laden with milk powder, Chinese training shoes and bolts of linen – all cheaper on the Tibetan side – and attempt to sneak them past the customs checkpost just south of Tatopani. Chinese brandy is also a good buy at the border, as it is highly sought-after in Kathmandu and makes a welcome gift if you've got friends there.

Tatopani

Until the mid-1980s, **TATOPANI** (1530m) enjoyed a small following among Westerners, who came to gaze into forbidden Tibet and soak in the village's hot springs (*taato paani* means "hot water"), but it has fallen out of fashion now that Tibet is open and the Arniko Highway has gone to hell. It remains a quiet, relaxing place – probably too dull for most, but a real find if you're into offbeat locales.

The village stretches along the highway for at least a kilometre, in two parts. Tamangs are in the majority at this altitude, and they maintain a small **gompa** five minutes' walk above the southern bazaar. The building is modest, but it looks out on a fine view of the valley and, up at the head of it, a smidgen of Tibet. The **hot springs** are at the northern end of the village, behind a wooden entrance and down steps towards the river. A hot tub it's not: the water splashes out of pipes into a concrete pool and is used strictly for washing. If you take the waters, remember that nudity offends in Nepal.

Western menus have virtually disappeared, but a few **lodges** limp on from the good old days. *Sonam Lodge* and *Tibet Lodge* (both ①), at the north end, are prob-ably the best. Hints of China's nearness are everywhere: you'll see chopsticks and Thermos flasks in every kitchen, and some places even sell Chinese beer.

Buses to Kathmandu originate at Kodari (see below) and so are often full by the time they reach Tatopani. To be sure of a seat, buy a ticket at the Kodari booking office the day before.

Kodari and the border

Disabuse yourself of any visions of high, snowy passes into Tibet. The border village of **KODARI** (1640m), 3km on from Tatopani, is just another bedraggled roadside bazaar at the bottom of a deep valley, with nary a yak in sight. The lowest point along the Nepal–Tibet border, Kodari has always been the preferred crossing for traders between Kathmandu and Lhasa. Its balmy elevation isn't as extraordinary as it might seem, though: the main Himalayan chain, which the border generally follows, is breached in several places by rivers that are older than the mountains themselves (the watershed, in fact, runs not along the highest peaks but as much as 100km to the north). In the case of Kodari, the border was actually shifted further south after an ill-advised war with Tibet in 1792.

Shared **taxis** ply between Tatopani and Kodari, and in good weather two **buses** a day make it up here from Kathmandu. Another long, drawn-out bazaar, Kodari is the Nepali equivalent of a service strip along a highway bypass, while old Kodari, a scattered village with a small *gompa*, perches on the ridge above. **Accommodation** is available at a few lodges along the road, the cleanest being *Lhasa Guest House* (②). Tatopani is the better bet, but if you're crossing into Tibet you'll want to stay here to get an early start.

The border is marked by the so-called **Friendship Bridge**, which spans the Bhote Kosi at the top end of town, guarded at either end by lackadaisical Nepali and Chinese soldiers. Up at the head of the valley, 600m higher than Kodari, the Chinese buildings of **Khasa** (or **Zhangmu**) cling to the side of a mountain – that's the extent of the view of Tibet from here.

Should you be **crossing the border**, the 9km between the Kodari and Khasa immigration posts is a no-man's-land which, when the road isn't washed out, will be traversed by some sort of shuttle vehicle. When the road is closed, you'll have to walk; you can hire a porter to carry your pack for about Rs150. If you were wondering how all that pink Chinese toilet paper gets to Kathmandu, here's your answer. Remember that Tibet is two hours and fifteen minutes ahead of Nepal, so you have to set off early to catch the bank in Khasa before it closes.

If you're entering Nepal from Tibet, set off from Khasa as early as possible, as it's a very full day's journey to Kathmandu. If you miss the direct Kodari–Kathmandu bus you'll probably have to take a taxi to Tatopani and then a bus to Barhabise, where there are more frequent connections. Better yet, *don't* go straight to Kathmandu: spend a night or two in Dhulikhel or Bhaktapur, which are much pleasanter places to wind down after China.

The Trisuli road

One of Nepal's earliest forays into road-building, the **Trisuli Road** was constructed in the mid-1960s as part of a hydroelectric project on the Trisuli River, northwest of Kathmandu. That's the official story, anyway, although the road probably owes its existence as much to historical nostalgia as progress: the route retraces the triumphal approach of Prithvi Narayan Shah, founding father of Nepal, from his fortress of Nuwakot to the Kathmandu Valley two centuries ago. It's since been extended north to a mining area in the Ganesh Himal. The majority of travellers passing this way are only concerned about getting to Dhunche, the usual starting point for treks to Langtang and Gosainkund, yet Nuwakot is sorely underrated as a stopover, and Kakani makes a serviceable destination in itself.

Nine express **buses** a day go from Kathmandu to Trisuli (4hr) and two to Dhunche (8hr). The road is slow and laborious: its endless zigzagging, potholes, fords and light traffic are all better appreciated on a **bike**.

Kakani

KAKANI (*Kaa*-kuh-nee), the closest mountain viewpoint to Kathmandu, straddles the valley's northwest rim at an elevation of 2070m. Like Nagarkot, Kakani is

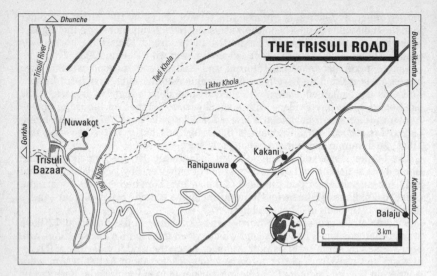

essentially a tourist invention, as opposed to a town, with mountain views and not much else. It's less developed than Nagarkot and the views are somewhat inferior, but it makes a nice halt along the Trisuli Road, particularly if you're biking.

Trisuli-bound **buses** drop you off at a gap in the valley rim, 24km from Kathmandu. From there, follow the paved road to the right for 3km (there are shortcuts), passing a large army barracks en route. In the days of Prithvi Narayan Shah, the Kakani pass was the Kathmandu Valley's Achilles' heel – by controlling it, he was able to besiege the valley for two years – but this hilltop post, like the one at Nagarkot, now seems a quaint throwback to the days of hand-to-hand combat.

Limited **accommodation** has for many years made Kakani a marginal destination. As of early 1996, Kakani's main place to stay was still the *Kakani Tara Gaon Resort* (☎290812; B⑦), discounts for stays of more than one night), just beyond the army base. It's fairly run-down and unwelcoming, but features a marvellous back lawn where you can lounge like a sahib, with the Ganesh and Langtang Himals splashed across the horizon and the Likhu Khola coursing through the valley 1000m below. *Bhanjyang Abode Restaurant*, located at the junction of the Trisuli and Kakani roads, has a couple of rooms that are similarly overpriced (⑤). However, competition may soon arrive in the form of at least two new guest houses – *Gorkha Resort* and *Kakani Hill Resort* – planned for sites along the ridge just below the *Tara Gaon*. For **food**, the *Tara Gaon* and the *Bhanjyang Abode* serve palatable lunches.

Other than the mountains, Kakani is short on sights. The yellow building next door to the *Tara Gaon* is the former British Resident's bungalow, whose grounds once boasted a miniature golf course. During the Rana era, when Residents were prohibited from travelling outside the Kathmandu Valley, this was their window on the rest of Nepal. Occupying a high point further to the east, the Kakani Memorial Park honours those who died in a 1992 airliner crash north of here.

From Kakani you can **walk back** to Balaju in three or four hours. Follow the dirt road east from Kakani past an agricultural station, then bear right and contour beneath the ridge before bending south and down along a spur. After passing a set of stupas, look for a fork to the left leading to Dharamthali and Balaju. **By mountain bike**, you can ride down to Budhanilkantha, a half-day descent requiring a good bike. Head east past the agricultural station and keep to the ridge: you'll have to carry your bike for about 2km before joining the Shivpuri Watershed road, which contours down to Budhanilkantha (see p.150). You may have to pay Rs250 to enter the watershed.

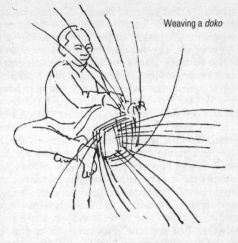

Weaving a *doko*

Trisuli Bazaar

TRISULI BAZAAR (540m) is just 17km from Kathmandu as the crow flies, but 70km – and a good four hours – as the bus crawls. Curled at the bottom of a deep, subtropical (and once malarial) valley, it was put on the map by the construction of the Trisuli River hydroelectric project and flourished for a time as the trailhead for Langtang treks. The development bandwagon has moved on, and nowadays most trekkers don't stop in Trisuli for longer than it takes to swill a bottle of Coke and get back on the bus to Dhunche. Indeed, there's little to see in this ramshackle township, with the possible exception of the old, stair-stepped **bazaar** (reached through a passage at the west end of the bridge) and a small **stupa** perched above the opposite bank. That said, staying overnight at Trisuli permits a visit to nearby Nuwakot, which, if you find yourself with an extra day at the end of a trek, is a good deal more enjoyable than killing time in Dhunche or returning to Kathmandu early. The trek to Gorkha and Pokhara begins here, following the lovely Samri Khola to the west.

For **accommodation**, a gaggle of trekking-standard lodges on the west side of the river offer ① rooms, or you can move up to *Hotel Trisuli*, which is very clean and has a nice little garden (③/B④; dorm beds ①). To return to Kathmandu, ticket offices for both private and *Sajha* **buses** are located across the street from the lodges (*Sajha* buses are faster).

Nuwakot

One of Nepal's proudest historical monuments, Prithvi Narayan Shah's abandoned fortress looms like a forgotten shipwreck on a ridge above Trisuli, casting a poignant, almost romantic spell over the tiny village of **NUWAKOT**. The **walk** from Trisuli takes less than an hour, although the trail is a tad tricky to find: climb a flight of steps from the water tap near the east side of the Trisuli Bazaar bridge to the Dhunche Road, walk up the road for about two minutes and make a right at the first group of houses. The path becomes wide and eroded as it climbs through a spindly forest of *sal* trees – the trees are coppiced for animal fodder – and reaches Nuwakot on the crest of a ridge about 300m above the valley floor. To **cycle**, take the dirt road that leaves the main road about 1km south of Trisuli.

The **fortress** stands to the right as you enter the village, consisting of three brick towers rising like Monopoly hotels within a walled compound. The tallest one is open to the public, though you may have to track down the caretaker to unlock it for you. The views from the top-floor windows are stupendous, looking out on Ganesh Himal and the pastoral Trisuli and Tadi valleys.

It was from this command centre that **Prithvi Narayan Shah**, the unifier of Nepal, directed his dogged campaign on the Kathmandu Valley from 1744 to 1769, and gazing out through these windows you can gain some insight into the mind of this obsessive but brilliant military tactician. In his determination to conquer the valley, Prithvi Narayan had **three other towers** built in the name of the three valley capitals, perhaps hoping to bring about their downfall by a kind of voodoo; the Kathmandu and Patan towers share the main compound, while the crumbling Bhaktapur tower stands on a rise just outside. After Kathmandu's fall, Nuwakot had just one more moment in the limelight. In 1792, attempting to extend Nepal's territory into Tibet, Prithvi Narayan's successor pushed his luck too far and was driven all the way back to Betrawati, the next village north of Trisuli. In the resulting **peace treaty**, signed at Nuwakot, Nepal ceded to Tibet the lucrative trading posts of Kyirong (north of Trisuli) and Khasa (north of Kodari), accounting for two southward lunges in the border that remain to this day.

Nuwakot's old main street runs south from the fortress along the spine of the ridge and suddenly dead-ends, the land falling away to reveal a vast **panorama** of the Tadi and Trisuli valleys. In the late eighteenth century, when Nuwakot enjoyed a brief flowering as the winter residence of the Kathmandu court, the houses along this boulevard must have looked considerably posher. The only building of note now is a two-tiered **Bhairabi Mandir**, which hosts a festival in honour of Bagh Bhairab in April.

On to Dhunche

Beyond Trisuli the road is unpaved, steep and agonizingly slow, buses taking four hours to cover this 40km stretch (you may prefer to close your eyes as the bus negotiates some of the switchbacks). Foreigners must show trekking permits at a couple of different army posts above Trisuli.

The road has replaced what used to be the first two days of the Langtang trek, and **DHUNCHE**, an unmemorable administrative centre, has boomed since its completion. Dhunche's guest houses are clustered around the main drag just past the town gate and are all ① – *Hotel Langtang View* has a good restaurant and hot water. To return to Kathmandu, make sure to book your seat as early as possible the day before.

The Tribhuwan Rajpath and Daman

Nepal's most magnificent and hair-raising highway, the **Tribhuwan Rajpath** (usually just called the Rajpath) heads west out of the Kathmandu Valley and then hurls itself, through an astounding series of switchbacks, straight over the

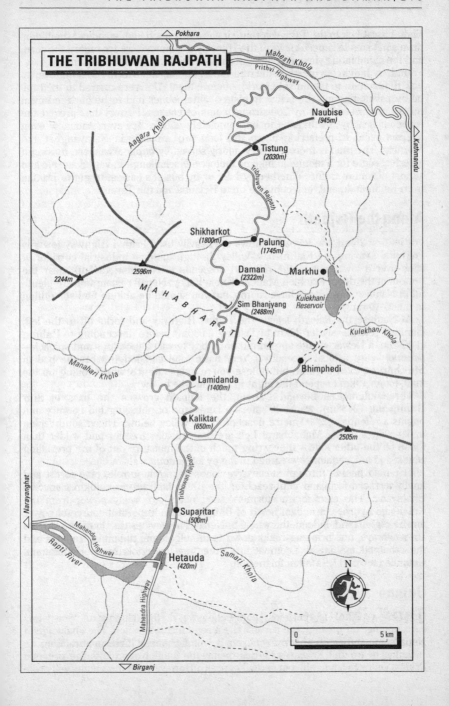

THE TRIBHUWAN RAJPATH

△ Pokhara

Mahesh Khola

Prithvi Highway

Naubise
(945m)

△ Kathmandu

Tistung
(2030m)

Tribhuwan Rajpath

Aagara Khola

Shikharkot
(1800m)

Palung
(1745m)

Daman
(2322m)

Markhu

2596m

2244m

M A H A B H A R A T   L E K

Sim Bhanjyang
(2488m)

Kulekhani
Reservoir

Kulekhani Khola

Manahari Khola

Lamidanda
(1400m)

Bhimphedi

Kaliktar
(650m)

2505m

Tribhuwan Rajpath

Narayanghat ◁

Suparitar
(500m)

Mahendra Highway

Rapti River

Hetauda
(420m)

Samari Khola

Mahendra Highway

N

0   5 km

▽ Birganj

Mahabharat Lek to the Tarai. En route it passes through lush stands of rhododendron and takes in superb views of the Himalaya. Mountain-bikers regard the road, and the culminating viewpoint of **Daman**, as something of a holy pilgrimage.

Built by Indian engineers in the mid-1950s, the Rajpath was the first highway to link Kathmandu to the outside world – before that, VIPs were carried to the capital by palanquin, and the prime ministers' automobiles had to be portered from India, fully assembled, by 200-strong teams of coolies. History has proved the route chosen by the Indians to be completely idiotic, however, and now even Nepalis avoid it, preferring to go the long way around via Narayanghat and Mugling. The road is therefore very poorly served by public transport, making it a perfect route for a mountain bike or motorcycle: challenging, varied, scenic and almost devoid of traffic. Whether by bike or by bus, it's easiest to get to Daman from Kathmandu and then continue on to Hetauda and the Tarai.

Along the Rajpath

For its first 26km, the Rajpath follows the heavily used Prithvi Highway towards Pokhara. Leaving the Kathmandu Valley through its most industrial corridor, it slips over a low point in the rim and descends to **Naubise** (945m), near the bottom of the deep, wrinkled Mahesh Khola Valley. Nepali restaurants are plentiful in Naubise; few places have rooms, but you should be able to find something in the ①–② range.

At Naubise the Rajpath leaves the Prithvi Highway and forks off to the left, climbing relentlessly for 30km to Tistung (2030m) before descending to **Palung** at 1745m, a Newar village spread out amid tidy terraces (potatoes and spinach – *paalung* – are a local speciality). Very basic food and lodging can be had in **Shikharkot**, 2km beyond, but unless you're desperate it's worth toiling up the final, tough 10km to spend the night in Daman (see below).

Three kilometres beyond Daman, the Rajpath crosses the pass of **Sim Bhanjyang** (2488m), where it enters a landscape of plunging hill country and begins a relentless, 2000-metre descent to the valley below. These south-facing upper slopes of the Mahabharat Lek are dramatically greener and wilder than those on the other side – they wring much of the moisture out of the prevailing winds, and are frequently wreathed in fog by afternoon.

The road passes through successive zones of mossy jungle, pine forest and finally terraced farmland until reaching the Bhimphedi turning, 40km from Sim Bhanjyang. The electric transformers seen near here relay power from the Kulekhani hydroelectric dam north of Bhimphedi, an important source of power for the region, and, indeed, the whole of Nepal. The devices that look like ski lifts are ropeways, one bringing rocks down to the big cement plant in Hetauda and the other taking finished cement and other raw materials up to Kathmandu. Hetauda (see p.311) is 10km further on.

Daman

DAMAN (2322m) is the most comprehensive of the Himalayan viewpoints surrounding Kathmandu, but it's also the most difficult to reach. The challenge of getting to it, and getting back down from it, is in fact one of its main attractions.

Sitting below the Rajpath's highest point, the hamlet overlooks the peaceful Palung Valley to a magnificent spread of peaks. However, the mountains will probably be in clouds when you arrive: an overnight stay is obligatory to see them in their best morning light. Bring a sleeping bag in winter, unless you've got reservations at the deluxe *Everest Panorama Resort*.

Getting there

The most useful and reliable (but unfortunately very local) **buses** to Daman are those operated by the *Sajha* cooperative. Plying the Rajpath in both directions, they depart simultaneously from

Technical difficulties

Hetauda and Kathmandu (Bhimsen Tower) at 7am, arriving at Daman by around 10am and noon respectively. Book early the day before, as seats on these buses go quickly. At least two private bus companies also provide services along the Rajpath through Daman, but their schedules are sporadic and prone to change. Another problem is that they break the journey up into two days, overnighting either in Markhu or Shikharkot (see map), which means that if you're coming from Kathmandu you won't get to Daman until the next morning. Departures tend to be around midday, but verify this at the Kathmandu or Hetauda main bus station.

If you're **cycling** from Kathmandu, you'll definitely want to skip the Kathmandu–Naubise stretch, which is horrendously busy with trucks and buses – take any bus bound for Pokhara or the Tarai and throw the bike on the roof. Naubise to Daman involves two separate climbs totalling 1700m of vertical gain – an exhilarating but (make no mistake about it) shattering all-day ride. Cycling up from Hetauda is an even more macho climb, gaining 2000m. An easier option is to bus up and pedal back down, but note that *Sajha* buses can't take bikes; coming from Kathmandu, take the bus to the Markhu turning or Shikharkot and pedal the final 500m ascent. Heads up for approaching vehicles, as the road is narrow and many corners are blind.

The village and around

A signboard announces you're in Daman, but blink and you'll miss it. The village consists of a loose gathering of houses, a couple of agricultural research facilities, a seismic station and – its one unmissable landmark – an enclosed **view tower** that looks as if it might have been built for air traffic control purposes. Operated by the adjacent *Daman Mountain Resort*, the tower offers the best views in the village (admission Rs20 for non-guests). Tourism boosters claim you can see seven 8000-metre peaks from here, which may be stretching it, but certainly Annapurna, Manaslu, Shisha Pangma and the distant plume of Everest are visible, along with the closer and hence more prominent 7000-metre peaks of Himalchuli, Ganesh Himal and Langtang. A couple of high-powered telescopes give awesome close-ups of the peaks: from this angle, the magnified view of Everest is almost identical to the one you get from Kala Pattar, ten days into the Everest trek. The view from the tower also gives you a good feel for the topography of the central hills and the Kathmandu Valley, from Phulchoki to the Trisuli Valley.

An even more sweeping (though unmagnified) vista can be had from the *Everest Panorama Resort*, a twenty-minute walk up the Rajpath, which also happens to be a fine spot for breakfast or lunch. One hairpin turn below the

Everest Panorama, a signposted path winds through oak and rhododendron forest to a Buddhist **gompa** in another twenty minutes. Run by a Bhutanese lama, the monastery is small and unembellished, but the view from its meditation perch is awesome.

Practicalities

Daman lacks the facilities for travellers that other viewpoints such as Nagarkot and Dhulikhel have. For **accommodation**, there's not much choice, and all of it is expensive for what you get. At the budget end, *Hotel Sherpa & Hill Side* (③) is little more than trekking digs: cold water, *daal bhaat* and not much English. If that's full, the truckers' haunts just downhill from the view tower should be able to put you up in rustic style. At the pricier *Dhulikhel Mountain Resort* (⑥), accommodation is in safari-style tents – as tents go they're cushy, with beds, electricity and hot water, but you still have to go outside to use the bathroom and it's really pretty cold sleeping in a tent at this elevation in winter. If you really want to go in style, book into the *Everest Panorama Resort* (Kathmandu office: ☎415372), 2km above Daman, where you can participate in organized activities ranging from hiking and rock climbing to pony riding and fishing. Rooms with central heating are B⑨, thatched-hut tents ⑧, and basic tents ⑦.

In all likelihood, you'll **eat** wherever you're staying. Besides the guest houses, the only other source of sustenance is *Hotel Daman*, a nightspot-cum-truckstop just down from the view tower.

Moving on

Leaving Daman by public transport can be difficult, as **buses** passing through are standing room only, and standing on a bus on this road is no fun. Sometimes they're so full they don't even stop. Getting to Kathmandu is further complicated by the fact that only the *Sajha* bus goes directly there, the others overnighting in Markhu or Shikharkot. Infrequent trucks take on passengers, but nearly all of them are heading south to Hetauda after delivering their cargo to Kathmandu (fully laden vehicles bound for Kathmandu take the safer Prithvi Highway).

These transport peculiarities make a good case for **walking** down instead. From Daman a trail descends to Markhu, on the western shore of the Kulekhani Reservoir, in three to four hours. From there you can catch a boat across the lake to Thulo Markhu, where there's basic lodging, and either catch a bus to Kathmandu the next morning or walk another full day to Pharping in the Kathmandu Valley (see p.174). A second option from Thulo Markhu is a two-day trek first to Chitlang and then to Thankot on the Prithvi Highway, from where it's a quick bus ride to Kathmandu.

Biking down, you'll probably just take the Rajpath. For a longer, more adventurous route to the Tarai, head north along the Rajpath 5km beyond the Palung bridge and turn right onto a graded unpaved road, which skirts the Kulekhani Reservoir, climbs over the Mahabharat Lek and descends to Bhimphedi before rejoining the Rajpath.

CHAPTER FOUR

THE WESTERN HILLS

The **western hills** are Nepal at its most outstandingly typical: roaring gorges, precariously perched villages and terraced fields reaching to unsupportable heights, with some of the most graceful and accessible peaks of the Himalaya for a backdrop.

In this, Nepal's most populous hill region, people are the dominant feature of the landscape. Magars and Gurungs, the most visible **ethnic groups**, live in their own villages or side by side with Tamangs, Hindu castes and the usual smattering of Newar merchants. Life is traditional and close to the earth, but relatively prosperous: the houses are tidy and spacious, and hill women are festooned with the family gold. The prosperity comes, indirectly, from an unlikely quarter, as the western hills were the original – and still are the most important – recruiting area for **Gurkha soldiers**. It's an often-quoted statistic that Gurkha salaries and pensions were, up until the mid-1970s, Nepal's biggest foreign-exchange earner; in many villages here they still are, and they're arguably the major source of development financing as well. Ex-Gurkhas command the highest respect within their communities, and young men look up to them as role models. They also speak English, happily, and wherever you go there will probably be an ex-Gurkha to help you over the language barrier.

History, too, figures prominently here, for the foundations of modern Nepal were laid in the western hills. While the kings of the Kathmandu Valley were building temples, the princes of the hills built forts – many of which still stand – and it's the hillmen who rule Nepal today.

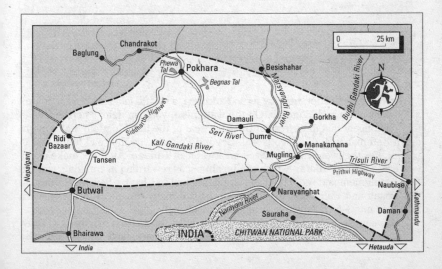

PUBLIC BUS SERVICES IN THE WESTERN HILLS

	Frequency (day)	Frequency (night)	Time (minimum)
To and from GORKHA			
Abu Khaireni	6		1hr
Birganj	4		7hr
Kathmandu	10#		5hr
Narayanghat	7		2hr 30min
Pokhara	2		5hr
Sunauli	1		7hr
To and from POKHARA			
Baglung	10		4hr
Biratnagar		1	18hr
Birganj	14	2	10hr
Butwal	17	8	7hr
Chandrakot	10		2hr
Dhangadhi		1	21hr
Gorkha	2		5hr
Janakpur		1	12hr
Kakarbitta		2	20hr
Kathmandu	21*#	14#	8hr
Narayanghat	12		4hr
Nepalganj		2	15hr
Sauraha/Chitwan	*		
Sunauli	6*	3	10hr
Tansen	3		6hr
To and from TANSEN			
Butwal	30		2hr
Kakarbitta		1	18hr
Kathmandu	1#	6	13hr
Pokhara	3		6hr
Ridi/Tamghas	6		2hr/6hr

* Tourist bus services also available – see p.246.
# *Sajha* service available.
Note: **Internal flights** from Pokhara are listed on p.246.

The chief destination here by far is **Pokhara**, a restful lakeside retreat as well as Nepal's major trekking hub. On the way there, you can detour northwards to the magnificent hilltop fortress of **Gorkha**, seat of the tiny kingdom that brought down Kathmandu and unified Nepal. Beyond Pokhara, on the road to the Indian border, lies the even less publicized backwater of **Tansen**. All three make excellent bases for **day hikes** – which can be almost as rewarding as trekking, without the commitment and red tape (treks are described in Chapter Seven). **Rafting** on the Trisuli and Kali Gandaki rivers also brings many travellers to the western hills (see pp.53–56 for river descriptions and advice).

Two main roads cut a swathe through the hills: the **Prithvi Highway** (Prithvi Rajmarg), running west from Kathmandu to Pokhara, and the **Siddhartha**

Highway (Siddhartha Rajmarg), which carries on from Pokhara to the Indian border. These and two spur roads (to Gorkha and Baglung) are literally the only paved roads in this region, and they're not always paved. Elsewhere, most journeys are made on foot – and you don't have to go far in this area to appreciate how blurred the distinction between "travelling" and "trekking" can be.

HEADING WEST: THE PRITHVI HIGHWAY AND GORKHA

If you take one of the **tourist buses** between Kathmandu and Pokhara you might think there's nothing worth stopping for en route, for there are few towns of any consequence along the 200-kilometre Prithvi Highway. Travelling by **local bus**, however, you get a healthy dose of roadside villages. **Biking** can't really be recommended, on account of all the traffic, though having your own wheels would allow you to explore a few offbeat sights along the way. Certainly the side trip to Gorkha makes a strong case for breaking the journey, even though it will mean giving up your seat on the bus.

Other activities might bring you in contact with the Prithvi Highway: **rafting** trips on the Trisuli River follow the road for about 50km, and **treks** around the Annapurna Circuit start on a side road from Dumre.

Along the Prithvi Highway

Bobbing and weaving through the heart of the hills, the **Prithvi Highway** (Prithvi Rajmarg) is most visitors' initiation into the pain and pleasure of Nepalese bus travel. You may find yourself on it several times, in fact, since besides linking Kathmandu and Pokhara it's also the first leg between either city and the Tarai. Mountain views are only intermittent, though, since the road careers along the bottom of deep valleys most of the way. Nepal's second trunk road when it was built by the Chinese in 1973, the Prithvi Highway has played a crucial role in modernizing the country, opening up the western hills and enabling Pokhara to develop into Nepal's second tourist city. More recently, the government and its foreign-aid bankers have rediscovered the highway's significance for industry as a link between Kathmandu and the Tarai, and have upgraded and widened it, at least as far as Mugling. Further progress is slow, though: much of the work is done by hand (you'll see crews of women and even children breaking up rocks for ballast), and every year the monsoon brings setbacks. Whenever you go, expect construction delays somewhere along the way.

After parting with the Tribhuwan Rajpath at Naubise (see p.216), the highway descends steadily along the south side of the Mahesh Khola, which soon joins the **Trisuli River**. Keep an eye out for magnificent, spidery suspension bridges and precarious ropeways spanning the Trisuli; you might also spot funeral pyres on the sandy banks, and rafting parties running the rapids. The high-water mark on the rocks shows how much the Trisuli, like all Himalayan rivers, swells and rages during the monsoon. The solid, three-storey farmhouses seen here generally belong to Bahuns and Chhetris, while the humbler mud-and-thatch huts are typical Tamang or Magar dwellings.

Tourist buses from Kathmandu make a mid-morning pitstop at **Malekhu** or **Kurintar**, quite developed roadside bazaars that specialize in fast food and provisions for foreigners. Nearby Charaundi and Fishling have facilities for rafters.

HILL CULTURE: GURUNGS AND MAGARS

Leavened with nothing but the water of God
Comes from Rumjatar the flour of millet pounded,
Gurungs have mastered the knowledge of God
And Brahmans are left astounded.

Nepali poet Jnandil (c.1821–83)

Hardy, self-sufficient peasant farmers, Gurungs and Magars are the "aboriginals" of the western hills. Both groups exhibit Mongoloid features and speak Tibeto-Burman dialects – signs that their ancestors probably migrated here from Tibet, though nobody's sure when. Together, they form the backbone of the Gurkha regiments (see p.250), and also account for a fair proportion of the Nepalese army.

Although **Gurungs** are a common sight around Pokhara, where many have invested their Gurkha pensions in guest houses and retirement homes, their homeland remains the middle elevations from Gorkha to the southern slopes of the Annapurna Himal (those living in the Gorkha area call themselves Ghale). The majority who don't serve in the military herd sheep for their wool, driving them to pastures high on the flanks of the Himalaya, and raise wheat, maize, millet and potatoes. Gurungs were once active trans-Himalayan traders, but the Chinese occupation of Tibet has put a damper on that, while other traditional pursuits such as hunting and honey-gathering are being encroached upon by overpopulation. Their unique form of **shamanism** is coming under pressure, too, as Hinduism advances from the south and Buddhism trickles down with Tibetan settlers from the north. Gurungs employ shamans to propitiate ghosts, reclaim possessed souls from the underworld, and guide dead souls to the land of their ancestors – rituals that contain clear echoes of "classic" Siberian shamanism and are believed to resemble those of the ancient Bon priests of pre-Buddhist Tibet. Some authorities see the ongoing power struggle between Tibetan lamas and Gurung shamans as a modern re-enactment of Buddhism's battle with Bon in seventh-century Tibet; in that instance, Buddhism won.

A somewhat less cohesive group, **Magars** are scattered throughout the lower elevations of the western hills (recently they've colonized parts of the eastern hills as well). A network of Magar kingdoms once controlled the entire region, but the arrival of Hindus in the fifteenth century brought swift political decline and steady cultural assimilation. Nowadays, after centuries of coexistence with Hindu castes, most employ Bahun *pujari* (priests) and worship Hindu gods just like their Chhetri neighbours, differing only in that they're not allowed to wear the sacred thread of the "twice-born" castes. Similarly, with farming practices, housing and dress, Magars are an adaptable lot and not easily distinguished from surrounding groups – the velvet blouses, coin necklaces and *pote* (thin strands of glass beads) worn by many Magar women, for instance, are also common to Gurungs and Chhetris. Even the Magar language varies from place to place, consisting of at least three mutually unintelligible dialects (most Magars speak Nepali). Despite the lack of unifying traits, however, group identity is still strong, and will probably remain so as long as Magars keep marrying only within the clan.

Mugling

Local buses and some tourist buses break for lunch at **MUGLING**, 110km from Kathmandu, whose wide main street and wood-fronted buildings give it the look of a wild-west town. Drivers get free meals for parking in front of certain **restaurants** – you can always check out the dozens of others, but there's little difference between one *daal bhaat* and another here. With buses coming and going twenty-four hours a day, Mugling would be an awful place to spend the night, and in any case only a few "hotels" have **rooms**. Names change often, but try *Naulo Hotel & Restaurant* or *Hotel New Bijay* (both ②),

Children swinging during the October Dasain festival

or splash out on *Motel du Mugling* (Kathmandu ☎01/225242; B⑦), located across the bridge and commanding a grandstand view of Mugling's latrines. At 280m, Mugling is the lowest point along the Prithvi Highway. Sugar cane is cultivated on a small scale around here, and you'll also see *simal*, a tall, angular Tarai tree that produces red flowers in February and pods of cotton-like seeds in May. Traffic bound for the Tarai turns left (south) at Mugling and continues along the Trisuli River, making the gradual 34-kilometre descent to Narayanghat (see p.282).

The Prithvi Highway crosses the Trisuli just past Mugling and heads upstream along the Marsyangdi River, passing the massive **Marsyangdi Hydroelectric Project** powerhouse 2km later. The dam and reservoir are 12km further on; water is diverted through a tunnel to the powerhouse and then channelled down to the turbines. Completed in 1990, the project is the single most expensive thing ever built in Nepal, costing $210 million of German, Saudi and World Bank money, and it generates nearly thirty percent of the country's electricity. (See "Development Dilemmas" in *Contexts* for a discussion of the problems surrounding hydroelectric development schemes.)

Manakamana

The spur road to Gorkha (see p.224) leaves the highway at **Abu Khaireni**, 7km west of Mugling and home to a big rubber factory. For a really off-the-beaten-track excursion, walk from here up to the hilltop holy site of **MANAKAMANA** (Maan-*kaam*-a-na), reached by a steep, 700-metre ascent that takes at least four hours up and back. The trail begins about 1km up the Gorkha road on the right, slipping through a gap in the bazaar and immediately crossing the Marsyangdi by footbridge. You can't get lost – just follow the tea stalls and puffing pilgrims. Every day hundreds make the journey to worship at Manakamana's **Bhagwati Mandir**, revered as one of Nepal's five great wish-fulfilling temples and especially popular with Newar newlyweds, who come to pray for sons. Morning animal sacrifices are an essential part of the ritual, and locals raise goats and chickens specifically for the sacrificial market. For Nag Panchami, in late July or early August, celebrants construct an entire shrine out of flowers and foliage. Visiting Manakamana is a very Nepali thing to do, and even if you don't sacrifice a goat you'll feel like you've received an initiation into the society.

Manakamana itself is a substantial little bazaar, with plenty of **lodgings** and **food**, electricity and bustle. It's far more pleasant and interesting to stay overnight here than in, say, Abu Khaireni. Options include *Malla Hotel* (②), *Manakamana Lodge* (②/B④, but still only cold water) and many others not advertised in English.

Dumre and Damauli

The views improve beyond Abu Khaireni: initially the closest peaks are Boudha and Himalchuli of the Manaslu Himal, while the Annapurna Himal takes over as you get closer to Pokhara. Trekkers tackling the Annapurna Circuit usually get off at **DUMRE** (450m), a drab roadside bazaar 18km past Mugling, and continue north to Besisahar by bus. If you're cycling from Kathamandu to Pokhara, this would be a marginally quieter place to stay than Mugling. *New Manaslu Guest House* and *Hotel Chhim Keshori* (both ①) are two of many trekkers' inns left over from Dumre's heyday as a trailhead.

West of Dumre, the hills get gentler and more heavily cultivated. It's 8km uphill and another 8km down from Dumre to **DAMAULI** (350m), a nondescript administrative town overlooking the confluence of the Madi and Seti rivers. A paved road runs south from the highway for 1km to the sadhu hangout of **Byas Gupha**, a cave where Byas (or Vyasa), the sage of the *Mahabharat*, is supposed to have been born and lived. One of the temples contains a life-size statue of Byas. After traversing the Madi, the highway rises and then descends gradually to rejoin the broad Seti Valley, finally reaching Pokhara 54km from Damauli.

FARMING IN THE HILLS

Most Nepalis live in countryside like that seen along this stretch of the Prithvi Highway, and the **farming** methods practised here are fairly representative of those employed throughout the hills. The land is used intensively but sustainably: trees and bamboo are pruned for fodder; livestock, fed on fodder, pull ploughs and provide milk and manure; and manure, in turn, is dolloped onto the fields as fertilizer (and used as fuel at higher elevations). Goats, chickens and pigs recycle scraps into meat and eggs, and even pariah dogs are tolerated because they eat faeces.

Nepali hill farmers have a harder go of it than their Tarai counterparts (see p.281): the average hill family's half-hectare holding is fragmented into several plots located at different elevations, often a half-hour or more apart. The typical household owns only simple hand tools – its only beast of burden a buffalo or ox – and grows just seventy percent of the food it needs each year. Most farmers barter surplus grain for odd essentials such as salt, sugar, pots and pans, and have little to do with the cash economy, though growing numbers near the highway are starting to raise vegetables for sale. Several research stations in this area are experimenting with improved seeds, but tractors and chemical fertilizers will probably never be appropriate for the vast majority of farms in Nepal's hills.

Gorkha

Despite being midway between Kathmandu and Pokhara, **GORKHA** (Gor-*kaa*) remains strangely untouristed, probably because of the longstanding difficulty of

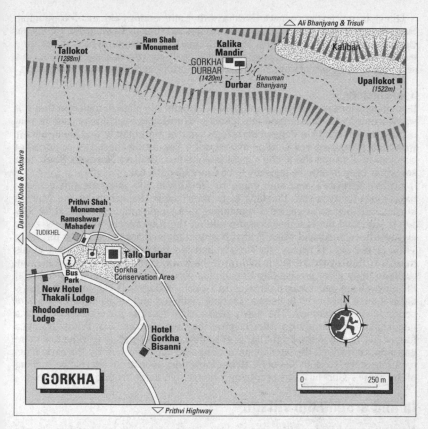

Map labels:
△ Ali Bhanjyang & Trisuli
Ram Shah Monument
Kalika Mandir
Kaliban
Tallokot (1288m)
GORKHA DURBAR (1420m)
Hanuman Bhanjyang
Durbar
Upallokot (1522m)
Daraundi Khola & Pokhara
Prithvi Shah Monument
Rameshwar Mahadev
TUDIKHEL
Tallo Durbar
Gorkha Conservation Area
Bus Park
New Hotel Thakali Lodge
Rhododendrum Lodge
Hotel Gorkha Bisanni
GORKHA
N
0 — 250 m
▽ Prithvi Highway

getting there. However, the surfacing of the 24-kilometre road up from Abu Khaireni now means it's a relatively painless half-day's ride from Pokhara, Kathmandu or Chitwan. The government is devoting a large chunk of its tourism budget to sprucing up Gorkha's monuments, and there seems to be some vague notion of putting the town on the tourist map. But for the time being, at least, Gorkha is suspended in a happy halfway state, with just enough basic facilities to get by, yet still primitive enough to keep the crowds away.

Cradle of a nation and the ancestral home of the Nepalese royal family, Gorkha occupies a central place in Nepalese history. The village itself is minuscule, but hunched on the hilltop above is its link with that splendid past, the **Gorkha Durbar**, an architectural tour de force worthy of the flamboyant Gorkha kings and the dynasty they founded. Unless you're setting straight off on a trek or just finishing one (the Pokhara–Trisuli trail passes through Gorkha), you'll have to spend the night here. Think about staying longer: the Durbar and environs could easily soak up a day, and hikes around the area could keep you busy for another day or two. The hill climate is agreeable, the pace is easy and, for the moment at least, there's not an apple pie or pizza in sight.

Direct **bus** services connect Gorkha with Kathmandu, Pokhara, Narayanghat, Sunauli and Birganj (see p.220 for frequencies and times). Coming from Chitwan, catch the Birganj-originating bus at Tadi Bazaar. All buses terminate at Gorkha's modest bus park at the lower edge of the village. If you're pedalling, note that it's a serious 900-metre ascent from Abu Khaireni to Gorkha, and it gets steeper as you go.

Some history

In a sense, Gorkha's history is not its own. A petty hill state in medieval times, it was occupied and transformed into a sort of Himalayan Sparta by outsiders who used it as a base for a dogged campaign against Kathmandu and then, having won their prize, restored Gorkha to obscurity. Yet during those two centuries of occupation, it raised the nation's most famous son, **Prithvi Narayan Shah**, and somehow bred in him the audacity to conquer all of Nepal.

Prithvi Narayan's ancestors came to Gorkha in the mid-sixteenth century, having been driven into the hills from their native Rajasthan by the Muslim horde, and they soon gained a reputation as a single-mindedly martial lot. His father launched the first unsuccessful raid on the Kathmandu Valley in the early eighteenth century, and when Prithvi Narayan himself ascended to the throne in 1743, at the age of twenty, he already had his father's obsession fixed in his mind*. Within a year, he was leading Gorkha in a war of expansion that was eventually to unify all of present-day Nepal, plus parts of India and Tibet. Looking at the tiny village and meagre terraces of Gorkha today, you can imagine what a drain it must have been to keep a standing army fed and supplied for 27 years of continuous campaigning. The hardy peasants of Gorkha got little more than a handshake for their efforts. After conquering the valley in 1769, Prithvi Narayan moved his capital to the bright lights of Kathmandu, relegating Gorkha to a mere garrison from which the later western campaign was directed. By the early nineteenth century, Gorkha had been all but forgotten, even as an alternative spelling of the name – Gurkha – was becoming a household name around the world.

In and around the village

Nestled on a shelf beneath a steep ridge, most of the village stretches along a single main lane, with buildings huddled close together to save space for farming. To get there from the bus park you'll first walk past or through the **Gorkha Conservation Area Project**, a newly developed zone consisting of gardens, walkways, monuments, an information centre and other as-yet-unbuilt facilities. The one historic building actually conserved by the project is the old **Tallo Durbar** (Lower Palace). Built in around 1750, this imposing Newar-style edifice served as the kingdom's administrative headquarters, while the upper Durbar housed king and court. Seen from above, Tallo Durbar indeed looks like a mini-Pentagon. Its fine brick and woodwork is getting a slow facelift, and the building

---

*An odd legend confirms Prithvi Narayan's destiny, but also puts the scale of his accomplishment into perspective. When still a prince he was approached by an old man, who took the boy's hand and spat in it. The spittle turned to yoghurt and the man ordered Prithvi to eat it; the prince, not unreasonably, flung the curd on the ground at his feet. At that, the old man revealed himself to be Gorakhnath, the demigod protector of the Shah kings, and pronounced that Prithvi Narayan would go on to rule wherever he placed his feet – but had he eaten the curd, he could have ruled the world.

is eventually supposed to be opened up as a museum of Gorkha history spanning the generations of Shahs leading up to Prithvi Narayan.

The main road into the village leads past Gorkha's modest Tudikhel (parade ground) and a small temple precinct. The gilded figure kneeling atop a pillar facing the onion-domed **Rameshwar Mahadev Mandir** is Prithvipati Shah; an early Gorkha king, he established most of the temples and shrines still in use around the town, including the Kalika temple in the upper Durbar.

Gorkha Durbar

It's a brisk, 250-metre ascent to the **Gorkha Durbar** along the main trail from Pokharithok, the junction just east of Tallo Durbar (figure on half an hour). At the top of this route – once the royal approach to the palace – you can marvel at the massive front stairway that's one of the Durbar's most distinctive features, despite its recent restoration into a retaining wall. Pure ostentation or cheeky bluff, either way it must have cowed visiting vassals into submission – a neat trick for a tinpot realm that could barely muster 150 soldiers at the time of Prithvi Narayan's first campaign.

The climb repays itself with more than history. Set on the ridge crest, the Durbar looks out on a broad **panorama** of the Himalaya from Dhaulagiri to Ganesh Himal, with Boudha and Himalchuli of Manaslu Himal occupying centre stage. Although the warlike Gorkhalis picked the site for its strategic position, they can't have been unmoved by the scenery.

Conceived as a dwelling for kings and gods, the fortress remains a religious place, and first stop in any visit is the **Kalika Mandir**, probably the most revered shrine this side of Kathmandu. Occupying the left (western) half of the Durbar building, its interior is closed to all but priests and the king of Nepal (others would die upon beholding Kali's terrible image, say the priests). Plenty of action takes place outside, though: sacrifices are made in the alcove in front of the entrance, and during the twice-monthly observance of Astami, which is celebrated with special gusto in Gorkha, the paving stones are sticky with blood. Most worshippers arrive cradling a trembling goat or chicken and leave swinging a headless carcass. Chaitra Dasain, Gorkha's biggest annual **festival**, brings processions and more bloodletting in late March or early May, as does the tenth day of Dasain in October.

The east wing of the Durbar is the historic **palace**, site of **Prithvi Narayan's birthplace** and, by extension, the ancestral shrine of the Shah kings. This accounts for King Birendra's regular visits (his helipad is just west of the complex) and the government's spare-no-expense renovation of the Durbar's exceptional eighteenth-century woodwork. Though predating the Gorkhali conquest of Kathmandu, the palace bears the unmistakeable stamp of Newar craftsmanship: the Gorkhalis, who never pretended to have any art or architecture of their own, imported workmen from Kathmandu. Upstairs are said to be Prithvi Narayan's **throne** and an **eternal flame** that's been burning ever since he unified Nepal. Sentries discourage photography in the courtyard and bar the interior to all foreigners – a vandal could kick out the fire and cast a serious hex on Nepal's monarchy.

The remaining space within the fortress walls is fairly littered with other Hindu shrines. By the main entrance is a small temple built around the holy **cave of Gorakhnath**, the centre for worship of the shadowy Indian guru who gave Gorkha its name and is regarded as a kind of guardian angel by the Shah kings. Sadhus of

The Gorkha Durbar

the Gorakhnath cult are known as *kaanphata* ("split-ears"), after an initiation ceremony in which they insert sticks in their earlobes – which is a walk in the park compared to some of the other things they get up to in the name of their guru.

Upallokot and Tallokot

The notch in the ridge just east of Gorkha Durbar is known as **Hanuman Bhanjyang** (Hanuman Pass), after the valiant monkey king whose image guards the popular shady rest stop. Cross the main trail (a branch of the Pokhara–Trisuli porter route) and follow a steep, stone-paved path up the ridgeline. Just above the crossing is a vantage point where you can stand in the stone "footsteps" of Ram, hero of the *Ramayan* and Hanuman's best buddy, and snap a postcard picture of the Durbar.

From Hanuman Bhanjyang it's another half-hour hike to **Upallokot** (Upper Fort), a 1520-metre eyrie at the highest, easternmost point of the ridge. Except for the slight intrusion of a microwave relay tower, the panorama here is total. If you can manage it, sunrise is the best time to visit: to the east, the ridge abruptly plunges 500m to misty depths while the sun's first rays play across the peaks. Late afternoon is pretty special, too, as the sun slants behind the Durbar and fills the Daraundi Khola Valley to the west with a golden haze. From this angle, looking down the spine of the ridge, the Durbar looks like Nepal's answer to Mad Ludwig's castle. The one thing lacking is a sense of wilderness: nearly every hill and valley is cultivated and tamed, except for **Kaliban**, the forest covering the northern crest of the ridge. Spookily alive with rhesus monkeys, this sacred grove supplies wood for the Durbar's eternal flame. Upallokot itself is more a hut than a fort, its thatched roof long gone. The small walled pen contains an old grinding wheel and a set of stones laid out in the shape of a reclining human figure – obscure icons of Bhairab and Kali.

At the other end of the ridge stands **Tallokot**, a watch post with more limited views north and west. You can easily stroll there from the Durbar's front entrance, passing a small but active Kali temple and a new monument to Ram Shah, the seventh-generation ancestor of Prithvi Narayan Shah who is reckoned by some to have been the progenitor of the Shah title. A rough track descends directly from Tollokot to Gorkha, tripping down terraces past small clusters of farmhouses and the odd communal spring.

Longer walks

If that circuit whets your appetite for **longer walks**, there are two main options. The high road through Hanuman Bhanjyang descends gently for about an hour and a half to **Ali Bhanjyang** (shops), then ascends along a ridge with fabulous mountain views, reaching **Khanchok Bhanjyang** two and a half hours later. This would be about the limit for a day hike, but given an early start you could continue down to the subtropical banks of the Budhi Gandaki at **Arughat**, a long day's 20km from Gorkha, and find basic lodging there – at this point you'd be a third of the way to Trisuli. Other, less distinct trails from Upallokot and the Ram Shah monument take roundabout routes to Ali Bhanjyang. Alternatively, follow the main trail west out of Gorkha village, which reaches the untrammelled **Daraundi Khola Valley** after about an hour and a half. You could continue on for another three hours to **Khoplang**, a beautiful hill village with lodgings. You could even do a two-day loop: Gorkha to Khanchok Bhanjyang, from there down to the Daraundi at Ulte, head downstream to Chorkate, and then back up to Gorkha. For trekking from here, see Chapter Seven.

Practicalities

Finding **accommodation** in Gorkha is fairly straightforward. The best in town, but not by much, is *Hotel Gorkha Bisauni* (☎064/20107; ③/B④, dormitory beds ①), 400m back down the road from the bus park. Though the building is rather run-down, the garden is nice and the staff speak some English. It's also the only place in Gorkha that can provide hot water for washing, albeit by the bucket. *Gorkha Hill Resort* (☎064/20325; Kathmandu office: ☎227929; B⑧) is more luxurious, but inconveniently located 3km down the road. (Another midrange option may be in the offing, as the Gorkha Conservation Area Project's master plan calls for the construction of a "tourist lodge complex" near the Tudikhel.) If money's the only object, there are half a dozen dives near the bus park – the cleanest and quietest are *Rhododendrum Restaurant & Lodge* (②) and *New Hotel Thakali Lodge* (①), both located just west of the bus park.

For **food**, the choice is similarly limited. The *Gorkha Bisauni*'s little diner does reasonably good Western fare, including seasonal fresh vegetable soups. Plenty of places near the bus park serve up the usual *momo*, *thukpa* or all-you-can-eat *bhaat*.

CHAUTAARA

A uniquely Nepali institution, the **chautaara** is more than just a resting place – it serves important social and religious functions as well. Every hill village has its *chautaara*, and you'll find them at appropriate intervals along any reasonably busy trail. The standard design consists of a rectangular flagstoned platform, built at just the right height for porters easily to set down their *doko*, and sometimes a smaller platform atop that. Two trees planted in the earthen centre provide shade for all who gather underneath: passing strangers, old friends, couples, village assemblies.

Chautaara are erected and maintained by individuals as an act of public service, often to earn religious merit or in memory of a deceased parent. Commonly they'll be found on sites associated with animist deities, indicated by sindur-coloured stones. The trees, too, are considered sacred. Invariably, one will be a **pipal**, whose Latin name (*Ficus religiosa*) recalls its role as the bodhi tree under which the Buddha attained enlightenment. Nepalis regard the pipal, with its heart-shaped leaves, as a female symbol, and women will sometimes fast and pray before one for children, or for success for the children they already have. Its male counterpart is the **banyan** (*bar* in Nepali), another member of the fig genus that sends down Tarzan-vine-like aerial roots which, if not pruned, will eventually take root and establish satellite trunks. A *chautaara* is incomplete without the pair; occasionally you'll see one with a single tree, but sooner or later someone will get around to planting the other.

POKHARA

The Himalaya form the highest, sheerest rise from subtropical base to icy peaks of any mountain range on earth, and nowhere is the contrast more marked than at **POKHARA** (pronounced *Poke*-rhuh). Sited at just 800m above sea level, it boasts a nearly unobstructed view of the 8000-metre-plus Annapurna and Manaslu *himal*, 25km north. Dominating the skyline, in beauty if not in height, is the double-finned summit of Machhapuchhre – "Fishtail" – only one of whose peaks is visible from Pokhara.

Basking in the view, Nepal's main "resort" area lolls beside the shore of **Phewa Tal** (Phewa Lake), well outside the actual town of Pokhara. This is Nepal's little budget paradise: carefree and culturally undemanding, though highly commercialized, with a steaks-and-cakes scene rivalling that of Kathmandu. Whatever you're looking for, it's a buyer's market here – everything comes so easily, the main challenge is sifting through the growing multitude of possibilities. New businesses pop up like mushrooms after each monsoon, and disappear just as quickly; cheap places have a habit of going upmarket, great views get blocked, and what's hot today may be dead tomorrow. No guidebook can hope to keep up with all the changes, so take all recommendations with a pinch of salt.

If you're spending more than a week in Nepal, chances are you'll touch down in Pokhara at some point. As the main destination served by tourist buses, it's usually the first place travellers venture to outside the Kathmandu Valley. For trekkers, Pokhara is the gateway to Nepal's most popular trails; for everyone else, it's the most beautiful place in Nepal that's accessible by public transport. Day trips around the Pokhara Valley beckon, and if the area is short on temples and twisting old alleys, you might find that a relief after Kathmandu's profusion. Despite its shallow hedonism – which definitely gets cloying after a while – Pokhara is an ideal place to recharge your batteries, especially after a trek, or time in India. By comparison, Kathmandu seems downright claustrophobic.

Because it's 500m lower than the capital, Pokhara is a better place to be in winter, but rather hot from April onwards. With lower foothills to the south, it's also less protected from the prevailing rains, and receives about twice as much precipitation as Kathmandu. Touring the valley, you'll be struck by the active, shaping presence of water everywhere: lakes and rivers are conspicuous features here, and the paddies are traced by canals of roiling mountain water.

Fittingly for a place that worships mammon, Pokhara's biggest annual event is a secular one designed purely to fill beds. Held in late March, the **Annapurna Festival** is dominated by sporting events such as a triathlon (swim across the lake, cycle around the valley and run up Sarangkot and back), marathon and boat race. Organizers plan to add folk music, dance, and ethnic cuisine demonstrations to the lineup.

Orientation and arrival

Pokhara's layout requires some explanation if you plan to do any sightseeing (an activity which, admittedly, isn't a top priority for most visitors here). To get your bearings, start with the tourist areas of **Lakeside** and **Damside**, set 1km apart on

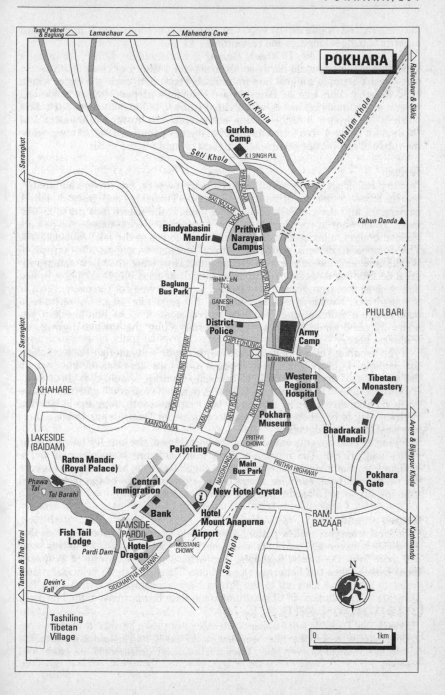

POKHARA

Tashi Palkhel & Baglung △ Lamachaur △ △ Mahendra Cave

Railechaur & Siklis

△ Sarangkot

Kali Khola

Bhalam Khola

Gurkha Camp
K I SINGH PUL

Seti Khola

BHIM BAZAAR

BAG BAZAAR

Kahun Danda ▲

Bindyabasini Mandir

Prithvi Narayan Campus

NADIPUR PATAN

PHULBARI

△ Sarangkot

Baglung Bus Park

BHIMSEN TOL

GANESH TOL

District Police

CHIPLEDHUNGA

Army Camp

MAHENDRA PUL

KHAHARE

POKHARA-BAGLUNG HIGHWAY

SIMAL CHAUR

MANSWARA

NEW ROAD

RATNA BAZAAR

Western Regional Hospital

Tibetan Monastery

△ Arwa & Bijaypur Khola

LAKESIDE (BAIDAM)

Pokhara Museum

Bhadrakali Mandir

Ratna Mandir (Royal Palace)

Paljorling

PRITHVI CHOWK

Phawa Tal
Tal Barahi

Central Immigration

NAGDHUNGA

Main Bus Park

PRITHVI HIGHWAY

Pokhara Gate

Bank

ⓘ New Hotel Crystal

RAM BAZAAR

Fish Tail Lodge

DAMSIDE (PARDI)

Hotel Mount Anapurna
Airport

△ Kathmandu

Pardi Dam

Hotel Dragon

MUSTANG CHOWK

Seti Khola

△ Tansen & The Tarai

Devin's Fall

SIDDHARTHA HIGHWAY

Tashiling Tibetan Village

N

0   1km

the eastern and southeastern edges of **Phewa Tal**, where you'll find the vast majority of budget lodgings and restaurants.

Northeast of the lake, **Pokhara Bazaar** is maddeningly diffuse, sprawling a good 5km along two main north–south roads and a ladder of cross streets – the map doesn't begin to suggest how interminably far it is to cycle the entire length of it. Roughly 1km east of Damside are Pokhara's **airport**, tourist office and several of the upmarket hotels, with **Prithvi Chowk**, home of the **bus park**, 1km north of the airport. A further 1.5km northwards, the bustling **Mahendra Pul** (Mahendra Bridge) area forms the heart of the new, southern end of town, while the subdued **old bazaar** occupies the highest ground further north.

Arrival

Due to a rather sly arrangement between lodge owners, taxi drivers and touts*, tourist buses refuse to drive on to Lakeside/Damside, and instead deliver passengers into the clutches of the hotel touts at the **main bus park**, 2–3km away. You'll want to spend as little time as possible here – unless you're on a skeletal budget, a taxi is the only sensible way to reach the lake (about Rs50). The touts and drivers really go into a feeding frenzy at the arrival of Westerners, and the only way to escape intact is to state your destination with great certitude and decide on a driver as quickly as possible. Don't be surprised if they insist that your guest house burned down last week or the owner died, or if your driver, having agreed to take you to a particular guest house, tries to take you to a different one. You'll be spared most or all of this hassle if you arrive by public bus; public services entering along the Prithvi Highway all terminate here.

If you're coming off a trek in the Annapurna region and entering Pokhara along the Baglung Highway, you'll be dropped at a separate, less frenetic bus park on the west side of town. A taxi ride to Lakeside/Damside should cost about Rs50. It's also possible to trek directly to Lakeside, in which case you'll enter it from the north via Khahare. If you're arriving by bus from the south along the Siddhartha Highway, ask to be let off at Pardi (the local name for Damside) and walk a short way west to get to lodgings.

Flying to Pokhara cuts out some of the hardships of the journey (see p.246 for routes and prices). The mountain views from aloft are stupendous; if you're coming from Kathmandu, take the earliest flight available, before clouds obscure the peaks, and book early for a seat on the righthand side of the plane. A taxi from the airport to Lakeside/Damside should cost about Rs50.

Getting around

Poor local transport makes getting around Pokhara time-consuming, widening the divide between lake and bazaar and making it that much harder to tear yourself away from the tourist fleshpots. A crosstown journey on one of Pokhara's **local buses** takes the better part of an hour. There are three principal routes (refer to map): Lakeside up to the Prithvi Narayan campus via Mahendra Pul; Damside to the campus via Chipledhunga; and Ram Bazaar (east of the bus park)

---

*Lakeside and Damside lodge owners each argue that they'd be unfairly discriminated against if buses went to the other area first, so the buses stop instead at a point that's equally inconvenient for everybody. Touts and taxi drivers, meanwhile, are guaranteed business.

to Mahendra Cave. Catch buses in Damside near *K.C.'s Restaurant* and in Lakeside near the *Hungry Eye* and the municipal campground.

Taxis are seldom there when you need one, but innkeepers will book one for you given a couple hours' notice. The nearest taxi hangout is the roundabout at the beginning of the Baidam (Lakeside) road, and taxis can also usually be found near the bus park and the airport. Taxis are unmetered and fares are always more expensive for foreigners. You can keep the price down by telling the driver you're willing to share.

A **bicycle**, rentable all over Lakeside and Damside, multiplies your mobility and flexibility tremendously. One-speed bikes go for Rs40–50 a day, mountain bikes with gears Rs60–100 – the latter being more practical for exploring the valley, which has a lot of slopes to it. For speedier zipping around the valley, consider renting a **motorcycle**, available from a few Lakeside outlets for about Rs400 a day (not including fuel). Pokhara has no tempos or rikshas.

Information

Staff at the sleepy **tourist information office**, opposite the airport, can answer simple, specific questions (Sun–Thurs 10am–5pm, 4pm in winter, Fri 10am–3pm). However, all the information you really need is contained in the standard tourist **map** of Pokhara, sold in most bookstores.

> The telephone code for Pokhara is ☎061.

The lake and the bazaar

Visitors to Pokhara typically spend most of their time within arm's reach of apple pie, which means staying close to the lake. This is not fertile territory for cultural interaction, but a number of activities on the lake will at least help you to work off the calories. Real life goes on in the bazaar, which, though it pales in any comparison with the lake area, deserves more attention than it usually gets.

Phewa Tal

According to a local legend, **Phewa Tal** covers the area of a once-prosperous valley, whose inhabitants one day scorned a wandering beggar. Finding only one sympathetic woman, the beggar warned her of an impending flood: as the woman and her family fled to higher ground, a torrent roared down from the mountains and submerged the town – the "beggar" having been none other than the goddess Barahi Bhagwati. The woman's descendants settled beside the new lake and erected the island shrine of **Tal Barahi**; for local innkeepers and restaurateurs, who've done rather well out of the lake, a few alms at her shrine still don't go amiss.

The other, geological explanation is that the entire Pokhara Valley, like the Kathmandu Valley, was submerged about 200,000 years ago when the fast-rising Mahabharat Lek dammed up the Seti River. Over time, the Seti eroded an ever-deeper outlet, lowering the water level and leaving Phewa Tal and several smaller lakes as remnants. However, the legend might contain a grain of truth, as

NAUTICAL PURSUITS

Boating (or just floating) on Phewa Tal is the easiest way to get away from the business of getting away from it all. Oversized **rowing boats** – they'll hold six easily – can be rented all along the eastern shore. Prices are supposed to be fixed at Rs100 per hour or Rs250 per day, but "discounts" are possible, especially at Damside. Wooden **sailboats**, available from *Hotel Fewa* and from a couple of freelances nearby, cost Rs150 per hour or Rs600 per day, somewhat more for fibreglass ones. At least one operator rents pedalos (Rs150 per hour), and rafting companies such as *Equator Expeditions* and *Ultimate Descents* might consent to rent out their kayaks if they're not being used (about Rs600 per day). You can even rent a **fishing rod** from some Lakeside shops, and try to land sporty *sahar*, *kande* and *dudhe* carp. Keep an eye on the **weather**, especially if sailing – wind squalls are common in late spring, and it's easy to be becalmed at other times of the year. (An Irish woman drowned in Phewa Tal in 1996 when her boat overturned.) The shore around the Royal Palace is off-limits, and if you see gesticulating security guards you're too close. **Swimming** is best done from a boat, as the shore is muddy, but the bacteria count doesn't bear thinking about.

An obvious first destination is **Tal Barahi**, the island shrine located a few hundred metres offshore from the palace. While the temple itself is modern and not much to look at, it's a busy spot on Saturdays, when the lake goddess exacts a steady tribute of blood sacrifices. If that doesn't put you off your lunch, the island makes a fine place for a picnic. During the spring wedding months you might find yourself caught up in a flotilla of merrymakers headed for the island, where music, dancing and *raksi*-drinking go on until all hours.

From the island it's about the same distance again to the far shore which, with dense jungle, manic monkeys and few places to put ashore, is most easily observed from the water. If you want to walk around on the other side, make for **Anadu**, the diffuse Gurung village that covers the hillside directly opposite Lakeside, twenty to thirty minutes' row from the palace. Food is available from a few lakeside establishments – best bets are *Kopila* and *Park Anadu Tip*, both with beautiful outdoor seating. Trails from various points along the shore climb up through Anadu's scattered houses and terraced fields to eventually reach the ridgetop for great views. For some real exercise, you could row clear to the opposite (northwest) end of the lake and up the meandering Harnan Khola, the main tributary feeding the lake.

submerged tree stumps at the lake's northern end indicate that the water level rose in the not-too-distant past, perhaps because an earthquake blocked the outlet. Phewa was further enlarged by the installation of Pardi Dam in 1967, which brought electricity and irrigation to the valley, and gave Damside its name. The dam, meanwhile, may be the death of the lake: some experts are predicting that siltation will fill it up in as little as thirty years.

Lakeside (Baidam)

Next to eating, promenading along **Lakeside**'s pipal-shaded main drag is the favourite pastime in Pokhara. It's a pleasant enough stroll in parts, but new construction in this area (known locally as **Baidam**) has largely spoiled the area's former rural character: they've literally paved paradise here. Although it's illegal to build commercial structures along the shore, shops and restaurants now crowd together so closely on the main strip that they effectively block off any lake views between the Royal Palace and the campground. There's talk of the World Bank funding a network of lakeside trails and parks, but in the meantime access to the shore is limited.

You don't have to be staying at the *Fish Tail Lodge*, on Phewa Tal's opposite shore, to take the rope ferry across and have a look. Further north at **Gauri Ghat**, where the Lakeside strip passes at its closest to the lake, a set of steps leads from a leafy *chautaara* down to a rocky outcrop marked by a *linga* shrine. Midway along the strip sits Ratna Mandir, the winter **Royal Palace**, a definite no-go area during the king's residence each February. At the palace's western

Traditional Gurung House

edge, a road leads down to the lake at a shady spot known as **Barahi Tol**, where Nepalis and visiting Indians often go to escape the Western-dominated strip. Numerous other lanes head back away from the lake into what was until recently lush farmland; the farmers have now all sold out to developers and speculators, although many of the family-run guest houses retain their traditional vegetable plots, sugar-loaf haystacks and banana-palm borders. North of Lakeside in the area known as **Khahare**, the strip reverts to a dirt track which can be followed along the less developed northern shore; side trails lead up to Sarangkot (p.248) from here.

Damside (Pardi)

In **Damside (Pardi)**, go for mountain views – the classic scene, captured in a ubiquitous Ministry of Tourism poster, can be viewed from a small Vishnu shrine in the triangle of land between the spillway and the lake.

Pardi Dam is of no intrinsic interest, and unfortunately you can't walk across it, but from the footbridge that crosses the Pardi Khola, downstream, trails lead south to Devin's Fall (see below) or up the ridge to the west. The ridge walk takes a good 45 minutes, passing through deep, monkey-populated jungle before reaching a Buddhist shrine at the top for phenomenal views of the lake and mountains.

Pokhara Bazaar

Most of **Pokhara Bazaar** was destroyed in a fire in 1949, leaving little of interest. The active, southern end of town around **Mahendra Pul** is new since the fire, while the remnants of the original Newar quarter begin 1km further northwest, running from Bhimsen Tol up to Bag Bazaar. Perched on a hillock in the middle of this area you'll find the **Bindyabasini Mandir**, Pokhara's main cultural attraction, a quiet temple complex more noteworthy for its sweeping mountain views than its collection of shrines. The featured deity, Bindyabasini, is an incarnation of Kali, the mother goddess in her bloodthirsty aspect, who is represented here by a *shali-gram* (see p.261). Animal sacrifices are common at this temple, particularly on Saturdays and the ninth day of Dasain in October. Bindyabasini has a reputation as a bit of a prima donna: in one celebrated incident, her stone image began to sweat mysteriously, causing such a panic that the late King Tribhuwan had to order special rites to pacify the goddess. The fire that swept the bazaar in 1949 allegedly started here, when an offering burned out of control.

The **Pokhara Museum** (daily except Tues 10am–5pm; Rs5), located south of Mahendra Pul, contains a small exhibit of photos and artefacts relating to Nepalese ethnic groups, haphazardly arranged and with minimal English commentary. Tucked away in one corner of the Prithvi Narayan Campus at the northeastern part of town, the **Annapurna Regional Museum** (daily except Sat 9am–12.30pm & 1.30–4pm; free) offers a similarly slapdash treatment of Nepal's natural history, the prize exhibit being a collection of Himalayan butterflies. An adjacent **information centre**, maintained by the Annapurna Conservation Area Project, contains some exhibits not found at the Central Immigration office and the ACAP headquarters in Ghandruk, but it's not worth a special trip.

Immediately east of town lies the mossy, almost invisibly narrow **Seti River gorge**, where the abrasive torrent has cut like acid though the valley's soft sediments. It can easily be seen from the bridge east of Mahendra Pul (*pul* means bridge) – there's something remarkable about witnessing natural forces at work so close to the bazaar – but the footbridge east of the airstrip, and K I Singh Pul at the northern end of town on the way to Mahendra Cave (see p.251), provide less rubbish-strewn vantage points.

Just west of Prithvi Chowk hides the smallest and least interesting of Pokhara's three former Tibetan refugee camps (see p.253). **Paljorling**, more commonly known as the **Tibetan Handicrafts Centre**, is now not so much a community as a factory with on-site housing. The emphasis is on retail sales, and its inhabitants work over any foreigners who inadvertently fall into their web from the nearby bus park. There's little reason to actually enter the compound, as handicrafts are sold in shops along the main road outside.

Accommodation

Pokhara is glutted with cheap and moderately priced **accommodation**. Scores of small lodges have been built in recent years by ex-Gurkhas and Thakalis (the enterprising innkeepers of the trekking region north of Pokhara), but things are getting way out of hand. At any given time there seem to be a dozen concrete behemoths in the pipeline, and every small lodge owner has a scheme to replace his perfectly nice building with an ugly new one. Even the places that don't redevelop often have to share the noise and dust of nearby construction, and then get their views blocked by taller neighbours. The result is that the homely establishments that brought travellers here in the first place are being steadily edged out, and the lakeside accommodation districts are going the way of Goa and Ko Samui. You have to wonder where it's all going to end. A shakeout seems inevitable: the desperation of the touts at the bus park shows how bad it's already got and, sad to say, it won't get any better until guest houses start going under.

But looking on the bright side, you'll never have any trouble finding a room. And given the oversupply in the middle price range, you'll seldom have to pay the published rate, even in high season (in the off-season, expect discounts of 75 percent or more). Indeed, Pokhara offers the cheapest hot-water lodgings in Nepal, as well as some of the friendliest. More expensive hotel rooms should be booked in advance, at least in the high season; Kathmandu phone numbers are given where relevant.

Just about all independent travellers stay in Lakeside or Damside. Far removed from the din of the bazaar, overlooking the lake and peaks, and awash with Western food and comforts, both areas certainly offer a numbingly easy exis-

---

ROOM PRICE SCALES

All guest houses and hotels have been price-graded according to the scale outlined below, which represents the cheapest available double room in high season; codes prefixed by B denote the cost of a room with attached bathroom. See p.35 for a fuller explanation of the system.

① Less than Rs100
    ($1.75 if quoted in US$)
② Rs100–175 ($1.75–3)
③ Rs175–300 ($3–5)
④ $5–8

⑤ $8–12
⑥ $12–20
⑦ $20–40
⑧ $40–70
⑨ Over $70

---

tence. If you're looking to get away from other tourists, however, consider staying in Khahare or Anadu, or in one of the outlying destinations described later, such as Begnas Tal or Sarangkot. As a rule, the older, family-run guest houses are best – they're more intimate, friendly and genuine. The new ones are generally soulless and tasteless, and shouldn't be encouraged.

Lakeside: Baidam

With its strip of high-rise guest houses, thatched-roofed restaurants and corrugated-tin curio shacks, the **Baidam** portion of Lakeside is like Robinson Crusoe meets Las Vegas. It's Thamel all over again, full of self-conscious idleness and obsessive eating, but it's more laid-back, and behind the main strip it still preserves echoes of its old rural character.

Baidam covers a large area. The northern half of it is the more Disneyesque part; things are quieter south of the Royal Palace. Bear in mind that the further south you are, the better the mountain views. Avoid guest houses overlooking the strip, as you'll be tormented by early-morning buses revving their engines and honking for passengers. Places on the main road leading east from the campground towards the bazaar are particularly to be avoided.

Inexpensive

Amrit Guest House (no phone). If you really want to be on the strip, this is a relatively cheap, quiet option. ③/B④.

Gauri Shankar Guest House (☎20422). Flowering hedges shade a small patio. Nice atmosphere. ③/B④.

Hotel Fewa (☎20885). The only budget lodge right on the lake, but the facilities are really suffering from lack of maintenance. ②/B④.

New Star Lodge/Nanohana Lodge (no phone). A range of rooms from traditional to modern, all clean, in a relatively uncommercialized area. ③/B④.

Noble House (no phone). Unpretentious outfit with an attractive traditional building and grounds, unchanged after 15 years. ②.

Pokhara Peace Home (☎21599). Quiet, restful grounds and big rooms on a less developed back lane. ③/B④.

Sanctuary Lodge (no phone). Tiny family-run place with traditional rooms and gardens. ②.

Shanti Guest House (no phone). Small garden, modest facilities, friendly and economical. ②/B④.

Staywell Guest House (☎210707). Small, friendly and quiet, with a view from the roof. B④.

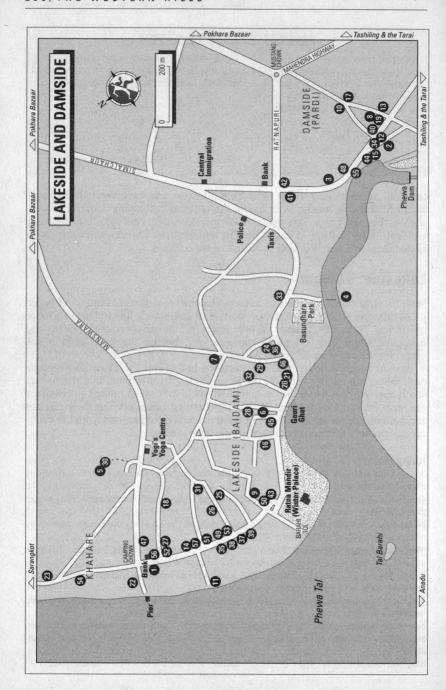

MAP KEY

GUEST HOUSES

1. Amrit Guest House
2. Ashok Guest House
3. City Annapurna Hotel
4. Fish Tail Lodge
5. Full Moon Lodge
6. Gauri Shankar Guest House
7. Gurkha Lodge
8. Hotel Anzuk
9. Hotel Barahi
10. Hotel Dragon
11. Hotel Fewa
12. Hotel Garden
13. Hotel Green View
14. Hotel Monal
15. Hotel Monalisa & Hotel Jharna
16. Hotel Nirvana
17. Hotel Pagoda
18. Hotel Temple Villa
19. Hotel Viewpoint
20. Lakeview Resort
21. Moonlight Resort
22. Municipal Campground
23. New Pleasure Home
24. New Star Lodge
25. Noble House
26. Pokhara Peace Home
27. Sanctuary Lodge
28. Shanti Guest House
29. Staywell Guest House
30. Sunset View Lodge
31. Teacher Krishna Lodge
32. Temple Guest House
33. Trekkers Retreat Lodge

RESTAURANTS

34. Bamboo Garden
35. Beam Beam
36. Bhanchha Ghar
37. Boomerang
38. Everest Steak House
39. Ganga Restaurant/Ganesh Bakery
40. German Bakery
41. Hotel Himalaya
42. Hotel Tragopan
43. Hungry Eye
44. K.C.
45. Laxman
46. Lhasa
47. Little Tibet Tea Garden
48. Loss Time
49. Maya Pub
50. Moon Dance
51. Nirula's
52. Old Blues Night
53. Once Upon A Time
54. Pink Elephant
55. Rodee Lakeview
56. 7-Eleven
57. Tea Time

Sunset View Lodge (no phone). The last word in seclusion, set on a hilltop with a magnificent view of the lake – but it's a longish hike to food or drink. ②.

Teacher Krishna Lodge (no phone). Farmhouse accommodation in a traditional old house: delightful but spartan, and it probably won't withstand modernization much longer. ②.

Temple Guest House (no phone). A mellow place with a nice garden, but otherwise basic. ③/B④.

Trekkers Retreat Lodge (☎21458). Views and garden at the quiet southern end of Lakeside. ②/B④.

Moderate and expensive

Fish Tail Lodge (Kathmandu office: ☎221711). Set amidst fabulous landscaping, the only hotel on the west side of Phewa Tal enjoys an unrivalled view of the lake and the classic profile of the mountains behind. Access by rope ferry. Two stars. B⑨.

Full Moon Lodge (☎21511). Supreme view of the lake and Baidam, located up a steep path. ④/B⑦.

Gurkha Lodge (no phone). Gardening buffs will love this place, tucked down a long Baidam lane, run by an ex-Gurkha and his English wife. B⑤.

Hotel Barahi (☎21879). Gorgeous grounds, surprisingly peaceful for such a central location. B⑥ (B⑧ with a/c).

Hotel Monal (☎21459). Good facilities, adequately set back from the strip. Nepali-Western management. B⑤.

Hotel Nirvana (☎20874). Huge, very clean rooms and spacious balconies in a rather pretentious building. Nepali-Western management. B⑤.

Hotel Temple Villa (☎21203). Immaculate place with spacious rooms and grounds. Nepali-Western management. ⑤/B⑥.

Lakeview Resort (☎21477). Nice grounds, right across from the lake, but a tad run-down. The bungalows (B⑥) are a better deal.

Moonlight Resort (☎21704). Good value for rooms so close to the lake. B⑤.

Lakeside: Khahare

Khahare, the area north of Camping Chowk (the main crossroads near the municipal campground), is well known to long-termers, hippies, Israelis and other bargain-hunters. It's also convenient if you're trekking directly into Lakeside, since it's the first lodging area you'll come to. Khahare's southern end is indistinguishable from Baidam, but further north, where the road and the shore start bending westwards (off the map), it preserves some of the undeveloped ambience of old, with several rough-hewn lodges and unmolested views of the lake. Restaurants and other facilities are few, but Lakeside proper is just a few minutes' walk away. Stay here to escape the tourist sound and fury, not for comfort.

Taxis can get reasonably close to any of the guest houses listed below; if you want total isolation, there are places located up on the ridge above Khahare that can be reached only on foot.

Banana Garden Lodge (☎21880). Lovely lake overlook, gardens and outside seating, standard rooms. Restaurant nearby. Claims to be the last pickup point for tourist buses. ①.

Blue Diamond Lodge (no phone). Rooms in a rustic private home. Cold water only. ①.

Hotel Sun Welcome (no phone). Small garden, restaurant, standard rooms. ①/B②.

Lonely View Lodge (no phone). Simple place, basic facilities, beautiful garden and lake views. Nepali-Western management. ②.

New Pleasure Home (no phone). Big rooms, lake views, small garden and the aptly named *Mellow Fellow* restaurant. ②.

Damside

If Lakeside is a rural Thamel, **Damside** is a suburban one. The mountain views are better, but it's questionable whether they compensate for the ugly foreground and lack of greenery. There's also less tourist razzamatazz than in Lakeside, making the streets quieter and the neighbourhood more residential, but the choice of restaurants and shops is correspondingly limited.

Inexpensive

Ashok Guest House (☎20374). Garden seating, and a good view of the lake and mountains from the roof. ③/B⑤.

Hotel Anzuk (☎21845). Good garden seating and unobstructed mountain views. ③/B④.

Hotel Garden (☎20870). Spacious, with a good location, greenery and view. ③/B⑤.

Hotel Green View (☎21844). Well-managed place, with a lovely, secluded garden restaurant and a roof view. The cheap rooms are in an older wing. ②/B③.

Hotel Pagoda (☎21802). Modest but friendly and spotlessly clean, with a small garden seating area. ③/B⑤.

Hotel Viewpoint (☎21787). Standard facilities, but a good view from roof. ③/B④.

Moderate and expensive

City Annapurna Hotel (☎21241). Clean, with well laid-out grounds, lawn seating and a great view from the roof. Breakfast included. B⑤.

Hotel Dragon (☎20391). Pretty garden with good views. Air-conditioned rooms with Tibetan furnishings. Two stars. B⑧.

Hotel Jharna (☎21925). Ideal location: overlooking the lake with the mountains behind. B⑤.

Hotel Monalisa (☎20863). Equally good location, but cleaner and friendlier than the *Jharna*. ④/B⑤.

Across the lake: Anadu

Anadu, directly across the lake from Baidam, is not one of Nepal's friendliest or best-kept villages, but there's a certain bohemian attraction to staying in a place that can only be reached by boat. (Actually, you can walk to Anadu from the highway on the other side of the ridge behind, but let's not spoil the atmosphere.)

If you're thinking of staying in one of the cheap places here, rent a boat and scout things out first, as new (hopefully better) places may have sprung up. The expensive places will of course arrange your boat passage. The nearest of the places listed here, the *Typical*, can be reached in about twenty minutes' rowing from the palace area of Lakeside. Following the shore to the right from there you'll reach the *Hotel Fewa Resort, Park Anadu Tip, Gurung Cottage* and *Monal Resort*, in that order.

Inexpensive

Gurung Cottage (no phone). Awfully primitive (cold water only), but certainly secluded. ①.

Park Anadu Tip (no phone). A pleasant shoreline restaurant that plans to build a few rooms in the ② range.

Typical Guest House (no phone). A slightly more developed version of *Gurung Cottage* (but still cold water only), with more variety in the food department. ③.

Moderate and expensive

Hotel Fewa Resort (☎20151). Green, quiet and roomy, with a fair restaurant. Operated by the Lakeside hotel of the same name. ⑤/B⑧.

Monal Resort (☎21459). A posh new hotel expected to be completed in early 1997, with a/c and a swimming pool. Operated by *Hotel Monal* on Lakeside. B⑨.

In the bazaar: Mahendra Pul and Prithvi Chowk

Pokhara Bazaar has little going for it, and its lodgings, catering mainly to Nepali and Indian businessmen, charge more for less. Realistically, you'd have to be either really stuck or really antisocial to stay here. That said, the **Mahendra Pul** area, Pokhara's main commercial centre, certainly has got spark, and you can get almost anything you need here. A messier, more organic locale, **Prithvi Chowk** seethes with a tumultuous melange of Nepalis, Indians and Tibetans; it happens to have a couple of new and rather posh guest houses, but otherwise it's grotty and takes its cues from the nearby bus park. If need be, you can find plenty of cheaper places than the ones listed here.

Hotel Anand, Prithvi Chowk (☎20029). Rooftop garden and TV. ②/B④.

Hotel Kailash, Mahendra Pul (☎21726). Clean, with a roof garden. ②/B④.

New Hotel Sunkoshi, Mahendra Pul (☎21569). Drab but adequate. ②/B③.

New Palace Hotel, Prithvi Chowk (☎20488). An Indian businessman's dream. ②/B③.

Other hotels

Several of Pokhara's older hotels are rather unhappily situated opposite the **airport**, relics of the days when the only way to get here was by air. A few posh new ones are being built south of the airport and in **Phulbari**, east of Mahendra Pul.

Bluebird Hotel, south of the airport (☎21007; Kathmandu office: ☎228833). Five-star hotel affiliated with *Bluestar Hotel* in Kathmandu. B⑨.

Hotel Dusit Fulbari, Phulbari (Kathmandu office: ☎52810). A new five-star hotel being built on a hillside with views. Affiliated with *Hotel Summit* in Patan. B⑨.

Hotel Mount Annapurna, opposite the airport (☎20037). Disappointing rooms, though the lawn is worthy of the Raj. Two stars. B⑧.

New Hotel Crystal, opposite the airport (Kathmandu office: ☎228561). Big hotel with a pool and tennis court. Three stars. B⑧ (B⑨ with a/c).

Shangri-La Village, south of the airport (Kathmandu office: ☎412999). Deluxe bungalows, with a pool and conference centre. Five stars. B⑨.

Tara Gaon Resort, opposite the airport (Kathmandu office: ☎470409). Part of the government-run chain and really forlorn. Two stars. B⑥.

Camping

Pokhara's **municipal campground** is right by the lake and not half bad. Charges are Rs20–40 per vehicle (depending on size), Rs40 per tent, Rs40 for a hot shower, and Rs40 to use the kitchen facilities. However, you'd probably be better off working out a deal with one of the guest houses along the back lanes of Lakeside.

Eating

Restaurants are everywhere in Pokhara, and food is a major preoccupation. Lakeside, in particular, is one long trough of feeding opportunities. Eating also sets the social agenda: there's not much nightlife after around 10.30pm, but the congenial restaurants and cafés around the lake are easy places to make friends and find trekking partners. Candlelight (often imposed by load-shedding) adds to the romance. Most tourist restaurants boast a more or less standard **menu**, featuring an implausibly international selection of dishes and local fish prepared umpteen different ways. The places recommended here pull it off with a bit more authenticity (or at least atmosphere) than the rest. What you get might not bear much resemblace to what you ordered, but it'll probably taste pretty good (especially after three weeks on the trail).

If pseudo-Western food gets you down, many restaurants do set **Nepali** meals and some pretty good **Indian** dishes. For something much cheaper, try one of the myriad **momo** shacks, where locals eat. Watch out for the **juice** sellers, though: they'll charge whatever they think they can get, and dilute the juice with water and sugar if you're not looking.

Prices are generally comparable to Kathmandu's Thamel area. Restaurants described here as cheap will charge less than Rs100 per person for a full dinner; inexpensive restaurants will run to Rs100–200; and moderately priced ones Rs200 or more.

Lakeside

Beam Beam. Lively place with a bar and back garden. Inexpensive.

Bhanchha Ghar. A humbler branch of the famed Kathmandu restaurant: fine Nepali and north Indian cuisine, nightly music and dance. Moderately priced.

Boomerang. Great for breakfast or an afternoon snack: seating under umbrellas and thatched pavilions on a vast lawn sloping down to the lake. There are several similar outfits nearby, but this is still the best. Inexpensive.

Everest Steak House. Lively rooftop place serving buffalo in every conceivable form; the huge garden is pleasant for daytime seating. Inexpensive.

Ganga Restaurant/Ganesh Bakery. Good bread and croissants; lively for dinner. Cheap.

Hungry Eye. Sit outside for sedate dining by candlelight, or indoors for the nightly culture show in an acoustic purgatory. Moderately priced.

Laxman. Funky, shoestring decor and a laid-back feel. Serious cakes and pies. Inexpensive.

Lhasa. Serene atmosphere, though Tibetan food is almost an afterthought. Inexpensive.

Little Tibetan Tea Garden. Tibetan and Western food in a lovely little bamboo grove. Inexpensive.

Maya Pub. Popular and efficient restaurant/bar serving good soups, pastas, sizzlers and vegetarian dishes. Loud music. Inexpensive.

Moon Dance. The epicentre of Lakeside eating, with reliable food (especially pizza), a great atmosphere, a roof terrace and a fireplace for winter evenings. Inexpensive to moderate.

Nirula's. A branch of the Indian fast-food-and-ice-cream chain (real sundaes and milk shakes). Inexpensive.

Once Upon a Time. Cosy Swiss Family Robinson decor, rooftop seating and loud tunes. The food is interchangeable with that of the neighbouring *Maya Pub*. Inexpensive.

Tea Time. One of Lakeside's original bamboo joints, good for daytime people-watching, drinks and snacks. Inexpensive.

Zorba (next to *Hotel Monal*). Classy decor and service, with some Austrian specialities. Moderately priced.

Damside

Damside's guest houses tend to have their own self-contained restaurants, so there are fewer separate eating places to recommend.

Bamboo Garden. Simple, friendly hangout. Cheap to inexpensive.

German Bakery. A fine candidate for breakfast or lunch ingredients: good views, tolerable croissants and wholegrain bread. Cheap.

K.C. Patio dining by the lake, or indoors by the fire in winter. Steaks, fish, cake and pie. No relation to the Kathmandu restaurant of the same name. Inexpensive to moderately priced.

Hotel Himalaya. Marwari restaurant specializing in south Indian dishes. Cheap to inexpensive.

Hotel Tragopan. Decent north Indian food in a vaguely upscale setting. Inexpensive to moderately priced.

Loss Time. Passable all-rounder, better for Indian food. Inexpensive.

Rodee Lakeview. Lovely patio seating right beside the lake, and the home of Damside's premier cake display. Excellent for breakfast. Inexpensive.

Pokhara Bazaar

Indian traders have moved in on Pokhara Bazaar, as they have wherever there's commercial potential, and Indian restaurants are a welcome result of their presence. You'll find several serviceable eateries around the northwest corner of Prithvi Chowk (west of the bus park), and a few others in Mahendra Pul and

Chipledhunga. One or two greasy spoons near the Paljorling entrance do Tibetan food. For tourist grub, try Mahendra Pul.

Nightlife

While nightlife around Pokhara usually just means a second helping of pie, a good way to break the routine is to catch a **culture show**. Several tourist restaurants put on free dinner music performances by local folk troupes. *Hotel Dragon* and *Fish Tail Lodge* host more elaborate music and dance programmes nightly in the high season. Tickets cost about Rs100 and are available through agents.

Pokhara **nightspots** regularly push back the usual 10pm bedtime barrier, at least during the high season. Their turnover rate is high, but the following were still raving as we went to press:

Beam Beam. Laid-back inside/outside affair with a nice belly-up bar. Occasional live music.

K.C. Damside's only nightspot to speak of.

Old Blues Night. Loud music, pool tables and a sociable atmosphere, but a slightly urban edge.

Maya Pub. Excellent rooftop bar and good music.

Moondance. Ever-creative music mixes and a comfortable atmosphere keep this place packed for after-dinner drinks.

Once Upon a Time. Eclectic music on two levels – the party never seems to stop.

Pink Elephant. A warehouse with a sound system and occasional live music.

7-Eleven. Cheesy Indian lounge with authentic *ghazal* enternainment.

Tea Time. Mellow place, popular for after-dinner drinks.

Shopping

Shopping is still a mainly outdoor activity in Lakeside and Damside, where laid-back curio stalls make a welcome change from the hard-driving salesmen of Kathmandu, even if their prices and selection don't quite compare. Specialities include **batiks**, wooden **flasks**, **dolls** in ethnic dress and fossil-bearing *shaligram* stones from the Kali Gandaki (note that the latter are illegal to export from Nepal). Hand-stitched **wall hangings** in simple Tibetan designs have been produced for the tourist market, but are attractive nonetheless. Persuasive Tibetans peddle their wares in Lakeside's cafés, but these aren't produced locally, and **carpets** are best purchased at the Tibetan villages. Hand-knitted **woollen** sweaters, socks and such aren't of very good quality here, but may fit the bill for trekking. Kashmiris have colonized Lakeside, as they have Thamel, with boutiques touting "Asian" art: mainly high-priced carpets and cheap **papier-mâché** and soapstone widgets. Other than that, you'll find the usual range of tourist bait, most of it imported from Kathmandu: ritual masks, *thangka*, embroidered T-shirts (wear that trek!), cloth bags and hippy clothes. Stalls along the strip opposite the palace are extremely competitive.

The **bookshops** and stalls around Lakeside and Damside are individually small, but collectively they can muster a good selection. Pokhara's **second-hand market** is very good.

Listings

Banks and moneychangers *Nepal Grindlays* in Lakeside handles foreign exchange and Mastercard/Visa cash advances, Sun–Fri 10am–4pm. *Rastriya Banijya*'s foreign-exchange counter, a short distance north of Damside, is open daily 7am–7pm. Several registered moneychangers operate in Lakeside and Damside, generally 8am–7pm. Some innkeepers will change dollars unofficially.

Car rental A taxi with driver will cost $25 a day for journeys within daytripping range of Pokhara.

Central Immigration A short walk north of Damside, it issues trekking permits (Annapurna and Rara treks only) and visa extensions. Application hours are daily except Sat 10.30am–1pm (12.30pm in winter); permits and visas are ready later the same day. For most trekking permits, an additional Annapurna Conservation Area fee is payable. Trekking or travel agents can handle the paperwork for a fee (about Rs50). Passport photos are available in minutes from studios near the office (about Rs75).

Dope is available, but sold more discreetly than in Kathmandu. If you're going trekking, you'll find it much cheaper on the trail.

Film and processing Films are available at roughly Kathmandu prices. A couple of places in Lakeside and Pokhara Bazaar do processing, and other tourist shops can send film out.

Health The *Western Regional Hospital* (☎20066), with Western and Nepali staff, handles emergencies and does stool tests. A few pharmas in Lakeside/Damside will send your stool to the lab for a fee (about Rs100), and one or two offer ayurvedic medicine. *Phan Dey Medical Centre*, across the road and up from the *Hungry Eye* in Lakeside, does Tibetan medicine.

Laundry Most lodges take laundry for a few rupees per item; the places calling themselves "dry cleaners" return your clothes dry, but wash as wet as the others.

Massage Various shacks advertise their services. *Natural Health Clinic*, opposite *Snowland Hotel* in Lakeside, can be recommended for Nepali hard massage and ayurvedic/aromatherapy massage. Jyoti at *Nightingale Lodge* (near *Bhanchha Ghar*) does deep tissue massage (women only). *Green Peace "M" Corner*, opposite *Tea Time*, does reflexology. For acupressure and shiatsu, ask at *Hotel Monal*. The neck-cracking that barbers do may be appropriate for some, but can result in temporary stiffness for others.

Meditation and yoga Most meditation courses in Pokhara are organized by centres in Kathmandu, but you may be able to join up on the spot – check the noticeboards around Lakeside/Damside. *Yogi's Yoga Centre* on Manswara (the road leading from the north end of Lakeside to the bazaar) does daily afternoon yoga classes, three-day introductory courses and one-week intermediate courses. The Osho (Rajneesh) people have a meditation centre east of the bus park.

Newspapers and magazines *International Herald Tribune*, *Time* and *Newsweek* are available in bookshops, usually one or two days late. *Yak Bookstore* in Lakeside gets the English-language Nepali papers in late afternoon of the same day.

Post Tourist book- and postcard shops sell stamps, and some will take mail to the post office for free. The main post office, in Mahendra Pul, is open Sun–Thurs 10am–5pm (4pm in winter), Fri 10am–3pm. They've got a poste restante department, but it may not be as reliable as the one in Kathmandu – don't have anything of value sent to you here.

Provisions Mini-supermarkets along the Lakeside strip anticipate your every need. Basically, everything you can get in Kathmandu, you can get in Lakeside/Damside: chocolate, dried fruit, tinned food, bread, cheese, muesli, toiletries, batteries, etc.

Teaching English *Pokhara English Language Institute* (☎21756), in Mahendra Pul opposite the GPO, needs native-speaking instructors.

Telephone calls As in Kathmandu, you'll find plenty of ISD/IDD businesses (most open 7am–11pm), plus many guest houses have international dialling facilities. International calls are charged at around Rs180–200 per minute, depending on country (shop around), trunk calls to Kathmandu about Rs15 per minute.

Tours *Sarangsar Tours & Travels* (☎21595) in Lakeside and *Pokhara Sightseeing* (☎21943) in Damside do tours of the valley for about Rs400 a day. Book through any agent.

Moving on from Pokhara

Buses link Pokhara with Kathmandu via the Prithvi Highway, and with the Tarai and India via the Siddhartha Highway. All four domestic airlines connect Pokhara with Kathmandu.

Buses

About a dozen companies operate **tourist buses** from Pokhara to Kathmandu. In addition, *Standard Travels* in Lakeside runs tourist services to Sauraha (for Chitwan National Park) and Sunauli (for India). Though roughly twice as expensive (Rs150–200) as public buses, they're more comfortable and somewhat faster, and – big advantage, this – they pick up passengers in Lakeside and Damside. Certain public **express buses** also do this, but then proceed to the bus park to take on more passengers. (See the box on p.220 for a summary of public bus services from Pokhara.)

All tourist buses and some public buses can be booked through ticket agents, but shop around since not every agent deals with every bus, and prices vary quite a bit. The agent's fee for obtaining a public bus ticket may be more than the ticket itself, but it's well worth it to avoid an extra encounter with the bus park. However, some buses aren't bookable in advance, in which case you're on your own. Tickets for buses travelling the Prithvi Highway (to Kathmandu or the Tarai, for example) are sold from a booking hall at the top of the steps on the west side of the **main bus park**. Services along the Siddhartha Highway (such as those to Tansen) are represented by a smaller booth at the southwestern edge of the bus park. For services along the Pokhara–Baglung Highway (including those to various Annapurna region trailheads), you need to buy tickets from the separate **Baglung bus park**, located on the western side of the bazaar.

If you're heading **to India**, read the section on ticket agents in *Basics* (p.29) first.

Flights

For **internal flights**, go through an agent or contact the airlines directly. See the box for frequencies and fares. Many agents can also book or reconfirm **international flights** by phone to Kathmandu – *Mountain Voyages Nepal* (☎21669), in Lakeside near the *Boomerang Restaurant*, is very professional.

Everest Air, Nagdhunga (☎21883).

Necon Air, Ratnapuri, west of the tourist office (☎20256).

Nepal Airways, Nagdhunga (☎20966).

RNAC, at the airport (☎21021).

INTERNAL FLIGHTS FROM POKHARA			
	Frequency	Time	Fare ($)
Bharatpur	1/day	25min	40
Dolpo	1/week	40min	72
Jomosom	2–5/day	25min	50
Kathmandu	5–8/day	35min	61
Manang	4/week	25min	50
Mountain	0–2/day	30–45min	50–60

Trekking

There are any number of ways to get to the start of a **trek** in the Annapurna region north of Pokhara. The completion of the Pokhara–Baglung Highway has opened up three major trailheads, **Suikhet (Phedi)**, **Chandrakot** and **Baglung**. A taxi to Chandrakot – the most popular gateway – should cost about Rs500. Alternatively, you can take any Baglung-bound bus, departing hourly from the Baglung bus park (Rs30). You can also enter the region by hiking straight in from Lakeside, via **Sarangkot** (see p.248), or by hiring someone to row you across the lake and upriver to a point below Naudanda. Those trekking the Annapurna Circuit typically start at Besisahar, reached by taking a bus to **Dumre** (on the way to Kathmandu), from where trucks shuttle the rest of the way; an alternative trailhead is **Begnas Tal**, reached by local bus from Chipledhunga in the bazaar.

Recommending **trekking agencies** in Pokhara is even riskier than in Kathmandu. Anyway, you don't need an agency to trek the Annapurna region unless you're doing something unorthodox – in which case, organize it in Kathmandu. Trekking **guides** and **porters** can be hired through almost any guest house or equipment-rental stall. The Chhetri sisters at *Yeti Guest House* (☎ 21423) in Khahare can arrange female guides and porters. See "Listings", above, for information on the local Central Immigration office, and Chapter Seven for full details on trekking preparations and routes. To find a **trekking partner** you could try putting up a message at the *Boomerang* or other Lakeside restaurant notice boards.

Pokhara's selection of rental **trekking equipment** pales beside Kathmandu's, but you'll pay for fewer days by renting locally. Sleeping bags, packs and parkas are easily obtainable.

Rafting

If you're going to go **rafting** from Pokhara, you'll probably do the Kali Gandaki. Many companies also raft the Trisuli, which can serve as a satisfying segue into the Tarai, though from Pokhara you will probably only run the tamer lower section. (See p.53 for more information on choosing a trip.)

Several **rafting operators** have offices in Lakeside, but, as in Kathmandu, most change personnel so often that it's not worth mentioning them by name. Two reputable companies with offices in Lakeside are *Equator Expeditions* (☎20688), near *Beam Beam*, and *Ultimate Descents* (☎20335), just up from the *Hungry Eye*.

THE POKHARA VALLEY

Day trips around the **Pokhara Valley** make excellent training for a trek, and serve as an effective antidote to lakeside idleness. Excursions generally entail a healthy amount of cycling or hiking, often both. Start early to make the most of the views before the clouds move in and the heat builds – it can get really sticky here in all but the winter months – and bring lunch and a full water bottle. If you're feeling adventurous (or running behind schedule), you can **stay overnight** at Sarangkot, Tashi Palkhel or, most promisingly, Begnas Tal.

Many of the **ethnic groups** that make treks north of Pokhara so popular – Gurungs, Magars, and Bahun and Chhetri Hindu castes – are equally well represented around the valley, and less touched by tourism here. In addition, the **Tibetan settlements** in the area are less commercial, and in their own way more instructive about Tibetan culture, than those in the Kathmandu Valley.

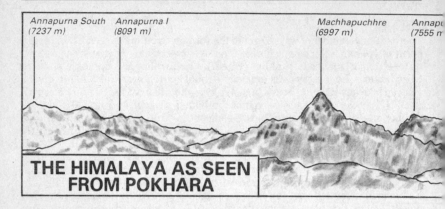

Annapurna South   Annapurna I   Machhapuchhre   Annapu
(7237 m)   (8091 m)   (6997 m)   (7555 m

THE HIMALAYA AS SEEN
FROM POKHARA

Sarangkot

For the classic, full-length spectacle of the Himalaya – featuring Dhaulagiri, the
Annapurnas, Manaslu and the graceful pyramid of Machhapuchhre – hike up one
of the hilltops north and east of Pokhara. **Sarangkot**, a high point (1590m) on the
ridge north of Phewa Tal, is the more popular and well developed of the two, with
food, refreshments and overnight facilities.

Two principal routes ascend the ridge, one directly from Lakeside, the other from
the Bindyabasini temple in the bazaar. The **Lakeside route** is much better for hiking,
but it's a longer, steeper climb, with no mountain views until the very top – if you're
running late you might miss them altogether. Follow the road north from Lakeside
until it becomes a trail, where it traverses a large cultivated area and then snakes alternately through jungle and pastures. When in doubt, stay on the flagstoned path and
keep heading generally towards the summit; you'll be doing well to make it to the top
in less than two and a half hours. This route is used by an increasing number of trekking parties, but usually on the descent, since it's awfully steep for a first day out.

The route **from the bazaar** follows a paved road for much of the way, which is a
good reason for cycling this first part. Compared to the Lakeside approach this is a
gentler ascent, and the scenery – both mountains and lake – gets better and better
as you go. The signposted road starts from just south of the Bindyabasini Temple,
and climbs for 5km until the pavement gives out. Someone will watch your bike
here for a small fee. A wide path leads up to the summit, a half-hour hike.

The **village** of Sarangkot, nestled just below the summit, has tea shops, handicrafts sellers and several trekking-standard **lodges**. If you're not planning to trek,
at least spend a night here: *View Top Lodge* and *New Tourist Lodge* (both ①) have
electricity but no hot water. For the **summit**, continue another ten minutes up to
a walled compound, where the local council will hit you for a donation for their
water supply. If you've hiked up from Lakeside, the sudden view here will come
as a staggering revelation. The peaks seem to levitate above their blue flanks, the
gathering clouds add a quality of raw grandeur, while to the south, Phewa Tal
shimmers in the hazy arc of the valley. If you hadn't been planning on trekking,
this is where you might change your mind.

Kaski, seat of the kingdom that once ruled the Pokhara Valley, lives on as a
village (with more basic lodges) about two hours further west, just below the
ridge. From there you can march up a long stone staircase to Kaskikot, where low

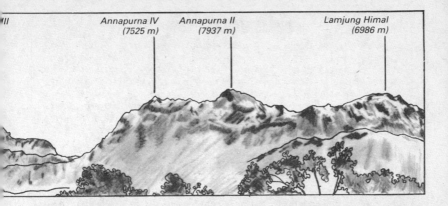

walls and a small Durga shrine are all that remain of the citadel of the Kaski kings, which fell to the Gorkhalis without a fight in 1781. Continuing west along the ridge for another hour and a half, the trail joins the Pokhara–Baglung Highway at **Naudanda** (or Nagdanda), a small bazaar on the Pokhara–Baglung Highway that's the first place from which Machhapuchhre's true fishtail profile can be seen. Though you can't continue any further west without a trekking permit, you can spend the night here or catch a ride back to Pokhara on the main road.

The road from the Bindyabasini temple is eventually supposed to be extended to Naudanda, and on a mountain bike it might already be possible to ride the unfinished Sarangkot–Naudanda section: inquire locally. If so, it would make a nifty all-day loop, returning along the Baglung Highway.

Kahun Danda and the Bhalam Khola

If the view from **Kahun Danda**, the hill east of Pokhara, is a shade less magnificent than Sarangkot's, a lookout tower near the top gives you a better crack at it. The trail up the ridge is totally uncommercialized and consequently hard to find. Although the furthest from Lakeside/Damside, the easiest and most interesting

---

HIKING AND BIKING AROUND THE VALLEY

Most outings in the Pokhara Valley involve biking to a destination and then exploring further on foot. Here are some suggested all-day itineraries (refer to the standard tourist map):

Sarangkot – Hike up from Lakeside, or bike/hike from the bazaar; continue along the ridge to Kaski or even to Naudanda, where you can catch a bus back.

North of the bazaar – Bike to Mahendra Gupha; from there you can hike to the head of the Kali Khola valley or bike past Lamechaur toward Lhachok. On the return, make a side trip up the Bhalam Khola.

Begnas Tal – Biking to the lake along the highway isn't much fun, but from that point on the possibilities are unlimited. On the way back, detour up the Bijaypur Khola.

Siddhartha Highway – The sinuous paved road is good for cycling, ascending about 700m to a saddle, with mountain views near the top. Return the same way.

THE GURKHAS

As I write these last words, my thoughts return to you who were my comrades: the stubborn and indomitable peasants of Nepal. Once more I hear the laughter with which you greeted every hardship. Once more I see you in your bivouacs or about your fires, on forced march or in the trenches, now shivering with wet and cold, now scorched by a pitiless and burning sun. Uncomplaining, you endure hunger and thirst and wounds; and at the last, your unwavering lines disappear into the smoke and wrath of battle. Bravest of the brave, most generous of the generous, never had a country more faithful friends than you.

Ralph Lilley Turner, *Dictionary of the Nepali Language* (1931)

Comprising an elite Nepalese corps within the British and Indian armies for over 175 years, the **Gurkha regiments** have been rated among the finest fighting units in the world. Ironically, the regiments were born out of the 1814–16 war between Nepal and Britain's East India Company: so impressed were the British by the men of "Goorkha" (Gorkha, the ancestral home of Nepal's rulers) that they began recruiting Nepalis into the Indian Army before the peace was even signed.

In the century that followed, Gurkhas fought in every major British military operation, including the 1857 **Indian Mutiny** and campaigns in Afghanistan, the North-West Frontier and Somaliland. More than 200,000 Gurkhas served in the two world wars, and, despite being earmarked for "high-wastage roles", earned universal respect for their bravery: ten of the one hundred **Victoria Crosses** awarded in World War II went to Gurkhas. Following India's independence after the war, Britain took four of the ten Gurkha regiments and India retained the rest. More recently, Gurkhas have distinguished themselves in Sarawak, Cyprus and the 1982 Falklands War, and are currently stationed in Hong Kong, Brunei, Belize and the UK.

Gurkhas hail mainly from the Magar, Gurung, Rai and Limbu hill tribes (growing up in the Nepal hills is ideal preparation for the army). Most boys from these groups dream of making it into the Gurkhas, not only for the money – the annual salary of £5000 is about fifty times the Nepalese average – but also for a rare chance to see the world and return with prestige and a comfortable pension.

The Gurkhas' long and faithful service to Britain is winding down, however. With Hong Kong (the Gurkhas' headquarters) to be handed over to China in 1997, and the Sultan of Brunei's contract for Gurkha protection due to expire in 1998, Britain's need for military forces in Asia is expected to decline. Anticipating this, the main Gurkha recruiting and training centre in Dharan was handed over to civilian use at the end of 1989, and all remaining operations are now carried out at the smaller facility in Pokhara. Would-be recruits can still try out for places in the lower-paid Indian regiments – which is what most who failed to make the cut for the British Gurkhas used to do anyway – but the gradual loss of salaries and pensions is apt to take the steam out of many Nepali hill communities.

starting point is the **Tibetan monastery** 2km east of Mahendra Pul. At the top of a breathless couple of hundred steps at the southern base of Kahun Danda, the Karma Dhubgyu Chhokhorling Nyeshang Korti Monastery occupies a breezy spot – always good for keeping the prayer flags flapping – with valley views east and west. Around thirty monks and monklets inhabit the monastery, which is modern and contains all the usual Vajrayana paraphernalia.

The trail to the lookout tower starts at the bottom of the steps, hugs the western base of the ridge for about 1km, and then climbs through several lazy settlements collectively known as **Phulbari**. Keep heading towards the tower (1460m), which is visible most of the way and can be reached in about an hour and a half from the monastery. From the half-finished concrete platform, you can contemplate the tremendous force of the Seti River and its tributaries, which tumble out of the Annapurna Himal clouded with dissolved limestone (*seti* means white) and, merging at the foot of the Kahun Danda, split the valley floor with a bleached chasm. Descending back to the monastery, paths bearing to the left may suggest a longer circuit via the valley and villages on the east side of the ridge.

Also eminently worth exploring is the tidily terraced side valley of the **Bhalam Khola**, immediately north of Kahun Danda. To get there directly from the tower involves some nasty bushwhacking, so it's better to backtrack towards the monastery until you pick up the first main northbound trail. It's also accessible by a rough (mountain-bikeable) track heading northwards on the east side of the Seti River. The power of erosion can readily be seen from this route as it passes the confluence of the Bhalam, Seti and Kali rivers, where they undercut old gravel beds, leaving sheer, mossy cliffs. The bikeable track continues at least another 3km to the village of Railechaur, and trails go further up the valley from there. This route can be linked with the one to Mahendra Cave (see below) by crossing two footbridges over the Bhalam and Kali rivers, but it's easier to visit the cave first.

Mahendra Gupha (Cave) and the Kali Khola

While it just about scrapes a description as a geological wonder, **Mahendra Gupha** (Mahendra Cave) is probably best thought of as a base from which to explore the snug hills and side valleys north of Pokhara, even though it's a long nine-kilometre haul from Lakeside/Damside. To get there, cross K I Singh* Pul (Bridge) at the top end of Pokhara and head north past the Gurkha camp, turn right up a paved road 600m beyond the bridge, and follow it for about 3km to the end. The climb is relentless and if you're on a one-speed bike you'll have to push some of the way (the reward comes on the way back). Some city buses come up this way from the bazaar east of the bus park, via Prithvi Chowk. A taxi will charge about Rs300 return.

Water percolating down from the limestone hills above has etched away at the valley's alluvial sediments, creating a honeycomb of caves extending up to 2km from the main entrance. Mahendra Cave used to be well known for its limestone stalactites, but these have unfortunately been ransacked by vandals; a few surviving **stalagmites** are daubed with red sindur and revered as *shivalinga* because of their resemblance to phalluses.

Admission is Rs15, which includes the services of a guide. Though the cave is neither dangerous nor vast – the accessible part takes about ten to fifteen minutes to tour – a guide is still useful, if only to show you which way to point your flashlight (a fairly essential item, since the electric generator rarely works and guides make do with feeble candles). They'll probably try to sell you a tour of **another cave** about ten minutes' walk away, promising a bigger chamber and better stalactites. It is, surprisingly, as advertised, but it's a hell of a scramble, and once inside it may strike you that, were it not for Nepalis' innate honesty, you could be rolled for everything you've got. For serious spelunkers only.

---

*A cross between Che Guevara and Houdini, **K I Singh** led the western insurgents in the 1951 overthrow of the Rana regime, twice being imprisoned and twice escaping. He later briefly served as prime minister.

Eastwards from Mahendra Cave, a trail beckons up the **Kali Khola,** a minor tributary of the
Seti, to the village of Armala. Adventurous types
might want to forge on. Scrambling up the cultivated slopes on either side of the valley might
make for some interesting encounters and good
views. By traversing the ridge to the south, you
should theoretically be able to return to Pokhara
the same day via the Bhalam Khola.

A *gaaine*

About 1km south of Mahendra Cave, the road
from Pokhara passes through **Batulechaur,** a
village locally famous for its **gaaine**. Wandering
minstrels of the old school, *gaaine* are still found
throughout the hills, earning their crust by singing ballads to the accompaniment of the *sarangi*, a
four-stringed, hand-hewn violin: "I have no rice to
eat/let the strings of the *sarangi* set to," runs the *gaaine*'s traditional opening coup-
let. These days, many find they can make better money down at Lakeside serenading tourists, spawning legions of inept imitators.

To vary the route on the way back, take a left onto a paved road just before K I
Singh Pul and then look for a pathway off to the left. From there you can cross
the Kali and Bhalam rivers by footbridges (you'll have to carry your bike a bit) to
get to the Kahun Danda area (see above).

The Pokhara–Baglung Highway

Heading northwest from the bazaar through the valley of the Yamdi Khola, the
Pokhara–Baglung Highway provides the chief access for treks in the
Annapurna region. Currently its endpoint is **Baglung,** a zonal headquarters
72km from Pokhara, but there are plans to extend it all the way up the Thak
Khola to Jomosom. Many trekkers use this road to get to various trailheads, but
other than that it sees few foreign faces. It would make a worthy **biking** route
for one or more days, but note that officially you're supposed to have a trekking
permit and ACAP receipt to proceed beyond Naudanda. The highway will serve
as the return route of a very interesting all-day loop when the
Sarangkot–Naudanda road is roughed in enough for mountain-biking (see
above). **Accommodation** is available at Tashi Palkhel (see p.254), Naudanda
and other villages en route.

As has happened elsewhere, the new highway is introducing enormous
changes to the local social order, bringing wealth and prosperity to a few – mostly
outside developers – and luring young people away to the cities. Only fifteen
years ago, Shining Hospital (now just an empty lot at the north end of Pokhara
Bazaar) was the end of the road, the region beyond accessible only by foot or
pack animal. Today, the Yamdi Khola has been transformed, not only by vehicles,
but also by a hydroelectric project and a roadside smattering of modern concrete
dwellings emanating like a comet's tail from Pokhara Bazaar. The old walking
route is falling into disuse, since trekkers and locals alike seldom walk when they
can ride a bus. Bazaars like Naudanda and Kaare are considerably less busy than
they were even five years ago – not only have they lost the trekkers' business,

they've also lost much of their former market in household provisions, since local residents can now easily do their shopping in Pokhara, previously a day or two's walk away.

The Tibetan settlements

If Tibet were free tomorrow, we'd drop our hammers and go. We wouldn't even think about it.

A Tibetan working on a building project at Tashi Palkhel

Thirty years ago, Dervla Murphy worked as a volunteer among Tibetan refugees in Pokhara, and called the account she wrote about her experiences *The Waiting Land* (see "Books" in *Contexts*). Pokhara's Tibetans are still waiting: three former refugee camps, now self-governing and largely self-sufficient, have settled into a pattern of permanent transience. Because Pokhara (unlike Kathmandu) has no Buddhist holy places, most Tibetans have remained in the camps, regarding them as havens where they can keep their culture and language alive. Many plainly don't see the point of moving out and setting up permanent homes in Nepal when all they really want is to return to their former homes in Tibet.

Two of the three settlements are located outside of Pokhara (a third, Paljorling, is described in the earlier "Pokhara Bazaar" section). They are open to the public, and a wander around one is an experience of workaday reality that contrasts with the otherworldliness of, say, Boudha or Swayambhu. You'll get a lot more out of a visit if you can get someone to show you around – and if the tour inevitably finishes with a sales pitch back at your guide's one-room home, so much the better.

TIBETANS IN EXILE

At the time of the Chinese invasion of Tibet in 1950 and the Dalai Lama's flight in 1959, the **Tibetans** now living in Pokhara were mainly peasants and nomads inhabiting the border areas of western Tibet. The political changes in faraway Lhasa left them initially unaffected, but as the Chinese occupation turned genocidal, thousands streamed south through the Himalaya to safety. They gathered first at Jomosom, where the terrain and climate were at least reminiscent of Tibet, but within months the area became overcrowded and conditions desperate. Under the direction of the Swiss Red Cross, three transit camps were established around low-lying Pokhara and about two thousand refugees were moved down. Thirty years on, the subtropical heat still heightens Tibetans' sense of displacement.

The first five years were hard times in the camps, marked by food rationing, chronic sickness and general unemployment. Relief came in the late 1960s, when the construction of Pardi Dam and the Prithvi and Siddhartha highways provided welcome work. Since then, the Tibetans' fortunes have risen with Pokhara's tourism industry, and carpet-weaving and other handicrafts have become the main source of income, especially for women. Many of the men work seasonally as trekking porters or guides, where they can make better money than in the camps. A small but visible minority have become smooth-talking curio salespeople, plying the cafés of Lakeside and Damside, but whereas Tibetans have by now set up substantial businesses in Kathmandu, opportunities are fewer in Pokhara, and prosperity has come more slowly. See p.401 for more on the lives of Tibetan exiles.

Tashi Palkhel (Hyangja)

With eight hundred residents – sixty of them monks – **TASHI PALKHEL** (also known as **Hyangja**, after the village 3km beyond) is the largest and also the least commercial of Pokhara's Tibetan settlements. The entrance is clearly marked, about 4km northwest of the north end of Pokhara Bazaar on the Pokhara–Baglung Highway. Get there by bike, taxi or a bus from the Baglung bus park. If you're doing the Siklis trek you can hit the trail not far from here.

As soon as you enter the village you'll be adopted by friendly but insistent saleswomen, who'll escort you to the **gompa** and wait to make their pitch as you come out. The *gompa* is of the Kagyu-pa sect, and portraits either side of the Buddha statue inside the hall depict the Dalai Lama and the late Kagyu leader, the sixteenth Karma Lama. A long **weaving hall** is the focal point of Tashi Palkhel's carpet industry, and forming the other sides of a quadrangle are wool dyeing and drying areas and a co-operative shop. The community also has a school, an old people's home (many of the original refugees are now getting on in years), a clinic and – the latest project – a community hall. **Handicrafts** can be purchased at the co-operative shop, whose profits support community projects, as well as a couple of private enterprises.

If you decide to stay overnight, the camp's co-operative **guest house** can supply rooms (②); hot showers are sometimes available, and camping is possible. Get **food** at the guest house or at one of the camp's smoky, buttery holes-in-the-wall.

Tashiling and Devin's Fall (Patale Chhango)

Much easier to reach, **TASHILING** lies about 2km west of Damside beside the Siddhartha Highway. On a bicycle you can be there in ten or fifteen minutes. With some 550 residents, Tashiling is smaller than Tashi Palkhel, but laid out on much the same lines. It's best to make straight for the weaving hall and wool-dyeing shed, a good 400m down the main drive at the far end of the camp. A short walk from here to the camp's southern edge brings you to an abrupt drop and a glorious panorama of the valley of the Phusre Khola, a Seti tributary. On the way back to the entrance are a *gompa*, a primary school, several rows of distinctly Tibetan barracks-style stone houses (the windows trimmed with characteristic orange and white skirts) and, in a separate compound, a school for Tibetan orphans from all over Nepal. The inescapable souvenir peddlers and **shops** near the entrance sell the usual wares. If you're planning to make any purchases while in Pokhara, it's worth coming here first to establish the going rate – and even if things aren't any cheaper here, you'll have the satisfaction of buying them in their natural environment.

On the opposite side of the highway, **Devin's Fall** (entrance Rs5) marks the spot where the Pardi Khola (the stream that drains Phewa Tal) enters a grottoed channel and sinks underground in a sudden rush of foam and fury. Given a good monsoon run-off in the autumn it can be damned impressive, as the green water corkscrews and thunders into the earth, forcing up a continuous plume of mist; in the spring it's a washout.

The spot is perhaps more interesting as a source of pop mythology: known to locals as **Patale Chhango** (roughly, "waterfall"), the sinkhole is said to have acquired its Western-sounding nickname when a "female European" was drowned while skinny-dipping with her boyfriend. An alternate spelling, David Fall, suggests it may have been the boyfriend who perished. The sign at the entrance reads "Devi's Fall", illustrating the Nepali propensity to deify everything that moves (*devi* means goddess). The whole story sounds like a fabrication to warn local youth to shun promiscuous Western ways.

Begnas Tal and Rupa Tal

With Lakeside and Damside approaching build-out, **Begnas Tal** and **Rupa Tal**, twin lakes lying 15km east of Pokhara, look destined to be the next big tourist discoveries. Begnas Tal, the bigger and better-known of the two, is framed by meticulously engineered paddy terraces marching right down to its shore, while Rupa, on the other side of an intervening ridge, remains pristinely hidden in a bushy, steep-sided valley. Come prepared to spend the night: several lodges can put you up, and roads and trails open up a wealth of outstanding mountain-biking and hiking opportunities.

Getting there is easier than it looks on the map. Buses, departing every hour or so from New Road just south of Chipledhunga, take 45 minutes and tend to be crowded. Cycling is more scenic, and with a mountain bike you'll be able to probe well into the countryside. After the first (mostly downhill) 10km along the Prithvi Highway, turn left at the sign onto a straight, paved road, and from there it's 3km to the end of the line at the hamlet of **Begnas**. You'd never guess it, but Begnas Tal is right around the corner from here. Begnas itself is a cipher: typical of so many roadhead towns, it seems to exist only as a conduit for corrugated roofing, bags of cement and other tools of progress for the surrounding hills.

The quick approach to Begnas Tal – not to be confused with the scenic one – is the dirt road to the left immediately before the cul-de-sac where the buses stop. It's not even five minutes' walk along here to the dam at the south end of the lake, below which the Ministry of Agriculture has built a huge **fish farm**, consisting of concrete holding tanks fed by water from the lake. Fish farming is getting to be big business here, with Chinese carp and native *sahar* and *mahseer* being raised for restaurants in Pokhara and Kathmandu. Phewa-style **boats** are rented out beside the lake just beyond the dam; with tent-shaped Annapurna II for a backdrop, the boating here is at least as scenic as at Phewa Tal, and you'll practically have the lake to yourself.

A better introduction to the lakes, although it involves a fair amount of up and down, is the trail along **Panchbhaiya Danda**. Starting at the bus turnaround, follow a graded dirt road north for about twenty minutes, then take the trail to the left, which ascends steadily along the ridge dividing the two lakes (mountain-bikers, stay on the road). Begnas is visible first, on the left, and then Rupa comes into view after the highest point of the ridge is passed, about 45 minutes from the bus stop. Local belief has it that the lakes are husband and wife, and that an object thrown into one lake will eventually appear in the other. What appear to be fences peeping above the water of both lakes are more fish farms – Rupa Tal is said to be particularly rich in nutrients. In another ten minutes or so the trail rejoins the road and then a

Harvesting rice

few minutes later reaches the half-dozen shops of **Sundari Dhaara**, and from here on it's follow-your-nose time.

A trail leading off to the right, signposted "Karputar", descends to the north end of Rupa Tal and the village of **Talbesi**, with the additional possibility of a steep side trip to the hilltop fortress of **Rupakot**. This trail makes an attractive alternative way into the Annapurna Circuit. Further down the road, a trail to the left leads down to the lake (from which you may be able to get a boat back to the dam area) and up to another Begnas village, and eventually joins up with the main trail north to the Siklis trekking area. The road itself swings around to Talbesi, and is eventually supposed to be pushed all the way through to Besisahar. When buses are able to negotiate this route, expect it to vie in popularity with the one from Dumre – but also to kill off the walking route.

Practicalities

Suddenly everybody's opening **guest houses** around Begnas Tal. Several are crowded near the dam, an easy walk from the bus stop – the location is good for access to the lake, but otherwise lacklustre. Others along the Panchbhaiya Danda trail are harder to get to and on the whole more primitive, but indescribably peaceful. The latter definitely have the better views. Meanwhile, at least two luxury resort hotels are being built below Panchbhaiya Danda on the Begnas side, and no doubt others will follow.

Obviously, the **food** served by the guest houses here is pretty unexciting compared to what's on offer in Pokhara, although it probably won't be long before tourist menus make their appearance. Apart from the guest houses, the only other eateries are a couple of *bhojanalaya* near the bus stop, serving typical Nepali food.

ALONG PANCHBHAIYA DANDA

Begnas Lake Viewpoint Lodge. Traditional cottage with lush gardens and an excellent view of Begnas. Absolutely idyllic, so long as you don't mind roughing it (no electricity or foam mattresses). ①.

Dinesh House. Fabulous views of both lakes, but somewhat less friendly. Electricity. ②.

P R Lodge. Again, great views, but very dreary facilities. ①.

NEAR THE DAM

Dolphin Lodge. Basic accommodation and food. ②.

Evergreen Lodge. Small place with basic rooms, outdoor seating and music. ②.

Happy Days. Accommodation in a family's house, with the best views from this area. ①.

Hotel Rupa & Begnas. A Lakeside-style tower block overlooking the fish ponds and a bit of the lake. The only lodge with hot water. ②/B③.

SOUTH OF POKHARA

The only through road beyond Pokhara, the **Siddhartha Highway** (Siddhartha Rajmarg), points south: a slow, uncomfortable, but occasionally rewarding journey to the Tarai. In 160km the highway traverses four major river drainages, negotiates countless twists and turns, and often claims a tyre or an axle. Six hours would be a fast run. Although it's the most direct route between Pokhara and the Indian border, give some thought to going via Chitwan if you're travelling by bus. Cyclists, however, will enjoy the variety, light traffic and relatively easy gradients.

From Pokhara, the road labours 800m up to a divide before descending to **Naudanda**, a little-used alternative starting point for treks into the Kali Gandaki/ Annapurna region; minibuses from Chipledhunga in Pokhara shuttle up here every half-hour or so. An old Kaski fortress guards the pass from the hill just to the east. Entering the **Amdhi Khola** watershed, the highway wriggles tortuously across the side of the valley, purposely avoiding the flat, straight valley floor – in a country so reliant on agriculture, you don't put a road through the best farmland. After the bazaar of **Syangja**, the valley draws in and the hills rear up spectacularly in places, although you can't help noticing how badly overworked and eroded the land is in settled areas. Public buses stop at **Waling**, a nondescript wayside that owes its existence to busloads of hungry travellers. Tourist buses take a break at **Ramdi Ghat**, where the road crosses the rugged canyon of the **Kali Gandaki** and rafting parties pull out, before climbing almost 1000m to its highest point. A few kilometres beyond is the turning for Tansen, the only town of note in this area. From there it's an hour's descent to Butwal and the Tarai (covered in Chapter Five). This last forty-kilometre stretch is prone to landslides and so is often in dreadful shape, but an ongoing project to build retaining walls should help reduce its vulnerability.

Tansen

TANSEN is sold as is, unvarnished for tourist sensibilities. Once the seat of a powerful kingdom and now a lowly district headquarters, it makes no attempt to be anything but a typical market town in the heartland of the western hills. Yet slowly, almost reluctantly, Tansen yields its secrets: clacking *dhaka* looms glimpsed though doorways; the potters of Ghorabanda; the view from Srinagar Hill. Above all, it makes a superb base for day hikes and bikes in the surrounding countryside. As long as you're passing by on the Siddhartha Highway it's well worth breaking the journey here – especially if you're coming from India, for Tansen makes a more authentic introduction to Nepal than Pokhara.

Tansen's **history** goes back to the early sixteenth century, when it was known as Palpa, and when the Sen clan of princes, already established at Butwal, chose it as a safer base from which to expand family holdings that soon covered the length of the lower hills, almost to Sikkim. Makunda Sen, Palpa's legendary second king, allegedly raided Kathmandu and carried off two sacred Bhairab masks, only to be cut down by a plague sent by the Pashupatinath *linga*. Chastened by the king's death, his successors settled for forming a strategic alliance with Gorkha, which bought them breathing space when the latter began conquering territory in the mid-eighteenth century. Aided by a friendly Indian rajah, Palpa staved off the inevitable until 1806, when it became the last territory to be annexed to modern Nepal. Tansen remains the headquarters of Palpa District, and many still nostalgically refer to it as Palpa. You might also hear it called Tansing, which was its original Magar name – the hills here are Magar country, although the town is now predominantly Newar.

Arrival

Public **buses** serve Tansen from Pokhara, Butwal, Kathmandu and Kakarbitta (see p.220 for frequencies and times); from other points in the Tarai, change at Butwal. Coming from Pokhara or Sunauli you've also got the option of taking a

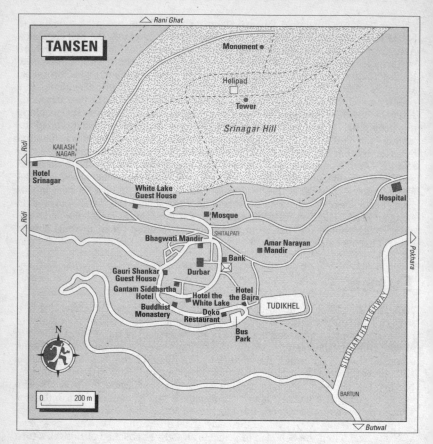

faster and more comfortable tourist bus. However, tourist buses don't leave the Siddhartha Highway, and instead drop you off at Bartun, the village at the start of the three-kilometre Tansen spur road. A Tansen-bound bus will take you the rest of the way, or you can hoof it up the steep one-kilometre short cut that starts immediately north of the intersection.

There are no taxis or rikshas in Tansen. However, **bicycle** rental can be arranged informally through most guest houses (mountain bikes may be available). *Gauri Shankar Guest House* has a motorcycle for rent.

The Town

Tansen spills down the flank of Srinagar Hill, with the **bus park** occupying the lowest, newest level, surrounded by a tacky bazaar area. Things improve once you've found your way to the **upper town**. The direct footpath up from *Hotel the Bajra* emerges at what English-speakers call Bank Street, home of a modest bazaar and a *Nepal Bank* branch; across the street is the prosaic twentieth-century

Durbar. Bank Street ends at Shitalpati, where you'll find the only visible reminder of Tansen's grand past – **Mul Dhoka** (Main Gate), tall enough for elephants and their riders to pass through, and reputedly the biggest of its kind in Nepal. West of here lie Tansen's oldest neighbourhoods, whose cobbled alleys and brick houses could pass for parts of Kathmandu, minus the crowds. An undistinguished **Bhagwati Mandir** enshrines the hostess of Tansen's biggest festival, the Bhagwati Jaatra (late Aug–early Sept), which, in addition to its religious function, also commemorates an 1814 battle in which Nepal routed British troops near here. The lane going east from Shitalpati leads down to the nineteenth-century **Amar Narayan Mandir**, a pagoda-style temple that's the stopping place for sadhus on their way to Janai Purnima festivities at Muktinath in late July or early August.

Wherever you wander, keep an eye out for **dhaka weavers**, who work at wooden treadle looms shaped like upright pianos. Woven in many hill areas, *dhaka* fabric is created by shuttling coloured threads back and forth across a constant vertical background to form repeating, geometric patterns. Palpali *dhaka*'s trademark is the use of brightly dyed *pashmina*, a fine goat's wool, against a white cotton background – it's famous throughout Nepal, and many *topi* (Nepali caps) are made from it. The simplicity of *dhaka* designs allows for almost infinite improvisation: each weaver decides without chart or counting threads where to lay the colours to form the patterns; many know a hundred or more basic designs and invent new ones all the time. The process is labour-intensive and the fabric doesn't come cheap: a good-quality Palpali weave will set you back Rs400 a metre, although you can get lesser quality for as little as Rs100. Many shops in the bazaar sell nothing but *dhaka*.

Accommodation

Tansen has several unassuming but adequate **guest houses**, though you have to search them out: refer to the map for locations. Don't settle for the lodges ranged around the bus park, which are noisy and a steep slog from the centre.

Gauri Shankar Guest House (☎075/20150). Big rooms, tolerably clean, but the immediate surroundings are marred by a vehicle repair shop and a noisy road. ②/B③.

Gautam Siddhartha Guest House (☎075/20280). Friendly, clean and fairly quiet. No hot water, however. ②.

Hotel Srinagar (☎075/20045). It's difficult to understand how this place keeps afloat. It's got great views nearby, but the facilities and service are terrible for the price. B⑦.

Hotel the Bajra (☎075/20443). A big place with decent rooms, just far enough from the bus park to provide some seclusion. Hot water only in rooms with attached baths. ②/B③; also dorm beds for ①.

Hotel the White Lake (☎075/20291). The in-town location makes it somewhat noisier than the *Hotel Srinagar*, but it's much better managed. Decent restaurant. B⑥.

Lumbini Rest House (no phone). A cheaper, cold-water place next door to the *Bajra*. ①/B②.

White Lake Bed & Breakfast (☎075/20174). A comfortable establishment in a very quiet location, with lovely grounds and a fine view of the town below. Brand new at the time of writing, it looks set to become Tansen's premier budget choice, but we'll see if it lives up to its promise. It's a long walk from the bus park, but a pickup service is available (Rs100). ②/B③.

Eating and other practicalities

If you haven't yet tested the waters of Nepali **restaurants**, here's your chance, since Tansen has little else. A modish *bhatti*, the *Doko Restaurant* serves a good range of *momo* and other Newari dishes. Loads of nameless *bhojanalaya* and *mithai pasal* around the bus park and in the old part of town do *daal bhaat*, road snacks and sweets. The guest house dining rooms have rudimentary menus with some Western items, but only *Hotel the White Lake*'s is a serious contender in the tourist food department.

The **bank** can only exchange US dollar travellers' cheques (Sun–Thurs 10am–2pm, Fri 10am–noon).

Around Tansen: Srinagar Hill and beyond

The best thing about Tansen is getting out of it and exploring the outlying hill country and unaffected Magar villages. People on the trail will likely greet you with delighted smiles and the full palms-together *namaste* – a sign of gratitude for the assistance provided by foreign doctors at the nearby United Mission Hospital, which they will tend to assume you work for.

First stop on most excursions is **Srinagar Hill** (Srinagar Danda), north of town. The most direct route, which takes about half an hour on foot, starts from a small Ganesh temple above Shitalpati, but you have to zigzag a bit to get to the temple. From *Hotel Srinagar* it's an easy twenty-minute walk east along the ridge. The top (1525m) is planted with thick pine forest – catch the view from the helipad or the open area west of *Hotel Srinagar*. Dhaulagiri and Annapurna are particularly dramatic from here; Machhapuchhre is less dominant than from the perspective of Pokhara, but its true "fishtail" profile is visible from this angle. On the other side, beyond Tansen, lies the luxuriant Madi Valley, which in autumn and on winter mornings is filled with a silver fog. The area north of the helipad, just below the summit, has been turned into a municipal park complete with nine-hole golf course.

Rani Ghat

For walks beyond Srinagar there are at least two strong options, the first being the fourteen-kilometre round-trip to **RANI GHAT**, site of a fantastically derelict palace along the Kali Gandaki. The trail begins 200m east of *Hotel Srinagar* (locals call this intersection Kailash Nagar) and descends through an immensely satisfying landscape of farmland, trailside hamlets and, finally, a jungly gorge with impressive waterfalls. The walk itself takes three or four hours, but you'll want to set aside the whole day.

Set in a tranquil spot beside the turquoise Kali Gandaki, Rani Ghat is the site of occasional cremations, as well as an annual **festival** on the *ekadashi* of Kartik (the eleventh day of the bright fortnight of October–November). But the main attraction here is the spooky old **palace**, which was built in the late nineteenth century by a former govern-

ment minister who, according to the custom of the day, was exiled to Palpa after a failed palace coup. Perched atop an outcrop directly overlooking the river, it's now nothing but an overgrown shell – the only part of it still maintained is a small Shiva shrine in the courtyard. You get a great view of it from the suspension bridge that crosses the river here.

Terraced fields in the western hills

Rani Ghat itself isn't really a village, just a couple of *chiya pasal* that offer only very limited food and emergency shelter. Bring a lunch and picnic on the tranquil, sandy beach.

To return to Tansen by a more adventurous route, follow the trail downstream through pleasant forest, reaching **Ramdi Ghat** beside the Siddhartha Highway in about three or four hours. You can get food here while you wait for a bus to take you back up to the Tansen turn-off.

To Ridi Bazaar

RIDI BAZAAR makes an equally eventful all-day outing, either on foot (13km one way, with the option of busing back) or by bike. From *Hotel Srinagar*, walk west to a fork at a police checkpost, bear right and in half an hour you'll reach Chandi Bhanjyang; turn left here and descend through a handsome canyon before rejoining the unpaved road for the last 7km. On a bike, stay on the main road all the way.

Set on the banks of the Kali Gandaki, Ridi is considered sacred because of the wealth of **shaligrams** – fossil-bearing stones associated with Vishnu – found in the river here. It used to be said that if a person were cremated at Ridi and his ashes sprinkled into the river, they would congeal to form a *shaligram*, and if the stone were then made into a likeness of Vishnu, the devotee would be one with his god. The spiral-shaped ammonite fossils typically found in *shaligram* are 150–200 million years old, dating from a time when the entire Himalayan region was submerged under a shallow sea.

Ridi has declined in importance over the years, but remains an occasional cremation ground and, during the **festival** of Magh Sankranti (January 14 or 15), a pilgrimage site for ritual bathing. The colourful commercial end of town lies across a stream that joins the Kali Gandaki here, while the magical eighteenth-century **Rishikesh Mandir** is south of the stream, just above the bus stop. According to legend, the idol inside the squat temple, a form of Vishnu, was fished out of the river and originally bore the likeness of a young boy, but over the course of years has matured into adult form.

Several **buses** a day head back to Tansen, taking two hours. The return journey can be combined with a visit to **Palpa Bhairab**, up a short path off the road 8km before Tansen. The Bhairab image here is supposed to be so scary that not even the priest is allowed to look at it (it's actually a replica of Kathmandu's easily viewable Kalo Bhairab), and the gilded *trisul* is claimed to be the biggest in Asia. Animal sacrifices are performed on Saturdays and Tuesdays.

Ghorabanda

The most fascinating of the villages east of Tansen, **GHORABANDA** is locally famous for its **potters**. It's just off the Siddhartha Highway, 3km north of the Tansen turning, but without your own wheels you'll have to walk. Take the dirt road from the Amar Narayan temple towards the United Mission Hospital, bear right onto a trail after about 500m, descend and then contour through extensive paddy – if you've done it right, you'll drop down to the highway after about 2km, with Ghorabanda another 1km further along the road. Ghorabanda's potters, members of the Kumal caste, throw their almost spherical water jugs on heavy clay flywheels, shaping them and adding a stipple pattern with a wooden paddle, then sun-drying and finally kiln-firing them. The farmhouses and potteries of Ghorabanda spread down the hill from the highway.

CHAPTER FIVE

THE WESTERN TARAI

I n a country best known for its mountains, the lowland **Tarai** often gets short shrift. A narrow strip of flatland extending along the entire length of Nepal's southern border – including several *dun* (inner Tarai) valleys north of the first range of hills – the Tarai was originally covered in thick, malarial jungle. In the 1950s, however, the government identified the fertile southern plains as a major growth area to relieve population pressure in the hills, and, with the help of liberal quantities of DDT, brought malaria under control. Since then the jungle has been methodically cleared and the Tarai has emerged as Nepal's most productive agricultural and industrial region, representing seventy percent of the country's arable land and accounting for more than half its GDP. The barrier that had once insulated Nepal from Indian influences as effectively as the Himalaya had guarded the north, making possible the development of a uniquely Nepali culture, has been replaced by the geographic and political equivalent of a welcome mat. An unmistakeable quality of Indianness now pervades the Tarai, as evidenced by the avid mercantilism of the border bazaars, the wearing of *lungyi* and the chewing of betel,

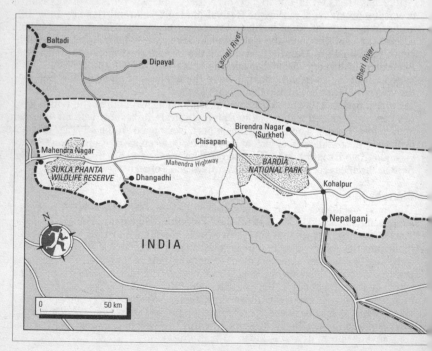

Muslim mosques and orthodox Brahmanism, the heat and dust, the jute mills and sugar refineries, and the many roads and irrigation projects built with Indian aid.

Fortunately, the government has set aside sizeable chunks of the **western Tarai** in the form of national parks and reserves, which remain as some of the finest **wildlife** and bird havens on the subcontinent. Dense riverine forest provides cover for predators like tigers and leopards, swampy grasslands make the perfect habitat for rhinoceros, and vast, tall stands of *sal*, the Tarai's most common tree, thronged with what at times seems to be the entire cast of Bambi. You'll probably only have the time to visit one national park. **Chitwan**, the richest in game and the most accessible, is deservedly popular, but if crowds bother you and you're willing to invest some extra effort, check out **Bardia** or **Sukla Phanta**.

The region's other claim to fame is historical: the Buddha was born 2500 years ago at **Lumbini**, and his birthplace – one of the four most important pilgrimage sites for Buddhists – is an appropriately serene place.

Bus connections to the Tarai from Kathmandu and Pokhara are well developed via Narayanghat; the two most common destinations are Sauraha for Chitwan and Sunauli for the **Indian border**. The Tarai itself is traversed by a single main road, the **Mahendra Highway** (Mahendra Rajmarg, also known as the **East–West Highway**), now paved nearly all the way to the far western border, making possible an adventurous backdoor route between Kathmandu and Delhi. Traffic drops off dramatically west of Butwal, which makes for great **cycling** but potentially long waits for bus connections. Internal **flights**, while expensive and not always reliable, can save a lot of time.

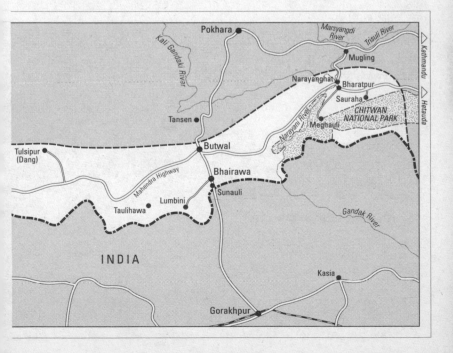

The **weather** in the Tarai is at its best from October to January – the days are more pleasantly mild during the latter half of this period, though the nights can be surprisingly chilly and damp. However, the wildlife viewing gets much better after the thatch has been cut, from late January on, by which time the temperatures are starting to warm up again. It gets really hot (especially in the far west) in April, May and June. The monsoon brings not only rain but mosquitoes and malaria, and many roads become impassable at this time.

PUBLIC BUS SERVICES IN THE WESTERN TARAI			
	Frequency (day)	Frequency (night)	Time (minimum)
To and from BHAIRAWA			
Butwal	24		1hr 30min
Janakpur	1		12hr
Kathmandu	1#	2#	9hr
Lumbini	18		1hr 30min
Taulihawa	2		3hr
To and from BUTWAL			
Bhairawa/Sunauli	24		1hr 30min
Biratnagar		2	14hr
Birganj	4	3	6hr
Dhangadhi		2	9hr
Janakpur		3	10hr
Kathmandu	5	17	8hr
Mahendra Nagar	1	2	11hr
Nepalganj	4		6hr
Pokhara	17	8	7hr
Tansen	30		2hr 30min
To and from DHANGADHI			
Baitadi	1		16hr
Dadeldhura	1		8hr
Dipayal	1		14hr
Kathmandu		2	21hr
Mahendra Nagar	10		3hr
Nepalganj	2		6hr
Pokhara		1	21hr
To and from JAGATPUR			
Narayanghat	10		2hr
To and from MAHENDRA NAGAR			
Banbasa (border)	20		30min
Birganj		1	22hr
Dhangadhi	10		3hr
Kathmandu		2	24hr
Nepalganj	3		8hr
To and from MEGHAULI			
Kathmandu	1#		7hr
Narayanghat	7		2hr

CHITWAN AND AROUND

Whatever your itinerary, **Chitwan National Park** is likely to be your first destination in the Tarai. The park is just a short detour off the Prithvi (Kathmandu–Pokhara) Highway, and if you're travelling to or from India it can be visited on the way.

	Frequency (day)	Frequency (night)	Time (minimum)
To and from NARAYANGHAT*			
Devghat	6		30min
Gorkha	7		3hr
Jagatpur	10		2hr
Kathmandu	9#		5hr
Meghauli	7		2hr
Pokhara	12		4hr
Tadi Bazaar	20		45min
To and from NEPALGANJ			
Birendra Nagar (Surkhet)	8		6hr
Butwal	4	5	6hr
Dhangadhi	2		6hr
Janakpur		2	16hr
Mahendra Nagar	3		8hr
Kathmandu	1#	6#	15hr
Pokhara		2	15hr
Thakurdwara	1		3hr
To and from SAURAHA (CHITRASARI)			
Kathmandu	*		
Pokhara	*		
To and from SUNAULI			
Butwal	24		2hr
Gorkha	1		7hr
Kathmandu	8	17	10hr
Pokhara	6*	3	10hr
To and from TADI BAZAAR*			
Kathmandu	1#		6hr
Narayanghat	20		45min
To and from TAULIHAWA			
Bhairawa	2		3hr
Kathmandu	1#		12hr
To and from THAKURDWARA			
Nepalganj	1		3hr

* Tourist bus services also available – see the respective sections for details.
** Many other buses pass through (in the case of Bhairawa, most originate in Sunauli).
# *Sajha* service available.

Chitwan is the name not only of the park but also of the surrounding *dun* valley and administrative district. The name means "heart of the jungle" – a description that, sadly, now holds true only for the lands protected within the park. Yet the rest of the **valley**, though it's been reduced to a flat, furrowed plain, still provides fascinating vignettes of a rural lifestyle that's different again from the hill-clinging existence of upland Nepal. Really ugly development is confined to the wayside conurbation of **Narayanghat/Bharatpur** – and even this has left the nearby holy site of **Devghat** unscathed.

Chitwan National Park

The best and worst aspects of **CHITWAN NATIONAL PARK** are that it can be done on the cheap and it's relatively easy to get to. In recent years the park has risen meteorically on the list of Things to Do in Nepal, so that these days, unless you go during the steamy season, you'll have to share your experience with a lot of other people.

You're forgiven if you thought **Sauraha** is where budget tourists stay in Chitwan. For all intents and purposes, it is. In the late 1970s some genius had the idea of setting up a little thatched-roof lodge just outside the Sauraha park entrance, and the place has basically had a monopoly ever since. But package trips have taken a lot of the spontaneity out of Sauraha, and in autumn, with the inhabitants of forty-odd lodges all converging on the same finite patch of park, the area can get uncomfortably crowded. If you don't mind roughing it a little, try **Gaighat**, **Jagatpur** or **Meghauli** instead. Or, if you've got the money – usually at least $100 a night, all-in – go for pampered seclusion at any one of half a dozen luxury lodges and tented camps **inside the park**.

Chitwan has perhaps been oversold in recent years, often with misleading promises of "safari adventure". While its **wildlife** is astoundingly concentrated, remember that the dense vegetation doesn't allow the easy sightings you get in the savannas of Africa. But go with realistic expectations, don't buy into the package-tour mentality, and it's still possible to enjoy yourself. **Elephant rides**, **jeep tours**, **canoe trips** and just plain **walks** each give a different slant on the luxuriant, teeming forest.

Park entry permits are valid for two consecutive days, which tends to dictate the length of most travellers' stays. Rushed as it is, this can work out quite reasonably, but don't be led into thinking that you can "do" Chitwan in two nights and three days.

About budget packages

Avoid them. Packaged Chitwan "safaris" booked in Kathmandu or Pokhara don't cost that much more than what you'd spend on your own, but truth be told, they don't save you much trouble, either. A three-day package only gives you a day and a half in the park, and you'll have little control over the if-it's-8am-it-must-be time-for-the-bird-walk programme of activities. You probably won't get to choose your guide, or even what to eat. If you must be bound by an itinerary, at least book it direct through the lodge's own office in Kathmandu or Pokhara, which will be more accountable for arrangements than an agent will be. You can get office addresses and phone numbers by collecting brochures from agents. Figure on $50 per person for a two-night stay in a budget lodge with common bath ($60

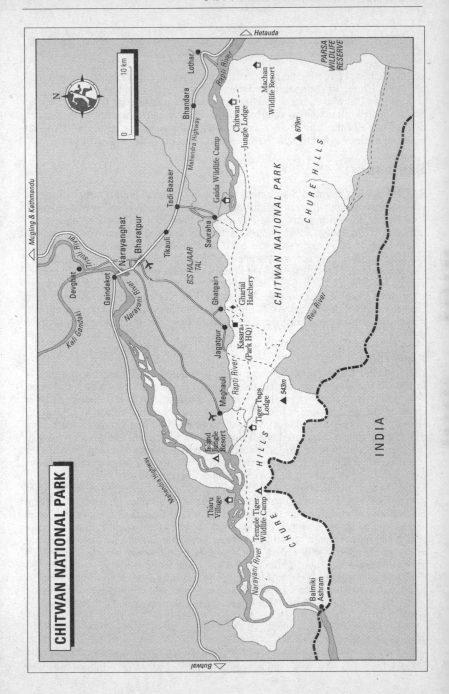

The telephone code for Sauraha and Chitwan District is ☎056.

with attached bath), including meals, bus transport, park entry permit and activities. (Doing the same thing independently will cost about $5 less.)

A visit to Chitwan can also be combined with a **raft trip** on the Trisuli River, bookable through rafting operators in Kathmandu and Pokhara. But while this can cut out some of the long drive, no matter what the salesman says, the raft won't take you all the way to the park: Narayanghat is normally the end of the line.

Sauraha

SAURAHA (pronounced *So*-ruh-hah), Chitwan's original budget safari village, is one of those unstoppably successful destinations at which Nepal seems to excel. It is, in fact, the spitting image of Pokhara's Lakeside a decade or so ago: quiet, unpaved lanes, folksy guest houses, a few restaurants and provisions stalls, a smattering of bikes for rent, the odd bookshop and ticketing office, and a growing number of concrete eyesores (as if in homage, there's even a *Hungry Eye Restaurant*). The village still retains much of its intimacy and its unhurried, almost soporific character, but each year, like Lakeside, it loses a little more of what once made it so enjoyable. The arrival of electricity looks likely to take Sauraha further down that road. Lights, refrigeration and sound systems will suddenly seem natural, even indispensable, but something special will have died.

Getting there

Daily **tourist buses** serve Sauraha from Kathmandu and Pokhara; the fare is Rs150–200 (minibuses are more expensive) and the journey takes about six hours. The buses don't actually go all the way to Sauraha, due to an unspanned river crossing, so the last stop is a dusty parking area near the village of Chitrasari, where the touts will have prepared the usual ambush for you. Cross the footbridge to the waiting fleet of battered guest house jeeps, which will take you the remaining 3km for a fixed price (Rs30). Each guest house has its own jeep, so whoever you ride with will probably make every effort to win your business – you don't have to stay at their place, of course, but count on being dropped off there.

The nearest **public bus** stop is Tadi Bazaar on the Mahendra Highway, 6km north of Sauraha. Tadi isn't a final destination for most services (the exception being *Sajha* from Kathmandu), but any bus passing by Tadi along the Mahendra Highway will let you off there. However, getting a ride from Tadi to Sauraha may be a problem. If you arrive by midday your chances of meeting up with a guest house jeep are pretty good (again, Rs30). Failing that, you may have to walk or cycle. The walk is pretty dull and takes about an hour and a half – just follow the road south from the Tadi bus stop and you'll enter Sauraha along its main drag. If you think you can pedal with a pack on, rent a bike in Tadi and have your guest house return it later.

It's also possible to **fly** to Bharatpur, about 15km west of Tadi Bazaar – see p.282.

Accommodation

Sauraha has a great tradition of "camp"-style **accommodation** – the best guest houses here are like rustic little country clubs, with simple bungalows, airy

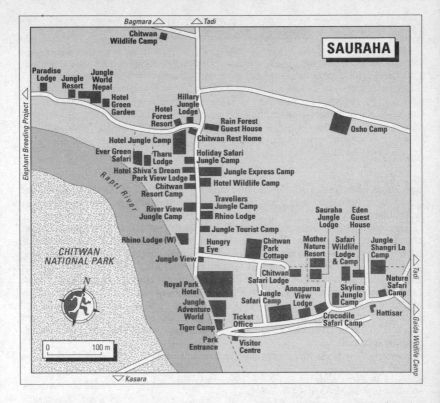

dining pavilions and shady gardens or open lawns. Unfortunately, many are forsaking traditional mud and thatch for concrete, and some of the newer places, with their regimental rows of bunkers and little or no shade, look more like prison camps than jungle camps.

Most lodges line up shoulder to shoulder along the village's main north–south strip, but other, more secluded ones are scattered in the area east of the park entrance. Newer outfits are proliferating along the road leading westwards to the elephant-breeding project – a quiet but rather lonely and inconvenient area. When deciding where to stay, aim for a place that isn't too far from the park entrance: after a four-hour jungle walk, the last thing you'll feel like doing is trudging an extra fifteen minutes along a road in the midday heat. It's also worth paying more to be beside the river.

BUDGET LODGES

Sauraha's **budget lodges**, which outnumber the rest by a wide margin, are the ones so aggressively promoted by the touts at the bus stop. They charge a fairly constant rate of Rs100–150 for bungalows with access to a common bathroom, or Rs350–400 for attached bath where available; add Rs100 for a room with a fan. Prices will often drop dramatically when occupancy is low, and **discounts** for singles can generally be negotiated. Common-bath huts typically have mud walls,

ROOM PRICE SCALES

All guest houses and hotels have been price-graded according to the scale outlined below, which represents the cheapest available double room in high season; codes prefixed by B denote the cost of a room with attached bathroom. See p.35 for a fuller explanation of the system.

① Less than Rs100   ⑤ $8–12
   ($1.75 if quoted in US$)   ⑥ $12–20
② Rs100–175 ($1.75–3)   ⑦ $20–40
③ Rs175–300 ($3–5)   ⑧ $40–70
④ $5–8   ⑨ Over $70

dirt floors and screen windows; the ones with attached baths are bigger and made of breezeblocks and glass. Hot water and mosquito netting should come with either category.

The lodgings are too spread out, and it's usually too hot, to do much comparison-shopping in Sauraha. The best strategy is to decide on a guest house in advance, and try to get a ride with a jeep that's going directly there. The following list is short, but highly selective. It specifically excludes several lodges that, for various reasons, should be avoided: *Crocodile Safari Camp*, *Holiday Safari Jungle Lodge*, *Jungle Tourist Camp*, *Rain Forest Guest House* and *Tharu Lodge*. Many others indicated on the map are perfectly fine, but can't be recommended because, frankly, they probably won't still be in business by the time you get there: the coming of electricity is expected to cause quite a shakeout in Sauraha's lodging sector.

Annapurna View Lodge (no phone). Nice location and grounds, with a short, shady walk to the park boundary. ②.

Chitwan Resort Camp (no phone). Close to the village but reasonably insulated from it. Standard facilities, sun and shade. B④.

Eden Guest House (☎29371). Friendly, with good music programmes. ②/B④.

Jungle Resort (Kathmandu office: ☎410303). Well-managed, traditional architecture but a bit short on vegetation. B④.

Rhino Lodge (☎29365). Bungalows in the riverside section have unbeatable views, though the facilities are rather dreary. B④.

River View Jungle Camp (no phone). It isn't actually on the river, but it's close enough. Pricier than most, but with pleasant, leafy grounds. ③/B⑤.

MODERATE AND EXPENSIVE LODGES

Price is not necessarily an indicator of quality in Sauraha. Some lodges charge deluxe prices for budget facilities, on the theory that package tourists will never know the difference. However, the ones listed here are a cut or two above the budget pack – you should be able to count on superior location or grounds, good (or at least better) food, reliable jeeps, and small touches like a library, slide shows and enough binoculars to go around.

These lodges get by mainly on package business, so their Kathmandu offices may not want

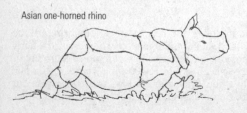

Asian one-horned rhino

to book accommodation only. However, they'll take you on an accommodation-only basis if you just show up, enabling you to save quite a bit of money by paying for activities à la carte.

Hotel Jungle Camp (Kathmandu office: ☎222132). Extensive forested grounds, nifty bamboo bungalows, two restaurants. Pool planned. B⑧.

Osho Camp (☎29367). Huge, shady and very peaceful grounds. Rates include vegetarian meals and meditation sessions. ⑤/B⑦.

Royal Park Hotel (Kathmandu office: ☎412987). River views, good restaurant, safari-style outdoor bar. B⑦.

Tiger Camp (Kathmandu office: ☎522641; Pokhara ☎21435). Possibly the best location in Sauraha, overlooking the river right at the park entrance. Good restaurant. Marvellous *machaan* (watchtower)-like huts (shared bath) and more run-of-the-mill bungalows. ⑦/B⑦.

Eating and drinking

Most people just eat what their **guest house** puts in front of them. In the budget category, food varies little from one place to the next, being limited to variations on cutlets, macaroni, chow mein and trusty *daal bhaat* – not very appetizing, by and large, but you get to hobnob with guides and fellow travellers, and dinner often ends with music and dance.

The **restaurants** in Sauraha's burgeoning little dining quarter are nowhere near as sophisticated as those in Nepal's other tourist hotspots, but they at least offer the chance to break free from the guest house routine and put a little variety in your diet. The *Jungle View* and *Hungry Eye* have the best views of the river. You could also visit one of the posher guest houses for a nice meal – *Tiger Camp* and *Royal Park Hotel* can be recommended – or go for really cheap local fare at one of the *bhatti* at the eastern edge of the village (around *Nature Safari Camp*).

Some of the tourist restaurants advertise "happy hours" and are beginning to acquire some of the trappings of actual **nightspots**. No doubt they'll become more proficient over time. *Jungle Pub*, a desert-island-castaway pub directly overlooking the river, is a particularly romantic place for an evening drink. Don't stay out after 10pm or so though, to avoid unplanned encounters with wildlife.

Entertainment

Sauraha's trademark entertainment is the **Tharu stick dance**, a mock battle in which participants parry each other's sticks with graceful, split-second timing. The original purpose of the dance, it's said, was simply to make a lot of racket to keep the wild animals away at night. On any given night in the high season, local villagers will perform at several Sauraha lodges for package groups or anyone prepared to stump up Rs500. (They do the dance for real during Faagun Purnima, the full moon of Feb–March.) Some lodges (notably *Eden Guest House*) also host informal folk-dancing sessions where audience participation is expected, if not coerced.

Two establishments in the village, *Chitwan Culture House* and *Nepali Culture House*, put on nightly **culture shows** featuring costumed programmes of regional music and dance for tourist consumption (Rs120).

Park practicalities

Park **entry permits** (Rs650 for 2 days, plus a Rs10 hotel association fee) are purchased at the ranger's office (daily 6–10am & 2–3pm) to the left of the visitor centre. (A park permit may also be required to enter certain forested areas outside the park, such as Bis Hajaar Tal, but this policy seems to be irregularly enforced.) The permit queue can be slow around opening time, so get there early, or pay someone at your lodge to wait for you (Rs50–100 surcharge). Elephant rides can be booked at the same time. Ask to see the ticket before setting off, as guides sometimes try to sneak tourists into the park with invalid tickets – if caught, you'd have to pay the fine. There's no formal park **entrance**; you enter by canoe or by wading across the river.

The **visitors' centre** (daily 6am–6pm) has a modest but informative display on the ecology of the park. The **maps** on the wall are useful for getting your bearings; park maps are also sold in Sauraha, but they're not very detailed.

Guides

Don't enter rhino or tiger habitat, inside or outside the park, without a **guide**. Sauraha's guides are some of the most keen, personable characters you'll meet in Nepal, on and off the job. Their knowledge of species, especially birds, can be encyclopedic. Guides are certified as "junior", "senior" or "advanced" under a Peace Corps-initiated programme, and should be able to show their credentials. Junior guides are not only less experienced, they also speak less English, so there's more risk of miscommunication in a dangerous situation. (If your guide yells *look*, that means

---

CHITWAN IN THE BALANCE

It's an open question whether Chitwan has been blessed or cursed by its own riches. Its big game couldn't escape the notice of trigger-happy maharajas for long: when Jang Bahadur Rana overthrew the Shah dynasty in 1846, one of his first actions was to make Chitwan a private hunting preserve for rulers and visiting dignitaries. The following century saw some truly hideous **hunts** – King George V, during an eleven-day shoot in 1911, killed 39 tigers and 18 rhinos. In those days the technique, if you could call it that, was to send *shikari* (trackers) into the forest to locate a tiger and set out a buffalo calf as bait. The sahibs were then alerted, loaded onto elephants and, joined by other huntsmen, the whole party of as many as 600 elephants and riders would approach the spot from all directions. As the circle closed, helpers would spread white sheets between the advancing elephants to keep the tiger from breaking through. High up in their howdahs, the sahibs could get off shots at point-blank range.

Still, the Ranas' patronage afforded Chitwan a certain degree of protection, as did malaria. That all changed in the early 1950s, when the Ranas were thrown out, the monarchy was restored, and the new government launched its malaria-control programme. Settlers poured in and **poaching** went unpoliced – rhinos, whose horns were (and still are) valued for Chinese medicine and Yemeni knife handles, were especially hard-hit. By 1960, the human population of the valley had trebled to 100,000, and the number of rhinos had plummeted from 1000 to 200. With the Asian one-horned rhino on the verge of extinction, Nepal emerged as an unlikely hero in one of conservation's finest hours. Chitwan was set aside in 1962 as a **rhino sanctuary** (it became Nepal's first national park in 1973) and, despite the endless hype about tigers, rhinos are Chitwan's biggest attraction and its greatest triumph.

Chitwan now boasts nearly 500 one-horned rhinos – a quarter of the species total – and numbers are growing healthily. Poaching isn't nearly the problem here that it is in India, no doubt thanks to the deployment of an entire army batallion in the park, although a recent rise in the number of killings is an ominous trend. (Many observers believe the poaching is an inside job.) About 100 **tigers** have been counted in the park; they, too, are on the rebound, and the establishment in 1984 of

"hide" in Nepali!) Oh, and lone women should watch out for those infamous "night walks".

Every lodge has its own **in-house guides**, but you can also hire one through any of the growing number of freelance **guide services**. If you sign up with an in-house guide you might get stuck trailing around with a group of package tourists, with little choice of departure time or itinerary. A freelance will let you call the shots, but his fee will probably work out more expensive unless you can put together a group of three or more. Hire a senior or advanced freelance guide if you want to do any non-standard walks or explore the park from any of the alternative bases listed below. See the box on p.274 for safety information.

Shopping and other practicalities

Small **shops**, stalls and "bakeries" stock basic food and other items: chocolate, jam, muesli, bread, buns, biscuits, rum, bottled water, film, batteries, toilet paper, postcards and so on. You can even buy and sell books.

Bikes can be rented from a few operators in the village for about Rs60 a day, and some guest houses have their own. A couple of offices provide international **telephone** services, though the rates from here are about Rs20–30 higher per minute

Parsa Wildlife Reserve, adjoining Chitwan to the west, secured a vital secondary habitat for them. Altogether, 51 mammalian species are found in Chitwan, including four kinds of deer, langur, gaur, sloth bear, leopard, the rare gangetic dolphin and an elusive herd of wild elephants that stomp around the southeastern corner. Chitwan is also an important sanctuary for **birds**, with more than 400 species recorded, as well as two varieties of **crocodile**.

But Chitwan's seesaw battle for survival continues. As the **population** of the valley swells to over 250,000, conservationists wonder how much longer residents will tolerate the setting aside of such fertile land, not to mention the destruction of their crops by the rhinos that are protected there. **Tourism** has undoubtedly helped make animals and trees worth more alive than dead, but only to those few in the tourist industry. Local people receive some small compensation in the form of a two-week open season on thatch-gathering in January, but even this benefit is being devalued year by year as tourist lodges use more thatch for themselves. Many feel cheated: the way they see it, the government is managing the park for foreign exchange, not conservation, and while it tells them they have to stay out of the park, it's actually *encouraging* foreigners to enter.

Recent initiatives offer some hope. One is **Parks and People**, a joint project of the UN Development Programme and HMG that's active in Chitwan as well as the other Tarai parks and wildlife reserves. Working from the grassroots up, the project organizes income-generating schemes and small-scale infrastructure improvements for communities inconvenienced by the park. Another effort by WWF–World Wide Fund for Nature and the King Mahendra Trust for Nature Conservation is helping establish **community forests** outside the park, which will provide villagers with an alternative to cutting fuel and fodder illegally inside the park. These projects should receive a boost from the 1995 **Buffer Zone Act**, which authorizes 30–50 percent of the revenues earned from entrance fees to be set aside for local use, though it remains to be seen whether this money will in fact be allocated. Such measures stand to give local people a real stake in the park's continued protection; without them, even an army batallion won't be enough.

For more detail on Tarai wildlife, see "Natural History" in *Contexts*.

STAYING ALIVE IN CHITWAN

Lodge owners and guides often play down the risks associated with tracking wild-life, so as not to scare off business. In fact, **safety** is a serious issue in Chitwan. Since record-keeping began in 1979, over 100 people have been killed by rhinos and 20 by tigers; sloth bears are also dangerous if surprised. Most of those killed have been locals during the January thatch-gathering, but it's unusual for a year to go by without two or three tourist maulings as well. There are no emergency medical facilities in or near the park – the closest hospital is in Bharatpur, a minimum two-hour evacuation when you add up all the stages, which means if there's major bleeding the patient is essentially out of luck.

The best safety tip is not to go into the jungle without a guide, but even a guide can't guarantee your personal safety. Most guides are young and gung-ho, and in their eagerness to please will sometimes encourage tourists to venture too close to animals. And no matter how competent, a guide can't know where all the animals are, nor can he, in an emergency, assist more than one person at a time. You can improve your chances by ensuring that the group is no bigger than four or five clients plus guide, though you must still be responsible for your own safety. A few **tips**: a rhino will lower its head and take a step back if it's about to charge; if it does, try to run in a zigzag path and throw off a piece of clothing (the rhino will stop to smell it), or better yet, climb the nearest big tree. If a bear or tiger charges, climb a *small* tree. Don't get anywhere near a mother with young ones of any of these species.

than they are from Kathmandu. There are no **banks** or registered moneychangers in Sauraha.

Moving on

Leaving Sauraha is easy **by tourist bus**. Your guest house or an agent can arrange the ticket to Kathmandu or Pokhara, and a guest house jeep will get you to the departure point in plenty of time. Just be sure to book as far in advance as possible to be sure of a seat.

Difficulties may arise if your next destination isn't along a tourist bus route. First, your guest house will probably be unable to get you a confirmed seat on a **public bus** from Tadi (the nearest stop), since they all originate elsewhere. Second, there may not be any jeeps going to Tadi when you want to go. The best solution is to get a ride in your guest house's jeep to Tadi whenever it's going (probably in the early morning), and from there catch any local bus heading to Narayanghat, a major transport hub. See p.264 for bus frequencies and journey times.

Agents in Sauraha can also arrange **air tickets** from Bharatpur to Kathmandu (2–3 daily; $50) or Pokhara (1 daily; $40).

Alternative bases

Two other areas outside the park's northern boundary have guest houses, but not, as yet, guides, elephants or other services available for budget travellers. Until they do – and keep your ear to the ground, because this could change – you're better off first going to Sauraha and hiring a guide who's familiar with these other less-trodden parts of the park.

Ghatgain and Jagatpur

Several lodges are located along or near the Rapti River between **GHATGAIN** and **JAGATPUR**, respectively 16km and 20km due west of Sauraha. All are within easy reach of the Kasara park headquarters, the gharial crocodile breeding project, Lami Tal and a good patch of jungle. The government is talking about establishing an official entrance station and possibly quartering elephants near Jagatpur. If you come **with a guide**, he'll probably bring you on foot from Sauraha through the park (see "Jungle Treks", below) and then back by bus via Bharatpur and Tadi. Alternatively, you can

Water buffalo

take a **jeep** tour to Kasara and walk from there, which shouldn't necessitate a guide. Local **buses** trundle to Jagatpur from Narayanghat every 45 minutes in the morning, less frequently in the afternoon. For Ghatgain lodges, ask to be let off at Patihari (if that doesn't ring a bell, ask for *Safari Narayani*), from where it's a 1.5-kilometre walk south on a side road.

The park starts on the other side of Rapti River: cross by dugout canoe from Jagatpur or Ghatgain and pay your entry fee (if you haven't already got a ticket) to one of the soldiers on the other side.

Gharial Safari Jungle Resort, between Jagatpur and Ghatgain. Luxury tented camp beside the Rapti River with a lovely garden and hot running water. It's 1km down a side road off the Bharatpur–Jagatpur road (the turning is about 1.5km east of Jagatpur). B⑦.

Ghumtee Riviera Lodge, Ghatgain. Sauraha-style mud-and-thatch bungalows and pretty, shady grounds. Cold water. ②.

Safari Narayani Lodge (☎20130; Kathmandu office: ☎525015), Ghatgain. Deluxe outfit with comfy rooms, fine food and its own elephants and jeeps. It's affiliated with the *Narayani Safari Hotel* in Narayanghat; most guests come here as part of a package. B⑨.

Rapti Riverview Lodge, Ghatgain. Simple rooms in a cottagey longhouse. Cold water. ②.

Tourist Hotel & Lodge, 300m west of the Jagatpur bus stop. A cheap but not very cheerful concrete guest house. ②.

Meghauli

MEGHAULI, 15km west of Jagatpur, is home to the **airstrip** used by guests visiting *Tiger Tops*, which all but owns this part of the park (daily flights from Kathmandu; $72). Consequently the village sees daily herds of upmarket tourists migrating back and forth on planes and jeeps, but has absolutely nothing to do with them. Few independent travellers make it here either, as it's two days' walk from Sauraha (see "Jungle Treks", below), or about two hours by **bus** from Narayanghat (hourly in the morning, less frequent after 10am). There's also a daily *Sajha* service between Kathmandu and Meghauli.

Buses stop at the newest, easternmost end of the village, known as Parsadhap Bazaar. Several separate settlements, all considered part of Meghauli, are dotted along the dirt road that leads westwards past the airstrip (which begins about 1.5km from the bus stop) and on to the Rapti River crossing (another 2km). Dugouts ferry *Tiger Tops* guests across here, but the boatmen are told not to assist independent travellers, so *bakshish* may be necessary. The Bhimle **guard post**, where you have to show your park permit or pay an entrance fee, is another 3km beyond, and the main rhino habitat for this area is beyond that.

Remarkably, Meghauli supports two crude but unmistakeably Sauraha-esque safari **lodges**.

Chital Lodge, located down a northbound lane between the bus stop and the airstrip. Mud-floored huts, cold water, no electricity, *daal bhaat*. ①.

Meghauli Jungle Lodge, just beyond the western end of the airstrip. Facilities are equally primitive, but the location is better for access to the park. ①.

Inside the park: luxury lodges and tented camps

Accommodation **inside the park** includes the most expensive lodgings in Nepal. They pay the government massive fees to stake out exclusive concession areas, with the result that you really feel like you've got the park all to yourself. Some are lavish **lodges** with permanent facilities, others are more remote **tented camps** – camping in the softest sense, with fluffy mattresses, solar-heated showers and fully stocked bars – and some are both. The prices quoted below, which are on a per-person basis, include all activities. **Book ahead** for these places, either through an agent or by calling directly. They arrange your travel there and back by private vehicle, plane or raft, which in most cases costs extra.

Chitwan Jungle Lodge (Kathmandu office: ☎228918). The biggest operator in the park, with 32 rooms. $260 per person for 2-night, 3-day package (includes transport).

Gaida Wildlife Camp (Kathmandu office: ☎220940). Lodge situated close to Sauraha, $245 for 2 nights; jungle camp 8km south at base of hills, $92 per night.

Island Jungle Resort (Kathmandu office: ☎220162). Tented camp on an island in the middle of the Narayani River. $220 for 2 nights.

Machan Wildlife Resort (Kathmandu office: ☎225001). Lodge with the only swimming pool in the park, $225 for 2 nights.

Temple Tiger Wildlife Camp (Kathmandu office: ☎221585). Tented camp at the west end of the park. $327 for 2 nights.

Tiger Tops (Kathmandu office: ☎423171). The first and still the most fashionable. Perched on stilts, the lodge is pure jungle Gothic, $566 for 2 nights; tented camp and *Tharu Safari Resort*, Tiger Tops' culture camp, both cost $175 per night.

Park activities

Most **activities inside the park** take place in early morning or late afternoon, when wildlife-viewing is best. All of the following can, and in most cases should, be arranged through your lodge or a guide service. It's essential to book the night before, or even earlier during the cut-throat months of October, November and March. All prices are in addition to the park entry fee.

Guided walks

Walking is the best way to observe the park's prolific **bird** life. The region is an important stopover spot for migratory species in December and March, as well as being home to many year-round residents – look for parakeets, Indian rollers, paradise flycatchers, kingfishers, hornbills, ospreys and literally hundreds of others. By walking you'll also be able to appreciate the smaller attractions of the jungle at your own pace: orchids, strangler figs, towering termite mounds, tiger scratchings, rhino droppings piled up like cannon balls. Experienced jungle-walkers say they get their best animal sightings on foot, although that usually doesn't apply when they've got four or five flat-footed neophytes in tow. Throw away that shopping list of animals; you have to be content with what's on offer. You are virtually guaranteed a **rhino** (probably several), and deer and monkeys are easy to spot, but tiger sightings are rare – maybe one or two a week.

The best **season** for walking is spring, when the grass is shorter, though at other times of year you can compensate by spending more time in the forest. The **cost** for a morning's walk is Rs150–400 per person (depending on the guide's certification level and the number of clients) and Rs300–500 for a full day with lunch, plus a few rupees for the guide's nominal entry fee. An all-day walk doesn't necessarily increase your chances of seeing game – most of the rhinos hang out close to Sauraha – but it gets you further into the park where you aren't running into other parties every two minutes. In cool weather some guides lead walks in the Chure Hills, where you may see gaur (Indian bison) in addition to deer, monkeys and birds.

One short walk you can probably chance **unguided** is to Isle Machaan, a hide overlooking a rhino wallow. The trail goes southeast from the visitors' centre, follows a creek and then crosses it to reach the *machaan* after half an hour.

Elephant rides

In terms of cost per hour the jeep's a better deal, but how often do you get to ride an **elephant**? The park keeps a dozen rideable animals and sends them out on one-hour-plus trips at around 8am and 4pm; the **cost** is Rs650, not including the Rs50–100 fee for your lodge to arrange the trip for you. During slack times you can sign yourself up at the ranger's office at 6am for one of that day's rides, but normally the queue starts forming in the wee hours. A word of warning: rides aren't held on major holidays (for instance, the eighth and ninth days of Dasain, and Lakshmi Puja), and the king has been known to spirit Chitwan's elephants away for months at a time for royal hunting expeditions.

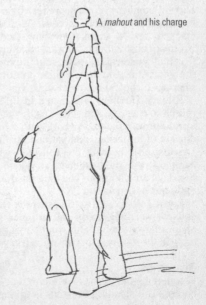

A *mahout* and his charge

The elephant's stately gait takes you back to a time, as recently as the early 1950s, when this was the way foreign delegations entered Nepal. The *mahout* (driver) sits astride the animal's neck, giving it commands with his toes and periodically walloping its huge skull, and attentively fending branches out of passengers' way. An elephant is the safest way to get around in the grasslands – especially in summer and autumn, when the grass towers 8m high – and it's the best way to observe **rhinos** and possibly wild boar or sloth bear. Rhinos have terrible eyesight and rely on their keen sense of smell, but since the elephant's scent masks your own it's possible to approach quite close and without fear of attack. From the height of an elephant's back you get a clear view of these prehistoric tanks, with their armour-plated skin, twitching ears and highly coveted horns.

Jeep rides ... and gharial crocodiles

A **jeep ride** is the closest thing to a tour of Chitwan, as it also takes in the park's two permanent sights, the gharial crocodile breeding project and Kasara Durbar, both about 20km west of Sauraha. For big game, however, you're limited to what you can see through the dusty wake of an army surplus vehicle in the afternoon (not the best time for wildlife viewing), which pretty much means **deer**. The whole trip takes three or four hours and **costs** Rs650, plus Rs15 to see the gharials. Most lodges have their own jeep; the park only allows four or five in at a time, but as long as you book early enough your lodge will get you a seat on whichever vehicle is going. The **best months** are from February to April, after the grass has been cut and the new shoots attract the deer. Note that jeeps can't cross the river after the monsoon until mid- or late November; during that time shorter trips may be run to the elephant-breeding project (see below).

The longest of the world's crocodiles – adults can grow to more than 6m from nose to tail – the **gharial** is an awesome fishing machine. Its slender, broom-like snout, which bristles with a fine mesh of teeth, snaps shut on its prey like a spring-loaded trap. Unfortunately for the gharial, its eggs are regarded as a delicacy, and males are hunted for their bulb-like snouts (*gharial* means bulb), which are believed to have medicinal powers. In the mid-1970s, the world suddenly realized there were only 1300 gharials left. Chitwan's **breeding project** was set up in 1977 to incubate eggs under controlled conditions, upping the survival rate, which is only one percent in the wild, to as high as 75 percent. A few gharials from the first (1978) hatch are kept here for breeding, though there has been no success with this yet. The majority of hatchlings are released back into the wild after three years, when they reach 1.2m in length; more than 500 have been released so far into the Narayani, Kosi, Karnali and Babai rivers. Unfortunately gharials are still rarely sighted in the wild, and without reliable estimates of current numbers (the most recent figure, from 1981, is 1367 individuals) it's hard to gauge the project's success. As if the gharials didn't already have the deck stacked against them, they now face a new threat: two paper mills on the Narayani upstream of Chitwan, which use little or no effluent controls. Biologists fear that chemicals released into the river from these mills, recently permitted by the government to double their production, will be the final nail in the Narayani gharials' coffin. So see them while you still can.

Kasara Durbar, constructed in 1939 as a royal hunting lodge, has now been rebuilt in concrete and serves as the park's administrative headquarters. Inside is a **museum** (daily except Sat), with a meagre collection of animal skulls, a small display of butterflies and various pickled reptiles, all accompanied by signs (in Devanaagari) bearing the collected wisdom of His Majesty. The lovely safari camp opposite the headquarters is kept ready for use by HM and his retinue for a few days each spring. (The king used to come here to hunt tigers, but has apparently given it up as bad PR.)

Lami Tal ("Long Lake"), a marshy oxbow lake about 1km to the east, is a prime spot for watching **birds** and **mugger crocodiles**. There's a rickety view tower about midway along. This would be a good place to wait for tigers or rhinos very early in the morning, but on a jeep trip you'll blow by in mid-afternoon.

River trips

Wooden dugout canoes are moored at the end of the lane in front of the visitors' centre. The standard itinerary is to depart after breakfast, float down the **Rapti**

River for 45 minutes and then walk back in time for lunch. Every package includes this trip, and since everybody has to walk back along the same trail, it's just a steady stream of tourists all morning – the animals know better than to hang out here. Either take the earliest possible morning trip, or go in the afternoon.

In **winter**, when the water's cool, your chances of seeing **mugger crocodiles** sunning themselves on the gravel banks are better than even; ruddy sheldrakes also winter here in profusion. In hot weather the outing is less rewarding, and the walk's a sticky chore, though you'll be assured of plenty of birds.

The canoe ride only **costs** Rs90, but the guided walk back is Rs150–250 (depending on guide experience), plus you have to pitch in for the guide's boat ticket.

Jungle treks

To get well clear of the Sauraha crowds you need to walk for two or more days, overnighting en route – think of it as a **jungle trek**. Staying with the trekking analogy, there's one "teahouse" route in the park, plus any number of other possibilities for those willing to camp.

The teahouse route follows the forest road from **Sauraha to Kasara** and on to **Mcghauli**, or vice versa. It takes two days of roughly equal length, or you could just do one half or the other. The Sauraha–Kasara leg is more commonly trekked, and is also the route taken by jeep tours out of Sauraha. There are of course no teahouses inside the park, but you can spend nights at Meghauli and Gaighat/Jagatpur (see p.275–276). It's possible to get another park permit at Bhimle (near Meghauli) and carry on trekking for a further two days, overnighting at Maadi (along the park's southern boundary) and then returning to Sauraha. Go with a senior or advanced guide who's done this trek before – many haven't.

Although it involves more logistics, **camping** gives you a much more intimate, exciting and – well, let's be honest – dangerous encounter with the jungle. (The government is considering setting up a network of permanent shelters in the park, which would reduce the risk.) Camping is permitted at designated sites inside the park (Rs300 per person per night), although local officials don't always consent to issue permits. Obviously, you'll need an experienced guide who's familiar with these sites, and you'll also have to fork out for a cook and/or porter(s), all of whom will expect hazard pay. Allow a couple of days for your guide to make all the arrangements. Tents, sleeping bags and other equipment are hard to come by here, so you're better off bringing them from Kathmandu.

Activities outside the park

After you've had your two days in the park, you might be reluctant to shell out for another permit. Here are a few (mostly) admission-free options.

The hattisar (elephant stables) and breeding project

The majority of Chitwan's elephant workforce is housed at the government *hattisar* (elephant stables), on the southeastern edge of Sauraha. The best time to catch them is mid-afternoon, when they're sure to be around for feeding time. In hot weather they're taken down to the river for a bath at midday – immensely photogenic. To the west of here, the **Nepal Conservation Research and Training Centre** functions as the base for animal research and monitoring, naturalist training and sustainable development programmes supported by the King Mahendra Trust for Nature Conservation.

Sauraha lodges offer jeep tours out to the **elephant-breeding project**, 4km west of the village, where baby elephants are the main attraction. You can visit the project independently either on foot or bicycle, though you have to cross a stream just before you get there; come with a guide, who can explain the goings-on and then take you on to Bis Hajaar Tal (see below). Until a decade or so ago, the parks department commonly bought its elephants from India, where they were captured in the wild and trained in captivity. But in recent years the price of elephants has skyrocketed – a trained animal now goes for upwards of Rs300,000, despite the fact that it may already be halfway through its working life. Feeling the pinch, the government began breeding and training its own elephants, first at the old *hattisar* and then, in 1988, establishing this separate facility, where elephants can mate in peace and mothers and babies can receive special attention. At any given time the project is home to three or four breeding bulls and about as many cows, and usually a couple of calves. The young elephants need to spend as much time as possible with their mothers to become socialized into elephant society. The best time to see them is in late afternoon, after they've returned from educational trips to the river and the jungle.

Bis Hajaar Tal

Large patches of jungle still exist outside the park, albeit in a less pristine state. The most easily accessible of these starts just west of the elephant-breeding project, reaching its climax about 5km to the northwest in the area known as **Bis**

ASIAN ELEPHANTS

In Nepal and throughout southern Asia, **elephants** have been used as ceremonial transportation and beasts of burden for thousands of years, earning them a cherished place in the culture – witness the popularity of elephant-headed Ganesh, the darling of the Hindu pantheon. Thanks to this symbiosis with man, Asian elephants (unlike their African cousins) survive mainly as a domesticated species, even as their wild habitat has all but vanished.

With brains four times the size of humans', elephants are reckoned to be as **intelligent** as dolphins; recent research suggests they may communicate subsonically. What we see as a herd is in fact a complex social structure, consisting of bonded pairs and a fluid hierarchy, usually headed by a female. Though they appear docile, elephants have strongly individual personalities and moods. They can learn dozens of commands, but they won't obey just anyone – as any handler will tell you, you can't make an elephant do what it doesn't want to do. That they submit to such apparently cruel head-thumping by drivers seems to have more to do with thick skulls than obedience.

Asian elephants are smaller than those of the African species, but their statistics are still formidable. A bull can grow up to 3m high and weigh four tons, although larger individuals are known to exist. An average day's intake is 200 litres of water and 250kg of fodder – and if you think that's impressive, wait till you see it come back out again. All that eating wears down teeth fast, which is why an average elephant goes through six sets in its lifetime, each more durable than the one before. The trunk is controlled by an estimated 40,000 muscles, enabling its owner to eat, drink, cuddle and even manipulate simple tools (such as a stick for scratching). Life expectancy is seventy to eighty years and, much the same as with humans, an elephant's working life can be expected to run from its mid-teens to its mid-fifties; training begins at about age five.

Hajaar Tal (Twenty-Thousand Lakes). The name refers to a maze of marshy oxbow lakes, many of them already filled in, well hidden among mature *sal* trees. Although the area is managed as a community forest, and you're always conscious of chopping and other human activity around the fringes, it's still favoured by deer, monkeys and even a few rhinos – especially during the January thatch-gathering, when animals in the park are disturbed and flee here.

Bis Hajaar Tal used to be a popular spot for free wildlife viewing, but community forest organizers have started demanding their own Rs650 **entrance fee**. Ask at your guest house whether this is still the case.

Jeep tours to the elephant-breeding project sometimes finish up with a toddle through this general area. To explore it more fully, have a guide lead you in **on foot** from the breeding project, and allow a full day. Without a guide, you'd be wise to take the long way round to avoid getting lost: **cycle** to Tadi Bazaar, from there follow the main highway 3km west to just before it crosses a canal (the village here is called Tikauli), then go southwest on a gravel road beside the canal for about 2km until you begin to see the lakes. This road continues along the canal for another 8km or so to Gita Nagar, on the Bharatpur–Jagatpur road.

Tharu villages and bike rides

Guided Tharu village walks out of Sauraha usually mean a loiter through the few houses around *Chitwan Park Cottage*, or out to Bachhauli, a village just to the east of Sauraha. It's all rather voyeuristic, especially when you consider how many tourists have trooped through before you, and the way guides point at residents and pick up their tools without asking is not something that should be encouraged.

You'll learn a lot more about real Tharu (and Bahun) life by hopping on a bike and just getting lost on the back roads to the east and west of Sauraha. In November, when the **rice** is harvested, you'll be able to watch villagers cutting the stems, tying them into sheaves and threshing them – or, since it's such a busy time of year, piling them in big stacks to await threshing. January is **thatch-gathering** time, when you'll see people bringing huge bundles out of the park, to be put by until a slack time before the monsoon when they can repair their roofs. In early March, the **mustard** or **wheat** that was planted after the rice crop is ready; **corn** is then planted, to be harvested in July for animal fodder, flour and meal. During each of these harvest seasons you'll hear the rhythmic toot-toot of local mills, hulling or polishing grain, or pressing oil.

From Sauraha, the most fertile country for exploration lies to the east: heading towards Tadi along the eastern side of the village, turn right after about 500m and you can follow that road all the way to **Parsa**, 8km away on the Mahendra Highway, with many side roads to villages en route. Given a full day and a good (mountain) bike, you could continue eastwards fom Parsa along the'highway for another 10km, and just before Bhandara turn left onto a track leading to **Baireni**, a particularly well-preserved Tharu village. Another 10km east of Bhandara lies **Lothar**, where by following a trail upstream you'll reach the waterfalls on the Lothar Khola, a contemplative spot with a healthy measure of birdlife.

For a short ride west of Sauraha, head north for 3km and take the first left after the river crossing, which brings you to the authentic Tharu villages of **Baghmara** and **Hardi**. If you're game for a longer journey, pedal to Tadi and west along the Mahendra Highway to Tikauli. From there the canal road (see "Bis Hajaar Tal", above) leads about 10km through beautiful forest to **Gita Nagar**, where you join the Bharatpur–Jagatpur road, with almost unlimited possibilities from there.

Two mysteries surround Nepal's second-biggest ethnic minority, the Tarai-dwelling **Tharus**: where they came from, and how they came to be resistant to malaria. Some anthropologists speculate that the tribe migrated from India's eastern hills, filtering across the Tarai over the course of millennia. This would account for their Mongoloid features and Hindu-animist beliefs, but it doesn't fully explain the radically different dialects, dress and customs of different Tharu groups. Isolated by malarial jungle for thousands of years, bands of migrants certainly could have developed their own cultures – but why, given such linguistic and cultural evolution, would the name "Tharu" survive with such consistency? Confusing the issue are the Rana Tharus of the far west, who claim to be descended from high-caste Rajput women who were sent north by their husbands during the Muslim invasions and, when the men never returned for them, married their servants. (There's some circumstantial evidence to support this, as Rana Tharu women are given extraordinary autonomy in marriage and household affairs.)

As to the matter of **malaria resistance**, red blood cells seem to play a role – the fact that Tharus are prone to sickle-cell anaemia might be significant – but very little research has been done. At least as important, Tharus boost their natural resistance with a few common-sense precautions, such as building houses with tiny windows to keep smoke in and mosquitoes (and ghosts) out.

As **hunter-gatherers**, Tharus are skilled at snaring pigs and other small animals, fishing, and using plants for myriad medicinal and practical purposes. Modern times have forced them to become **farmers** and livestock raisers, clearing patches in the forest and warding off wild animals from flimsy watchtowers called *machaan*. Their whirling stick dance evokes their uneasy but respectful relationship with the spirits of the forest, as do the raised animal emblems that decorate their doorways. **Fishing** remains an important activity – given the Tarai's high

Narayanghat, Bharatpur and Devghat

It's hard to travel very far in Nepal without at least passing through **NARAYANGHAT**: the construction of the Mugling–Narayanghat highway has made it the gateway to the Tarai and the busiest crossroads in the country. What was once a far-flung intersection is now a 500-metre strip of diesel and *daal bhaat*, and it's said that real estate changes hands here for almost as high stakes as in Kathmandu. **BHARATPUR**, its sister city to the east and the headquarters of Chitwan District, can muster a large regional college, a couple of breweries and an airstrip. Unflattering as all that may sound, you may have occasion to stay, or at least eat, in the area; the side trip to Devghat may provide an incentive.

Buses to Pokhara, Gorkha and Devghat have their own bus park at the north end of Narayanghat on the road to Mugling. All other express buses stop at the fast-food parade just east of Pulchowk (the intersection of the Mugling and Mahendra highways). There are two additional bus parks for local services: buses and minibuses to Tadi Bazaar and eastern Chitwan District start from a point about 500m east of Pulchowk, on the south side of the highway;

water table, it's easy enough to scoop out a pond and stock it – and you're likely to see fisherwomen wielding hand-held nets between crossed poles, or carrying their catch home in wicker boxes.

Tharu **houses** are made of mud and dung plastered over wood-and-reed frames, giving them a distinctive ribbed effect. Traditionally, western Tharus built communal **longhouses**, big enough for a half a dozen families or more and partitioned by huge vial-shaped grain urns, but most have now moved up to detached models. While **clothing** varies tremendously by area, Tharu women often wear thick silver bracelets above the elbow; tattooing of the forearms and lower legs is common among older women but is falling out of fashion with the younger generation.

The Tarai has long been viewed as Nepal's frontier and the Tharus dismissed as primitive aboriginals. Since the turn of the century – when, as a preliminary step to abolishing slavery, the government encouraged **slaves** to homestead in the Tarai – it's been seen as a place where a settler can clear the land and start a new life. The government's malaria-control programme accelerated the process, and several million gung-ho **immigrants** from the hills and India (the border is highly porous) have now cleared, tamed and transformed the Tarai into the breadbasket of Nepal, felling much of the valuable timber in the process. The migration is far from over – the Tarai's population is doubling every twenty years (some urban areas are doubling twice as fast). Prosperity has probably peaked, however, and since productivity isn't keeping up with population, the Tarai's agricultural surplus is steadily declining.

In one generation, the Tharus have been outflanked, outfarmed and in many cases bought out and reduced to sharecropping. Traditional culture is still strong in the far west, particularly among the Dangauria and Rana groups, but in other areas it's been all but drowned by a tide of hill, Indian and Western tendencies. Like indigenous peoples the world over, Tharus know more about their own environment than anyone, but they're not being listened to.

minibuses to Meghauli and Jagatpur start from the "Gita Nagar Bus Park" – in reality little more than a stop – across the highway and about 200m to the north. Bharatpur's **airstrip** is just south of the Mahendra Highway; *RNAC* (☎20326) and *Everest Air* (☎21093) each fly daily to Bharatpur from Kathmandu ($50).

Rikshas should take you anywhere within the two towns for Rs10 or less.

Accommodation

Bharatpur caters for well-heeled tourists, offering a few resort-style hotels near the airstrip. Budget travellers would do better to head for Narayanghat.

Eagle Rest House, Pulchowk. The largest of several inns here, cavernous and noisy but with good food. ②/B③.

Hotel Chitwan Keyman (☎056/20200). Air conditioning, restaurant. B⑦.

Hotel Narayani Safari (☎056/20130; Kathmandu office: ☎525015). Air conditioning, pool, tennis courts. B⑨.

Hotel River View, behind the Pokhara bus park. The most palatable budget option, it really does have a river view and makes the best base for visiting Devghat. ②/B③.

Island Jungle Resort Bharatpur Heights (Kathmandu office: ☎220162). Air conditioning, restaurant. B⑦.

Quality Guest House, Sanghamchowk (the next major intersection to the east of Pulchowk). Basic Nepali lodge. ②/B③.

Eating

Food, plentiful but not wildly exciting, can be found around Pulchowk. Standing out slightly from the greasy spoons and whisky shacks are *Royal Restaurant* and, further east and across the street, *Amrit Sagar Restaurant*, with English menus and Indian/Chinese/"Continental" (ie everything with chips) food. *Hotel Narayani Safari*'s dining room does astonishingly good meals that run to about Rs250 a head.

Devghat

DEVGHAT (or Deoghat), 5km northwest of Narayanghat, is a lot of people's idea of a great place to die. An astonishingly tranquil spot, it stands where the wooded hills meet the shimmering plains, and the Trisuli and the Kali Gandaki merge to form the Narayani, one of the major tributaries of the Ganga (Ganges). Some say Sita, the heroine of the *Ramayan*, died here. The ashes of King Mahendra, the present king's father, were sprinkled at this sacred *tribeni* (a confluence of three rivers: wherever two rivers meet, a third, spiritual one is believed to join them), and scores of *sunyasan*, those who have renounced the world, patiently live out their last days here hoping to achieve an equally auspicious death and rebirth. Many have retired to Devghat because they have no children to look after them in their old age and to perform the necessary rites when they die. *Pujari* (priests) also practise here – their professional signs are the only advertising you'll see – and often take in young candidates for the priesthood as resident students.

Occasional **buses** shuttle between Narayanghat and Devghat, taking about half an hour, but the one-hour **walk** along the footpath that parallels the river through the woods is much more pleasant. In either case, you come to the Trisuli and cross it by a footbridge (immortalized in the Nepali film *Kanchhi*, in which a heartbroken lover attempts suicide here), then bear left to the village. You can also cross the river further downsteam by **dugout canoe** – for the return trip, the ferryman, if he thinks he can be spared from his duties, might consent to take you all the way back to Narayanghat for Rs50 or so.

Though dozens of small shrines lie dotted around the village, none is big or particularly interesting: you come here more for the atmosphere than the sights. Devghat is home of a well-known guru, the one-armed **Ashori Baba**, who gives audiences to serious seekers; a statue of his late predecessor, Jaleshwar Baba, is usually surrounded by a congregation of devotees. Rafting guides are fond of telling stories about the "Crazy Baba", a now deceased guru who was famed for his penile performances. A huge **pilgrimage**, the Tribeni Mela, is held here on the new-moon day of January/February, and Shiva Raatri, one lunar month later, brings many Indian devotees. At other times, sadhus and pilgrims do *puja* at the point where the rivers meet – cremations are also held here – and old-timers meditate outside their huts in the sun. Be sensitive to the residents, and don't disturb them or touch anything that might be holy: many are orthodox Bahuns and your touch would be polluting. There's **no lodging** at Devghat, but it wouldn't be appropriate to stay overnight anyway.

LUMBINI TARAI

Hordes of travellers hurry through this ancient part of the Tarai, west of Chitwan; few take the time to look around. It's best known, unfairly, for **Sunauli**, the main tourist border crossing between Nepal and India. Yet only 20km away is one of Nepal's premier destinations, **Lumbini**, birthplace of the Buddha and the site of ruins going back almost three thousand years.

Two main highways – the Siddhartha and the Mahendra – connect the region with Pokhara and the rest of the Tarai, and buses to Sunauli are frequent. The journey to Lumbini is a bit taxing, but well worth the extra effort. Accommodation and food here, as in most other parts of the Tarai, are readily available but usually very simple.

Butwal

Westwards from Narayanghat the Mahendra Highway runs across a washboard of cultivated fields, skirts the occasional cemetery of charred stumps, and briefly climbs over a jungle-cloaked spur of the Chure Hills. It's a relatively painless, if dull, three hours to **BUTWAL**. Crouching uninvitingly at the mouth of a canyon, Butwal is the hub of the Lumbini administrative zone: north lies Pokhara; south is Sunauli and the Indian border; and to the west, the Mahendra Highway barrels along towards Nepalganj and Nepal's western border.

Placed at the start of an important trade route to Tibet as well as the pilgrim trail to Muktinath, the **tax post** at Butwal was for centuries a tidy little earner for Palpa (Tansen) and then Kathmandu. Much later, it came to be a staging post for Nepal's most lucrative export: Gurkha soldiers, bound for the recruiting office at Gorakhpur in India. In the early nineteenth century, Nepal and the East India Company fell into a dispute over the territory around Butwal, and the murder of some British police here touched off a two-year **war with Britain**. Nepal scored several improbable early victories here and elsewhere but, outnumbered four to one, was eventually forced to surrender. Under the terms of the resulting treaty, the Tarai territories from Butwal west had to be ceded to the British (Nepal struck a deal to get the disputed land around Butwal back the same year). Any reminders of the past are, however, conspicuously absent in modern Butwal.

Many **buses** originate or terminate at this busy crossroads – see p.264 for routes and frequencies. Most express services stop at "Traphik Chowk", a bazaar area on the Siddhartha Highway as it skirts the east side of town. Local buses use the bus park at the west end of town, a few hundred metres south of the bridge over the Tinau River.

Accommodation and eating

As in many Tarai cities, Butwal's **accommodation** is all either cheap in a very Nepali way or upscale in a more Indian style; there's not much middle ground for budget foreign travellers. The more expensive hotels are your best bet for **food**.

Hotel Hillsun, at the bus park (no phone). Basic bus-park cheapie. ②; dorm beds ①.

Hotel Kandara, Traphic Chowk (☎073/20175). Clean place with hot water, a small garden, and vegetarian restaurant. B④.

Hotel Siddhartha, Traphic Chowk (☎071/20380). Large, well-appointed outfit, with hot water, a good restaurant, and some a/c rooms. B⑤/B⑦.

Hotel Sindoor, just south of the bus park (☎073/20189). Butwal's best: river views and a decent restaurant. B⑦.

Santosh Guest House, two blocks west of Traphic Chowk (no phone). The most palatable budget option: basic, but in a relatively quiet part of town. ②; dorm beds ①.

Bhairawa, Sunauli and the border

Half an hour south by bus, **BHAIRAWA** (officially, the name has been changed to **SIDDHARTHA NAGAR**, but it's not catching on) is a virtual rerun of Butwal. The bazaar, west of the main roundabout on the Siddhartha Highway, supports a sizeable minority of Muslim traders and, like so many border towns, exists primarily to peddle mundane Western goods to acquisitive Indians. As a base camp for Lumbini, though, it does the job, and it certainly beats Sunauli.

For **orientation** purposes, think of Bhairawa's three main streets forming a triangle: the eastern side is the highway to the border, the other two comprise the bazaar. Buses stop on the border highway near the *Hotel Yeti* (a handy landmark), which stands at the southeastern apex of the triangle; rikshas and jeeps bound for Sunauli wait here, and the bazaar lies to the west. The road to Lumbini leaves the border highway about 1km north of the *Hotel Yeti*, just north of the triangle's northern apex.

Places to stay include – in descending order of price and hygiene – *Hotel Yeti* (☎071/20551; B⑥, B⑦ with a/c); *Hotel Himalayan Inn* (☎071/20347; B⑤), on the border road about 500m north of the *Yeti*, towards Butwal; *Hotel Shantanu* (B⑤), opposite the *Himalayan*; or *City Guest House* (②/B③) or *Centaur Guest House* (①/B②), both in the bazaar west of the *Yeti*. *Hotel Himalayan Inn*'s dining room does competent Indian and Chinese **meals**.

You might be able to rent a **bike** informally through your guest house. For **onward bus tickets**, the private and *Sajha* offices are located at the main intersection near *Hotel Yeti*. Most long-distance buses originate at Sunauli, but getting a seat from Bhairawa is no problem as long as you book it the day before.

Sunauli and the border

Four kilometres south of Bhairawa, **SUNAULI** (Soo-*no*-li) is the most convenient border crossing between Nepal and most parts of India. (The portion of Sauraha on the Nepal side of the border is locally referred to as Belhiya.) Bus and train package deals to or from India usually involve an overnight here – see p.131 for more on these. It's a good place to glean information from travellers coming the other way or meet up with people going in your direction, but when the bus leaves the next morning you'll definitely want to be on it.

Only budget **accommodation** is available in Sunauli, and it tends to be noisy, dirty and redolent of toilets. It would be an exercise in futility to make recommendations, as standards rise and fall (mostly fall) so rapidly here. The half-dozen guest houses are close enough together so you can shop around to see which one's been remodelled most recently. They're all around ①/B②, and should be able to provide hot water by the bucket. Better accommodation is available in Bhairawa and on the Indian side of the border, if you're willing to spend more. The **food** in Sunauli's guest houses and local restaurants isn't bad – whichever way you're heading, the menus give a taste of what's in store further on (if you're coming from India, you might welcome the sight of Coca-Cola).

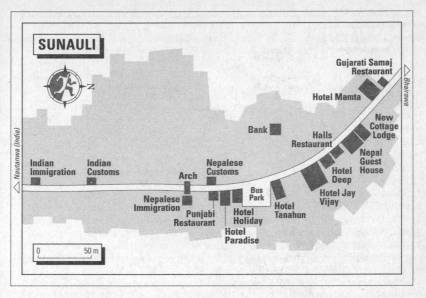

As a funnel for traffic from India, Sunauli is well served by **buses**, but be sure to book ahead, since an empty seat in Sunauli might be spoken for in Bhairawa. Each guest house has its own man-and-a-desk "travel agency" that can book onward tickets or provide general advice. If you're heading from here to Lumbini, catch a jeep opposite the bus park (Rs3) to Bhairawa, where local minibuses start.

Government-registered **moneychangers** in Sauraha keep long hours (some round the clock), so there's no problem exchanging money. Indian rupees are readily accepted in Sunauli but not beyond. International **telephoning** is possible from here, but it's considerably more expensive (about Rs250 per minute) than from Kathmandu or Pokhara.

The Nepalese **immigration office** is open daily from 6am to 6pm. Figure on half an hour to get through Nepalese and Indian border formalities, and remember that Nepal time is fifteen minutes ahead of India. The offers of riksha rides across the border aren't to be taken seriously, since from start to finish it's only a distance of about 200m.

Buses from the Indian side make for Gorakhpur (hourly; 3hr), Varanasi (3 daily; 8hr) and Delhi (5 daily; 22hr). "Deluxe" buses to Gorakhpur go straight to the railway station; from there you can make broad-gauge **train** connections throughout India.

Lumbini

After I am no more, Ananda! Men of belief will visit with faithful curiosity and devotion to the four places – where I was born . . . attained enlightenment . . . gave the first sermons . . . and passed into Nirvana.

The Buddha (c.543–463 BC)

For the world's 300 million Buddhists, **LUMBINI**, 22km west of Bhairawa, is where it all began. **The Buddha's birthplace** is arguably the single most

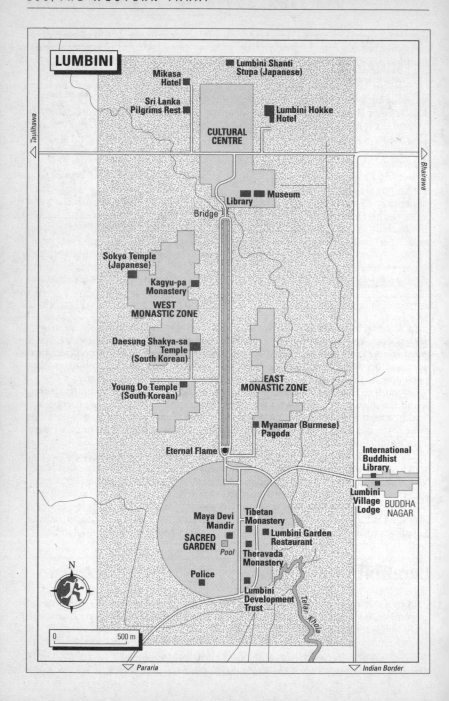

LUMBINI

Mikasa Hotel

Sri Lanka Pilgrims Rest

Lumbini Shanti Stupa (Japanese)

Lumbini Hokke Hotel

CULTURAL CENTRE

Museum

Library

Bridge

Sokyo Temple (Japanese)

Kagyu-pa Monastery

WEST MONASTIC ZONE

Daesung Shakya-sa Temple (South Korean)

Young Do Temple (South Korean)

EAST MONASTIC ZONE

Myanmar (Burmese) Pagoda

Eternal Flame

International Buddhist Library

Lumbini Village Lodge

BUDDHA NAGAR

Maya Devi Mandir

Tibetan Monastery

Lumbini Garden Restaurant

SACRED GARDEN

Pool

Theravada Monastery

Police

Lumbini Development Trust

Telar Khola

Taulihawa

Bhairawa

N

0   500 m

Pararia

Indian Border

important historical site in Nepal – not only the source of one of the world's great reli-gions but also the centre of Nepal's most significant **archeological finds**, dating from the third century BC. With only modest ruins but powerful associations, it's the kind of place you could whizz round in two hours or soak up for days.

The Buddha has long been a prophet without much honour in his own country: the area around Lumbini is now predominantly Muslim, while the main local **festival** is a Hindu one, commemorating the Buddha as the ninth incarnation of Vishnu – it's held on the full moon of the Nepali month of Baisakh (April–May). Celebrations of **Buddha Jayanti** (the Buddha's birthday) are comparatively meagre because, as the local monks will tell you with visible disgust, Buddhists from the high country think Lumbini is too hot in May.

But big changes are in store. The government has set aside land and author-ized a hugely ambitious **master plan** for a five-square-kilometre religious **park** consisting of monasteries, cultural facilities, gardens, fountains and a tourist village. The Lumbini Development Trust, charged with carrying out the plan, has the backing of the United Nations and has raised piles of cash from Japan, Korea and other Buddhist countries. Several buildings have already been completed, 600,000 trees have been planted, and since the construction of a deluxe hotel, Japanese tour groups have begun to add Lumbini to their whirlwind tours of the Buddhist holy sites. An international airport has even been mooted. Of course there is ample cause for scepticism, yet if the remaining plans come off, Lumbini could grow to be quite a cosmopolitan religious site – the only one of its kind in the world.

Getting there

Dust off your Buddhist tolerance, because public transport connections to Lumbini are slow. Decrepit **minibuses** from Bhairawa (approximately every 30min) take an interminable hour to ninety minutes, depending on stops. Most are bound for Pararia, the village immediately south of the master plan area, which means you'll want to hop off earlier, near the Tibetan monastery; the last bus back is at 5.30pm.

You can speed the journey by renting a **jeep** with driver through any of the "travel agents" in Sunauli or *Hotel Yeti* in Bhairawa (Rs300–400 return), but you'll have to make separate arrangements if you want to stay at Lumbini more than an hour or two. If possible – and if it's not too hot – go by **bike**: head west out of Bhairawa, turn left onto a paved side road after 20km, and turn right onto a dirt track about 2km later.

An **information** booth has been temporarily erected near the bus stop. Guide service may be available – it's well worth hooking up with one of the Lumbini Development Trust's archeologists, who freelance as guides.

The Sacred Garden

The **"Sacred Garden"**, where the Buddha reputedly was born, contains all of Lumbini's ancient treasures in an area no bigger than a football pitch. By all accounts a well-tended grove in the Buddha's day, the spot was consecrated soon after his death, and at least one monastery was attached to it by the third century BC when Ashoka, the great north Indian emperor and Buddhist evangelist, made a well-documented pilgrimage to the spot. Ashoka's patronage established a thriv-ing religious community, but by the time the intrepid Chinese traveller Hiuen

The Buddha's birth

Tsang visited in the seventh century it was limping, and must have died out after the ninth century.

The garden was lost for six hundred years and its **rediscovery**, in 1895, was one of the greatest (and luckiest) finds of the century. Armed with archaic and often contradictory accounts, the German archeologist A A Führer had managed in the previous year to unearth some separate but related relics near Taulihawa. Believing he was on the Buddha's trail, he arranged to return to the same spot, but at the last minute his Nepali escort requested a more convenient meeting place about 25km to the east. By sheer coincidence, the party made camp practically on top of the garden. While Führer slept, a porter – no doubt answering the call of nature – stumbled upon the ruins, which had been obscured by thick jungle.

The Maya Devi temple and sculpture

Centrepiece of the site, the **Maya Devi Mandir** features brickwork dating back to the third century BC, although subsequent layers were added through the fifth or sixth centuries AD. In an ongoing restoration that probably won't be completed before 1997, archeologists are dismantling the temple brick by brick to separate the ancient from the merely old (an ugly twentieth-century addition was the first to go), and are rebuilding the walls to illustrate the original structure's 800-year architectural evolution. Until 1993 the temple was shaded by a majestic *pipal* (*bodhi*) tree which, though not in fact ancient, was regarded by many as a living link with the Buddha's day. However, its roots had for many years been interfering with the temple, and in a controversial move officials had the tree cut down.

The temple derives its name from Maya Devi, the Buddha's mother, for until its restoration it housed a famous bas-relief **sculpture** depicting her and the newborn Buddha in the Mathura style (second or third century AD). The sculpture is now on view at a nearby temporary building. So worn are the features, from centuries of *puja*, that archeologists at first dismissed the temple as Hindu because locals were worshipping the image as a fertility goddess (they still do). A recent replica reconstructs the tableau: Maya Devi grasping a tree branch for support, a tiny Buddha standing fully formed at her feet, and (ecumenical, this) the Hindu gods Indra and Brahma looking on. The sculpture illustrates an elaborate Buddhist nativity story, according to which the baby Buddha leapt out of the womb, took seven steps and proclaimed his world-saving destiny.

The Ashokan pillar and other remains

West of the temple, the **Ashokan pillar** is the oldest monument in Nepal. It's not much to look at – it looks like a smokestack – but the inscription (also Nepal's oldest), recording Ashoka's visit in 249 BC, is the best available evidence that the

THE BUDDHA: A LIFE

The year of the Buddha's **birth** is disputed – it was probably 543 BC – but it's generally accepted that it happened at Lumbini while his mother, Maya Devi, was on her way to her maternal home for the delivery. He was born Siddhartha Gautam ("he who has accomplished his aim"), the son of a king and a member of the Shakya clan, who ruled the central Tarai from their capital at Tilaurakot (see below). Brought up in his father's palace, Prince Siddhartha lived a sheltered life until, at the age of 29, he made a fateful trip into town where, according to legend, he encountered an old man, a sick man, a corpse and a hermit: old age, sickness and death were the end of life, he realized, and contemplation seemed the only way to understand the nature of suffering.

Siddhartha fled the palace and spent five years as an ascetic before concluding that self-denial brought him no closer to the truth than self-indulgence. Under the famous *bodhi* tree of Bodh Gaya in India, he vowed to keep meditating until he attained **enlightenment**. This he did after 49 days, at which time Siddhartha became the Buddha, released from the cycle of birth and death. He made his way to Sarnath (near modern Varanasi in India) and preached his **first sermon**, setting in motion, Buddhists believe, *dharma*, the wheel of the truth. Although he's said to have returned to Kapilvastu to convert his family, and according to some stories he even put in an appearance in the Kathmandu Valley, the Buddha spent most of the rest of his life preaching in northern India. He **died** at the age of 80 in Kasia (Kushinagar), about 100km southeast of Lumbini. For a fuller account of Buddhism, see "Religion" in *Contexts*.

Buddha was born here. Split by lightning sometime before the seventh century, its two halves are held together by metal bands. Pillars were a sort of trademark of Ashoka, serving the dual purpose of spreading the faith and marking the boundaries of his empire: this one announces that the king granted Lumbini tax-free status in honour of the Buddha's birth. The carved capital to this pillar, which early pilgrims such as Hiuen Tsang describe as being in the shape of a horse, has never been found; the weathered stone lying on the ground beside the pillar is the lotus-or bell-shaped "bracket" upon which it would have rested.

The square, brick-sided **pool** just south of the Ashokan pillar is supposed to be where Maya Devi bathed before giving birth to the Buddha. Heavily restored **brick foundations** of buildings and stupas around the site, dating from the second century BC to the ninth century AD, chart the rise and fall of Lumbini's early monastic community. The two mounds north and south of the garden aren't ancient – they're archeological debris removed during particularly careless excavations in the 1930s led by Field Marshal Kesar Shamsher Rana.

The Tibetan and Theravada monasteries

Two active monasteries face the Sacred Garden and are open to the public; neither is tremendously old, and like all the modern buildings in the area they're slated for eventual demolition to make way for the master plan. The soaring **Tibetan monastery**, built by the king of Mustang, displays a typical array of prematurely aged frescoes and gilded Buddhas and *bodhisattva* in glass cabinets. It provides a winter residence for up to fifty monks from an affiliated monastery in Boudha, who can be heard chanting in the early morning and mid-afternoon; only a skeleton crew stays on during the hot months.

The more austere **Theravada** establishment offers less to look at, but its solitary gold-robed monk, the Venerable Vimalananda, speaks good English. Built by the government of Nepal, the monastery has the feel of something designed by a civil servant, with an eclectic mix of Newar woodwork, Burmese and Thai images and Tibetan-style paintings.

Around the master plan area

A walk northwards from the Sacred Garden, pleasant for its own sake, hits the highlights of the slowly unfurling master plan. An elevated path passes through what will be a reflecting pool encircling the Sacred Garden, and beyond burns an **eternal flame**, a symbolic remembrance of the "Light of Asia". From here you can follow the kilometre-long central canal past the **East and West Monastic Zones**, where 41 plots have been set aside for monasteries representing each of Buddhism's major sects and national styles of worship. A dozen organizations have signed agreements to build monasteries here, at least five of which have already been built or are under construction (see map).

The canal, now largely dry after a decade of disuse, ends at what is being billed as Lumbini's **Cultural Centre**, which at the time of writing was decidedly lacking in culture, or for that matter, any sign of life at all. The tubular buildings of the Indian-funded museum and Japanese-built library/research institute were in place, but forlornly vacant, while a planned auditorium, restaurants and shops remained stubbornly on paper. It goes to show that it's easier to build buildings in a place like Lumbini than it is to fill them with books or people.

Practicalities

Lumbini's **lodgings** are spread thinly over a wide area. Ideally you want to stay as close as possible to the Sacred Garden, but the only options here are the monasteries, which shelter pilgrims informally for a modest donation but are sorely lacking in things like bedding or hot water. The Theravada monastery has a tranquil *dharmsala* set in a mango garden, while, outside of the busy winter months, the Tibetan monastery can put visitors up in its monks' quarters. Since facilities inside the master plan area are controlled, the only other budget accommodation is in Buddha Nagar, the hamlet just outside the east entrance: the bare-bones *Lumbini Village Lodge* is overpriced (③), but growing demand is likely to spur competition.

Offically sanctioned lodgings are all at the north end of the master plan area, nearly a half-hour's walk from the Sacred Garden. Cheapest is *Sri Lanka Pilgrims Rest* (☎071/20009; ⑤), a huge, 188-bed hostel that looks a bit like a minimum-security jail, though it does have hot water, a restaurant and a shady grove nearby. *Mikasa Hotel*, nearing completion as this book went to press, will have rooms in the B⑦ range, while the crypt-like *Lumbini Hokke Hotel* (Kathmandu ☎521348; B⑨) is patronized almost exclusively by Japanese tour groups.

The only sources of **food** around the Sacred Garden area are *Lumbini Garden Restaurant*, which charges rather a lot for unexceptional tourist and Indian dishes, and a couple of grass-shack eateries attached to the monasteries, which serve much simpler, cheaper fare. *Lumbini Garden Restaurant* has a **foreign exchange** facility.

Tilaurakot

A dusty 24km west of Lumbini, **TILAURAKOT** is believed to have been the capital of ancient **Kapilvastu**, and the Buddha's childhood home. Although it's yielded more relics than Lumbini, due to its back-of-beyond location it's recommended only for real archeology buffs.

Admission to the **excavation** site is free, and the lonely guards will probably be happy to give you a sign-language tour around the shaded grounds. Among the visible remains are a couple of stupa bases, thick fortress walls and four gates – the **eastern gate** being of great metaphorical significance to Buddhists, as it was the start of the Buddha's journey in search of enlightenment. It's doubtful that this is literally the ruins of the palace of King Suddhodana, the Buddha's father, for the style of bricks used aren't thought to have been developed until the third century BC, but it may well have been built on top of it; assuming the earlier structure was made of wood, no trace of it would remain. Archeologists working in the area are now focusing their attention on a number of other **outlying digs** where objects dating back to the Buddha's time have been unearthed, as well as two **Ashokan pillars** erected to commemorate the birthplaces of mythical Buddhas of previous ages.

A small **museum** (daily except Tues, 10am–5pm; Rs15), opposite the start of the side road to the Tilaurakot site, displays some of the three thousand coins found in the area (including one bearing the Shakya name), together with Lumbini and Kapilvastu pottery spanning three distinct periods and a thousand years. Even older pottery discovered in caves near Jomosom, high in the Himalaya, is for some reason also displayed here. The contents of this museum may eventually be transferred to Lumbini's new museum.

Practicalities

The easiest way to get to Tilaurakot is by **jeep** from Sunauli or Bhairawa, though this is expensive (around Rs500), and it tends to lock you into a rushed half-day tour of Lumbini and Tilaurakot. Of course you can always stay longer if you're willing to find your own way back. Getting there by public transport, you're stuck with the two morning **minibuses** which make their way from Bhairawa to **Taulihawa**, 22km beyond Lumbini on the same road; you could try flagging these down from Lumbini at the intersection near the *Lumbini Hokke Hotel*, but don't expect to get a seat. From the centre of Taulihawa, walk 3km along the main (paved) northbound road until the pavement gives out, where a short track to the right leads to Tilaurakot. If you've got a bicycle you could pedal from Lumbini to Tilaurakot in about two hours, but the road is very bumpy.

Basic **food** is available at Taulihawa – if you get stuck and need a place to **stay**, there are a couple of Nepali inns a short distance north of the town centre along the road to Tilaurakot.

THE FAR WEST

Until recently, the sheer misery of travelling the Mahendra Highway was enough to deter all but the most dedicated from entering Nepal's remote **far west**. Now, with the highway largely completed, this once-neglected quarter of the country looks poised to open its doors to travellers. It's still a hell of a haul to get here, and not for the faint of heart, but the new highway makes this an up-and-coming route to or from Delhi (which is just ten hours by bus from the far western border crossing).

As word gets out, expect the sights described in this section to grow in popularity and sophistication. Two in particular, **Bardia National Park** and **Sukla Phanta Wildlife Reserve**, may someday become serious rivals to Chitwan National Park.

Nepalganj and Birendra Nagar

The Mahendra Highway makes good time to Nepalganj, 190km west of Butwal, crossing a spur of the Chure Hills and following the pleasingly rural Rapti Valley (no relation to the river of the same name in Chitwan). North of here lies Dang, home of the white-clad Dangaura Tharus and fine cycling country. Nearing Nepalganj on the main highway, the hills to the south peter out and the highway emerges from semi-forest into the bleached vastness of the Indian plains.

Nepalganj

Trade and transport hub of the far west – for what little trade and transport there is in the far west – **NEPALGANJ** is, more interestingly, Nepal's most Muslim city. The presence of Muslims in the Tarai is hardly surprising, of course, since the border with India, where Muslims comprise a significant minority, was only determined in the nineteenth century. Until just prior to the 1814–16 war with the British, this part of the Tarai belonged to the Nawab of Oudh, one of India's biggest landowners; after Nepal's defeat it was ceded to the East India Company and only returned to Nepal as a goodwill gesture for services rendered during the Indian Mutiny of 1857. A fair few Muslims fled to Nepalganj during the revolt – Lucknow, where the most violent incidents occurred, is due south of here – and

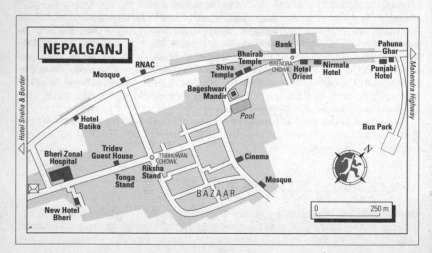

others filtered in during the Rana years, seeing chances for cross-border trade. The result is a permanent Muslim community, self-contained but maintaining business and family links with India. Indeed, the entire city feels overwhelmingly Indian, with its cheap neo-Mughal architecture and frenetically mundane bazaar. Imperious warnings against trade in Indian rupees ("by order of the Nepal Rastra Bank") are a further reminder that India is just a betel-spit down the road.

Nepalganj sprawls more than a city of 50,000 should, thanks in part to an influx of labourers and project managers working on the Mahendra Highway in the early '90s. Its heart is **Tribhuwan Chowk**, the lively but dilapidated intersection of the city's two main shopping thoroughfares, south of which rikshas wait beneath an Indian-style Hindu temple that sits in the middle of the road like a toll booth. The **Muslim quarter** lies northeast of Tribhuwan Chowk – "picturesque" is probably too strong a word, but one canopy-shaded section is almost like a souk, with bearded traders wearing crocheted caps and pyjama-like clothes, and transactions conducted on wooden benches in the street. The mosques in this area are disappointingly modern, and at any rate out of bounds to nonbelievers. Hindu worship and trade is centred around the nondescript **Bageshwari Mandir**; behind the temple is a large pool with a jaunty statue of Mahadev (Shiva) in the middle – marvellously kitsch.

Practicalities

Hardly anybody sets out to see Nepalganj, but a few people heading further west end up spending an unintended night here. If you're flying to any of the far-western airstrips there'll be a change in Nepalganj and, all too often, some problem or other with the onward flight. Nepalganj's **airport**, the country's third busiest, is a six-kilometre plod north of town by *tonga* (horse-drawn cart) or riksha – see the next page for flight details. The **bus park** has been inconveniently banished to the extreme north end of the city, and it might be a good idea to buy an onward ticket when you arrive to avoid the extra trip later on. The **border**, which is open to tourists, is 6km south of town.

Nepalganj has a surprisingly good selection of cheap and moderately priced **accommodation**. Top of the line is *Hotel Batika* (☎081/21360; B⑦, B⑧ a/c), which is reasonably sound-proofed and even has a pool (non-guests can use it for Rs200). Similarly green and secluded, *Hotel Sneha* (☎081/20119; B⑥, B⑦ a/c) is a favourite with Western project workers. *Punjabi Hotel* (☎081/20818; ②/B③, B⑥ a/c) runs a distant third, but is priced more reasonably. Closer to town but correspondingly noisier, several cold-water lodges are grouped between Birendra Chowk and the bus park: best of these are *Hotel Orient* (①/B③), *Nirmala Hotel* (①/B②) and *Pahuna Ghar* (②/B③). Another option is *Tridev Guest House* (②; dorm beds ①), south of Tribhuwan Chowk.

If you don't speak Nepali, **eating** in Nepalganj is pretty much a smile-and-point operation at roadside carts or *bhojanalaya*. North of the Bageshwari temple, a couple of holes in the wall run by displaced Sherpas and Humla Bhotiyas do terrific *momo*, but that's all they do. Out towards the bus park, the popular and efficient *Punjabi Hotel* specializes in "daal-fried-roti" and fish curry. For more conventional food, try the better hotels.

Moving on from Nepalganj

Bus services out of Nepalganj are patchy (see p.265 for a rundown of routes). Only a handful of buses a day head west, and of these only the Thakurdwara and

FLIGHTS FROM NEPALGANJ			
	Frequency	**Time**	**Fare**
Bhairawa	3/week	45min	$77
Jumla	1–3/day	45min	$44
Kathmandu	2–4/day	1hr 10min*	$99
Mahendra Nagar	1/week	1hr 30min	$77
Sanfebagar	1/day	35min*	$61
Silgadhi Doti	2/week	40min*	$66
Simikot	5–7/week	50min*	$88
* Indirect flights will take longer.			

Mahendrea Nagar ones are likely to be much help. Eastbound, most buses travel at night becasue of the long distances involved. The only day bus to Kathmandu is the daily *Sajha* run, which you'll have to book first thing the day before to have any hope of getting a seat.

If you're moving west, consider renting a vehicle or flying. **Jeeps**, which can be arranged through any of the fancier hotels in town for about Rs1200 per day, are highly recommended for exploring Bardia or Sukla Phanta. **Motorcycles** can also be rented for about Rs400 per day.

Far western Nepal is where domestic **flights** really come into their own, and Nepalganj is the hub for all air services in the region. *RNAC*'s Mahendra Nagar flight will cut out eight hours in a bus, and if you're planning to trek around Jumla, Simikot or Dolpo, flying from here saves a good deal of money over flying from Kathmandu (see box); charter helicopters are also available. All domestic airlines cover the Kathmandu–Nepalganj route. *RNAC*'s office (☎20239) is out on the highway that bypasses town, west of Tribhuwan Chowk. The queue for tickets starts forming early and there's a mad dash when the doors open, but foreigners paying dollar fares can get "preferred" service upstairs. Other airlines with offices in Nepalganj are *Asian Airlines Helicopter* (☎20085), *Everest Air* (☎21482), *Necon Air* (☎20307) and *Nepal Airways* (☎20646).

Birendra Nagar (Surkhet)

Ninety kilometres northwest of Nepalganj – way, way off the beaten track – **BIRENDRA NAGAR** (as often as not called by its old name, **SURKHET**) comes as a pleasant surprise. Placed in the middle of an undulating *dun* valley, it's neither as hot, flat nor Indian as towns closer to the border. It's also managed to escape the usual shabby fate of Tarai boomtowns, thanks, surprisingly, to government planning: HMG has transferred its western regional headquarters from Nepalganj to here, a move that has created plenty of jobs and trade. A good deal of development effort is going into the valley, too, as evidenced by the gaggle of American, British, Japanese and other volunteers.

You might find yourself in Birendra Nagar for the start of a trek – from here it's a week to Rara Lake – or to raft in the Bheri River, which is half an hour south of town. By **bus**, it's a rugged six-hour trip from Nepalganj (afternoon buses break the journey overnight), though the road is supposedly slated for improvement. No one seems to have tried it yet, but this route would make an excellent two-day ride on a **mountain bike** – and once here, the bike would come in handy for getting around the valley. A trekking permit is required for travel north of the valley.

While in Birendra Nagar, you might as well see **Karki Bihar**, 2km out of town on a wooded knoll in the middle of the valley, which houses the remains of an ancient Buddhist temple. In town, the only real attraction is **Bulbule Tal**, a new but agreeably cool and shady park that's good for bird-watching.

A typical Tarai shop

Food and **lodging** in Birendra Nagar are of the most basic sort, with plenty of Nepali inns in the bazaar.

Bardia National Park

With Chitwan becoming increasingly mass-market, **BARDIA NATIONAL PARK**, northwest of Nepalganj, beckons as an unspoiled alternative. Hard to get to and still barely developed, it's the largest area of undisturbed wilderness left in the Tarai. Budget lodging is available, but there's nothing like the commercialism of Sauraha here. Indeed, if this section oversells the comparisons with Chitwan, it's because Bardia has everything Chitwan has – except Sauraha. As the word gets out about Bardia, transport connections may get easier and facilities cushier, but its distance from Kathmandu should shield it from the masses for many years to come.

Ecologically, Bardia spans an even greater range of habitats than Chitwan, from thick riverine forest and *sal* stands to *phanta* (isolated pockets of savannah) and dry upland slopes. The **Geruwa**, a branch of Nepal's biggest river, the awesome **Karnali**, forms the park's western boundary and major watering hole, and the density of wildlife and birds along this western edge is as great as anywhere in Asia. The less accessible eastern portion of the park is drained by the **Babai River**, which forms a sanctuary-like *dun* valley teeming with game.

Like Chitwan, Bardia is widely hailed as a conservation success story. **Rhinos**, hunted to extinction here earlier this century, have been reintroduced since 1986 and now number about fifty individuals – still not nearly as many as in Chitwan, but enough for most visitors to see one. About forty **tigers** inhabit the park, and are sighted fairly frequently, especially during their mating season (April–May). As many as thirty or forty **wild elephants** – Nepal's largest herd – crash around Bardia's western side, though they sometimes wander off into India for extended periods. The Karnali/Geruwa is probably the best place in Nepal to get a peep at rare **gangetic dolphins**, which favour the river's deep channels, and to fish for **mahseer**, a form of carp that can weigh up to 40kg. Mugger (and, increasingly, gharial) **crocodiles** can also be spotted in winter. Five species of **deer** – spotted,

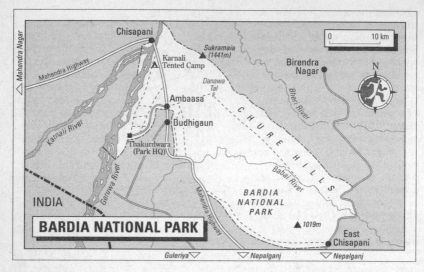

Chisapani

Mahendra Nagar

Mahendra Highway

Karnali
Tented Camp

Sukramaia
▲ *(1441m)*

Birendra
Nagar

Danawa
Tal

Ambaasa

CHURE

Bheri River

Budhigaun

Katnali River

Thakurdwara
(Park HQ)

Geruwa River

HILLS

Babai River

INDIA

Mahendra Highway

BARDIA
NATIONAL
PARK

BARDIA NATIONAL PARK

▲ 1019m

East
Chisapani

Guleriya▽   ▽ Nepalganj   ▽ Nepalganj

0   10 km

N

sambar, hog, barking and swamp – can be seen in abundance, along with **langurs** and **wild pig**. **Nilgai** ("blue bull"), bovine-looking members of the ante-lope family, roam the drier upland areas, while graceful, corkscrew-horned **black-buck** (featured on the back of Nepal's ten-rupee note) graze an area south of the park. More elusive are sloth bear, leopard and other nocturnal creatures, as well as the endangered hispid hare, which survives in Bardia's grasslands. The park is also home to 250 bird species, three of which – the Bengal florican, the lesser florican and the sarus crane – are endangered. The commonest sight of all around Bardia are **termite mounds**, looking like sand-coloured volcanoes, which reach their greatest height – up to 2.5m – here.

Thakurdwara

Virtually all of Bardia's lodgings are within walking distance of the park head-quarters at **THAKURDWARA**, 12km off the highway in a game-rich corner of the park near the Geruwa River. A sleepy Tharu farming settlement, Thakurdwara is archetypal Tarai. It has no centre, unless you count the cluster of mud houses just south of the HQ, or the microscopic bazaar where the bus stops, at the edge of the clearing another 1km to the east. It supports no tourist facilities other than its guest houses, and precious few even for locals. A small temple near the bus stop serves as the focus of activities for a big *mela* (religious fair) held on Magh Sankranti (Jan 14 or 15). A few other park-related points of interest are scattered in and around the village, notably the leafy headquarters compound, but most of the action is inside the park. In short, it's a lot like Sauraha was in the good old days: quiet, remote and adventurous.

Tourism will inevitably change Thakurdwara, but conservationists are already taking steps to ensure it doesn't repeat Sauraha's mistakes. Efforts are under way to create regulations to pre-empt inappropriate growth, and the Parks and People project (see "Chitwan in the Balance", p.272) is working on ways to help local people literally make money from the park.

Getting there

A daily afternoon **bus** runs directly from Nepalganj to Thakurdwara, following the Mahendra Highway to Ambaasa – nothing more than a tea shack at a crossroads – and then heading south on a dirt access road for another 12km. However, it's slow and crowded, so you might as well take any express day bus passing Ambaasa and get off there: the Thakurdwara local should pass through at around 5 or 6pm (but check to make sure the schedule hasn't changed). Day buses serving this stretch of the Mahendra Highway all ply between Nepalganj and Dhangadhi or Mahendra Nagar (see the box on p.264); coming from points east of Nepalganj, you'll have to change at Kohalpur, the turning for Nepalganj on the main highway. You should be able to get to Thakurdwara from Butwal if you make an early start, but any further east and you'll either have to overnight somewhere or travel by night. A night bus from Kathmandu or Pokhara will drop you off at Ambaasa in the early morning, but that's a hell of a way to get there.

Guest-house **touts** will probably board the bus at Ambaasa and quickly befriend you. You'll need them, as it may well be dark by the time the bus gets to Thakurdwara, and it's a long walk to lodgings.

If you can afford it, consider renting a **jeep** in Nepalganj or Mahendra Nagar. Besides making for a more comfortable journey and greater flexibility, the vehicle will enable you to explore the park more fully (see "Jeep Rides", below). It'll cost you Rs1000 to drive into the park, on top of the Rs1200 daily rental charge plus fuel, but split between four people it works out to about the cost of an elephant ride.

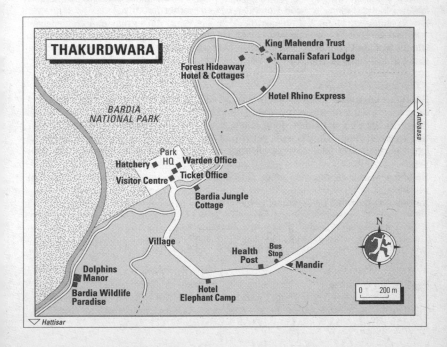

Accommodation

Until recently, the only way to experience Bardia was to stay in an exclusive safari lodge costing upwards of $350 for a two-night package. That's all changed with the opening of several budget operations in and around Thakurdwara, offering simple alternative lodging for a tiny fraction of the price.

BUDGET LODGES

Thakurdwara's **budget lodges** are spread out along the park boundary north and south of the HQ (refer to the Thakurdwara map for locations). They're all very similar, being based on the formula pioneered in (and steadily disappearing from) Sauraha: mud-and-thatch huts, kerosene lamps (there's no electricity), a simple dining pavilion, a separate toilet/shower block and, in a few cases, solar hot water. The food is simple: mainly *daal bhaat*. By far the biggest variable is the staff – turnover is high – so heed word-of-mouth referrals. Room **prices** are high by Chitwan standards, but you're paying for an elite experience, and in any case accommodation makes up only a small part of the cost of visiting Nepal's wildlife parks.

The lodges with phone numbers offer **packages**, which can take a lot of the sweat out of getting to the park – a much greater consideration for Bardia than for Chitwan – but will end up costing you quite a bit more than doing it yourself. Some operators and agents offer packages that combine a seven-day raft trip down the Karnali with a wildlife programme at a Bardia lodge.

Bardia Jungle Cottage (book through *Lucky Travel Service*, Kathmandu: ☎214769). Thakurdwara's original budget lodge, run by a former park warden, with a great location and atmosphere. Hot water in the common bathroom only. Bikes for rent. ④/B⑤.

Bardia Wildlife Paradise (book through *Rhino Lodge*, Kathmandu: ☎416918). Serviceable facilities, though lacking in shade. Hot water, bikes for rent. ③.

Forest Hideaway Hotel & Cottages (book through *Shiva's River Adventure*, Kathmandu: ☎417685). Businesslike operation with a jeep and probably the best food in Thakurdwara. ④.

Hotel Elephant Camp. Small and primitive (cold water only). ③.

Hotel Rhino Express. Ditto. ③.

EXPENSIVE LODGES

Bardia's **expensive lodges** deal mainly in all-inclusive packages, which work out to at least $100 a night per person. The extra money buys you access to the full range of Bardia's activities (jeep rides, rafting, fishing), plus marginally better facilities and food. They'll pick you up at the Nepalganj airport (usually for an extra charge) and take care of all your arrangements for the duration of your stay.

Dolphins Manor (Kathmandu office: ☎417191). Deluxe concrete bungalows; swimming pool planned. B⑨.

Karnali Safari Lodge (book through *Link Travel & Tours*, Kathmandu: ☎230318). Mutton dressed as lamb: the only difference between this outfit and the better budget lodges is a bar. ⑧.

Tiger Tops Karnali Tented Camp and **Karnali Lodge** (Kathmandu office: ☎423171). These high-class outfits actually aren't anywhere near Thakurdwara: the tented camp overlooks the Geruwa in the northern part of the park, and the lodge is just outside the park near its southernmost point. B⑨.

Park practicalities

Park **entry permits** cost Rs650 and are valid for three consecutive days. Buy them from the **ticket office** inside the headquarters compound, or have your guest house do it for you. Elephant ride tickets and fishing permits (see below) are also booked here. Park brochure/maps may be available from the nearby **warden's office**, but don't count on it.

While you're at the HQ, stop by the park's reptile **hatchery**, a small, zoo-like facility where gharial and mugger crocodiles, turtles and a few monitor lizards are raised from eggs. Like a similar effort at Chitwan (see p.278), this project greatly ups the chances of these endangered and sensitive species living to maturity, at which point they're released into local waters. Also in the HQ compound, a **visitor centre** is being constructed to house a small exhibit on Bardia's ecology.

Guides

Although the rhino danger is somewhat lower here than in Chitwan, it would still be extremely foolish to enter the park without a **guide**. Hire one informally through your guest house; the price will be around Rs400 per person per day. Although guides here speak less English and are less well trained than those at Chitwan, they know the territory and can keep you out of harm's way.

See "Staying Alive in Chitwan" (p.274) for jungle safety tips.

Moving on

The daily **bus** to Nepalganj leaves Thakurdwara at around 8 or 9am. If you're heading east, you could stay on board to Kohalpur (the turning for Nepalganj), where you ought to be able to book a confirmed seat on a day express bound for Butwal. If you're in a hurry to get to Kathmandu or Pokhara, carry on to Nepalganj where several night buses originate. Heading west, get off at Ambaasa and flag down any bus that's going to Chisapani and then size up your options from there. You should be able to get to Mahendra Nagar before dark, though may end up having to change buses again at Atariya, the turning for Dhangadhi.

Park activities

Bardia's menu of activities is similar to Chitwan's; you'll find lengthier descriptions of walks and elephant rides in that section.

Walks

Most of your forays into the park will be on foot with a guide. Most **walks** from Thakurdwara take a northerly bearing, roughly paralleling the river through mixed grassland and jungle. You could see anything here: deer, monkeys and all manner of birds are assured, and rhinos, tigers, elephants, bears, boars, nilgai and (in the river) dolphins are often sighted. The view tower at Bagaura Phanta, about 7km north of Thakurdwara, is a prime bird-watching spot. The best rhino habitat is 10–15km north of Thakurdwara – a full-day hike. A much shorter walk southwards to the river offers good opportunities to see dolphins and rhinos.

Elephant rides

Arrange **elephant rides** at the headquarters ticket office, or have your guest house do it. The charge is Rs650 for a standard one-hour-plus ride. It's advisable to reserve the day before, or even two days before if there are many other tourists in the village, as only eight rideable elephants are kept here, and not all of them may be on duty on any given day. Departures are in the early morning and late afternoon. The usual route heads west and north from the HQ into deep jungle; you can go further into the park by special arrangement (and extra payment)

Jeep rides

At the time of writing, *Forest Hideaway* was the only budget lodge with its own **jeep**, which it was renting out at extortionate rates – Rs6000 for a half day, Rs10,000 for a full day. No doubt the price will come down as other lodges follow suit. In the meantime, you'll save money by renting a jeep in Nepalganj (see p.296).

A jeep might or might not increase your chances of surprising game, but it will certainly enable you to penetrate remoter parts of the park where the game isn't as wary of humans. Tops on any itinerary would have to be the edenic Babai Valley, reached via Danawa Tal, a favourite wallowing place for wild elephants. You could also explore the network of roads in the park's western sector, which gives access to pristine stretches of river and rich wildlife habitat, and continue north to Chisapani to look for gharials and dolphins. Another road heading north from Ambaasa dead-ends at the base of the Chure Hills, from where you can hike up to the summit of Sukramala, which at 1441m is the highest point around. Finally, you could head south to look for blackbuck antelope (see "Activities outside the park", below).

Rafting

A few **rafting** companies do week-long trips down the Karnali, pulling out at Chisapani, and a couple run the Babai, a two- or three-day float right through the park. However, these trips are all organized out of Kathmandu – try the operators listed on p.128. Once you get to Bardia your options are limited to day trips on the Geruwa, and only if you're staying in the right lodge. Currently only *Tiger Tops* has its own rafts, but *Forest Hideaway* is supposed to be getting one, and other lodges may eventually offer raft trips as well. It won't come cheap, though: *Forest Hideaway* is talking about charging Rs3500 per person for a half-day float.

Once on the river, you've got a good chance of seeing dolphins, muggers, monkeys and birds, and some people have seen elephants and even tigers from the water. It's also a great way to fish.

Fishing

The Karnali/Geruwa is renowned for its **mahseer**, a sporting fish related to carp that can weigh up to 40kg. If you catch one, release it: the *mahseer* population is declining due to pollution, dams, barriers and a general lack of headwaters protection.

Fishing is allowed only on the Karnali and Geruwa rivers – the Babai is off-limits because it's a gharial release area. You'll need a fishing **permit**, which costs Rs300 per day and can be obtained from the ticket office at park HQ. Bring your own tackle (you can buy simple gear in Pokhara and Kathmandu).

Activities outside the park

In addition to the reptile hatchery and visitor centre at park headquarters (see above), Thakurdwara offers two other quickie sightseeing possibilities. About twenty minutes' walk north of the park HQ, the **King Mahendra Trust for Nature Conservation** maintains an educational and research centre where the main attraction is a pair of orphaned leopards. Researchers and community-development workers based here are good sources of information on local conservation matters. To watch Bardia's hardest-working employees enjoying some down time, visit the government *hattisar* (elephant stable), about forty minutes south of the HQ. Although it's not set up as a breeding centre, this *hattisar* usually has a baby elephant or two in residence, thanks to the nocturnal visits of wild bulls.

Some guest houses in Thakurdwara rent **bicycles**, which opens up a host of possiblities for exploring the surrounding countryside. The traditional **Tharu villages** dotted along the Thakurdwara–Ambaasa road make worthy destinations. Given more time and a packed lunch, you could conceivably cycle to Chisapani or some of the other spots normally only reached by jeep (see above).

Nepal's only herd of blackbuck antelope congregates around a big *phanta* at **Khairi Panditpur**, 30km southeast of Thakurdwara. The government is attempting to buy the land to create a separate wildlife reserve to protect the herd, which numbers 100 to 150 animals. If you take a local bus from Budhigaun (3km east of Ambaasa on the Mahendra Highway) south to Gulariya you'll see them off to the left.

West of the Karnali

When it's finally completed, the Mahendra Highway from Nepalganj to the far western border post of Mahendra Nagar will be, for Nepal, something of an engineering marvel. Laying down 240km of asphalt was easy; building bridges over the countless streams that dice the route (not to mention spanning the Karnali) has been the real challenge. At the time of writing, the bus ride from Nepalganj to Mahendra Nagar took about nine hours – down from twelve just two years earlier – but when all the bridges are passable that time should drop to six or seven.

The Karnali Bridge and Chisapani

The Mahendra Highway emerges from Bardia National Park to vault the mighty **Karnali River**, surging out of a gap in the rugged foothills, on what is reputed to be the longest single-tower suspension **bridge** in the world. Before the completion of the bridge, in 1993, the Karnali effectively formed the western border of Nepal: those living on the other side maintained stronger links with Delhi than with Kathmandu. The World Bank-funded bridge won't automatically bring the far west back under Kathmandu's sway – Delhi is still closer – but when the highway is finished it will enable a lot more heavy-goods traffic to pass through here on its way between the two capitals, which is likely to give an important boost to Nepal's trading relationship with India. (The World Bank appears to have permanently shelved another, even bigger project for this area: the Karnali Dam would, if fully configured, have been the biggest hydroelectric dam in the world.)

As for the bridge's exotic design, it appears to have been dictated mainly by the foreign contractors' need for a showcase project. Alas, after crossing this gleaming, state-of-the-art span, the paved highway promptly reverts to a four-wheel-drive track, illustrating the politically sensitive nature of development in Nepal. China was contracted to build this section of the Mahendra Highway, but in 1994, with the work nearing completion, India became nervous about the presence of Chinese so close to its border and offered to buy out the contract. Nepal took India's money, the Chinese went home, the contractor chosen to finish the job didn't come through, and the money was spent on other projects. The result: a jarring eight-kilometre gap just west of the Karnali, followed by nine temporary river crossings between there and the Dhangadhi turnoff.

Overlooking the forested west bank of the Karnali, the shacks of **CHISAPANI** look like they were erected yesterday in the expectation that they'd be dismantled tomorrow. Nevertheless, this polyglot little bazaar does a steady trade with shoppers from the hills, some of whom walk a week or more to buy basic provisions here. If you're stuck, there are a few makeshift bunkhouses at the north end of the bazaar.

Dhangadhi

Another 100km west and back out of the trees, **DHANGADHI** is a flatter, duller and altogether more conventional border town sitting 12km south of the highway, off a paved spur road to India. Unless you're heading for India's Dudhwa National Park (which is just south of the border) or catching a bus to Dipayal or one of the other hill towns to the north, there's little reason to be here. The new **bus park** is about 1km east of the main roundabout, and the breezeblock bazaar about 500m east of that. The **airstrip** ($159 to Kathmandu) lies 10km north of town on the way back to the highway – rikshas are plentiful – and the **RNAC office** (☎091/21205) is by the main roundabout. The Indian **border**, 2km south of the roundabout, is open to foreigners.

Lodgings are for the most part cheap and modest, the best being *Hotel Afno Ghar* (☎091/22959; B④), with air-cooled rooms, hot water and a nice garden. *Sangam Lodge*'s (②/B③) facilities are nearly as good, and its restaurant is better. *Hotel the Lonely Plannet* (②/B④), located in the quieter aid enclave of Hasanpur, about 1km east of the main bazaar, also has a fair restaurant. A half-dozen other places in the bazaar and around the bus park offer cold-water facilities. The guest houses do the best **food**, though *Marina Mistan Bhandar* is worth checking out for sweets. There's a **bank** in Hasanpur, next to the *Lonely Plannet* (Sun–Thurs 10am–2pm, Fri 10am–noon).

Mahendra Nagar

The end of the line is **MAHENDRA NAGAR**, another border town but with a good deal of spark, thanks to daytripping shoppers from India. The town is laid out in an unusually logical grid south of the highway, with the **bus park** at the northwestern end. Walking south from the bus park, the first landmark you'll come to is Chattari Chaura, the umbrella roundabout at the intersection of the town's main east–west street. Mahendra Nagar's **airstrip** is a long, clattering riksha ride to the southwest, almost at the entrance to Sukla Phanta Wildlife Reserve (see below). *RNAC* flies here once or twice a week from Kathmandu ($160) and Nepalganj ($77).

Budget **lodgings** are scattered along the main drag and a few side streets to the east of Chattari Chaura. *New Hotel Anand*, overlooking the central market area, is noisy and stark, but very helpful with arrangements for Sukla Phanta and India (B③). *Apee Guest House*, at the east end of the main street, is dingy but quieter and friendly (B②). Both of these can provide hot water by the bucket. Mahendra Nagar's finest accommodation, *Hotel Sweet Dream* (☎099/22313; B⑦), sits out on the highway east of the bus park – it offers air-cooled rooms, hot running water and a tourist restaurant, but suffers from early-morning noise from the highway. Local **places to eat**, concentrated mainly along the side street one block east of Chattari Chaura, do a fair range of Nepali and tandoori food.

Any of the guest houses mentioned above can fix you up with a **jeep** for exploring Sukla Phanta or Bardia (Rs1200 per day plus fuel). The **bank**, just south of

Chattari Chaura, is unpredictable about exchanging foreign currency other than Indian rupees (Sun–Thurs 10am–2pm, Fri 10am–noon). IC is readily accepted and unofficially exchanged everywhere in Mahendra Nagar. You'll find the **RNAC office** (☎099/21196; erratic hours) one block east of Chattari Chaura.

Mahendra Nagar's bustle is only a border aberration, for the outlying region is one of the more traditional parts of the Tarai. Rana Tharu sharecroppers work the fields, maintaining an apparently happy symbiosis with their old-money landlords, and their **villages**, scattered along dirt tracks north of the Mahendra Highway, still consist of traditional communal longhouses. Villagers go completely over the top for visitors and positively preen for the camera – a Polaroid would be a *big* hit – but it's bad manners to breeze in without at least enough Nepali to repay them with thanks and a little conversation.

A Rana Tharu girl

The border

The **border** lies 6km west of Mahendra Nagar, at the Mahankali River, with Nepalese and Indian immigration posts separated by a 300-metre no-man's land. Buses shuttle between Mahendra Nagar and the border approximately every half hour during the day, and slower horse-drawn *tonga* make the trip on demand. The Nepalese immigration post keeps strange **opening hours** (at last check 6–7am, noon–2pm & 5–6pm) – and the bureaucrats there demand Rs50 for an "arrival sticker". There are no exchange facilities at the border. It's a fifteen-minute riksha ride to Banbasa, the border town on the Indian side, with narrow-gauge rail service to Bareli.

There's more to this lonely border post than meets the eye: it's said to be the number-one entry point into India for smuggled **computer chips**. India assiduously protects its domestic electronics industry with high duties on imports; Nepal doesn't, fuelling a black-market flow of parts from the Far East to Delhi via Kathmandu and Banbasa. Since a single suitcase can hold $1 million worth of chips, there's potentially more profit these days in silicon than in heroin.

Sukla Phanta Wildlife Reserve

In Nepal's extreme southwest, a different feature appears on the land: *phanta*, great swathes of natural grassland that could almost be mistaken, albeit on a smaller scale, for the savannas of East Africa. **SUKLA PHANTA WILDLIFE RESERVE**, south of Mahendra Nagar, is dotted with them, and touring it is, for once, really like being on safari. The reserve is home to the world's largest population of swamp deer – sightings of 1000 at a time are common – as well as a good concentration of tigers. Seeing Sukla Phanta independently is relatively expensive,

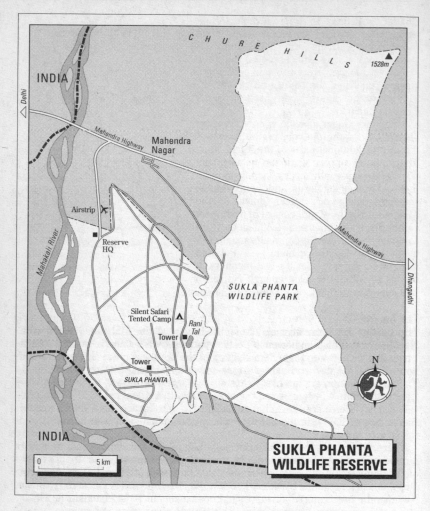

SUKLA PHANTA
WILDLIFE RESERVE

as it entails renting a vehicle, but you'll have the satisfaction of going where few have gone before. In addition, a lone in-park operator offers luxury safaris.

Several four-wheel-drive tracks crisscross the reserve, making itineraries flexible, but first stop is bound to be *the* **Sukla Phanta** at the southwestern end, a rippling sea of grass that turns silvery-white in October (*sukila* means white in the local Tharu dialect). You're guaranteed **swamp deer** here, and in quantity – make for the view tower in the middle and scan for them with binoculars. As *barasingha* ("twelve points"), the swamp deer was one of Kipling's beloved *Jungle Book* animals – "that big deer which is like our red deer, but stronger" – and common throughout the plains and hills. Today it's an endangered species, finding safety in numbers in the *phanta* and particularly the boggy parts where seasonal fires don't burn off the grasses. The species' high density in Sukla Phanta assures plenty of prey for the reserve's thirty-odd **tigers**, which for the time being seem healthy. However, a question mark hangs over their long-term survival, as habitat outside the reserve is steadily disappearing, and Sukla Phanta alone isn't large enough to support an independent breeding population. Meanwhile, poaching is a growing threat. As India's tiger numbers dwindle, poachers are increasingly targeting Nepal's animals, and Sukla Phanta, which borders India, is right on the front line of this battle: the sound of gunshots coming from the southern (Indian) end is distressingly frequent.

Having seen your obligatory *phanta*, make a beeline for **Rani Tal** (Queen's Lake), near the centre of the reserve. Surrounded by riotous, screeching forest, the lake – a lagoon, really – is like a prehistoric time capsule, with trees leaning out over the shore, deer wading shoulder-deep around the edges and crocodiles occasionally peering out of the water-hyacinth-choked water. The **birdlife** is like nothing you've ever seen, a dazzling display of cranes, cormorants, eagles and scores of others. You can watch all the comings and goings from a tower by the western shore. Nearby is an overgrown **brick circle**, 1500m in circumference, which locals say was the fort of Singpal, an ancient Tharu king (Rani Tal is said to have been his queen's favourite spot); the fact that the remains have never been excavated shows how little historical research has been done in western Nepal.

Though you'd think they'd be hard to miss, chances are Sukla Phanta's **elephant herd** will give you the slip – they seem to spend an increasing amount of their time south of the border. Evidence of their passage is abundant, however, especially along the road south from the entrance, where in places the forest looks like it's been hit by a tornado. The dominant male of this herd, dubbed Thulo Hatti ("Big Elephant"), was killed in 1993 by a homemade mine, planted either by poachers or by a farmer trying to protect his crops. Before his demise, Thulo Hatti was believed to be the world's biggest Asian elephant, and was even featured in a BBC documentary.

Practicalities

The reserve **entrance** is 10km southwest of Mahendra Nagar, not far from the airstrip (see p.304). The Rs650 **entry fee** is good for three consecutive days.

The nearest budget lodgings are in Mahendra Nagar, which seriously blunts the reserve's appeal as well as adding considerably to the cost of visiting it **independently**. The only feasible way to enter the park – and certainly the best way to track game across the *phanta* – is by jeep, rentable in Mahendra Nagar for around Rs1200 a day. Although rikshas will take you to the reserve entrance, you won't be allowed to enter alone on foot, and there are no guides or elephants for hire.

There is another way to visit Sukla Phanta, but it involves more money – still, even if you hate the idea of a **luxury safari**, this might be the place to do one. An unpretentious family outfit, *Silent Safari* (☎099/21230; fax ☎099/22220; Kathmandu office: ☎527708), runs customized trips in the park for about $140 per person per night, and can also arrange Tharu village treks. It's a one-man operation – Col. Hikmat Bisht, former hunter, retired military attaché, patrician landowner and self-styled man of the forest – and a trip with him is one of the most delightfully idiosyncratic experiences in Nepal. His **tented camp** is pitched next to a waterhole in deep jungle – real Tarzan country – and there's also the unique opportunity to spend a night or two in a *machaan* (tree-top blind) for nocturnal sights and sounds. He is considering building a more moderately priced lodge just outside the park entrance, with rooms in the $20 range.

CHAPTER SIX

THE EASTERN TARAI AND HILLS

A s with the west, the **eastern Tarai** – the portion east of Chitwan – is where Nepal dovetails with India, and in many ways it offers the best of both worlds. Overwhelmingly rural, the plains have a timeless, almost genteel quality: thatched houses perch on stilts, clumps of bamboo and palms erupt in green explosions, and the foothills, if not the Himalaya, are always within sight. Most travellers only flit through here on their way to the border crossings of **Birganj** (for Patna) and **Kakarbitta** (for Darjeeling), and outside these places you

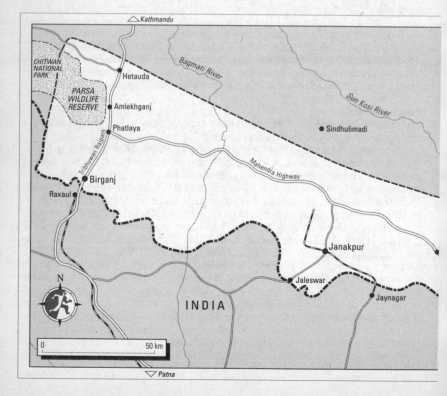

won't find a speck of commercialism. The cities are admittedly awful, but with one outstanding exception: **Janakpur**, a pilgrimage centre that's immensely famous among Hindus but seldom visited by Westerners, which provides all the exoticism of India without the attendant hassles. Although large tracts of jungle are less common east of Chitwan, birdwatchers can check out **Koshi Tappu Wildlife Reserve**, straddling the alluvial plain of the mighty Sapt Koshi River.

What few visitors the **eastern hills** get tend to be trekkers bound for the Everest or Kanchenjunga massifs, which rear up like goalposts on the northern horizon. But while the prospect of travelling twenty-plus hours by bus from Kathmandu puts most people off, this isn't a problem if you're already in the eastern Tarai. By turns riotously forested and fastidiously terraced, the hills are great for day-hiking, even if you've vowed not to trek (but get a permit anyway, just in case you change your mind). At least two towns here are worth visiting in their own right: **Hile**, a rowdy frontier bazaar with a Tibetan ambience, and **Ilam**, Nepal's tea-growing capital.

Both the eastern Tarai and hills are noticeably better off than the non-touristed parts of the west; **travel connections** are (by Nepali standards) comprehensive, and even in remote places you should be able to **eat** well, if not Western. A phenomenon specific to eastern Nepal is the **haat bazaar**, or weekly market, and it's worth trying to coincide with one or two of these pan-cultural extravaganzas.

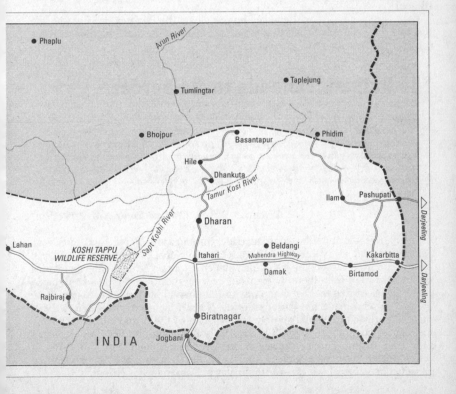

THE EASTERN TARAI

For travellers coming by road from other parts of Nepal, Hetauda is the gateway to the eastern Tarai: from Narayanghat (Chitwan) it's an easy two-hour bus ride to Hetauda along the **Mahendra Highway**, hugging the hills as it follows the attractive *dun* (inner Tarai valley) of the Rapti River; the **Tribhuwan Rajpath** (see p.216) enters the town from the north and continues south to the Indian border at Birganj.

Both west and east of Hetauda, **buses** along the Mahendra Highway are frequent and relatively fast. If you're **cycling**, many of the small bazaars en route can provide basic food and, at a pinch, lodging.

The Rajpath: Hetauda to the border

There is something peculiarly sinister and ominous about the jungle of the Tarai. You have that feeling that danger in one form or another lurks around every corner . . . Over everything a strange, oppressive silence broods . . . A big gray ape chatters at us maliciously from his perch on an overhanging rock. A leopard, camouflaged almost to invisibility by his spotted hide, steals on stealthy feet across the road. There is a sudden crash of underbrush behind the jungle wall – an elephant or a tiger perhaps.

E Alexander Powell, *The Last Home of Mystery* (1929)

For centuries the only developed corridor through the Tarai, this route was, before air travel, every foreigner's introduction to Nepal. A narrow-gauge railway used to run from Raxaul, the last Indian station, as far as Amlekhganj; dignitaries were transported from there by elephant over the first band of hills to Hetauda before being carried the rest of the way to Kathmandu by donkey or sedan chair. Those few who made the journey during Nepal's isolation years before 1951, such as our Mr Powell, did so only by invitation of the prime minister or king. The construction of the **Rajpath** in the 1950s eliminated the need for elephants and sedan chairs, but the railway wasn't decommissioned until the 1970s. If you're driving your own vehicle in from India, the Rajpath makes an exhilarating introduction to Nepal, with an overnight stay in Daman (see p.216).

Hetauda

Clumped around the junction of the Mahendra Highway and the Rajpath, **HETAUDA** is still a staging-post on the India–Kathmandu route, but whatever romance it may once have had has long gone. Indian trucks rumble through with fuel and bulk goods for Kathmandu, while buses stop here at all hours: it's a restless, transient place. Among Nepalis, Hetauda is probably most famous for its cement plant, whose output is transported to the Kathmandu Valley by ropeway (visible from the Rajpath). The smoke from its chimneys may be the shape of things to come. The government is making noises about encouraging the carpet industry to move to Hetauda from the Kathmandu Valley, where effluents from the washing process are polluting the water. And where would the effluents go if the factories moved to Hetauda? Down the Rapti River into Chitwan National Park. It might sound preposterous, but the Department of Roads has even gone so far as to propose a new highway from Kathmandu to Hetauda via a tunnel through the Mahabharat Lek – any donors?

Practicalities

Hetauda's **bus park** is located southwest of the main intersection; the main entrance is from the north. Many buses pass through here bound for destinations to the east and west. If you're trying to get to Daman or Kathmandu, only one daily *Sajha* bus travels the Rajpath in each direction (two other private buses also serve this route, but they overnight in Markhu and Shikharkot respectively – see p.217).

Cyclists will probably **spend the night** here, as there are no other worthwhile places to stay between Daman and the border or Chitwan. Fortunately, *Motel Avocado* (☎057/20429; ③/B⑤, ⑦ with a/c) more than compensates for Hetauda's shortcomings. Located in a quiet compound well north of the bazaar (get there by tempo if you're not cycling), the grounds are shaded by a small grove of avocado trees planted by displaced Californians when this was the USAID guest house. In late autumn practically everything on the menu has avocado in it. Running a distant second is *Hotel Rapti* (☎057/20882; B④), south of the main intersection, which is the only place in the bazaar with a little sound-deadening space around it. There are several cheaper choices north of the crossroads (such as *Neelam Lodge*, ①), but they're apt to be very noisy. **Food** outside the guest houses is unexceptional, but you'll find a number of tea stalls and a couple of serviceable *sekuwa* restaurants near *Neelam Lodge*.

South to Birganj

Heading south over the low **Chure Hills**, the Rajpath, perpetually unfinished here, enters a strange landscape of stunted trees, wide gravel washes and steeply eroded pinnacles. These hills are the newest wrinkle in the Himalayan chain, heaved up as the 30-million-year-long collision between the Indian and Asian continental plates ripples southwards – less than half a million years old, they're so young that the surface sediments haven't yet been eroded to expose bedrock.

Leaving the hills once and for all, the road passes Amlekhganj, the former rail terminus (now Nepal's main fuel depot), and 4km further on, the entrance to **Parsa Wildlife Reserve**. An annexe of Chitwan National Park, providing secondary habitats for many of its sub-adult tigers, the reserve isn't developed for tourism; no food or lodgings are available, and visitors aren't allowed in on foot without

PUBLIC BUS SERVICES IN THE EASTERN TARAI AND HILLS			
	Frequency (day)	Frequency (night)	Time (minimum)
To and from BASANTAPUR			
Dharan	9		5hr
To and from BIRATNAGAR			
Butwal		2	14hr
Dharan	20		1hr 30min
Janakpur	5		8hr
Kakarbitta	12		4hr
Kathmandu		12	18hr
Pokhara		1	18hr
To and from BIRGANJ			
Butwal	4	3	6hr
Dharan	1		10hr
Gorkha	4		7hr
Janakpur	7		5hr
Kathmandu	8#	26#	10hr
Pokhara	14	2	10hr
To and from BIRTAMOD			
Ilam	5		6hr
Kakarbitta	20		30min
Phidim	2		12hr
To and from DHANKUTA			
Basantapur	9		2hr
Dharan	18		3hr
Hile	18		30min
Kathmandu		2	20hr
To and from DHARAN			
Basantapur	9		5hr
Biratnagar	20		1hr 30min
Birganj	1		10hr
Dhankuta	18		3hr
Hile	18		3hr 30min

a guide (who may also be unavailable). Accompanied by a guide brought from Sauraha, you could do day trips from Birganj and have the run of the whole place, though you'd need a jeep to get into interesting habitat. The entrance fee is Rs650.

The Mahendra Highway branches off to the east at **Phatlaya**, 3km south of the Parsa entrance, and **Simara**, another 3km south, heralds a dreary succession of factories and fields that continues all the way to Birganj. For obscure reasons of national security, Nepal passed a law in the mid-1980s requiring that all new factories must be built at least 10km from the Indian border, which is causing the major border cities to flare northwards. Simara has an **airstrip** (daily flights to Kathmandu, $44).

	Frequency (day)	Frequency (night)	Time (minimum)
Kakarbitta	4		4hr
Kathmandu		10	18hr
To and from HETAUDA*			
Kathmandu (via Rajpath)	1#		8hr
To and from HILE			
Basantapur	9		1hr 30min
Dhankuta	18		30min
Dharan	18		3hr 30min
Kathmandu		2	21hr
To and from ILAM			
Birtamod	5		6hr
Phidim	2		6hr
To and from JANAKPUR			
Bhairawa		1	12hr
Biratnagar	5		8hr
Birganj	7		5hr
Butwal		3	10hr
Jaleswar	10		30min
Kakarbitta	4	4	9hr
Kathmandu	2#	10#	12hr
Nepalganj		2	16hr
Pokhara		1	12hr
To and from KAKARBITTA			
Biratnagar	12		4hr
Birtamod	20		30min
Dharan	4		4hr
Janakpur	4	4	9hr
Kathmandu		21	20hr
Pokhara		2	20hr
Tansen		1	19hr

* Many other buses pass through.
# *Sajha* service available.

Birganj and the border

Nepal's busiest port of entry, **BIRGANJ** is a thoroughly disagreeable place – an unflattering introduction to Nepal if you're just arriving and a rude send-off if you're leaving. The latest census (1991) puts Birganj's population at 69,000, but like most of the Tarai's urban centres it must be growing at an annual clip of at least five percent. A new highway bypass has made the main street south of the prominent clocktower vastly more liveable, but all traffic to and from the border still converges on the city's northern approach, reducing it to an uncrossable torrent of lurching trucks, buses and ox carts.

Nevertheless, some travellers may have to pass this way, and if you're touring India and Nepal by bicycle you might want to cross here once to avoid backtracking. Buses connect Birganj with Kathmandu, Pokhara and a few major Tarai cities (see box on p.312). The efficient new **bus park** is located almost 1km east of the clocktower, beyond the bypass and off the map. Rikshas and tempos provide transport from there.

If you're stranded in Birganj, you could probably kill a few hours in the old-ish market area around **Maisthan**, a mother-goddess temple just off the main drag. Beyond that, though, the city has little to offer: **Adarsh Nagar** is a fairly humdrum market area that's unlikely to appeal to anyone except Indian consumers, and the new (and as yet unfinished) west side of town is devoid of interest.

Practicalities

You can manage quite comfortably for food and **lodging** in Birganj (but note that there are no facilities at the border). At the top end, *Hotel Makalu* (☎051/23054; B⑥) has air conditioning and a phone in every room, and *Hotel Samjhana* (☎051/22122; B⑤, or ⑦ with a/c) has a nice garden and facilities, though it's in a terrible location way north of the centre, off the map. Best of the midrange choices, *Hotel Cottage Fulbari* (B④) and the older *Hotel Kailas* (③/B③) both have good restaurants. *Hotel Prakash* (②/B③) and *Nabin Hotel* (②/B③) are about as cheap as guest houses get in Birganj; the *Prakash* is marginally the better of the two, but no great shakes.

Both the *Kailas* and the neighbouring *Diyalo* have fine, if seedy, Indian **restaurants**, while *Kanchha Sweets*, nearby, serves up a miraculous assortment of Indian goodies. *Hotel Samjhana's Hariyali Restaurant* prepares admirable Continental and Indian food in pleasant surroundings. You'll also find *sekuwa*, fried fish and other street food in stalls around the town centre.

Cross-border commerce supports numerous **banks** in Birganj, at least five of which do foreign exchange. The most useful are *Rastriya Banijya* (Sun–Thurs 10.30am–4.30pm, Fri 10.30am–1.30pm) and *Nepal Bank* (Mon–Fri 11am–6pm, Sat 11am–3pm). Nearly all businesses in Birganj accept Indian rupees at the official rate.

THE ETHNIC SCENE

There seems to be an unwritten rule in Nepal that all migrations have to be from west to east, with the result that contingents of almost every Nepalese ethnic group now jostle together in the eastern quarter of the country.

The original inhabitants of the eastern hills were the **Kirantis** (or Kiratas), a warlike tribe mentioned in the *Mahabharat* who may well have been the same Kiratas who ruled the Kathmandu Valley in semi-mythological times. The Kiranti nation long ago fragmented into several tribes, the most important ones being the **Rais** and **Limbus**. Like the Magars and Gurungs of the west, members of these dauntless hill groups make up a significant portion of the Gurkha regiments; similarly, they follow their own form of shamanism, but increasingly embrace Hindu or Buddhist practices, depending on their location. Unusually, the Kiranti clans bury their dead (as opposed to cremating, which is the usual practice throughout the subcontinent), and Limbus erect distinctive rectangular, whitewashed grave markers. Rais, who have a reputation as a staunchly independent people, traditionally occupy the middle-elevation hills west of the Arun River, while Limbuwan, as the Limbu homeland is sometimes still called, is centred around the lower slopes of the Tamur Kosi Valley, further east.

Rais and Limbus had the hills virtually to themselves until a spate of migrations, beginning in the late eighteenth century, completely transformed the ethnic map of eastern Nepal. The Gorkhali army marched in and annexed the region in 1776; in their wake, **Bahuns** and **Chhetris** began infiltrating the Arun basin and **Newars** took over the trading crossroads. At about the same time, **Sherpas** and **Tamangs** were steadily elbowing the Rais out of Solu, and more recently, **Magars** and **Gurungs** have hopped across from their traditional homelands in the west. Little wonder, then, that when the Rais and Limbus were recruited by the British in the last century to pluck tea in Darjeeling, they too headed east.

Even more than in western Nepal, the clearing of the eastern Tarai during the past three decades has spurred a feverish new land rush, as hill people in turn displace native **Tharus** (see p.282), **Danuwars** and the Maithili-speaking **Hindus** who predominate between Janakpur and Biratnagar. Meanwhile, **Biharis** and **Bengalis** keep arriving in droves from India. Bouncing along the Mahendra Highway, where housing and dress styles change from one village to the next, you almost feel as if you're watching the migration in motion.

The border

The **border** is 4km south of Birganj, and **Raxaul**, the first Indian town, sprawls for another 2km south of the border. Horrendous traffic jams are a regular occurrence here – if you're driving it can take hours to get through physically, leaving aside the paperwork. Rikshas charge about Rs40 to ferry passengers from Birganj to Raxaul (make sure the price quoted is in Nepalese rupees). Horse-drawn *tonga* are cheaper, but they probably won't wait while you go through customs and immigration. Nepalese immigration is open 24 hours a day for foreigners; if you're entering Nepal and you don't already have a visa, make sure you have the correct change in cash (dollars).

From Raxaul, buses run infrequently to Patna (5hr), where you can catch broad-gauge trains to most parts of northern India.

Janakpur

JANAKPUR, 165km east of Birganj, is indisputably the Tarai's most fascinating city. Often called **Janakpurdham** (*dham* denoting a sacred place), it's a holy site of the first order, and its central temple, the ornate Janaki Mandir, is an obligatory stop on the Hindu pilgrimage circuit. Although Indian in every respect except politically, the city is, by Indian standards, small and manageable: motorized traffic is all but banned from the centre, tourist hustle is largely absent, the poverty isn't oppressive, and the surrounding countryside is delightful. To top it all, Janakpur's railway, the only one still operating in Nepal, makes an entertaining excursion in itself. There's so much going on, both in and around Janakpur, that it's worth setting aside a few days to absorb it all – though bear in mind that there are no tourist-style lodgings, restaurants or other facilities.

Hindu mythology identifies Janakpur as the capital of the ancient kingdom of **Mithila**, which probably controlled a large part of north India between the tenth and third centuries BC. The city features prominently in the *Ramayan*, for it was in Janakpur that **Ram** – the god Vishnu in mortal form – wed **Sita**, daughter of the Mithila King Janak. Recounting the divine couple's later separation and heroic reunion, the *Ramayan* holds Ram and Sita up as models of the virtuous husband and chaste wife; in Janakpur, where the two command almost cult status, the chant of "Sita Ram, Sita Ram" is repeated like a Hindu Hail Mary, and sadhus commonly wear the tuning-fork-shaped *tika* of Vishnu. Mithila came under the control of the Mauryan empire around the third century BC, then languished for two millennia until Guru Ramandanda, the seventeenth-century founder of the sect of Sita that dominates Janakpur, revived the city as a major religious centre.

Despite the absence of ancient monuments to confirm its mythic past – no building is much more than a century old – Janakpur remains a strangely attractive city. Religious fervour seems to lend an aura to everything; the skyline leaves a lasting impression of palm trees and the onion domes and pyramid roofs of local shrines. Most of these distinctively shaped buildings are associated with **kuti** – self-contained pilgrimage centres and hostels for sadhus – some five hundred of which are scattered throughout the Janakpur area. Janakpur's other distinguishing feature is its dozens of **sacred ponds** (*sagar* or *sar*), which here take the

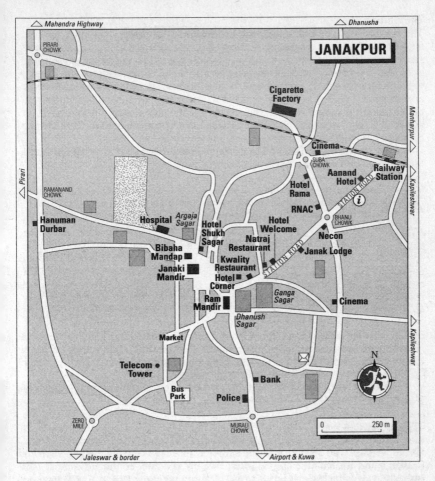

place of river ghats for ritual bathing and *dhobi*-ing. Clearly man-made, the roughly rectangular tanks might, as locals claim, go back to Ram's day, although it's more likely that they've been dredged over the centuries by wealthy merit-seekers.

Arrival and information

Janakpur lies 30km off the Mahendra Highway, so it's not on the way to anywhere else, and most day **buses** come from Birganj. A few come from Kakarbitta and Biratnagar each day, but only two (both *Sajha*) from Kathmandu. The rest are night buses. Try for *Sajha* first, but if you can't get a ticket you'll have to do penance on a night bus or take your chances with Birganj. The bus park is an easy riksha ride from lodgings. You could conceivably **fly** here from Kathmandu ($55), in which case you'll land at the airstrip 2km south of town.

JANAKPUR'S FESTIVALS

At any time of year, Janakpur's atmosphere is charged with an intense devotional zeal. New shrines are forever being inaugurated and idols installed, while *kuti* loudspeakers broadcast religious discourses and the mesmerizing drone of *bhajan*. Pilgrimage is a year-round industry, marked by several highlights in the **festival** calendar:

Bibaha Panchami – The culmination of this five-day event is a re-enactment of Ram and Sita's wedding at the Janaki Mandir, which draws hundreds of thousands of pilgrims on the fifth day after the new moon of November–December.

Ram Navami – Ram's birthday, celebrated on the ninth day after the full moon of March–April, attracts thousands of sadhus, who receive free room and board at the city's temples.

Parikrama – As many as 100,000 people join the annual one-day circumambulation of the city on the day of the full moon of February–March, many performing prostrations along the entire eight-kilometre route. The pilgrimage coincides with the festival of Holi, when coloured water is thrown everywhere and on everyone.

Diwali (Tihaar) – The popular "Festival of Lights", held around the new moon of October–November, is celebrated here, as elsewhere, with oil lamps, singing and special daily *puja*. Lakshmi Puja, the third day, inspires creative wall murals in the villages surrounding Janakpur.

Chath – Women bathe in Janakpur's ponds and line them with elaborate offerings to the sun god Dinanath a few days after Diwali.

The **tourist office** (Sun–Thurs 10am–4pm, Fri 10am–3pm) has brochures on Janakpur and can answer questions about the complex religious goings-on. It's on Station Road, east of Bhanu Chowk (named after Bhanu Bhakta Acharya, a much-loved Nepali poet, whose statue graces the intersection).

The **bank** at the southern end of town exchanges some foreign currencies (Sun–Thurs 10am–2pm, Fri 10am–noon).

The City

Janakpur has to be one of the world's most car-free cities. Unlike other Tarai and Indian cities, it's founded not on commerce but religion, so there just aren't that many private vehicles, and buses are kept out of the core area by a well-sited bus park and a ring road. It's a joy to get around here – just watch out for all the cyclists. Though the city is easy enough to get around on foot, **rikshas** are a terrific deal; they wait in efficient ranks all over town and are supposed to stick to a fixed-price structure, though it may be hard for a foreigner to get them to abide by it. You should be able to rent a **bicycle** informally through your hotel.

The Janaki Mandir

A palatial confection of a building in the Mughal style, the **Janaki Mandir** (pronounced *Jaa*-nuh-ki) is supposed to mark the spot where a golden image of Sita was discovered in 1657 and, presumably, where the virtuous princess actually lived. The present plaster and marble structure, erected in 1911 by an Indian queen, is already looking a little mouldy. The outer building encloses a courtyard and inner sanctum, where at least twice a day (generally 8am and 4pm) priests draw back a

curtain to reveal an intricate silver
shrine and perform various rituals for
attending worshippers; non-Hindus
are allowed to watch, and the priests
even seem willing to bestow blessings on unbelievers. It's an enchant-
ing place at night and early in the
morning, when the devout gather in
lamplit huddles and murmur haunting hymns. The temple is also a traditional place for boys to undergo the
ritual of *chhewar* (the first shaving of
the head), and male dancers in drag
(*natuwa* in Nepali), who are often
hired to perform at the ceremony,
may sometimes be seen here.

The Janaki Mandir

Climb the stairs to the roof of the
outer building for a view of the
central courtyard and the dense, brick-laned Muslim village butting right up
against the temple's rear wall: one of Janakpur's most extraordinary aspects is the
way rural life can be seen almost in the heart of the city. North of the temple, the
modern, Nepali pagoda-style **Ram Janaki Bibaha Mandap** (Ram Sita Wedding
Pavilion) houses a turgid tableau of the celebrated event.

Other temples and sights

The city's oldest, closest quarter lies to the south and east of the Janaki Mandir –
making your way through this area, with its sweet shops, *puja* stalls and quick-
photo studios, you begin to appreciate that Janakpur is as geared up for Indian
tourists as Kathmandu is for Western ones. The main landmark here, the pagoda-
style **Ram Mandir**, isn't wildly exciting except during festivals. Immediately to
the east, **Dhanush Sagar** and **Ganga Sagar** are considered the holiest of
Janakpur's ponds. The sight of Hindus performing ritual ablutions in the fog at
sunrise here is profoundly moving, and during festivals the scene is on a par with
Varanasi's famed ghats in India.

Walk westwards from the Janaki Mandir to the highway and you reach
Ramanand Chowk, the nucleus of many of Janakpur's *kuti* and a major sadhu
gathering place during festivals. In an alcove at the southwest corner of the intersection, devotees have been chanting the names of Ram and Sita continuously
since 1986 (the vigil, sponsored by wealthy individuals, is to last a total of twelve
years). Two well-known establishments, Ramanand Ashram and Ratnasagar Kuti –
the latter, rising grandly in the midst of farmland, looking uncannily like a Russian
Orthodox church – are located west of here, but like most *kuti*, they are closed to
non-Hindus, whose presence would necessitate all sorts of ritual cleansing.

If by this time you're tiring of the serious side of Hinduism, head to **Hanuman
Durbar**, a small *kuti* 150m south of Ramanand Chowk on the west side, to see
the **world's biggest rhesus monkey**. Bauwa Hanuman weighs 55kg, and he's
been certified as the world's biggest by the Triflorous Explorers Association,
whatever that is – a certificate is on display near the cage. It's a gross sight if ever
there was one. By the way, *bauwa* is a pet term for a baby monkey.

Around Janakpur

The Tarai is full of great little villages, but Janakpur makes a particularly good base for visiting them. The holy city's traditionalism extends into the surrounding countryside, which is inhabited by Hindu castes and members of the Tharu and Danuwar ethnic groups, and features some of the most meticulously kept farmland you'll see anywhere. You can ride the narrow-gauge railway east or west, or bike along several roads radiating out from the city. (Needless to say, winter is a much more comfortable time for biking.)

The Janakpur railway

If you've already had dealings with Indian trains, Janakpur's **steam railway** will be less of a thrill, but it's still an excellent way to get out into the country. On a misty winter's morning, the ride past sleepy villages and minor temples is nothing short of magical. Built in the 1940s to transport timber to India from the now-depleted forest west of Janakpur, the narrow-gauge railway these days operates primarily as a passenger service.

Janakpur is the terminus for two separate lines, each about 30km long: one eastbound to Jaynagar, just over the border in India, and the other westbound to Bijalpura. New diesel locomotives donated by India now run on the more popular Jaynagar service, but trains to Bijalpura are still pulled by steam engines. **Trains for Jaynagar** depart at 6am, 10.30am and 3pm (but check: times may vary); and trains coming the opposite way are supposed to leave Jaynagar at the same time. You'll doubtless be stopped by Nepalese customs at Khajuri, about two hours from Janakpur (if not, you could have trouble re-entering Nepal). For a shorter trip, get off at Baidehi, about an hour from Janakpur, and catch the train coming the other way about half an hour later – or you could walk or bike the 12km back. The **Bijalpura service** runs only once a day each way, departing at 2.45pm at either end, so you'll have to alight at Loharpati in order to return to Janakpur the same day. Alternatively, you could walk or cycle to Khurta (7km; see p.322) or Loharpati (12km) by way of Ramanand Chowk, and return by train.

Detail from a Maithili painting

The **fare** to Jaynagar is Rs9 in second class or Rs15 in first, the latter being far from luxurious but perhaps a shade less crowded. Arrive early for a seat; on the way back you'll probably end up riding on the roof.

The Janakpur Women's Development Center

Hindu women of the deeply conservative villages around Janakpur are rarely spared from their household duties, and, once married, are expected to remain veiled and silent before all males but their husbands. Fortunately, their rich tradition of folk art (see opposite) offers them an escape from this isolated existence. The non-profit **Janakpur Women's Development**

MAITHILI PAINTING

For three thousand years, Hindu women of the region once known as Mithila have maintained an unbroken tradition of **painting**, using techniques and ritual motifs passed down from mother to daughter. The colourful, almost psychedelic images can be viewed as fertility charms, meditation aids or a form of storytelling, but on a deeper level they represent, in the words of one critic, "the manifestation of a collective mind, embodying millennia of traditional knowledge".

From an early age Brahman girls practise drawing complex symbols derived from Hindu myths and folk tales, which over the course of generations have been reduced to *mandala*-like abstractions. By the time she is in her teens, a girl will be presenting simple paintings to her arranged fiancé, perhaps using them to wrap gifts; the courtship culminates with the painting of a **kohbar**, an elaborate fresco on the wall of the bride's bedroom, where the newlyweds will spend their first four nights. Depicting a stylized stalk of bamboo surrounded by lotus leaves (symbols of male and female sexuality), the *kohbar* is a powerful celebration of life, creation and everything. Other motifs include footprints and fishes (both representing Vishnu), parrots (symbolic of a happy union), Krishna cavorting with his milkmaids, and Surabhi, "the Cow of Plenty, who inflames the desire of those who milk her". Perhaps the most striking aspect of the *kohbar* is that, almost by definition, it's ephemeral: even the most amazing mural will be washed off within a week or two. Painting is seen as a form of prayer or meditation; once completed, the work has achieved its end.

Women of all castes create simpler **wall decorations** during the autumn festival of Diwali (Tihaar). In the weeks leading up to the festival they apply a new coat of mud mixed with dung and rice chaff to their houses and add relief designs. Just before Lakshmi Puja, the climactic third day of Diwali, many paint images of peacocks, pregnant elephants and other symbols of prosperity to attract a visit from the goddess of wealth. Until Nepali New Year celebrations in April, when the decorations are covered over with a new layer of mud, they're easily viewable in villages around Janakpur.

Paintings **on paper**, which traditionally play only a minor part in the culture, have grown to become the most celebrated form of Maithili art – or Madhubani art, as it's known in India, where a community-development project began turning it into a marketable commodity in the 1960s. More recently, the Janakpur Women's Development Center (see opposite) has helped do the same in Nepal, making Maithili paintings a staple of Kathmandu tourist gift shops. When working on paper, the artist first outlines the intended design in black, then adds a border and embellishes every remaining space with fantastic detail, and finally illuminates it with brilliant, posterpaint colours. Many artists concentrate on traditional religious motifs, but a growing number are depicting people – mainly women and children in domestic scenes, always shown in characteristic doe-eyed profile.

Center (Sun–Thurs 10am–5pm/4pm in winter; free), 3km south of Janakpur provides a space for women from nearby villages to develop personally and artistically. Founded in 1989, with assistance from several international aid organizations, the artists' co-operative helps its fifty-odd members turn their skills into income – and the fact that some have gone on to start their own companies is a sure sign of the project's success. But more importantly, the centre empowers women through training in literacy and business skills, and support sessions in which they can share their feelings and discuss their roles in family and society.

Initially specializing in Maithili paper art, the centre has since branched into other media and now has separate buildings for sewing and screen printing, ceramics, painting, mirrors and tapestries. Visitors are welcome to tour the beautiful, mango-shaded facility, and to meet the artists and learn about their work and traditions. A gift shop sells crafts made on the premises, as well as the JWDC's own booklet, *Janakpur Art: A Living Tradition*, a sensitive treatment not only of Maithili art but also of the women who make it here.

The centre is a fifteen-minute bike or riksha ride from Janakpur. Head south towards the airport and make a left turn about 1km after Murali Chowk (look for a mural painted on a brick wall that says "JWD Center"). Bear right after about 200m, keeping a small, white temple on your right, and pass through the well-kept village of **Kuwa**. The centre, in a walled compound, appears on the right after about 300m. If in doubt, ask for Neri Bikas Kendra. Or just have a riksha wallah take you – they all know the way.

Other villages

Dozens of villages dot the land around Janakpur at regular intervals, each with its own mango grove and a *sagar* or two. Subsistence farming – livestock, grains, vegetables and fish – is virtually the only occupation here: you'll rarely see even the smallest shop. Perhaps the most eligible direction for exploring is **westwards** from Ramanand Chowk, where you can follow a dirt lane through the huts of Pirari, over the train tracks and through some nice shady groves, and finally to **Khurta**, a substantial community with grain mills and a Friday-afternoon market.

North from Suba Chowk, a road passes through the villages of Bhenga and Thumana and, after 15km, reaches **Dhanusha** (Dhanushadham), an important pilgrimage site. According to the *Ramayan*, it was here that King Janak staged an Arthurian contest for the hand of his daughter, Sita, declaring that the successful suitor would have to prove himself by lifting an impossibly heavy bow. After all others had given up, Ram picked up the bow with ease, and broke it in two for good measure. Villagers can point out a rock that's said to be a piece of the bow. There are also several good villages on either side of the main road that connects Janakpur to the Mahendra Highway. Loveliest is **Kumrora**, on the right about 4km north of Pirari Chowk, a tidy Brahman settlement of one- and two-storey houses and particularly expressive wall murals. To avoid the worst of the roadside grunge around Pirari Chowk, take a back way just to the east, via Rajol, which joins the main road halfway.

South from Murali Chowk, past the turnings for Kuwa and the Janakpur Women's Development Center (see above) and the airport, you can carry on to Deupura, Ganguli and, about 10km from Janakpur, larger and more prosperous **Nagrain**. This rather shadeless road, which is served by infrequent, claptrap buses, continues to the Indian border, 3km beyond Nagrain. Other roads heading **east** go to the villages of Kapileshwar and Manharpur, but the Jaynagar railway is a better way to explore in this direction.

Accommodation

Janakpur's few **lodgings** cater mainly to Indian pilgrims, so consequently are not too well versed in what Westerners want: they're all of the crummy, concrete variety. Bus and truck noise isn't a problem, for once, but the *kuti* around the Janaki Mandir manage to create a hell of a racket over their loudspeakers. While the scarcity of accommodation normally doesn't present a problem, you need to book well ahead during the big festival times. Refer to the map for locations.

Aanand Hotel (☎041/20562). A perpetually half-completed building with the rudiments of a garden seating area, located in a lively part of town. Hot water is available in the more expensive rooms. ②/B④.

Hotel Rama (☎041/20059). Quiet, though it's rather far from the sights. The upstairs rooms are quite spacious and have hot water. B② (B④ with hot water).

Hotel Shukh Sagar (☎041/20488). Great (but noisy) location overlooking the Janaki Mandir. Good vegetarian restaurant. ①/B③.

Hotel Welcome (☎041/20224). The most experienced at dealing with foreigners, but in a state of decline. ②/B③.

Janak Lodge (no phone). Cheap and dingy. A few comparable places without English signs can be found nearby. ①.

Eating

If you enjoy Indian **food**, you'll eat like a rajah in Janakpur. *Hotel Welcome*'s and *Hotel Rama*'s restaurants and *Hotel Corner* all do beautiful veg and non-veg meals, or for pure vegetarian food hit the *Shukh Sagar*. For Nepali food, the *Natraj Restaurant* (no English sign), around the corner from *Hotel Welcome*, is the ticket. If you like Indian sweets or *chiura dahi* (beaten rice and curd) you can take your pick from a host of *mithai pasal* around the Janaki and Ram temples. To sample the local brew, ask for *sophi* or *dudhiya*, fennel- and aniseed-flavoured spirits that are just about drinkable when mixed with Sprite.

Moving on from Janakpur

For **bus** frequencies and travel times from Janakpur, see p.313. Note that *Sajha* tickets are purchased at Ramanand Chowk, not at the bus park, and the *Sajha* bus to Kathmandu originates there (another *Sajha* service, originating in Jaleswar, also stops there). Tickets for night buses to Kathmandu are also sold from desks along Station Road near *Aanand Hotel*. Two **airlines** – *RNAC* (☎20185) and *Necon Air* (☎20688) – fly from here to Kathmandu most days of the week ($55), and both have offices near Bhanu Chowk in town.

There is a small-time **border crossing** about 20km east of town at Jaleswar, and another at Jaynagar (reached by railway), but neither of these is officially open to foreigners.

Koshi Tappu Wildlife Reserve

East of the Janakpur turnoff, the Mahendra Highway rolls along uneventfully all the way to the Sapt Koshi River. The latter half of this section passes through long stretches of farmland punctuated by bamboo thickets and idyllic little villages – the kind of places you can't imagine anyone would ever leave – which probably explains why cyclists passing through here sometimes complain of being stared at by locals.

The landscape changes markedly at the Sapt Koshi, eastern Nepal's biggest river. Crossing the **Koshi Barrage** – not a dam, but a network of dykes and flood-control gates – you can look in amazement at the immense body of water that squeezes through here before fanning out again into the shimmering haze of India. A short stretch of highway just west of the barrage remains unpaved and very rough on account of a long-running dispute over who's responsible for finish-

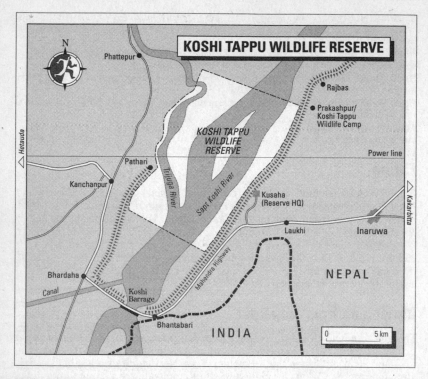

KOSHI TAPPU WILDLIFE RESERVE

ing it, Nepal or the Indian contractor who built the embankment it runs along. Reaching the far side, the highway bends north and runs parallel to a disused railway: keep an eye out for the rusty old steam engines which, until the railway tracks were severed in the 1988 Dharan earthquake, hauled rubble to build up the seven- to ten-metre embankments that keep the Sapt Koshi in check during the monsoon.

Straddling a floodplain of shifting grassland and sandbanks north of the barrage, **KOSHI TAPPU WILDLIFE RESERVE** is the most low-key of the Tarai's parks. It's not bound to appeal to most travellers – there are no tigers or rhinos, nor even any jungle – but birdwatchers can have a field day here, for Koshi Tappu is one of Asia's most important stopping places for migratory **birds**: the Arun River, the Sapt Koshi's main tributary, forms one of the few breaches in the Himalayan barrier north of here. Though other parks can claim more species, Koshi Tappu hosts nearly all of Nepal's long list of wildfowl, waders, egrets, storks, ibises, terns and gulls, and you're certain to tick off several varieties here that you haven't seen anywhere else.

The reserve was established to protect one of the subcontinent's last surviving herds of **wild buffalo** (*arnaa*), believed to number 160 animals. However, wildlife experts are concerned about the number of domestic buffalo getting into the reserve and mating with the wild ones: if this is allowed to continue, the result could be a semi-domestic herd whose continued protection would be hard to justify. Also inhabiting the reserve are blue bull (*nilgai*), wild boar, langur and spotted deer (*chital*). In addition, eighty gharial crocodiles from the Chitwan hatchery have been relocated here from Chitwan – at last count, only four or five were known to have survived – and a small number of gangetic dolphins are reportedly trapped upstream of the barrage. Koshi Tappu's most famous resident, a semi-wild bull elephant dubbed Ganesh Maharaj, was killed by a poacher's poisoned spear in 1991; his skull is on display at the reserve headquarters.

Visiting Koshi Tappu

The reserve is marked by a yellow sign beside the Mahendra Highway about 12km east of the barrage – or, if you're coming from the other direction, 3km west of Laukhi – and from here an access road leads 3km north to the **reserve headquarters** (generally known as the *warden ophis*). An **entry permit** costs Rs650 and is valid for two days.

However, the only **accommodation** in the vicinity is provided by *Koshi Tappu Wildlife Camp* (book through *Victoria Travels* in Kathmandu: ☎226130; ⑧), located at the northeast corner of the reserve and reached by a separate access road (packages include transport from Biratnagar). To visit Koshi Tappu independently, you'd either have to do it as a day trip from Biratnagar, which requires a vehicle, or be prepared to **camp** at the headquarters (Rs300 per night). Vehicles aren't allowed inside the park, although you could cycle for miles along the eastern embankment. Park rangers, with limited English, can **guide** you if they're free, otherwise they might be able to put you onto a local English-speaking guide (about Rs300 per day). Koshi Tappu's *hattisar* (elephant stables) is located near here, but its contingent of ten **elephants** is usually on loan to Chitwan. You can get *daal bhaat* and tea at the minuscule hamlet of **Kusaha**, just to the east of the headquarters.

With no rhinos or large carnivores, Koshi Tappu is comparatively safe for wandering around **on your own**. Two rivers join at the reserve: the Trijuga generally hugs the western embankment, while the Sapt Koshi has formed two main channels, along the east side and down the middle, and tends to shift from one to the other every couple of monsoons. Between these three channels lie a number of semi-permanent islands of scrub forest and grassland that are the main stomping ground for blue bull. (*Tappu* means "islands" in Nepali, which is an accurate description of this floodplain in the wet summer months.) Birds and buffalo are best viewed along the Sapt Koshi, but given the way the rivers change course it's impossible to give specific advice on where to look. It may be necessary to cross one or more channels to reach the current hot area, in which case you should be able to hitch a ride in a canoe. Stalking the wild cousins of common water buffalo is sometimes hard to take seriously – especially when they moo – yet these are big animals that can make a thunderous noise when frightened; and while they normally run away at the first scent of humans, you have to make sure not to block their escape route.

Biratnagar

About 200km east of the Janakpur turnoff, **BIRATNAGAR** (population 130,000) is Nepal's second-biggest city, and growing at a galloping rate. Though the city is prospering as a magnet for industry and trade – it's on a direct line to the port of

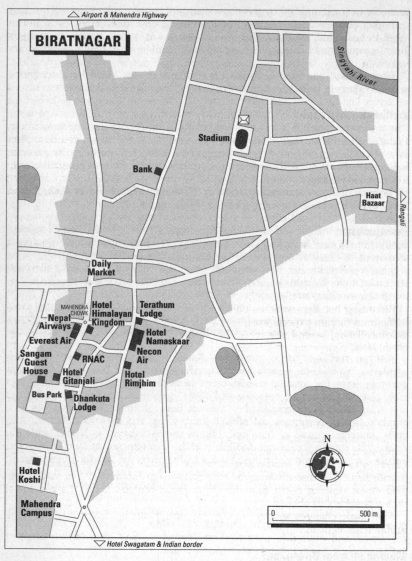

Calcutta – foreign observers foresee major growth-related problems in the coming years. Jute is in decline, Birganj is muscling in on trade with Calcutta, government offices have been shifted north to Dhankuta, and the bonanza of the $770 million Arun III hydroelectric project north of here has failed to materialize – yet immigrants from the hills and India keep pouring in looking for work. You still see ox carts hauling raw jute to the mills near the border, but modern Biratnagar is probably best exemplified by the prosaic zipper factory north of town. The city's one other claim to fame is as a political hotbed: thanks to its proximity to India's West Bengal state, Biratnagar has long been a sort of safe house for many of Nepal's communist parties, which were banned until the restoration of democracy in 1990.

More Indian than Nepali, Biratnagar's streets are lined with an uninspiring array of concrete buildings and border-bazaar shops. That said, the city centre is relatively laid-back and traffic-free. There are few sights, but if you're here on a Wednesday don't miss Biratnagar's **haat bazaar**, held in a field east of town, where you can count on a colourful assembly of Tharus, Rais, Limbus and various Indian castes. In the countryside surrounding Biratnagar, Tharus and Danuwars (a related group, whose women wear their homespun saris like togas) are indigenous: to sample **village life**, head out on the road towards Rangali, east of town, or visit the area around Duhubi, off the main road about halfway between Biratnagar and the Mahendra Highway. The Jogbani **border crossing**, 5km south of town, is closed to foreigners (officially, anyway).

Practicalities

Kathmandu–Kakarbitta buses don't go through Biratnagar, but stop at **Itahari**, a crossroads bazaar on the Mahendra Highway; Biratnagar is 23km south, and Dharan (covered later in this chapter) lies to the north. Direct buses to Biratnagar let you off at the dismal **bus park** southwest of the city centre. The **airport** is 4km north of town (Rs20 by riksha).

Biratnagar hoteliers went on a building binge in anticipation of fat profits to be made from foreign experts working on the Arun III hydroelectric project. Since its cancellation, several new swish **hotels** vie for a very few customers, among them *Hotel Swagatam* (☎021/22299; B⑤, B⑥ with a/c), *Hotel Koshi* (☎021/24408; B⑤, B⑥ with a/c) and *Hotel Himalayan Kingdom* (☎021/27172; B④, B⑥ with a/c). For a mid-range choice, try *Hotel Gitanjali* (③/B④) or *Hotel Rimjhim* (③/B③). At the budget end, *Sangam Guest House* (B②), *Dhankuta Lodge* (①/B②) and *Terathum Lodge* (①) are the brightest and least smelly of the lot. Be sure to request mosquito netting.

For tourist **food**, *Hotel Koshi*, *Hotel Namaskaar* and *Hotel Himalayan Kingdom* all have good restaurants, the last specializing in Indian and Nepali cuisine. For cheap local fare, make for one of the rough-and-ready eateries north of Mahendra Chowk, which do tasty *sekuwa* and *maachhaa masaala* (local carp fried in a spicy tomato sauce); try also *dudhiya*, the local aniseed-flavoured *raksi*. The main shopping street running north from the *Namaskaar* contains a few unexceptional *mithai pasal* (sweet shops).

The **bank** changes money Sunday through Thursday from 10am to 2pm, Friday 10am to noon.

Moving on from Biratnagar

Biratnagar being the air hub of eastern Nepal, you will have to pass through here to **fly** to Taplejung (for Kanchenjunga). Flights to other hill airstrips and Kathmandu may be of interest – see the box on the next page. The offices of *RNAC* (☎25335), *Everest* (☎25345) and *Nepal Airways* (☎25324) are all at or near Mahendra Chowk, while *Necon Air* (☎25988) is on the next major street to the east.

Onward **bus** connections from Biratnagar are fairly limited (see p.312).

FLIGHTS FROM BIRATNAGAR			
	Frequency	Time	Fare ($)
Kathmandu	3–5/day	50min*	77
Lamidanda	5/week	30min	50
Phaplu	2/week	35min	66
Taplejung	5/week	30min	50
Tumlingtar	4–6/week	30min	33
* Indirect flights will take longer.			

East to the border

From Itahari, the Mahendra Highway's final 100-kilometre leg crosses the frontier districts of **Morang** and **Jhapa**. Once renowned for its virulent malaria, Morang remains untamed in parts, but hill settlers, encouraged by the government, are steadily moving in, and logging companies are whittling away at the jungle. Jhapa, further east, is already largely cultivated and dotted with monotonously similar villages, each containing a wide, dusty bazaar full of people selling delicious oranges and cheap bangles; the half-timbered houses on stilts are the work of transplanted Limbus. The latest and most numerous immigrants in these

BHUTANESE REFUGEES

The plight of **Bhutanese refugees** in Jhapa and Morang – who numbered nearly 90,000 as of early 1996 – has scarcely been acknowledged outside of Nepal. The remoteness of the refugee camps only partly explains how such a large-scale tragedy could go unreported. A greater factor has been the international community's fuzzy romanticism about tiny Bhutan, a kingdom of misty mountain monasteries and dashing archers, whose leader says all the right things about sustainable development and the "gross national happiness" of his subjects. It's hard to believe that the torture, rape and forcible expulsion of ethnic Nepalis could be happening in such an idyllic land.

Members of Nepali hill groups began migrating into Bhutan in significant numbers as long ago as the mid-nineteenth century, eventually accounting for at least a third of Bhutan's population and earning the designation **Lhotshampas** (southerners), after the southern hill areas where they came to predominate. Right up to the early 1980s, multicultural government policies encouraged their integration with Bhutan's ruling **Drukpas**. However, during the mid-1980s, the continued influx of ethnic Nepalis and a rise in Nepali militancy in neighbouring Darjeeling and Sikkim gave rise to a wave of Drukpa nationalism. The Drukpas, believing their language and unique Kagyu Buddhist tradition to be under threat, were quick to make scapegoats of the Lhotshampas – who, not coincidentally, controlled lands that were emerging as the economic powerhouse of Bhutan.

In 1986, King Singye Wangchuk, apparently under pressure from the family of his four wives, instituted the **Drig Lam Namzha** code of cultural correctness, which among other things required all residents of Bhutan to wear traditional heavy wool garments that were neither natural nor practical for the southerners. In 1988, after a national **census** was taken, the government began a process of systematic discrimination against anyone who couldn't provide written proof of residency in Bhutan in 1958. A campaign of ethnic cleansing gathered momentum, culminating in 1992

parts are refugees from Bhutan – the majority live in three big refugee camps, Beldangi I, II and III, located up a side road north of the Mahendra Highway at Damak. Jhapa's tea plantations, though flat and not much to look at, are a reminder that Darjeeling is barely 50km away as the crow flies, and Ilam, Nepal's prize tea-growing region, sits in the hills just north of here.

Kakarbitta and the border

A border crossing with a real backwoods flavour, **KAKARBITTA** feels like one of those all-night shantytowns that Indian buses always seem to stop at, where you wake up to men selling peanuts and bidis by candlelight and ask "where the hell are we?" Unlike other border towns, it's too far out in the sticks to be much of a trading centre, and the only apparent link with the rest of the world is the fleet of night buses that roars in from Kathmandu every morning and roars out again every afternoon. You don't want to stay here any longer than necessary.

Kakarbitta's finest **accommodation** is *Hotel Rajat* (B⑤), where all rooms have phones and TVs, while at the other end of the scale, *Hotel Kathmandu & Lodge* is noisy but cheap (①). *Kanchan Hotel* strikes a good balance between quality and economy (②/B③). All three are located on the highway between the bus park and the border. Most guest houses have their own **restaurants**, but assuming you're only going to be eating one hot meal in Kakarbitta, you might as well eat it at *Hotel Rajat*'s *Hariyali Restaurant*. Lodges and restaurants will swap Nepalese

when "illegal" families were forced to sign **"voluntary leaving certificates"** and evicted from their lands with little or no compensation, while those identified as "anti-nationals" (and their families) were harassed, imprisoned, tortured and violated.

Receiving little encouragement from India, most refugees continued on to their ethnic homeland, Nepal. During the height of the exodus, as many as 25 trucks a day arrived at the Kakarbitta border post, overburdened with refugees and the few possessions they had managed to flee with. As their numbers swelled, the Nepalese government, wanting to keep the problem out of sight, established **refugee camps** at Timai and Goldhap (south of Birtamod), Pathari (southeast of Itahari) and, biggest by far, Beldangi I, II and II (north of Damak). The UN High Commission on Refugees (UNHCR) has put the Lutheran World Service in charge of running the camps; the UN World Food Program distributes food rations, while Save the Children and other organizations have built housing, schools, health posts and other essential facilities.

The Nepalese government feels a reluctant responsibility for the refugees, but has no intention of harbouring them indefinitely. India, which has its own fears of pan-Nepali resurgence, is disinclined to take them. All parties agree that **repatriation** to Bhutan is the only permanent solution to the problem, but as this book went to press the Nepalese and Bhutanese governments remained deadlocked over terms. In early 1996, several hundred refugees set off on a peace march to Thimpu to deliver a petition to the king and were promptly arrested in India. The king was quoted as claiming that "99 percent" of the refugees in the Nepalese camps weren't Bhutanese, yet at the same time his government was attempting to negotiate an extradition treaty with India that would define the marchers as Bhutanese nationals and subject them to charges of treason. Fearing imprisonment or worse, most refugees were remaining in the camps, unwilling to return until they could be assured of their democratic rights in Bhutan – a prospect that looks unlikely in the foreseeable future.

For more information or to get involved in the cause, contact the Bhutanese Refugee Support Group, 5 Little Twye, Buckland Common, Tring, Herts HP23 6PB (☎01494/758106).

and Indian rupees at the market rate, but to change hard currency you'll have to use the **bank** (*Nepal Rastra Bank*, a pink building signposted only in Nepali; daily 8am–5pm). The tourist office is useless.

The wide Mechi River forms **the border**, about 500m east of town. Nepalese immigration is open from 8am to 5pm. As it's a fifteen-minute walk between Kakarbitta and Raniganj, the first Indian village, you might as well take a riksha (not that you'll be able to fend them off anyway). Foreigners driving their own vehicles are allowed through this crossing, which is pleasantly low-key for border formalities. Jeeps and buses to Siliguri/New Jalpaiguri (the train station for Darjeeling and Calcutta) depart from the junction just east of Raniganj; touts offer to "guide" travellers to Darjeeling for Rs150 or so, but you can easily do it yourself for half that. If you're coming from India and planning to catch one of the night buses to Kathmandu, they leave Kakarbitta in staggered intervals between 3 and 5pm, but try to arrive a couple of hours early to be sure of a good seat. That said, you'll be much happier sticking to day buses: Dharan and Janakpur make good intermediate destinations from here (see p.313 for a rundown of services).

THE EASTERN HILLS

Two main roads link the Tarai with the hills east of the Sapt Koshi – the **Dhankuta road**, leaving the Mahendra Highway at Itahari, and the **Ilam road**, beginning at Charali. Bus services are more fickle on these than along the Mahendra Highway, so it's always wise to make an early start. Either road would make a superb jaunt on a mountain bike. While this section describes short hikes in the area, remember that you're officially supposed to have a trekking permit to go more than a day's walk off a road.

The Dhankuta road

Call it development or call it colonialism by another name, but the big donor nations have staked out distinct spheres of influence in Nepal, and nowhere is this more apparent than in the British bailiwick around Dhankuta. Britain's interest in this area has not been without ulterior motives: roughly half the recruits for the Gurkha regiments have traditionally come from the eastern hills, and the biggest Gurkha training camp was, until 1989, in Dharan. In the 1970s, no doubt pricked by a sense of obligation to the people of the area, Britain initiated a series of projects based in Dhankuta that are now administered by the **British Aid Project Support Office (BAPSO)**. Agriculture, forestry, health and cottage industries have all been funded by British aid through this programme (Princess Di lent royal support to these projects with a visit in 1993), but the biggest and most obvious undertaking has been the **road** to Dharan, Dhankuta, Hile and Basantapur. Constructed with £50 million of British taxpayers' money, it's almost absurdly luxurious for a hill region with minimal traffic, though in fairness it must be seen in the context of the entire integrated development programme. The road was also to have been extended northwards to access the massive Arun III hydroelectric project at Num, 30km from the Tibetan border; in 1995 the World Bank withdrew its portion of the $770 million in funding for the hydro project, citing environmental and fiscal concerns (see p.410).

From the Mahendra Highway, the road winds languidly through forest as it ascends the Bhabar, the sloping alluvial zone between the Tarai and the foothills. Dharan, 16km north of the highway, sits a slightly cooler 300m above the plain.

Dharan

Noisy and tawdry, **DHARAN** isn't much of a place to linger – unless, that is, you're a member of the development elite and staying out at the former Gurkha Camp, the closest thing in Nepal to Calcutta's Tollygunge Club. If you're heading for Dhankuta or Hile, though, you'll have to stop here (and perhaps spend the night).

Dharan hit world headlines in 1988 when a powerful **earthquake** killed 700 people and flattened most of the town – the main bazaar has been rebuilt, but things look decidedly ramshackle. Disaster struck a second time at the end of 1989 when the **British Army**, foreseeing forces reductions, pulled out of Dharan and handed the Gurkha Camp back to HMG. The withdrawal dealt a blow to would-be recruits here, who must now travel all the way to Pokhara to compete for even fewer places in the regiments (for more on the Gurkhas, see p.250); most of Dharan's *khukuri* smiths disappeared overnight, and shopkeepers still bemoan the loss of Gurkha trade.

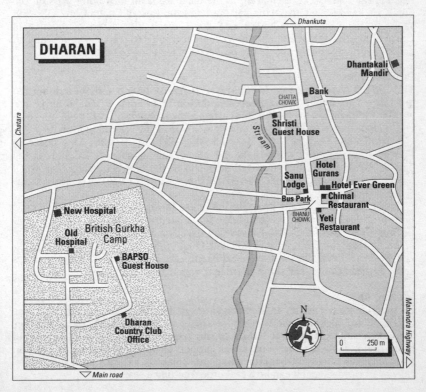

Yet the **bazaar** continues to do a bustling business, since for people through-out the eastern hills Dharan is the proverbial Bright Lights where they come to sell oranges by the sackload and spend their profits on kitchen utensils, provisions and bottles of *Urvashi* from the bazaar's well-stocked spirits stalls. In the area northeast of the central Bhanu Chowk you'll see hill women investing the family fortune in gold ornaments – the age-old safe haven – and shops selling fantastic Raj-era silver coins to be strung into necklaces. If you happen to be in the market for a cauldron, check out the brass-workers' quarter further east.

The most amazing thing about Dharan is the sheer contrast between the bazaar and the **British Gurkha Camp** (as it's still called), a Rs20 tempo or riksha ride west of the bus stand. You can wander freely around the grounds now, which you wouldn't have been allowed to do when the Gurkhas occupied it, and although there's not much to see, the long, tree-lined lanes are blessedly quiet – it's like a university campus during summer break. The camp has been handed over to the B P Koirala Institute of Health Sciences, which runs an extensive medical teaching facility and, rolling in Indian aid, is throwing up new buildings all over the place. BAPSO leases part of the camp for its project staff, and maintains for their benefit the quaintly colonial **Dharan Country Club**, with a golf course, tennis and squash courts and a swimming pool. Visitors can use the facilities for a daily guest fee.

Chatara, 15km west of Dharan, is the finishing point for rafting trips on the Sun Kosi; Land Rovers make the trip starting from west of Chatta Chowk (Rs25). Walk an hour north of Chatara and you'll reach the sacred confluence of **Barahakshetra**, site of a temple to Vishnu incarnated as a boar (Barahi) and an annual pilgrimage on the day of the full moon of October–November.

Practicalities

The *BAPSO Guest House* (☎025/20978 or 21019; ⑤/B⑤) is without a doubt the quietest, cleanest and cosiest **accommodation** in Dharan, or indeed anywhere east of Kathmandu – it's like an honest-to-goodness English B&B (well, maybe a cheap one). However, at the time of writing it was facing relocation from its premises within the Gurkha Camp to somewhere almost certainly less peaceful. Priority goes to project workers, so call ahead. Among cheaper lodgings in the bazaar, *Shristi Guest House* (②/B③) seems to be the best bet; failing that, you'll have to settle for *Hotel Ever Green* (B②), *Hotel Gurans* (②/B③) or *Sanu Lodge* (B②), all fairly smelly and dark.

Hooliganism periodically prompts the police to impose a curfew on Dharan's taverns and **restaurants**, so don't leave it too late to eat. *Chimal Restaurant* and *Gurans Guest House*'s *Bamboo House* do excellent Indian and Nepali food; the *Mona Lisa* and the *Yeti* are less proficient. Other, more local-oriented *bhojanalaya* just west of Chatta Chowk serve *daal bhaat*, *sekuwa* and *sokuti*. Street vendors around Bhanu Chowk sell some weird and wonderful fried morsels.

Moving on

Buses run from Dharan to Biratnagar every half hour during the day, less frequently to Kakarbitta and Birganj (see p.312 for route details). To reach other Tarai destinations, change at Itahari or Biratnagar. If you want to go straight to Kathmandu, you'll have to book ahead on one of the night buses that leave in mid-afternoon. Buses to Dhankuta and points north are basically local and chronically overcrowded, and it can be a real ordeal getting a seat.

Dhankuta

From Dharan the road switchbacks abruptly over a 1420-metre saddle with dramatic views and the very competent *Arun Valley Hill Top Restaurant*, then descends to cross the Tamur Kosi at Mulghat (280m) before climbing once again to **DHANKUTA**, stretched out on a ridge at 1150m.

Though you'd never guess it by looking at it, Dhankuta is the administrative headquarters for eastern Nepal. There are of course bigger, more developed cities in the eastern Tarai, but Nepal is after all a hill country run by hill people, and so the job of administering the region must fall to a hill town. This political promotion, and the road that came with it, has decisively shifted Dhankuta's economic base from trade to **bureaucracy**: bypassed by the road, the bazaar is withering, while a whole new suburb of government and aid agency offices has sprung up along the road above town.

A *jhankri* (shaman) of the hills

But for travellers who make it this far, it's an easy-going, predominantly Newar town, with pedestrian-only streets, smartly whitewashed houses and shady *chautaara*. The outlying area is populated by Rais, Magars and Hindu castes, who make Dhankuta's **haat bazaar**, on Thursday, a tremendously vivid affair.

Although you can't see the Himalaya from here, the area makes fine **walking** country, and you're bound to run into chatty aid workers or ex-Gurkhas on the trail. In **Santang**, a Rai village about 45 minutes southeast of town, women can be seen embroidering beautiful shawls and weaving *dhaka*, which is as much a speciality of the eastern hills as it is in the west (see p.259). You can walk to Hile in about two hours by taking short cuts off the main road: stick to the ridge and within sight of the electric power line.

Practicalities

Project workers get first priority at the *BAPSO Guest House* (☎026/20259; B⑤), Dhankuta's most salubrious **place to stay**, but it doesn't hurt to ask or call ahead. Located 200m south of the bus park, it features a garden, solar hot water, real furniture, two sitting rooms, and stodgy Western fare. Cheapies in the bazaar are cold-water, trekking-standard outfits: *Hotel Parichaya* (①), near the upper (north) end, is friendly and clean; *Hotel Suvatri* (②/B④) is comparatively overpriced. Plenty of **eateries** in the bazaar do *daal bhaat, pakauda* and the like. *Sayapatri Restaurant*, just down from the *Parichaya*, the only one with a menu, can rustle up *momo, thukpa* and curries.

Hile

If you're here to start (or finish) a trek – and you'd be crazy to come all this way and *not* trek – **HILE** (pronounced *Hee*-lay) might seem anticlimactic. Yet this spirited little pioneer settlement would merit a stay even if it weren't a trailhead. One of the most important staging areas in eastern Nepal, Hile is a melting pot of ethnic groups and commercial interests, and, in a sense, a microcosm of Nepal.

Most buses to Dhankuta continue as far as Hile. Seemingly teetering over the deep, often fog-shrouded Arun Valley, the village huddles along the main road, 15km beyond Dhankuta and 750m higher up along the same ridge. A straggling strip of shops, a few hotels and a couple of one-room *gompa* just about sum up the **bazaar**; you can walk the length of it in five minutes. The shops bristle with commodities like plastic containers, readymade clothes, metal pots and salt, all bound for the hinterland: porters gather in Hile by the hundreds, and the trail to Tumlingtar, three days up the Arun Valley, is like a *doko* highway.

Local Rais, Newar merchants and Indian entrepreneurs are all dicing for a piece of Hile's action, but its most visible minority are Bhotiyas (see p.358), who have relocated en masse from the highlands near Kanchenjunga. Undoubtedly one of the most exotic things you can do in Nepal is to spend an evening in a flickering Bhotiya kitchen sipping hot millet grog from an authentic **tongba**: unique to this area, these miniature wooden steins with brass hoops and fitted tops look like they were designed for Genghis Khan. Hile's **haat bazaar**, on Thursday, is lively, but not as big as Dhankuta's.

Magnificent **views** (even by trekking standards) can be had just a half-hour's hike from Hile. Walk to the north end of the bazaar, bear left up a dirt lane and after 250m go up a set of steps to join the Hattikharka trail, which contours around the hill, skirts an army base and finally reaches a grassy plateau. The panorama spreads out before you like a trekking map: to the northwest, the Makalu Himal floats above the awesome canyon of the Arun (though Everest is hidden behind the crest, you can see its characteristic plume); the ridges of the Milke Danda zigzag to the north; and part of the Kanchenjunga massif pokes up in the northeast. It's heaven – pity about the army base, though. The trail to Tumlingtar angles to the left near the north end of the bazaar, passing the British-funded agricultural research station at Pakhribas en route.

Practicalities

Hile's Bhotiya **lodges** are pretty savvy about catering to foreigners, though innkeepers don't speak much English. *Hotel Gajur*'s rooms are clean (②) and its kitchen is legendary for *momo, sokuti* and *tongba* (there's also a small garden seating area). In addition to the guest houses, many stalls at the north end of the bazaar do *momo, sokuti* and chow mein. The rooms are somewhat bigger at *Hotel Himali* (①), but the walls are thinner and the dining area isn't so cosy. Lodges and shops are well stocked with tinned food, chocolate, instant coffee and other trekking **provisions**.

When it's time to **move on**, you can get a night bus direct to Kathmandu if you're in a hurry, but it's a rough ride. If possible, break the journey into two or more days, with stops in Janakpur and/or Chitwan. Buses leave Hile every half hour for Dharan, where you can pick up onward connections.

Basantapur and beyond

Most buses rumble on as far as **BASANTAPUR**, a dusty hour and a half from Hile. You get tremendous views of the Makalu massif for much of the way, and Kanchenjunga manages to pop into view near the end. Encouraged by a recently liberalized market, some landowners along this route are now beginning to cultivate tea, which is already big business to the east of here in Ilam (see opposite).

Basantapur's dank, muddy, almost Elizabethan bazaar sits in a saddle at 2400m – it's exotic or godforsaken, depending on how you cock your head. This, for the moment, is where the frontier has moved to. Besides being a main supply line for the entire northeast corner of Nepal, Basantapur plays host to trekking groups bound for Kanchenjunga and the Milke Danda. Several **lodges** offer basic accommodation, *Hotel Yak* and *Laxmi Lodge* (both ①) being the most proficient in the food department (*tongba* available).

Scurvy as Basantapur is, the hills above it are a delight for **walking**: mixed pasture and dense mossy forest, rhododendrons, orchids, jasmine, and friendly villages. Likely targets are Tinjure (lodging available), situated at a high point on the ridge (great views) two to three hours above Basantapur, and Chauki, an hour further on. Anything beyond that is a trek.

The road has been extended beyond Basantapur to Terathum, 25km to the east and 700m lower. Trucks already use it, and a bus service can't be far behind. **Mountain-bikers** could have a blast on this stretch, or explore the few miles of road that were roughed in from Basantapur towards Tinjure to access the now-cancelled Arun III project.

The Ilam road

Like the Dhankuta road, the Ilam road keeps getting longer: originally engineered by the Koreans to connect the tea estates of Kanyam and Ilam with the Tarai, it now reaches Phidim and is in the process of being extended to Taplejung.

Buses to Ilam start at Birtamod, located on the Mahendra Highway 8km west of the actual start of the road at Charali – they tend to be very crowded, and the last one leaves at 10am or 11am. The journey takes about six hours by bus; by bike it would probably be a two-day trip. After traversing lush lowlands, the road begins a laborious 1600-metre ascent to Kanyam and its undulating monoculture of tea. At Phikal, a few kilometres further on, a side road heads east to the obscure border crossing of Pashupati Nagar, which unfortunately is closed to foreigners (should it ever open, it would make an intriguing short cut to Darjeeling). Beyond Phikal the road descends 1000m in a series of tight switchbacks – where it hasn't been cleared, the forest here is magnificent – to cross the Mai Khola before climbing another 500m to Ilam (1200m).

Ilam

To Nepalis, **ILAM** (Ee-*laam*) means tea: cool and moist for much of the year, the hills of Ilam district (like those of Darjeeling, just across the border) are perfect for it. Ilam town, headquarters of the district, is a tidy little bazaar whose colourfully painted wooden houses, featuring prim balconies and decorated eaves, give it an unmistakeably alpine air. It looks a lot like Darjeeling, in fact, without all the hype and new construction, and if it only had better food and mountain views Ilam would make a terrific alternative hill resort.

Settled by Newars, Rais and Marwaris (a business-minded Indian group with interests in tea), Ilam was at one time eastern Nepal's main centre of commerce. While hill towns like Ilam have lost much of their trading importance to the Tarai in recent years, its exuberant **haat bazaar** (held on Thursdays) still draws

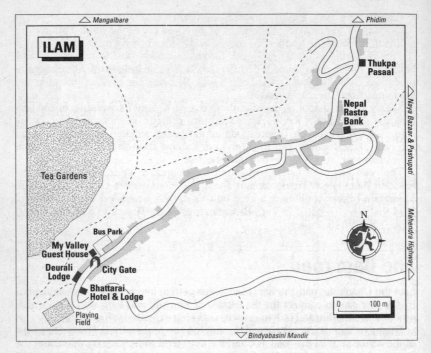

shoppers from a wide radius, and of course tea cultivation provides an anchor for the local economy. Unaccustomed to dealing with foreign travellers, **accommodation** here is on the spartan side. *My Valley Guest House* (②/B②) is the best of the lot, although rooms in front suffer from bus-park noise. *Bhattarai Hotel & Lodge* (①) is adequate but similarly noisy, *Deurali Lodge* (①) quieter but crummier. Simple **meals** are available at the guest houses and in several nameless eateries along the main drag – mostly it's just *daal bhaat* and packaged noodles, but you can get tasty *thukpa* at a place near the top of the bazaar. Change money at *Nepal Rastra Bank* (Sun–Thurs 10am–2pm, Fri 10am–noon), not at *Nepal Bank*.

The tea gardens

The most pleasant thing to do in Ilam is stroll around the **tea gardens**, which carpet the ridge above town and tumble down its steep far side; between April and December you can watch the pluckers at work, and at other times it's just a relaxing place to be. Nepal's first tea estate, it was established in 1864 by a relative of the prime minister after a visit to Darjeeling, where tea cultivation was just becoming big business. Marwaris, who had already cornered the cardamom trade here, soon assumed control of the plantation on a contract basis, an arrangement that lasted until the 1960s, when the government nationalized this and six other hill estates under the direction of the Nepal Tea Development Corporation. Since its re-privatization in 1992, the industry has experienced a small renaissance, as evidenced by the explosion of designer tea packages now sold in Kathmandu. But privatization also spelled the death of the NTDC tea factory on the hill above Ilam, and although it has spawned several new factories, none can easily be visited from here.

Ilam tea is graded by quality, ranging from the coveted TGFOP (Tippy Golden Flower Orange Pekoe, "tippy" referring to the tenderest new leaves) to the lowly PD (Pekoe Dust). Ilam's TGFOP compares favourably with the best of Darjeeling, and indeed most of it is exported to Germany to be blended into "Darjeeling" teas. A 500g bag costs about Rs350 here – much less than the comparable grade in Darjeeling. That's still too expensive for most Nepalis, though, who typically brew their *chiya* from tea dust processed by Tarai plantations.

Beyond Ilam: walks and the road to Phidim

The Ilam area is noted for its greenness – higher up, the jungle is profuse and exuberant, and even the terraced slopes are teemingly fertile. Keep an eye out for **cardamom**, which grows in moist ravines and has become an important cash crop here. This black cardamom (*sukumel*), which is an inferior form of the tropical green variety (*elaichi*) grown in Kerala, is shipped through India to Singapore where it's sold on the world market. Another common cash crop cultivated in this area is broom grass (*umsilo*), which is used to make traditional Nepali whisks. Rais make up the majority of villagers, followed by Bahuns, Chhetris and Limbus.

Rewarding **walks** set off in at least three directions. From the tea gardens, you can contour westwards and cross the Puwamai Khola, ascending the other side to Mangalbare, site of a Wednesday **haat bazaar** even bigger than Ilam's (there are supposed to be views of Kanchenjunga from further south along this ridge). A trail heading east from Ilam descends to cross the Mai Khola, where the annual **Beni Mela** attracts thousands of Hindus on the first day of Magh (January 14 or 15), and continues on to Naya Bazaar. A sacred pond atop a wooded ridge north of Ilam, **Mai Pokhri** can be reached by walking or hitching along the road towards Phidim and making a right at Bibliarti, from where it's another two or three hours' ascent. **Sandakpur**, a superb viewpoint on the Indian border, is a day's walk further, which suggests an illicit trek from here to Darjeeling. Finally, if you're looking for a quick leg-stretch, check out the small but attractively sited **Bindyabasini Mandir**, about 1km down the main road from bus park.

Buses ply the road north of Ilam as far as **Phidim**, a run-of-the-mill district headquarters deep in Limbu territory, six hours further on. Although there's no checkpost, you're supposed to have a trekking permit to travel here. The road has been extended all the way to **Taplejung**, but a major bridge about midway along is not expected to be completed until 1997.

CHAPTER SEVEN

THE HIMALAYAN TREKKING REGIONS

A hundred divine epochs would not suffice to describe all the marvels of the Himalaya.
Hindu proverb

Rearing up over the subcontinent like an immense, whitecapped tidal wave, the **Himalaya** (Hi-*maal*-aya) are, to many travellers' minds, the whole reason for visiting Nepal. Containing eight of the world's ten highest peaks – including, of course, Everest – Nepal's 800-kilometre link in the Himalayan chain puts all other attractions in the shade. More than just majestic scenery, though, the "Abode of Snow" is also the home of Sherpas, yaks, yetis and snow leopards, and has always exerted a powerful spiritual pull: in Hindu

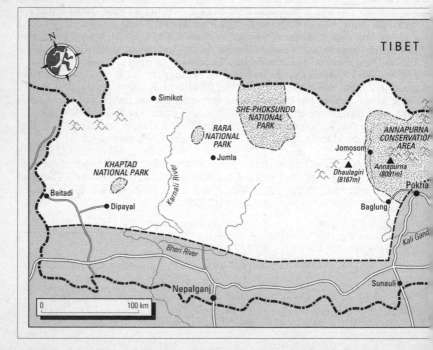

mythology the mountains are where gods meditate and make sacrifices, while the Sherpas hold certain peaks to be the very embodiment of deities; mountaineers are often hardly less mystical.

Nepal's **trekking regions**, as defined by the government, take in all parts of the country more than about a day's walk from a main road – a huge area covering nearly the entire northern half of Nepal, and including not only the Himalaya but also large sections of the hills. These regions span an incredible diversity of terrain and cultures, but one thing they all have in common is that you need a **trekking permit** to travel there.

Trekking needn't be expensive nor agonizingly difficult. Most treks follow established routes where you can eat and sleep in simple inns for less money than you'd spend in Kathmandu. Trails are often steep, to be sure, but you walk at your own pace, and no standard trek goes higher than about 5500m (the *starting* elevation for most climbing expeditions). That said, trekking is not for everybody – it's demanding, sometimes uncomfortable, and it does involve an element of risk. This chapter is organized to help you decide if you want to trek, and if so, how and where you might like to do it. The first section covers things you need to know about trekking in general, and the second gives overviews of the most popular, and a few of the more notable out-of-the-way, treks. It is *not*, however, intended to take the place of a trekking guidebook.

Seasonal considerations

Where you go and how you do it will depend to a great extent on the time of year. **Autumn** (October–November) is normally dry, stable and very clear, although

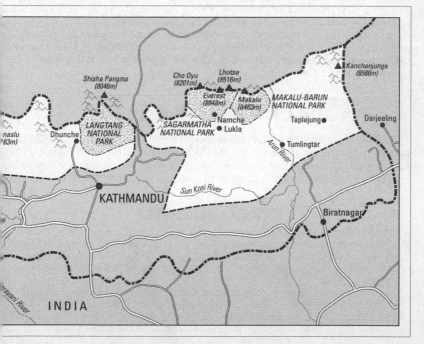

bear in mind that bad weather can strike at any time of year (a disastrous storm in November 1995 brought up to three metres of snow in the high country and claimed dozens of trekkers' lives). This is a good time for higher treks: it can be cold at night, but not as cold as it gets later on, and the daytime temperatures are pleasantly cool for walking. At low elevations it may still be quite hot during the day. Of course this is also the most popular season for trekking, so all standard routes – especially Annapurna and Everest – will be maxed. Don't expect solitude.

Winter (Dec–Jan) is for the most part dry and settled. When precipitation does fall, however, the snow line may drop to 2500m and sometimes even lower. Passes over 4000m may be blocked by snow and ice, and some settlements described in trekking guidebooks may be uninhabited. High-altitude treks, such as Everest, require good gear and experience in cold-weather conditions during this period. Below 2000m, temperatures can be quite spring-like, though valleys are often filled with fog or haze. The teahouses are much quieter than in the autumn, and proprietors have more time to chat.

Temperatures moderate during **spring** (Feb to mid-April), but the likelihood of precipitation increases – snow may be encountered above 3000m – and the haze level rises as the weather warms. This is Nepal's second trekking season, so the main trails can again get crowded, but not as much as in autumn.

It gets that much hotter, hazier and unsettled as spring gives way to the **pre-monsoon** (mid-April to early June). Avoid low elevations, and be prepared for rain, especially in traditionally wet areas such as Annapurna and eastern Nepal. The most colourful rhododendrons bloom in April between 2000m and 3000m.

Few foreigners trek during the **monsoon** (June–Sept) because of the rain, leeches and general lack of mountain views. However, treks in the Himalayan rain shadow and in Nepal's far west are largely sheltered from the monsoon. Even in wet areas, gaps in the clouds occasionally reveal dramatic, mist-wreathed peaks, and wildflowers and butterflies can be seen in abundance. Note that the monsoon isn't consistently rainy – it builds up to a peak in July and August, then tapers off again.

TREKKING BASICS

This section runs through the different **styles** of trekking, **preparations** you'll have to make before setting off, **health** matters to be mindful of, and other factors of **life on the trail**. It's designed to complement the information given in standard trekking guides, with particular emphasis on the nuts and bolts of independent trekking.

WHY TREK?

Most Nepalis will admit to only three reasons for walking around in the mountains with a load on their back: to go home to their village, to make a religious pilgrimage, or to earn money. Those in the trekking business are used to the idea that foreigners will spend huge sums to play the part of a lowly porter, but even they don't necessarily understand *why*.

The reason, of course, is that trekking is the best way to experience Nepal's incredible beauty, both natural and man-made. Explaining this to Nepalis, when appropriate, will not only help them to understand you better, it will also remind them that they have much to be proud of, and much that is worth preserving.

Trekking styles

How you choose to trek will depend on your budget, your time frame, and what sort of experience you're after. Trekking independently saves money and gives you a more individualized experience, but involves more preparation. Joining an organized trek minimizes hassles and enables you to reach remote backcountry areas, but you pay dearly for it.

Trekking independently

Trekking independently means making all your own arrangements instead of going through a trekking company. Most budget travellers trek this way, carrying their own packs and staying in teahouses, simply because it's cheaper.

The **cost** of lodging is negligible, and there's very little else to spend your money on besides food. Even in the Annapurna and Everest regions, where trekker menus may tempt you to order relatively expensive items, the average tab for three meals a day is unlikely to go over Rs400 ($7). Along other standard routes you'll probably find you spend Rs250–350 ($4–6) a day, and off the beaten track it may actually be impossible to spend more than Rs200 ($3.50) a day. These guidelines don't take into account such non-essentials as beer, soft drinks and chocolate, but even these will probably add no more than about Rs100 ($2) to your daily budget. Hiring a porter to carry your stuff will add about Rs300 ($5) a day, a guide Rs600 ($10) a day.

Doing it yourself gives you more **control** over many aspects of the trek: you can go at your own pace, stop when and where you like, choose your travelling companions and take rest days or side trips as you please. The downside is that you have to spend two or three days lining up trekking permits and bus tickets, renting equipment, buying supplies and perhaps tracking down a porter or guide. A further drawback is that you're effectively confined to **teahouse routes**; trekking to remote areas is difficult unless you speak Nepali or you're prepared to deal with considerable porter logistics.

Life on the trail is described later, but suffice it to say that an independent trek is **less comfortable** than one arranged through an agency. Lodges can be noisy and lacking in privacy, while the food is often fairly uninteresting. The active teahouse **social scene** goes some way to compensating for this, however – even if you start out alone, you'll quickly meet up with potential trekking companions.

By not being part of a group, you're better placed to learn from Nepali ways rather than forcing Nepalis to adapt to yours. Equally important, a high proportion of the money you spend goes directly to the local economy (whereas most of the money paid to trekking agencies goes no further than Kathmandu, and often finds its way overseas). However, as an independent trekker you must guard against contributing to **deforestation**. If you stay in teahouses and order meals cooked over wood fires you encourage innkeepers to cut down more trees, and if you bring along a guide or porter, so do they. Fortunately, kerosene has largely replaced wood in the most popular areas. See the box on p.351 for tips on minimizing your environmental impact.

Hiring porters and guides

Porters are an important part of the Himalayan economy and there's no shame in hiring one. With a porter taking most of your gear, you only have to carry a small pack containing the things you need during the day; this can be a great relief at high elevations, and it's essential when trekking off established routes, where tents, food and cooking equipment have to be brought in. As porters rarely speak much English, you might want to pay more for a **guide** who does. An increasing number of them are willing to carry gear as well, but this isn't always the case: ask. Guides are really only necessary on esoteric routes, but any trek will be enlivened by the company and local knowledge of a guide, who may well take you on unusual side trips to visit the homes of family and friends.

Hiring a porter or guide is simple enough – just ask your innkeeper, or try any trekking agency or equipment-rental shop. If you're not sure you need a porter, or you think you'll only need one for a few tough days of a trek, you can usually hire someone on the spot at Namche, Jomosom or other major towns along the established routes. The business is very informal and not always reputable, so shop around and interview more than one candidate if necessary. A bad guide can be

Anything can fit in a *doko*

worse than useless. Be clear whether or not the agreed wage includes food – a porter can run up a huge bill if you're paying – and don't pay too much of it up front. Expect also to give your guide or porter a tip of gear, clothing (make sure it's clean) or a few hundred rupees at the end of the trek, assuming the work was well done.

However, the **responsibilities** of employing a porter or guide cannot be overstated. Several porters die needlessly each year, typically because their sahib (pronounced "sahb") thought they were superhuman and didn't mind sleeping outside in a blizzard. You *must* make sure your employees are adequately clothed for the journey – on high-altitude treks, this will mean buying or renting them good shoes, a parka, sunglasses, mittens and a sleeping bag. Establish beforehand if something is a loan. If they get sick, it's up to you to look after them, and since most porters hired in Kathmandu and Pokhara are clueless about altitude-related problems, it's your responsibility to educate them. Don't let a porter carry a double load, even if he volunteers, and don't hire anyone who looks underage.

If you've never trekked before, don't try to organize a trek off the teahouse routes. Finding a guide familiar with a particular area will be hard, and transporting him with a crew of porters and supplies to the trailhead a major (and expensive) logistical exercise. Getting a trekking agency to do it might not cost much more.

Organized trekking

Organized treks are for people who haven't got the time or inclination to make their own arrangements, or who want to tackle ambitious routes that can't be done independently. They **cost** from $15 to $150 a day, depending on the standard of service, size of the group, remoteness of the route, and whether you book the trip

---

A FEW BAD APPLES

This is an advisory notice for women contemplating trekking alone with a male guide: reports in the past few years suggest that two or three Kathmandu-based guides make a practice of raping their female clients. These men have not been brought to trial – perhaps because of bribes, perhaps because their victims have been unable or unwilling to remain in Nepal long enough to bring legal action. In the absence of convictions, this book cannot name names. The vast majority of Nepali guides are good as gold, but women should be aware that there are a few bad apples. The best way to avoid them is to hire your guide on the recommendation of someone you trust, and bring along a trekking partner. Consider hiring a female guide - see p.247.

---

in your home country or in Kathmandu. The price should always include a guide, porters, food and shelter, although cheap outfits often charge extra for trekking permits, national park fees and transport, and may cut other corners as well. The cheaper the price, the more wary you need to be.

A trek is hard work however you do it, but a good company will help you along with a few **creature comforts**: you can expect appetizing food, "bed tea" and hot "washing water" on cold mornings, camp chairs and a latrine tent with toilet paper. Depending on the size of your party, a guide, *sirdar* (guide foreman) or "Western trek leader" (native-English-speaking guide) will be able to answer questions and cope with problems. Trekking groups usually sleep in **tents**, which, while quieter than teahouses, may be colder and are certainly more cramped. The daily routine of eating as a group can get monotonous, and gives you **less contact** with local people. There's something to be said for safety in numbers, but trekking with a group imposes a somewhat **inflexible itinerary** on you, and if you don't like the people in your group, you're stuck.

In theory, organized treks are more **environmentally sound**, at least in the Everest and Annapurna areas, where trekkers' meals are required to be cooked with kerosene. Sometimes, however, cooks use wood so they can sell the kerosene at the end of the trek – and, worse still, for each trekker eating a kerosene-cooked meal, there may be two or three porters and other staff cooking their *bhaat* over a wood fire.

But the main advantage of organized trekking is it enables you to get **off the beaten track**: there's little point in using an agency to do a teahouse trek.

Budget operators

Small **budget operators** in Kathmandu and Pokhara, charging $15–25 a day, are notoriously hard to recommend: most are fly-by-night operations offering mainly customized treks, but they're rarely competent to handle anything off the mass-market routes. Names change and standards rise and fall – if you hear of a good one by word of mouth, try it. A few of the more established budget companies run scheduled treks, but again, usually only to the most popular areas.

Bigger operators

Kathmandu's **big operators** mainly package treks on behalf of overseas agencies, but they may allow "walk-ins" to join at a reduced price, and some offer cheaper treks specifically for the local market (typically $30–60 a day). A list of recommended companies is given on p.129. Write or fax for brochures to make sure your schedule coincides with theirs; for customized treks to exotic areas,

> ## QUESTIONS TO ASK TREKKING COMPANIES
>
> Trekking companies in Nepal speak the green lingo as fluently as anyone, but in many cases their walk doesn't match their talk. Here are some specific questions to put to them to find out what they're actually doing to mitigate their impact on the environment. You probably won't find a company able to answer every question satisfactorily, but the exercise should help establish which outfits are genuinely concerned.
>
> • Do they carry enough kerosene to cook all meals for all members of the party, including porters?
>
> • What equipment do they provide to porters – tents, proper clothing, shoes, UV sunglasses?
>
> • Do they separate trash and carry out all non-burnable/non-biodegradeable waste?
>
> • How many of their staff have attended the *Kathmandu Environmental Education Project*'s annual Ecotrek workshop on responsible trekking? (Attendees will be able to show a certificate.)
>
> • Do staff have wilderness first-aid training?

contact them several months in advance, or be prepared to wait up to a week in Kathmandu while arrangements are being made.

Overseas agencies
Booking through an **overseas agency** lets you arrange everything before you leave home, but expect to pay £50–100/$75–150 per day. Some agencies have their own Nepali subsidiaries in Kathmandu, others use independent outfitters like those listed on p.129. The overseas agency will look after all your arrangements up till the time you leave your home country, and will also play a part in maintaining quality control in Nepal. Some may allow you to join up in Kathmandu at a reduced price. See p.55 for names and addresses.

Preparations

Arranging a trek is like anything else in Nepal: complications arise, things inevitably take longer than planned, but it's unquestionably worth it in the end. Obviously, trekking independently involves more preparation than joining an organized group. The remainder of this chapter is geared specifically to independent trekkers, although most of the information will apply to groups as well.

Permits and other formalities
A **trekking permit** is required for entry into any of the areas described in this chapter. Apply at the Central Immigration offices in Kathmandu or Pokhara (details on p.125 and p.245). Pokhara is generally easier to deal with than Kathmandu, but both are frantic during October – especially just before and after the week-long Dasain holiday. Note that Pokhara issues permits only for Annapurna and Rara treks. Application forms are colour-coded by region, so be sure to fill in the correct one. Two passport-sized photos are required with your application, but you can get these from nearby fast-photo studios.

For the most popular trekking areas, permits **cost** $5 per person per week (payable in rupee equivalent) for the first thirty days, $10 per week thereafter.

Permits for Lower Dolpo and Kanchenjunga cost double, for Manaslu they're $75–90 per week (depending on season), and for Mustang and Upper Dolpo they're $700 for the first ten days, $70 per day thereafter. If your trek goes through any of the national parks or conservation areas, you'll have to purchase a separate Rs650 entry ticket at the time of application.

A trekking permit still doesn't give you free run of the country – most border areas are closed, and peaks are restricted. Two dozen peaks, ranging in elevation from 5587m to 6654m, can be attempted with a separate **trekking peak** permit ($150–300 per party). Trekking peak expeditions must be organized by a registered trekking company, which will arrange the permit as well as the mandatory insurance ($100 per party).

Before setting off on any trek, **register with your embassy** in Kathmandu, as this will speed things up should you need rescuing. You can have the *Kathmandu Environmental Education Project* (see below) forward the details to your embassy. It's also advisable to be **insured** for trekking – note that travel-insurance companies may add a surcharge to their rates to cover "hazardous sports" such as trekking.

Information, maps and books

The best sources of current trekking **information** are the *Kathmandu Environmental Education Project* (☎410303) and the *Himalayan Rescue Association* (☎418755), with offices just off Tridevi Marg west of the Kathmandu Central Immigration office. Both keep logbooks full of comments from returning trekkers – invaluable for tips on routes and trekking agencies – and can advise on trail conditions and equipment. Both have small libraries, and *KEEP* also sells some books and other trekking-related items. *KEEP* doesn't take a position on independent versus agency trekking, but encourages trekkers to use their clout as consumers to effect changes in the trekking industry; exhibits in the office give a primer on trekkers' impact on the environment and culture. *HRA* provides information on altitude sickness and health posts. Noticeboards outside both offices are good for finding **trekking partners** and used equipment.

Nepal's trekking regions are fairly well **mapped**, although the rule, as always, is you get what you pay for. The locally produced *Mandala* and *Nepa* series include colour maps of the most popular routes, and *Mandala* does dyeline versions of many more obscure areas. Better, though pricier, are the *Schneider* maps of the Everest and Langtang/Helambu areas and the *ACAP* map of Annapurna, all of which are available in the bigger tourist bookshops. Specific titles are recommended in the area descriptions given later in this chapter. Trekking **guidebooks** and general books on the Himalaya are listed in *Contexts* (p.428); all can easily be bought in Kathmandu or Pokhara.

What to bring

Having the right **equipment** on a trek is obviously important, though when you see how little porters get by with you'll realize that high-tech gear isn't essential – bring what you need to be comfortable, but keep weight to a minimum. The equipment list given here is intended mainly for independent trekkers staying in teahouses. If you're planning to camp, you'll need quite a few more things, and if you're trekking with an agency you won't need so much.

By **renting** bulky or specialized items in Nepal, you'll avoid having to lug them around during the rest of your travels. Kathmandu has dozens of rental shops, and Pokhara a somewhat more limited selection; if you're trekking in the Everest region, you can rent high-altitude gear in Namche. However, you might have trouble finding good gear during the busy autumn trekking season. You'll be expected to leave a deposit of money or an international air ticket. Inspect sleeping bags and parkas carefully for fleas (or worse) – if there's time before setting off, have them cleaned – and make sure zippers are in working order. You can often **buy** equipment quite cheaply (see p.121). If you buy or rent boots, obviously make sure they fit properly, and break them in before hitting the trail.

Clothes must be lightweight and versatile, especially on long treks where conditions vary from subtropical to arctic. Many first-time trekkers underestimate the potential for extremes in temperature. What you bring will depend on the trek and time of year, but in most cases you should be prepared for sun, rain, snow and very chilly mornings; dress in layers for maximum flexibility. As explained in "Cultural Hints" in *Basics*, Nepalis have innately conservative attitudes about dress: in warm areas, women should wear calf-length dresses or skirts with demure tops; men should wear a shirt and long pants (not shorts) wherever possible, and both sexes should wear at least a swimsuit when bathing.

For **footwear**, running shoes will suffice for most trekking situations, and serve as a good backup for evenings. However, hiking boots, by providing better

---

EQUIPMENT CHECKLIST

Items marked (*) can be purchased in Nepal and those marked (**) can also be rented, but if you want to be absolutely sure of having it, bring it with you.

ESSENTIALS
Backpack** – one with an internal frame and hip belt is best.
Sleeping bag** – a three-season bag is adequate for hill treks; above 4000m, or in winter, you'll need a four-season bag and possibly a liner.
Medical kit – see p.349
Water bottle*
Toiletries*
Toilet paper* – see "Conservation Tips", p.351.
Towel*
Flashlight (torch)* – remember that batteries run down faster in the cold.
Pocket knife*
Sunglasses* – a good UV-protective pair, ideally with side shields if you expect to be in snow.
Sunscreen/lip balm – at altitude you'll need a high protection factor or zinc oxide.

FOOTWEAR
Hiking boots** – leather or *Gore-Tex* boots are best if wet or snowy conditions are expected.
Trainers – okay for most low-elevation trails, handy for evenings.
Flipflops* – may be useful for evenings at low elevations.

CLOTHES
Shirts/T-shirts*
Trousers* – baggy (to leave room for thermal underwear) and with plenty of pockets; separate lightweight pair for warm days.
Skirt/dress* – mid-calf length is best.
Shorts – not recommended on off-the-beaten-track routes.

traction, ankle support and protection, will take you through a greater range of the sort of conditions you're likely to encounter. Leather boots are heavier than synthetic ones, but, being sturdier and more easily waterproofed, are recommended for treks at high elevations or during the winter or monsoon. Bring plenty of socks, because you'll be changing them often.

Bringing **camera** equipment involves a trade-off between weight and performance – a pocket 35mm model may be a good compromise. An SLR body with long and short zoom lenses will produce much better results, especially with a tripod and polarizing filters, but it's heavy and obtrusive. You'll find more general tips on photography in *Basics*.

Health and emergencies

Guidebook writers tend to go overboard about the **health** hazards of trekking, particularly altitude sickness. Don't be put off – the vast majority of trekkers never experience anything worse than a mild headache. That said, health is of

Sweat pants – can be worn over shorts in the morning; also good for evenings.
Socks – several thin cotton/blend and thick woollen* pairs.
Underwear – thermal underwear essential for high-altitude or winter treks.
Sun hat* – helpful at low elevations.
Wool sweater* – or a synthetic pile jacket.
Bandana – to use as a handkerchief, sweatband or scarf.
Parka** – preferably filled with down or lightweight fibre.
Wool hat* – one that covers the ears is best.
Wool mittens* – ski gloves are warmer, but bulkier.
Rain shell/poncho – breathable waterproof material (such as *Gore-Tex*) is best. An umbrella* will suffice at lower elevations, and can also function as a parasol.

HIGH-ALTITUDE GEAR – OPTIONAL
Gaiters** – worth having for passes where snow is likely.
Down pants** and booties – welcome luxuries on cold evenings.
Ski poles** – may be useful for keeping your balance in snow.
Ice axe** – may be needed for icy passes in winter.
Crampons** – ditto.

OTHER USEFUL ITEMS
Day pack
Foam mat** – optional for teahouse treks on the main routes.
Camera equipment
Sewing kit
Stuff sacks – handy for separating things in your pack and for creating a pillow when filled with clothes.
Plastic bag* – to put over your pack in the rain.
Candles*
Emergency snack food* – biscuits and chocolate can be bought along the way on teahouse routes.
Entertainment* – book, cards, musical instrument, etc.

paramount concern when doing any strenuous physical activity, and all the more so when trekking, which routinely takes you a week or more from the nearest medical facilities. Stomach troubles can spoil a trek, while injuries or altitude sickness, if untreated, could prove fatal. It's best to err on the side of caution.

Children, seniors and people with disabilities have all trekked successfully, but a minimum **fitness** level is required. Needless to say, the better prepared you are physically, the more you'll enjoy the trek. If you're in any doubt about your ability to cope with strenuous walking, see your doctor. It's also worth seeking advice if you have any allergies, especially to antibiotics.

Stomach troubles

The risk of **stomach troubles** is particularly high while trekking, and water is the usual culprit: you need to drink lots of fluids on the trail. Innkeepers normally boil water and tea, but not always for the statutory ten minutes, and at high altitudes the boiling point of water is so low that germs might not be killed. All running water should be assumed to be contaminated – wherever you go, there will be people, or at least animals, upstream.

Treating the water is not only the best line of defence against illness, it also reduces your reliance on boiled water. Iodine is the safest method, either in tablet or crystal form or, more commonly, as a two-percent liquid solution: use two to five drops per litre, depending on the cloudiness of the water, and wait at least twenty minutes before drinking. You might want to cover up the taste with powdered fruit drink. Chlorine-based tablets may not be effective against amebas and giardia. Ceramic filter pumps produce pure water without the aftertaste, although they're expensive and take up space.

See pp.22–23 for tips on treating stomach upsets.

Minor injuries

Most minor injuries occur while walking downhill; **knee strains** are common, especially among trekkers carrying their own packs. If you know your knees are weak, bind them up with crepe (ace) bandages as a preventative measure, or hire a porter. Good, supportive boots reduce the risk of **ankle sprains** or twists, but the best prevention is just to pay careful attention to where you put your feet: don't try to admire the scenery and walk at the same time.

It's hard to avoid getting **blisters**, but make sure your boots are well broken in and always wear two pairs of socks, changing them regularly (especially if they get wet). Apply moleskin to hotspots as soon as they develop, making sure to clean and cover blisters so they can heal as quickly as possible.

Acute mountain sickness

Barraged by medical advice and horror stories, trekkers all too often develop altitude paranoia. The fact is that just about everyone who treks over 4000m experiences some mild symptoms of **acute mountain sickness (AMS)**, but serious cases are very rare, and the simple cure – descent – almost always brings immediate recovery.

At high elevations there is not only less oxygen but also lower atmospheric pressure, which can have all sorts of weird effects on the body: it can cause the brain to swell, fill the lungs with fluid, or play havoc with the body's digestive processes. The syndrome varies from one person to the next, and strikes without regard for fitness – in fact, young people seem to be more susceptible, possibly because they're more hung up about admitting they feel rotten.

FIRST-AID CHECKLIST

Most of the following items can be purchased in Kathmandu or Pokhara for much less then they cost back home. This is a minimum first-aid kit – trekking guide-books usually give much longer lists. See p.22 for tips on self-diagnosis, and use antibiotics advisedly.

FOR INJURIES

Band-Aids – large and small sizes.
Gauze pads
Sterile dressing
Surgical tape
Moleskin – synthetic adhesive padding for blisters.
Elastic support bandages – for knee strains, ankle sprains.
Antiseptic cream – for scrapes, blisters, insect bites.
Tweezers
Scissors
Thermometer – one that also reads low temperatures, in case of hypothermia.

FOR ILLNESSES

Aspirin/Paracetamol
Cold medicine
Throat lozenges – sore throats are common at high elevations.
Diarrhoea tablets
Jeevan Jal – a Nepali brand of oral rehy-dration formula for diarrhoea.
Tinidazole – an anti-protozoan, for giardia.
Antibiotic – Ciprofloxacin, Norfloxacin or Cephalosporin for intestinal bacteria, Erythromycin for throat/bronchial infections. Other drugs may also be used – consult a doctor or trekking guidebook.
Diamox – for treatment of mild AMS symptoms (optional).

PREVENTION

Most people are capable of acclimatizing to very high elevations, but the process takes time and must be done in stages. The golden rule is **don't go too high too fast**. Above 3000m, the daily net elevation gain should be no more than 500m; take mandatory acclimatization days at around 3500m and 4500m – more if you're feeling unwell – and try to spend these days day-hiking higher. These are only guidelines, and you'll have to regulate your ascent according to how you feel. Trekkers who fly directly to high airstrips have to be especially careful to acclimatize.

Drink plenty of **liquids** at altitude, since the body tends to retain water, and the air is incredibly dry. The usual adage is that you're not drinking enough unless you pee clear. Keeping warm, eating well, getting plenty of sleep and avoiding alcohol will also help reduce the chances of developing AMS.

SYMPTOMS

AMS usually gives plenty of warning before it becomes life-threatening. Mild **symptoms** include headaches, dizziness, insomnia, nausea, loss of appetite, short-ness of breath and swelling of the hands and feet; one or two of these shouldn't be cause for panic, but they're a sign that your body hasn't yet adjusted to the elevation. You shouldn't ascend further until you start feeling better, or, if you do keep going, you should be prepared to beat a hasty retreat if the condition gets worse. Serious symptoms (persistent vomiting, delirium, loss of co-ordination, bubbly breathing and bloody sputum, rapid heart rate or breathlessness at rest, blueness of face and lips) can develop within hours, and if ignored can result in death.

CURE

The only effective cure for advanced AMS is **descent**. Anyone showing serious symptoms should be taken downhill immediately, regardless of the time of day or night – hire a porter or pack animal to carry the sufferer if necessary. Recovery is usually dramatic, often after a descent of only a few hundred vertical metres.

Some doctors recommend acetazolamide (a diuretic better known under the brand name **Diamox**) to relieve mild AMS symptoms, although it has to be stressed that this does nothing to treat the underlying cause of AMS; the dose is 250mg twice a day. For further advice on AMS, visit the *Himalayan Rescue Association*'s aid posts at Manang (on the Annapurna Circuit) and Pheriche (on the Everest trek).

Other dangers

Other altitude-related dangers such as hypothermia and frostbite are encountered less often by trekkers, but can pose real threats on high, exposed passes or in bad weather.

The symptoms of **hypothermia** are similar to those of AMS: slurred speech, fatigue, irrational behaviour and loss of coordination. Low body temperature is the surest sign. The treatment, in a word, is heat. Get the victim out of the cold, put him in a good sleeping bag (with another person, if necessary) and give him warm food and drink.

Frostbite appears initially as small white patches on exposed skin, caused by local freezing. The skin will feel cold and numb. To treat, apply warmth (*not* snow!). Avoid refreezing, which can lead to permanent damage.

Common-sense **precautions** bear repeating: wear or carry adequate clothing; keep dry; cover exposed extremities in severe weather; eat lots and carry emergency snacks; and make for shelter if conditions get bad.

Snowblindness isn't a worry as long as you're equipped with a good pair of sunglasses.

Emergencies

Ninety-nine percent of the time, trekking in Nepal is a piece of cake and it's hard to imagine something going wrong. But while few trekkers ever have to deal with **emergencies** – illness, AMS, storms, missteps, landslides and avalanches are the main causes – they can happen to anyone.

Bezruchka's *A Guide to Trekking in Nepal* (see "Books" in *Contexts*) gives full advice on emergency **procedures** and a rundown of hospitals, aid posts, airstrips and radio transmitters found near the main trekking routes. In non-urgent cases, your best bet is to be carried by porter or pack animal to the nearest **airstrip** or **hospital**, although bear in mind that medical facilities outside Kathmandu and a few other major cities are very rudimentary. Where the situation is more serious, send word to the nearest village equipped with a radio to request a **helicopter rescue**. A typical rescue costs upwards of $1000, and they won't come for you until they're satisfied you'll be able to pay; being registered with your embassy will speed the process of contacting relatives who can vouch for you.

Trekking life

A trek, it's often said, is not a wilderness experience. Unlike other mountain ranges, the Himalaya are comparatively well settled, farmed and grazed – much of their beauty, in fact, is man-made – and the trails support a steady stream of local traffic. If you're trekking independently, you'll be sleeping and eating in teahouses and making equal contact with locals and other foreigners. You'll need a good deal of adaptability to different living situations, but the payback comes in cultural insights, unforgettable encounters, and of course breathtaking scenery.

The trailhead is typically reached at the end of a long, bumpy bus ride, and **getting there** is an integral part of the experience. This is also a big factor in deciding where to trek, as the going and returning can eat up two days (or more) and, in the case of far-flung treks reached by air, can represent the single biggest expense. See *Basics* for general information on bus and air travel.

Trails

Trekking in the Himalaya is no stroll in the park. If you're not an experienced outdoors person, prepare yourself for serious, strenuous **walking**. Most trekkers take it in easy stages, from one glass of *chiya* to the next – there's no race to the top. It's best to set off early each morning to make the most of the clear weather, as clouds usually roll in around midday. Pad your schedule for rest days, weather and contingencies, and make time for at least one unusual side trip – that's when things get really interesting.

Trails are often steep and rough, and bridges precarious. You may occasionally **get lost**, but not for long: stopping to chat and ask directions is part of the fun, and a good opportunity to learn some Nepali. Don't **trek alone**, or at least stay within sight of other people and spend nights in the company of others, as they can help you if you get hurt and can detect signs of AMS or hypothermia. Nepalis think all lone travellers are a bit odd, so you might find it worthwhile teaming up with others just to avoid the constant question, *Eklai?* ("Alone?"). Be sure to read

---

CONSERVATION TIPS

The main environmental problem in the Himalaya is **deforestation**, and trekking puts an additional strain on local wood supplies: it's been estimated that one trekker consumes, directly and indirectly, between five and ten times more wood per day than a Nepali. In addition, trekkers leave litter, strain local sanitation systems and contribute to water pollution. The following are suggestions on how to minimize your impact on the fragile Himalayan environment.

- Where the choice exists, eat at teahouses that cook with kerosene or electricity instead of wood.
- Bring plenty of warm clothes so you (and your porter) are less reliant on wood fires to keep warm.
- Try to time your meals and co-ordinate your orders with other trekkers; cooking food in big batches is a more efficient use of fuel.
- If trekking with an agency, see that all meals are cooked with kerosene, and complain if they aren't.
- Decline offers of hot showers except in inns where the water is heated by electricity, solar panels or fuel-efficient "back boilers".

- Treat water with iodine instead of asking innkeepers to fill your canteen with boiled water.
- Use latrines wherever possible. Where there's no facility, go well away from water sources, bury your faeces and burn your toilet paper. Better yet, don't use toilet paper at all – use water, as Nepalis do.
- Use phosphate-free soap and shampoo, and don't rinse directly in streams.
- Deposit litter in designated rubbish bins, where they exist. Elsewhere, carry all non-burnable litter back out – that includes tins and especially batteries.

"Cultural Hints" in *Basics*; again, *don't* give pens or rupees to children, whether they ask or not – if you do, every trekker that comes after you will be hounded for handouts.

Teahouses
Teahouses along the major trekking routes are efficient little operations, with English signs, menus and usually an English-speaking proprietor. Although they cater exclusively to trekkers and their porters, these tourist inns follow the Nepali tradition of providing practically free lodging (usually Rs30 or less per bed) to dinner customers. Private rooms are available along the most popular routes, but elsewhere dormitory accommodation is the rule. The beds will normally have some sort of padding, but a foam mat may come in handy, and a sleeping bag is obligatory. Many places have wood stoves, and a growing number have electricity.

You'll find fewer comforts on **less-trekked trails**, however, where lodgings are likely to be private kitchens and meals are eaten by the fire amid eye-watering smoke, and you may have to sleep on the floor. Such places rarely advertise themselves, but once you've spent a little time off the beaten track you'll start realizing that almost every trailside house with an open front is potential shelter.

Recommending specific trekking lodgings is beyond the scope of this book. At any rate, they come and go so quickly that your best recommendations will be from trekkers coming the other way.

Food and drink
Trekking cuisine is a world unto itself. Although teahouses' plastic-coated cardboard menus promise tempting international delicacies, items often turn out to be permanently *paindaina* (unavailable), and you'll notice that the "spring roll" wrappings, "enchilada" tortillas, "pizza" crusts and "pancakes" all bear more than a passing resemblance to chapatis. But at any rate, eggs, porridge, custard and even (sometimes) apple pie are all reassuringly familiar, and goodies like chocolate and muesli are available on the main trails.

However, many trekkers order "Western" food simply because it's there, not because it's good, and indeed it costs much more than **local food**. In highland areas you'll be able to eat such Tibetan dishes as *momo, thukpa* and *riki kur*, and instead of porridge you might be served *dhedo* or *tsampa* (see "Eating and Drinking" in *Basics*). At lower elevations, *daal bhaat*, chow mein, packet noodles and potatoes are the standard offerings. A further advantage of eating local fare is that it's almost always quicker: there are usually unlimited quantities of *daal bhaat* steaming away on the back burner, whereas foreign food has to be made specially. On less-travelled routes, where *daal bhaat* and potatoes are often the only food available, you'll have to force yourself to eat large amounts to get enough calories and protein (you might also want to bring vitamin tablets).

When **ordering**, bear in mind that the cook can only make one or two things at a time, and there may be many others ahead of you: simplify the process by co-ordinating your order with other trekkers. Most innkeepers expect dinner orders to be placed several hours in advance, and there's usually a dog-eared notepad floating around on which you're meant to keep a tally of everything you've eaten. Pay when you leave, and be sure to bring plenty of small money on the trek, since innkeepers often have trouble changing anything over Rs100.

Tea and "hot lemon" are the main **drinks** on the trail. Bottled soft drinks, water and even beer are common along the popular routes, but the price of each bottle rises by about Rs10 for each extra day it has to be portered from the nearest road. Don't miss trying *chhang*, *raksi* and *tongba* – again, see *Basics* for fuller explanations of these alcoholic specialities.

Sanitation

Washing and toilet facilities, where they exist, range from primitive to modern. Off the established routes or at higher elevations, you'll have to bathe and do laundry under makeshift outdoor taps in freezing cold water (which explains why hot springs are such major attractions). Some teahouses in the Annapurna and Everest regions have solar or electric-heated showers. Others will offer washing water that has been heated on a wood fire, but this is an environmentally dubious practice. Most teahouses provide outdoor latrines (*chaarpi*), and a few even have indoor flush toilets, but don't be surprised if you're pointed to a half-covered privy hanging over a stream, or simply to a paddock.

THE TREKS

Nepal's mountains can be divided into five regions, the first three being most suitable for first-time independent trekkers. On a limited budget and schedule, you'll be restricted to the **Annapurna** and **Helambu–Langtang** regions, north of Pokhara and Kathmandu respectively. Given more time or money, you'll be able to tackle **Everest** or some of the longer Annapurna routes. With experience, or a sense of adventure, you should consider treks in the more remote regions of **eastern** and **far western Nepal**.

The sections below give overviews of the areas and describe the major trekking possibilities within them, but for a step-by-step route description you'll need a full-blown trekking guidebook. The box on the next page summarizes the major teahouse treks.

North of Pokhara: Annapurna

Nearly sixty percent of all trekking permits are issued for the **Annapurna** region north of Pokhara. The popularity is well deserved, since nowhere else do you get such a rich feast of spectacular scenery and varied hill culture. Compared to most other regions, **logistics** are simple: treks all start or finish close to Pokhara, and transportation to trailheads is well developed; with great views just two days up the trail, short treks are particularly feasible. Pokhara is the only place outside Kathmandu with a Central Immigration office that issues **trekking permits**, and the Pokhara office is, if anything, saner than Kathmandu's. If your trek starts and ends in Pokhara, you'll be able to store excess luggage and **rent equipment** there as well.

That said, the popular treks in the Annapurna region have become highly **commercialized** and culturally rather tame – this is the Costa del Trekking. To be fair, most trekkers regard familiar food, mattresses, English signs and Western company as pluses, but if you're looking to get away from it all, look elsewhere.

The **Annapurna Himal** faces Pokhara like an enormous sofa, 40km across and numbering nine peaks over 7000m, with Annapurna I above all at 8091m. It's

TREKS AT A GLANCE

Trek	Days*	Best Months	Elevation (m)	Difficulty	Comments
Helambu	3–10	Oct–April	800–3600	Moderate	Easy access, uncrowded, varied; only modest views.
Gosainkund	5–7	Oct–Dec, Feb–May	1950–4380	Strenuous	Sacred lakes; festival in July–August.
Poon Hill	5–8	Oct–April	1100–3200	Moderate	Easy access, excellent views; very commercial.
Siklis	4–7	Oct–April	1100–2200	Moderate	Easy access; need 2 days' supplies.
Rara	6–8	Oct–Nov, April–June	2400–3500	Moderate	Fly in; must be prepared to camp; pristine lake and forest.
Pokhara – Trisuli	7–10	Nov–March	400–1450	Easy	Pleasant hill walk, snow-free in winter; basic teahouses.
Dolpa	7–14	April–Sept	2100–5110	Strenuous	Fly in; remote and rugged, must be self-sufficient.
Langtang	8–12	Oct–May	1700–3750	Moderate	Beautiful alpine valley close to Kathmandu.
Lower Kali Gandaki	8–12	Nov–March	900–3200	Moderate	Longer version of Poon Hill, returning a less commercial way.
Annapurna Sanctuary	9–12	Oct–Dec, Feb–April	1100–4130	Moderate/Strenuous	Spectacular scenery, easy access; acclimatization necessary.
Dhorpatan circuit	10–14	Oct–April	470–3400	Moderate	May need guide, shelter and food.
Jomosom/Muktinath	12–16	Oct–April	1100–3800	Moderate	Spectacular, varied; very commercial.
Everest (Lukla fly-in)	14–18	Oct–Nov, March–May	2800–5550	Strenuous	Superb scenery, flights a problem; acclimatization necessary
Annapurna circuit	16–21	Oct–Dec, March–April	450–5380	Strenuous	Incredible diversity and scenery; high pass requires care and acclimatization.
Everest (Jiri walk-in)	26+	Oct–Nov, March–April	1500–5550	Very strenuous	Wonderful mix of hill and high-elevation walking, but with a lot of up and down.
Everest (E. approach)	30+	Nov, March	300–5550	Very strenuous	Similar, but with an even greater net vertical gain.

* Not including transport to and from the trailhead.

	Buses		Flights	
	Frequency	Time	Frequency	Time
To and from POKHARA				
Baglung	1/hr	4hr		
Begnas Tal	1/hr	45min		
Chandrakot	1/hr	2hr		
Dumre/Besisahar	*			
Gorkha	2/day	5hr		
Jomosom			2–5/day	25min
Manang			4/wk	25min
Phedi	1/hr	1hr		
Tansen	3/day	6hr		
To and from KATHMANDU				
Gorkha	10/day	6hr		
Jomosom			0–2/wk	40min**
Pokhara	21/day	8hr	5–8/day	35min
	(2–12/day)#	7hr		
Trisuli	9/day	4hr		

ANNAPURNA TRAVEL CONNECTIONS

* No direct buses: take any eastbound bus from Pokhara, get off at Dumre (2hr), from where buses run to Besisahar (another 4hr).
** Indirect flights will take longer.
\# Number in parentheses refers to tourist buses.

an area of stunning diversity, ranging from the sodden bamboo forests of the southern slopes (Lumle, northwest of Pokhara, is the wettest village in Nepal) to windswept desert (Jomosom, in the northern rain shadow, is the driest). The region is covered by ACAP's reasonably accurate "Annapurna" (1:125,000) **map**; cheaper, but less reliable, is the *Mandala* "Round Annapurna" (1:150,000).

The *himal* and adjacent hill areas are protected within the **Annapurna Conservation Area Project** (ACAP), for which you have to pay a Rs650 **entry fee** when applying for your trekking permit. The money goes to a good cause. A quasi-park administered by a non-governmental trust, ACAP has won high praise for its holistic approach to tourism management. Its twofold aims are to protect the area's natural and cultural heritage, while at the same time ensuring sustain-able economic and social benefit for local people. To take the pressure off local forests, the project has set up kerosene depots and installed microhydroelectric generators to provide alternative fuels, and has supported the creation of tree nurseries and reforestation efforts. Lodge owners benefit from small-business training and low-interest loans, enabling them to invest in things like solar water heaters and efficient stoves, while rubbish pits, latrines, health posts and even a telephone service have been established with ACAP entry fees.

The Jomosom trek

JOMOSOM TREK is an acknowledged classic: an ideal sampler of Himalayan scenery and culture, and, not surprisingly, the most developed stretch of trail in

Nepal. A guide definitely isn't necessary. **Food and lodging** are of a relatively high standard: many lodges have electricity and hot showers, and some look like they've been imported wholesale from Thamel. All have English menus and outdo each other with the Westernness of their cuisine.

The full Jomosom trek takes ten to twelve days, but the trail network is extensive, so shorter and longer variations are possible; the first half of the trek, which can be done on its own, is described first. The usual **starting point** is Chandrakot, reached by bus or taxi from Pokhara; it's also possible to start from Lakeside, Suikhet or Baglung (see p.247 for transport advice).

To Poon Hill

If you haven't time to do the full Jomosom trek, you can get a taster of it by turning the first half into a circuit of four to six days. The route ambles through steep, lush hill country, taking in some lovely Gurung villages and, weather permitting, rewarding you with outstanding views of the Annapurnas and Machhapuchhre. The **trails** are wide and well maintained, though steep in places. The highest point reached is 3200m, which shouldn't present any altitude problems, but it's high enough that you'll need **warm clothes** at night. Rain gear is also advisable.

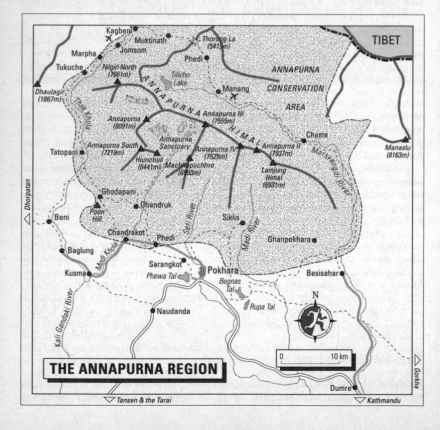

THE ANNAPURNA REGION

Poon Hill, a day and a half northwest of Chandrakot and 2000m higher, is literally the high point of this instant-gratification route: watching the mountains at sunrise from here is probably the single most done thing in the trekking universe. If clouds block your view, as they often do, it's well worth hanging on for an extra day. You can vary the return trip by heading east through magnificent stands of giant rhododendrons dripping with orchids to the pretty Gurung town of **Ghandruk**, headquarters of the ACAP, with a visitor centre and museum. From Ghandruk, trails head up to the Annapurna Sanctuary and down to Chandrakot and Suikhet.

The Thak Khola

A lead donkey heading up the Thak Khola

North of Poon Hill, the trail drops into the valley of the Kali Gandaki (locally called the **Thak Khola**) and the fun really begins: as you follow the course of the world's deepest gorge – the 8000-metre hulks of Dhaulagiri and Annapurna tower on either side – the scenery changes by the mile. The valley is also famous for its ethnic diversity, Thakalis being the dominant group. Make way for their jingling donkey trains, which feature so prominently in this area.

The walking actually gets easier after Poon Hill (and by this time you should be in better shape), and the trail stays below 3000m until the last day's climb to Muktinath at 3800m. There's essentially only one route through the Thak Khola, so unless you carry on up over the Thorung La (described in "The Annapurna Circuit", below) or fly back from Jomosom, **backtracking** is unavoidable; but by the same token, you can walk as far as you like and head back when you need to. The round trip from Pokhara to Muktinath takes ten to twelve days. If you **fly** from Pokhara to Jomosom, or vice versa, you cut the time in half; there are up to five scheduled flights a day in the high season ($50), weather permitting.

The towns of the Thak Khola are worthy destinations in their own right. **Tatopani** is renowned for its Western food, videos (cringe) and **hot springs** (*taato paani* means "hot water"). Further up, the trail passes through thick, monkey-infested forest to Tukche, once the main Thakali trading centre, and **Marpha**, a tidy, stone-clad village surrounded by apple and apricot orchards. **Day hikes** and overnight trips up from the valley floor are the best way to appreciate the incredible dimensions of the Thak Khola and the peaks around it: little-trekked trails lead to North Annapurna Base Camp, the Dhaulagiri Icefall and Dhampus Pass. Above Tukche, the vegetation dies out as you begin to enter the Himalayan rain shadow, and a savage, sand-blasting wind from the south makes it unpleasant to trek after midday. **Jomosom**, though it gives its name to the trek, is no place to linger unless you've got business at the airstrip – far more romantic is the fortress town of **Kagbeni**, only a couple of hours further on, with its medi-eval ruins and terracotta Buddhist figures. Geographically speaking,

BHOTIYAS AND THAKALIS

Bhotiya is the Nepali term for all northern border peoples of Tibetan descent. Unfortunately, Bhotiyas themselves have tended to resent the label ever since an 1854 government edict, intended to find places for all minority groups in the Hindu caste system, placed them in the lowly category of "enslavable alcohol-drinkers" because they ate yak meat (which Hindus regarded as being almost as bad as eating beef). Most prefer to identify with a specific regional group, of which there are at least a dozen in Nepal; Sherpas, the best-known Bhotiya group, are highlighted in the Everest section later in this chapter.

In most ways, Bhotiyas are indistinguishable from Tibetans. Except in certain areas in the far west, where some have been influenced by Hinduism, they are exclusively **Buddhist**, and their *chorten* (stupa-like cremation monuments), *mani* walls (consisting of slates inscribed with the mantra *Om mani padme hum*), *gompa* (monasteries) and prayer flags (*lung ta*: literally, "wind horse") are the most memorable man-made features of the Himalaya. Farmers, herders and trans-Himalayan traders, they always settle higher and further north than other ethnic groups. The climate there is harsh, and life is a constant struggle to eke out a living. Bhotiya villages vary in appearance, but those in the Annapurna region are strongly Tibetan, with houses stacked up slopes so that the flat roof of one serves as the grain-drying terrace of the next. Like Tibetans, they like their tea flavoured with salt and yak butter, and married women wear trademark rainbow aprons (*pangden*) and wrap-around dresses (*chuba*).

Unencumbered by caste, Bhotiyas are noticeably less tradition-bound than Hindus, and **women** are better off for it: they play a more nearly equal role in household affairs, speak their minds openly, are able to tease and mingle with men publicly, and can divorce without stigma. Having said that, even Bhotiyas tend to consider a female birth to be the result of bad karma, and during death rites lamas customarily urge the deceased to be reincarnated as a male.

A hill group with influence far beyond their small numbers, **Thakalis** are the ingenious traders, innkeepers and pony-handlers of the Thak Khola, the valley followed by the Jomosom trek. Their entrepreneurial flair goes back at least to the mid-nineteenth century, when the government awarded them a regional monopoly in the salt trade; since then, many have branched out into more exotic forms of commerce – importing electronics from Singapore and Hong Kong is a popular wheeze – while others have set up efficient inns in many parts of the western hills. Similarly, the **Manangis** of the upper Marsyangdi have built early trading privileges into a reputation for international smuggling and other shady activities. Women run most of the trekking lodges in both of these valleys, while their well-travelled husbands spend most of their time away on business.

you're on the edge of the Tibetan plateau here, with the main Himalaya chain looming magnificently to the south.

Finally, it's a 1000-metre climb up a side valley – out of the wind, thankfully – to poplar-lined **Muktinath**, one of the most important religious sites in the Nepal Himalaya. The *Mahabharat* mentions Muktinath as the source of mystic *shaligram* fossils (see p.261); a priest will show you around the Newar-style temple and its wall of 108 water spouts, while further down the trail you'll find a Buddhist shrine that shelters two miraculous perpetual flames. Yartung, a madly exotic **festival** of horse-riding, is held at Muktinath around the full moon of August–September.

The lower Kali Gandaki

On the return journey, if you don't feel like slogging back up the ridge south of Tatopani, you can keep following the Kali Gandaki River south from Tatopani, a low-key **valley walk** with occasionally impressive views; since there's little up and down, it's possible to make good time. This route sees far fewer trekkers than the main Jomosom trail, so **accommodation** and **food** are cheap but rudimentary. At this low elevation the weather is balmy in winter, but in spring and early autumn the heat and mosquitoes are unpleasant. The trail passes through cultivated land and villages, where Magars and Gurungs are the dominant **ethnic groups**, as well as the big Newar bazaars of Beni and Baglung.

The Pokhara–Baglung Highway is being extended northwards, bound eventually for Jomosom, but progress is slow. For the time being, buses for Pokhara depart from Baglung.

The Annapurna Sanctuary

The aptly named **ANNAPURNA SANCTUARY** is the most intensely scenic short trek in Nepal. From Ghandruk on the Jomosom route, the trail bears singlemindedly north into the very heart of the Annapurna range: following the short, steep Modi Khola, it soon leaves all permanent settlements behind, climbs through dense bamboo jungle and finally, rising above the vegetation line, makes for a narrow notch between the sheer lower flanks of Machhapuchhre and Hiunchuli. Once past this sanctuary "gate", it stumbles across moraines to a cluster of huts (often still called "Machhapuchhre Base Camp") and, further on, to the so-called **Annapurna Base Camp**. Wherever you stand in the sanctuary, the 360-degree views are unspeakably beautiful, and although clouds roll in early, the curtain often parts at sunset to reveal radiant, molten peaks. The altitude is 4100m: bring warm gear.

The sanctuary can be treated as a side trip from the Jomosom trek, adding five to seven days, or a six- to nine-day round trip from Pokhara, accessed from Chandrakot or Suikhet (Phedi). The actual distance covered isn't great, but **altitude, weather** and **trail conditions** all tend to slow you down – the trail gains more than 2000m from Ghandruk to the sanctuary, so unless you're already well acclimatized you'd be wise to spread the climb over four days. Frequent precipitation makes the trail extremely slippery at the best of times, and in winter it can be impassable due to snow or avalanche danger.

The Annapurna Circuit

The **ANNAPURNA CIRCUIT** is a challenging but rewarding three-week trek with excellent views, plenty of cultural contact and the greatest net vertical gain of all the popular routes. Starting in subtropical paddy at about 500m, the trail ascends steadily to the 5415-metre **Thorung La** (Thorung Pass) before returning along the previously described Jomosom route. A minimum of sixteen days is required, but a few extra days should be set aside for digressions, acclimatization and other contingencies. The trek is strenuous, and you'll need boots, gloves and very warm clothes for the pass, and a good four-season bag for a night spent at 4400m.

Although the eastern half of the circuit is less developed for trekkers than the Jomosom side, **food and lodging** are always available, and somewhat cheaper. A guide isn't necessary. The full circuit is best done between mid-October and mid-December – crossing the Thorung La is iffy from late December till March, though

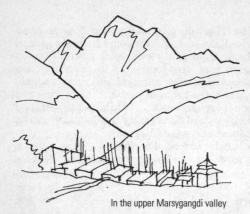

In the upper Marsygangdi valley

not out of the question, while the lower parts of the trek are uncomfort-ably warm from April on. Snow can block the pass at any time of year, so be prepared to wait it out or go back down the way you came. You can **fly** in or out of Manang ($50 from Pokhara), saving a week of walking.

Nearly everyone goes around the circuit anticlockwise, the only reason being that the Thorung La makes a longer climb from the Jomosom side, requiring an extra acclimatization day above Muktinath. The upshot of this is that if you go anticlockwise you'll be in step with the same people for the entire trek, whereas if you go clockwise you'll be constantly passing people coming the other way. The usual **starting point** is Besisahar, a ghastly four-hour bus or jeep ride (Rs100) north of Dumre on the Kathmandu–Pokhara highway; if all goes well, you can leave Kathmandu in the morning and be in Besisahar that night. If you're coming from Pokhara, you can avoid Dumre and instead follow the Pokhara–Trisuli trek (see below) to Besisahar in two days.

The circuit follows the Marsyangdi Valley north and then west all the way to the pass. The first few days are a long preamble through terraced farmland and frequent villages, with only fleeting views to whet your appetite, but then, in the course of two days, the valley constricts and the trail climbs steeply, leaving the paddy behind and passing through successive climatic zones: temperate forest, coniferous forest, alpine meadows and finally the arid steppes of the rain shadow. The walk from Chame to **Manang** is spectacular and shouldn't be rushed. The sight of the huge, glacier-dolloped Annapurnas towering almost 5000m above the valley will stay with you forever. Manang's architecture, like that of all the older villages here, is strongly Tibetan; *gompa* at Manang and Braga are well worth visiting. Manang also has an airstrip and a **Himalayan Rescue Association post**, where they give daily talks on AMS. If you're going for the Thorung La, the next night will probably be spent at **Phedi**, a grotty place where you'll be woken up at 4am by trekkers who've been told (wrongly) that they have to clear the pass by 8am. The climb up the pass, and the knee-killing 1600-metre descent down the other side to Muktinath, is a tough but exhilarating day. The remainder of the circuit follows the Jomosom trek (see above).

Other Annapurna treks

Aside from the fact that they share some of the same trails, the following treks have nothing in common with the razzle-dazzle teahouse trails in the Annapurna area. You'll typically find only Nepali food and lodging along these trails, and except for the Pokhara–Trisuli route, you'll need to be equipped to spend nights out and cook for yourself. If you're not trekking with an agency, you'll probably want to go with a **guide**.

Pokhara–Trisuli

The old **POKHARA–TRISULI** trail is little trekked now that it's been superseded by the Prithvi Highway, and that's its chief recommendation. A gentle, low-altitude trek, it wanders through typical hill country and dozens of laid-back ethnic villages, with Annapurna, Manaslu and Ganesh Himal popping up often enough to keep things ticking over scenically. This is the only serious trek that's guaranteed to be snow-free all year, making it a good choice for winter.

The trek can be done in six days, but allow eight or ten; many trekkers start or finish at Gorkha, the midway point, for an easy outing of four to five days. There are any number of ways to get started from Pokhara, but to bypass a lot of road-walking, take a bus to Begnas Tal and take any trail heading east and north towards Besisahar on the Annapurna Circuit – try to go by way of **Ghanpokhara**, a lovely Gurung village – finally reaching **Gorkha** in a minimum of three days (more like five via Ghanpokhara). From there it's another four days or so of undulating between subtropical valleys and scenic ridges to Trisuli, which is linked by road with Kathmandu.

The Siklis trek

An alternative to other short treks in the region, the **SIKLIS TREK** probes an uncrowded corner of the Annapurna Conservation Area under the shadows of Lamjung Himal and Annapurnas II and IV. The main teahouse itinerary takes about a week, starting at Begnas Tal and heading north to the Madi Khola, then following the river's west bank up to well-preserved **Siklis** (1980m), Nepal's biggest Gurung village. From here you strike westwards over the thickly forested ridge that separates the Madi and Seti drainages and then descend via Ghachok, another Gurung settlement, to reach the Pokhara–Baglung Highway. Variations on this route are often touted as the "Royal Trek", after a rally-the-troops swing Prince Charles took through the area in 1980 to visit the villages of Gurkha recruits. As part of an effort to develop this into a model ecotrekking route, ACAP has funded the construction of a small museum and cultural facility in Silkis.

The Dhorpatan circuit

The **DHORPATAN CIRCUIT** breaks away from the lower Kali Gandaki (see p.359) at Beni and wanders westwards up into high, open hill country with commanding views of Dhaulagiri Himal. The trail climbs crosses a tough but beautiful 3400-metre pass and reaches the broad Dhorpatan Valley in about four days, where the attraction isn't the valley itself but the opportunities for exploring the huge **Dhorpatan Hunting Reserve** to its north. In a day, you can get up onto the 4100-metre summit immediately north of the valley for dynamite views; if you're prepared for a few nights out you can continue into the rugged Dhaulagiri area, check out mountaineering base camps and maybe even see some **blue sheep** or **tahr**. Leaving Dhorpatan, two lower, less dramatic routes complete the circuit, one returning to Baglung and the other finishing at Tansen.

Two weeks would be a realistic time frame for Dhorpatan. The circuit is fairly demanding, taking you a long way from conventional tourist places. Lodging is available throughout, but you'll have greater flexibility if you **bring your own equipment**. Anytime between October and April is fine for Dhorpatan, although in winter the high route may be blocked by snow.

Around Manaslu

It takes three weeks to trek **AROUND MANASLU**, a challenging circuit east of the Annapurna area that ventures into extremely remote country and over a 5200-metre pass. Government restrictions on travel in this area mean you need a special trekking permit ($75 per week; $90 in Sept–Nov), plus you must be self-sufficient for a full week of the trip. The trek usually starts in Gorkha, first heading east and then north up the valley of the Budhi Gandaki, finally rounding behind Manaslu (8163m) over the Larkya La (5213m). From there it's two days down to Bagarchap on the Marsyangi River. The rest of the trek follows the Annapurna Circuit in reverse to Besisahar.

Mustang

Since 1991 trekkers have been allowed in limited numbers into **MUSTANG**, the high desert region north of Jomosom that still has its own nominal king. ACAP has taken over the management of the area for tourism purposes, but it's expensive to visit ($700 for ten days). The starting point is Jomosom – groups usually fly in and out – and the trip takes a minimum of ten days, following the Thak Khola north to two walled cities before doubling back on the same trail.

North of Kathmandu: Helambu, Langtang and Gosainkund

Trekking **north of Kathmandu** is curiously underrated and uncrowded. The most accessible of all the trekking regions, it's well suited to one- or two-week itineraries, which is handy if you're trying to cram a trek into a short stay in Nepal or you don't want to stray far from Kathmandu. What it lacks in superlatives – there are no 8000-metre peaks in the vicinity (unless you count Shisha Pangma, across the border in Tibet) – it makes up for in base-to-peak rises that are as dramatic as anywhere. Langtang, in particular, delivers more amazing views in a short time than any other walk-in trek in Nepal, with the possible exception of the Annapurna Sanctuary.

Two distinct basins and an intervening *lek* (ridge) lend their names to the major treks here; each stands on its own, but given enough time and good weather you can mix and match them. **Helambu** is closest to Kathmandu, comprising the rugged north–south valleys and ridges that lie just beyond the northeast rim of the Kathmandu Valley. North of Helambu, running east–west and tantalizingly close to the Tibet border, lies the high, alpine **Langtang Valley**, which in its upper reaches burrows spectacularly between Langtang and Jugal Himals. **Gosainkund** comprises a chain of sacred lakes nestled in a rugged intermediate range northwest of Helambu. One practical inconvenience is that the connections between these three treks aren't reliable – winter snow may block the passes between Helambu and the other two – and done on their own, the Langtang and Gosainkund treks require you to retrace your steps for much of the return journey.

Food and lodging here is less luxurious than in the Annapurna and Everest regions, but never a problem on the usual routes. The area is covered by *Mandala*, *Schneider* and *Nepa* **maps**, all on the scale 1:100,000.

Helambu

HELAMBU (or Helmu) is great for short treks: access from Kathmandu is easy, and an extensive trail network enables you to tailor a circuit to your schedule. The area spans a wide elevation range – there's a lot of up and down – but the highest point reached is only 2700–3200m (depending on route), so acclimatization is rarely a consideration. Winter treks are particularly feasible. The peaks of Langtang Himal are often visible, but the views aren't as close-up as those in other areas. Helambu was once considered a hidden, sacred domain, and its misty ridges and fertile valleys are still comparatively isolated; relatively few people trek here, and with so many trails to choose from, they tend to spread themselves out. Helambu's Bhotiyas call themselves **Sherpa**, although they're only distant cousins of the Solu-Khumbu stock (see p.369): their ancestors probably migrated from Kyirong, the area just north of the Kodari border crossing. Tamangs are also numerous, while the valley bottoms are farmed mainly by Hindu castes.

Sundarijal, a local bus or taxi ride from Kathmandu, is the most common **starting point**, but alternative trailheads include Budhanilkantha, Sankhu,

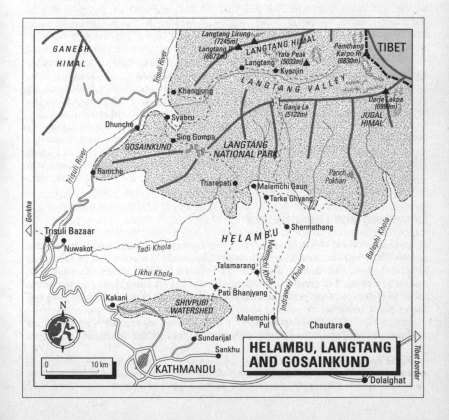

NORTH OF KATHMANDU BUS CONNECTIONS		
To and from Kathmandu	Frequency	Time
Dhunche	2/day	8hr
Malemchi Pul*		
Sundarijal	4/day	1hr
Trisuli	9/day	4hr

* No direct buses: take any bus up the Arniko Highway to Panchkal (3hr), from where buses run to Malemchi Pul (another 2hr).

Kakani, Nagarkot and Malemchi Pul. However you go, first impressions are somewhat dispiriting – the Kathmandu Valley approaches are heavily populated, and the route from Malemchi Pul involves a rather tedious local bus ride from Panchkhal on the Arniko Highway – but things quickly improve as you get up onto the ridges. Entering the region from the Kathmandu Valley takes you through the Shivpuri Watershed (entry fee Rs250). Most trekkers make a loop around two main ridges and the valley of the Malemchi Khola, trying to stay as high as pos-sible and taking in the villages of **Malemchi Gaun**, **Tarke Ghyang** and **Shermathang**. The walk between the second two is especially rewarding, passing picturesque monasteries and contouring through forests of oak, rhododendron and daphne, whose bark is used to make paper. Countless other trails strike west and east to villages that see few trekkers.

Other variations on Helambu are more challenging. Gosainkund can be reached by a long, rugged day's walk from Tharepati, via a 4600-metre pass, but an overnight stop at Gopte or Phedi to acclimatize is advisable. The route to Langtang heads north from Tarke Ghyang over the 5122-metre **Ganja La**, a very tough three-day hike for which you'll need a tent, food, crampons and ice axe (it may be impassable Dec–March). From Tarke Ghyang, lesser trails lead to **Panch Pokhri** (3800m), a set of lakes two or three days to the east, and from there you could continue east or south to the Arniko Highway. All these routes take you into **Langtang National Park** (entry fee Rs650).

Langtang and Gosainkund

In contrast with Helambu, the Langtang and Gosainkund treks make straight for specific destinations, gaining elevation quickly and then leaving you to explore at your own pace. To return, a certain amount of backtracking is unavoidable, unless you cross into Helambu. Culture is not a big part of either, except during Janai Purnima, a massive Hindu **pilgrimage** held at Gosainkund during the full moon of July–August.

Both treks **start** at Dhunche (see p.214), about eight hours by bus from Kathmandu, and fall within **Langtang National Park** (entry fee Rs650).

Langtang
The **LANGTANG TREK** can be done in as little as a week, but day hikes in the upper valley are sure to detain you for at least another two or three days, and

given more time you'll want to add Gosainkund to the itinerary. It takes about a day to get interesting, first following the continuation of the Dhunche road (a spectacularly destructive feat of engineering, built to reach a lead and zinc mine in the Ganesh Himal) up the unpromising valley of the Bhote Kosi before leaving the road and rounding a bend to Syabru in the Langtang Valley. The next two days are spent climbing briskly up the gorge-like lower valley, where oaks and rhododendron give way to peaceful hemlock and larch forest; after ascending an old moraine, snowy peaks suddenly loom ahead and the gorge opens into a U-shaped glacial valley. Springtime is excellent for flowers here, and in autumn the berberis bushes turn a deep rust colour.

Two Bhotiya villages occupy the upper valley: **Langtang** (3300m), the bigger of the two, makes a good place to spend a night and acclimatize, while **Kyangjin** (3750m) boasts a small *gompa*, a cheese "factory" (fabulous yoghurt) and an attractive chalet-lodge. The Langtang Glacier is a full day's walk further up the valley. You'll want to spend at least a couple of nights in the upper valley to explore the glaciers and ascend **Tsergo Ri** (5033m), from which you can view an awesome white wilderness of peaks, including 8013-metre Shisha Pangma.

You can **return** by crossing into Helambu over the Ganja La (see above), but most people go back down the valley, varying the trip by going via Khangjung, high up on the grassy northern side, and Syabrubensi, site of a Tibetan resettlement project. To link up with Gosainkund, you have to backtrack to Syabru.

Gosainkund

GOSAINKUND can be trekked on its own in as little as four days, but because of its rapid ascent to high elevation – 4380m – it's best done after acclimatizing in Langtang or Helambu. Combined with either of these, it adds three or four days; a grand tour of all three areas takes sixteen or more days.

From either Dhunche or Syabru, trails ascend steeply through mossy rhododendron forest to the monastery and cheese factory of **Sing Gompa** at 3250m (the climb from Dhunche is particularly brutal). Above here, the trail climbs through tall fir stands before emerging above the tree line for increasingly panoramic views of the high peaks (Laurebinayak is a great place to stop) and finally entering the barren upper reaches of the Trisuli River, where glacial moraines and rockslides have left a string of half a dozen **lakes** (*kund*). Several lodges sit by the shore of **Gosainkund**, the most sacred of the lakes and renowned among Nepali Hindus. A famous legend recounts how Shiva, having saved the world by drinking a dangerous poison, struck this mountainside with his *trisul* to create the lake and cool his burning throat. In good weather you can climb a nearby summit (5144m) for superb views.

Pilgrims walking to Gosainkund

Everest (Solu-Khumbu)

Everest – or to give it its proper Nepali name, **Sagarmatha** ("Brow of the Ocean"), or its even more proper Sherpa name, **Chomolungma** ("Mother Goddess of the World") – is more a pilgrimage than a trek. As with all pilgrimages, it is a tough personal challenge with a clear goal at the end. Lasting images, however, are of the revelations along the way: remote monasteries, irrepressible Sherpas, and peaks with almost human moods and personalities. Prior experience isn't strictly necessary, but treks in this region require extra effort.

The Everest region is the main trekking destination east of Kathmandu, and in terms of popularity it runs second to Annapurna. It divides into two distinct areas, the lower, greener and more populous country to the south known as **Solu** – if you're not flying in, you'll probably begin at Jiri and spend the first week of your trek walking eastwards across Solu's deep canyons and tall ridges – and **Khumbu**, wedged between Solu and the Tibetan border, comprising the spectacular, harsh landscape of Everest and the surrounding peaks and glaciated valleys.

The challenge of **getting there** puts many people off. The choice is between **flying** into Lukla, at 2800m on the doorstep of Khumbu ($83 from Kathmandu; note the wrecked planes beside the runway), and taking the **bus** to Jiri in Solu (which adds 5–7 days' walking each way). In an ideal world, you would walk in from Jiri to get acclimatized and fly out of Lukla to avoid backtracking, but it

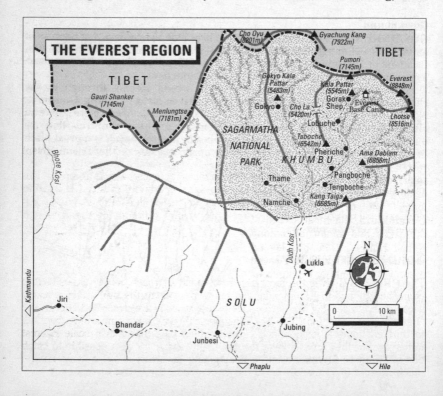

EVEREST REGION TRAVEL CONNECTIONS				
	Buses		Flights	
	Frequency	Time	Frequency	Time
To and from Kathmandu				
Jiri	4/day	11hr		
Lamidanda			3/wk	35min
Lukla			2/day	40min
Phaplu			4/wk	25min

seldom works out that way, as high-season flights may be booked up by organized trekking parties or grounded due to bad weather. Largely for this reason, more than half the people who trek Everest go with a group.

The walking in Solu is very strenuous, while in Khumbu, **altitude** is the overriding factor: to get a good look at Everest, you'll have to spend at least four nights above 4000m and at least one at around 5000m. There is a risk of developing acute mountain sickness (AMS) and you must know the signs. Not only is this the highest of the standard treks, it's also the **coldest**, so you'll need a good four-season bag, several layers of warm clothes, and sturdy boots that will keep out mud and snow. A great help on this front are the rental shops of Namche, in Khumbu, where you can stock up on high-altitude gear and return it on the way back down. Because of weather, the **trekking "window"** is especially short in Khumbu – early October to mid-November, and late March to late April – and this, in turn, creates a seasonal stampede on the trails and at the Lukla airstrip. Winter isn't out of the question, but it's just that much colder.

While Everest isn't as heavily trekked as Annapurna, its high-altitude **environment** is even more fragile. Khumbu, with only four thousand inhabitants, receives more than nine thousand trekkers a year (plus probably twice as many porters); locals spend three times longer collecting firewood than they did a decade ago, and the demand for wood is now estimated to be three times the regeneration capacity of the area. Even some trek leaders privately admit that the best thing for Khumbu would be to give it a rest from trekking for a few years. Most of Khumbu is protected within **Sagarmatha National Park**, which is helping to preserve the remaining forest, but it can't be said often enough: have as little to do with wood-burning as possible.

The popular trails through Solu-Khumbu are all equipped with **teahouses**. The main Jiri–Lukla–Namche–Base Camp route is very straightforward, but a **guide** is advisable if you're planning to do anything unusual. Solu-Khumbu is the easiest area in Nepal to hire a **woman porter** – a Sherpani – although few speak enough English to serve as guides.

Solu: the Jiri walk-in

The **JIRI WALK-IN** is the most popular Everest approach, as Jiri (see p.209) is connected by bus to Kathmandu, and innkeepers along the trail are reasonably accustomed to serving Westerners (other approaches are described later in the "Eastern Nepal" section). The **bus** is no picnic though, taking anywhere from ten to thirteen hours – experienced climbers often joke that they'd scale Everest tomorrow but they'll never take the bus to Jiri again. It's also possible to catch one of the three **flights** a week to Phaplu, four days east of Jiri, though it's not much cheaper ($77) than flying all the way to Lukla, three days further on.

EVEREST

In 1849, while taking routine measurements from the plains, members of the Survey of India logged a previously unnoted summit which they labelled simply Peak XV. Three years later, computations revealed it to be the world's highest mountain, and the British subsequently named it after **Sir George Everest**, head of the Survey of India from 1823 to 1843. Politically off-limits until the early twentieth century, the climb to the summit was first attempted from the Tibetan side in 1922 by a British party that included **George Mallory**, who coined the famous "because it is there" phrase. Two years later, Mallory and Andrew Irvine reached at least 8500m – without oxygen – before disappearing into a cloud; their bodies were never found, but some believe that they reached the summit. Several more attempts were made until World War II suspended activities, and climbs were further hampered by the Chinese invasion of Tibet in 1950, which closed the northern approach to mountaineers.

With the opening of Nepal in 1951, however, attention turned to southern approaches and a race between the Swiss and the British was on. The mountain was finally scaled, using a route via the South Col, by New Zealander **Edmund Hillary** and Sherpa **Tenzing Norgay** in a British-led expedition in 1953. On the morning of May 29, Hillary planted the Union Jack, the Nepalese and United Nations flags on the summit; Tenzing left an offering of sweets and biscuits to the mountain's gods.

Throughout the next two decades, increasingly big expeditions put men and women on the top by various routes, and sometimes got carried away in their bids for lucrative sponsorship – in 1970 a Japanese, **Yuiichi Miura**, skied most of the way down the mountain, breaking a number of bones in the process. Since the mid-1970s the trend has been away from large-scale assaults in favour of small, quick "alpine-style" ascents. Dominating the field for more than a decade, Italian **Reinhold Messner** was one of two climbers to reach the summit without oxygen in 1978, and in 1980 he made the first successful solo ascent of Everest.

Nowadays, new routes on Everest are rare, but other records continue to fall. Frenchman **Marc Batard** achieved the fastest ascent – 22.5 hours – in 1988, following the southeast ridge. In 1995, Briton **Allison Hargreaves** became the first woman to reach the summit without oxygen (tragically, she died on K2 later the same year). Meanwhile, **Ang Rita Sherpa** notched up his ninth successful climb of Everest in 1995 – a record that is likely to stand for a long time to come.

One record that can only be broken is the number of people who have reached the summit. At the time of writing, 615 climbers had successfully ascended Everest, and with "commercial" Everest expeditions opening up the mountain to less experienced climbers (who pay upwards of $40,000 for a place) the number is rising rapidly. So, too, is Everest's death toll. In May 1996, eight mountaineers died when they were caught in a sudden blizzard, bringing the total number of people who have died on Everest to 142. The bodies of nearly 100 of those lost remain on the mountain, buried under ice and snow.

Cutting across the lay of the land, the trail bobs between valleys as low as 1500m and passes as high as 3500m: the ups and downs can be disheartening, but the fitness and acclimatization gained come in handy later on. A few glimpses of peaks – notably Gauri Shankar (7145m) – urge you along during the first five or six days, although Solu's lasting images are of tumbling gorges, rhododendron forests and terraced fields hewn out of steep hillsides. Solu has benefited from

THE SHERPAS

Nepal's most famous ethnic group, the **Sherpas** probably migrated to Solu-Khumbu four or five centuries ago from eastern Tibet; their name means "People from the East". They were originally nomads, driving their yaks to pasture in Tibet and wintering in Nepal, until change came from an unlikely quarter: the introduction of the potato in the 1830s is believed to have been the catalyst that caused Sherpas to settle in villages, and the extra wealth brought by this simple innovation financed the building of most monasteries visible today.

Sherpas maintain the highest permanent settlements in the world – up to 4700m – which accounts for their legendary hardiness at altitude. Their mountaineering talents were discovered as early as 1907, and by the 1920s hundreds of Sherpas were signing on as **porters** with expeditions to Everest and other Himalayan peaks – from the Tibet side, ironically, as Nepal was closed to foreigners at the time. When mountaineering expeditions were finally allowed into Nepal in 1949, Sherpas took over the lion's share of the portering work, and four years later **Tenzing Norgay** reached the top of Everest, clinching Sherpas' worldwide fame. The break couldn't have come at a better time, for trans-Himalayan trade, once an important source of income, was cut short by the Chinese occupation of Tibet in 1959. Since then, Sherpas have deftly diversified into tourism, starting their own trekking and mountaineering agencies, opening lodges and selling souvenirs. Conveniently, the trekking season doesn't conflict with summer farming duties.

Like Tibetans and other Bhotiya groups, Sherpas are devout Buddhists, and most villages of note support a *gompa* and a few monks (or nuns). But in a throwback to animism that's perfectly permissible in Lamaist Buddhism, they revere **Khumbila**, a sacred peak just north of Namche, as a sort of tribal totem, and regard fire as a deity (it's disrespectful to throw rubbish into a Sherpa hearth). Sherpas eat meat, of course, but in deference to the *dharma* they draw the line at slaughtering it – they hire Tibetans to do that.

several projects funded by **Edmund Hillary's Himalayan Trust**; groups of children may accompany you on their way to one of the "Hillary" schools in the area.

The route passes through some important Sherpa villages, notably **Bhandar** and **Junbesi**, the latter with an active monastery. Most trekkers are understandably impatient to get up to Everest or back to Kathmandu, but side trips to the cheese "factory" at **Thodung** and **Thubten Chholing Gompa** north of Junbesi are fascinating. From **Jubing**, a Rai village five days in, the trail finally bends north towards Everest, following the valley of the Dudh Kosi. Two days later, it sidesteps **Lukla** and joins the well-trodden route to Khumbu.

The bulk of traffic through Solu consists of porters humping in gear for trekking groups and expeditions flying into Lukla, and this is reflected in the no-frills **food and lodging** available. Solu is covered by the *Mandala* "Lamosangu to Mount Everest" **map** (1:110,000), though *Schneider*'s "Tamba Kosi" and "Shorong/Hinku" (both 1:50,000) show the route in greater detail.

Khumbu: the Everest trek

The trail north from Lukla is the trunk route of the **EVEREST TREK**: everyone walks it at least once, and all but a few backtrack along it as well. Most trekkers

follow it to the end at Kala Pattar
(the classic viewpoint of Everest)
and Everest Base Camp, both
about eight days northeast of
Lukla; quite a few combine this
with a trip to the beautiful Gokyo
Lakes, about the same distance
north of Lukla.

Khumbu **lodges** are heavily
geared for trekkers, and you
should have no trouble getting a
bunk and a good meal wherever
you go along the busier trails.
Prices aren't unreasonable,
considering the distance supplies
have to be carried, but they do
rise steadily as you go up. An additional expense is the Rs650 entry
fee for **Sagarmatha National
Park**.

Namche bazaar

Khumbu is well **mapped**. By far the best for the area north from Namche is
Schneider's "Khumbu Himal" (1:50,000), while *Mandala*'s "Khumbu Himal"
(1:50,000) covers the route from Lukla north. An even more detailed map of the
immediate Everest area, originally created for *National Geographic* and now
reprinted, is available in some Kathmandu bookshops.

Lukla to Everest Base Camp and Kala Pattar

From Lukla the trail meanders north along the Dudh Kosi before bounding up to
Namche (3450m), where Khumbu and the serious scenery start. Nestled handsomely in a horseshoe bowl, the Sherpa "capital" has done very well out of mountaineering and trekking over the years. Besides trekking equipment, Namche's shops
sell absolutely anything a trekker could desire – film, maps, batteries, Mars bars
from around the world, a dozen styles of Swiss Army knife, albeit all at inflated
prices. There's also a bank and post office. Most lodges have electricity and some
even have microwaves. Try to make your trip coincide with the pan-cultural
Saturday market, or visit the national park **visitors' centre**, perched on the ridge
east of town, which contains an informative museum.

Beyond Namche, the trail veers northeast into a tributary valley and climbs to
Tengboche, surrounded by protected juniper forest and commanding a show-
stealing view of everybody's favourite peak, Ama Dablam (6828m). Tengboche's
much-photographed monastery, which burned down in 1989 when its newly
installed electrical wiring malfunctioned (is there a lesson in this?), has now been
rebuilt. Mani Rimdu, the Sherpa dance-drama **festival**, is held here on the full
moon of November–December. The trail continues to **Pangboche**, containing
Khumbu's oldest *gompa*, where for a donation the lama will show you some yeti
relics, and on to **Pheriche** (4250m), site of a **Himalayan Rescue Association
post** (AMS talks every afternoon during the trekking season). From here up,
settlements are strictly seasonal, and their stone enclosures and slate-roofed huts
are reminiscent of Scottish crofts.

From Pheriche the route bends north again, ascending the moraine of the Khumbu Glacier and passing a series of monuments to Sherpas killed on Everest, to reach **Lobuche** (4930m). Another day's march along the glacier's lateral moraine brings you to **Gorak Shep** (5180m), the last huddle of teahouses – and a cold, probably sleepless night. The payoff comes when you climb up the grassy mound of **Kala Pattar** (5545m): the extra height provides an unbelievable panorama, not only of **Everest** (8848m) but also of its neighbours Lhotse (Nepal's third-highest peak, at 8516m) and Nuptse (7861m), as well as the sugarloaf of Pumori (7165m). A separate day trip can be made across the amazing Khumbu Glacier to **Everest Base Camp**. You may encounter a half-dozen or more expedition parties here, constantly ferrying supplies up the dangerous Khumbu Icefall to higher camps; the climbers may be happy to have well-wishers, but if they seem wary of trekkers you can't blame them.

Gokyo Lakes

The scenery is every bit as good at **Gokyo Lakes**, in the next valley to the west, and other trekkers are noticeably fewer. If you're equipped to spend a night out in a yak-herder's hut and are good at route-finding (the *Schneider* map will help), you can be there in two days from Gorak Shep, crossing the strenuous **Cho La** (5420m) west of Lobuche and descending a treacherous scree slope. Otherwise, you'll have to backtrack almost to Tengboche, and then follow the Dudh Kosi north for two days to Gokyo, set beside the immense Ngozumba Glacier (the biggest in Nepal). Several brilliant blue lakes, dammed up by the glacier's lateral moraine, dot the west side of the valley above and below Gokyo. The high point of Gokyo is an overlook called, again, **Kala Pattar**, surveying a clutter of blue teeth – Cho Oyu, Everest and Lhotse are just the ones over 8000m – and the long grey tongue of the Ngozumba Glacier. You can also scramble north beside the glacier as far as Cho Oyu Base Camp.

Eastern Nepal

Treks in **eastern Nepal** are hampered by a fundamental problem of access: Hile, the principal trailhead, is a 21-hour bus journey from Kathmandu. However, it's possible to enter (or leave) this region by way of Everest, which cuts out the long ride in one direction. Flights are also good value for money here – the one from Kathmandu to Tumlingtar costs only $44. **Food and lodging** is patchy, though, and seldom geared for trekkers.

You're supposed to have a white "mixed-area" **permit** to trek in this region, but no one is going to hassle you if you've got an Everest permit and you're just passing through on your way down. The only trekking **map** of the area is the *Mandala* "Dhankuta to Kanchenjunga, Mt Everest, Makalu & Arun Valley" (1:192,500).

Ethnically, eastern Nepal is even more diverse than the Annapurna region: Rais and Limbus are dominant in the hills, Gurungs and Magars are found in smaller numbers, while Sherpas, Tamangs and other Bhotiyas inhabit the high country and Hindu castes the valleys. Makalu and Kanchenjunga provide stunning **views** from most high points. Flora and fauna are also of great interest to specialists, especially the **butterflies** and other insects of the upper Arun Valley, and the **rhododendrons** of the Milke Danda.

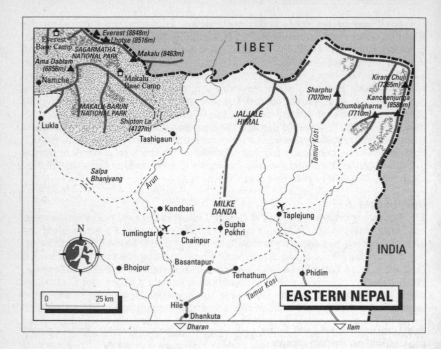

The Everest eastern approach

While still not nearly as developed as the Jiri walk-in, the **EASTERN APPROACH** to Everest is becoming more popular and facilities along it are expanding yearly. It's usually treated as an "escape route" from Everest by trekkers who want to avoid the long backtrack to Jiri; there's no reason why the itinerary can't be done in reverse, except perhaps that it's better to gain some confidence on the more developed Everest trails before tackling this less-trekked region. Another factor to consider is the **season**: try to do the lower section of the trek when it's cooler.

The **route** leaves the Jiri walk-in at **Kharte**, about a day south of Lukla, and heads southeastwards to reach Tumlingtar five to seven days later. Part of this stretch traverses the Makalu-Barun Conservation Area (see below), and an entrance fee may be required. The first half of the trek passes through tangled hills inhabited mainly by Rais; after reaching a high point at the lush Salpa Bhanjyang (3350m), it descends steadily to the deep, hot and predominantly Hindu Arun Valley. **Tumlingtar** is a busy bazaar overlooking the Arun; *RNAC* flies from there to Kathmandu about four times a week ($44). If you're returning to Kathmandu by bus, carry on to Hile (see p.333), two days south and 1400m higher. The route is equipped with **teahouses** and a guide isn't needed, but don't expect English signs or fancy food. You'd be wise to bring a few provisions just in case.

For more adventure, you could carry on walking from Tumlingtar **to Phidim** (see p.337) by way of Chainpur, a tidy village renowned for its brassware, and the Milke Danda (see below). Another route aims roughly due south from Lukla **to Lamindanda** (three times a week to Kathmandu; $66). If you can't get on a flight

THE YETI

The **yeti** ("man of the rocky places") has been a staple of Sherpa and Tibetan folklore for centuries, but stories of hairy, ape-like creatures roaming the snowy heights first came to the attention of the outside world during the early days of British rule in India. Explorers in Tibet reported seeing mysterious moving figures and large, unidentified footprints in the snow – captivated by the reports, an imaginative Fleet Street hack coined the term "abominable snowman" – but it wasn't until 1951, during the first British Everest expedition from the Nepal side, that climber Eric Shipton took clear photographs of yeti tracks. Since then, several highly publicized yeti-hunts, including one led by Sir Edmund Hillary in 1960, have brought back a wealth of circumstantial evidence but not one authenticated sighting.

Sceptics dismiss the yeti as a straightforward myth, of course, arguing that the hairy creatures in question are more likely bears, and that the oversized footprints could be any animal's tracks, melted and enlarged by the sun. Meanwhile, relics kept at the *gompa* of Pangboche and Khumjung have failed to provide scientific proof of the yeti's existence. The "skulls" have been examined by experts and deemed to be made of serow (Himalayan wild goat) skins, while the skeletal hand at Pangboche is presumed to be human. Yet yaks continue to be mauled, and Sherpas insist the yeti isn't a hoax. Perhaps the most significant aspect of the yeti is humans' reaction to it: we want it to exist, like the Loch Ness Monster – some secret part of the world that mankind hasn't yet discovered and explained – yet in our endless curiosity we want to find and dissect it. Thankfully, it has eluded us so far.

there, trails continue south to the Tarai or east to Hile via Bhojpur, Nepal's most famous *khukuri*-making centre.

Other treks in eastern Nepal

Many hill treks north of Hile and Ilam are probably feasible without supplies. Development workers in the area rave about a circuit from Phidim to Basantapur via Taplejung. Bhojpur, Chainpur and Khadbari, quintessential Newar hill towns within two or three days' walk of Hile, also make great targets. This is fine country for adventurous trekkers who like exploring places that aren't written up in guidebooks, and this book isn't going to spoil that pleasure by writing about them.

However, here are three more conventional treks which, though they would be difficult to do independently, are finding their way into agency brochures.

The Milke Danda

A long north–south ridge famed for its rhododendrons, the **MILKE DANDA** can be linked up with a visit to Chainpur for a seven- to ten-day trek that combines spectacular flora with one of Nepal's best bazaars. The route goes no higher than 3500m, but takes in plenty of mountain views. From Basantapur (see p.334) the route heads north, initially following the main porter trail to Taplejung and then continuing north through the lush cloud forest of the Milke Danda. Various trails to **Chainpur** branch off to the east; from there you can continue to the airstrip at Tumlingtar ($44 to Kathmandu) or return to Hile.

Basic **food** and **lodging** can be found along most of this route, but the absence of teahouses north of Gupha Pokhri limits an independent trekker's ability to explore the Milke Danda. Groups with porter support can continue north into the Jaljale Himal.

EASTERN NEPAL TRAVEL CONNECTIONS

To and from Kathmandu	Buses		Flights	
	Frequency	Time	Frequency	Time
Basantapur	*			
Bhojpur			2/wk	45min
Hile	2/night	21hr		
Ilam/Phidim	**			
Taplejung			5/wk	2hr#
Tumlingtar			3–4/wk	55min

* No direct buses: change at Dharan or Hile.
** No direct buses: change at Birtamod.
# Via Biratnagar.

Makalu Base Camp

MAKALU BASE CAMP, a three-week trek from Hile up the Arun Valley and over the Shipton La (4127m), requires a tent and food for ten days; the last teahouse is at Tashi Gaun, less than a day beyond where the trail leaves the Arun. Much of this trek passes through the wild and remote **Makalu-Barun National Park** and the contiguous **Makalu-Barun Conservation Area**, which forms a protective buffer zone in the inhabited area to the south and east. Established in 1992, the park is intended to stem the growing human pressure around the base-camp area and preserve what is regarded as one of the most biologically diverse areas in the Himalaya. The conservation area, meanwhile, is supposed to be modelled on the Annapurna Conservation Area Project and operate on similar principles of involving locals in conservation.

Kanchenjunga

The most incredible trek in this part of Nepal is to the foot of **KANCHENJUNGA**, at 8586m the third-highest peak in the world. Because of its remote location in the extreme northeastern corner of the country, Kanchenjunga is an expensive trek. Most groups fly in and out of Taplejung ($110 from Kathmandu), which requires a plane change in Biratnagar. To save money and take in some pretty hill country, you could walk to Taplejung from Basantapur (see p.334) in three days, but you'd still have to have a couple of porters toting two weeks' worth of supplies. Two separate routes head northeastwards from Taplejung, one to the so-called North Base Camp and Pang Pema, the other to the South Base Camp and the Yalung Glacier; these routes can be combined into a circuit.

Far western Nepal

West of Dhaulagiri, the Himalaya subside somewhat and retreat north into Tibet, and the band of foothills flares out to become an almost impenetrable jumble. The northern third of the region, left in the rain shadow of the foothills, receives little monsoon moisture – in every way but politically, this highland strip is part of Tibet. Jagged Himalayan grandeur isn't so much in evidence, but there's a wildness and a vastness here, and the feeling of isolation is thrilling. The **far west** is the deep end of trekking in Nepal, and the treks here are well off the beaten track: they're a chore to get to, they require a lot of preparation and, with the exception of Rara Lake, you'll find that very few Westerners have gone before you. All that might appeal if you're an experienced trekker looking for new challenges, but if you're a first-timer, forget it.

Logistics make or break a trek in the far west. Given the distances involved, you'll need to fly to the starting point, but **flights** from Kathmandu are few and often delayed. Connections from Nepalganj are more frequent and considerably cheaper, though no more reliable, and Nepalganj isn't a great place to be stuck waiting for a plane. **Food and lodging** are in uncomfortably short supply, so you'll need to bring a tent, cooking utensils and at least some provisions. You should be prepared to carry it all yourself, because **porters** here are a fickle lot and often can't be spared from their farmwork. **Guides** are also scarce, so you shouldn't venture out without a reasonable command of Nepali. If you go on an **organized trek** you may not be entirely insulated from these inconveniences, and for this reason agencies will probably try to steer you towards more easterly destinations.

As roads gradually penetrate into the far west, trekking might become easier. In the meantime, the four treks described below are the most realistic possibilities. Three require a white "mixed area" **permit**; the fourth, Dolpo, requires a special permit. For **maps**, see the *Mandala* "Jumla to Api & Saipal Himal" and "Jomosom to Jumla & Surkhet" (both 1:250,000).

Rara National Park

RARA NATIONAL PARK is the best known – and for the non-specialist, probably the least daunting – of the far western treks. The usual itinerary is a loop that starts and ends at Jumla, 150km north of Nepalganj, and takes about ten days.

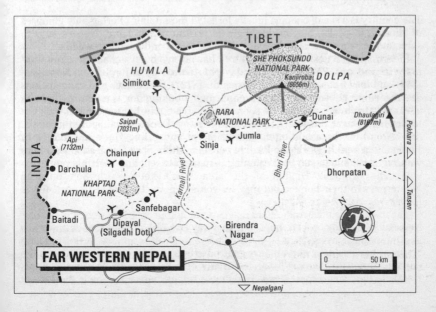

FAR WESTERN TRAVEL CONNECTIONS

	Buses		Flights	
	Frequency	Time	Frequency	Time
To and from POKHARA				
Bajhang			3/wk	*
Bajura			3/wk	*
Birendra Nagar (Surkhet)	**			
Dolpo (Dunai)			1/wk	40min
Jumla			1–3/day	*
Sanfebagar			1/day	*
Silgadhi Doti (Dipayal)	#		2/wk	*
Simikot			5–7/wk	*
To and from KATHMANDU				
Bajhang			3/wk	*
Bajura			3/wk	*
Birendra Nagar (Surkhet)	**			
Dolpo (Dunai)			5/wk	*
Jumla			1–2/wk	1hr 15min
Sanfebagar			1/day	*
Silgadhi Doti (Dipayal)	#		2/wk	*
Simikot			5–7/wk	*

* Indirect flight: total travel time will vary considerably due to stopover in Nepalganj (or Pokhara, in the case of Dolpo).
** No direct buses: change at Nepalganj.
\# No direct buses: change at Dhangadhi.

The country is a sea of choppy, mostly forested mountains, offering only glimpses of Himalayan peaks, but the highlight is pristine **Rara Lake**, Nepal's largest, surrounded by a wilderness area of meadows, forest and abundant wildlife.

In terms of practicalities, the Rara trek has always been a challenge. You want to **fly in and out**. *RNAC, Everest* and *Nepal Airways* fly to Jumla from Nepalganj ($44) and less frequently from Kathmandu ($127), but delays and cancellations are the rule and you can't get a confirmed booking for the return flight in advance – try to arrange this as soon as you arrive, but be prepared to walk out to Birendra Nagar (Surkhet), a week's hike away. **Food** can be bought in Jumla, but beyond the bazaar is often unavailable at any price. There are **lodges** in Jumla and a bunkhouse at the lake; in between, there are a few teahouses where you might be able to stay, but camping is more pleasant and certainly more reliable. The orthodox Hindus of the area aren't keen on having outcaste Westerners in their homes, but may let you sleep on the roof. The **park fee** is Rs650.

Technical difficulties aside, Rara makes a fair compromise between the popular treks and the really obscure ones, and in a way combines the best of both worlds: like the popular treks, Rara is given detailed route descriptions in the trekking books so you can do it without an organized group or even a guide, yet it's remote enough to ensure that you'll see few if any other foreigners. Starting at Jumla (2400m), the route crosses two 3500-metre ridges before reaching the lake at

3000m. The park is one of the best places in Nepal to see mountain **wildlife**, including Himalayan black bear, tahr, goral, musk deer and the rare red (lesser) panda. Autumn and spring are the **best seasons**, and Rara is particularly worth considering in May and June, when the weather elsewhere is getting too hot or unpredictable. Winter flights are unreliable – a pity, since the far northwest offers the best potential skiing in the country. A day and a half south of the lake is **Sinja**, where the ruins of the capital of the twelfth- to fourteenth-century Khasa dynasty (see "The Historical Framework" in *Contexts*) can be viewed across the river.

Dolpo (She-Phoksundo National Park)

DOLPO (sometimes written Dolpa) is an enormous, isolated district northwest of Dhaulagiri and bordering Tibet, the western half of which has been set aside as **SHE-PHOKSUNDO NATIONAL PARK**, Nepal's biggest. The park, established in 1984, protects an awe-inspiring region of deep valleys, unclimbed peaks, remote monasteries and rare fauna. Dolpo was the setting of Peter Matthiessen's *The Snow Leopard* (see "Books" in *Contexts*), and until recently the book was as close as most foreigners were allowed to get to it. Southern ("Lower") Dolpo is now open to independent trekkers, but it's a food-deficit area, so you will need to be self-sufficient. (Northern, or "Upper", Dolpo is also open, but much more expensive – $700 for a ten-day permit.) Guides and porters, pretty well essential here, can be hired in Dunai. The climate is continental and only slightly affected by the monsoon, so the **best time to go** is May to September.

Dolpo lies between Dhorpatan and Rara, and two of these treks, or even all three, could be combined into a single tour from Pokhara to Jumla – but this would take a minimum of four weeks. Dolpo on its own takes one to two weeks, assuming you fly in and out of **Dunai** ($77 each way from Nepalganj). Everyone heads north from there, entering the park after about a day (Rs650 **entry fee**) and reaching Ringmo and the stunningly blue **Phoksundo Tal** after another two days. There are plenty of day-hiking opportunities around the lake. From there you can retrace your route to Dunai or, given an extra week, take a much longer, harder route westwards over the Kagmara La (5114m), returning eastwards over the Balangra La (3837m).

Other treks in far western Nepal

These last two treks are so out of the way that even trekking agencies don't touch them, and they haven't yet been described in any trekking guidebook. They're only recommended for experienced trekkers, though either one can be done independently with only a couple of days' worth of supplies.

Humla

Tucked away in the extreme northwest corner of Nepal, **HUMLA** is high, dry and strongly Tibetan. Rounded, snowcapped peaks hem the district in on three sides and shut out most outside influences, including the monsoon. Trekking facilities are nonexistent, but the Buddhist highlanders are more accommodating to strangers than the caste-conscious Hindus further south.

RNAC **flies** from Nepalganj to **Simikot** (Humla's district headquarters) most days of the week ($88). From there it's seven to nine days to Jumla, stopping at Rara Lake along the way. Doing it vice versa – going towards the mountains – would seem more natural, but bear in mind that Jumla is easier to get out of than Simikot. The trail involves a good deal of up and down, but goes no higher than 3600m. In May–June, which is the **best time** to go, the wildflowers are out of this world. Most of the country north and east of the route is out of bounds to foreigners, which knocks out a few tempting side trips, but one allowable exception is **Raling Gompa**, the most sacred of Humla's many Buddhist monasteries, a tough, full-day's climb north of Simikot.

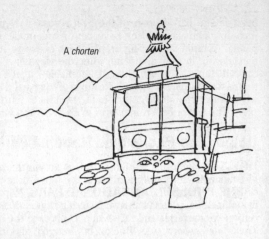

A *chorten*

Some companies now run treks from Simikot to sacred Mount Kailas and Lake Manosarovar in **Tibet**, about three days' walking via the 4600-metre Nara La.

Khaptad National Park

Set on a plateau in the middle of the foothills, **KHAPTAD NATIONAL PARK** is, for lack of a better term, a spiritual park. A five-square-kilometre core area has been set aside for "meditation and tranquility", comprising a pilgrimage spot of Hindu shrines and sacred streams. The centrepiece of the park, literally, is the Khaptad Baba, a famous holy man in the grand old mountaintop-guru tradition.

Two year-round **airstrips** – at Silgadhidoti ($66 from Nepalganj) and Sanfebagar ($61 from Nepalganj) – are within one or two days' walk of the park, making it possible to do this trek in as little as a week. **Food and lodging** are available at the airstrip towns, the southern park entrance and the park HQ. The food is poor and you'll want to bring as much of your own as possible, but you should be able to get by without a porter. The park **entry fee** is Rs650.

Hovering at about 3000m, the **central plateau** consists of rolling, open grassland and forest, with views of Saipal (7031m) and Api (7132m), the far west's tallest peaks. The attractions of the plateau are a sacred confluence, site of the Ganga Deshara **festival** in May–June, and the Baba's hut. Numerous tales surround the **Khaptad Baba**, all impossible to substantiate because he declines to answer questions about himself. His followers swear he's over 100 years old (he doesn't look it) and that he used to be a doctor in Kashmir before moving up to Khaptad forty years ago to meditate. He speaks excellent English and, hardest to explain, always seems mysteriously well informed about any subject, however esoteric. A surprising cross-section of the Nepalese intelligentsia follows the Baba, and even the king has been known to fly in for consultation; no doubt thanks to his pull with HM, the Baba won a long campaign to establish Khaptad as a national park in 1985.

PART THREE

THE
CONTEXTS

THE HISTORICAL FRAMEWORK

For a tiny Himalayan backwater, Nepal has played a surprisingly pivotal role in Asian history. In its early days it reared the Buddha and hosted the great Indian emperor Ashoka; much later, its remarkable conquests led it into wars with Tibet and Britain, and during the past three decades it has come to be regarded as a vital buffer state by both India and China. Its name and recorded history go back nearly 3000 years, although it has existed as a nation for barely 200: before 1769, "Nepal" referred only to a kingdom based in the Kathmandu Valley.

BEGINNINGS

Neolithic tools found in the Kathmandu Valley indicate that humans have inhabited parts of Nepal for tens of thousands of years – and the fact that the shrines of Swayambhu and Changu Narayan are located on hill tops suggests that ancient animists may have lived and worshipped there as much as 200,000 years ago, while the valley floor was submerged under a primordial lake. The Newar creation myth, which tells of the *bodhisattva* Manjushri releasing the waters and establishing Swayambhu, perhaps preserves a dim racial memory of that prehistoric era.

Nepal's early semi-mythological genealogies aren't borne out by any archeological evidence, but at some points they tally with other sources. The **Kirata** (or Kiranti) tribe pops up in several Hindu texts – and even in Ptolemy – although the term might well have applied to all hill people in the first millennium BC. Significantly, the Kirata were often described as a warlike people known for carrying deadly knives. Whoever they were, by the sixth or seventh century BC the Kirata appear to have divided into two distinct groups, one controlling the eastern hills and the other the Kathmandu Valley.

Hindus were by this time encroaching on the less malarial parts of the Tarai and founding the citystates of **Mithila** (modern Janakpur), the scene of many of the events in the *Ramayan* epic, and **Kapilvastu** (now Tilaurakot), where the Buddha spent his pre-enlightenment years during the sixth century BC. North India was unified under the **Mauryan empire** (321–184 BC), whose most famous ruler, Ashoka, was responsible for spreading Buddhism throughout the subcontinent, including Nepal. Following the fall of Maurya, north India was again divided among a number of states and Hinduism began a slow but inexorable comeback in the Tarai.

EARLY DYNASTIES

Nepal's history comes into sharper focus with the arrival of the **Lichhavis**, a north Indian clan who overthrew the Kiratas around 200 AD and established their capital at Deopatan (modern Pashupatinath). Exploiting Nepal's position as a trading entrepôt between India and Tibet, the Lichhavis founded a strong, stable and culturally sophisticated dynasty. No buildings from the period survive, but contemporary accounts by Chinese travellers describe "multi-storeyed temples so tall one would take them for a crown of clouds" – perhaps a reference to the pagoda style that was to become a Nepali trademark. Under Lichhavi sponsorship, artisans ushered in a classical age of stone sculpture and produced Nepal's most acclaimed pieces, many of which still casually litter the Kathmandu Valley. Although Hindus, the Lichhavis endowed both Hindu and Buddhist temples – Pashupatinath and Swayambhu were built, or at least expanded, during their rule – and established a policy of religious tolerance that has been maintained to the present day.

Much of what we know about the Lichhavis comes from a handful of stone inscriptions whose authors were probably more intent on self-praise than historical accuracy. The earliest inscription, dated 464 AD and still on view at Changu Narayan, extols **Manadeva**, the legendary builder of the Boudha stupa. The greatest of the Lichhavi line, **Amsuvarman** (605–621) is said to have composed the first Sanskrit grammar and built a splendid palace believed to have been located at present-day Naksal in Kathmandu. "Down to the reign of this monarch the gods showed themselves plainly in bodily shape," intone the Nepalese chronicles, "but after this they became invisible." By this time Nepal had become a vassal of Tibet, and Amsuvarman's daughter Bhrikuti, who was carried off by the Tibetan king, is popularly credited with introducing Buddhism to Tibet.

The Lichhavi era came to a close in 879, and the three centuries that followed are sometimes referred to as Nepal's "Dark Ages". The Nepalese chronicles record a long list of **Thakuri kings**, although the title was probably a Hindu honorific and not the name of an hereditary dynasty; these kings may well have been puppets installed by one or more of the powers controlling the Tarai at the time. Nonetheless, learning and the arts continued to thrive, and from the eleventh century onwards the valley became an important centre of tantric studies (see "Religion", p.388).

THE KHASAS AND MALLAS

While the Thakuris were ruling central Nepal, yet another Hindu clan, the **Khasas**, were migrating up from the plains and carving out a small fiefdom in western Tibet. In the early twelfth century a Khasa king, Nagaraja, moved his capital down to Sinja in the Karnali basin and established a powerful dynasty which at its height controlled a broad sector of the Himalaya from Kashmir to present-day Pokhara. The history of the Khasas is little understood, for they left few written records and only minor ruins at Sinja (now Hatsinja) and Dullu, south of Jumla.

Nepal entered a new and much better documented period of its history when the Thakuri king of Bhaktapur, Arideva, took the title **Malla**, probably in the year 1200. Malla was, in fact, a popular form of royal address in India at the time – the Khasa kings also called themselves Mallas – but the name has come to be associated with at least three separate dynasties, lasting more than five centuries, that presided over the renaissance of Nepali culture during which most of the temples and palaces still on display in the Kathmandu Valley were built.

The early Malla era was marked by great instability: the Khasas mounted several raids on the valley, although they were never able to gain a ruling foothold, and in 1349 Muslims swept up from Bengal and pillaged both Hindu and Buddhist holy sites in a brief spree of destruction and violence. Despite these disruptions, trade flourished, many of the valley's smaller cities were founded, and Arniko, the great Nepali architect, was dispatched to the Ming court to instruct the Chinese in the art of building pagodas. **Jayasthiti Malla** (1354–95) inaugurated a period of strong central rule from Bhaktapur, but his most lasting contribution was to dragoon his Buddhist subjects into the Hindu hierarchy by dividing them into 64 occupational castes – a system which remained enshrined in Nepali law until 1964. Malla power reached its zenith under **Yaksha Malla** (1428–82), who extended his domain westwards to Gorkha and eastwards as far as present-day Biratnagar. Upon his death, the kingdom was divided among three sons, and for nearly three centuries the independent city states of Kathmandu, Patan and Bhaktapur (and occasionally others) feuded over lucrative trade arrangements with Tibet. Judging by the opulent durbars built during this period, there must have been enough to go around, and the intense rivalry seems to have been good for both art and business.

The Khasa kings didn't fare so well, and by the late fourteenth century their empire had fragmented into a collection of petty provinces. The Muslim conquest of north India during the early part of the century figured indirectly in Khasa's downfall: a steady stream of princes from Rajasthan, which had borne the brunt of the invasion, limped into the Khasa hills in search of consolation prizes, and rapidly wheedled their way into positions of power. Those who took the reins of the Khasa provinces came to be known as the **Baaisi Raja**

(Twenty-two Princes), while others who subjugated Magar and Gurung states to the east became the **Chaubisi** (Twenty-four).

UNIFICATION

For three centuries the Chaubisi and Baaisi confederacies were able to maintain an uneasy status quo, forming numerous defensive alliances to ensure that no one state could gain control over the rest. Divided, they were small, weak and culturally backward. **Gorkha**, the most easterly territory, was no different from the rest, except that it was that much closer to the Kathmandu Valley and that much more jealous of the Mallas' wealth. Under the inspired, obsessive leadership of **Prithvi Narayan Shah** (1722–75), Gorkha launched a campaign that was to take 27 years to conquer the valley, and as long again to unite all of modern Nepal.

At the time of Prithvi Narayan's rise to the throne, in 1743, rivalry between the three Malla kings had reached an all-time high. Still, Gorkha wasn't nearly strong enough to invade Nepal outright; Prithvi Narayan first captured Nuwakot, a day's march northwest of Kathmandu, and from there directed a ruthless twenty-year **war of attrition**. By 1764 he was able to enforce a total blockade, starving the valley and at the same time replenishing Gorkha's coffers with Tibetan trade. Kirtipur was targeted for the first major battle, and surrendered after a six-month siege. Answering a plea from the Kathmandu king, Jaya Prakash Malla, the East India Company sent in 2400 soldiers against the Gorkhalis, who proceeded to cut them to shreds; only 800 returned. On the eve of Indra Jaatra in 1768, Jaya Prakash, by now rumoured to be insane, let down the city's defences and **Kathmandu fell** to the Gorkhalis without a fight. They took Patan two days later, and Bhaktapur the following year, and by 1774 had marched eastwards all the way to Sikkim.

Suspicious of Britain's growing influence in India, Prithvi Narayan adopted a closed-door policy that was to remain in force until the 1950s. Missionaries were thrown out forthwith: "First the bible, then the trading station, then the cannon," he warned. The bloody **battle for succession** that followed Prithvi Narayan's death set the pattern for

Nepali politics well into the twentieth century. Yet when they weren't stabbing each other in the back, his successors managed to subdue Gorkha's old Chaubisi and Baaisi rivals in the west, so that by 1790 Nepal stretched far beyond its present eastern and western borders. Lured on by promises of land grants – every hillman's dream – the Nepali army became a seemingly unstoppable fighting machine, with Kashmir in its sights.

Westward progress was interrupted, however, by a brief but chastening **war with Tibet**. Troubles had been brewing for some time over trade relations, and the Tibetans were growing alarmed by Nepal's encroachments on their ally, Sikkim. In 1788 and again in 1791, Nepal invaded, plundered a few monasteries and exacted tribute from Tibet, but in 1792 the Tibetans launched a counterattack, penetrating as far as Nuwakot and forcing Nepal to accept harsh terms.

Nepal's further adventures in the west brought it into increasing **conflict with Britain**'s East India Company, which by now controlled India, and open hostilities broke out in 1814 when Nepal annexed the Butwal sector of the Tarai. For the British, the dispute provided a perfect pretext to "open up" Nepal, which had been so tantalizingly closed to them, and thus to muscle in on trade with Tibet. Britain attacked with a force of 50,000 men against Nepal's 12,000, expecting an easy victory; in the event it took two years and heavy losses before Nepal was finally brought to heel. The **Treaty of Segauli** forced Nepal to accept its present eastern and western boundaries and surrender much of the Tarai, and worst of all, to admit an official British "resident" in Kathmandu. Yet so impressed were the British by "our valiant opponent" – as a plaque at an Indian battle site still proclaims – that they began recruiting Nepalis into the Indian Army before the treaty had even been signed. These companies formed the basis for the famed **Gurkha regiments** (see p.250). Britain restored Nepal's Tarai lands in return for its help in quelling the Indian Mutiny of 1857.

THE RANA YEARS

The Kathmandu court was practically paralysed by intrigue and assassinations during the first half of the nineteenth century, culminating in the ghastly **Kot massacre** of 1846, in which more than fifty courtiers were butchered in a courtyard off Kathmandu's Durbar Square. In the ensuing upheaval, a shrewd young general, **Jang Bahadur**, seized power, took the title **Rana** and proclaimed himself prime minister* for life, an office which he later made hereditary by establishing a complicated roll of succession. For the next century, the kings of Nepal were nothing more than puppets, while Ranas ruled like shoguns and packed the palace with their ever-increasing offspring. Authoritarian and blatantly exploitative, they built grandiose palaces while putting virtually no money into public works, suppressed education for fear it would awaken opposition, and remained firmly isolationist to avoid losing control to the British. (Ironically, an impoverished Nepal suited Britain, since it assured a steady supply of willing Gurkha cannon fodder.) Only a handful of foreign dignitaries were allowed to enter – usually only as far as Chitwan – and even the British resident wasn't allowed to venture beyond the Kathmandu Valley. To survey Nepal and Tibet, Britain had to send in Indian spies disguised as Buddhist monks.

Yet Jang Bahadur knew the value of staying on good terms with the British Raj, now at its zenith; in 1850 he broke with tradition and travelled to England, where he met Queen Victoria and by all accounts cut a dashing figure. He returned with several Western affectations, including a fondness for neoclassical architecture and epaulettes; soon after, to his credit, he abolished the practice of *sati*.

Other Ranas continued in the same vein. **Chandra Shamsher Rana**, who came to power in 1901 by deposing his brother, is best known for building the thousand-roomed Singha Durbar and (belatedly) abolishing slavery. He also made some feeble attempts at modernization, including the construction of Nepal's first college, railway, hydroelectric plant and paved roads. By 1940, underground resistance against the regime was developing,

and **Juddha Shamsher Rana** had four plotters executed; after the fall of the Ranas these men were declared martyrs and a monument south of Kathmandu's Tudikhel was erected in their honour.

THE MONARCHY RESTORED

The Ranas' anachronistic regime wasn't able to survive long after World War II, from which over 200,000 soldiers returned with dangerous ideas of freedom and justice. In 1948 the British quit India, and with them went the Ranas' chief support. The new Indian government mistrusted the Ranas, and became genuinely worried about Nepal's weakness as a buffer state after the Communist takeover of China in 1949. Seeking stability, India signed a far-reaching **"peace and friendship" treaty** with Nepal in 1950 which, despite the upheavals that were to follow, remains the basis for all relations between the two countries.

Later the same year the strategic balance shifted again as a result of the Chinese invasion of Tibet, and the **Nepali Congress Party**, recently formed in Calcutta, called for an armed struggle against the Ranas. Within a month, King Tribhuwan had requested asylum at the Indian embassy and was smuggled away to Delhi; the next morning, the Nepali Congress Party launched simultaneous assaults on Birganj and Biratnagar. Sporadic fighting continued for two months until the Ranas, internationally discredited, reluctantly agreed to enter into negotiations. Brokered by India, the so-called **Delhi Compromise** arranged for Ranas and the Congress Party to share power under the king's rule, with Nepalis given the right to vote in the parliamentary-style democracy.

The compromise was short-lived. **Tribhuwan**, a previously retiring figure, emerged as a "hero of the revolution" and an adroit politician, and before the end of 1951 he had dismissed the Rana prime minister. This was an end to the Rana regime, but not Rana influence: by an agreement that has never been made public, the Shah royal family continues to appoint Ranas to most key military posts, and the families are inseparably tied by marriage (the queen is a Rana, and two of her sisters are married to two of the king's brothers). In his four years as king, however, Tribhuwan neither

---

*Though the "Rana" title has generally been equated with that of a prime minister, technically it conferred a grade of kingship. The holder's full title was Shri Tin Maharaja (short for Shri Shri Shri Maharaja; "Shri" is an honorific prefix). The king's was, and still is, Shri Paanch (Five Shri) Maharajdhiraj.

consolidated his power nor delivered the elections he promised. Unaccountable to the voters, the party bosses who controlled the interim government weren't much of an improvement over the Ranas.

PANCHAAYAT POLITICS

Crowned in 1955, **King Mahendra** lost no time in offsetting the parties' power by developing his own grassroots network of village leaders, forcing the parties to do likewise. They demanded elections; the king stalled, but finally agreed to a vote in 1959. Amazingly, the Nepali Congress Party swept seventy percent of the seats, and under Prime Minister **B P Koirala** began bypassing palace control and creating a party machine very much like India's. Mahendra was none too pleased with this **"experiment with democracy"**, as it came to be called – the following year he sacked the cabinet, banned political parties and threw the leaders in jail. For the rest of his reign he relied on heavy police measures to quell dissent.

In place of democracy, Mahendra offered the **"partyless" panchaayat system**, a uniquely Nepali form of government that grew out of the king's old-boy village network. Village councils (*panchaayat*) were established to look after local affairs; these were to send one representative on to a district council, which in turn elected members to a national assembly. The king chose the prime minister and cabinet and appointed one fifth of the national assembly, which served as a rubber stamp for his policies. "Partylessness" meant, of course, one party – the king's. The *panchaayat* system conveniently preserved an illusion of democracy while silencing opposition and ensuring loyalty to the king: in other words, it was a new and improved version of absolute monarchy. Corruption was the same as before, only now more decentralized, as every village *panchaayat* wallah had a tiny piece of the pie.

India was unhappy with the changes, but Mahendra, unlike his father, didn't owe his crown to India, and sought wider international support. He threw open Nepal's doors to **foreign aid**, which endeared him to the major powers, enriched the state's coffers and swelled the bureaucracy (see "Development Dilemmas"). After the 1962 Sino-Indian border war, Mahendra was able to exploit Nepal's buffer position with particular skill, alternately playing off the two powers against each other to obtain economic and military aid; no sooner had India completed the Rajpath, Nepal's first highway from the plains to Kathmandu, for example, than Mahendra persuaded the Chinese to extend the road to Tibet, much to India's horror. The **"China card"** became an important unofficial strand of foreign policy, but ultimately it was to help bring about the downfall of the *panchaayat* system.

The present king, **Birendra**, assumed power after Mahendra's death in 1972, although for astrological reasons wasn't crowned until 1975. Educated at Eton and Harvard, the young king set out as an enlightened reformer, taking steps to curb the bureaucracy and cronyism that had flourished under his father. Reacting to Mahendra's laissez-faire policies on tourism – which had become Nepal's major industry – he cracked down on the growing hippy population by tightening visa restrictions. In 1975 he made the shrewdest and most popular move of his career when he proposed designating Nepal a **Zone of Peace**, a Swiss-style neutrality pledge that would at first glance appear to be completely unassailable. India, however, has consistently opposed the measure as a violation of the 1950 "peace and friendship" treaty, which provides for mutual defence, while cynics like to point out the irony of Nepal – home of the Gurkhas, the world's most formidable mercenary soldiers – declaring itself a peace zone.

Birendra's domestic reforms soon ran out of steam, and discontent grew over corruption and the slow pace of development. Widespread uprisings broke out in 1979, forcing the king to promise a national **referendum** in which voters could choose between the *panchaayat* system and multiparty democracy. Democracy lost by a margin of 55 to 45 – many say the vote was rigged – and the *panchaayat* system was retained.

During the 1980s Birendra proved himself to be an earnest but weak leader, easily manipulated by advisers and the queen – forever chaperoned by minders with walkie-talkies, he simply fell out of touch with the people. Despite token tinkerings with the system, the gravy train got more crowded throughout the decade, and insiders, sensing that the regime's days were numbered, tried to grab everything they could in the time remaining. In 1988 the king's brother, Dhirendra, was forced to relinquish his title as prince to avoid wide-ranging corruption charges. The king himself was rumoured to have Swiss bank accounts and an island in the Maldives (or Greece). Political opponents were imprisoned, while freedom of speech and the press was nonexistent. Diplomats insist Birendra was uninvolved with any shady dealings, but he would have had to be incredibly naive not to have known what was going on in his name.

DEMOCRACY RESTORED

The chickens started coming home to roost in March 1989, when India, outraged by (among other things) Nepal's purchase of anti-aircraft guns from China, retaliated with a crippling **trade embargo**. Indian Prime Minister Rajiv Gandhi – who had long professed a deep distaste for Birendra's antiquated monarchy – apparently believed shortages of fuel and medicines would touch off a popular uprising and topple the regime in a matter of weeks. Only his timing was off. The government rode out the immediate crisis by closing the universities, rationing fuel and whipping up traditional anti-Indian sentiment, until the Indian elections in December, when Gandhi's more conciliatory successor, V P Singh, eased the embargo.

But after eight months of hardship, inflation and police action, Nepalis were fed up, and India could no longer be cast as the villain. The previous year had witnessed China's failed pro-democracy movement at Tiananmen Square and the spectacularly successful revolutions in Eastern Europe: Nepalis were enormously stirred by these examples. Seeing their chance, the banned opposition parties united in the so-called **Movement to Restore Democracy**, demanding an end to the *panchayaat* system and the creation of a constitutional monarchy. They called for a national day of protest on February 18, 1990 – a date already designated by the government, with unintended irony, as Democracy Day. Hundreds of opposition members were duly placed under house arrest, and the planned revolt got off to a shaky start. Yet Faagun 7 (the Nepali date of Democracy Day) marked the true launch of the **Jana Andolan** ("People's Movement"), which in subsequent weeks gathered strength, resulting in violent clashes and deaths in Bhaktapur,

Narayanghat and Hetauda. Even while under detention, opposition leaders were able to call strikes and blackouts at will. The king, counselled by hardliners, kept silence.

On April 3, protesters overran Patan, and three days later an estimated 200,000 people marched up Kathmandu's Durbar Marg towards the Royal Palace. The army fired into the crowd, killing at least 45 people, and an ominous shoot-on-sight curfew was imposed. Finally moved to action by the **massacre**, the king dissolved his cabinet, legalized political parties and invited the opposition to form an interim government with Bhattarai as prime minister. The *panchaayat* system was dead.

After a few hiccups, the changeover to democracy proceeded in an orderly, if leisurely, fashion. By November 1990 the interim government had ratified a **new constitution** guaranteeing free speech, human rights and a constitutional monarchy. Under its provisions, the king remains the commander-in-chief of the armed forces, but cannot make any executive decisions without consulting the prime minister and cabinet; the old Rastriya Panchaayat was replaced by a Parliament consisting of a directly elected House of Representatives and a smaller National Assembly.

After a suitable interval to allow the news of democracy to percolate into the remoter regions, Nepal's first free **elections** in more than thirty years were held in May 1991. The Nepal Congress Party, which had paid its dues in exile for three decades and could claim much of the credit for bringing down the *panchaayat* system, won a majority – but not by much. While the rest of the world was backpedalling from communism as fast as it could, Nepal's several Communist parties put in a strong showing, maintaining their traditional strongholds in the east and, incredibly, sweeping the comfortable Kathmandu Valley. The National Democratic Party, largely packed with former *panchaayat*-wallahs, went down in a ball of flames. It was a clear referendum against the old guard, but a less than enthusiastic vote of confidence for the Congress Party.

CONGRESS, COMMUNISM AND COALITION

Any government inheriting such immense challenges with so slender a mandate was probably doomed to disappoint, and the first **Nepali Congress** government's honeymoon was short-lived. Prime Minister Girija Prasad Koirala, brother of the late B P Koirala, Nepal's first democratically elected prime minister, lost little time not only in attracting the enmity of the opposition Communists but also alienating many in his own party. The fragmentation of party power left the prime minister vulnerable to numerous political distractions.

Antagonism between the Indian-sponsored Congress Party and the Communists, who looked to China as their only remaining ideological mentor, produced strong political polarities on almost every issue. For example, Congress supported the cause of Tibetan refugees in a way that the *panchaayat* regime never did, which the Communists viewed as provocative to China. Yet the Communists certainly spoke for many Nepalis when they accused Congress leaders of selling out Nepal's interests to India. This frustration coalesced into a long and still unresolved squabble over the **Tanakpur project** – a $65 million hydroelectric diversion built by India on the Mahakali River, which forms the western border between the two countries – in which the government was accused of signing away most of Nepal's rights to the water and power generated from the river.

The Communists set up a steady drumbeat of criticism, and early on began calling for Koirala's resignation. Given their strength in the increasingly important urban areas, they adopted a style of taking their political gripes to the streets through black-flag marches, general strikes (*bandh*) and other actions. One such uprising on the 1992 anniversary of the *andolan*, later euphemistically referred to as the **April 6 "incidents"**, resulted in a mini-revolution in Kathmandu and Patan in which government security forces again opened fire on unarmed citizens, killing twenty-three. In May 1993, two Communist leaders were killed in a car accident in suspicious circumstances, leading opposition members to suspect a government conspiracy.

Over the next year, unemployment, unrest, Indianization and political infighting produced widespread disillusion, and steadily undermined the government's ability to manage the country's affairs. In July 1994, Koirala stepped down and the King dissolved Parliament, paving the way for new elections in November. This time no party emerged with a majority, but the **Communist Party of Nepal–United Marxist-Leninist,** the largest of several communist parties, narrowly edged out the Nepali Congress with a populist, Nepal-for-Nepalis platform summed up by the slogan *Aafno Gaun, Aafai Banaun* (roughly, "Build Your Own Village").

Among supporters, Asia's first democratically elected Communist government kindled much idealism. But lacking a parliamentary majority, the CPN–UML could only pursue a modest programme of reform: Prime Minister Manmohan Adhikari vowed to halt the sell-off of state-owned enterprises and made noises about overhauling the 1950 treaty with India, yet the government pragmatically continued Congress's economic liberalization policies and actively courted Indian investment in Nepalese industry. Land reform – the most radical item on the CPN–UML's agenda – was introduced cautiously, but even so it drew accusations of favouritism which helped bring the government down in September 1995.

After just nine months in office, the CPN–UML had built up considerable good will with the country, leading many observers to predict that the party would be returned to power with an outright majority in a future election; critics charged that the Communists had bought their popularity by making promises they couldn't afford to keep. At any rate, the Nepali Congress stepped into the vacuum, forming a centre-right **coalition government** with the National Democrats (in Nepali, the Rastriya Prajatantra Party, or RPP). Coming from a younger generation of Congress leaders, Prime Minister Sher Bahadur Deuba had fewer enemies than his predecessor, G P Koirala, but internal disputes within the party continued to fester.

The fragile Congress–RPP alliance is unlikely to last out its term, and if the recent past is any guide, Nepal can look forward to further periodic political upheavals. The likely result will be weak government preoccupied by short-term concerns and petty crises, making it that much harder for Nepal to achieve long-term development.

RELIGION: HINDUISM, BUDDHISM, SHAMANISM

To say that religion is an important part of Nepali life is a considerable understatement: it *is* life. In the Nepali world view, just about every act has spiritual implications; the gods are assumed to have a hand in every success or misfortune and must be appeased continuously. Belief and ritual form the basis of the whole social order, governing the way husbands relate to wives, parents to children and even the king to his subjects.

Three religious strands intertwine in Nepal: Hinduism, Buddhism and shamanism. In theory, these faiths are philosophically incompatible, but Nepalis, being an exceptionally tolerant lot, tend to overlook the differences. As practised by the masses, each employs superstition and rites of passage to get followers through the present life, and codes of behaviour to prepare them for the next; Hindu priests, Buddhist lamas and tribal shamans play similar roles in their respective communities. Indeed, it's really only outside observers who bother to distinguish between the religions and dwell on their outward differences – most Nepalis find such distinctions needlessly academic.

Hinduism is the state religion of Nepal, and the government claims that ninety percent of the population is Hindu. However, there are social advantages to professing Hinduism in Nepal, and official statistics don't reflect the extent to which many Nepalis blithely combine Hinduism with Buddhist or shamanist beliefs. In general, Hinduism prevails at the lower elevations and Buddhism in the Himalaya, while shamanism is strongest among the ethnic minorities of the hills.

HINDUISM

Hinduism doesn't conform to Western notions of what a religion should be, and indeed the word "religion" is totally inadequate to describe it. Hindus call it *dharma*, a much more sweeping term that conveys faith, duty, a way of life and the entire social order. Having no common church or institution, its many sects and cults preach different dogmas and emphasize different scriptures. On social matters, Hinduism can be tragically rigid – witness the caste system – and when it comes to rituals, rather petty. Yet it's a highly individualistic system, offering worshippers an almost limitless choice of deities and admitting many paths to enlightenment. By absorbing and neutralizing opposing doctrines, rather than condemning them as heresies, it has flourished longer than any other major religion.

Hinduism has been evolving since approximately 1600 BC, when **Aryan** invaders swept down from central Asia and subjugated the native Dravidian peoples of the Indus and Ganges plains. They brought with them a pantheon of nature gods and goddesses, some of whom are still in circulation: Indra (sky and rain) is popular in Kathmandu, while Surya (sun), Agni (fire), Vayu (wind) and Yama (death) retain bit parts in contemporary mythology. These so-called Vedic gods were first immortalized in the *Vedas* ("Books of Wisdom"), which were probably written between the twelfth and eighth centuries BC, and it was during this period that most of the principles now identified with Hinduism were thrashed out.

To make sure they stayed on top of the conquered Dravidians, the Aryans banned intermarriage and codified the apartheid-like **caste system**; *varna*, the Sanskrit word for caste, means "colour", and to this day members of the higher castes generally have lighter skin. Initially, four castes were established: Brahmans (priests), Kshatriyas (warriors and rulers), Vaisyas (traders and farmers) and Sudras (artisans and menials); over time, the lower two divisions spawned innumerable occupational subcastes. The *Rig Veda*, Hinduism's oldest text, put a divine seal of approval on the arrangements by proclaiming that Brahmans had issued from the mouth of the supreme creator, Kshatriyas from his arms, Vaishyas from his thighs and Sudras from his feet.

Brahmans (called Bahuns in Nepal), entrusted with the brain work, proceeded to exploit their position by inventing preposterously complex rituals and sacrifices, and making themselves the indispensable guardians of these mysteries (cow-worship probably dates from this period). Despite this stagnation, the philosophical foundations of Hinduism were laid during the late Vedic period and recorded in a series of discourses known as the **Upanishads**. Ever since, Hinduism has run along two radically different tracks: the Brahmans' hocus-pocus popular religion, with its comic-book deities and bloody sacrifices, and the profound, intuitive insights of gurus and *rishi* (teachers).

The essence of Hinduism, unchanged since the *Upanishads* were written, is that the soul (*atman*) of each living thing is like a lost fragment of the universal soul – **brahman**, the ultimate reality – while everything in the physical universe is mere illusion (*maya*). To reunite with *brahman*, the individual soul must go through a **cycle of rebirths** (*samsara*), ideally moving up the scale with each reincarnation. Determining the soul's progress is its **karma** – its accumulated "just deserts" – which is reckoned by the degree to which the soul conformed to **dharma**, or correct Hindu behaviour, in its previous lives. Thus a low-caste

Hindu must accept his or her lot to atone for past sins, and follow *dharma* in the hopes of achieving a higher rebirth. The theoretical goal of every Hindu is to cast off all illusion, achieve release (*moksha*) from the cycle of rebirths, and dissolve into *brahman*.

Hinduism has assembled a vast and rich body of mythology over the past three millennia, largely in an effort to personalize *brahman* for the masses. Early on, a few of the Vedic gods were renamed, relieved of their old nature associations and given personalities to illustrate divine attributes. The concept of the **Hindu "trinity"** – Brahma the creator, Vishnu the preserver and Shiva the destroyer – was developed, and the process of god-creation was speeded by the invention of numerous **avatar**, or manifestations of gods. Hinduism's best-loved epics, the *Mahabharata* (pronounced *Mahabharat* in Nepal) and the *Ramayana* (*Ramayan*), portray two of Vishnu's *avatar*, Krishna and Ram, as models of human conduct (although as often as not Hindu gods, like their Greek counterparts, are made out to be vain and foolish).

The explosion of deities has given rise to a succession of **devotional cults** over the centu-

---

AUM

"AUM" is a word that represents to our ears that sound of the energy of the universe of which all things are manifestations. You start in the back of the mouth, "ahh," then "oo," you fill the mouth, and "mm" closes the mouth. When you pronounce this properly, all vowel sounds are included in the pronunciation. AUM. Consonants are here regarded simply as interruptions of the essential vowel sound.

All words are thus fragments of AUM, just as all images are fragments of the Form of forms. AUM is a symbolic sound that puts you in touch with that resounding being that is the universe. If you heard some of the recordings of Tibetan monks chanting AUM, you would know what the word means, all right. That's the AUM of being in the world. To be in touch with that and to get the sense of that is the peak experience of all.

A-U-M. The birth, the coming into being, and the dissolution that cycles back. AUM is called the "four-element syllable." A-U-M – and what is the fourth element? The silence out of which AUM arises, and back into which it goes, and which underlies it. My life is the A-U-M, but there is a silence underlying it, too. That is what

we would call the immortal. This is the mortal and that's the immortal, and there wouldn't be the mortal if there weren't the immortal. One must discriminate between the mortal aspect and the immortal aspect of one's own existence . . . that's why it is a peak experience to break past all that, every now and then, and to realize, "Oh . . . ah . . ."

From "The Power of Myth", by Joseph Campbell, reproduced by permission of Bantam Doubleday Dell.

ries, the most important of which nowadays are Vaishnava (followers of Vishnu), Shaiva (Shiva) and Mahadevi (the mother goddess); the last often goes by the name Shakti, a tantric term explained below. Brahma is rarely iconographically depicted and consequently not widely worshipped.

THE HINDU PANTHEON

If you're daunted by Hinduism's technicolour array of gods and goddesses, don't worry: your average Hindu would be hard pressed to name most of them. While Hinduism is said to boast of 33 million deities, they can all be thought of as representations of the one supreme god – a paradox which isn't hard to deal with if you've been trained that everything is illusion anyway. The most important gods, described below, can easily be identified by certain trademark implements, postures and "vehicles" (animal carriers). As for gods' multiple arms and heads, these aren't meant to be taken literally: they symbolize the deity's "universal" (omnipotent) form, while severed heads and trampled corpses signify ignorance and evil.

VISHNU

Vishnu (often known as Narayan in Nepal) is the face of dignity and equanimity, typically shown standing erect holding a wheel (*chakra*), mace (*gada*), lotus (*padma*) and conch (*sankha*) in his four hands, or, as at Budhanilkantha, reclining on a serpent's coil. A statue of **Garuda** (**Garud** in Nepal), Vishnu's bird-man vehicle, is always close by. Vishnu is also sometimes depicted in one or more of his ten incarnations (*das avatar*), which follow an evolutionary progression from fish, turtle and boar to man-lion, dwarf, axe-wielding Brahman and the legendary heroes **Ram** and **Krishna**.

Ram is associated with **Hanuman**, his loyal monkey-king ally in the *Ramayan*, while Krishna is most commonly seen on calendars as a chubby blue baby, flute-player or charioteer. Interestingly, Vishnu's ninth *avatar* is the Buddha – this was a sixth-century attempt by Vaishnavas to bring Buddhists into their fold – and the tenth is Kalki, a messiah figure invented in the twelfth century when Hindus were being persecuted at the hands of Muslim invaders.

Vishnu's consort is **Lakshmi**, the goddess of wealth, to whom lamps are lit during the festival of Tihaar. Like Vishnu, she assumed mortal form in two great Hindu myths, playing opposite Ram as the chaste princess Sita, and opposite Krishna as the passionate Radha.

SHIVA

Shiva's incarnations are countless, ranging from the hideous Bhairab, who alone is said to take 64 different forms, to the benign Pashupati ("Lord of the Animals") and Nataraj ("King of the Dance"). To many devotees he is simply Mahadev: Great God. The earliest and still the most widespread icon of Shiva is the *linga*, a phallic stone fertility symbol* commonly housed in a boxy stone *shivalaya* ("Shiva home"). Shiva temples can be identified by the presence of a *trisul* (trident) and the bull **Nandi**, Shiva's mount, who is himself something of a fertility symbol.

Many sadhus worship Shiva the *yogin* (one who practises yoga), the Hindu ascetic supreme, who is often depicted sitting in meditative repose on a Himalayan mountaintop, perhaps holding a *chillam* of *ganja*. Pashupatinath is the national shrine to Shiva as **Pashupati**, and is patronized by Pashupata, Kaplika and other Shaiva sects, who take it to be Shiva's winter home. Another popular image of Shiva is as the loving husband with his consort, Parvati: the two can be seen leaning from an upper window of a temple in Kathmandu's Durbar Square. Nearby stand two famous statues of **Bhairab**, the tantric (see below) interpretation of Shiva in his role as destroyer: according to Hindu philosophy, everything – not only evil – must be destroyed in its turn to make way for new things.

MAHADEVI

The mother goddess is similarly worshipped in many forms, both peaceful and wrathful, and many of these are reckoned to be the consorts of corresponding Shiva forms. As **Kali** ("Black") she is the female counterpart of Bhairab, wear-

---

* The phallic aspect of the *linga* is perhaps overplayed by non-Hindus. Gandhi wrote: "It has remained for our Western visitors to acquaint us with the obscenity of many practices which we have hitherto innocently indulged in. It was in a missionary book that I first learned that the Shiva *linga* had any obscene significance at all." Then again, Gandhi denied most things to do with sex.

ing a necklace of skulls and sticking out her tongue with bloodthirsty intent; as **Durga** she is the demon-slayer honoured in the great Dasain festival. In Nepal she is widely worshipped as **Bhagwati**, the embodiment of female creative power. In all these forms, the mother goddess is appeased by sacrifices of uncastrated male animals. On a more peaceful level, she is also Parvati ("Hill", daughter of Himalaya), Gauri ("Golden") or just **Mahadevi** ("Great Goddess").

GANESH AND OTHERS

Several legends tell how **Ganesh**, Shiva and Parvati's son, came to have an elephant's head: one states that Shiva accidentally chopped the boy's head off, and owing to an obscure restriction on the god's restorative powers, was forced to replace it with that of the first creature he saw. The god of wisdom and remover of obstacles, Ganesh must be worshipped first to ensure offerings to other gods will be effective, which is why a Ganesh shrine or stone will invariably be found near other temples. Underscoring Hinduism's great sense of the mystical absurd, Ganesh's vehicle is a rat.

Of the other Hindu deities, only **Annapurna**, the goddess of grain and abundance (her name means "Full of Grain"), and **Saraswati**, the goddess of learning and culture, receive much attention in Nepal. Saraswati is normally depicted holding a *vina*, a musical instrument something like a sitar.

BUDDHISM

The Buddha was born Siddhartha Gautama in what is now Nepal (see p.287) in the fifth or sixth century BC, and his teachings were in many ways a protest against the ritualism to which popular Hinduism had by then been reduced. The Buddha rejected the Hindu caste system and the belief in a creator God, while adapting its doctrines of reincarnation and *karma*, along with many yogic practices; the result was a non-theistic, pragmatic philosophy that placed a greater emphasis on the active pursuit of enlightenment.

Whereas the Hindu ideal is to reunite with the Creator, the Buddhist goal is **nirvana**, a state of being where wisdom and compassion have completely uprooted the "three poisons" of greed, hatred and delusion. The essence of the Buddha's teaching is encapsulated in the **four noble truths**: existence is suffering; suffering is caused by desire; the taming of desire ends suffering; and desire can be tamed by following the **eightfold path**, a set of deceptively simple guidelines for achieving *dharma*. He called the whole prescription the **Middle Way** because it avoided the extremes of sensual indulgence and asceticism, both of which were popularly believed to lead to enlightenment if pursued with sufficient vigour (and the Buddha had tried them both pretty vigorously before rejecting them).

As it developed, Buddhism became for many followers a full-time monastic pursuit. But for most lay people, the lonely quest for enlightenment was too hard-core and impersonal; to restore emotional elements that had been lost in the monastic movement, Buddhism evolved a populist strand known as **Mahayana** ("Great Vehicle"). Reintroducing elements of worship and prayer, Mahayana Buddhism developed its own pantheon of *bodhisattva* – enlightened intermediaries, something akin to Catholic saints, who have forgone *nirvana* until all humanity has been saved. Many of these were a repackaging of older Hindu deities, who were now given new names and roles as protectors of the *dharma*.

Followers of the original teachings called their school **Theravada** ("Way of the Elders"), but to Mahayana Buddhists it came to be known, somewhat disparagingly, as **Hinayana** ("Lesser Vehicle"). This tradition remains active in Sri Lanka and much of southeast Asia. It was the Mahayana doctrine that came to Nepal, around the fifth century, and also spread to China, Korea and Japan, adapting differently to each. Buddhism in India was dealt a death blow in the seventh century by Muslim invasions, which destroyed the great monastic universities and the thousands of monks who lived in them; what was left of Buddhism was effectively absorbed into the ocean of Hinduism.

TANTRA AND VAJRAYANA

Even as Hinduism was on the wane in India, a new religious movement was developing in Bengal and Bihar that would give a radically new bent to both Buddhism and Hinduism. **Tantra** erupted like the punk rock of religion, proclaiming that *everything* in life can be used to reach enlightenment: the five things normally shunned in orthodox Hinduism and Buddhism as poisons – meat, fish, parched grains, alcohol and sex – are embraced wholeheartedly on the tantric path. Sex, in particular, is regarded as the central metaphor for spiritual enlightenment, and it is this inversion of the sacred and profane that has given *tantra* its somewhat risqué reputation. *Tantra* abounds in esoteric imagery, *mantra* (verbal formulas) and *mandala* (diagrams used to aid meditation), which together make up a sort of mystic code intended only for initiates.

According to **Hindu *tantra***, the female principle (*shakti*) possesses the creative energy which is capable of activating the male force. The gods are powerless until joined with their female counterparts – in tantric art, Bhairab is often shown locked in a fierce sexual embrace – and in many of her guises the mother goddess has become Shakti, one half of a tantric union of sexual opposites. The human psyche, too, is held to consist of male and female forces that must be harnessed: followers of Hindu *tantra* are trained to visualize the body's female energy rising like a snake from the level of the sexual organs, ascending the seven psychic centres (*chakra*) of the spinal column to reach the male principle at the top of the head, resulting in realization.

Buddhist *tantra*, known as **Vajrayana** ("Thunderbolt Way"), reverses the symbolism of these two forces and makes the male principle of "skill in means" or compassion the active force, and the female principle of "wisdom" passive. In tantric rituals, these forces are symbolized by the the hand-held "lightning-bolt sceptre" (*vajra*; *dorje* in Tibetan), which represents the male principle, and the bell (*ghanti*), representing the female. Expanding on Mahayana's all-male pantheon, Vajrayana introduces female counterparts to the main Buddha figures and some of the *bodhisattva*, and sometimes depicts them in sexual positions.

LAMAISM (TIBETAN BUDDHISM)

Vajrayana Buddhism found its greatest expression in Tibet, which it reached (by way of Nepal) in the eighth century. At the time, Tibet was under the sway of a native shamanic religion (see below) known as **Bön**; Vajrayana eventually overcame Bön*, but only by taking on board many of its symbols and rituals, thus creating the spectacularly distinct branch of Buddhism that outsiders call **Lamaism**.

Lamaism turned Bön's demons into fierce guardian deities (*dharmapala*) – these can usually be seen flanking monastery (*gompa*) entrances – and incorporated elements of Bön magic into its meditational practices. Since blood sacrifices were out of the question, they were adapted into "vegetarian" offerings in the form of conical dough cakes called *torma*. The *Bardo Thödol* ("Tibetan Book of the Dead") is basically a shamanic guide to the after-death experience that probably owes much to Bön.

While its underlying principles aren't much different from that of Mahayana Buddhism, Lamaism has a tendency to express them in incredibly esoteric symbolism. The **Wheel of Life**, often depicted in *thangka* and frescoes at monastery entrances, is an intricate exposition of the different levels of rebirth and the limitations of the unenlightened state. The **stupa** (*chorten* in Tibetan), an ancient abstract representation of the Buddha, is developed into a complex statement of Buddhist cosmology, and Buddhahood is refracted into five aspects, symbolized by the five transcendent or *dhyani* (meditating) Buddhas, which can be seen in niches surrounding the Swayambhu stupa. **Prayer wheels**, usually bearing the *mantra*, *Om mani padme hum* ("Hail to the jewel in the lotus"), are Tibetan innovations that aid meditative concentration, and **prayer flags** also bear *mantra* and wishes for compassion which are meant to be picked up and spread by the wind.

By far the most important feature of Tibetan Buddhism are its ***bodhisattva***, which are often mistaken for deities. Held to be emanations of the *dhyani* Buddhas, they are used in meditation and rituals to help develop the qualities they symbolize, and also serve as objects of devotion. The most popular figures are **Avalokiteshwara** (**Chenrezig** in Tibetan), a white male figure with four arms (or, sometimes, a thousand), who represents

---

* Unrepentant Bön priests were banished to the Himalayan periphery, and even today vestiges of the Bön tradition may be encountered while trekking in Nepal: for example, a follower of Bön will circle a religious monument anticlockwise, the opposite direction to a Buddhist.

compassion; **Tara**, a white or green female figure, also representing compassion; and **Manjushri**, an orange-yellow male youth gracefully holding a sword above his head, who represents wisdom. Though these figures are peaceful and benign, there are also wrathful ones with bulging eyes, often wearing human skins and drinking blood, who symbolize the energy and potency of the enlightened state and the sublimation of our crudest energies.

From the beginning, Tibetan Buddhism placed great emphasis on close contact with a **lama**, or spiritual guide, who can steer the student through the complex meditations and rituals. Teachings were passed on orally from lama to disciple, so the divergence of various sects over the centuries has had more to do with different lineages than with major doctrinal differences. The leader of each sect, and indeed of each monastery, is venerated as the reincarnation (*tulku*) of his or her predecessor, and is expected to carry on the same spiritual tradition. Of the **four main sects**, the oldest is the Nyingma-pa ("Red Hats"), founded in the eighth century by Guru Padma Sambhava, who, if all the stories told about him were true, meditated in every cave in Nepal. The Sakya-pa broke away in the eleventh century, tracing their line from the second-century Indian philosopher Nagarjuna. The Kagyu-pa order emerged in the eleventh and twelfth centuries, inspired by the Tibetan mystic Marpa and his enlightened disciple Milarepa, who also meditated his way around Nepal. The Gelug-pa ("Yellow Hats") sect, led by the Dalai Lama, is the only one that takes a significantly different theological line; born out of a fifteenth-century reform movement to purge Lamaism of its questionable religious practices, it places greater emphasis on study and intellectual debate.

THE NEWAR SYNTHESIS

Ask a Newar whether he's Hindu or Buddhist, the saying goes, and he'll answer "yes": after fifteen centuries of continuous exposure to both faiths, the Newars of the Kathmandu Valley have concocted a unique **synthesis** of the two. To religious scholars, the Newar religion is as exciting as a biologist's missing link, for some believe that it provides a picture of the way Mahayana and Vajrayana Buddhism functioned historically in India.

Until only the past two centuries, the Newars held fast to the original monastic form of tantric Buddhism – as the *bahal* of Kathmandu and Patan still bear witness – while their rulers pursued the Hindu tantric path. However, the Kathmandu Valley has become progressively "Hinduized" since the unification of Nepal in the eighteenth century: the monasteries have largely disappeared, their monks have married, and the title of **Vajracharya** (Buddhist priest) has become a hereditary caste like that of the Bahun (Brahman) priests. Today, Newar Buddhists are perhaps the only Buddhist culture that no longer maintains active communities of monks or nuns. Although the acceptance of caste and the decline of monasticism have shifted the balance in favour of Hinduism, at the popular level the synthesis remains as well bonded as ever.

When Newars refer to themselves as **Buddha margi** (Buddhist) or **Shiva margi** (Hindu), they often do so only to indicate that they employ a Vajracharya or Bahun priest; even this doesn't always hold true, though, as many *jyapu* (farmers) call themselves "Hindu" and attend Hindu festivals, yet still use Vajracharyas. In any case, Newar rituals vary little from Hindu to Buddhist.

Puja (an act of worship) is performed to gain the favour of deities for material requests as often as for "spiritual" reasons. It is a profound and very personal ritual. An integral part of all Newar rituals is the "*puja* of five offerings", consisting of flowers (usually marigolds), incense, light (in the form of butter lamps), *sindur* (coloured powder) and various kinds of purified food (usually rice, dairy products, sometimes sweets). Before **darshan** (audience with a deity), the devotee or the priest uses consecrated water to wash him or herself and to bathe the deity. After the deity has symbolically accepted and eaten some food, the remainder is taken back by the devotee as **prasad** (consecrated food). This, along with a **tika** made with the coloured powder, confers the deity's blessing and protection.

Priests are ordinarily engaged for the more important **life-cycle rites** (birth, marriage, death) or for larger seasonal festivals; wealthier Newars may also seek private consultations at times of illness or important decisions. Bahun priests don't perform animal **sacrifices**, but they do preside over the rituals that precede them. This brings up one of the rare differences between Hindu and Buddhist Newars: while Hindu Newars are enthusiastic sacrificers – they call the bloody ninth day of the Dasain festival *Syako Tyako* (roughly, "the more you kill, the more you gain") – Buddhists seldom participate. During Dasain, Tibetan monasteries in Nepal hold special services to pray for good rebirths of the sacrificed animals.

THE NEWAR PANTHEON

All the Hindu and Buddhist deities already discussed are fair game for Newars, along with a few additional characters of local invention. Some deities specialize in curing diseases, others bring good harvests – as far as Newars are concerned, it doesn't matter whether they're Hindu or Buddhist so long as they do the job. The following are some of the figures uniquely adapted by the Newars.

Machhendranath, honoured as a rainmaker par excellence, typifies the layering of religious motifs that so frequently takes place among the Newars. To be accurate, only Hindus call the god Machhendranath; Buddhist Newars know him as **Karunamaya** or by any of a number of local names. He is commonly associated with Avalokiteshwara, the *bodhisattva* of compassion, who is invoked by the mantra *Om mani padme hum*. Depending on his incarnation (he is said to have 108), he may be depicted as having anything up to a thousand arms and eleven heads. While it's unclear how Avalokiteshwara came to be associated with the historical figures of Machhendranath and Gorakhnath – who are considered saints by Hindus – it was certainly in part the result of a conscious attempt by

---

A VISIT TO THE ASTROLOGER

His name is Joshi – in Newar society, all members of the astrologer subcaste are called Joshi – and to get to his office I have to duck through a low doorway off a courtyard in the old part of Patan and feel my way up two flights of wooden steps in the dark, climbing towards a glimmer of light and the sounds of low murmuring. At the landing I take off my shoes and enter the sanctum. Joshi-ji doesn't even look up. He's sitting cross-legged on the floor behind a low desk, glasses perched on the end of his nose, scowling over a sheaf of papers and, except for his Nepali-style clothes, looking exactly the way I'd always pictured Professor Godbole in *A Passage to India*. Shelves of books and scrolls are heaped behind him, and over in one corner a small shrine is illuminated by a low-watt bulb and a smouldering stick of incense. An older couple is seated in front of Joshi-ji's desk, nervously asking a question of the great man; he pushes his glasses up on his forehead, scribbles something, then pulls himself up to answer in melodic, nasal tones. I settle down on the floor next to two other waiting couples and together we keep a respectful silence.

To Newars, the **astrologer** is a counsellor, confessor, general practitioner and guide through the maze of life. With the priest and the doctor, he acts as mediator between the self and the universe (which are one); and since astrology is but one branch of Hindu knowledge, his prognostications on important occasions are considered as important as a priest's blessings, and he is often called upon to provide a second opinion on a doctor's diagnosis. He knows most of his clients from birth. For new parents, the astrologer will prepare complex planetary charts based on the baby's precise time and place of **birth**, together with a lengthy interpretation detailing personality traits, health hazards, vocational aptitude, characteristics of the ideal marriage partner, and a general assessment of the newborn's prospects. When a **marriage** is contemplated, he will study the horoscopes of the prospective couple to make sure the match is suitable, and if so, he'll perform further calculations to determine the most auspicious wedding date. During an **illness**, he may prescribe a protective amulet, gemstone or herbal remedy corresponding to the planets influencing the patient. He may also be consulted on the advisability of a business decision or a major purchase.

While Western astrology is well suited to an independent, egocentric culture, **Hindu astrology** is much more at ease with the insignificance of the individual in the midst of the vast cosmos. And unlike the Western system, which is regarded more as a tool for personal fulfilment, the Hindu tradition emphasizes external events and how – and when – to deal with them. The

Hindu rulers to establish religious and social bonds by grafting two Hindu saints on to a local Buddhist cult.

Kumari, the "Living Goddess", is another often-cited example of Newar syncretism (religious fusing): although acknowledged to be an incarnation of the Hindu goddess Durga, she is picked from a Buddhist-caste family. **Bhimsen**, a mortal hero in the Hindu *Mahabharat*, who is rarely worshipped in India, has somehow been elevated to be the patron deity of Newar shopkeepers, both Hindu and Buddhist.

Manjushri, the *bodhisattva* of wisdom, has been pinched from the Buddhist pantheon to play the lead role part in the Kathmandu Valley's creation myth (although he is often confused with Saraswati, the Hindu goddess of knowledge). He is always depicted with a sword, with which he cuts away ignorance and

attachment, and sometimes also with a book, bow, bell and *vajra*. Likewise **Tara**, the embodiment of the female principle in Vajrayana Buddhism, assumes special meaning for Newars, who consider her the deification of an eighth-century Nepali princess.

Quintessentially tantric, the **Bajra Joginis** (or Vajra Yoginis) command their own cult centred at four temples around the Kathmandu Valley. They are regarded as the female aspect of the Buddha and are the subjects of esoteric cults and closely guarded secrets. Harati, the Buddhist protector of children, is zealously worshipped by Newars under the name **Ajima**, the grandmother goddess.

Throughout Nepal, stones and trees marked with *sindur* may be seen: vestiges of older animist practices, these may mark the place where a nature goddess (generically known as **Mai**), local spirit or serpent (**nag**) is supposed

horoscope represents a snapshot of the subject's *karma*: at the precise moment of reincarnation, the planets display the tally, and although it's misleading to speak in terms of planetary "influences", the *karma* that they reveal strongly implies the future course of one's life. The astrologer's role, then, is to suggest the best way to play the hand one was dealt.

The Hindu method of generating horoscopes follows the same essential principles as in the Western tradition, although technical differences between the two will produce somewhat different results. Hindu astrology recognizes the same twelve **signs of the zodiac**, albeit under different (Sanskrit) names, and assigns many of the same attributes to the planets and houses. The basic **birth chart** indicates the **sun sign** (the sign corresponding to the sun's position at the time of birth), the ascendant or **"rising" sign** (the sign rising above the eastern horizon at the time of birth) and the positions of the moon and the five planets known to the ancients, plus a couple of other non-Western points of reference. The positions of all of these are also noted in relation to the twelve **houses**, each of which governs key aspects of the subject's life (health, relationships and so on). The chief technical difference between Western and Hindu horoscopy is in how they line up the signs of the zodiac with respect to the earth. Western astrologers use the **tropical zodiac**, in which Aries is always assumed to start on the spring equinox

(March 21, give or take a day), even though a wobble in the earth's axis causes the actual constellations to drift out of sync by about 30° (one sign) every 2000 years or so – that's why it's now Pisces that the sun enters on March 21, and pretty soon, New Agers say, we'll be into the age of Aquarius. Hindu astrologers, on the other hand, go by the **sidereal zodiac**, which takes all its measurements from the *actual* positions of the constellations. (Technically speaking, this is a pretty profound difference, but since the Western and Hindu methods of interpretation are different, it all comes out in the wash.) If you have a horoscope done in Nepal, you'll probably be presented with a beautifully calligraphed scroll detailing all these measurements in chart and tabular form, using both tropical and sidereal measurements.

If charting a horoscope is largely a matter of mathematical donkey work, **interpretation** is an intuitive art requiring great eloquence and finesse. The astrologer can draw on numerous texts describing every conceivable conjunction of planets, and the positive and negative effects of every planet on every house; but at the end of the day, the usefulness of the reading must come down to the astrologer's own skill and experience. As I found out on my visit to Joshi-ji, the specifics aren't everything. The astrologer isn't peddling facts; he's offering insight, hope, reassurance, and a dash of theatre.

David Reed

to live. There are many types of these lesser spirit beings who require offerings to safeguard passage through their respective domains.

SHAMANISM

More ancient than Hinduism or Buddhism, **shamanism** is followed in diverse ways throughout the world by peoples fortunate enough to have been overlooked by the institutional religions. Variously described as medicine men, witch doctors or oracles, shamans perform mystical rituals to mediate between the physical and spiritual realms on behalf of their flock. (Western society has its "shamans", too – faith healers and mediums, for example.)

Shamanism is the traditional religion of most of Nepal's native ethnic groups, and while many have adopted at least outward forms of Hinduism or Buddhism (depending on their location), it is still widely practised in the eastern and western hills. In Nepali, the generic words for shaman are *jhankri* and *dhami*, although each ethnic group has its own term as well. Forms and practices vary from one tribe to another, but a *jhankri* – usually carrying a double-sided drum and often wearing a headdress of peacock feathers – is always unmistakeable.

The *jhankri*'s main job is to maintain spiritual and physical balance, and to restore it when it has been upset. As a healer, he may examine the entrails of animals for signs, gather medicinal plants from the forest, perform sacrifices, exorcize demons, chant magical incantations to invoke helper deities, or conduct any number of other rituals. As an oracle, he may fall into a trance and act as a mouthpiece of the gods, advising, admonishing and consoling listeners. As the spiritual sentry of his community, he must ward off ghosts, evil spirits and angry ancestors – sometimes by superior strength, often by trickery. All this, plus his duties as funeral director, dispenser of amulets, teller of myths and consecrator of holy ground and so on, put the *jhankri* at the very heart of religious and social life in the hills. Little wonder that Hinduism and Buddhism have been so shaped in Nepal by these shamanistic traditions, producing a unique melting pot of religions.

Charles Leech and David Reed

MUSIC AND DANCE

Nepali music hasn't exactly swept the world-music charts. Nepal's recording artists have a hard enough time holding their own against imports from India, let alone exporting their product overseas. Complicating matters is the fact that there are as many styles of Nepali music and dance as there are ethnic groups, and at any rate most of them can only be appreciated live – but all of this puts you in a position to appreciate some wonderfully rare sounds and sights while you're travelling around the country.

CLASSICAL AND RELIGIOUS

Little attempt has been made to chart the history of Nepali music. However, one of the earliest influences surely must have been **Indian classical music**, which goes back to a time when there was no distinction between India and Nepal, and to a region that extended well beyond the present borders of India. Classical music of the north Indian style flourished at the courts of the Malla kings and reached its zenith in Nepal under the Rana prime ministers, who patronized Indian musicians in their court to the exclusion of Nepali folk performers. Though it was always primarily an aristocratic genre, there is still a lively classical music network in Kathmandu, with tourist culture shows supplementing public performances and private recitals (for example, bimonthly at the royal palace).

Newar Buddhist priests still sing esoteric **tantric hymns** which, when accompanied by **mystical dances** and hand postures, have immense occult power. The secrets of these are closely guarded by initiated priests, but a rare public performance is held on Buddha Jayanti, when five *vajracharya* costumed as the Pancha Buddha dance at Swayambhu.

The contemporary layman's form of sacred music is ***bhajan*** – devotional hymn-singing, usually performed in front of temples and in rest houses. *Bhajan* groups gather on auspicious evenings to chant praises to Ram, Krishna or other Hindu deities; during festivals they may carry on through the night, and round-the-clock vigils are sometimes sponsored by wealthy patrons. Like a musical *puja*, the haunting verses are repeated over and over to the mesmeric beat of the tabla and the drone of the harmonium.

Sherpas and other Bhotiyas have their own ritualistic music rooted in **Tibetan Buddhist** traditions. Rhythm is more important than melody in this crashing, banging music, which is the exclusive preserve of monks. There's a hierarchy of instruments in the lamaist orchestra, from the *ghanti* (bell), *sankha* (conch shell) and *jhyaamta* (small cymbals), through the *bugcham* (large cymbals), *kangling* (small trumpet, made from a human thigh bone) and *dhyangro* (bass drum), to the *gyaling* (jewel-encrusted shawm, or oboe) and *radung* (a ten-foot-long telescopic trumpet, which looks like a Swiss alpenhorn and produces a sound like a subsonic fart). The human voice forms a separate instrument in the mix, as monks recite prayers in deep, dirge-like, "self-harmonizing" chanting – a unique practice lately introduced to the West by touring Tibetan ensembles.

FOLK

For Nepalis where electricity and videos haven't yet reached, **folk music** and dancing is still just about the only form of entertainment available. On holidays and festival days, the men of a village or neighbourhood will typically gather in a circle for an evening session of singing and socializing; as a rule only the men perform on these occasions, while the women look on.

The musical backing always consists of a ***maadal*** (horizontally held two-sided drum), and often also includes other drums, harmonium and *murali* (bamboo flute). After some preliminary tapping on the *maadal*, a member of the group will strike up a familiar verse, and all join in on the chorus; the first singer runs through as many verses as he can remember, at which point someone else takes over, often making up comical verses to suit the occasion. Members of the group dance to the music one at a time, each entertaining onlookers with his interpretation of the song in swirling body movements, facial expressions and hand gestures.

Young men and women sing and dance together (though again, not at the same time) at **rodi ghar**, the Nepali equivalent of a sock hop. Originally a Gurung institution, *rodi* has been embraced by many other hill groups as an informal, musical means of courtship. Young men and women of the hill tribes also sing improvised, flirtatious duets; the woman may even take the lead in these, forcing the man to come up with rejoinders to her jesting verses. In addition, women also sing in the fields, where singing lightens the burden of manual work – especially during *ropai* (rice transplanting), which has its own traditional songs.

Folk musical traditions vary among Nepal's many ethnic groups, but the true sound of Nepal may be said to be the soft and melodic music of the hills. Of several hill styles, **jhyaure**, the *maadal*-based music of the western hills, has emerged as the most popular. **Selo**, the musical style of the Tamangs that's performed to the accompaniment of the *damphu* (a one-sided, flat, round drum), has also been adopted by other ethnic communities. The music of the **Jyapu** farming caste has a lively rhythm, provided by the *dhime* (big two-sided drum) and a host of other drums, percussion instruments and woodwinds, though the singing has an extremely nasal quality that's hard for outsiders to appreciate.

Although folk music is, by definition, a pursuit of amateurs, two traditional castes of professional musicians exist in Nepal. **Gaaine** – wandering minstrels – have always served as an important unifying force in the hills, relaying not only news but also songs and musical styles from village to village. Accompanying themselves on *sarangi* (four-stringed fiddles), *gaaine* once thrived under patronage from local chieftains, whose deeds were the main topics of their songs. They're on the decline nowadays, but a few still ply their trade in the villages north of Pokhara, in the far west, and in Kirtipur in the Kathmandu Valley (needless to say, the so-called *gaaine* in Thamel and Lakeside aren't worthy of the title). Their repertoire includes sacred songs in praise of Hindu deities, bittersweet ballads of toil and triumph, great moments in Nepali history and, increasingly, political commentary and even government propaganda.

Much more numerous are the **damai**, members of the tailor caste, who for generations have served as the exclusive guardians of the *paanchai baajaa* (see below), and may also be employed at shrines to play during daily offerings and blood sacrifices. The tailor-musician combination isn't as strange as it might sound: Nepalis traditionally used to have just one set of clothes made each year, for the autumn Dasain festival, so tailors needed an occupation to tide them over during the winter and spring. Handily, that's the wedding season, when musicians are much in demand.

WEDDINGS AND FESTIVALS

No wedding would be complete without the **paanchai baajaa** (five instruments), a traditional Nepali ensemble of *sahanai* (shawm), *damaha* (large kettledrum), *narsinga* (C-shaped horn), *jhyaali* (cymbals) and *dholaki* (two-sided drum). ("They got married without *paanchai baajaa*" is a euphemism for living together.) Despite the name, bands ideally number nine members – eleven is the legal maximum, set to keep wedding costs down (similarly, the number of wedding guests is limited to 51). In the Kathmandu Valley, *paanchai baajaa* musicians have largely traded in their traditional instruments for Western brass horns and their ceremonial dress for fanciful, military-style uniforms, but the music remains distinctly Nepali.

Raucous and jubilant, *paanchai baajaa* music is considered an auspicious accompaniment to processions, Hindu rituals and life-cycle rites. During a **wedding**, the band accompanies the groom to the home of the bride, plays during the wedding ceremony, and again during the return procession. Apart from playing popular folk songs and film favourites, the musicians have a traditional repertoire of numbers for specific occasions – for example, the "bride-requesting tune", in which the shawm player mimics the bride's wailing as she departs from her family home, and the music of the rice-transplanting season, which imitates the body rhythm of the workers.

Festivals bring their own interwoven forms of music and dance, especially in the Kathmandu Valley. The Newars of the valley are renowned for their spectacular **masked dances**, in which the dancers enter a trance-like state to become the embodiments of the gods they portray, gesturing and gyrating behind elaborately painted (papier mâché masks. Best known of these are Bhaktapur's Nawa Durga dancers and their supporting musicians: their vigorous dance-drama, held on the tenth day of Dasain, recounts the victory of the goddess Durga over a buffalo demon. In Kathmandu, several different troupes take the stage during Indra Jaatra, performing the famous dance of the demon Lakhe, the sword-spinning Sawo Bhaku dance, and tableaux of the Das Avatar (ten incarnations) of Vishnu. The dancing is in a more humorous vein during Gaai Jaatra, when boys and young men play female roles in drag, since women aren't normally supposed to dance in public.

Virtuoso **drummers**, the Jyapus (Newar farmers) of the valley provide the rolling beat for processions on festival days: generally they beat enormous cylindrical drums (*dhime baajaa*) in groups with two sizes of cymbal. At some shrines, in addition to a singing group, there is a complement of nine drums (*nawa daaphaa*), which are played in sequence during festivals with various accompanying instruments. Another type of popular processional band (*bansuri baajaa*) combines flutes and barrel drums.

Tibetans and Bhotiyas have their own form of dance-drama, *cham*. Tengboche hosts the most famous of such performances, Mani Rimdu, on the day after the full moon of October–November (another performance is held at Thami in May), when monks wearing masks and costumes represent various good and bad guys in the story of Buddhism's victory over the ancient Bön religion in Tibet. Monasteries at Boudha also present *cham* dances around Losar (Tibetan New Year).

MODERN MUSIC

Pre-1951, Nepal had no radio and no recording industry, and those few artists who travelled to Calcutta to record their songs on 78rpm were known only to a handful of aristocrats with record players. The dawn of modern Nepali music came in 1952, the year after the fall of the Ranas, when **Radio Nepal** was established; only a year later, Dharma Raj Thapa made recording history, selling 3000 copies of a novelty song about the conquest of Everest by Hillary and Tenzing Norgay.

A homegrown **recording industry** took root under King Mahendra (1955–72), himself something of a patron of the arts, and with it came Nepal's first wave of **recording stars**. Still the best loved of these, though he died in 1991, is Narayan Gopal, whose songs are praised for their poignant *sukha-dukha* (happiness-sadness). Aruna Lama remains popular for her renditions of sad and sentimental songs, and Kumar Basnet for his folk songs, while Meera Rana is still in her prime, belting out classical, folk and even pop tunes. Several of Nepal's foremost composers also came out of this era, including Amber Gurung (now music director at the Royal Nepal Academy), Nati Kazi and Gopal Yonjan.

More recently, the growth of the Nepali **film industry** has opened up new horizons for composers and singers; television, introduced in the mid-1980s, has provided a further boost. These have in turn contributed to the establishment of new recording studios and cassette-reproduction concerns. That said, cinema and TV have also done their share of harm. By copying third-rate Indian productions, Nepali films have mainly enlarged the market for lowest-common-denominator music, turning audiences and musicians away from traditional styles and opening the floodgates to slick Indian-produced *masaala* ("spicy": a little of this . . . a little of that).

Other recent developments have cut both ways, too. Tourist culture shows have inevitably led to the commercialization of Nepali culture and music, yet they've also helped preserve folk arts by providing a source of income for musicians and dancers. *Ghazal*, another Indian import (see p.118), has done nothing for Nepali music, but it too pays the rent for Nepali musicians. Even Radio Nepal gives with one hand and takes away with the other, by providing an important outlet for musicians but at the same time blurring regional differences.

A few Nepali groups have recently achieved crossover success with what might be called East-meets-West **mood music**, employing traditional instruments in non-traditional arrangements and recording to high production standards. The tabla-sitar-flute trio Sur Sudha (see box) has defined this sound. **Pop music** is of course a growing proposition with young urban Nepalis. Locally produced material is pretty unlistenable, and with music videos now available in Nepal via satellite dish, we can only expect quantity (if not quality) to increase.

**Gopal Yonjan, Carol Tingey
and David Reed**

DISCOGRAPHY

Sur Sudha *Images of Nepal*. New-agey instrumental renditions of Nepali folk songs.

The Feeling *On Classical Instruments*. More new-agey ragas on tabla, flute and other traditional instruments.

Homnath Upadhyaya *Prastar Improvisation III: Towards the Peace*. East–West fusion music on traditional Nepali and Indian instruments.

Various artists *Typical Folk Tunes*. Compilation of music from various ethnic groups of the hills, including *paanchai baajaa* wedding tunes.

Amber Gurung *Kahiry Lahar Kahiry Tarang*. Good lyrics and music, although Gurung is a better composer than singer.

Narayan Gopal Gurubacharya *Jeevan Yatra*, vols 1, 2 and 3. Songs expressing life's sentiments by the late number-one vocalist.

Gopal Yonjan *Kanchi* and *Sindoor*. Nepali film music.

Prem Raj Mahat & Rekha Shaha *Simsimi Panima*. Nepali pop rooted in the folk tradition, by a male–female duo.

Prakash Gurung *Jhooma*. Nepali film music.

Ranjit Gazmer *Chino* and *Lahuray*. Nepali film music.

Prem Avatari *Flute Recital*.

Tarabir Tuladher *Sitar Recital*.

Stefano Castelli *Folk Songs of Nepal* (Albatros). *Jhyaure*, Tamang and shaman songs; sleeve notes in Italian.

John Melville Bishop *Music of a Sherpa Village* (Folkways). Introduction to folk music from Helambu.

Caspar Cronk *Songs and Dances of Nepal* (Folkways). A varied collection of short samples of Bhotiya, Thakali, Newar and Sherpa songs; excellent sleeve notes.

Laurent Aubert & M Lobsiger-Dellenbach *Musique de Fête chez les Newars* (Archives Internationales de Musique Populaire). Varied collection of 1950s and contemporary recordings.

TIBETAN EXILES IN NEPAL

On October 7, 1950, the People's Republic of China, which had concluded its own communist revolution only a year earlier, invaded – or, as Beijing still insists, "liberated" – Tibet. The Tibetan Army was easily overpowered, and by May 1951 Tibet was forced to sign a treaty accepting Chinese rule, on the understanding that China would not interfere with Tibetan government or culture.

During the following eight years, however, Chinese troops gathered in increasing numbers in Lhasa, the Tibetan capital; Tibetan monks were tortured, women raped and children taken from their homes for "re-education" in China. The Chinese imposed disastrous new agricultural methods on Tibetans, causing widespread famine. Tension mounted, fighting flared up in the east, and in March 1959 a full-scale **uprising** erupted in Lhasa. It was brutally crushed by the Chinese and thousands of Tibetans were executed or imprisoned, while Tibet was formally annexed to China. The **Dalai Lama**, Tibet's spiritual and political leader, fled to India; he still resides in Dharmsala, where the Tibetan government-in-exile is based. Tens of thousands of Tibetans followed, making their way into Nepal and India by various routes through the Himalaya.

For three decades, Tibet has endured outright **genocide** at the hands of the Chinese: the Dalai Lama's Bureau of Information calculates that 1.2 million Tibetans have been executed, tortured, killed in battle, starved or died in Chinese labour camps; during the 1966–76 Cultural Revolution, virtually every monastery was deliberately destroyed. An organized **guerrilla movement**, supported by the CIA, fought the Chinese along the Nepalese border until the early 1970s, when the US–China thaw led to its dissolution. Until a few years ago, Tibet's plight was largely ignored by the major powers, but China's Tiananmen Square massacre and the Dalai Lama's receipt of the 1989 Nobel Peace Prize put discussion of Tibetan independence back on the agenda.

Today, 15,000 out of a total of 110,000 **Tibetan exiles** live in Nepal, predominantly in the Kathmandu and Pokhara valleys. A large number of these industrious immigrants have by now achieved success in the carpet and handicrafts businesses, to the point where they can no longer be regarded as an underprivileged group. Many are playing an active role in establishing Boudha as a centre of Buddhist study, thus sustaining Tibetan religion and culture until the Chinese occupation of Tibet is ended.

Given Nepal's reliance on Chinese aid, the Tibetans are a source of discomfort for the government. China regards the exile communities as potential counter-revolutionary hotbeds, and exerts pressure on Nepal to supress any political activities there. While the "Free Tibet" movement is much bigger in India, where the Dalai Lama and the Tibetan government-in-exile are based, a **Tibetan underground** does exist in Nepal, chiefly among the disaffected youth of the former refugee camps. Don't expect anyone to discuss it openly, however, since Tibetan leaders have been warned that any "political" remarks could be grounds for prompt eviction. Recent political changes don't appear to have benefited the Tibetans, either. Nepal's powerful Communist Party has links with Beijing and is therefore keen to help keep Tibetan nationalism in check.

The following profiles contrast the experiences of two Tibetans now living in Nepal.

CHOKYI NYIMA RINPOCHE: A LAMA

Chokyi Nyima Rinpoche ("Sun Lotus of the Precious One") was born in Runying, a village about 150 miles north of Lhasa, in the year of the Iron-Hare, 1951, the son of a recognized *tulku* (reincarnate lama) and an aristocratic mother. At the age of one and a half, after successfully completing numerous tests prescribed by Tibetan Buddhist tradition, he was identified as the seventh incarnation of Gar Druchen, a spiritual emanation of Nagarjuna, the second-century Indian Buddhist philosopher. Soon after, the young *rinpoche* ("precious one", a title given to revered Tibetan Buddhist teachers) was enthroned at his predecessor's monastery, Drong Gon Thubten Dargyeling, in central Tibet.

Chokyi Nyima recalls how 35 of the monastery's 500 monks were involved in lifelong retreats, as opposed to the more common three- to nine-year retreats, living in caves with "no door, only a window to pass food through, and they would never come out for the rest of their life" – a testament to the extreme faith with which some 200,000 monks and nuns devoted their lives in over 6000 monasteries and nunneries prior to China's occupation of Tibet.

Following the failed Tibetan uprising and subsequent upheavals of 1959, Chokyi Nyima and his family were whisked into exile in Gangtok, Sikkim, where, along with 53 other young *rinpoche*, he studied briefly in an English boarding school. He soon resumed his traditional monastic education, however, and for the next fifteen years studied under a series of famous Buddhist teachers.

Chokyi Nyima relates how one day, when he was nineteen or twenty, he and another young *tulku* approached their tutor, Gyalwa Karmapa, head of the Kagyu-pa sect of Tibetan Buddhism, with the intention of entering a three-year retreat. "He scolded us, saying, 'You are foolish, you just want to go in a cave to sleep. You are *tulku*, you need to save and help the sentient beings . . . why do you think you are being educated like this? Even though I am very happy that you have a willingness to go on a retreat at such a young age – on the one hand it is a good quality, but on the other hand it is not good *enough!*'" Finally sealing Chokyi Nyima's future, Gyalwa Karmapa said, "I think it is your *karma* to teach, especially to foreigners. You will go to Nepal and help your father (Urgyen Rinpoche) build a monastery." Chokyi Nyima still fondly recalls the wisdom of his teacher: "His mind was like the ocean, whereas our minds were but a drop in that ocean."

In 1974, Chokyi Nyima came to Boudha to help his father build the Ka Nying Shedrupling Monastery, and soon after, on the instructions of Gyalwa Karmapa, was made its abbot. Ka Nying Shedrupling today houses some 120 monks and lay people, who are dedicated to preserving and spreading Tibetan Buddhism through traditional wood-block printing of *pechha* (Tibetan liturgical texts), translating and publishing Buddhist books in English, and maintaining a large library of books on Buddhist topics.

Following the wish of his tutor, Chokyi Nyima began teaching not only the local community but also a growing number of foreigners. "I like to find out what kind of people they are, why they came here and what they are searching for," he says. In fact, one of his first Western *dharma* students is now undertaking a three-year retreat at a Buddhist centre in Scotland. Tibetan Buddhists aren't surprised by the spread of Buddhism in the West, for they regard it as the fulfilment of an eighth-century prophecy attributed to Guru Padma Sambhava, the legendary founder of Buddhism in Tibet: "When the iron bird flies and horses run on wheels, the Tibetan people will be scattered across the face of the earth, and the *dharma* will come to the land of the red men."

One morning, during one of his daily public audiences, where there are invariably two or three Westerners, Chokyi Nyima explains his thoughts on the increasing number of Westerners interested in Tibetan Buddhism. Throughout the informal talk he is occasionally interrupted by pilgrims and the faithful coming to receive his blessings and exchange *kata*, the white scarves Tibetans give as an offering of good luck. "I've found that the teachings are touching more and more people from different countries, because they ring true," he says. "Many Westerners, especially the younger generation, are putting more faith in Western science only to discover that there are still many unexplained things. But because they have grown up with the idea of always searching for new answers to old phenomena, they usually have a very open mind. This is very much like what the Buddha said: 'Don't take my word for it, but find out the truth for yourself.'"

To this end, one of the aims of Ka Nying Shedrupling, as well as of many other monasteries, is to make Mahayana Buddhism readily available in the West. In Chokyi Nyima's words, "If peace comes to every individual, then there will be no conflicts, no problems, because nowadays too many people think often only of themselves. That's why we train more monks to be sent all over the world to help others to share their knowledge of the peace and caring message of the Buddha."

The often serious tone that Chokyi Nyima uses to make a point never overshadows his humble and good-natured personality. As we leave the morning teaching, he gives us a mischievous look and says, "You must meditate! Don't be lazy and forget what I've said," throwing three oranges at us from a pile given as offerings.

Andy Balestracci

GEN TASHI: A KHAMPA

A boyishly trim man with a chiselled jaw is making the last stitches on a brown *chuba* (Tibetan wrap-around dress). "There! In time for Losar (Tibetan New Year)," he says to a Manang woman, who is wearing several raw-looking chunks of turquoise and coral strung around her neck.

"Please, won't you —"

"No, I said *no*. Your aunt will just have to wear something else. It's two days to Losar, and you want me to stitch another *chuba*? It's Losar, woman; we Tibetans drop all work. You go home and get the altars prepared, and leave me to my preparations."

Gen Tashi takes off his thick glasses, revealing curiously brown-bluish eyes. He bought the round-cut glasses in Lhasa on his way back from his hometown a few years ago; folding them, he puts them away with great care.

In the same room sits a younger man, Karma, shaking out black snuff onto his thumb from an aspirin bottle. He inhales with gusto, then digs out a square piece of woollen cloth from under the rug on his bed to blow his nose. "Drop everything, do your *puja*, and enjoy yourself at Losar — it's only once a year," he tells the woman.

"All right, all right. Losar is Losar I know," she says, laughing. "I won't bother you anymore. *Tashi delek* (Good day) to you — but please, after Losar . . ." And with her new *chuba* wrapped in newspaper under her arm, she leaves Gen's workroom.

For a man of 70, Gen Tashi cuts a trim figure. He sits cross-legged, ramrod straight. When people comment about his lithe figure, he says he is light because of his daily *kora* (circumambulations) around the Swayambhu hill. "The *kora* make you feel you can walk on and on," he says.

Considering his present occupation and boyish good nature, it's hard to believe that Gen spent more than a decade as a guerrilla fighter just south of the Tibetan border. He was born to a peasant family in the valley of Gyelthang, at the southeastern edge of the Tibetan plateau (the district is today part of the so-called Tibetan Autonomous Prefecture of Dechen). At the age of 14 he became a monk at Gyelthang's Sumtseling Monastery, which at the time supported 2000 monks, and for the next 18 years spent at least part of each year at the monastery observing special prayers and liturgies. For the rest of the year, when he was old enough, Gen went on family trading trips east to Dali and Lijiang in Yunnan (China), and west to Lhasa and southwest Kalimpong in Sikkim, where Chinese tea and Indian cotton and manufactured goods were traded. The trade helped finance Gen's monastic exams and initiations.

Chinese troops marched into Gen's district in 1954 and began imposing exorbitant taxes on traders, though they held back from enforcing immediate political changes. At the time of the 1959 uprising, Gen — who had just turned 36, an age considered inauspicious by Tibetans — and his family were on a butter-buying trip near Lhasa, attempting to raise money for their lama's examinations. Joining other Khampas (people of Kham, a province in eastern Tibet) caught away from home by the uprising, Gen rushed to help guard the Norbu Lingka, the Dalai Lama's summer palace in Lhasa, until the Dalai Lama could escape. Anticipating reprisals from the Chinese after the uprising, Gen fled south to Gangtok, Sikkim, where he and many compatriots found work building mountain roads.

Later the same year, the news of a reformed guerrilla movement known as the "Four Rivers and Six Ranges" reached Sikkim. Gen and a dozen fellow Gyelthangbas quickly joined up and were deployed to Mustang, the arid, rugged area north of Pokhara, where he participated in a variety of sabotage activities against the Chinese garrisoned across the border in Tibet. "I became good at hiding arms and ammunition underground," he says, not with bravado but with a sigh at being engaged in martial activities anathema to his vows as a Buddhist monk. (Several years have passed since he relinquished his vows.)

But lacking in international support, the guerrilla operations in Nepal gradually petered out, and the military camps became semipermanent settlements. Gen dropped out of the movement and took up tailoring, earning a living by sewing *chuba* for the camp. Finally, after twelve years in Mustang, he and Karma, a fellow Khampa, together with Karma's wife, decided to move down to Kathmandu: their lives and the struggle didn't seem to be leading anywhere.

What had it all been for? "Well, we carried the hope that we could return to our fatherland," says Gen, for the first time showing emotion.

For their new lives in the capital, they found themselves hopelessly handicapped. By then, the efforts of other Tibetans to turn the folk art of carpet-weaving into a commercially viable venture was paying off; most of them were no longer refugees. In contrast, Gen, Karma and his wife had to adjust to a new environment, learn a new language and start from scratch. The only livelihood they could turn to was stitching *chuba*.

For years they were barely able to make ends meet, but recently Karma has started earning large commissions selling antique carpets. Now only Gen needs to stitch *chuba*, while Karma's wife manages the household. She and Karma have a twelve-year-old son, Dhendup, who attends a Tibetan school in the valley. Unlike Gen and his parents, Dhendup can write and speak in English, Tibetan and Nepali. He calls Gen grandfather.

Among the shrinking number of first-generation Tibetan exiles in Nepal, especially those of Kham, Gen's story is a common one. Many spent a large part of their adult lives fighting for their country. Now, with just as much hope, though perhaps with less urgency, they still look to the day when they can return to their homeland. Until then, they continue to circumambulate and pray and work for their younger ones.

Kesang Tseten

To get involved in the Tibetan cause, contact:

Tibet Information Centre, 14 Napier Close, ACT 2600 (☎06/285 4046).

Friends of Tibet New Zealand, PO Box 5991, Auckland (☎09/436 066).

International Campaign For Tibet, 1735 "I" St NW, Suite 615, Washington DC 20006 (☎202/785-1515).

Office of Tibet, 241 E 32nd St, New York, NY 10016 (☎212/213-5010);1 Culworth St, London NW8 7AF (☎0171/722 5378).

Tibet Support Group Ireland, 120 Upper Glenageary Rd, Glenageary, Dublin (☎01/285 3443).

Tibet Support Group UK, 9 Islington Green, London N1 2XH (☎0171/359 7573).

DEVELOPMENT DILEMMAS

This is How a Nation Pretends to Survive

This is Machhapuchhre, Your Excellency!
And that's Annapurna.
And, beyond that are
The ranges of Dhaulagiri.
You can see them with your naked eyes.
I don't think you'll need any binocular, sir.
We want to open a three-star hotel, Your
  Excellency!
Will you give us some loan?

Your Excellency!
This is Koshi, that's Gandaki
And, that one, yes, that blue one, is Karnali.
You might have read in some newspapers
That rivers in Nepal are on sale.
But that's not true, sir.
In fact, we have named our zones
In the name of these rivers.
It's our plan to generate electricity from them.
Will you give us some loan?

This is Kathmandu Valley, Your Excellency!
I mean country's capital,
Which contains three cities –
Kathmandu, Lalitpur and Bhaktapur.
Please mind the smell!
You may use your handkerchief, if you like.
It's true we have not been able to build
Either the sewer or public lavatories.
But in the next five-year plan
We are definitely going to introduce
"Keep the City Clean" programme.
Will you give us some loan, Your Excellency!

Min Bahadur Bista (1989).

With a per-capita income of just $200, Nepal is one of the world's poorest nations. Its population of 21 million is rising at an annual rate of 2.1 percent, and is expected to triple by the middle of the next century. With agriculture unable to keep pace with demand, Nepal's "food deficit" is widening yearly and the country has little hope of ever feeding three times as many people – indeed, because of erosion due to overuse and deforestation, productivity may actually decline.

However, there are silver linings to all these dark clouds.

Nepali schoolchildren are frequently asked to write essays on "What I Would Do if I Were King". There are, of course, no right answers. Nepal is sloshing with foreign experts, all clamouring to offer their suggestions – and money – yet despite the efforts of the past four and a half decades the country remains economically poor. Some say Nepal's underlying problems, and the inefficacy of foreign aid, will keep it forever backward. Others point to tangible improvements that have been made, such as increases in life expectancy and literacy. Still others claim that Nepal's problems have been vastly overstated by the government (to ensure continued aid) and development agencies (to justify their payrolls).

"Development" is a word like "progress": it means different things to different people, and all too often is assumed uncritically to be a desirable end in itself. Throughout the world – not only in Nepal – no one has yet worked out whether development is in fact a Good Thing, and if so what form it should take. But after spending time in the field, many aid workers conclude that Nepalis – who lead rich and elegantly simple lives, nearly self-sufficient and unencumbered by many modern problems – have more to teach the "developed" (some would say overdeveloped) world than it has to teach them.

Pragmatists usually argue that development is going to come anyway, and communities should at least be given a fair choice as to what kind of development they want, rather than being forced to choose between development and non-development. But while no one advocates withholding aid or denying Nepalis' aspirations to certain material improvements, many in the development world reckon that Nepali schoolchildren are probably better able to solve their own problems than foreign experts, and that Nepalis ought to be the ones who decide what is appropriate development for Nepal.

Most people agree that Nepal's overarching problem ("challenge", in development parlance) is **poverty**, which can be traced to a number of factors: steep terrain, which makes farming inefficient and communications difficult; landlocked borders; few natural resources; a rigid social structure that entrenches the rich against the poor; and a comparatively late start (the Nepalese government did essentially nothing for its people before 1951). Unable to do anything about these causes, most development organizations have devoted themselves to alleviating symptoms.

All too often, foreigners (and, it has to be said, some Nepalis) have tended to view Nepal's situation as a set of problems that could be identified, measured and solved in isolation. Trouble is, life isn't like that: tackling one problem often only succeeds in shifting it to another area. For example, better health and sanitation are obvious requirements, but providing them increases the rate of population growth, at least in the short term. Curbing population is no simple task, for it is rooted in poverty and the low status of women. In the meantime, agriculture has to be improved to feed the growing population, deforestation reversed to stop the fuel wood crisis, and industry developed to provide jobs. Irrigation projects, roads, hydroelectric diversions are needed . . . you get the idea. Even if you resolve that development should be left to Nepalis, education, or at least "awareness-raising" programmes, will be required to get the ball rolling, and that means not so much building schools as addressing the poverty that keeps children from attending classes.

To take a more holistic approach, the big donor countries have come up with the idea of **integrated rural development projects (IRDPs)**, in which various sub-projects are coordinated to complement each other. The Swiss IRDP at Jiri and the British one in Dhankuta are prominent examples. Unfortunately, projects like these run counter to the "small is beautiful" maxim: they're terribly expensive (and therefore unlikely ever to be successfully passed on to Nepali management), prone to corruption and, in the end, limited to tiny geographic areas. Again, there are no easy, pat answers – only dilemmas.

The following sections only scratch the surface of complex issues. Many simplifications have been made. Some dilemmas are unique to Nepal, but many – if not most – are common to the entire "developing" world. The vast majority of people in the "developed" world are dangerously ignorant of the terrible pressures building in the poorer nations; travelling in Nepal affords a chance to witness the inequities first hand and grapple with some of the dilemmas, which cannot help but make you re-examine your own lifestyle.

HEALTH

People rarely starve to death – usually **malnutrition** weakens their systems to a point where simple infections prove fatal. It may seem hard to believe, but 80 percent of Nepal's cute little children are undernourished, and up to 15 percent are clinically malnourished. As a result, **child mortality** (ages 0–5) is estimated at 165 per 1000, although this is an improvement over 1960, when the figure was 300 per 1000 – almost one in three. The introduction of cheap oral rehydration packets, together with simple immunization programmes, are largely responsible for saving these lives.

Nepal is one of the few countries in the world where men live longer than women: **life expectancy** is 55 for males, 54 for females. Females are the last in the family to eat (one study found that Nepali girls under the age of five suffer 50 percent higher malnutrution than boys) and are expected to work harder (another study estimated women do 57 percent of all farm work in Nepal).

Poor sanitation, unsafe water and crowded, smoky conditions contribute to Nepal's high incidence of **disease**. Up to 80 percent of the population are reckoned to be suffering from parasitic infections at any one time, and 8 percent have TB. Nepal's per-capita leprosy rate is among the highest in the world – higher, even, than India's – with an estimated 24,500 cases. On the bright side, mosquito spraying in the Tarai has reduced malaria cases to about 25,000 annually, compared with two million a year during the 1950s (but even this is on the way back up). Improved public **sanitation** is gradually being introduced, but in the booming Tarai cities covered sewers are barely keeping pace with growth, while village latrines are still rarely found off the popular trekking routes. Communal taps and wells have been built in many villages to provide **drinking water**, yet as of 1991 (the latest year for which such figures are available) only 37 percent of Nepalis had access to safe water.

Although the government, aided by United Mission to Nepal and others, has constructed over 110 hospitals to date, Western-style facili-

THE DEVELOPMENT INDUSTRY

Everyone loves to give aid to Nepal. Although carpet manufacture is officially listed as the country's top source of foreign exchange, the development industry is even bigger. Aid to Nepal brings in around $250 million annually in direct grants and concessionary loans, not counting the value of technical assistance.

Foreign development projects in Nepal fall roughly into three categories. **Bilateral** (and multilateral) aid – that is, money given or lent by foreign governments directly to Nepal – has financed most of the infrastructure (roads, dams, airports), as well as the biggest IRDPs. Many smaller projects are carried out by hundreds of international **non-governmental organizations (NGOs)**; some of these are well known, such as Oxfam, CARE and Save the Children, while others are just one person doing fieldwork and raising sponsorship money in his or her home country. Voluntary NGOs, such as Britain's Voluntary Service Overseas (VSO) and the US Peace Corps, generally don't run their own projects, but instead slot volunteers into existing HMG programmes. Finally, **international lending bodies** like the World Bank and Asian Development Bank act as brokers to arrange loans for big projects with commercial potential – usually irrigation and hydroelectric schemes.

Many of these organizations do excellent work; almost all are motivated by the best possible intentions. However, money cannot automatically solve Nepal's problems, as some of the biggest projects have learned to their cost. By paying their imported experts ten or twenty times more than Nepalis to do the same job, the big bilateral missions can cause resentment or, worse, encourage Nepalis to gather round the aid trough instead of doing useful work. And to the extent that they import experts and materials, they undermine Nepalis' ability to do things for themselves, fostering a crippling **aid dependency** that now permeates almost every level of society. In 1983, foreign handouts made up forty percent of Nepal's development budget; in 1993 it was up to sixty percent. Some wags joke that the country can't *afford* to develop, lest it jeopardize development funding.

So why is everybody clamouring to give aid to Nepal? For bilateral donors, foreign aid is a handy way of buying **political influence**. China and India are forever one-upping each other with offers to Nepal, which they regard as a crucial buffer state; and while Nepal is of less strategic interest to the main Western powers, they're happy to throw some small change Nepal's way just to ensure a compliant regime.

Aid is also a means of stimulating the donor country's own domestic economy: for example, more than half of British aid to Nepal (which amounts to £10 million annually) is paid directly to British **contractors**. Thus the emphasis of aid is usually on Western-style techno-fixes and economic growth, rather than appropriate technology and self-sufficiency. Encouraging farmers to, say, irrigate and buy fertilizers to grow cash crops may raise their income, but not necessarily their quality of life. It will, however, give Western banks a capital project to finance, Western contractors an irrigation system to build, Western chemical companies a new market for fertilizers, and Western consumer-goods companies new consumers. Meanwhile, Nepalese cash crops may be exported out of the area (probably to India), even as Nepalis suffer malnutrition.

For their part, institutions like the World Bank and its sister organization, the International Monetary Fund, have reputations for pushing expensive **megaprojects** that often prove inappropriate for their impoverished recipients, and for imposing harsh "structural adjustment" programmes when debtor nations can't repay their loans. Fortunately, these institutions finally seem to be moving with the times. In 1995 the new head of the World Bank scrapped plans for a mega-hydroelectric project in eastern Nepal (see p.410), in what seems to be an effort to steer the Bank towards smaller, more environmentally sensitive projects.

But even when foreign governments and agencies try to step back and do the right thing, their charity may still have a corrupting influence. The latest fashionable philosophy is that the best way to get things done is to finance **local NGOs**, which, it's assumed, have a better handle on local problems and solutions than foreign experts. Sounds great in theory, but what's the result? An explosion in local NGOs for every conceivable cause, all sounding just as right-on as could be: "small-scale" this, "women's development" that, "environmental" whatever. (There are now so many local NGOs in Nepal that at least one exists simply to co-ordinate them all.) Unfortunately, some of these organizations aren't doing much besides writing grant proposals, and the only development they're assisting is their director's bank balance.

ties are neither affordable nor appropriate for most villages. A better measure of progress on this front has been the creation of some 800 primary **healthcare posts**, where health assistants (often local people) are trained in traditional ayurvedic practices.

POPULATION

Slowing **population growth** isn't just a matter of passing out condoms. In Nepal, as in other countries, children are relied on to do many time-consuming chores – fetching water, gathering fuel, tending animals – and are also considered an investment for old age, since there's no state pension to draw on. Moreover, Nepalis tend to have large families because they can't be sure all their children will survive. Hindus, especially, keep trying until they've produced at least one son, who alone can perform the prescribed rites (*shradha*) for his parents after they've died.

While it's not the place of aid workers to contradict Hindu beliefs, population-control efforts can have little impact unless the **status of women** (see p.411) is raised, which to a great extent is a matter of providing them with paid employment opportunities. Earning income doesn't merely empower women; it makes it more expensive for them to have children, since to do so means stopping work. Education can also play an important part in bringing down birth rates – but the education must be targeted not so much at women, who already know they're repressed, but at men, who do the repressing. Many "women's programmes" have failed because they've assumed that women only need to be provided with the awareness and skills to improve their situation; in fact they can do little if their husbands still hold the power.

The other reasons for **high fertility** could be removed by reducing the current high levels of poverty and child mortality, and by providing ready sources of fuel and water to reduce the usefulness of extra hands. It's often said that "development is the best contraceptive", and indeed, there is a close correlation between rising standards of living and declining birth rates. Unfortunately, in most countries this so-called **demographic transition** involves a period of rapid population growth until the birth rate settles down to match the lower death rate. Some East Asian countries have seen their birth rates fall more or less simultaneously with their economies' rise, but Nepal is not, alas, in the same economic league.

At the moment, Nepal's population is still very much in growth mode. Currently doubling every 34 years, the population has a biological momentum that is unlikely to be checked in the present generation, simply because of the number of girls already approaching child-bearing age. Meanwhile, the government's **family planning** efforts are still woefully inadequate: only fifteen percent of Nepalis practise any form of contraception at all. The remoteness of villages makes it all the more difficult to get the message out.

If Nepal's population doubles or triples, where will all the extra people live? As it happens, this is not a brand-new situation, for some parts of the middle hills have probably been overpopulated for the past century. **Emigration** – to the Tarai, India and, more recently, to Kathmandu and overseas – has always regulated the people pressure. Significantly, the latest census (1991) shows a dramatic decline in the annual rate of population growth – to 2.1 percent, down from 2.6 percent a decade earlier – most of which is probably due to emigration. Even so, it's estimated that the country's urban population will double in the next decade, and most of this increase will be taken up by the Kathmandu Valley and a half-dozen Tarai cities.

AGRICULTURE

If Nepal's population doubles, **food production** must theoretically double, too – a seemingly unattainable goal, given that in the past decade the country has gone from being a net exporter of food to a net importer.

Nepal's farmland is already among the most intensely cultivated in the world. A mere 20 percent of the country's land area is arable; clearing new land for cultivation only adds to deforestation, so it's preferable to find ways of increasing the productivity per acre. Various methods have been tried in Nepal, as in other countries. Agriculture experiment stations, such as the British-funded facility at Pakhribas in the eastern hills, have achieved some success in showcasing **high-yielding seeds** and animal breeds. **Pesticides** and chemical **fertilizers** are now heavily used in the Kathmandu Valley and Tarai, thanks to government encouragement, but unfortunately neither users nor sellers have much training in proper application, resulting in an alarming recent rise in health problems. (Meanwhile, Kathmandu Valley produce, which used to be organic by default, is now sometimes laced with unhealthy levels of agricultural chemicals.) Pesticides and fertilizers are beyond the means of most Nepali farmers, so average yields on staple crops such as rice and wheat have shown little improvement in the past decade. It is those farmers well-off enough to move into **cash crops** who have been able to make use of these inputs, more than doubling their yields in the same period.

Irrigation is another high priority for improving productivity, since it permits an extra crop to be grown during the dry season. Small-scale community projects are now being built with generally good results, but the government's inefficient and poorly maintained projects have resulted in benefit to relatively few farmers (usually the best-off ones). It's been estimated that a big government-built system costs at least eight times more per acre than a community-built one.

Stark inequities prevail in Nepal's agriculturally based economy. Controlled by vested interests, the government has done a poor job of enforcing **land reform**, with the result that 63 percent of cultivable land is still owned by 16 percent of the population. Despite a 1964 law prohibiting landlords from charging tenant farmers annual rents of more than 15 percent of their crop, many farmers are locked in a hopeless cycle of debt and victimized by unscrupulous lenders. **Credit** is therefore a pressing need. Various government programmes extend credit to poor farmers to tide them over lean months, with variable success, but the official Agriculture Development Bank, which was created to make loans for simple improvements, has unfortunately grown so bureaucratic that only wealthier farmers can avail themselves of it.

Most people agree that agriculture must receive the main thrust of development efforts in Nepal. With over 80 percent of Nepalis still making their living from the land, it's unrealistic to look for miracles elsewhere.

DEFORESTATION AND EROSION

In the Nepal hills, population, agriculture and environmental damage combine in a worrying vicious cycle: the need for more food leads to more intensive use of the land, which degrades the environment and lowers productivity, which further increases pressure on the land. An expanding population needs not only more **firewood**, but also more **fodder** for animals, which provide manure to maintain soil fertility. Overuse of firewood and fodder results in **deforestation**, as does any expansion of farmland, and as a result Nepal's forest area is shrinking by as much as one percent per year. Trees help anchor the fragile Himalayan topsoil – removing them causes **erosion** and landslides, which not only reduce the productivity of the land but also send silt down to the Bay of Bengal, contributing to disastrous **floods** in Bangladesh.

Or so goes the theory. In practice, emigration seems to stabilize the cycle, and studies give wildly differing estimates for the rate of deforestation. The most that can be said is that the situation is definitely bad in some areas, but not so bad in others. Experts still don't know to what extent deforestation contributes to erosion, but most agree that the prime cause is simply the natural sloughing and shifting of very young mountains.

Even the government now admits it got it wrong in the 1950s when it **nationalized the forests** to protect them. Before that, the forests had been competently managed by local communities; but when the trees were taken away from them, locals felt they had no stake in their preservation, and because government enforcement was weak they easily plundered them. HMG's current policy of **community forestry** is supposed to give the forests back to the people, recognizing that villagers are in fact very ecologically minded and will manage their forests responsibly and sustainably so long as they don't fear re-nationalization. While foreign development projects have concentrated mainly on **reforestation**, newly planted areas account for only about one percent of Nepal's forest cover.

Deforestation is a separate issue **in the Tarai**, where the trees have been felled as a matter of policy, to make way for settlers and to earn money for the government through state-sanctioned timber sales. Although the vast majority of the Tarai's magnificent native forest has gone in the past four decades, the clearing continues. Nepal has won praise abroad for setting aside large chunks of the Tarai's forests as **national parks** and wildlife reserves, but the government can expect mounting resistance from its own people, who question why such valuable land should be set aside for tourists and crop-destroying animals (see p.272).

ELECTRICITY, ROADS AND OTHER TECHNOLOGY

Many see **electricity** – specifically hydroelectricity – as Nepal's greatest natural resource and a vital engine for development. The country's steep, mountain-fed rivers are estimated to have hydroelectric potential to the tune of 83 million megawatts – enough to power the British Isles. Unfortunately, due to the cost of getting materials and technical experts into Nepal's rugged backcountry, this potential is rather expensive to harness. Ironically for a

country so richly endowed, only 10 percent of Nepalis have access to electricity, and the supply falls so short of demand that grid managers must resort to frequent load-shedding (scheduled power cuts) during the dry season.

Yet Nepal's electricity use is soaring at an annual clip of 15 percent, fuelled mainly by demand from industry and urbanites' growing reliance on electrical appliances. Most economic planners see this as a healthy trend, and regard a growing supply of electricity as essential for stimulating domestic industry and creating employment. This, however, locks Nepal into an expensive quest for power.

Fortunately, Nepal has always been able to rely on foreign donors to finance the showcase **large-scale hydroelectric** projects which provide most of its electricity. Diversions have been built on the Kulekhani (south of Kathmandu) and the Marsyangdi (along the Prithvi Highway), and further medium-to-large-scale projects are planned for other rivers. Such major diversions have serious drawbacks –

DEATH OF A MEGAPROJECT

In 1987, the World Bank selected the upper reaches of the Arun River in eastern Nepal to be the site of a world-class hydroelectric diversion projected to cost $770 million. The so-called **Arun III** project was conceived as a strategic effort for Nepal not only to meet its growing demand for electricity but also to earn significant revenue by exporting surplus power.

Early concerns about the environmental consequences of building an access road to the site were silenced by the establishment of the huge Makalu–Barun National Park and Conservation Area, to the west of the Arun. Some observers questioned the wisdom of a poor country like Nepal putting all its eggs into such a costly basket, but no organized opposition surfaced until 1993, when the small **Alliance for Energy** charged that HMG had failed to properly investigate more appropriate alternatives to Arun III. The following year another ad-hoc organization, **Arun Concerned Group**, lodged a formal appeal with the World Bank's newly formed Inspection Panel. It was a David-versus-Goliath proposition if ever there was one: Arun III was precisely the sort of Third World megaproject the World Bank had been sponsoring for decades over the objections of the world's biggest environmental groups.

But change was afoot within the lending giant, and Arun III was to become one of the first indicators of it. Reassessing every aspect of the project, the Inspection Panel concluded that it was **too big** an undertaking for Nepal, allowing too little margin for error and claiming too great a share of the country's slender development budget. The panel also found that Arun III would probably drive up Nepal's electricity tariffs – already the highest in South Asia – by 50 percent, calling into question the economic justification for building it. In 1995, incoming World Bank president James Wolfensohn **cancelled** Arun III, pledging to redirect the Bank's share of the funding towards eighteen small- and medium-scale hydro projects and a package of development assistance to the Arun region.

The decision rocked Nepal's political establishment and, for many, underscored the humiliating extent to which outside interests control Nepal's development agenda. Some warned that the loss of Arun III would mean even more serious power shortages and economic stagnation in the coming decade. Others expressed relief that Nepal would now be free to pursue smaller, less sophisticated projects that it could build, operate and maintain with less foreign involvement. The new-look World Bank seems to favour the latter view. Let's hope they're right.

they're environmentally disruptive, require vast inputs of foreign aid to build, and put Nepal at the mercy of foreign experts to operate and maintain them – but if Nepal is to keep up with its demand for electricity they are probably a necessary evil. **Microhydro** projects can't deliver the kind of power industry needs, but they are appropriate technology for mountain villages too remote to be economically connected to the grid. Scores of these have been installed (both with foreign and private Nepalese funding) to supply electricity for a few hundred households each.

Rural electrification, both on and off the grid, can encourage local economic development, reduce fuel wood use, and benefit women and children by freeing up time otherwise spent gathering wood. However, electricity is no use to the majority of Nepalis who can't afford it, and it can only play a limited role in offsetting deforestation: as far as most rural Nepalis are concerned, wood is free, whereas electricity costs rupees – and electric appliances cost dollars. Some observers reckon that providing electric lights only encourages people to stay up later and burn more wood to keep warm. In trekking villages like Namche and Tatopani, however, where innkeepers cook with electricity, the net wood saving is probably worthwhile.

The introduction of relatively cheap, domestically produced **solar water heaters** promises to take some of the pressure off the electric grid and the forests; the price of photovoltaic panels may soon become cheap enough to do likewise. But at the household level, appropriate technology has to be something the average Nepali peasant can afford, which isn't much. Several groups have worked hard to introduce "**smokeless**" *chulo* (stoves), which burn wood more efficiently and reduce unhealthy kitchen smoke. Yet even this simple innovation illustrates the dilemmas of tampering with traditional ways: Nepalis complain that the new stoves aren't as easy to regulate and don't emit enough light, while the lack of smoke allows insects to infest their thatched roofs; thus many Nepalis are converting from thatch to corrugated metal.

Roads, like big hydroelectric and irrigation projects, don't come out well in cost-benefit analyses in Nepal, though planners insist that they're necessary for development. They cost far more than Nepal could ever afford without aid, and are almost as expensive to maintain;

many are hastily built, only to wash away with the next monsoon. The wealthy – bus owners, truckers, merchants, building contractors – benefit from road-building, while porters and shopkeepers along the former walking route lose out. Nevertheless, roads form an important part of Nepal's development strategy because it's virtually impossible to deliver services, administer projects, maintain order or even collect taxes in areas not served by roads. By contrast, **footbridges** put villages within easier reach of jobs and health facilities, and enable villagers to get their produce to market more efficiently, making them perhaps the most useful and popular type of public-works project.

WOMEN AND CHILDREN

Outside the relative sophistication of Kathmandu, Hindu **women** are a long, long way from liberation. In remote rural areas, they're considered their husband's or father's chattel, given or taken in marriage for the price of, say, a buffalo – a status reinforced by law. Orthodox Bahuns, while in the minority, reveal the extent of female subjugation. They believe a woman is ritually unclean during menstruation and for ten days after giving birth, and that she must remain apart during that period and drink cow's urine to cleanse herself. Polygamy, though officially outlawed, is widely practised in the hills, and if a woman doesn't produce a son she's liable to be replaced. Sherpanis and other Buddhist women are treated much more equally, and high-caste Hindu women may easily flout conventions, but even these women don't enjoy true power-sharing. (Indeed, when it comes to gender roles, the wealthy and sophisticated of Kathmandu can be as traditional as any villager: the sudden popularity of foetal ultrasound testing services in the capital suggests that some couples are seeking to eliminate unwanted females.)

Several development problems already touched on – inequities between the sexes in health care and education, and the failure of population-control efforts – arise directly from the low status of women in Nepal. Another tragic consequence is the **trafficking** of Nepali girls for Indian brothels. It's estimated that 200,000 Nepalis have been sold into sexual slavery in India – a third of them in Bombay alone – where patrons prize them for their beauty and supposed lack of inhibitions. To

THE END OF THE ROAD

Anna Robinson worked for three years as a VSO volunteer in Doti District, in the far western hills, and is now field officer for VSO Nepal.

Gazing down from the hill, over terraces of paddy fields, we could see the first truck making its hesitant journey up the spiralling new dust road. Local people ran down the main street of the bazaar to meet the first iron monster to complete the ascent.

For them it was the excitement of seeing a machine that moved along the ground. For me it was the feeling that here, at last, was a link with the outside world. There was the weekly plane to Kathmandu, of course. But with only eighteen seats – and $30 a seat at that – it was hardly significant to most people.

Excitement about the road lasted quite a while. Then people became less frightened and awe-struck, and the verges were no longer dotted with rapt, admiring observers. Those who could afford the fare became seasoned travellers and were no longer to be seen vomiting out of the windows as the truck lurched along. In fact it became an accepted part of daily life – rather like the plane, it came and went, affecting few people.

Goodies

But down by the airstrip, a shantytown of temporary shacks sprang up overnight with the coming of the road. Here was where all the goodies that came by truck from India were to be found: plastic snakes that wriggled, gilt hair-slides, iron buckets, saucepans and – best of all – fresh fruit and vegetables.

For us foreigners, and the paid office workers, accustomed to going for weeks with nothing but potatoes and rice in the shops, it seemed like paradise. Every day more and more apples, oranges, onions, cabbages and tomatoes would make their way up the hill. There was even a rumour that ten bottles of Coca-Cola had been sighted in the bazaar.

One morning, as I was eyeing a big plastic bucket full of huge Indian tomatoes in a local shop, a woman pulled my arm. "Don't you want to buy mine?" she asked. And there, in her *doko*, were a few handfuls of the small green local tomatoes.

Just a fortnight earlier I would have followed her eagerly, begging to be allowed to buy some. Now the shopkeeper laughed at her: who would want to buy little sour green tomatoes when there were big sweet red ones to be had?

For women like her, trudging in for miles from one of the surrounding villages to sell her few vegetables, there was no longer a market. The influential bazaar shopkeepers negotiated deals with the Indian traders with their truckloads of vegetables. The new road meant new money for the shopkeepers – but less for the poor, whose livelihood was undermined and who had no way of buying the wonderful new merchandise.

Casualties

There were other casualties, too. Gaggles of poor women, who had made a living out of carrying people's baggage from the airstrip to the bazaar, were once a common sight, haggling in angry, spirited voices over the price of their services. But with the coming of the new road, people simply boarded one of the trucks – baggage and all. Ragged and downtrodden at the best of times, these women were reduced to silently and gratefully accepting any rate people were prepared to pay for their help.

I began to wonder about the road. But I needn't have worried. Soon the monsoon rains arrived and the swelling river took charge of things. Within days the bridge was completely washed away, leaving several trucks stranded on the wrong side of the river, never to return to India.

After the monsoon

The original truck continued to creak up and down the winding road between the airstrip and the bazaar, its fuel being hoisted across the river by rope-pulley, but became so overcrowded that one day it broke down halfway up the hill. As the road had been almost completely washed away by the rain, it was simply left there in the middle of the road.

When the monsoon ended, it was overgrown with creepers and made a very pleasant home for a local family.

By then the grand new road was little more than a memory. The women porters went back to climbing regularly up and down the hill; the shantytown vanished as quickly as it had appeared; and everyone went back to eating rice and potatoes as before.

Last I heard, a foreign-aid agency had decided to rebuild the road, with a proper bridge this time: in the interests of development.

Anna Robinson

Reproduced by permission of New Internationalist Publications.

poor Hindu families in Nepal, daughters are often regarded as burdens, costing money to be married off and then becoming another family's asset; when a middleman comes offering, say, Rs15,000 for a pubescent daughter, many readily agree. A prostitute may eventually buy her freedom, but ordinarily she won't be released until she's been "damaged" – which these days means she has AIDS (the World Health Organization estimates that 100,000 Nepalis will be infected by the year 2000). So far the Nepal government, which has its hands full with other public health matters such as TB and malaria, has shown little inclination to act on the growing problem. Concerned NGOs have been left to set up homes for former prostitutes, who would otherwise be shunned by family and friends if they returned to their villages.

The **women's movement** is embryonic in Nepal. Women weren't granted the vote until 1948, and though the All Nepal Women's Organization was formed in 1951, women working for social change were forced to operate underground until the 1990 restoration of democracy. Aid projects and agencies have been chiefly concerned with setting up cottage-industry employment for women, so they can earn spare cash as a first step to some sort of self-determination. Two very successful efforts, the Bangladesh-based Grameen Bank and the Nepalese government's Production Credit for Rural Women programme, have targeted women's development by making "**microenterprise loans**" to small, self-organizing groups of women and supporting the borrowers with literacy, family-planning and other training.

Children, like women, are often victims of poverty in Nepal. As already mentioned, however much their parents love them, in poor familes they are counted as an economic resource from an early age. **Child labour** has always been essential in agriculture, and in the past it was common for children to work as unpaid servants for village landowners simply so there would be one less mouth to feed. In the growing cash economy, however, children are increasingly being relied on to earn wages as porters, *kanchha* ("boys"), carpet-weavers or tea-pluckers. One survey suggests that two-thirds of the carpet industry's labour force is made up of children under the age of 16. Not only are these youngsters forced to work long hours in unhealthy conditions, and are frequently abused, they are deprived of their childhood – the right to play, be loved and be educated. The government has passed laws against child labour, but this is yet another problem that can only be effectively addressed by attacking its root cause: poverty. (See p.96 for information on Kathmandu's street children.)

EDUCATION

Nepal's education system has come a long way in a short time. There were few state **schools** before 1951, and they were open only to the children of elites – now there are primary schools within walking distance of most villages, and legions of private schools in the Kathmandu Valley. However, primary-school enrolment is probably well below the official figure of 80 percent, and actual attendance may be less than 25 percent. Only 13 percent of boys – and just 3 percent of girls – finish secondary school. The trouble is that "free" public education is actually quite expensive for families who depend on their children for labour, and so in a poor country like Nepal, government-subsidized schools tend to benefit the well-off more than the poor. The country has made great strides in increasing **literacy**, though the gulf between adult males (55 percent) and females (25 percent) is telling.

Nepal's proportion of qualified **teachers** is very low (only 39 percent are trained), so most aid programmes have focused on teacher training. Low pay is another problem, sapping teachers' motivation and contributing to an estimated 50-percent *teacher* absentee rate. Western workers believe education could be a powerful catalyst for change in Nepal, but many complain that the current curriculum is geared for churning out bureaucrats and should be made more vocational and relevant to a peasant population. Others worry that the sponsorship of education programmes by foreign agencies leads to a lack of accountability and a sense that the curriculum is externally designed.

Those who do finish high school and go on to one of Nepal's many **colleges** or **universities** often find that there's no work for them when they graduate – a common problem in most countries, but all the more acute in Nepal, whose non-agricultural sectors are particularly poorly developed. A further cultural complication is the prevalent attitude towards education in Nepal: equated with high status, it is all too often pursued merely to avoid physical labour, which carries low status. This, ironically, has the effect of removing many of Nepal's most highly trained people from the productive workforce. Frustrated by a lack of opportunities or just plain bored, the educated youth of the Kathmandu Valley make up a growing class of angry young men given to revolutionary talk and *goonda* antics.

INDUSTRY AND TRADE

Nepal needs to create jobs – agriculture simply cannot absorb all of its growing workforce. Moreover, a developing nation like Nepal has to produce things, not only for domestic consumption but also for export, so that it can earn foreign exchange to pay for the imported technology and materials it needs for development. That means boosting **industry**, which in Nepal's case accounts for a relatively low 16 percent of gross domestic product.

Carpets are Nepal's great rags-to-riches story, having now exploded into a $200 million industry employing (directly and indirectly) 300,000 people. Some analysts believe carpet manufacture has the potential to be Nepal's economic salvation: highly labour-intensive, it generates plenty of employment and adds lots of value to relatively cheap materials; it's also helping to diversify the economy away from an overreliance on tourism. But all this comes at a very high price in terms of exploitation, social disruption and pollution – see p.168.

Similarly, **tourism** has its drawbacks. The industry creates tens of thousands of much-needed jobs, plus indirect employment in related industries, but this work tends to be menial and seasonal. Moreover, the economic benefits of tourism are highly localized, and an estimated 80 percent of the foreign exchange earned from tourism goes right back out of the country to pay for imported materials. True, tourism can claim some credit for shaping HMG's mostly progressive environmental record – but it's an open question whether the revenue earned really offsets the ecological and cultural costs. The fruits of tourism, so arbitrarily awarded, have turned legions of Nepalis into panhandlers, in much the same way that aid has done to politicians and institutions.

In many other industries, Nepal finds itself in a classic Third World bind. It can't profitably produce things like vehicles and computers because its domestic market is so small (and poor), and importing even modest amounts of these items quickly runs up a nasty **trade deficit**. The government has therefore put much of its energy into stimulating the production of run-of-the-mill goods for domestic consumption, achieving dubious successes in some sectors. Beer production, to take one example, has increased 400 percent in the past decade. In development economics, this is known as **import substitution**: for a country short on foreign exchange, a penny saved is a penny earned. Washing powder, paper, cement and shoes have seen similarly dramatic increases in output. Many of these factories have been set up as licensed **monopolies**, which give the government more control over the pace of development, but tend to concentrate wealth in the hands of a few Kathmandu fat cats (the law requires that all businesses have a majority Nepali ownership, which makes for some very well-off silent partners). A few essential industries are still run as state-owned enterprises, but the government is gradually privatizing these poorly managed and typically loss-making concerns.

The presence of **India** as Nepal's neighbour to the south inevitably complicates matters. Nepal's main trading partner, India has traditionally levied high import duties to protect its own industries, thus benefiting Nepali border traders (who can sell imported goods for less than their Indian competitors), but crippling Nepali exporters (whose goods become uncompetitive with duty added on). Fortunately, Nepal's closer ties with India's leadership since the restoration of democracy have resulted in more favourable **terms of trade**, and the decision of both countries to make their currencies fully convertible has begun to make their goods more competitive in the world market. However, critics charge that the Congress Party, when it has been in power, has tended to turn a blind eye while Indian entrepreneurs bought up Nepal's choicest businesses.

ECONOMIC REFORM

Development workers advocate all sorts of wonderful-sounding ways to bring Nepal out of poverty; economists ask: how do we pay for it? Hard work and good ideas will amount to nothing unless they're accompanied by a sound economic strategy.

Central to Nepal's strategy since 1991 has been a policy of **economic liberalization**, which has meant selling off loss-making state enterprises, reducing restrictions and tariffs on imports, making the currency fully convertible, and allowing for easier licensing of banks and other businesses. These actions have helped open the door to a flood of foreign goods and capital, resulting in a dramatic increase in wealth and economic activity in the Kathmandu Valley and to a lesser extent in the urban centres of the Tarai. However, it should be noted that such policies are designed by and for those who already have the capital, and they offer little benefit to Nepal's subsistence farmers and labourers. Wealth is slow to trickle down in a country like Nepal.

Meanwhile, the government has not been adept at tackling its own fiscal shortcomings. During the 1990s its tax **revenues** have been rising only a tenth as fast as its expenditures (when expressed as a proportion of GDP), leading to a growing deficit and, consequently, less money to finance development. On a related note, one measure of **national debt** more than doubled between 1983 and 1993 (the latest year for which figures are available). Chronically short of funds, the government is unable to operate its infrastructure efficiently, makes short-sighted decisions, and has little left over to invest in improvements; indeed, the government's fiscal inefficiency is such that it can't even utilize much of the foreign aid being offered to it.

KATHMANDU VALLEY PROBLEMS

Solutions often create their own problems. For forty years, people have been trying to get Nepal to develop – now that it has, in the **Kathmandu Valley**, many are nervously fumbling for the "off" switch.

Kathmandu appears to be following in the footsteps of other Asian capitals like Bangkok, Taipei and Seoul, albeit on a smaller scale. Overpopulation is driving a growing **rural exodus**; new roads and bus services are carrying the landless poor away from their villages, while jobs in the carpet and tourism industries

attract them to the Kathmandu Valley. Many immigrants land jobs and begin the difficult process of finding a place for themselves in the **big city**, and a few even find their fortune there. But there's no safety net for those who don't. They may end up squatting in the most primitive conditions imaginable – in unhealthy shacks by the river, in empty buildings, in the streets – and scrounging a living from the rubbish heaps or prostitution.

While poverty is a perennial problem in the valley, it's prosperity that's creating the brand-new headaches, starting with **traffic** and **pollution**. Industrial workers get to their factories by tempo or bus. The more affluent drive their own motorbikes or cars. Goods must be moved by truck. Tourists take taxis. The result is ever-growing gridlock and an increasing smog problem from a fleet of vehicles that is doubling every two to three years. In addition, carpet-washing factories release toxic chemicals into the environment, and the tide of raw sewage being dumped into streams rises ever higher with the population. Those who can afford to are moving out to the suburbs, and their commuting only worsens the problem.

Meanwhile, sheer numbers of people are taxing the valley's other infrastructure. In Kathmandu, demand for **drinking water** is about three times higher than supply, with the result that residents in most neighbourhoods have pressure only on alternate mornings or evenings – most pump what water they can get up to rooftop storage tanks, and supplement it with deliveries by tanker. (The government and the UN Development Programme are studying the feasibility of diverting water from the Malemchi Khola, northeast of the valley, to augment the supply.) Similarly, the valley accounts for a disproportionate amount of Nepal's energy demand, thanks to personal affluence (videos and refrigerators) as well as industrial growth – which, as already discussed, means rationing in the form of **load shedding**. **Garbage** is another problem, not only because the valley's growing population is generating more of it, but also because its municipalities still haven't agreed on a permanent dumping site.

The damage that has been done to the valley's **culture** in the name of progress is less easy to quantify, but is arguably more profound. Traditional architecture is no longer valued. Members of the younger generation are drifting away from the religion of their parents. *Guthi* (charitable organizations) are in decline and have been forced to leave the upkeep of many temples to foreign preservationists. Tourism has robbed crafts of their proper use, and many performance arts of their meaning. Work outside the home has disrupted family life, and the influx of strangers has introduced social tensions and crime.

But perhaps we shouldn't be unduly pessimistic. The government and aid agencies are working to address all of these problems, or at least the more tangible ones. And what may seem horrendous to an outsider may well be cheerfully accepted by Kathmandu residents as the price of progress – indeed, a little pollution or crime will seem a small price to pay for improvements that are able to keep children from dying and give people greater control over their lives.

BUREAUCRACY, CORRUPTION AND FATALISM

Many aid workers identify the root cause of Nepal's slow development as "institutional problems", a euphemism that covers a multitude of sins. They speak of management bottlenecks, where **bureaucrats** hoard power to such an extent that project managers have to spend most of their time in Kathmandu queueing for signatures instead of getting things done in the field. They complain that Nepali managers are overly fond of desk jobs in the capital, regarding remote hill postings as punishment and making no secret of their disdain for the local people they're supposed to be helping. (The most coveted position in Nepal is a job that involves no work and produces a regular pay cheque.) Managers frequently leave the important work to untrained underlings, preferring instead to pass their time in seminars. Slogans and planning targets are more in evidence than action, while planners tend to favour rigid, "top-down" approaches without consulting experts in the field. These traits aren't unique to Nepal, of course, and indeed many aid organizations are themselves centralized and top-down-oriented.

Unfortunately, though, there is little tradition of public service in Nepalese government, and the free-for-all of **corruption** was particularly

bad during the 1980s. Development agencies routinely had to pad their budgets by as much as 30 percent to allow for "leakage" – it's been estimated that $1 billion went missing during the decade. The graft has been perpetuated by artificially low salaries and, no doubt, by the sight of apparently limitless piles of development loot. Government regulations seem to have been devised to streamline the process – most bilateral aid, for instance, is required to be disbursed by HMG "line agencies".

These institutional problems are themselves only projections of Nepal's culture, elements of which seem almost designed to thwart Western-style development. One of Nepal's foremost anthropologists, Dor Bahadur Bista, argues compellingly that Nepal's greatest handicap is the **fatalism** peddled by its Bahun (Brahman) elite. According to Bista, along with Nepalis' admirable *ke garne* ("what to do?") attitude comes an exasperating apathy, and an obstructive suspicion that development efforts are merely futile attempts to resist fate. Responsibility for actions and decisions is often passed on to higher-ups (whether a boss, an astrologer or a deity), and the relationship between present work and future goals (at least in this life) is glossed over, resulting in haphazard planning and follow-through. Moreover, Nepali society places a great emphasis on connections and old-boy networks (called *aafno maanche* in Nepali: "one's own people"), which make it hard for members of ethnic minorities to advance, and on patronage, in which dependents are rewarded for loyalty rather than skill or innovation. Invaluable as these traits may be in a traditional village society, in a modern nation they tend to produce inept government, and foster a grovelling dependency on foreign patrons.

PROSPECTS

The foregoing isn't intended to make it sound as if Nepal's situation is hopeless, nor that there is no way for outsiders to help. Newcomers to the field tend to be the gloomiest ones, while people with a longer perspective are able to cite many major improvements. The country probably lost some ground during the greedy 1980s, and the restoration of democracy in 1990 hasn't proved the great watershed many had hoped – yet Nepal seems more in control of its own development than at any other time in its history, which has to be a change for the better. And given a more open political climate, responsible aid agencies stand a much better chance of achieving the work they've set out to do.

As a traveller, you too are playing a part in Nepal's development. With the right mixture of know-how and humility, you can be an agent of social change just by being yourself. Spent wisely, your money can bring tangible improvements to villages and families. In addition, there are plenty of good causes you may feel inclined to donate money to when you get home: with a little effort you should be able to see a few in action during your travels, and judge them by their fruits. (For a list of recommended charities, see p.x.)

NATURAL HISTORY

The Himalaya are not only the world's tallest mountains, they're also the youngest – and still growing. Because of them, most of Tibet and parts of northern Nepal are high-altitude deserts, hidden in the Himalayan rain shadow, while many southern slopes, which bear the full brunt of the monsoon, are rainforest: nowhere in the world is there a transition of flora and fauna so abrupt as the one between the Tarai and the Himalayan crest, a distance of as little as 60km. As a result, Nepal can boast an astounding diversity of life, from rhinos to snow leopards.

GEOLOGY

The Himalaya provide graphic evidence for the **plate tectonics** (formerly known as continental drift) theory of mountain-building. According to this theory, the earth's crust is divided into a dozen or so massive plates which collide, separate and grind against each other with unimaginable force. The Himalaya are the result of the Indian subcontinental plate ramming northwards with particular force into the Asian plate – something like a car smashing into the side of a truck. It has been estimated that a 2000-kilometre cross-section of land along the collision zone has been compressed into 1000km, doubling the thickness of the crust and producing not only the Himalaya but also the vast Tibetan Plateau.

The shallow **Tethys Sea**, which once covered the entire region, was the main casualty in the process; its sedimentary deposits, now contorted and metamorphosed, can be seen at all elevations of the Himalaya. The first phase of mountain-building began around 45 million years ago, as the edge of the Asian plate, buckling under pressure from the advancing Indian plate, rose out of the sea to a height of about 2000m. Although it has since been lifted much higher, this **Tibetan Marginal Range**, which parallels the main Himalayan chain to the north, still stands as the divide between the Ganges and Tsangpo/Brahmaputra rivers. Unique among the world's major mountain ranges, the Himalaya don't form a watershed: rivers like the Kali Gandaki, Bhote Kosi (there are several by that name) and Arun cut right through the Himalaya because their courses were established by this earlier Tibetan Marginal Range.

The next major uplift occurred between 10 and 25 million years ago, when great chunks of the Asian plate were thrust southwards on top of the Indian plate, creating a low-altitude forerunner of the Himalayan range. Things appear to have remained more or less unchanged until just 600,000 years ago – practically yesterday, in geological time – when what is now the **Tibetan Plateau** was suddenly jacked up to an average elevation of 5000m, and the Tibetan Marginal Range to about 7000m. From this point on, monsoonal rains became an important erosive force on the south (Nepalese) side of the mountains, while the north, left in the rain shadow, turned into a high desert. Southward-flowing rivers, fuelled by phenomenal gradients of up to 6000m in 100km, further eroded the landscape.

Most of Nepal's present features were created at the geological last minute. Beginning around 500,000 years ago, the Tibetan rim lunged forward along numerous separate fronts to form the modern **Himalaya**. Averaging 8000m, Nepal's *himal* (massifs) show a freeze-frame of the current state of play; geologists calculate that parts of the range are still rising at a phenomenal rate of up to 1cm a year.

But mountain-building produces downs as well as ups: around 200,000 years ago, a broad belt of foothills subsided, creating Nepal's **midland valleys**, while the southern edge of this zone curled up to form the **Mahabharat Lekh** and, still further south, the **Chure Hills** (called the Siwaliks in India). These ridges rose so rapidly that they forced many southbound rivers to make lengthy east–west detours and permitted only three principal outlets to the Tarai; the Bagmati and Seti rivers were initially dammed up by the Mahabharat Lekh, flooding the Kathmandu and Pokhara valleys respectively.

The Himalaya are believed to be rising still, albeit at a slower rate than previously. Periodic and severe **earthquakes** demonstrate that the earth continues to rearrange itself – one in eastern Nepal in 1988 killed 700 people – while **hot springs**, sometimes found near streams along trekking trails, are indicators of tectonic faultlines. **Erosion** is a particular problem in the Himalaya, where the mountains are continually sloughing off their skins, and landslides occur regularly during the monsoon. While **glaciers** play a part in shaping the terrain above about 5000m, the Himalaya aren't highly glaciated due to their sheer slopes (which can't support glacier-breeding snowfields) and relatively low precipitation at high elevations. On the whole, Himalayan glaciers are in a retreating phase, as they are in most parts of the world, and old moraines (piles of rubble left behind by melting glaciers) are commonly seen above 4000m.

Nepal's valleys are like vast cutaway diagrams of geological history, and trekking or rafting in them you'll be able to imagine the forces that have shaped the Himalaya. Igneous intrusions (usually granite) are common, but most outcrops consist of metamorphic rocks (schist, gneiss, limestone and dolomite), deposited as underwater sediments and later mashed and contorted under tremendous pressure; the wavy light and dark bands of the Lhotse-Nuptse Wall, in the Everest region, illustrate this. **Fossils** found in many of these layers have helped geologists date the phases of Himalayan mountain-building. The famous *shaligram* stones of Muktinath in the Annapurna region contain fossilized ammonites (spiral-shaped molluscs) dating from 150–200 million years ago. Of a much more recent origin, the bones of Peking Man and primitive stone tools have been found in the Chure Hills – proving that the Himalaya are so young that early humans were present during their creation.

FLORA

Nepal's **vegetation** is largely determined by altitude and can be conveniently grouped into three main divisions. The lowlands include the Tarai, Chure Hills and valleys up to about 1000m; the midlands extend roughly from 1000m to 3000m; and the Himalaya from 3000m to the upper limit of vegetation (typically about 5000m). Conditions vary tremendously within these zones, however: south-facing slopes usually receive more moisture, but also more sun in their lower reaches, while certain areas that are less protected from the summer monsoon – notably around Pokhara – are especially wet. In general, rainfall is higher in the east, and a greater diversity of plants can be found there.

THE LOWLANDS

Most of the Tarai's remaining forest consists of *sal*, a tall, straight tree much valued for its wood – a factor which is hastening its steady removal. *Sal* prefers well-drained soils and is most often found in pure stands along the Bhabar, the sloping alluvial plain at the base of the foothills; in the lower foothills, stunted specimens are frequently lopped for fodder. In spring, its cream-coloured flowers give off a heady jasmine scent. Other species sometimes associated with *sal* include *saj*, a large tree with crocodile-skin bark; *haldu*, a tree used for making dugout canoes; and *bauhinia*, a strangling vine that corkscrews around its victims.

The wetter **riverine forest** supports a larger number of species, but life here is more precarious, as rivers regularly flood and change course during the monsoon. *Sisu*, related to rosewood, and *khair*, an acacia, are the first trees to colonize newly formed sandbanks. *Simal*, towering on mangrove-like buttresses, follows close behind; also known as the silk-cotton tree, it produces bulbous red flowers in February, and in May its seed pods explode with a cottony material that is used for stuffing mattresses. *Palash* – the "flame of the forest tree" – puts on an even more brilliant show of red flowers in February. All of these trees are deciduous, shedding their leaves during the dry spring. Many other species are evergreen, including *bilar*, *jamun* and *curry*, an understorey tree with thin, pointed leaves that smell just like their name.

Grasses dominate less stable wetlands. Of the more than fifty species native to the Tarai, several routinely grow to a height of 8m. Even experts tend to pass off any tall, dense stand as "elephant grass", because the only way to get through it is on an elephant; the most common genera are *Phragmites*, *Saccharum*, *Arundo* and *Themeda*. Most grasses reach their greatest height just after the monsoon and flower during the dry autumn months. Locals cut *khar*, a medium-sized variety, for thatch in winter and early spring; the official thatch-gathering season in the Tarai parks (two weeks in January) is a colourful occasion, although the activity tends to drive wildlife into hiding. Fires are set in March and April to burn off the old growth and encourage tender new shoots, which provide food for game as well as livestock.

THE MIDLANDS

The decline in precipitation from east to west is more marked at the middle elevations – so much so that the dry west shares few species in common with the moist eastern hills. Central Nepal is an overlap zone where western species tend to be found on south-facing slopes and eastern ones on the cooler northern aspects.

A common tree in dry western and central areas is **chir pine** (needles in bunches of three), which typically grows in park-like stands up to about 2000m. Various **oak** species often take over above 1500m, especially on dry ridges, and here you'll also find *ainsilo*, a cousin of the raspberry, which produces a sweet, if rather dry, golden fruit in May.

Although much of the wet midland forest has been lost to cultivation, you can see fine remnants of it above Godavari in the Kathmandu Valley and around the lakes in the Pokhara Valley. Lower elevations are dominated by a zone of **chestnut** and *chilaune*, the latter being a member of the tea family with oblong concave leaves and, in May, small white flowers. In eastern parts, several species of **laurel** form a third major component to this forest, while alder, cardamom and tree ferns grow in shady gullies.

The magical, mossy oak-rhododendron forest is still mostly intact above about 2000m, thanks to the prevalent fog that makes farming unviable at this level. *Khasru*, the predominant

oak found here, has prickly leaves and is often laden with lichen, **orchids** and other epiphytes, which grow on other plants and get their moisture directly from the air. It's estimated that more than 300 orchid varieties grow in Nepal, and although not all are showy or scented, the odds are you'll be able to find one flowering at almost any time of year. **Tree rhododendron** (*lali guraas*), Nepal's national flower, grows over 20m high and blooms with gorgeous red or pink flowers in March–April. Nearly thirty other species occur in Nepal, mainly in the east – the Milke Danda, a long ridge east of the Arun River, is the best place to view rhododendron, although impressive stands can also be seen between Ghodapani and Ghandrung in the Annapurna region. Most of Nepal's 300 species of **fern** are found in this forest type, as are many medicinal plants whose curative properties are known to ayurvedic practitioners but have yet to be studied in the West. Also occurring here are **daphne**, a small bush with fragrant white flowers in spring, whose bark is pulped to make paper, and **nettles**, whose stems are used by eastern hill-dwellers to make a hard-wearing fabric.

Holly, magnolia and maple may replace oak and rhododendron in some sites. **Dwarf bamboo**, the red panda's favourite food, grows in particularly damp places, such as northern Helambu and along the trail to the Annapurna Sanctuary. Cannabis thrives in disturbed sites throughout the midlands.

THE HIMALAYA

Conifers form the dominant tree cover in the Himalaya. Particularly striking are the forests around Rara Lake in western Nepal, where **Himalayan spruce** and **blue pine** (needles grouped in fives) are interspersed with meadows. Elsewhere in the dry west you'll find magnificent **Himalayan cedar** (deodar) trees, which are protected by villagers, and a species of cypress. Two types of **juniper** are present in Nepal: the more common tree-sized variety grows south of the main Himalayan crest (notably around Tengboche in the Everest region), while a dwarf scrub juniper is confined to northern rain-shadow areas. Both provide incense for Buddhist rites. In wetter areas, hemlock, fir (distinguished from spruce by its upward-pointing cones) and even the deciduous larch may be encountered.

One of the most common (and graceful) broadleafed species is **white birch**, usually found in thickets near the tree line, especially on shaded slopes where the snow lies late. **Poplars** stick close to watercourses high up into the inner valleys – Muktinath is full of them – while **berberis**, a shrub whose leaves turn scarlet in autumn, grows widely on exposed sites. Trekking up the Langtang or Marsyangdi valleys you pass through many of these forest types in rapid succession, but the most dramatic transition of all is found in the valley of the Thak Khola (upper Kali Gandaki): the monsoon jungle below Ghasa gives way to blue pine, hemlock, rhododendron and horse chestnut; then to birch, fir and cypress around Tukche; then the apricot orchards of Marpha; and finally the blasted steppes of Jomosom.

Alpine vegetation predominates on the forest floor and in moist meadows above the treeline, and – apart from the **dwarf rhododendron** (some species of which give off a strong cinnamon scent and are locally used as incense) – many **flowers** found here will be familiar to European and North American walkers. There are too many to do justice to them here, but primula, buttercup, poppy, iris, larkspur, gentian, edelweiss, buddleia, columbine and sage are all common. Most bloom during the monsoon, but rhododendrons and primulas can be seen flowering in the spring and gentians and larkspurs in the autumn.

MAMMALS

Most of Nepal's rich **animal life** inhabits the Tarai and, despite dense vegetation, is most easily observed there. In the hill regions, wildlife is much harder to spot due to population pressure – along trekking trails, at least – while very few mammals live above tree line. The following overview progresses generally from Tarai to Himalayan species.

The **Asian one-horned rhino** (*gaida*) is one of five species found in Asia and Africa, all endangered. In Nepal, about 400 rhinos – a fifth of the species total – live in Chitwan, and about a dozen have been introduced to Bardia; they graze singly or in small groups in the marshy elephant grass, where they can remain surprisingly well hidden.

Although trained **elephants** (*hatti*) are a lingering part of Nepali culture (see "Chitwan National Park"), their wild relatives are seen only rarely in Nepal. Since they require vast territory for their seasonal migrations, the settling of the Tarai is putting them in increasing conflict with man, and the few that survive tend to spend most of their time in India.

Koshi Tappu is the only remaining habitat in Nepal for another species better known as a domestic breed, **wild buffalo** (*arnaa*), which graze the wet grasslands in small herds. Majestic and powerful, the **gaur** (*gauri gaai*), or Indian bison, spends most of its time in the dry lower foothills, but descends to the Tarai in spring for water.

Perhaps the Tarai's most unlikely mammals, **gangetic dolphins** – one of four freshwater species in the world – are present in small numbers in the Karnali, Narayani and Sapt Koshi rivers. Curious and gregarious, dolphins tend to congregate in deep channels where they feed on fish and crustaceans; they may betray their presence with a puffing sound which they make through their blow-holes when surfacing. They're considered sacrosanct by Nepali Tharus, but are cruelly hunted in India.

The most abundant mammals of the Tarai, *chital*, or **spotted deer**, are often seen in herds around the boundary between riverine forest and grassland. Hog deer – so called because of their porky little bodies and head-down trot – take shelter in wet grassland, while the aptly named barking deer, measuring less than two feet high at the shoulder, are found throughout lowland and midland forests. Swamp deer gather in vast herds in Sukla Phanta, and males of the species carry impressive sets of antlers (their Nepali name, *barasingha*, means "twelve points"). *Sambar*, heavy-set animals standing five feet at the shoulder, are more widely distributed, but elusive. Two species of antelope, the graceful, corkscrew-horned **blackbuck** and the ungainly **nilgai** (blue bull), may be seen at Bardia and Koshi Tappu respectively; the latter was once assumed to be a form of cattle, and thus spared by Hindu hunters, but no longer.

Areas of greatest deer and antelope concentrations are usually prime territory for **tiger** (*bagh*), their main predator. However, your chances of spotting one of Nepal's endangered Bengal tigers are slim: they're mainly nocturnal, never very numerous, and incredibly stealthy. In the deep shade and mottled sunlight of dense riverine forest, a tiger's orange- and black-striped coat provides almost total camouflage. A male may weigh 250kg and measure 3m from nose to tail. Tigers are solitary hunters; some have been known to consume up to twenty percent of their body weight after a kill, but they may go several days between feeds. Males and females maintain separate but overlapping territories, regularly patrolling them, marking the boundaries with scent and driving off interlopers. Some Nepalis believe tigers to be the unquiet souls of the deceased.

Leopards are equally elusive, but much more widely distributed: they may be found in any deep forest from the Tarai to the timber line. As a consequence, leopards account for many more maulings than tigers in Nepal, and are more feared. A smaller animal (males weigh about 45kg), they prey on monkeys, dogs and livestock. **Other cats** – such as the fishing cat, leopard cat and the splendid clouded leopard – are known to exist in the more remote lowlands and midlands, but are very rarely sighted. Hyenas and wild dogs are scavengers of the Tarai, and **jackals**, though seldom seen (they're nocturnal), produce an eerie howling that is one of the most common night sounds in the Tarai and hills.

While it isn't carnivorous, the dangerously unpredictable **sloth bear**, a Tarai species, is liable to round on you and should be approached with extreme caution. Its powerful front claws are designed for unearthing termite nests, and its long snout for extracting the insects. The **Himalayan black bear** roams midland forests up to tree line and is, if anything, more dangerous. **Wild boars** can be seen rooting and scurrying through forest anywhere in Nepal.

Monkeys, a common sight in the Tarai and hills, come in two varieties in Nepal. Comical **langurs** have silver fur, black faces and long, ropelike tails; you'll sometimes see them sitting on stumps like Rodin's *Thinker*. Brown **rhesus macaques** are more shy in the wild, but around temples are tame to the point of being nuisances. Many other small mammals may be spotted in the hills, among them porcupines, flying squirrels, foxes, civets, mongooses and martens. The **red panda**, with its rust coat and bushy, ringed tail, almost resembles a tree-dwelling fox; like its Chinese relative, it's partial to bamboo, and is very occasionally glimpsed in the cloud forest of northern Helambu.

Elusive animals of the rhododendron and birch forests, **musk deer** are readily identified by their tusk-like canine teeth; males are hunted for their musk pod, which can fetch $200 an ounce on the international market. Though by no means common, **Himalayan tahr** is the most frequently observed large mammal of the high country; a goat-like animal with long, wiry fur and short horns, it browses along steep cliffs below the tree line. **Serow**, another goat relative, inhabits remote canyons and forested areas, while **goral**, sometimes likened to chamois, occurs from middle elevations up to the tree line.

The Himalaya's highest residents are **blue sheep**, who graze the barren grasslands above the tree line year-round. Normally tan, males go a slaty colour in winter, accounting for their name. Herds have been sighted around the Thorung La in the Annapurna region, but they occur in greater numbers north of Dhorpatan and in She-Phoksundo National Park. Their chief predator is the **snow leopard**, a secretive cat whose habits are still little understood.

AMPHIBIANS AND REPTILES

Native to the Tarai's wetlands, crocodiles are most easily seen in winter, when they sun themselves on muddy banks to warm up their cold-blooded bodies. The endangered **mugger crocodile** favours marshes and oxbow lakes, where it may lie motionless for hours on end until its prey comes within snapping distance. Muggers mainly pursue fish, but will eat just about anything they can get their jaws around – including human corpses thrown into the river by relatives unable to afford wood for a cremation. The even more endangered **gharial crocodile** lives exclusively in rivers and feeds on fish; for more on its precarious state, see p.278.

Nepal has many kinds of **snakes**, but they are rarely encountered: most hibernate in winter, even in the Tarai, and shy away from humans at other times of year. Common cobras – snake charmers' favourites – inhabit low elevations near villages; they aren't found in the Kathmandu Valley, despite their abundance in religious imagery there. Kraits and pit vipers, both highly poisonous, have been reported, as have pythons up to twenty feet long. However, the commonest species aren't poisonous and are typically less than two feet long.

Chances are you'll run into a **gecko** or two, probably clinging to a guest house wall. Helpful insect-eaters, these lizard-like creatures are able to climb almost any surface with the aid of amazing suction pads on their feet. About fifty species of **fish** have been recorded in Nepal, but only *mahseer*, a sporty relative of carp that attains its greatest size in the lower Karnali River, is of much interest; most ponds are stocked with carp and catfish.

BIRDS

Over 800 **bird species** – one tenth of the earth's total – have been sighted in Nepal. The country receives a high number of birds migrating between India and central Asia in spring and autumn and, because it spans so many ecosystems, provides habitats for a wide range of year-round residents. The greatest diversity of species is found in the Tarai wildlife parks, but even the Kathmandu Valley is remarkably rich in birdlife. The following is only a listing of the major categories – for the complete picture, get hold of *Birds of Nepal* (see "Books").

In the **Tarai** and lower hills, raptors (birds of prey) such as ospreys, cormorants, darters, gulls and kingfishers patrol streams and rivers for food; herons and storks can also be seen fishing, while cranes, ducks and moorhens wade in or float on the water. Many of these migratory species are particularly well represented at Koshi Tappu, which is located along the important Arun Valley corridor to Tibet. Peafowl make their meowing mating call – and peacocks occasionally deign to unfurl their plumage – while many species of woodpeckers can be heard, if not seen, high up in the *sal* canopy. Cuckoos and "brain fever" birds repeat their idiotic two- or four-note songs in an almost demented fashion. Parakeets swoop in formation; bee-eaters, swifts, drongos, swallows and rollers flit and dive for insects, while jungle fowl look like chickens as Monet might have painted them. Other oddities of the Tarai include the paradise flycatcher, with its lavish white tailfeathers and dragonfly-like flight; the lanky great adjutant stork, resembling a prehistoric reptile in flight; and the giant hornbill, whose beak supports an appendage that looks like an upturned welder's mask.

Many of the above birds are found in **the midlands** as well as the Tarai – as are mynas, egrets, crows and magpies, which tend to scavenge near areas of human habitation. Birds of prey – falcons, kestrels, harriers, eagles, kites, hawks and vultures – may also be seen at almost any elevation. Owls are common, but not much liked by Nepalis. Babblers and laughing thrushes (genus name *Garrulax*!) populate the oak-rhododendron forest and are as noisy as their names suggest. Over twenty species of flycatchers are present in the Kathmandu Valley alone.

Nepal's national bird, the iridescent, multicoloured *danphe* (impeyan pheasant), can often be spotted scuttling through the undergrowth in the Everest region; a range of house paints has been named after it. *Kalij* and *monal*, two other native pheasants, also inhabit the higher hills and lower **Himalaya**. Migrating waterfowl often stop over at high-altitude lakes – Brahminy ducks are a trekking-season attraction at Gokyo – and snow pigeons, grebes, finches and choughs may all be seen at or above the tree line. Mountaineers have reported seeing choughs at up to 8200m on Everest.

INVERTEBRATES AND INSECTS

Perhaps no other creature in Nepal arouses such squeamishness as the **leech** (*jukha*). Fortunately, these segmented, caterpillar-sized annelids remain dormant underground during the trekking seasons; during the monsoon, however, they come out in force everywhere in the Tarai and hills, making any hike a bloody business. Leeches are attracted to body heat, and will inch up legs or drop from branches to reach their victims. The bite is completely painless – the bloodsucker injects a local anesthetic and anticoagulant – and often goes unnoticed until the leech drops off of its own accord. To dislodge one, apply salt or burn it with a cigarette; don't pull it off or the wound could get infected.

Over 600 species of **butterflies** have been recorded in Nepal, with more being discovered all the time. Although the monsoon is the best time to view butterflies, many varieties can be seen before and especially just after the rains – look beside moist, sandy banks or atop ridges; Phulchoki is an excellent place to start in the Kathmandu Valley. Notable hill varieties include the intriguing orange oakleaf, whose markings enable it to vanish into forest litter, and the golden birdwing, a large, angular species with a loping wingbeat. **Moths** are even more numerous – around 5000 species are believed to exist in Nepal, including the world's largest, the giant atlas, which has a wingspan of almost a foot.

Termites are Nepal's most conspicuous social insects, constructing towering, fluted mounds up to eight feet tall in the western Tarai. Organized in colonies much the same as ants and bees, legions of termite workers and "reproductives" serve a single king and queen. The mounds function as cooling towers for the busy nest below; monuments to insect industry, they're made from tailings excavated from the colony's galleries and bonded with saliva for a wood-hard finish. **Honey bees** create huge, drooping nests in the Tarai and especially in the lush cliff country north of Pokhara. **Spiders** aren't very numerous in Nepal, although one notable species grows to be six inches across and nets birds (it's not poisonous to humans). **Fireflies**, with orange and black bodies, give off a greenish glow at dusk in the Tarai. For many travellers, however, the extent of their involvement with the insect kingdom will be in swatting **mosquitoes**: two varieties are prevalent in the lowlands, one of them *Anopheles*, the infamous vector of malaria.

BOOKS

Most of these books are a lot easier to come by in Kathmandu, and some will be available only in Nepal. Where the UK and US publishers are different, the UK publisher is given first – books published in other countries are indicated accordingly. Out of print (o/p) books may still be found in Nepal, or in your library.

GENERAL

Lynn Andrews *Windhorse Woman* (Warner, US). One woman's spiritual quest in Nepal; very new age.

Barbara Crossette *So Close to Heaven* (Knopf, US). A survey of the "vanishing Buddhist kingdoms of the Himalayas", including a chapter focusing on Nepal's Tibetans, Bhotiyas and Newars.

Jeff Greenwald *Mister Raja's Neighborhood: Letters from Nepal* (John Daniel, US). The author went to Kathmandu to write the Great Asian Novel and ended up writing a series of letters – though perhaps contemplating his navel a bit too much in the process. *Shopping for Buddhas* (Harper & Row, US) is something of a sequel.

Harka Gurung *Vignettes of Nepal* (Sajha Prakashan, Nepal). Probably the best book written by a Nepali in English about his country, a vivid travelogue illuminated by a native's insights.

Pico Iyer *Video Night in Kathmandu* (Black Swan/Random House). A collection of essays on popular traveller hang-outs in Asia that are stronger on style than substance.

Peter Matthiessen *The Snow Leopard* (Collins Harvill/Viking Penguin). Matthiessen joins biologist George Schaller in a pilgrimage to Dolpo to track one of the world's most elusive cats, and comes up with characteristically Zen insights. A magnificent piece of writing, filled with beautiful descriptions of the landscape – and ever-perceptive observations of how Matthiessen's quest for the snow leopard became one of self-discovery.

Dervla Murphy *The Waiting Land* (Overlook Press, US). A personal account of working with Pokhara's Tibetan refugees in 1965, written in the author's usual entertaining and politically on-the-ball style.

COFFEE-TABLE BOOKS

Kevin Bubriski *Portrait of Nepal* (Chronicle Books, US). An extraordinary collection of large-format portraits that does for Nepal's indigenous peoples what E S Curtis's photography did for Native Americans. With great subtlety and dignity, Bubriski has documented cultures and lifestyles that are passing within our generation. A truly important book.

Kevin Bubriski and Keith Dowman *Power Places of the Kathmandu Valley* (Inner Traditions International, US). A collaboration by two eminently qualified authorities: rich colour photographs accompanied by well-researched text.

Jim Goodman and Thomas Kelly *Kathmandu Valley* (Book Faith India). A collection of sumptuous photos and accompanying cultural essays.

Thomas Kelly and Patricia Roberts *Kathmandu: City at the Edge of the World* (Weidenfeld & Nicolson/Abbeville Press). Stunning photography and extensive essays on culture and religion.

Eric Valli and Diane Summers *Caravans of the Himalaya* (Thames & Hudson). Travelogue of a journey along the Nepal–Tibet trade route, packaged for maximum armchair impact. Valli and Summers have collaborated on several other books of the same lavish ilk, notably *Honey Hunters of Nepal* (Thames & Hudson, o/p), which features amazing photos of Gurung men clinging to rope ladders while raiding beehives.

HISTORY

Byron Farwell *The Gurkhas* (Penguin). One of many books lionizing Nepal's famous Gurkha soldiers.

Percival Landon *Nepal* (Ratna Pustak Bhandar, Nepal). In two volumes, this was the most comprehensive study of the country at the time (1928) and is regarded as a classic – but having been commissioned by the Maharaja, it has a distinct political bias.

Ludwig Stiller *The Rise of the House of Gorkha* (Ratna Pustak Bhandar, Nepal). An academic but readable account of Nepal's unification and war with Britain, written by a Jesuit priest turned Nepalese citizen.

CULTURE AND ANTHROPOLOGY

Mary M Anderson *The Festivals of Nepal* (Rupa, Nepal). Despite the title, this only covers the Kathmandu Valley's festivals, but it's quite readable.

Dor Bahadur Bista *Peoples of Nepal* (Ratna Pustak Bhandar, Nepal). The standard overview of Nepal's ethnic groups, though much of the information is now superseded by more recent work.

Jim Goodman *Guide to Enjoying Nepalese Festivals* (Pilgrims Book House, Nepal). All the arcane whys and wherefores of the Kathmandu Valley's festivals: authoritative, though not very user-friendly.

BHOTIYAS

Christoph von Fürer-Haimendorf *Himalayan Traders* (John Murray, US). An anthropological study of the impact of China's occupation of Tibet on Bhotiya and Sherpa traders.

David L Snellgrove *Himalayan Pilgrimage* (Shambhala). An insightful travelogue/anthropological account of a trip through north-western Nepal in the 1950s.

CHHETRIS

Monica Connell *Against a Peacock Sky* (Penguin/Viking Penguin). Beautiful, impressionistic rendering of life among the *matawaali* (alcohol-drinking) Chhetris of Jumla District, capturing the subtleties of village life in Nepal.

GURUNGS

Broughton Coburn *Nepali Aama: Portrait of a Nepalese Hill Woman* (Moon Publications, US). Delightful study of a Gurung woman in a village south of Pokhara, in her own words, with photos.

Stan Royal Mumford *Himalayan Dialogue: Tibetan Lamas and Gurung Shamans in Nepal* (University of Wisconsin Press). An account of myths and rituals practised in a village along the Annapurna Circuit – fascinating, once you get past the anthropological jargon.

MAGARS

Gary Shepherd *Life Among the Magars* (Sahayogi, Nepal). A personal account, with plenty of pertinent insights.

SHERPAS

Hugh R Downs *Rhythms of a Himalayan Village* (Harper & Row, US). An extraordinarily sensitive synthesis of black-and-white photos, text and quotes, describing rituals and religion in a Solu village.

James F Fisher, *Sherpas: Reflections on Change in Himalayan Nepal* (University of California Press, US). A before-and-after account, written by a member of Edmund Hillary's 1964 school-building team, who concludes that Sherpas are more resilient than we give them credit for.

RELIGION

HINDUISM

P Lal (trans) *The Ramayana of Valmiki* (Tarang, Nepal). A condensed version of the classic epic.

K M Sen *Hinduism* (Penguin/Viking Penguin). An accessible survey, explanatory without being too obscure.

Shri Purohit Swami (trans) *The Geeta* (Faber & Faber, UK). A portable, robust translation of the *Bhagavad Gita*.

TIBETAN BUDDHISM

Tenzin Gyatso (the Dalai Lama) *The Way to Freedom: Core Teachings of Tibetan Buddhism* (HarperCollins, US). Good primer, though perhaps a bit evangelical.

Christmas Humphries *Buddhism: An Introduction and Guide* (Penguin). First published in 1951, this classic but demanding overview puts all the major sects into perspective.

Vicki Mackenzie *Reincarnation: The Boy Lama* (Bloomsbury, UK). An intriguing book, recounting the lives of Lama Yeshe, the abbot of Kopan Monastery, who died in 1984, and Osel Hita Torres, who was born in 1985 and enthroned as Yeshe's reincarnation at the age of two.

Robert A F Thurman *Essential Tibetan Buddhism* (HarperCollins, US). A survey of basic teachings, weaving together classic texts with modern commentary. Not for beginners.

Chögyam Trungpa *The Myth of Freedom* (Shambhala, Nepal). A useful primer on the metaphysics of Buddhist meditation, one of a welter of books by a master who was instrumental in packaging Buddhism for the West.

ART AND ARCHITECTURE

Lydia Aran *The Art of Nepal* (Sahayogi, Nepal). Surprisingly good overview of Nepalese religion as well as stone, metal and wood sculpture and *thangka* paintings.

Claire Burkert *Janakpur Art: A Living Tradition* (Janakpur Women's Development Center, Nepal). As simple and understated as its subject, this slim booklet highlights the dignity of the women who create Maithili art.

Susi Dunsmore *Nepalese Textiles* (British Museum Press, UK). A labour of love, this handsome, full-colour book details the history, patterns and techniques of all of Nepal's major ethnic groups.

Handicraft Association of Nepal *A Short Description of Gods, Goddesses and Ritual Objects of Buddhism and Hinduism in Nepal* (Handicraft Association of Nepal). An inexpensive booklet that may help in sorting out iconography.

Michael Hutt *Nepal: A Guide to the Art and Architecture of the Kathmandu Valley* (Kinscadale, UK). An in-depth discussion of iconography, design and construction, in hard cover.

Philip Rowson *The Art of Tantra* (Thames & Hudson/Norton). A survey of the iconography and the theology behind it.

FICTION AND POETRY

W E Bowman *The Ascent of Rum Doodle* (Pimlico, UK). Reprint of the classic 1956 parody of the mountaineering-account genre.

Laxmi Prasad Devkota *Muna Madan* (Nirala, India). The most famous work by Nepal's best-loved poet recounts the tragic (almost Shakespearean) tale of a young Newar trader who leaves his young wife to travel to Lhasa.

Kesar Lall and Tej R Kansakar (trans) *Forbidden Fruit and Other Stories* (Ratna Pustak Bhandar, Nepal). Some of these stories, translated from the Newari, are better than others, but all shed light on Nepali culture, dealing with themes of family duty, class relationships, fate and the ever-present spectre of *dukha* (sadness).

Greta Rana *Guests in This Country* (Book Faith India). A wicked spoof about a junior development worker's encounters with aid red tape and government mismanagement in the fictional (but oh-so-Nepali) land of Lapalistan.

Kim Stanley Robinson *Escape From Kathmandu* (Unwin/Tor). Pure potboiler, but it might be fun for the real-life *mise en scène* (action starts at the *Hotel Star* in Thamel).

Tara Nath Sharma *Blackout* (Nirala, Nepal). A dark novel of life in the Nepal hills, by an author who has served time in jail for his views.

NATURAL HISTORY

Robert Fleming Jr *The General Ecology, Flora and Fauna of Midland Nepal* (Tribhuwan University, Nepal). A simple ecology text drawing on examples mainly from around the Kathmandu Valley.

Robert Fleming Sr, Robert Fleming Jr and Lain Singh Bangdel *Birds of Nepal* (Nature Himalayas, Nepal). The authoritative field guide.

K K Gurung *Heart of the Jungle* (André Deutsch, US). The essential guide to Chitwan's flora and fauna, written by the former manager of Tiger Tops Jungle Lodge.

Carol Inskipp *A Popular Guide to the Birds and Mammals of the Annapurna Conservation Area* (ACAP, Nepal). A slim volume with some colour plates.

Dorothy Mierow and Tirtha Shrestha *Himalayan Flowers and Trees* (Sahayogi, Nepal). A pocket-sized guide with colour plates and some useful information at the back.

George Schaller *Stones of Silence: Journeys in the Himalaya* (University of Chicago Press, US). Written by the wildlife biologist who accompanied Peter Matthiessen on his quest for the snow leopard, this book provides a detailed view of ecosystems of the high Himalaya.

Colin Smith *Illustrated Checklist of Nepal's Butterflies* (Rohit Kumar, Nepal). Beautiful colour plates showing nearly 600 species, by the curator of the Annapurna Regional Museum.

Martin Woodcock *Birds of India* (HarperCollins, US). A stand-in for Fleming (see above) if the latter is unavailable.

DEVELOPMENT AND POLITICS

When you're in Nepal, look out for *Himal*, a bimonthly magazine devoted to development and environmental issues. It's published in Kathmandu and available in many bookshops there.

Lynn Bennett *Dangerous Wives and Sacred Sisters* (Columbia University Press, US). Good insight into the life and position of Hindu women in Nepal.

Dor Bahadur Bista *Fatalism and Development* (Orient Longman, India). An insightful analysis of the cultural factors that stand in the way of Nepal's development, by the country's best-known anthropologist.

Indra Majpuria *Nepalese Women* (M Devi, Nepal). Though it wanders quite a bit, this forcibly gets across the hardships and problems facing women in Nepal.

Charlie Pye-Smith *Travels in Nepal* (Penguin/ Viking Penguin). A cross between a travelogue and a progress report on aid projects, this succeeds in giving plenty of facts and analysis without getting bogged down in institutional waffle.

David Seddon *Nepal: a State of Poverty* (Vikas, Nepal). A hard look at the issues by one of the longest-serving foreign critics of Nepal's development efforts.

Ludmilla Tüting and Kunda Dixit *Bikas-Binas, Development-Destruction* (Ratna Pustak Bhandar, Nepal). Excellent collection of articles which covers the whole gamut of dilemmas arising out of development, environmental degradation and tourism. It's supposed to speak for the entire Himalayan region, but it really focuses on Nepal.

HEALTH

Jim Duff and Peter Gormly *The Himalayan First Aid Manual* (World Expeditions, Nepal). Handy pocket-sized booklet.

Dr Ravi P Thapaliya *Your Health in Nepal* (Musk, Nepal). A thorough manual on health and safety for travelling, trekking, rafting and visiting the Tarai wildlife parks.

MOUNTAINS AND MOUNTAINEERING

Chris Bonington *Everest South West Face* (Hodder & Stoughton, UK, o/p). An exhaustive tome covering every aspect of a major Himalayan assault – in this case, an unsuccessful one. Also look out for Bonington's *The Everest Years* (Hodder, UK) and his retrospective, *Mountaineer* (The Mountaineers, US).

Maurice Herzog *Annapurna* (Paladin, US). Reprint of one of the earliest accounts of mountaineering in the Himalaya, describing the first successful ascent of an 8000-metre peak.

Reinhold Messner *The Crystal Horizon* (Crowood Press/The Mountaineers). Not very well written (or maybe it's the translation), but a nonetheless compelling account of Messner's 1980 solo ascent of Everest. Messner's *All 14 Eight-Thousanders* (Crowood Press, UK) has awesome photos and an interesting appendix of Himalayan mountaineering statistics.

H W Tilman *Nepal Himalaya* (Cambridge University Press, UK, o/p). A chatty account of the first mountaineering reconnaissance of Nepal in 1949–51, reprinted as part of *The Seven Mountain-Travel Books* (Diadem/The Mountaineers). Though crusty, and at times racist, Tilman was one of the century's great adventurers and his writing remains fresh and witty.

Walt Unsworth *Everest* (Grafton/Cloudcap). Exhaustive history of mountaineering on the world's highest peak.

TREKKING GUIDES

Stan Armington *Trekking in the Nepal Himalaya* (Lonely Planet). A less perceptive, but more portable, alternative to Bezruchka (below). Some people prefer its "Day 1–Day 2" route descriptions.

Stephen Bezruchka *A Guide to Trekking in Nepal*, 6th Ed. (Cordee/The Mountaineers). The most thorough, even-handed and sensitive book on trekking, containing background pieces on Nepali culture and natural history.

Alton C Byers III *Treks on the Kathmandu Valley Rim* (Sahayogi, Nepal). Mainly day hikes and overnights.

Amy R Kaplan and Michael Keller *Nepal: An Essential Handbook for Trekkers* (Mandala, Nepal). A primer on trek preparations and cultural and environmental sensitivity. Includes tips on health, porters and trekking with kids.

Wendy Brewer Lama *Trekking Gently in the Himalaya* (Sagarmatha Pollution Control Project, Nepal). An excellent, concise pamphlet on trekkers' environmental and cultural responsibilities.

Jamie McGuinness *Trekking in the Everest Region* (Trailblazer, UK). Exhaustive and perceptive guide to all the routes in the region.

Bill O'Connor *The Trekking Peaks of Nepal* (Crowood Press, UK). Describes climbing routes and trek approaches for eighteen trekking peaks.

Kev Reynolds *Annapurna: A Trekker's Guide* (Cicerone, UK). Short on context, but a lightweight option if you only intend to trek in this region.

Hugh Swift *Trekking in Nepal, West Tibet and Bhutan* (Hodder/Sierra Club). Gives vivid area accounts instead of hour-by-hour route descriptions; good for obscure treks.

OTHER GUIDES

John Burbank *Culture Shock! Nepal* (Graphic Arts Center, US). Sensitivity training for tourists, with valuable insights into social mores, religion, caste and cross-cultural relations.

Lisa Choegyal (ed) *The Insight Guide to Nepal* (APA). Great pictures and informative cultural essays, but short on practical information.

James Giambrone *Kathmandu Valley Bikes & Hikes* (APA). Two dozen itineraries, accompanied by an excellent fold-out route map.

Peter Knowles and Dave Allardice *White Water Nepal* (Rivers Publishing, UK). An indispensable companion for all river-runners, written with great wit and no nonsense; useful maps, stream profiles and hydrographs. *Rafting Nepal: A Consumer's Guide* is a cheaper, locally printed version.

John Sanday *Odyssey Guide to the Kathmandu Valley* (Collins, UK). The author is the leading authority on restoration of the valley's monuments.

LANGUAGE

Nepali is surprisingly easy to learn, and local people are always thrilled when travellers make the effort to pick up a few phrases. Knowing a little bit of the language certainly comes in handy, too, since while nearly all Nepalis who deal with tourists speak English, few people do off the beaten track.

Nepali (sometimes called *Gurkhali*) is closely related to Hindi and other Sanskrit-based languages, so Nepali-speakers and Indians can usually catch the gist of what each other is saying. However, nearly half of all Nepalis speak Tibetan, Sherpa or one of several dozen other Tibeto-Burman dialects, which are completely unrelated to Nepali – almost all speak Nepali as a second language, but sometimes with difficult to understand regional accents.

Nepali is written in a script known as **Devanaagari**: there's fortunately no need for travellers to learn it since signs, bus destinations and so on are usually written in Roman script. This transliteration, though, often leads to problems of inconsistency – see the note in "Information and Maps" in *Basics* for more on this. For a **glossary of food terms**, see "Eating and Drinking" in *Basics*.

The most useful **phrasebooks** on the market are Lonely Planet's *Nepal Phrasebook* and Shyam P Wagley's *Nepali Phrasebook* (Ratna Pustak Bhandar, Nepal). *A Simple Nepali for Trekkers* (Rupa, Nepal), available only in Nepal, goes a little deeper into grammar, but isn't as good for quick reference. For a full-blown **teach-yourself book**, try David Matthews' *A Course in Nepali* (School of Oriental and African Studies, UK).

PRONUNCIATION

Even when Nepali is transliterated from the Devanaagari script into the Roman alphabet using phonetic spellings, there are a number of peculiarities in pronunciation:

A as in *a*lone
AA as in f*a*ther
B sounds like a cross between "b" and "v"
E as in caf*é*
I as in pol*i*ce
J as in *j*ust
O as in n*o*te
R sounds like a cross between "r" and "d"
S sounds almost like "sh"
U as in b*oo*t
W sounds like a cross between "w" and "v"
Z sounds like "dj" or "dz"

The "a" and "aa" distinction is crucial. *Maa* (in) is pronounced as it looks, with the vowel stretched out, but *ma* (I) sounds like "muh" and *mandir* (temple) like "mundeer". The accent almost always goes on the syllable with "aa" in it, or if there's no "aa", on the first syllable.

Some Nepali vowels are nasalized – to get the right effect, you have to block off your nasal passage, producing a slightly honking sound like a French "n". Nasalized vowels aren't indicated in this book, but they're something to be aware of. To hear how they should sound, listen to a Nepali say *tapaai* (you) or *yahaa* (here).

ASPIRATED CONSONANTS

The combinations "ch" and "sh" are pronounced as in English, but in all other cases where an "h" follows a consonant the sound is meant to be aspirated – in other words, give it an extra puff of air. Thus *bholi* (tomorrow) sounds like b'*holi* and Thamel sounds like T'*hamel*. Note these combinations:

CHH sounds like a very breathy "ch", as in pi*tch h*ere
PH makes an "f" sound, as in *ph*one
TH is pronounced as in pu*t h*ere, not as in *th*ink

RETROFLEX CONSONANTS

Finally, the sounds "d", "r" and "t" also occur in retroflex forms – ie they're pronounced by rolling the tip of the tongue back towards the roof of the mouth. Again, it's not worth going into too much detail about this here, but it's a safe bet that whenever these letters are followed by an "h" they'll be retroflex – an obvious example is *Kathmandu*, which sounds a little like "Kardmandu". Sometimes retroflexion results in a difference in meaning: *saathi* means friend, but with a retroflex "th" it means sixty.

A BRIEF GUIDE TO SPEAKING NEPALI

GREETINGS AND BASIC PHRASES

For advice on the nuances of some of these basic phrases, see "Cultural Hints" in *Basics*.

Hello, Goodbye	*Namaste* (said with palms together as if praying)	I didn't understand that	*Maile tyo bujina*
		Please speak more slowly	*Bistaarai bolnus*
Hello (very formal)	*Namaskar*	I only speak a little Nepali	*Ma ali ali Nepali bolchhu*
Yes/No (It is/isn't)	*Ho/Hoina*		
Yes/No (There is/isn't)	*Chha/Chhaina*	Pardon?	*Hajur?*
Thank you (formal)	*Dhanyabaad*	Please	*Kripaya*
How are things?(informal);	*Kasto chha?*	No thanks	*Nai; Pardaina* (I don't want it)
(polite)	*Sanchai chhu?*		
Okay, Fine	*Thik chha*	I'm sorry	*Maph garnus*
What's your name?	*Tapaaiko naam ke ho?*	Let's go	*Jaun*
(to an adult);		It was an honour to meet you	*Hajur lai bhetera dherai kushi laagyo*
(to a child)	*Timro naam ke ho?*	Thank you (very much) for everything	*Sapai kurako laagi (dherai) dhanyabaad*
My name is . . .	*Mero naam . . . ho*		
My country is . . .	*Mero desh . . . ho*	See you again	*Pheri betaunla*
I don't know	*Malaai thaahaa chhaina*		

FORMS OF ADDRESS

Excuse me . . .	*O . . .*	Father (a man old enough to be your father)	*Bua*
(more polite)	*Hajur . . .*		
Elder brother (said to men your age or older)	*Daai; Daaju* (more respectful)	Mother (women old enough to be your mother)	*Aama*
Elder sister (women your age or older)	*Didi*	Grandfather (old men)	*Baje*
		Grandmother (old women)	*Bajei*
Younger sister (women or girls younger than you)	*Bahini*	Shopkeeper, Innkeeper (male)	*Saahuji*
		Shopkeeper, Innkeeper (female)	*Saahuni*
Younger brother (men or boys younger than you)	*Bhaai*		

BASIC QUESTIONS AND REQUESTS

Whether you're making a statement or asking a question, the word order is the same in Nepali – to indicate that you're asking, not telling, make sure you raise your voice at the end.

Do you speak English?	*Tapaai Angreji bolnuhunchha?*	Is/Isn't there a . . .?	*. . . chha/chhaina?*
		Is . . . available?	*. . . painchha?*
Is there someone who speaks English?	*Angreji bolne kohi chha?*	Is . . . okay?	*. . . hunchha?*
		Please help me	*Kripaya malaai madhat garnus*
I don't speak Nepali	*Ma Nepali boldina*		

Please give me . . .	*Kripaya . . . dinus*	What's this called in	*Nepali maa ke*
I'm (hungry)	*Malaai (bhok) laagyo*	Nepali?	*bhanchha?*
I'm not (hungry)	*Malaai (bhok)*	What does . . mean?	*. . . ko mane ke ho?*
	laageko chhaina	Really?	*Saachinai?* or *Hora?*
I like . . . (very much)	*Malaai . . . (dherai)*	How	*Kasari*
	manparchha	What	*Ke*
I want/don't want	*Ma . . . chaahanchhu/*	When	*Kahile*
	chaahunna	Where	*Kahaa*
What's this for?	*Ke ko laagi?*	Who	*Ko*
What's the matter?	*Ke bhayo?*	Why	*Kina*
		Which	*Kun*

NEGOTIATIONS

How much does this cost?	*Esko kati parchha?*	I don't have any change	*Masanga khudra*
How much for a (room)?	*(Rum) ko kati parchha?*		*chhaina*
How many people?	*Kati jana?*	Please use the meter	*Malaai meter-maa*
For (two) people	*(Dui) jana ko laagi*		*laijaanus*
Only one person	*Ek jana maatrai*	Just a moment	*Ek chin* (literally, "One
Can I see it?	*Herna sakchhu?*		blink")
It's very/too expensive	*Dherai mahango*	I'll come back	*Ma aunechuu*
	bhayo	Good job, Well done	*Kyaraamro*
Is there a cheaper one?	*Kunai sasto chha?*	Don't worry	*Chinta nagarnus*
I don't need it	*Malaai chahindaina*	The bill, please	*Bil dinus*

DIRECTIONS

Where is the . . . ?	*. . . kahaa chha?*	Here	*Yahaa*
Where is this (bus) going?	*Yo (bas) kahaa*	There/Yonder	*Tyahaa/Utyahaa*
	jaanchha?	(To the) right	*Daayaa (tira)*
Which is the way to . . . ?	*. . . -jaane baato kun*	(To the) left	*Baayaa (tira)*
	ho?	Straight	*Sidhaa*
Which is the best way?	*Kun baato sabhanda*	North	*Uttaar*
	raamro chha?	South	*Dakshin*
How far is it?	*Kati taadhaa chha?*	East	*Purba*
Where are you going?	*Tapaai kahaa jaadai*	West	*Pashchim*
	hununchha?	Near/Far	*Najik/Taadhaa*
I'm going to . . .	*Ma . . . jaadai chhu*		
Where are you coming	*Tapaai kahaabaata*		
from?	*aaunu bhayeko?*		

TIME

What time is it?	*Kati bajyo?*	(Five) past (six)	*(Chha) bajer*
What time does the bus	*Yo bas kati baaje*		*(paanch) minet gayo*
leave?	*jaanchha?*	(Ten) to (eight)	*(Aath) bajana (das)*
When does it arrive?	*Kati baaje*		*minet bakichha*
	pugchha?	Minute	*Minet*
How many hours does it	*Kati ghanta*	Hour	*Ghanta*
take?	*laagchha?*	Day	*Din*
(Two) o'clock	*(Dui) bajyo*	Day (of week)	*Bar*
(Nine)-thirty	*Saadhe (nau)*	Week	*Haptaa*
	bajyo	Month	*Maina*

Year	*Barsa*	Next week	*Aarko haptaa*
Today	*Aaja*	Last month	*Gayeko maina*
Tomorrow	*Bholi*	(Two) years ago	*(Dui) barsa agi*
Yesterday	*Hijo*	Morning	*Bihaana*
Now	*Ahile*	Afternoon	*Diuso*
Later	*Pachhi*	Evening	*Belukaa*
Ago, Before	*Pahile*	Night	*Raati*

DEALING WITH KIDS

There's no foolproof way to silence pesky kids, but the following phrases might help you parry the taunts.

Begging is bad	*Maagnu raamro hoina*	Go back/Go away	*Pharka/Jaaun*
Don't beg	*Namaago*	Rude boy/person	*Naraamro keta maanchhe*
I don't give to beggars	*Maagnelai dinna*	Don't you have any manners?	*Bhudi chhaina?*
So loud!	*Kasto karaieko!*	Don't you have anything better to do?	*Aru kaam chhaina?*
Am I deaf?	*Ma bahiro chhura?*	Don't do that	*Teso nagara*
Be quiet	*Chup laaga*	Don't touch that	*Tyo nachalau*

NOUNS

Bag, Baggage	*Jholaa*	Money	*Paisa*
Bed	*Bistaara*	Mother	*Aama*
Blanket, Quilt	*Sirak*	Mouth	*Mukh*
Boy	*Keta*	Nose	*Naak*
Bus	*Bas*	Pain	*Dukhyo*
Candle	*Mainbatti*	Paper	*Kaagat*
Children	*Bachha*	Person	*Maanchhe*
Clothes	*Luga*	Place	*Thau*
Daughter	*Choraa*	Problem	*Samasya*
Ear	*Kan*	Restaurant	*Resturent, Bhojanalaya*
Eye	*Ankha*		
Family	*Pariwaar*	Road	*Baato, Rod*
Father	*Buwa*	Room	*Rum, Kothaa*
Fever	*Joro*	School	*Skul*
Foot	*Khutta*	Seat	*Sit*
Friend	*Saathi*	Shoe	*Jutta*
Food	*Khaanaa*	Shop	*Pasal*
Girl	*Keti*	Son	*Chori*
Hand	*Haat*	Stomach	*Pet*
Head	*Taauko*	Success	*Safal*
Hotel/Lodge	*Hotel/Laj*	Teahouse	*Chiya pasal, Chiya dokan*
House	*Ghar*		
Husband	*Srimaan*	Ticket	*Tiket*
Job, Work	*Kaam*	Toilet	*Chaarpi, Toilet*
Lamp	*Batti*	Town, Village	*Gaaun*
Mattress	*Danlap*	Trail/Main trail	*Baato/Mul baato*
Medicine	*Ausadhi*	Water	*Paani*
Mistake	*Galti*	Wife	*Srimati*

ADJECTIVES AND ADVERBS

One tricky thing about Nepali adjectives: the ones that describe feelings are actually nouns. Thus to express the notion "I'm thirsty", you have to say *Malaai thirkaa laagyo* ("To me thirst has struck").

A little	*Alikati*	Early	*Chaadai*	Only	*Maatrai*
Already	*Pahilei*	Easy	*Sajilo*	Open	*Khulaa*
After	*Pàchhi*	Empty	*Khali*	Often	*Kahilekahi*
Again	*Pheri*	Enough	*Prasasta*	Quickly	*Chitto*
All	*Sabai*	Expensive	*Mahango*	Right (Correct)	*Thik*
Alone	*Eklai*	Far	*Taadhaa*	Rude	*Naraamro, phohori*
A lot	*Dherai*	Full (thing)	*Bhari*	Sad	*Dukhi*
Always	*Sadai*	Full (person)	*Agaayo*	Same	*Eutai*
Another	*Aarko*	Fun	*Majaa*	Similar	*Ustai*
Bad	*Kharaab, Naraamro*	Good	*Raamro*	Slowly	*Bistaarai*
Beautiful	*Raamro*	Happy	*Kushi*	Small	*Saano*
Best	*Sabhanda raamro*	Heavy	*Garungo*	Soon	*Chaadai, Chittai*
Better	*Ajai raamro*	Hot (person or weather)	*Garam*	Stolen	*Choreko*
Big	*Thulo*			Strong	*Baliyo*
Cheap	*Sasto*	Hot (liquid)	*Taato*	Stupid	*Murkha*
Clean	*Safaa*	Hungry	*Bhokayeko*	Tall	*Aglo*
Clever	*Chalakh*	Interesting	*Majaa*	Tasty	*Mitho*
Closed	*Bhanda*	Late	*Dhilo*	Terrible	*Jhur*
Cold (person or weather)	*Jaado*	Less	*Thorai*	Thirsty	*Tirkha*
		Lost	*Haraayeko*	Tired	*Thakai*
Cold (liquid)	*Chiso*	Loud	*Charko*	Too much	*Asadei*
Crazy	*Paagal*	More (quantity)	*Aru*	Uphill	*Ukaalo*
Dark	*Adhyero*	More (degree)	*Ekdum, Ajai*	Very	*Dherai*
Different	*Pharak*	Near(er)	*Najik(ai)*	Wet	*Bhijyo*
Difficult	*Gaaro*	Never	*Kahilei*	Worse	*Khattam*
Dirty	*Phohor*	New	*Naya*	Worst	*Sabhanda naraamro*
Dishonest	*Bemaani*	Noisy	*Halla*		
Downhill	*Oraallo*	Old (thing)	*Purano*		
Dry	*Sukeko*	Old (person)	*Budho* (male), *Budhi* (female)	Wrong	*Galti*

VERBS

The following verbs are in the infinitive form. To turn a verb into a polite command (eg, "Please sit"), just add -*s* (*Basnus*); for an informal command, replace the -*nu* with -*un* (*Basun*). For an all-purpose tense, drop the -*u* ending and replace it with -*e* (eg *Jaane* can mean go, going or went, depending on the context). The easiest way to negate any verb is to put *na*- in front of it (*Nabasnus, Ma najaane*).

Arrive	*Aaipugnu*	Forget	*Birsanu*	Lose	*Haraunu*
Ask	*Sodhnu*	Get	*Paunu, Linu*	Make	*Banaunu*
Believe	*Biswas garnu*	Give	*Dinu*	Need	*Chaahinu*
Break	*Bhaanchnu*	Go	*Jaanu*	Put	*Raakhnu*
Buy	*Kinnu*	Hear, Listen	*Sunnu*	Receive	*Paunu*
Carry	*Boknu*	Help	*Madhat garnu*	Remember	*Samjhinu*
Come	*Aunu*	Hurry	*Hatar garnu*	Rent	*Bhadama linu*
Cook	*Pakaaunu*	Learn	*Siknu*	Rest	*Aaram garnu*
Do	*Garnu*	Leave	*Chodnu*	Return	*Pharkanu*
Eat	*Khaanu*	Lie (speak untruthfully)	*Jhutho bolnu*	Run	*Dagurnu*
Feel	*Mahasus garnu*			Say, Tell	*Bhannu*
Fix	*Thoknu*	Look, See	*Hernu*	Sit	*Basnu*

Sell	Bechnu	Think	Bichaar garnu,	Walk	Hidnu
Sleep	Sutnu		Sochnu	Want	Chahanu
Speak	Bolnu	Try	Kosis garnu	Wash	Dhunu (face,
Steal	Chornu	Understand	Bujnu		clothes), Nuhaaunu
Stop	Roknu	Use	Prayog garnu		(body)
Take	Linu	Wait	Parkhinu	Work	Kaam garnu

OTHER HANDY WORDS

Most of the following words are what we would call prepositions. However, those marked with an asterisk (*) are actually postpositions in Nepali, meaning they come *after* the thing they're describing (eg "with me" comes out *masanga*).

Above, Over, Up	Maathi*	In front of	Agaadi*
And	Ra	If	Yedi
Below, Under, Down	Talla*	Or	Ki
Because	Kinabhane	Out, Outside	Bahira*
Behind	Pachhadi*	To, Towards	Tira*
But	Tara	With	Sanga*
From	Baata*	Without	Chhaina*
In, Inside	Bhitra*		

NUMBERS

Unlike the English counting system, which starts using compound numbers above 20 (twenty-one, twenty-two, etc), Nepali numbers are irregular all the way up to 100 – the following are the ones you're most likely to use. A slight further complication is the use of "counters" when quantifying nouns. In English, we sometimes use counters – for example, two pieces of paper, five plates of rice – but in Nepali the use is more systematic. Fortunately, you can get by with just two counters: *wotaa* for things, *jana* for people. Thus "five books" is *paanch wotaa kitaab*, "twelve girls" is *baahra jana keti*. But note these irregular counters: *ek wotaa = euta; dui wotaa = duita; tin wotaa = tintaa.*

half	aada	12	baara	50	pachaas
1	ek	13	tera	60	saathi
2	dui	14	chaudha	70	sattari
3	tin	15	pandra	80	asi
4	chaar	16	sora	90	nabbe
5	paanch	17	satra	100	ek sae
6	chha	18	athaara	1000	ek hajaa
7	saat	19	unnais	first (time)	pahilo (palta)
8	aath	20	bis	second	dosro
9	nau	25	pachhis	third	tesro
10	das	30	tis	fourth	chautho
11	eghaara	40	chaalis	fifth	paachau

DAYS AND MONTHS

It's unlikely you'll ever have to use these. Nepali months start around the middle of our months, and vary from 27 to 32 days.

Sunday	Aitabar	Jan–Feb	Magh	Aug–Sept	Bhadau (or
Monday	Sombar	Feb–March	Faagun		Bhadra)
Tuesday	Mangalbar	March–April	Chaitra	Sept–Oct	Ashoj (or
Wednesday	Budhabar	April–May	Baisakh		Ashwin)
Thursday	Bihibar	May–June	Jeth (or Jestha)	Oct–Nov	Kartik
Friday	Sukrabar	June–July	Asaar (or Ashadh)	Nov–Dec	Mangsir
Saturday	Sanibar	July–August	Saaun (or Shrawan)	Dec–Janu	Puus

SOME NEWARI PHRASES

Newari is still the first language for many in Kathmandu Valley. It's a difficult language to learn, with many local dialects, and knowing it is no more necessary than, say, knowing Welsh in Wales, yet trying out even the tiniest smidgen of it will astound and delight your innkeeper. The following phrases will get you going.

Hello	*Namaste*	No thanks	*Mha*
Yes/No	*Ji/Maji*	Please give me that	*Wo chhaka biya deshang*
Thank you	*Dhanyabaad*		
How are things?	*Chhitang gaya chong?*	Begging is bad	*Phonegu jya baamalaa*
Fine	*Bala*	A little	*Bhachaa*
What's your name?	*Chigu naang chhu?*	Bad	*Mabaalaa*
My name is . . .	*Jigu naang . . . kha*	Cheap	*Dang*
My country is . . .	*Jigu chhey . . . kha*	Good	*Baalaa*
I don't understand	*Jing mathu*	Hungry	*Naiya pityaa*
Can you repeat	*Chhaka dhaya dishang*	Thirst	*Pyaas*
Do you speak English?	*Chhi Englis kha lhayadhiya?*	Tired	*Thakejula*
		1	*Chharkaa*
I don't speak Newari	*Jing Newa kha lhayemasa*	2	*Nirkaa*
		3	*Sorhkaa*
Please help me	*Jitang gwali yana dishang*	4	*Perkaa*
		5	*Nyarkaa*
Excuse me	*Maph biya*	6	*Khurkaa*
Can I go in?	*Ji wone jilaa?*	7	*Nerkaa*
What's this called in Newari?	*Thuyatang chhu dhaigu?*	8	*Chyarkaa*
How far is it?	*Guli taappaa?*	9	*Gurkaa*
How much does this cost?	*Thukiya guli?*	10	*Jhirkaa*

NEPALI NUMERALS

१	२	३	४	५	६	७	८	९	१०
1	2	3	4	5	6	7	8	9	10

A GLOSSARY OF NEPALI, NEWARI AND TIBETAN TERMS

ANNAPURNA goddess of grain and abundance (literally, "Full of Grain"); form of Lakshmi.

ASHTA MANGALA the eight auspicious symbols of Buddhism.

AVALOKITESHWARA the *bodhisattva* of compassion (also known as Chenrezig).

AVATAR bodily incarnation of a deity.

BAGH tiger.

BAHAL buildings and quadrangle of a former Buddhist Newar monastery (a few are still active).

BAHUN Brahman, Hindu priest.

BAJRA see "Vajra".

BAJRA JOGINI (or **VAJRA YOGINI**) female tantric counterpart to Bhairab.

BAKSHISH not a bribe, but a tip in advance.

BAN forest.

BARAHI (or **VARAHI**) Vishnu incarnated as a boar.

BAZAAR commercial area of a town – not necessarily a covered market.

BENI confluence of rivers.

BETAL symbol of death, often represented by a pair of skeletons flanking a temple entrance.

BETEL see "Paan".

BHAAT cooked rice; food.

BHAIRAB terrifying tantric form of Shiva.

BHANJYANG a pass (Nepali).

BHARAT India.

BHATTI simple tavern, usually selling food as well as alcohol.

BHIMSEN patron god of Newar merchants.

BHOJANALAYA Nepali restaurant.

BHOT Tibet.

BHOTIYA highland peoples of Tibetan ancestry.

BIDESHI foreigner (but many Nepalis call all foreigners *Aamerikan* – even Japanese).

BIDI cheap rolled-leaf cigarette.

BODHISATTVA in Mahayana Buddhism, one who forgoes *nirvana* until all other beings have attained enlightenment.

BRAHMA the Hindu creator god, one of the Hindu "trinity".

BRAHMAN member of the Hindu priestly caste (*bahun* in Nepali); metaphysical term meaning the universal soul.

CHAARPI latrine.

CHAITYA small Buddhist monument.

CHARES hashish.

CHAUTAARA resting platform beside a trail with trees for shade.

CHHETRI member of the ruling or warrior caste.

CHHANG (or **CHHYANG**) homemade beer brewed from rice or other grains.

CHILLAM vertical clay pipe for smoking tobacco or *ganja*.

CHOLO traditional half-length woman's blouse.

CHORTEN another name for a *chaitya* in high mountain areas.

CHOWK intersection, square or courtyard (pronounced "choke").

CHUBA Tibetan sheepskin coat; Tibetan dress.

CHULO clay stove.

DAMARU two-sided drum.

DAADA (or **DANDA**) a ridge.

DANPHE Nepal's national bird, a pheasant with brilliant plumage.

DAPHNE shrub used in paper-making.

DAURA SURUWAL traditional dress of hill men: wrap-around shirt and jodhpur-like trousers.

DEWAL stepped temple platform; temple with prominent steps.

DEVI see *mahadevi*.

DHAARA communal water tap or tank.

DHAKA colourful hand-loomed material made in the Nepalese hills.

DHAMI shaman, similar to *jhankri*.

DHARMA religion; correct behaviour (applies to both Hinduism and Buddhism).

DHARMSALA rest house for pilgrims.

DHOKA gate.

DHOTI Indian-style loincloth; Nepali slang for Indian person.

DHYANI BUDDHAS four (sometimes five) meditating figures representing aspects of Buddha nature.

DOKO conical cane basket carried by means of a headstrap.

DORJE Tibetan word for *vajra*.

DUN low-lying valleys just north of the Tarai (sometimes called inner Tarai, or *bhitri madesh* – "inner plains").

DURBAR palace; royal court.

DURGA demon-slaying goddess.

DYOCHHEN tantric temple or meeting hall.

DZOPKIO sturdy yak-cattle crossbreed; the female is called a *dzum*.

GAIDA (or **GAINDA**) rhinoceros.

GAAINE wandering minstrel of the hills.

GAJUR brass or gold finial at the peak of a temple.

GANESH elephant-headed god of wisdom and remover of obstacles.

GANJA cannabis, marijuana.

GARUD Vishnu's man-bird carrier.

GAUN village, town.

GELUG-PA one of four main Lamaist sects.

GHANTA a bell, usually rung at temples as a sort of "amen".

GHAT riverside platform for worship and cremations.

GIDDA vulture; Nepali slang for Israeli.

GOMPA Buddhist monastery.

GOONDA hooligan, thug.

GURKHAS Nepali soldiers who serve in special regiments in the British and Indian armies.

GUTHI Newar benevolent association that handles upkeep of temples, organizes festivals, etc.

HANUMAN valiant monkey king in the *Ramayan*.

HATTI elephant.

HIMAL massif or mountain range with permanent snow.

HITI Newari word for *dhaara*.

HMG His Majesty's Government.

JAAND unstrained *chhang*.

JAATRA festival.

JAL holy water.

JANAI sacred thread worn over left shoulder by high-caste Hindu men.

JHANKRI shaman, or medicine man, of the hills.

JYAPU member of the Newar peasant farming caste.

KAGYU-PA one of four main Lamaist sects.

KALI the mother goddess in her most terrifying form.

KARMA the soul's accumulated merit, determining its next rebirth.

KAROD 10 million (*crore* in India).

KATA white scarf given to lamas by visitors.

KHOLA stream or river.

KHUKURI curved knife carried by most Nepali hill men.

KIRTIMUKHA common temple motif, a gargoyle-like face grappling with a snake.

KOT fort (pronounced "coat").

KRISHNA one of Vishnu's *avatar*, hero of the *Mahabharat*.

KUMARI a girl worshipped by Nepalis as the living incarnation of Durga.

KUNDA pond, water tank.

LA pass (Tibetan).

LALI GURAAS tree rhododendron.

LAKH 100,000.

LAKSHMI consort of Vishnu, goddess of wealth.

LAMA Tibetan Buddhist priest: hence Lamaism.

LEK mountain range without permanent snow.

LHAKANG interior of a *gompa*.

LINGA (or **LINGAM**) the phallic symbol of Shiva, commonly the centrepiece of temples and sometimes occurring in groups in the open.

LOKESHWAR see Avalokiteshwara.

MACHAAN watchtower used by Tarai farmers to ward off wild animals.

MACHHENDRANATH rain-bringing deity of the Kathmandu Valley; also known as Karunamaya or Bungadeo.

MAHABHARAT (or **MAHABHARATA**) Hindu epic of the battle between two families, featuring Krishna and containing the *Bhagavad Gita*.

MAHABHARAT LEK highest range of the Himalayan foothills.

MAHADEV "Great God", an epithet for Shiva.

MAHADEVI mother goddess.

MAHAYANA non-monastic form of Buddhism followed in Nepal, Tibet and east Asia.

MAHOUT elephant driver.

MANDALA mystical diagram, meditation tool.

MANDAP pavilion.

MANDIR temple.

MANI STONE slate inscribed with the mantra *Om mani padme hum*.

MANTRA religious incantation.

MASAN riverside cremation platform.

MATH Hindu priest's home.

MELA religious fair or gathering.

NADI river.

NAG snake or snake spirit, believed to have rain-bringing powers.

NAGAR city.

NAK female yak.

NAAMLO tumpline, headstrap for carrying a *doko*.

NANGLO cane tray, used for winnowing.

NANDI Shiva's mount, a bull.

NARAYAN common name for Vishnu.

NATH "Lord".

NIRVANA in Buddhism, enlightenment and release from the cycle of rebirth.

NYINGMA-PA one of four main Lamaist sects.

OM MANI PADME HUM the mantra of Avalokiteshvara, roughly translating as "Hail to the jewel in the lotus".

PAAN mildly addictive mixture of areca nut and lime paste, wrapped in a leaf and chewed, producing blood-red spit.

PADMA SAMBHAVA alias Guru Rinpoche, the eighth-century saint who brought Buddhism to Tibet.

PAHAAD hill.

PANCHAAYAT council or assembly, the basis for Nepal's pre-democratic government.

PARBAT mountain.

PARBATI (or **PARVATI**) Shiva's consort.

PATAKA (or **DHWAJA**) necktie-shaped brass ornament hanging from a temple, to be used by the deity when descending to earth.

PATI Open shelter erected as a public resting place.

PAUBHA Newar scroll painting.

PIPAL common shade tree of the fig genus; also known as *bodhi*, the tree under which Buddha attained enlightenment.

POKHRI pond, usually man-made.

PRASAD food consecrated after being offered to a deity – a sort of spiritual souvenir.

PUJA an act of worship.

PUJARI Hindu priest who tends to a particular temple.

PUL bridge.

PURETH Hindu priest who makes house calls.

RAJPATH, **RAJMARGA** "King's Way", "King's Road".

RAKSI distilled spirit.

RAM mortal *avatar* of Vishnu, hero of the *Ramayan*.

RAMAYAN (or **RAMAYANA**) popular Hindu epic in which Sita, princess of Janakpur, is abducted and eventually rescued by Ram and Hanuman.

RATH chariot used in religious processions.

RINPOCHE "precious jewel": title given to revered lamas.

RUDRAKSHA furrowed brown seeds, prized by *Shaivas*; it's said that the wearer of a *rudraksha* necklace must always tell the truth.

SADHU Hindu ascetic.

SAHIB honorific term given to male foreigners, pronouced "sahb"; women are called *memsahib*.

SAJHA co-operative; the name of a quasi-government bus company.

SAKYA-PA one of four main Lamaist sects.

SAL tall tree of the Tarai and lower hills, valued for its timber.

SARANGI Nepali four-stringed violin.

SARASWATI Hindu goddess of learning and the arts.

SATI (or **SUTTEE**) practice of Hindu widows throwing themselves on their husbands' funeral pyres.

SHAIVA member of the cult of Shiva (pronounced "Shaib").

SHAKTI in Hindu *tantra*, the female principle that empowers the male; the mother goddess in this capacity.

SHALIGRAM fossil-bearing stones found near Muktinath, revered by *Vaishnavas*.

SHIKRA Indian-style temple, shaped like a square bullet.

SHIVA "the destroyer", one of the Hindu "trinity" – a god of many guises.

SHIVALAYA one-storey Shiva shrine containing a *linga*.

SHIVA MARGI a Hindu Newar.

SHRI an honorific prefix.

SINDUR red paste used in making *tika* and decorating idols.

SIRDAR Nepali trek leader.

SITA Ram's wife, princess of Janakpur, heroine of the *Ramayan*.

STOL "short takeoff and landing" (read "hairraising") landing strip.

STUPA large dome-shaped Buddhist monument, usually said to contain holy relics.

SUDRA member of the lowest, menial caste of Hinduism.

TAAL lake.

TANTRA esoteric psycho-sexual path to enlightenment, a major influence on Nepali Hinduism and Buddhism.

TARA Buddhist goddess; female aspect of Buddha nature.

TASHI DELEK Tibetan for welcome, *namaste*.

TEMPO three-wheeled scooter, autoriksha.

THAKURI very orthodox Chhetri subcaste.

THANGKA Buddhist scroll painting.

TIKA auspicious mark placed on the forehead during *puja* or festivals or before making a journey.

TOL neighbourhood.

TOLA traditional unit of weight (11.5g); precious metals are sold by the *tola*, as is hashish.

TOPI traditional Nepalese cap.

TORANA elaborate wooden carving, or metal shield, above a temple door.

TORMA dough offerings made by Buddhist monks.

TRISUL the trident, a symbol of Shiva.

TSAMPA toasted barley flour, a staple food of Tibetans and Bhotiyas.

TUDIKHEL parade ground.

TULKU lama considered a reincarnation of a late great teacher.

VAISYA (or **BAISYA**) Hindu caste of traders and farmers.

VAJRA sceptre-like symbol of tantric power (pronounced "bajra").

VAJRACHARYA Buddhist Newar priest.

VAJRAYANA "Thunderbolt Way": tantric Buddhism.

VAISHNAVA follower of the cult of Vishnu (pronounced "Baishnab").

VEDAS oldest Hindu scriptures; hence Vedic gods, which were worshipped at the time.

VISHNU "the preserver", member of the Hindu "trinity", worshipped in ten main incarnations (pronounced "Bishnu").

YONI symbol of the female genitalia, usually carved into the base of a *linga* as a reservoir for offerings.

INDEX

HELP US UPDATE

We've gone to a lot of effort to ensure that this third edition of *The Rough Guide to Nepal* is completely up-to-date and accurate. However, things do change – places get "discovered", transport connections change, restaurants and guest houses get renamed – and any suggestions, comments or corrections would be much appreciated. We're particularly keen to hear of accounts of travels to remote and untried destinations.

We'll credit all contributions, and send a copy of the next edition (or any other Rough Guide if you prefer) for the best letters. Please mark letters "Rough Guide Nepal Update" and send to:

Rough Guides, 1 Mercer Street, London WC2H 9QJ
or
Rough Guides, 375 Hudson Street, 9th Floor, New York NY 10014
or
nepal@roughtravl.co.uk

direct orders from

Amsterdam	1-85828-086-9	£7.99	US$13.95	CAN$16.99
Andalucia	1-85828-094-X	8.99	14.95	18.99
Australia	1-85828-141-5	12.99	19.95	25.99
Bali	1-85828-134-2	8.99	14.95	19.99
Barcelona	1-85828-221-7	8.99	14.95	19.99
Berlin	1-85828-129-6	8.99	14.95	19.99
Brazil	1-85828-102-4	9.99	15.95	19.99
Britain	1-85828-208-X	12.99	19.95	25.99
Brittany & Normandy	1-85828-224-1	9.99	16.95	22.99
Bulgaria	1-85828-183-0	9.99	16.95	22.99
California	1-85828-181-4	10.99	16.95	22.99
Canada	1-85828-130-X	10.99	14.95	19.99
China	1-85828-225-X	15.99	24.95	32.95
Corsica	1-85828-089-3	8.99	14.95	18.99
Costa Rica	1-85828-136-9	9.99	15.95	21.99
Crete	1-85828-132-6	8.99	14.95	18.99
Cyprus	1-85828-182-2	9.99	16.95	22.99
Czech & Slovak Republics	1-85828-121-0	9.99	16.95	22.99
Egypt	1-85828-188-1	10.99	17.95	23.99
Europe	1-85828-159-8	14.99	19.95	25.99
England	1-85828-160-1	10.99	17.95	23.99
First Time Europe	1-85828-270-5	7.99	9.95	12.99
Florida	1-85828-184-4	10.99	16.95	22.99
France	1-85828-124-5	10.99	16.95	21.99
Germany	1-85828-128-8	11.99	17.95	23.99
Goa	1-85828-156-3	8.99	14.95	19.99
Greece	1-85828-131-8	9.99	16.95	20.99
Greek Islands	1-85828-163-6	8.99	14.95	19.99
Guatemala	1-85828-189-X	10.99	16.95	22.99
Hawaii: Big Island	1-85828-158-X	8.99	12.95	16.99
Hawaii	1-85828-206-3	10.99	16.95	22.99
Holland, Belgium & Luxembourg	1-85828-087-7	9.99	15.95	20.99
Hong Kong	1-85828-187-3	8.99	14.95	19.99
Hungary	1-85828-123-7	8.99	14.95	19.99
India	1-85828-200-4	14.99	23.95	31.99
Ireland	1-85828-179-2	10.99	17.95	23.99
Italy	1-85828-167-9	12.99	19.95	25.99
Kenya	1-85828-192-X	11.99	18.95	24.99
London	1-85828-231-4	9.99	15.95	21.99
Mallorca & Menorca	1-85828-165-2	8.99	14.95	19.99
Malaysia, Singapore & Brunei	1-85828-103-2	9.99	16.95	20.99
Mexico	1-85828-044-3	10.99	16.95	22.99
Morocco	1-85828-040-0	9.99	16.95	21.99
Moscow	1-85828-118-0	8.99	14.95	19.99
Nepal	1-85828-190-3	10.99	17.95	23.99
New York	1-85828-171-7	9.99	15.95	21.99
Pacific Northwest	1-85828-092-3	9.99	14.95	19.99

In the UK, Rough Guides are available from all good bookstores, but can be obtained from Penguin by contacting: Penguin Direct, Penguin Books Ltd, Bath Road, Harmondsworth, West Drayton, Middlesex UB7 0DA; or telephone the credit line on 0181-899 4036 (9am–5pm) and ask for Penguin Direct. Visa, Access and Amex accepted. Delivery will normally be within 14 working days. Penguin Direct ordering facilities are only available in the UK and the USA. The availability and published prices quoted are correct at the time of going to press but are subject to alteration without prior notice.

Paris	1-85828-235-7	8.99	14.95	19.99
Poland	1-85828-168-7	10.99	17.95	23.99
Portugal	1-85828-180-6	9.99	16.95	22.99
Prague	1-85828-122-9	8.99	14.95	19.99
Provence	1-85828-127-X	9.99	16.95	22.99
Pyrenees	1-85828-093-1	8.99	15.95	19.99
Rhodes & the Dodecanese	1-85828-120-2	8.99	14.95	19.99
Romania	1-85828-097-4	9.99	15.95	21.99
San Francisco	1-85828-185-7	8.99	14.95	19.99
Scandinavia	1-85828-039-7	10.99	16.99	21.99
Scotland	1-85828-166-0	9.99	16.95	22.99
Sicily	1-85828-178-4	9.99	16.95	22.99
Singapore	1-85828-135-0	8.99	14.95	19.99
Spain	1-85828-240-3	11.99	18.95	24.99
St Petersburg	1-85828-133-4	8.99	14.95	19.99
Thailand	1-85828-140-7	10.99	17.95	24.99
Tunisia	1-85828-139-3	10.99	17.95	24.99
Turkey	1-85828-242-X	12.99	19.95	25.99
Tuscany & Umbria	1-85828-243-8	10.99	17.95	23.99
USA	1-85828-161-X	14.99	19.95	25.99
Venice	1-85828-170-9	8.99	14.95	19.99
Vietnam	1-85828-191-1	9.99	15.95	21.99
Wales	1-85828-245-4	10.99	17.95	23.99
Washington DC	1-85828-246-2	8.99	14.95	19.99
West Africa	1-85828-101-6	15.99	24.95	34.99
More Women Travel	1-85828-098-2	9.99	14.95	19.99
Zimbabwe & Botswana	1-85828-186-5	11.99	18.95	24.99

Phrasebooks

Czech	1-85828-148-2	3.50	5.00	7.00
French	1-85828-144-X	3.50	5.00	7.00
German	1-85828-146-6	3.50	5.00	7.00
Greek	1-85828-145-8	3.50	5.00	7.00
Italian	1-85828-143-1	3.50	5.00	7.00
Mexican	1-85828-176-8	3.50	5.00	7.00
Portuguese	1-85828-175-X	3.50	5.00	7.00
Polish	1-85828-174-1	3.50	5.00	7.00
Spanish	1-85828-147-4	3.50	5.00	7.00
Thai	1-85828-177-6	3.50	5.00	7.00
Turkish	1-85828-173-3	3.50	5.00	7.00
Vietnamese	1-85828-172-5	3.50	5.00	7.00

Reference

Classical Music	1-85828-113-X	12.99	19.95	25.99
Internet	1-85828-198-9	5.00	8.00	10.00
Jazz	1-85828-137-7	16.99	24.95	34.99
Opera	1-85828-138-5	16.99	24.95	34.99
Reggae	1-85828-247-0	12.99	19.95	25.99
Rock	1-85828-201-2	17.99	26.95	35.00
World Music	1-85828-017-6	16.99	22.95	29.99

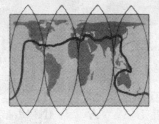

SLEEP EASY
BOOK AHEAD

AUSTRALIA
02 261 1111

CANADA
FREEPHONE 0800 663 5777

DUBLIN
01 301766

LONDON
0171 836 1036

BELFAST
01232 324733

GLASGOW
0141 332 3004

WASHINGTON
0202 783 6161

NEW ZEALAND
09 379 4224

IBN INTERNATIONAL BOOKING NETWORK

Call any of these numbers and your credit card secures a good nights sleep ...

in more than 26 countries

up to six months ahead

with immediate confirmation

HOSTELLING INTERNATIONAL

*Budget accommodation you can **Trust***